CW01081259

The Millennium Maritime Trade Revolution 700–1700

Praise for *How Maritime Trade and the Indian Subcontinent Shaped the World*

'Remarkable and fascinating…History with a capital H…the author's capacity to make effective use of archaeological and scientific data, alongside the economic, cultural and linguistic is impressive…a remarkable achievement well-worth investigating…this reviewer will be looking forward to the appearance of the next two volumes…definitely recommended.'
Professor Geoffrey Till, The Naval Review

'I am utterly astonished by it…clearly a most important work…the control of detail is remarkable…most enlightening.' Dr Ronald Hyam

'This book deserves to be read widely…fascinating and convincing…written with skill and enthusiasm…makes rather complex topics both interesting and coherent…Both remarkable and more importantly enjoyable.' Emeritus Professor Malcolm Falkus

'Well written, comprehensive and informative…While I can single out many other issues and topics the thing that impressed me the most was [the] attempt to put India on the map of world history.' Alfons van der Kraan

'An epic tome that sets out to put merchant history at the centre of world history…an interesting work, ambitious in scale but accessibly written and divided into manageable chunks…and will surely encourage readers to return to the author when he brings out his two upcoming books covering later periods. This book is Nautilus Book of the Month for September 2022.' Nautilus International

'Well written…very readable…the author has done a good job in taking such a large subject, breaking it down into the relevant parts…vast amounts of information…the author is to be congratulated.' ARRSE Review

'The book is immense in breadth and detail.' Charles Winder. The Bugle

The Millennium Maritime Trade Revolution 700–1700

How Asia Lost Maritime Supremacy

Nick Collins

Pen & Sword
MARITIME

First published in Great Britain in 2023 by
Pen & Sword Maritime
An imprint of Pen & Sword Books Limited
Yorkshire – Philadelphia

ISBN 978 1 39906 012 7

Typeset by Mac Style
Printed in the UK by CPI Group (UK) Ltd, Croydon, CR0 4YY.

Pen & Sword Books Limited incorporates the imprints of After
the Battle, Atlas, Archaeology, Aviation, Discovery, Family History,
Fiction, History, Maritime, Military, Military Classics, Politics,
Select, Transport, True Crime, Air World, Frontline Publishing, Leo
Cooper, Remember When, Seaforth Publishing, The Praetorian Press,
Wharncliffe Local History, Wharncliffe Transport, Wharncliffe True
Crime and White Owl.

For a complete list of Pen & Sword titles please contact

PEN & SWORD BOOKS LIMITED
47 Church Street, Barnsley, South Yorkshire, S70 2AS, England
E-mail: enquiries@pen-and-sword.co.uk
Website: www.pen-and-sword.co.uk
or
PEN AND SWORD BOOKS
1950 Lawrence Rd, Havertown, PA 19083, USA
E-mail: Uspen-and-sword@casematepublishers.com
Website: www.penandswordbooks.com

In memory of two shipping professionals:

Captain David Mockett, my cousin, murdered in 2011 in Aden while investigating a maritime fraud, by someone known to police and judiciary but never prosecuted.[1]

Essam Bella, good friend and entrepreneurial colleague, MD of Clarkson Dubai, died in 2021 of coronavirus, far too young.

Contents

Acknowledgements

Many historians have spent lifetimes researching original documents to piece together vital fragments of this contextual story, which otherwise could not be told with necessary certainty. I am awed by historians like Shlomo Goitein, Ralph Davis, Charles Boxer, Fernand Braudel, and those who painstakingly researched aspects of medieval Baltic trade in documents in multiple languages, those who research the far fewer Asian inscriptions and documents, and many, many more. Thanks to all. I reviewed early drafts of John Pike's *Thirty Years War*, now due to be published in three or more volumes. They gave interesting insights but, as yet unpublished, I am unable to acknowledge book and page, thus do so generally here. Once again I thank my Bolton School teachers Richard Wilkinson and Alan Benson, Magdalene College Cambridge supervisors, Ralph Bennet and Ronald Hyam and of course my parents who sacrificed much for my education. Thanks to many shipping and trading colleagues who shaped my views on the commercial maritime world, to my editor Lester Crook, the Pen and Sword team, graphic designer Sam Musgrove for the maps, the Baltic Exchange for their assistance in promoting this series' first book and my sons' continual support.

Names and Spellings

There are many ways names are spelt when Anglicised. I use the most recognisable, with the possible exception of Guangzhou, Canton to earlier historians, itself a corruption of Portuguese attempts to say Guangzhou.

Introduction: Themes

While this book may be read as a stand-alone volume, it may be more profitably appreciated after reading *How Maritime Trade and the Indian Subcontinent Shaped the World*, which starts in the deepest antiquity of Indian Ocean seafaring and maritime trade, gradually diffusing into the Mediterranean, linking with north European trade, eventually culminating in the maritime connected Roman Empire and its trade with the Indian Ocean. Its collapse meant European maritime trade all but ceased, stuttering to life by 670–700, whereas Indian Ocean trade continued, short and long-haul, in essentials, food and luxuries. This book continues the story, charting Asia's maritime trade acceleration and Europe's slow recovery. By 1700 Asian trade was still more voluminous, more controlled by Asians and Europe's ships were smaller, but northern Europe's merchants had expanded into the Baltic, Mediterranean, Indian Ocean and the Americas, which itself traded directly with Europe, Asia and Africa. This then, is partly the story of Europe's maritime trade's rebirth. The title 'Revolution', from revolve, thus refers to a reversal rather than dramatic short political or social change.

Maritime trade encompasses many industries, finished goods and raw materials, shipbuilding, ship owning, navigation, finance, repair, provisioning, warehousing, lodging, entertaining, buying and selling with merchants as intermediaries, operating in peace and war, sometimes encouraged, supported, ignored, or persecuted by governments. They continued reacting to ever-changing supply and demand, irrespective of national boundaries.

Historians have different priorities and philosophies. John Seeley (1834–1895) stated, 'history is past politics and politics, present history.' By contrast, economic historian George Unwin (1870–1925) thought history 'an account of the things that mattered most in the past,'[1] a philosophy more to this author's taste. He counselled, 'the serious student of history must learn as his primary duty to question all conventional views and values,'[2] something the first book took to heart. Political history is deeply ingrained at many universities. Shlomo Goitein rescued many boxes of the valuable Geniza documents, (Chapters 7 and 8) labelled by a Cambridge archivist 'commercial papers of no importance,'[3] yet it was from merchants that European medieval kings and princes borrowed to finance wars, buy allies and mercenaries.

Maritime trade largely drives world history. For example, in this period Asia's traders kept Indian Ocean societies rich. Trade led Europe's economic recovery, trade in crusader states opened Europe's eyes to a wider world, it was England's motivator in the Hundred Years War, a major issue in the Thirty Years War and motivated the Portuguese, Dutch and English push into Asia. The themes and philosophy of the series, outlined in some detail in the earlier book's Chapter 1, here recapped briefly, continue; the importance of maritime trade in world history, the cultural differences between maritime-influenced and continental regions, that maritime trade promotes economic development, wealth creation, toleration, creative, intellectual and practical progress and that choke points are key drivers in the story. How the maritime revolution happened was due to multiple destructive continental influences in Asia and the Mediterranean and fiercely independent, competitive north European merchants, increasingly encouraged by government.

As Henri Pirenne observed over a century ago, capital accumulates in cities, and 'when unimpeded by prince or other governmental authority, capital always exerts its power in favour of liberty...reflected in the advance of personal and political freedom,' especially in ports.[4] Fernand Braudel states 'the miracle of toleration... [occurred] wherever the community of trade convened.'[5] Options trader turned philosopher, Nassim Nicholas Taleb makes the same point. 'Money and transactions' he writes, 'purify relations...commerce, business, Levantine souks...are activities and places that bring out the best in people, making most of them forgiving, honest, loving, trusting and open-minded...commerce, particularly small commerce, is the door...to any form of tolerance.'[6] Experimenting in ports; shipbuilding, design, marketing, seeking technical or commercial solutions, he says 'depends on artificial tinkering,' and 'risk taking is largely responsible for innovation and growth.'[7] In the early-1660s, Thomas Sprat thought, 'the genius of experimenting is so much dispersed that...all places and corners are now busy and warm about this work.'[8] Contemporaneously it was missing in Asia and the Mediterranean; partly why maritime north Europe began its ascent.

There is a qualitative difference between maritime societies, experimentative, innovative, inclusive, wealth creating and tolerant, and continental societies, conservative and hierarchical. Gujarati, Tamil, Omani and Southeast Asian maritime Austronesians continued producing tenacious merchants and seafarers. Not all maritime societies are moulded in the same pattern, however. Some adapt more easily than others. Venetian commerce was conducted in its golden age mainly by Venetians. Hansa ports tried to enforce a north Europe-Baltic monopoly. Bruges, Antwerp, Amsterdam and London were more open and inclusive. Amsterdam and London merchants had substantial fleets, Bruges' and Antwerp's insignificant. Portuguese 16th-century Indian Ocean expansion was initially imbued with aggressive Reconquista character. Both they and the 16th-17th-century Dutch sought monopoly. Merchants fighting monopoly did so tenaciously, for example Dutch, English and Scandinavian Baltic merchants against the Hansa and those nations against each other. After Hansa collapse, Hamburg allowed foreign traders to settle with 50–60% of its 17th-century resident merchants foreign, its commercial infrastructure similar to Amsterdam and London. It thrived. Lubeck pursued xenophobic, intolerant religious policies forbidding foreigners to trade. It withered. Even in this diversity, the difference with continental powers, Mongols, Ming, France, Castile which influenced Spain after the 1469 union, Turks and Holy Roman Empire for example, in which conquest, not wealth creation was the aim, is striking. Sixteenth-century Fujian was densely populated, progressive and prosperous. Further inland was inward-looking and poor; one economy thriving, another stagnating. The principle operates virtually everywhere.[9]

Many hierarchical, continental powers feared maritime societies, which allowed enterprising, low-status men to discuss new, foreign ideas, disrupting traditional practices. Plato's city Magnesia was ten miles from the sea, away from moneymaking and foreign ideas. Aristotle suggested creating a break between port and city. Polybius and Isocrates were suspicious and Cicero feared imported ideas so 'none of the ancestral rules can remain intact.' Biblical writers viewed maritime trade negatively. St. Augustine's negativity about earthly civilisation's value and thus of trade and seafaring, influenced by Roman slow-motion collapse, continued in most of Catholic Europe. Merovingian Franks, concerned only with land, let ports decline. By 700 few survived. New Frisian, Scandinavian and English ports were primitive, but offered the greatest opportunity for human and material capital concentration. Indifference to trade, aristocratic, hierarchical, continental attitudes permeate French history, explaining its trajectory. Inland Berlin reflects central European and Prussian origins of the conservative German state. Inland Warsaw and Madrid, Poland and Spain's capitals, were conservative and aristocratic. By contrast, Dorestad, Quentovic, Bruges, Danzig, Bilbao, Marseilles, La Rochelle, Barcelona, London, Antwerp, Amsterdam, Venice, Genoa, Livorno and Hamburg were, bubbling maritime centres of trade, innovation, toleration and culture. The continental uniformity imperative was especially strong in China, where Confucianism discouraged travel and emphasised hierarchy.

This series' previous volume demonstrated two types of continental mentalities, that of the mobile steppe nomad and the immobile peasant. In this period, it is again sharply delineated. Robert Marshall describes Mongols, who conquered Eurasia from Poland to Korea, 'living in their pastoral wilderness for century upon century, trapped within a perennial struggle against climate and the fluctuations of tribal power...[they] developed no technologies, produced no manufactures, nor even learned simple mining.' But they viewed their nomadic culture as superior, so they and China's rulers 'surveyed one another with mutual arrogance,' mutual contempt.[10]

John Beckwith by contrast, portrays central Asians, not all nomads, more as traders, custodians of the Silk Road, an important riposte to simplistic categorisation of central Eurasia as a nomadic backwater, but there is a problem. Take his comparison of 16th-century Portugal's attempted Indian Ocean trade take-over with central Eurasians. 'The only significant difference was,' he says, that 'Europeans used ships and cannon instead of horses and compound bow to force the opening of trade when negotiation failed.'[11] But Huns, Jurchen, Mongols and Turks didn't aim to force trade, but conquer land and people. Central Asia never produced intellectual or practical achievements that maritime trade did. Steeped in Mongol slaughter and mounds of skulls, he concedes that Portuguese aggression, which horrified many was, 'on the whole …remarkable for…restraint.'[12] There are huge qualitative differences between benefits brought by maritime trade and continental nomad destruction, usually with long-lasting detrimental demographic and environmental effects. Mongols finally settled as Mughals, conquering much of India, a land empire, overtaxing peasants alien to Gujarati and Tamil merchant maritime cultures.

Islam religiously united an area from Iberia to the Indian Ocean. But it was divided between maritime-inspired Abbasid Baghdad, Oman and Yemen and continental-inspired areas where conquest and conversion motivated. China has a long coast and vast land. Having to spend much energy and treasure defending its frontiers from steppe nomads, it was doubly disadvantaged. But for much of this thousand years, T'ang, Song and Yuan dynasties had the strength and confidence to increasingly concentrate on maritime trade, producing the world's most advanced civilisation between 700 and about 1430. It sailed the world's technically best, largest ships. Its ports hosted foreign merchants' enclaves. But in 1372 the new Ming dynasty banned foreign private trade, choosing the road to decline, self-delusion and revolution. Great reformer Deng Xiao-ping explained the lesson. 'No country that wishes to become developed today can pursue closed-door policies. We have tasted the bitter experience as our ancestors tasted it…China was made poor and became backward and mired in darkness and ignorance.'[13] Since Deng, it developed faster than any nation, including second-half 20th-century Japan and Korea. It interacted with the world, not demanding tribute, but on a willing buyer-seller basis, relying on huge import and export volumes to maintain growth and social stability. Human choices battling geographical determinism in this period are displayed by Russia's Ivan IV and Peter the Great, trying to turn it towards the maritime west for economic benefit. Religiously narrow Castile contrasted with merchant-driven Aragon-Catalonia. When any militant religion drives leaders, its spells disaster for trade and wealth creation. French kings never understood the maritime merchant-driven world, the dynamic of ports and trade, instead concentrating on dynastic goals, whereas late-medieval England began the journey to a national maritime merchant future, encapsulated in the late-1430s *Libelle of Englyshe Polycye*,

The *leitmotif* of continental outlooks is a striving for uniformity. Charlemagne said conquered pagans refusing baptism or assisting cremation should die. For not baptising children, they were heavily fined.[14] Notker noted 'Charlemagne… grieved that the provinces and even the regions and cities differed in divine service, namely the manner of chant.' His and successors aim was 'absolute uniformity… an idea towards which ever closer approximations were made,'[15] as Spanish and Slavonic liturgy was suppressed from the 10th century. As Franks expanded, they equated east Europe's non-Christians with Celtic Christian variants.[16] In 849 a monk who thought men were predestined to heaven and hell irrespective of good or bad deeds was summoned to a synod, flogged almost to death, and ordered to keep quiet. When he died, his books and authorities cited were publicly burned.[17] In the

1230s Peter des Roches, bishop of Winchester thought Europe's enemies should be subjected to 'one Catholic Church...one shepherd and one fold.'[18] The papacy authorised the Albigensian Crusade, the largest, bloodiest Christian persecution. In the 1200s, the Inquisition burned philosophical books.

Many European countries expelled Jews, most significantly, Spain in 1492, shortly thereafter Portugal and forced conversion of Muslims in Grenada in 1499, Castile in 1502 and Aragon in 1526. But it was not uniform enough. Muslim and Jew converts were also expelled. Obsession with purity of religion and blood was absurd since huge swathes of Iberia's population were Phoenician/Carthaginian Semite descendants who converted to Judaism, many then to Catholicism, marrying indigenous Iberians, including nobles. In the Americas, burning native books and symbols, conversion rather than trade opportunities, were the goals. Spain's warmongering Philip II aimed to rule as 'one monarchy, one empire and one sword,' while overtaxing his subjects in repeated famines. His equally warmongering Ottoman opponent's aim was 'one empire, one faith, one sovereignty for the world.' Mughal monarch Aurangzeb tested the Muslim uniformity model to destruction, costing millions of lives and his dynasty. Loss of life in wars between merchant states was negligible compared with religious and dynastic wars and steppe nomad conquests.

Merchants and monarchs had different world views, aims and means of exercising power. Ports offered the greatest opportunity for concentration of human and material capital. Monarchs saw opportunities to take money from merchants, exchanged for privileges. Merchants aimed for profit, monarchs at power extension, regardless of the cost in lives or material losses. Food supply drove much of the shipping market; necessities like grains, fish and salt and desirables like fruit, nuts, sugar, spices, cacao, coffee and tea. Maritime merchants created networks, law codes and systems transcending rulers' territories, cooperating to take products to where they were needed, based on pragmatism, trust and tolerance, enhancing people's lives, sometimes saving them; Mediterranean grain to north Europe in 1317 and north Europe's grain to the Mediterranean in the 1590s. Fujian province's 1594 famine, ignored by its government, was rescued by maize and sweet potato shipments.

Shipping and maritime trade also opened minds. Europe's Renaissance, the re-learning or rebirth of classical enquiry, happened in maritime, not continental Europe. Ports were the gateway to new ideas brought by merchants. Frederick II Hohenstaufen encouraged new ideas at Messina, but it was Venice's, Genoa's and Pisa's trade with the Muslim world that helped Europe re-learn commercial practices. Its merchant enclaves in Alexandria and Constantinople brought wealth, benefitting hinterlands; Florence, Lucca and southern Germany. Practical, problem-solving, maritime trading environments were inimical to authoritarian popes demanding unquestioning obedience and uniformity. North Europe's Renaissance was also concentrated in Netherlands' ports, brought by sea by the first Genoese and Venetian ships to discharge in Bruges and London, just as France destroyed Champagne's great medieval fairs, the previous north-south European merchant interchange. Guilds educated its members in apprenticeships and sponsored schools.[19] The first insurance, banking, bourses, double-entry bookkeeping and other commercial solutions started in ports. Late-17th century English scientific discoveries and simultaneous commercial expansion was also no coincidence. Political stability and enquiring minds fostered such mentality.

Practical, intellectual innovation and cultural advance as part of maritime culture was a major theme in *How Maritime Trade and the Indian Subcontinent Shaped the World*. It is universally true. Robert Lopez persuasively points out that European medieval merchants, especially Italians and north Europeans, were in the vanguard of cultural, mathematical and scientific advance, but finds no 'consistent correlation between economic and cultural peaks', noting that Victorian England was richer and more powerful than Elizabethan England but Kipling was not as good as Shakespeare.[20] To expect an equation of trade volumes with literature's creativity, depicted by one Victorian and one Elizabethan author, is surely misguided. Throughout Britain's maritime ascendancy, she produced Marlowe, Milton, Swift, Byron, Defoe, Shelley, Blake, Burns, Keats, Coleridge, Southey, Wordsworth, Austin, Dickens, many others plus numerous creative scientists and philosophers. The spirit of Francis Bacon's demand for planned investigation, scientific method and inventions spilled over into a broader cultural advance, leading to the scientific revolution, commercial revolution, technical revolution, financial revolution and industrial revolution, all stemming from a maritime outlook. Consistently, cultural, scientific, engineering and intellectual advances were products of maritime orientated societies. Lopez puzzles however, that 'the Renaissance came later than the economic spurt of the Middle Ages.'[21] But he wrote when the Renaissance was seen as a late-15th to early-16th century north Italian phenomenon. Modern historians like Felipe Fernandez-Armesto see it more evolving from the 13th century,[22] in which case, it is logically consistent. Lopez' caveats to his main point are thus misguided. He was 100% correct without them. Fewer cultural luminaries in Portugal were probably because its years of maritime curiosity were imbued with religious Reconquista fervour and extinguished very quickly.

Choke points continued to be important. Battles occurred there when those regions and sea-lanes had economic importance; Sluys (1340), the Armada (1588), many Anglo-Dutch wars' battles, and those against France; Beachy Head (1690), Barfleur (1692), La Hoge (1692) and Malaga (1704). Hundred Year War land battles, Agincourt and Crecy for example, are often characterised as part of a dynastic war. Not so. Location, as with Sluys, was key. Northern Europe's most important trade, especially for England and the Netherlands was wool. France's continuing late-13th to early-19th century aim to acquire control of Flanders would have destroyed it. England had to defend it. In doing so, it began its journey from an agricultural economy to one of trade. By the mid-16th century, its foreign policy and maritime trade were two sides of the same coin, briefly lost by early Stuart kings. In the Channel, the Battle of the Downs (1639), the Thirty Years War's most decisive naval battle, another vain Spanish attempt to smash the commercial Dutch, confirmed the irretrievable decline of Spain, Dutch pre-eminence, and soon

Portuguese independence. Medieval concentration on the Baltic entrance reflected its ports' hinterlands and products importance. The Kra Isthmus, Malacca and Sunda Straits, Hormuz Straits, Bosporus and Dardanelles continued their role. Islam's locking of the Mediterranean-Indian Ocean choke point was the main reason for Europe's slow recovery.

This book's main theme also relates to the subject, when, how and why did Europe dominate in the last 300 years. Many historians have made contributions but none have concentrated on maritime trade and few offer an analysis further back than 1700. Nevertheless, such wide-ranging studies contrast with historical specialisation. As Janet Abu-Lughod pointedly remarks in support of tackling wider subjects, 'the price of concentration is often a loss of peripheral vision.'

The book continues examples of ideas diffused through maritime trade routes, the Renaissance to north Europe, Protestantism to the Baltic and North Sea, Islam in Southeast Asia and at the end of this period, the scientific revolution developed by Dutch and English, the two foremost 17th-century maritime nations. The Americas were influenced by its English, Spanish and Portuguese settlers and their homelands' values and institutions. Their products influenced European fashions; tobacco, beaver skin hats, potatoes and chocolate. Asian trade influenced Europe's obsession with spices, tea, coffee, silk, cotton cloth and porcelain.

Stopping trading, interacting and learning leads to stagnation. Maritime commerce involves interaction with culturally, racially and linguistically different people. It promotes creative thinking, seen in China until the mid-14th century, maritime India, Southeast Asia, Abbasid Baghdad, Genoa, Venice, Barcelona, Antwerp, Amsterdam and London. These were dynamic, challenging, problem-solving places where improvements in navigation, understanding distant markets, insurance, currencies, law codes and tastes were tackled, literature and other art-forms encouraged, compared to conservative agricultural areas where life was governed by seasons and literacy was a luxury. Shipping and trading created employment for sail and ropemakers, chandlers, shipbuilders, innkeepers and architects, creating vibrant, tolerant, educated, wealthy societies. Merchants had always invested profits in community religious devotion. Fortunes made from the medieval wool trade are demonstrated in small English villages with huge churches erected by wool merchants. European Protestant merchant philanthropy switched to secular education. Tamil merchants generously donated to temples serving their communities in banking, lending and charity.

In these 1,000 years, an apparent new factor made important contributions; Jewish merchants and artisans in Iberia, Egypt, India, Anatolia, Italian ports, the Netherlands, England and the Americas. These were ancient Phoenician and Carthaginian descendants from North Africa and Iberia. After the Third Punic War they converted to Judaism; their own gods discredited by defeat. Their enterprising culture was however, never compromised and was essential to Europe's economic recovery. While the narrative endeavours to be accessible, those unfamiliar with shipping terms are recommended to read the Glossary before reading what follows.

Part I

Vibrant Indian Ocean and Dark Age Europe Trade

Chapter 1

China's T'ang Dynasty and the Rise of Srivijaya

Indian Ocean and South China Sea 7th-8th-century regional and long-haul trade was much influenced by China, unified by the Sui Dynasty (587–617) whose austere programme, banning luxury aromatics and spices from Southeast Asia, reduced demand. T'ang Dynasty emperors after 617 however, despite official Confucian disdain for foreign luxuries, became interested and as demand increased, Southeast Asian exporters became richer and formed polities. China's population was already drifting south towards the coast. The Sui's Grand Canal (605–609) consolidated by the T'ang, linked Hangzhou with Chang'an (Xi'an) which had one to two million people, 106 walled districts and nine markets specialising in east African, Persian, Arabian, Indian and Southeast Asian products; pistachios, frankincense, myrrh, dates, birds' nests, benzoin, cotton cloths, saffron, pepper, fragrant woods and ambergris from multiple origins. Thus by 700, already vibrant maritime trade from the Gulf and east Africa to China accelerated, bringing wealth and rising populations, especially on China's south coast. By the mid-8th century, there were an estimated 200,000 Persian, Arab, Indian and Malay merchants living in Guangzhou who self-regulated internal disputes. China's ancient seafaring merchants, Austronesian Yue, may have remained until the 8th century before being fully sinicised.[1] The story of Aunt Yu's huge coastal trading ship on which people were born, married and died with hundreds of crew, 'reaping enormous profits',[2] sounds reminiscent of them. The 742-census recorded half of China's population in the south compared with only a quarter in the early-600s. Increased maritime trade was both cause and effect. The 754-census documented 1,859 cities and 50 million people. Art, poetry and literature were encouraged. Many of China's great poets lived at this time; 48,900 poems by 2,200 poets survive.[3] Calligraphy was refined, printed books appeared, block-painting introduced, history promoted and there were medical and astronomical advances. Churches, mosques and synagogues were allowed; in short, the familiar juxtaposition of maritime trade, toleration, cultural and intellectual progress.

The Mekong delta port, Oc-Eo, had been Southeast Asia's main entrepot for China between the 2nd and 5th centuries. Thereafter, no Southeast Asian polity dominated until Palembang sent its first embassies to China about 670–673. Its heart was a 10–15-kilometre, deep-drafted stretch of the Musi River, protected by defensible mangrove swamps. It accessed upstream forest products and was close to the Malacca Straits, convenient while waiting for changing monsoon winds. In 682, its ruler Jayanasu conquered Malayu's capital Jambi, its northern neighbour on the Batang Hari River, which had gold and forest products. A 683 Chinese visit seemingly formalised tributary status of this enlarged, newly forming polity to the Chinese emperor, Son of Heaven, presenting its products in return for presents. This was Srivijaya, 'radiant' in Sanskrit, to the Chinese, Sanfotsi, to Arabs, Zabag. To ensure economic stability, it needed control of the Kra Isthmus and Malacca and Sunda Straits, the region's maritime choke points. In 686, it annexed tin-rich Bangka Island, off east coast Sumatra and Tarumanagara on Java, controlling the Sunda Strait's east bank. Taruma means indigo. India was its first producer and exporter. Tarumanagara thus presumably indicates a major indigo import and distribution port. Colonising south Sumatra, Palembang took control of the west bank too. Kedah on the Kra Isthmus, en route to India, became subservient around 685–689. Barus in north Sumatra followed. By the 750s, central Java's Holing kingdom, which controlled Molucca's spice exports was also conquered. Panpan, controlling the short trans-Kra Isthmus route from Takua Pa to Chaiya was added about 775, which developed high-volume trade. Srivijaya's tributary status to China was convenient fiction. Its exchange of tribute for presents; trade masquerading as tribute, paid well. It was also good for China's economy. The Grand Canal enabled southern rice and imports to be shipped north. Its rivers enabled east-west transport. River traffic was so heavy that storms in Yangzhou in 721 and 751 led to the destruction of over 1,000 boats each time.[4] Jingdezhen's porcelain industry, started in the 3rd century, was enlarged, improved and became a major export.

Srivijaya's maritime empire was a federation built on cooperation. Its dependent entrepots collected cargo bound to China, India and the Gulf; pepper from Sunda in west Java, considered the best quality, camphor, aloes, cloves, sandalwood, nutmeg, cardamom, ivory, gold and tin. They were transferred to larger ships for long-haul transport to main markets, similar to today's container and tanker feeders consolidating in Singapore. Traders found all regional products in Palembang, also a centre of Buddhist learning. Chinese pilgrim I-Tsing recommended those wanting to study Buddhist texts in India, should spend a year there first.

The rise of T'ang China and Srivijaya increased Indian Ocean trade opportunities. Toleration, porcelain and silk attracted more Indian, Arab and Persian merchants, living in Guangzhou's merchant enclaves for centuries. A Chinese document from 727 reads, 'the Po-ssi [Persians] being by nature bent on commerce...are in the habit of sailing in big craft...enter the Indian Ocean to Sri Lanka, where they get precious stones...also to the K'unlun country [Sumatra] to fetch gold. They also sail in big craft to China for silk piece goods.' Persians dominated Gulf-China trade. In 671, before Palembang's first embassies to China, I-Tsing, sailing in a Persian ship from Guangzhou to Palembang, noted over 1,000 ships there. A 717 Indian 35-ship convoy was recorded sailing from Sri Lanka to Palembang, arriving at Guangzhou in 720. From 671 to 748 Persians, Indians and Southeast Asians were listed in Chinese documents as Guangzhou shipowners. In 748, Chinese monk Jian Zhen, said that on a trip between Hainan and Guangzhou he saw countless vessels

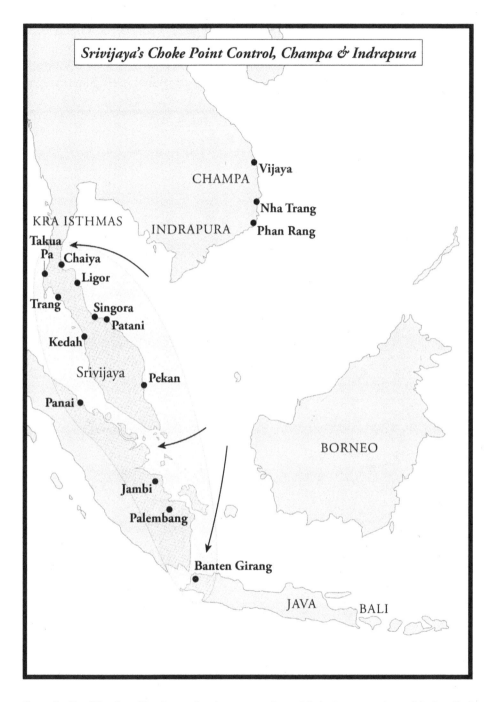

Srivijaya's Choke Point Control, Champa & Indrapura

CHAMPA

Vijaya

Nha Trang

KRA ISTHMAS   INDRAPURA   Phan Rang

Takua Pa

Chaiya

Ligor

Trang

Singora

Patani

Kedah

Srivijaya   Pekan

Panai

BORNEO

Jambi

Palembang

Banten Girang

JAVA   BALI

from India, K'unlun, Persia, and other countries with 'spices, pearls and jade piled up mountains high'. There was a Persian enclave in Hainan in 748.[5] Quanzhou and Fuzhou also grew as trade expanded. The 9th-century *Ling Biao Lu Yi* (*Strange Things Noted in the South*) described Arab ships with planks 'strapped together with coir palm fibre. All seams…caulked with an olive paste', also described in the mid-1st century *Periplus of the Erythraean Sea*, identified as an Omani speciality.[6]

The 2013 discovery of the 35 metre-long, mid-8th century Phanom Surin wreck, south of Bangkok altered previous impressions of a mainly Gulf-China trade, to

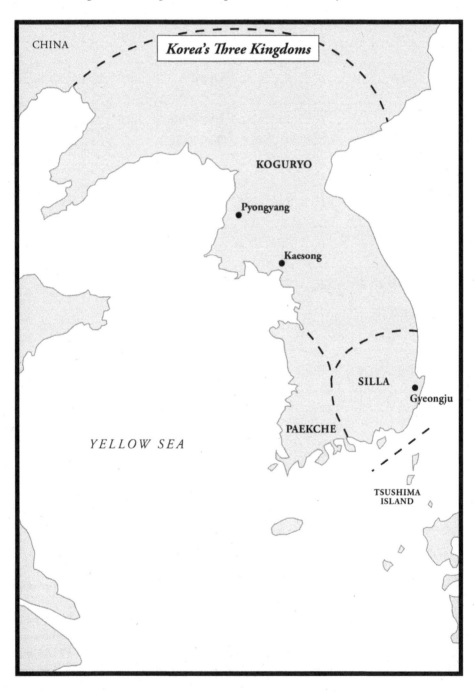

one encompassing all maritime areas between. Chinese, Mesopotamian and local Mon ceramics onboard apparently belonged to the crew. Its cargo was ivory, local antler horn and Mesopotamian torpedo-type jars, also found in an Abbasid palace built in 836 in Samara, an east African 8th-century coastal settlement, Basra, Siraf, Bushehr, Sri Lanka and China. A 6th-century mural at Ajanta, western India, depicts a three-masted ship carrying similar jars, used until the 11th century. The mural's narrative concerns a virtuous sandalwood merchant from the Buddhist *Purnavadana*. The jar's Persian Pahlavi inscription concerns Zoroastrian themes.

A Chinese-Pahlavi bi-lingual inscription of 874 from a Persian woman's tomb in a merchant enclave in Tumon, Shangxi province, northwest China, also appears in the 849–850 west coast India Quilon copper plate recording trading privileges granted by a local Malayalam ruler to Levantine merchants, written in Tamil and witnessed with Arabic, Pahlavi and Judeo-Persian names, contemporary with the wreck, and a Pahlavi inscription from near Palembang confirms Persian merchants in Palembang, Quilon, Chinese ports and southern Siam, an extensive maritime network linking regional inland trade. The wreck, between the Tha Chin and Chao Phraya rivers, linked Phetchaburi, Kha Bua, Ratchaburi, Nakhon Pathom, Pong Tuck, Lopburi, U Thong and Si Thep with Gulf of Thailand ports. Guangdong Yue ceramics on-board suggest it had already visited Guangzhou.[7]

Korean and Japanese trade was controlled mainly by Korea's Silla and Paekche kingdoms' merchants, mainly silk, porcelain, sandalwood, pepper, incense, camphor, musk, spices, horses, ivory, cotton textiles and slaves. Its Koguryo kingdom's trade was conducted by several hundred Fujianese. T'ang goods spread to Southeast Asia, India, Sri Lanka, the Gulf, Red Sea, Fustat (Old Cairo), Antioch, Constantinople, the Comoros islands and Zanzibar. Chinese inbound cargo entered customs sheds and 30% duty taken, the remainder bought by the government. The Chinese Inspector of Maritime Trade registered each foreign master, checked manifestos, collected duties and forbade the export of rare products. It took six months from Siraf in Persia to Guangzhou, where the summer was spent and six months back. Arabs and Persians competed with Tamils and Southeast Asians for Bay of Bengal trade.

Chinese trade restrictions and inland problems caused setbacks. In 684 K'unlun merchants killed Guangzhou's governor. In 755, Luoyang and Chang'an were conquered by rebel An Lushan, triggered by the 751 defeat at Talas in Kazakhstan by an Islamic army interested in Silk Road riches.[8] North China became independent from south China, whose port Hangzhou, southern terminus of the Grand Canal, was made the new capital. The victorious Islamic army took papermakers from Talas to Baghdad. With Chinese forces occupied in the north, in 758 Arab, Persian and other merchants plundered Guangzhou, probably connected with corrupt Chinese officials, laws restricting contact with Chinese women and high duties; enduring themes. The rebellion lasted until 763 and Tibet raided it until 777. Guangzhou was therefore closed between 758 and 792, but trade continued via Champa's ports, central in a trade network covering Indo-China, north Borneo, the Philippines and

Cambodia, all alternative forest product sources for China; aloes, eaglewood, rhino horn, ivory, etc. competing with Srivijayan products.

Champa's ports, Phan Rang and Nha Trang, as entrepots for Chinese ports, must have significantly disadvantaged Srivijaya, which was presumably why it conducted 35 years of raids from 767.[9] Most were unsuccessful, although Phan Rang was destroyed in 787. One resulted in the lower Mekong's Indrapura's conquest.[10] Srivijaya's other choke points were ruled by loyal subordinates. Indrapura was given to Jayavarman II, possibly a former hostage, seemingly remotely linked to the old Khmer dynasty[11] giving local legitimacy. He had apparently been indoctrinated in the benefits of Srivijayan overlordship, but on arrival in 802, he established an inland kingdom away from its maritime reach. Angkor Wat was later built there. With Guangzhou re-opened in 792, Champa's ports weakened, ending Srivijaya's attacks in 802. Guangzhou's Arab, Persian and Indian merchant enclave re-formed.

Another disruption was in central Java, where family factions including a Sailendra, related to Palembang's Sailendras, ruled. One of them completed Borobudur in 825, an outstanding Buddhist monument, with carvings of ships showing masts, rudders and outriggers, an evolution from original Austronesian designs. Java's Sailendras lost influence to the Sanjayas and Srivijaya lost direct control in 856, although the Sanjayas may also have been related. They continued to dominate spice distribution with Srivijayan cooperation.[12] Confusion arises because of the paucity of evidence and various spellings from different sources in

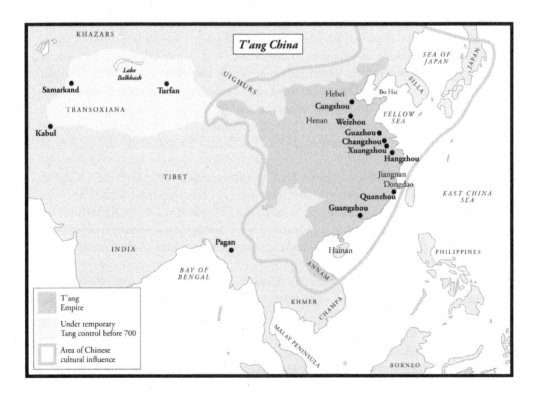

multiple languages. That Jambi sent its own missions to China in 852 and 871 suggests political difficulties, and that strong commercial imperatives were the main motivations. From around 900 an inscription found close to Manila in Sanskrit, old Javanese, Malay and Tagalog indicates 8th-9th century Javanese trade enclaves on Luzon. Little is known about Srivijaya between 860 and 990. The long period of economic expansion must have eased tensions with Champa,[13] whose capital in 877 moved to Quang Nam (Da Nang).

Despite the loss of Indrapura and direct central Javan control, Srivijaya prospered because of continued strong Chinese demand. It also received many enthusiastic endorsements from Gulf traders and travellers. One from Siraf wrote *Sulayman's Travels in India and China* (c. 851). He described a Javanese port. 'The city of Kalah is a market in which are concentrated the trades of sandalwood, ivory, tin, ebony, brazilwood and all kinds of spices and herbs which would be too long to describe.' Others noted Srivijaya's maharajah's custom of daily collecting gold ingots to place in water. On his death they were distributed. 'Among the kings of Zabag, it is a glory to have a long life and to leave…the greatest number of gold ingots.'

Chinese ceramic exports probably only re-started after Guangzhou's re-opening in 792. Ninth-century volumes grew significantly. Abbasid copies were exported to east Africa. All long-haul trade to and from China was in non-Chinese ships, the largest from Sri Lanka, up to 70 metres long. The Chinese called the South China Sea 'Bahr Sankhai', Spice Sea, denoting the cargoes most demanded.[14] Indian cotton cloth, frankincense, indigo, ivory, precious woods, tortoiseshell and aromatic oils were also popular. A shipwreck off southeast Sumatra near Belitung Island, which ceramic stamps and carbon dating suggest sank between 826 and 838, demonstrates rich maritime trade. An 18 by 8 metre teak-built Arab ship with planks stitched together with coir palm fibre, carried over 63,000 gold, silver and ceramic plates and vessels, among which the largest T'ang gold cup found and some fine Yueware from Zhenjiang province, a porcelain whose delicacy the Chinese compared to snow. But most cargo was mass-produced; 40,000 painted and decorated Changsha bowls from Hunan kilns, 1,000 miniature funeral urns, gold cups, bronze mirrors, silver boxes and 800 inkpots; testimony to literacy in maritime areas. Some had Islamic and Manichaean writing, probably bound for Basra and Baghdad. It also carried gemstones, three Persian blue and white dishes decorated with cobalt, a Persian import, aromatic resins and spices probably loaded en route from China. Maritime trade fostered more than luxury goods. It was well-organised, large-scale, customer-specific export production. The ship probably foundered approaching Palembang.

Al-Masudi (896–956) wrote, 'in the sea of Champa is the empire of the Maharaja, the king of the islands, who rules over an empire without limit and has innumerable troops. Even the most rapid vessels could not complete in two years, a tour round the isles…under his possession. The territories of this king produce all sorts of spices and aromatics and no other sovereign…gets as much wealth from the soil.' Srivijayan merchants were in India, settled Madagascar over centuries and competed in east Africa, trading and raiding, unsuccessfully in the case of Qanbalu on Pemba Island in 945. They wanted ivory, tortoiseshell, panther skins, slaves and ambergris,[15] a sperm whale excretion, then ubiquitous, as valuable as gold, found on beaches, which 'fixed' perfumes, scented oil lamps, and in China was considered an aphrodisiac.[16] African slaves were taken to Madagascar for agricultural labour in terraced rice fields, similar to those in Indonesia and Philippines. Vestiges of Hinduism and Sanskrit are found in Madagascan religion and language, indicating Indian influence. A Malagasy language study found the greatest affinities with south Kalimantan languages, that is from forest-dwelling dayaks rather than maritime Malays, concluding that dayaks were probably slaves, crew or labourers. Isolated in Madagascar, they tended to use the language of the majority, absorbing influences from other groups.[17]

While encouraging this exceptional trade growth, the Chinese were passive recipients. Guangzhou's foreign trader enclaves thus stoked resentment and xenophobia. As early as 840 emperor Wuzong blamed foreign ideologies and foreign trader enclaves for tough times. In 878, rebel Huang Cho sacked Guangzhou and, according to Abu-Zayd, slaughtered 120,000 Muslims, Zoroastrians, Jews and Christians, the number known due to the Chinese census of foreigners for taxation. Many moved to other ports, but some stayed as he said the rebels oppressed them, imposing legal burdens, appropriating their wealth.[18] They also tried to destroy mulberry groves providing its silk exports. After this, foreign trade concentrated more at Quanzhou on the Taiwan Strait, further from inland political interference with a better harbour and long-standing connections with Japan and Korea, attracting foreign traders.[19] In 880, Chang'an was destroyed and the T'ang collapsed in 907 with inflation, drought and plague, resulting in various unstable northern dynasties and ten small southern kingdoms, including in Guangdong and Fujian provinces, the Nan Han and Min, increasing demand for spices and exotic goods. Foreign traders continued living in Guangzhou, Quanzhou and Fuzhou. The kingdoms lasted 50–60 years until reunified by the Song, continuing growth in trade, industry and agriculture. They were a major turning point in Fujian's history, emphasising maritime trade, its major strength, essential to its future prosperity.[20] North Java's Intan wreck, about 300 tons, 30 metres long, from about 942 had a cargo of Chinese ceramics, Thai ceramics, bronze, tin, lead and silver ingots, gold jewellery, mirrors and Arab glass.[21] West Java's smaller Cirebon shipwreck, Southeast Asian in origin, dated to 968 carried over 300,000 Yue celadon vessels, pearls, precious stones, Indian and Javanese bronzeware, Egyptian glassware and Islamic jewellery. Overall, Arab, Persian, Indian and Southeast Asian ships carried hundreds of thousands of varied objects, probably also perishable cargo considerable distances; a rich, voluminous trade.

Chapter 2

Baghdad, Persian Gulf and Omani Trade with East Africa and India

C hristianity promoted poverty's 'virtues'. 'Blessed are the poor for yours is the kingdom of Heaven.' The idea originated from Hebrew anti-trade, anti-Phoenician prejudices, much voiced by *Ezekiel*, for example, originating in Indian asceticism.[1] Some Muslim ideology however, was from the Prophet's own trading background. The *Koran* praises fair market practice and merchants' ships are mentioned as a sign of God's bounty. 'Surely in the creation of the heavens and the earth, in the alteration of night and day; in the sailing of ships through the ocean for the profit of mankind...here are signs for a people who understand.'[2] 'You see ships ploughing in it that you may seek [profit] from his abundance and that you may give thanks.'[3] 'He sends the winds as tokens of glad tidings so that you may sample this mercy; that ships may sail by His command so you may see His bounty and be grateful.'[4] There are many more passages on trade in the *hadith*, stories of Mohammed's life.

The Prophet's actions had partly been a reaction against Persian aggression in Yemen to protect Arab Red Sea trading interests in economic depression. But when the first Umayyad caliph chose Damascus as the caliphate's capital to concentrate war against Constantinople, he strengthened the overland Persian Gulf-Levant route, further side-lining the Red Sea, declining since the mid-2nd century collapse of Roman-Indian Ocean trade.

Growing T'ang China-Srivijaya trade led Caliph al-Mansur (r. 754–775), after overthrowing the Umayyads in 750, to search for a new capital for his Abbasid Dynasty in Mesopotamia, which could be strengthened by importing east African slaves to make southern marshes agriculturally productive. The chosen site, 20 miles either side of the Tigris and Euphrates, was ideal. Canals to both gave it access to seaborne commerce. Named Madinat al-Salam, 'the City of Peace', it continued to be called its village's original name; Baghdad. Completed in 766, it was circular, the Round City, two miles across, surrounded by three walls, up to 112 feet, encircling gardens and bazaars. The population grew fast inside and outside the walls, then to the other side of the Tigris. By 800 it had around a million people.

Baghdad became a thriving inland port, a centre of wealth, luxury, culture and intellectual endeavour. Geographer al-Ya'qubi put these words into al-Mansur's mouth. 'It is an island between the Tigris and Euphrates...a waterfront for the world...[ships] can come....and unload here', transferring cargo to river boats for further distribution. He boasted, 'there is no obstacle between us and China, everything on the sea can come to us on it.'⁵ Al-Mansur's much-quoted 766 boast demonstrates the reason for his choice. He deliberately targeted rich Indian Ocean trade to China. Srivijaya had consolidated 70 years before. Al-Mansur initiated an equally bold plan for the same reasons, despite Guangzhou's 758 closure.

Mesopotamia and Persia became great demand centres for imports. Basra, Bahrain, Siraf and Hormuz continued the role of ports en route to India and east Africa via Oman. Early Islamic historian Sayf ibn Uamr (d. 796) described Dibba, a port beyond the Hormuz Straits, as 'a large settlement thronged with people and thriving with trade.' Mecca's importance as the birthplace of Islam led to the annual 'hajj' influx of pilgrims, fed by Egyptian wheat exports to Jeddah, its port. The Indian Ocean's vast trade area became open to Islam with Omanis and Yemenis gradually overtaking Persians as the main carriers. By contrast, desert nomads were North Africa's Islamic conquerors, their culture, pastoralism and the 'ghazu', caravan raiding. Raiding not trading was Mediterranean Muslims' imperative. Continental Islamic armies attempted conversion by force. Islam was culturally split between a militant continental and tolerant maritime mentality. The Prophet's pro-trade words inspired Muslim merchants. Abu al-Fadl's late-9th-century *The Beauties of Commerce* cautions, 'excessive pursuit of gain is the road to loss' and quotes the Prophet, 'whoever is blessed with fortune in one enterprise should devote himself to it.'⁶

As always, trade and intellectual endeavour went hand-in-hand. Al-Mansur according to historian al-Masudi (896–956) 'was the first caliph to have books translated from foreign languages into Arabic' including 'Aristotle on logic and other subjects, and ancient books from classical Greek, Byzantine Greek, Pahlavi, neo-Persian and Syriac.' He had three astronomers and pioneered remaking the ancient Greek astrolabe. One practical reason to translate world knowledge was caliphate administration. State secretaries learned arithmetic, geometry, astronomy, surveying and civil engineering. Al-Mansur encouraged the study of medicine and oversaw Baghdad's first hospital. It imported pepper, cinnamon, ginger, coconuts, cloves, nutmeg, mace, camphor and sandalwood from Southeast Asia, Egyptian linen and grain, Armenian carpets, Levantine glass and fruit, Arabian perfumes, Sri Lankan rubies, Chinese silks and porcelain, Persian metalwork, gold, ivory and slaves. Arabs took-over trades from Indians. Even Chinese goods to India went in Arab or Persian vessels. Ships sailed up the Tigris and Euphrates and sometimes merchants continued to the Caspian and Black Seas where Swedish/Rus traders came with furs, wax, honey, ivory, iron, animal skins and amber. (Chapter 3) Harun al-Rashid (r. 786–809) brought Baghdad to the height of trade-created wealth, power and creativity. It was a city of canals, scholars, specialty markets and over 800 book sellers. Siraf's abu-Zayd wrote, 'sea-traffic at that time [851] was regular because of the great exchange of merchants between al-Iraq and those countries [India and China].'⁷

Al-Mamun (r. 813–833) continued al-Mansur's and al-Rashid's work. Their agents in Constantinople, Armenia, the Levant and Egypt collected Greek

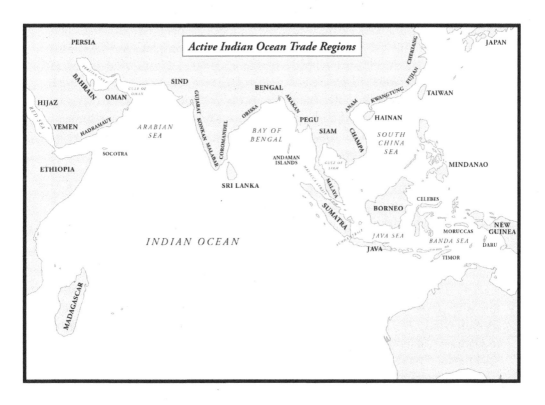

manuscripts to translate, some the only surviving record. Atomic theory re-emerged, influenced by both Greek and Buddhist writings. The preface of Al-Khwarizmi's (c. 780–847) treatise on algebra (al-jabr) said Al-Mamun 'encouraged me to compose a compendium work on algebra, confining it to the fine and important parts of its calculations, such as people constantly require in cases of inheritance, legacies, partitions, lawsuits and trade and in all their dealings with one another or where surveying, the digging of canals, geometrical computation' is concerned. He wrote *Concerning the Hindu Art of Reckoning*, based on a translation of Indian mathematician Brahmagupta and on astronomy using Greek and Indian works, laying the foundation of modern mathematics, introducing the Indian place system and algorithmic calculations. He built the first Arabic observatory in 828, wrote on geography, revised Ptolemy's work and drew new maps. Only Constantinople's 600,000 people in 800 rivalled Baghdad's one million, perhaps 1.5 million by the 10th century, when all classic trigonometric functions were defined and tabulated.

The idea of reason, 'ijtihad', that god could only be understood through unaided, individual reason, was expounded by al-Kindi (800–873), al-Razi (865–925), al-Farabi (873–950) and others. Ibn Rushd (1126–98) thought scientific enquiry could only be achieved by separation from religious dogma. They challenged ancient Greek thought by reason. Better instruments and methods would get more accurate results. Books on optics, medicine, astronomy and hygiene were produced. Science based on experiment was an early Islamic renaissance, an intellectual revolution[8] predating 17th-century maritime Europe's similar breakthrough by half a millennium. This 'falsafa' movement, from Greek 'philosophia', was ascendant against the 'ulama', religious scholars rejecting rational science as a threat to revelatory 'religious science'. Damascus and Cordoba were also hubs of art, literature, maths and astronomy, the latter, more due to ex-Carthaginian Jews, carrying the same ethos. Commercial lending, banks and cheques developed. Polo, backgammon and chess became popular. Thanks to Baghdad's scientists, Arabic scientific words entered the English language; alchemy, algebra, algorithm, alcohol, alembic, alkali, azimuth, borax, camphor, cipher, elixir, nadir, zenith. Religious toleration was normal. Christians and Jews, if competent and learned, were promoted. Jews produced their Phoenician-heritage glassware in various colours, shapes and designs.

Paper manufacture, started in Baghdad in 794, helped increase book circulation and spread literacy. Persecuted by Byzantines, Nestorian and Monophysites translators moved to Baghdad to pursue their studies and religion. Abbasid schools offered Greek studies in medicine, philosophy, music, maths, geography, zoology, botany, meteorology, astronomy, grammar and rhetoric. Nestorian Hunayn ibn Ishaq (809–873) travelled to Byzantium to search for Galen's 2nd-century medical book, *On Demonstration*. He found half of it 'in disorder and incomplete in Damascus'. His *On the Anatomy of Nerves* was also translated. They helped Arab scientists and philosophers break new ground. Al-Harun founded the world's first free public hospital. Al-Razi experimented for the healthiest place to locate it. Ibn-Sina (980–1037) wrote a medical encyclopaedia and the first clinical account of smallpox. *The Qanun* described diseases and how to use 760 drugs. Later translated into Latin, it dominated European medical studies. Baghdad had 860 licensed physicians. Libraries of Arab scholars had almost all the great ancient Greek works in translation, available to everyone.

Stories in *The Thousand and One Nights* show Baghdad as a city of glamour, intrigue, magic, philosophers, mathematicians and astronomers, reflecting marvellous new sciences, inventions and discoveries by wizard-scientists in which fictional Sinbad gave an accurate account of trade. 'I bought...merchandise all needed for a voyage and impatient to be at sea, I embarked...on board a ship for Basra...and sailed many days and nights, and we passed from isle-to-isle and sea-to-sea and shore-to-shore, buying...selling and bartering everywhere the ship touched' and 'I have traded fabrics for ginger and camphor; cinnamon and spiked cloves for ambergris, ivory and pearls.'

At the mouth of the Tigris-Euphrates, Basra, between Baghdad and northwest India, was the main Abbasid port and intellectual centre, 'seaport of the world, goldmine of trade and capital,' mainly with Indian goods and merchants, so much that Arabs said it belonged to 'Al-Hind'; India. Its late-9th century Al-Jahiz's *The Investigation of Commerce* lists elephants, rubies, ebony, sandalwood, coconuts, Chinese silk, porcelain, pepper, ink, cinnamon, gold, silver, Yemeni skins and incense, Maghrib panthers, Arab horses, Egyptian papyrus, topazes and much more from surrounding areas, mainly Indian Ocean goods, a sophisticated,

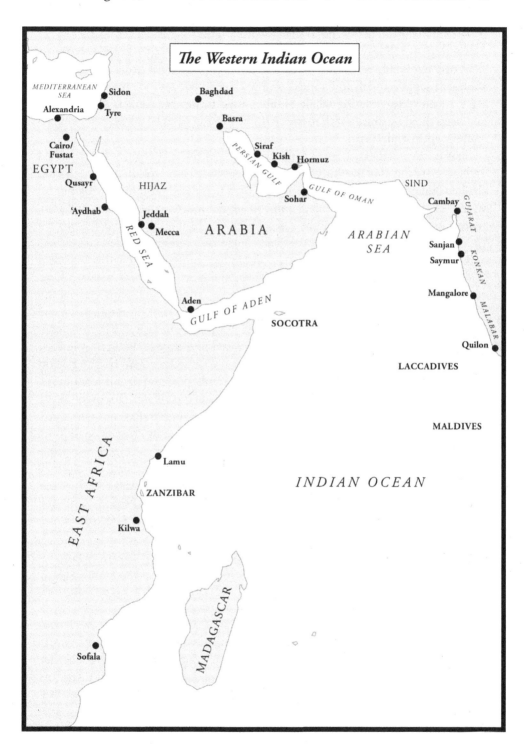

The Western Indian Ocean

MEDITERRANEAN SEA
Sidon
Alexandria
Tyre
Baghdad
Basra
Siraf
Kish
Hormuz
Cairo/ Fustat
EGYPT
PERSIAN GULF
GULF OF OMAN
SIND
Qusayr
HIJAZ
Sohar
Cambay
GUJARAT
'Aydhab
Jeddah
ARABIA
ARABIAN SEA
Sanjan
KONKAN
Mecca
Saymur
RED SEA
Mangalore
MALABAR
Aden
GULF OF ADEN
SOCOTRA
Quilon
LACCADIVES
MALDIVES
EAST AFRICA
Lamu
ZANZIBAR
INDIAN OCEAN
Kilwa
MADAGASCAR
Sofala

prosperous world,[9] including Indian swords, reflecting India's long history of pioneering metallurgy. Al-Muqaddasi (c. 945–991) thought Basra's resources exceeded Baghdad, producing silk, and sourcing pearls and gems. Ubullah had shipyards supplied with Indian teak and Maldivian coconut for masts, ropes and sails, a factory for treating whale blubber, used to protect timbers from rotting and keep them flexible, watch towers with beacons used as lighthouses and signal stations against pirates.

Siraf in the northeast Persian Gulf originated in the 2nd century, had declined and was re-founded in the 8th, becoming among the world's wealthiest ports. Basra's shallow draught explain its rise. Despite its barren, isolated position in a kilometre-wide coastal strip, mountains rising immediately behind, it had deep water and good protection from storms. In 250 hectares, multi-storied merchants' and shipowners' Indian and African teak-built houses had courtyards, fountains, gilded chandeliers and teak-panelled walls, with libraries containing translated works from ancient Greece. An industrial quarter produced pottery and glass. There was metal working, textile and jewellery manufacturing. Horses, pearls, dates, henna, gems, carpets and linens were shipped to India and China. It dealt with Baghdad, Shiraz and Fars and had over a hundred resident Indian merchants.[10] Many more visited. Pirate-bases in Bahrain, Qatar and Persian harbours were crushed by a large Abbasid fleet in 825.

Muslim influence seeped along east Africa's coast, from where traders bought ivory, gold, slaves and iron, selling Arabian rugs, tools, pots and pans, Indian bread, oil, butter, dyes, muslins, jewellery, cloth, metal implements, Maldivian cowrie shells, Thai and Burmese stone jars, Moluccan spices and Chinese silks and porcelains. Eighth-century Arabs and Persians ruled 200 miles of east Africa's coast from Somalia to Sofala. Ninth-century merchants ate off floral-patterned or opaque white Chinese porcelain, drank out of Persian glass goblets, had tortoiseshell combs and cosmetics, and traded leopard skins, ivory, rhino horn and gold. In short, east Africa had wealthy, autonomous ports visited by Indian, Persian, Arab and Southeast Asian merchants. For Arabs it was Zanj, its inhabitants zanj, from which Zanzibar is named. Some went as far as Sofala for gold.

Al-Muqaddasi said of Yemen 'the commerce of this province is important,' describing interlocking Egyptian, Levantine, Mesopotamian and Omani trade in carnelian, leather, slaves, drugs, perfumes, saffron, teak, ivory, pearls, brocade, onyx, rubies, ebony, coconut, sugar, aloes, iron, canes, earthenware, sandalwood, glass, pepper, ambergris, linen, clothes, eunuchs, tiger skins and 'other articles which were we to mention them in detail would unduly prolong the book.'[11] African slaves, worth over five-times white eunuchs in Mesopotamia, built cities, tended plantations, dug canals and mines. There were 11,000 slaves in Baghdad including 7,000 Africans. Iberian Ibn-Jubayr (1145–1217) claimed, 'they are a breed of no regard, and it is no sin to pour maledictions upon them.'[12] In 689 and 694, slave uprisings were suppressed, the last by 4,000 black troops who massacred 10,000 men, women and children. India bought African ivory for its superior carving qualities for jewellery and ornaments. Omanis had long organised east Africa's slave exports to the Gulf.

They settled Mombasa and Lamu, ruled Zanzibar and imported Chinese porcelain, carpets, silks, damasks, perfumes, pearls and glass beads. Persians and Indians also settled east Africa. A Persian ruled in Kilwa in 975, one of his sons in Mafia and his brothers in six other locations in the Comoros and mainland. Kilwa thrived on gold and ivory exports. New towns, mosques and palaces were built on offshore islands or mainland strong points. Eleventh-century Bahrainis founded Mogadishu. Leaders called themselves sultans and minted silver, sometimes gold coins.

The anonymous *Relation of China and India* (851) and Ibn Khordadbeh's *Book of Roads and Kingdoms* (846–85) described sailing routes followed by Siraf's masters en route to China. Ships loaded at Basra and Siraf, sailed to Muscat or Sohar then to the Malabar coast, any imports taxed, then across the Bay of Bengal, provisioning in the Andaman Islands, landing in Kedah to cross the Kra Isthmus, finally to Guangzhou. Cargoes were loaded en route; in Oman frankincense and myrrh, in Gujarat cotton cloths and indigo, in east Africa gold, ivory and slaves, sold in Palembang for Southeast Asian produce and in Guangzhou for porcelain and silk. The Red Sea also sent fleets to Asia. Aden at its entrance was described as 'the gateway to China.'[13] Ibn Khordadbeh described Jewish merchants' alternative Red Sea and Persian Gulf loadports depending on cargo origins.

Northwest Indian ports, trading with the Gulf for millennia, especially strong in the Roman Empire's golden age, were a continuing magnet for Arabs and Persians. Several major land routes converged at Cambay, a major port. Arab and Persian sources mention leather sandal exports, much in demand in Baghdad from Cambay and Sanjan, and emeralds exported to Aden and Mecca.[14] Sanjan in Gujarat, on the River Varoli, founded by Zoroastrian refugees, Parsis, in 698, was frequented by Persian, Arab, Jewish and native traders. Archaeological excavations revealed 8th-13th-century brick buildings, beads, bangles, ceramics, metal objects, glass and coins, indicating a lively economy and sustained contact with the Gulf and China in both luxury and mass-market goods. It was famous for teak and bamboo exports.[15] Ibn Hawqal's *Regions of the World* in 982 described it as a great, vibrant city.

Saymur, today's Chaul was, according to Arab writers, five days further south, populous and full of industrious, intelligent people. Most native Indian merchants tended to be Buddhists or Jains. Malabar coast ports, today's Kerala, welcomed Omanis and Yemenis, whose seafaring and trading tradition continued after Islamic conversion, settling there, as for millennia. Their new religion praising trade resonated with locals and were allowed to build mosques. Some influenced peaceful conversion of some low-caste locals. Ibn-Shahyar's 919 *Wonders of India* described three ships which foundered entering Saymur's harbour.[16] Al-Masudi in 915 in *Fields of Gold* described it as west coast India's largest port with '10,000 Muslims,' from Oman, Yemen, Basra, Siraf and Baghdad, 'who had married and settled… including some outstanding merchants,' interacting with Hindus, Parsis, Jains and Jews; distinct merchant communities.[17] All described mosques, Zoroastrian fire temples, synagogues and a church, indicating Arab and Persian traders,[18] enjoying the rich trading heritage of Tamil India's many ports, pearl fishing centres and trades, with 'conch bangles, many varieties of grain, white salt, tamarind and dried fish' according to the *Maduraikkanchi*.[19] Omani-Yemeni descendants, Mappilas, are 25% of Kerala's present population,[20] demonstrating their former importance. Some still wear a turban, lungi (waist cloth) and knife, traditional Yemeni dress. Al-Masudi in 917 said the best Indian Ocean seamen were Oman's Azd tribe.[21]

At Tondi 'merchants bring eaglewood, camphor and other fragrant substances.' The east coast's Chola kingdom's capital and main port, Kaveripattinam (Poompuhar or Puhar) 'is filled with horses, sacks of pepper…gemstones and gold, sandalwood and eaglewood…pearls… coral…wheat…rice' from east coast hinterlands, according to the *Silappathikaram*. Spikenard from northwest India was exported from southern Indian ports, confirming literary descriptions of heavy coastal shipping. Similar descriptions of trades in food, including up to 18 grain varieties, fragrant woods, gems and pepper indicate a rich literary civilisation of sophisticated consumption and lifestyle. Many poets were merchants. Satthanar, a grain merchant, wrote the *Manimekalai* and gold merchant Napputanar the *Mullaippattu*, two of many.[22] Although the *Maduraikanchi* and *Silappathikaram* have 1st-century origins, possibly earlier, they continued to be updated and were still revered in the 8th century, despite the pre-6th-century Kalabhra interregnum, described as an evil force in Tamil literature. Economic activity does not seem to have been adversely affected.[23] Kaveripattinam (pattinam is Tamil for commercial town or port) was one of six mentioned in the 1st-century's *Milinda Panha*. It hosted 8th-century enclaves of Muslim, Jewish, Parsi and Christian merchants. Traditionally Tamil kings protected trade routes and merchants, who were honoured and honourable in Tamil society.

Competition for control of south India between Cholas and Pandyas from Tamil Nadu and Pallavas and Cheras from Kerala, stretched into deep antiquity. A 1st-century Chola king built a 329-foot stone dam on the Kaveri River, their tribal heartland, with a canal network for water storage and irrigation; a sophisticated heritage. Cholas allied with Pallavas against Pandyas with their capital at Kanchipuram and its ancient main port, Mamallapuram near Chennai, centre of Tamil Sangam literature. It flourished in the 7th and 8th centuries, superseding Kaveripattinam in the early-8th century under Pallavan King Rajasimha Narasimhavarman II (r. 691–729), selling cinnamon, ginger, pepper, turmeric, paprika and cloves to Arabs for cream of tartar (grapes plus tamarinds) from east Africa. Elaborately carved 7th-century Tantric Buddhist shrines, cave temples, rock-cut art, requiring hundreds of skilled sculptors, still to be seen, attests to the wealth generated. An 8th-century Tamil text described an anchored ship 'bent to the point of breaking' and 'gems of nine varieties in heaps.'

The first references to Nagapattinam, 50 kilometres south, are from the 7th century but probably developed in the 6th or earlier.[24] It was vibrant, fortified, with major roads, busy with large ships. In the mid-7th century it attained similar cargo and passenger volumes to and from Sri Lanka and Srivijaya. The Pallavas built dockyards there, developed a navy and its guilds traded with Srivijaya, Kra

Isthmus kingdoms, Cambodia and Champa. Emissaries were exchanged with China,[25] which requested a temple/pagoda for Chinese visitors. In 731 the direct Pallava line died out and a collateral branch, ruling in Champa was elected by city officials and succeeded, emphasising its close maritime links with Southeast Asian Hindu kingdoms and impressive administration. Chinese sources indicate that in 692, five Indian kingdoms sent tribute to T'ang China and Chinese missions visited India in 643, 646 and 657.[26] King Rajasimha (r. 691–729) built the requested Chinese pagoda in Nagapattinam, indicating the port's importance in Chinese cargo exchange.[27] For Srivijayan and Chinese Buddhists, India was a holy land and commercial destination. Buddhist pilgrims had visited for centuries. An 860 Bihar inscription tells of a Srivijayan king building a monastery at Nalanda, site of the famous Buddhist university.[28] Early-9th-century Buddhist literature show Nagapattinam as a city illuminated all night, presumably because of heavy maritime traffic, including gold, camphor and elephants.[29]

Some Arabs settling south India created a mixed Tamil-Arab culture; Arwi. Kilakarai's Arwi community history, told generation-to-generation,[30] is that they descended from a group of 9th-century Omani pearl traders. Pearls were a millennia-old, major Indian Ocean activity, found in the UAE and Kuwait dating to 5500–5400 BC and 5000 BC respectively,[31] but Indian pearls had a higher reputation. Unhappy with an Omani ruler, they moved to Yemen and were equally unimpressed. They may have been part of a larger group recorded in 842 from Cairo between the tyrannical rules of Caliph Al-Multhazim and Al-Wathiq. They sailed in a four-ship convoy. One got lost en route and may have landed in Calicut in Kerala or Bhatkal in Karnataka, whose community has more in common with Kilakarai's Arwis in dress and speech. The second landed in Kayalpattinam where Muslim traders had settled from the mid-7th century, the Malabar's coast's most important pearl fishing and trading port since at least the 1st century. The third landed in Thondi in Tamil Nadu. The last ship, overseeing the landings, sailed to Kilakarai in south Tamil Nadu. All were pearl fishing and trading ports, which 4th-century BC Megasthenes had noted as the basis of Pandya kings' wealth. Cosmos of Alexandria about 530–550 also mentioned its pearl markets. Marco Polo later noted the pearl industry flourishing under the Pandyas, and thought 'Malabar' the world's richest country. Today, Kilakarai is predominantly Muslim with Christians and Hindus living separately and peacefully. Its Pannattar Street means 'People of different countries Street.' They speak Tamil with an Arabic script with some Arabic words and phrases, similar to Swahili's Bantu grammar and Arabic words. Cultural heritage in dress and speech is preserved with women wearing Arabic-style black coverings, their culture still trading and shipping, members based from the UAE to Singapore with Kilakarai the central family base. They regard themselves separate to north Indian Muslims, descendants of forced converts, one clear difference, the importance Arwi give to education.

The *Arthashastra* listed shells, diamonds, other gems and gold products as traded items but also included rice, beryls, pearls, sandalwood, teak, ebony and textiles.

Religious schools and temples were often endowed by wealthy merchants. The earliest evidence of merchant guilds, 'vanigrama' in Sanskrit, appear at this time, although it would be unsurprising if entrepreneurial, seafaring Tamils had them much earlier. One, the Manigramam, mentioned in six copper plates from 849 found near Quilon, recorded a contract in Malayalam, Arabic, Persian and Hebrew with Christian merchants allowing access to a fort protecting the port's market, apparently operated by them. The Manigramam apparently extended its influence to the east coast shortly thereafter. The Ayyavole guild from the Konkan coast, north of Kerala was seemingly the most powerful. The Manigramam, Nanadesi and at least 46 other professional bodies of artisans and mercenaries were apparently affiliated to it.

Pallava power was built on maritime trade revenues. A Tamil inscription from Southeast Asia from the 3rd-4th centuries and six from the 9th-13th show Tamil merchant and artisan activity, three with merchant guilds. A mid-9th-century Pallava inscription at Takua Pa on the Kra Isthmus's west coast, recorded building a tank used by a Vishnu Manigramam-owned temple. Merchants were patrons of religious establishments named Avaninaranam, Pallava king Nandivarman III's title. Tamils obviously settled here, at Pagan and Barus where inscriptions are also found, probably since antiquity. The presence of troops and merchants suggest an attempted outflanking of Srivijaya. However, in the late-9th century, Pallavan power declined. Other subcontinent polities were also active. The 909 Kaladi inscription in north Java's Brantas delta, mentions Klings, Sinhalese, Dravidians, Chams, Khmer and Mon and an earlier copper plate, Bengalis, Malabaris, and Khmer.[32]

Meanwhile Baghdad weakened. Al-Mamun (r. 813–833) came to power after civil war with his half-brother, in which much of the Round City was destroyed. He promoted translations, learning and sciences, commissioned a world map drawing on classical and current Arab seafaring knowledge. But the 'ulama' religious movement became stronger, including ibn Hanbal's severe Sharia law, Wahabi Islam's inspiration; xenophobic, hostile, intolerant and suspicious. Al-Mamun's execution of ibn Hanbal was the rallying point for anti-progressives. As reason was marginalised, Arab sciences stagnated, once the glory of its enlightenment. Abbasid cohesion weakened. For much of the 9th century they ruled from Samara further north. Thereafter they received two serious shocks at either end of the Baghdad-China trade route. As already related, in 878 T'ang rebel, Huang Cho's forces sacked Guangzhou killing 120,000, mainly foreign, merchants. In the 880s Chang'an, the T'ang capital was destroyed. The dynasty ended in 907. Thereafter Gulf-China voyages tended to end on the Kra Isthmus in a two-part journey, increasing Srivijaya's importance, reducing risk for shipowners specialising in one sector. When al-Masudi visited Srivijaya in 916, cargoes from Siraf and Hormuz, unaffected by zanj rebellion, continued in Srivijayan ships. Bay of Bengal trade fed into the east-west route, as Coromandel coast trading guilds increased their activities. Tenth-century Persian explorer, Ibn Rustah believed there was no richer or stronger kingdom than Srivijaya.

The second shock was more serious. The Abbasid empire was built on slavery, for marshland drainage, date palm cultivation, pearl-fishing, domestic use and the military, managed by an elite corps of Eurasians, Turkic horsemen and zanj. Conditions for harem girls were privileged, but agricultural slaves were harshly treated. In the 870s, 15,000 sacked Ubullah and Basra. Cut-off from the Gulf, Baghdad's merchants never fully recovered, though the city continued to be a cultural beacon. Baghdad's slave trade declined. Persia had conquered Yemen in the 6th century. In the mid-10th, al-Istakhri noted Jeddah's main commerce was still with Persia; 'Persians are the ruling class and live in splendid palaces.'[33] Moreover, Persian Buyids became the power behind the 10th-century Abbasids.[34]

Baghdad declined but Siraf and southern Gulf ports continued prospering. Al-Istakhri thought Siraf almost equalled Shiraz's size and splendour, 'the houses... several stories high built to overlook the sea.'[35] After retiring to Siraf, Buzurg ibn Shahriyar wrote *The Wonders of India*, stories of shipwrecks, giants and an island of sex-starved women. It assumed however, that merchants of any origin or faith were given fair and equal treatment, avoiding ports where not so. In his 912 story, a poor Jewish merchant returned to Sohar with a huge cargo of Chinese goods. Envious rivals persuaded the Caliph to confiscate the cargo, but Oman's governor, knowing it would damage Sohar's reputation, summoned merchant community heads and reversed the decision.[36] His 123 stories from sailors and traders, written about 950 thought Hormuz, where 'everything most rare and valuable' is brought, with 'many people of all religions...nobody is allowed to insult their religions...this city is called the citadel of security.' Ibn Hawqal described it as 'the emporium of the merchants in Kirman and their chief seaport.'

As a result of Abbasid trade decline, many Mesopotamian Jewish merchants moved to Fustat and Aden in the mid-10th century, (Chapter 8) a flight of capital and expertise benefiting the Red Sea-Mediterranean route, especially Egypt which became a major textile producer, its wealth spent partly on Chinese porcelain and Aksum's gold. Al-Muqaddasi (945–991) thought Baghdad 'once a magnificent city...is now fast falling into ruin and decay and has lost all its splendour...Fustat... is like Baghdad of old. I know of no city in Islam superior to it.'[37] It was, he said, 'the centre of the world's commerce...the treasure house of the west and the emporium of the east.' By contrast, Ibn Hawqal about 977 thought Cordoba half Baghdad's size, Fustat only a third. He said Siraf was the main departure port for China-bound ships, its population 'very rich', some living in east African and Indian ports. 'They abound in marine productions and commodities brought by sea, such as aloes, ambergris, camphire, pearls, canes, ivory, ebony, pepper, sandals and various kinds of drugs and medicines are sent...to all quarters of the world.' An earthquake badly damaged it in 977, increasing the importance of Hormuz and Sohar further south.

Southern Gulf ports, Sohar, Kis (sometimes Kish or Quays) and Dibba also increased in importance. Al-Muqaddasi listed Oman, Aden and Fustat as commercially rich and called Sohar 'the vestibule of China and the emporium of the east', exporting drugs, perfumes, saffron, teak, ivory, pearls, onyx, rubies, sugar, aloes, iron, lead, pottery, sandalwood, glass and pepper; except for pearls, all re-exports![38] The main imports were Malabar pepper, cloves, nutmeg, cinnamon, silk, Indian cotton textiles and Indian and east African iron. Al-Muqaddasi thought 'no distinguished city...in the China Sea is considered better than Sohar; it is prosperous, densely populated and honourable. It is a refined city, stretching along the coast. Its inhabitants have houses constructed of brick and teak...prepossessing in appearance they...enjoy an abundance of all things...It is the antechamber to China, the treasures of the east and Iran, the helpmate of Yemen...the emporium of the whole world...there is not a town where merchants are wealthier than here and all commodities of east, west, south and north are brought.' Omani pearl traders were famous. Omani enclaves in Sri Lanka sent back its gems and ivory. Omani ports were rich because they were strategically located between Mesopotamia and Persia further north, and east Africa in the south, for gold, ivory, ambergris, tortoiseshell, skins and timber, and to the east, India, Southeast Asia and China for rice, silk, spices and ceramics. Oman's Qalhat, Muscat, Dibba, Khor Fakkan and Fujaira also traded with India, Southeast Asia and China. In 999 al-Masudi copied al-Muqaddasi's description of Sohar.

In short, there was a change in emphasis from northern to southern Gulf ports, to Oman, Yemen and the Red Sea-Fustat route as the Indian Ocean-Mediterranean conduit, benefiting an impoverished Europe. Concluding Chapters 1 and 2, Indian Ocean and China Sea trade thrived, reflecting vigorous economies, rising trade volumes and intellectual endeavour, the only significant negative, declining Abbasid commercial and intellectual vigour.

Chapter 3

Frisian, English and Scandinavian Trade

Unlike Indian Ocean trade, with ships each carrying tens of thousands of ceramic, porcelain and gold plates, gems, ivory and necessities like rice, vigorous 1st-2nd century European trade had by 650 virtually ceased. Interconnectivity broke down. Without food imports and exports, Europe reverted to subsistence farming, became less productive, depopulated, poor and illiterate. Farm animals regressed to prehistoric, not even Iron Age sizes. Ports had already declined. Many were abandoned. Europe's tentative recovery was spearheaded by a few north European and Mediterranean ports but initially more vigorously in north Europe. Franks did not participate. The Rhine ceased to be civilisation's frontier. Instead, former Roman Belgica became the hub of an extended Europe, through which exchanges, material and intellectual, were transmitted.[1] Christianity was commercially negative. Lending money, even at modest interest rates, fair remuneration for a service, was equated with usury and condemned, a view not shared by Byzantine Christians. Most people were poor, needing basic necessities only, thus lending for investment in production ended. Scripture idealised poverty. 'Blessed are the poor in spirit for theirs is the Kingdom of Heaven,' to which the rich might gain entry by almsgiving. St. Augustine emphasised it. 'When we have food and raiment let us content ourself therewith…for covetousness is the root of all evil.' His doctrine of original sin, devised when the Roman world was collapsing, taught the poor to accept their position. The world was wicked and unreformable, merchants less useful than farmers.

Static, pessimistic beliefs encouraged indifference towards rational enquiry, unnecessary because of divine revelation through Christ. Miracles via martyr's relics replaced rational scientific medicine, suffering welcomed as a test of faith. Horizons were local. Trial by ordeal consisted of lowering suspects into a pool blessed by a priest, thus if he floated the holy water rejected him as guilty, if he sank it accepted him as innocent. Healing time determined guilt or innocence after pulling stones from boiling water or holding red-hot metal. All replaced Roman law, adjudicating facts, testing evidence, challenging witnesses.[2] Ordeals were only banned by the Church in 1215, long after Roman law was rediscovered in the 11th century, and had to keep banning them, as they stubbornly continued.[3]

Europe slowly recovered economically, intellectually and culturally in ports in Flanders, Brabant, Frisia, the Baltic and southeast England. Climatic warming from the mid-first millennium allowed Scandinavian farming areas to become more productive and marginal land brought into use, so unlike much of Europe, its

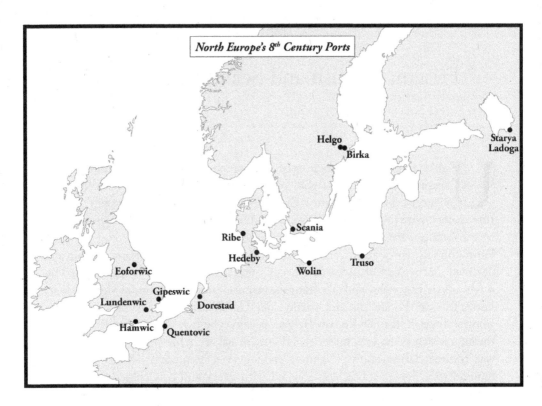

North Europe's 8th Century Ports

population grew. Maritime trade in the North Sea and Baltic rested on millennia of interconnectivity. Demand from east Saxons, east Angles, Lindsey, Deira, Jutes and Danes helped Frisian merchants spread economic activity inland.

Quentovic, near today's Calais, was probably the largest 7th-century Channel port. Fifty miles up the Rhine at its Lek confluence, Dorestad, first known from the 630s, expanded quickly from the 720s, overtaking it. By the 830s its kilometre waterfront, 50-hectare (123 acres) site had 15 jetties, each 6–8 metres wide, extending up to 200 metres from the Rhine to warehouses,[4] although its population probably never exceeded 2,000. Both were Frisian ports. The Rhine, Meuse and Scheldt deltas favoured sheep and cattle farming, dye and vegetable cultivation. They made parchment, instruments, leather, and from sheep's wool, brightly-coloured fine cloth, their main export, buying glass, weapons and metalwork. Dorestad also exported Rhine wines, other luxury goods and imported British slaves and cloaks, Baltic amber and, from the Loire, Noirmoutier's salt. Dorestad and Quentovic's Frisians became north Europe's leading maritime traders, albeit in small volumes, with 70 European coins, the farthest from Venice, found there. It minted silver coins, found in England, the Rhineland, Marseilles and Aquitaine, the silver from Byzantium and the Abbasid world via the Baltic. They were also artisan production centres. Commercial life developed sooner than most of north Europe because Frisian lands were river mouths of the Rhine, Ems, Meuse, Scheldt, Weser and Elbe, accessing Europe's interior and adjacent to England and the Baltic.

The association of Frisians with England was noted by Procopius about 553 in *Gothic War* 4.20. Informed by Angles, he wrote 'three very populous nations inhabit the island of Brittia, and one king is set over each of them. And the names of these nations are Angles, Frisians and Britons.' About 700, other Frisians settled in Gipes<u>wic</u> (Ipswich), establishing the first large-scale potteries since the Romans. Coiled pots were finished on wheels and kiln-fired. Elsewhere in England they were hand-made and fired on bonfires.[5] Gipes<u>wic</u> traded with Dorestad and various Scandinavian ports at the Baltic entrance. Other 'wics' like Ham<u>wic</u> (Southampton), the 16-hectare (40 acres) West Saxon port near its capital Winchester, Lunden<u>wic</u> (London) for both East Saxons and Mercia, its quays along today's Strand in the 670s, and Eofor<u>wic</u> (York) for Northumbria, were established. Proximity to capitals demonstrate importance. These wics/vics were not unique. From Germanic languages there were also Bruns<u>wick</u> and Schles<u>wig</u>, denoting where merchants lived, with no connection with the Latin 'vicus'. Port dues were an important revenue source. Ham<u>wic</u>, which gave its name to Hampshire, had a mint, metalled roads, metal and glass workers and merchants trading with Scandinavia, Frisia, Flanders and the Rhineland. Dorestad, Quento<u>vic</u>, Lunden<u>wic</u>, Gipes<u>wic</u>, Eofor<u>wic</u>, Jutland's Ribe, after 770 Hedeby, occasionally called Haithabu, and Bergen were interconnected. Flat-bottomed boats loaded and discharged on beaches where quays were unavailable.

Who were Frisians? Frisia is the coastal region from the Netherlands including modern Friesland and Groningen, parts of north Germany and Schleswig-Holstein. Some Frisian dialects are still spoken in southern Denmark and Holland. In north Germany these dialects are called Low Saxon or Friso-Saxon, hence the historical confusion about Anglo-Saxon identity. Ancient authors made little distinction between Saxons and Frisians. There are three existing Frisian languages with numerous dialects, mutually unintelligible. Others apparently became extinct. The former Roman province of Belgica, whose boundary was the rivers Marne and Seine, delineated Frisian language groups from Romance-speaking Gaul. The Frisian coast is adjacent to southeast England and many Frisian words are similar to English; see is sea, buter is butter, rein is rain, boat is boat, brea is bread and greine is green. West Flemish, now spoken around Bruges and as far south as Calais in the Middle Ages is also similar to English, for example beuter is butter, hille is hill and dinne is thin. Under the influence of modern Dutch, Danish, German and Norman French, they became less mutually intelligible, but the North Sea and English Channel was a millennia-old economic, linguistic and cultural zone of traders, raiders and settlers. Various imperatives drove different activities. The sea was no barrier. The Danish *Knutsdrapa* about Knut used 'Frisian' and 'English' synonymously.

In almost constant Frisian-Frankish conflict from at least the time of Chilperic (561–584), 'Terror of the Frisians', fortunes waxed and waned. Frisian commercial wealth induced the Franks to conquer Dorestad in 690, annexing more land in 734. It was fully conquered by Charlemagne in the 770s, Radbod their last independent king; two culturally distinct people, pagan, seafaring and merchant-driven against land-hungry, primitive Christians. Frisian merchants linked Europe's heart with the Baltic entrance and southern England with enclaves in Hedeby, York, Ribe, Lundenwic, Duisburg, Cologne, Mainz and Worms. After conquest, Christian propaganda reflected their reach inland. A story of a Frisian merchant with silk, carried down the Rhine onto the Lorelei rocks asked St. Goar's assistance and was saved, another left a pound of silver because of the saint's intervention. Frisian merchants were recorded in Paris trading wine.[6] When Worms had a large fire in 886, a chronicler reported the burning of the town's best part, 'where the Frisian merchants live.' They had the best quarters in Cologne and Mainz.[7] In contrast, Franks were uninterested in maritime trade's opportunities. French historian Robert Latouche laments, 'From that time dates that French indifference to the things of the sea with which we have so often been reproached.'[8]

Lundenwic had a mid-7th century mint and a modest trade until the 8th century when wine, querns and some luxury goods were imported, wool and cloaks, exported. Wars between English kingdoms produced slaves. One in 679 was recorded 'sold at Lundenwic to a Frisian'.[9] Bede mentioned them there in 731, 'a market for many people who come by land and sea.' Lundenwic was Mercia's port and minted coins for Kings Offa (757–96) and Coenwulf (796–821). The 8th-century North Sea probably had more commercial shipping than the Mediterranean after Marseilles' decline. Frisians sailed in convoys and were organised in guilds. In Sigtuna in the Baltic, a Frisian guild erected stones in memory of members.

For Scandinavia's extensive coast, ships were the best way to access hinterlands, the sea its natural environment, and where convenient or necessary, an escape. Like Bronze Age Greece, poor soil, mountains and indented coast encouraged a maritime outlook. Ships were the means of livelihood and power. About 705–710 Ribe was built on Jutland's west coast, ideally located to benefit from expanding North Sea trade. It and Lundeborg were trade and shipbuilding centres. In 726 a canal was built across the small island of Samso opposite Aarhus in eastern Jutland. Furs, walrus ivory, eiderdown and amber were gathered in ports like Birka on an island in Lake Malar, close to where Stockholm was later built, a maritime entrepot for millennia, attested by numerous prehistoric ship-shaped stones, usually denoting burials. It was defended by earth ramparts 20–40 feet wide, probably with palisade and watch towers and had oak jetties and breakwaters inside the fortified area,[10] guaranteeing merchant lives and property. Merchants and soldiers' graves contained balances, weights, weapons, Rhineland pottery and glassware, furs, walrus ivory, reindeer horn, silk, silver and carnelian beads, goods exchanged with Dorestad, Quentovic and English ports. Birka's relationship with Helgo, ten miles away is uncertain, but dominating the water route to central Sweden, it smelted iron and was a port for luxury goods. Other Baltic ports developed on its south coast like Wolin, four kilometres along the Oder and Truso on the Vistula with access to the interior.

Pepin's son, Charlemagne (r. 771–814) waged 47 years of war on Frisia, Wends, Saxons, Avars and Lombards, aspiring to a continental vision of power, to extend Christianity by force. The so-called Carolingian Renaissance's aim was to spread Christianity, but was a world without schools. He conquered Istria and Croatia in 809, but failed against Venice, and turned from the Mediterranean to push his frontiers east to the Elbe and Bohemia. Horizons hardly stretched beyond the locality or at best the local lords' boundaries. Charlemagne, the west's Christian emperor, enslaved eastern lands and people but was powerless to prevent enslavement of some of his own subjects, who after castration at Verdun, were taken to Muslim Iberia. At the same time literate, cultured Arabs, Persians and Indians sailed to China trading luxuries and necessities, creating prosperity and real intellectual renaissances.

Charlemagne, Europe's strongest king, wrote to Offa of Mercia, England's strongest, suggesting full protection for English and Frankish merchants, and regarding 'the dark stones which you asked us to send, have a messenger come to choose which kind you want...we will gladly order them to be given and help you with transport' and in return the lengths of English cloaks should be the same as last. This sounds like gift exchange, not independent trade. The 'dark stones' were probably Rhineland lava querns found at a watermill at Tamworth, a Mercian royal centre. He also sent church vestments, cloth for bishops, silk for Offa, swords and booty from his Avar wars.[11] This monarch-to-monarch correspondence about querns and the measurement of cloaks illustrates catastrophic decline since Europe's mid-2nd-century trade-zenith, and the huge gulf in quality and quantity compared with Indian Ocean trade. Harun, Caliph of Baghdad, probing the possibility of an alliance against Byzantium in 802, sent Charlemagne jewels, ivory, chessmen, an embroidered silk gown, a water clock and a tame white elephant. Charlemagne's gifts were red, white and blue Frisian cloth, products of his maritime-orientated subjects.

After Frisia's conquest, Charlemagne launched war against their Saxon neighbours in 772. Victory took 30 years and involved transportation of every third Saxon, uprooting settlements in merciless Christianising campaigns. Some fled to adjacent Denmark. On the Schleswig isthmus, Hedeby from 770, developed impressively as the region's main port for amber, boneware, shipbuilding and repair, helping open up the Baltic. Charlemagne's wars with Saxons and Wends meant Godfred of Denmark's (c. 804–810) trade routes and economic interests were threatened. By 804, Charlemagne's armies were at the Saxon-Danish border.[12] Godfred retaliated by harrying the Frankish-ruled Frisian coast in 810 with 200 ships before a peace treaty was signed in 811.[13] Charlemagne also needed a fleet and organised coastal defences north of the Seine estuary against pirates 'who infect the Gallic Sea.' By 810, he had ships on all navigable rivers[14] and restored Boulogne's Roman lighthouse so ships could return safely. Godfred built the 'Danevirke', a ten-kilometre, two-metre-high oak palisade in 808 against Charlemagne, improving a nearly hundred-year-old defensive wall and moved Reric's merchants in Charlemagne's Abodrit ally territory, probably near modern Lubeck, to Hedeby to concentrate trade in <u>his</u> port. It was inspired. At the Baltic end of the Danevirke, Hedeby increasingly commanded trade with Prussian, Pomeranian and Swedish ports and was intermediary between the North Sea and Baltic, of huge significance to Denmark, avoiding the risk of sailing around Jutland.[15] A six-hectare (15 acres) area surrounded by a wall in a half circle, still in places ten metres high, heavily defended against frequent attack, had a peak population of 1,000–1,500 people. By 900 it covered, with harbour and quay, 24 hectares (60 acres). Its early-9th-century coins featured sailing ships similar to the one found at Oseberg dating to about 820, part of a royal ship burial. Twenty metres long and over five metres wide with 15 pairs of oars, it carried 40–100 men or equivalent cargo. In 838 Danish King Horik demanded from Louis the Pious, that 'the Frisians be given over to him' and was refused.

Danes defended Frankish aggression in Saxony by protecting their Jutland base as the Baltic choke point and raided Frankish Dorestad and Quentovic. Norway's Atlantic coast orientation was west to Scotland, Iceland and Greenland. Its people needed land and pasture to settle. Swedes who sailed east Europe's rivers in adjacent areas, less rich than its homeland, had different motives. They knew that silver came from the south and went to find its source. Late-7th-century semi-legendary Swede, the 'Far Reacher', sailed and rowed the rivers, hauling his boats overland where necessary to the Black Sea and Caspian Sea. Trade created wealth and the new elites were given lavish boat burials, the practice transferred to England when they arrived to help natives defend against rival English tribes and 5th-century Scot/ Pict invaders. Sutton Hoo's contents contained imports including superb Byzantine silver plate. At Helgo in Sweden, 47 5th-6th-century Byzantine coins reflect these early links. A 6th or 7th-century north Indian Buddha has even been found. Iron ore, furs, leather, amber, antler horn, seal skins, walrus ivory, slaves, honey, fish glue, wax, steel swords and eiderdown were attractive products to Constantinople, traded for Byzantine and Egyptian goods. Scania was a gold and slave-trade centre and Bornholm Island between Scandinavia and Pomerania had a good harbour if needed for those heading to Poland, Russia and the Black Sea.[16]

These 'Rus', rowers, although some think Rus derived from ruddy or red haired, set-up trading posts at Staraya Ladoga on Lake Ladoga, near St. Petersburg in the 750s, later at Gorodische, then Novgorod about 860, Smolensk and Kyiv around 900, using the Don, Dnieper and Volga rivers, the 'water road', to the Black and Caspian Sea, trading as far as Uzbekistan for Islamic silver coins. Many have been found in Sweden, about two tons on the island of Gotland, whose burials date from about 650, and at Birka seven-times more Islamic coins than western.[17] There are over 1,000 silver coin hoards in Scandinavia, more than 100,000 coins, and many in Poland, Russia, Belarus and Ukraine. The Abbasid silver transfer was crucial for developing north European trade. Kaupang near Oslo also loaded high-quality goods to England and France.[18] The 6th century Atlantic maritime route from Byzantine North Africa to western British Celtic lands declined fast after Muslim armies took North Africa and ceased after about 700, so the Baltic became the hub of a more extensive trade network linking the Black Sea, Caspian Sea and Baghdad to the British Isles and northern Europe. North Sea and Channel ports helped disperse silver inland via Europe's rivers, but Mediterranean trade by contrast, stagnated. (Chapter 4)

Wealthy Constantinople attracted attack. An 860 raid of 200 ships, 'a thunderbolt from God,' said Patriarch Photius, was perhaps by Pechenegs or Magyars.[19] Kyiv developed as the main Rus merchant hub. Constantinople appreciated them as traders, mercenaries, protectors of their northern flanks and were given a special enclave to trade Baltic goods for silver coins, silk, pottery and glass from Byzantine and Abbasid worlds. In 922 Ibn Fadlan recorded a Viking prayer. 'I wish that you send me many merchants with many dinars and dirhams who will buy from me whatever I wish and will not dispute anything I say.' By the 1030s Kyiv's hold on Dnieper trade was absolute and national coffers overflowed.

*   *   *

Jute, Saxon, Angle and Frisian nobles helped defend British 4th-5th-century kingdoms. Integrating with locals, a different identity developed from Jutland's Jutes, who in the 790s suddenly arrived in the British Isles and north Europe for plunder. Leaders sought fame, power and wealth to reward and enlarge their followers by raiding, trading, then settling. Carolingian sources refer to all Scandinavians as Northmen, English ones as 'Vikings'[20] probably from Vik, frequent in Scandinavian place-names. In Icelandic, place-names ending vik are by the sea or bay's end,[21] related to Germanic wic or vic for towns, markets and especially ports. Despite their popular violent reputation, they were no more so than contemporaries and vital for east-west European integration via Scandinavia, drawn-into mainstream Europe for the first time; silver transfer the key.

Longships were intended for trade as much as, if not more than, raiding. 'It is wrong,' writes Chris Wickham, 'to see merchants and pirates as too sharply distinct; any raider becomes a trader if the port is too well-defended and many traders… readily raid if the port…seems weak, and then sell-off the booty elsewhere.'[22] Gwyn Jones similarly explains that both trade and piracy 'were essential to the Viking movement. When circumstances favoured, they were…merchants but when seas were undefended and towns lay open, they turned privateer.'[23]

In 790, Dorset's coast was attacked and in 792, Kent. The only places in 8th-9th-century northern Europe that had moveable wealth were monasteries and ports. At Charlemagne's Court, Alcuin recorded the 793 Lindisfarne raid. 'Never would one have believed in the possibility of such a voyage.'[24] His surprise showed how far Europe had regressed. This was a simple North Sea crossing! In 795 it was the turn of Skye, Iona and Rathlin in the kingdom of Dalriada, controlling Irish Sea shipping. In 799 Noirmoutier was attacked, continuing opportunistic, easy pickings. A French monk relating how Norse ships sailed up the Seine in 854, over 60 years after Alcuin's surprise, wrote 'one had never heard speak of such a thing or read anything like it;'[25] extraordinary parochialism. Belief that it was divine punishment, led to resignation.

Jutes/Danes attacked and settled eastern England; Norwegians the Orkneys, Shetlands, Faroes and the Irish Sea about 800, and Iceland in the 870s. For them, north Scotland was their Southlands (Sutherland). For Orkney and north Scotland-based Vikings, farming and raiding was part of the annual cycle. Raids disrupted trade. Hamwic's mint moved to Winchester. Lundenwic was sacked in 764, 798, 801, 841 and 852, and its mint stopped production between 851 and 861.[26] In 871, Lundenwic was occupied. Danes also raided north Europe during post-Charlemagne civil war between Louis the Pious and son Lothar; Dorestad in 834, 835 and 836, Rouen in 841, Quentovic and Hamwic in 842, Nantes in 843, although Baldwin I and II, Counts of Flanders, retaliated. When Louis died in 840 his three sons fought each other. The empire was divided into three kingdoms in 843, each weaker, inviting attack. Danes continued raiding, sacking Hamburg in 845 with sixty ships.[27] Instead of common defence, Frankish dynastic interests were paramount so when Louis the German tried to make his son king of Aquitaine, Viking raids assisted. Charles responded by persuading Bulgars to attack Louis' eastern frontier. Pepin II allied with Bretons in 859 and Norse in 864 in the Loire.[28]

Vikings over-wintered in Ireland from about 835 and in Noirmoutier in 843, then sacked Toulouse, Galicia, Arab-ruled Seville, and Lisbon and in 846 sailed back to Bordeaux. They used rivers to penetrate inland as far as Cambrai on the Scheldt, Sens on the Yonne, Chartres on the Eure, Fleury on the Loire, York on the Ouse and Reading on a Thames tributary, and from there overland.[29] In 845, 120 ships threatened Paris and were bought-off by Charles the Bald for 7,000 lbs. of silver. A monk at Noirmoutier, which exported salt and Loire Valley wine, in about 860 wrote, 'the number of ships grows, the endless stream of Vikings never ceases to increase...they seize Bordeaux, Perigueux, Limoges, Angouleme and Toulouse. Augers, Tours and Orleans are annihilated...Rouen is laid waste ... Paris, Beauvais and Meaux taken...Chartres occupied.' They returned to Bordeaux in 848 and sacked it so thoroughly that 30 years later, 'none of the faithful any longer have a roof over their head,' according to Pope John VIII's bull authorising the bishop to move to Bourges in central France. In centuries of decline, Bordeaux was sacked in turn by Vandals, Visigoths, Franks, Muslims and Vikings.

From 851 mainly Danish Vikings started to over-winter on the Isle of Thanet and Seine islands, launch pads for raids over the whole region, especially Paris. In 853 they sacked Nantes, Tours, Blois, Angers, Orleans and Poitiers, taking ecclesiastics for ransom and sale. They were so numerous in north France that in 858 one Seine-based group agreed to fight for Charles and in 862 others on the Somme agreed to attack those on the Seine. From 865 attacks on Anglo-Saxon kingdoms intensified and Danes in Ireland fought Norwegians. Dublin-based Vikings attacked Wales, northern England, the Cotentin peninsula and Normandy. Further south, Lisbon and Seville were briefly taken. In 859, 62 ships sailed from the Loire, attacking Iberian ports, into the Mediterranean, raiding North Africa and the Balearics, then settled in the Camargue to raid Arles, Nimes and Valence 100 miles north. They sacked and plundered Pisa. Norse shipbuilding skills spread to Basques, who adopted the overlapping plank technique for their whalers, trading blubber meat and oil. By 875 Basques reached the Faroe Islands fishing for cod, using indigenous sun-dried salt to preserve it. Almost fat-free, salted cod outlasted salted whale and herring. At Noirmoutier, Bourgneuf and Isle de Re, Vikings settled and increased salt-production, the northern-most port sunny enough to evaporate salt water. They traded it into north Europe and the Baltic, establishing a key medieval trading route. Robert Latouche, still lamenting Frankish maritime indifference, identifies all French marine and seafaring vocabulary from Norse; seamanship, ship's parts, rigging, even 'vague' (wave), 'additional and decisive proof of Frankish indifference to things of the sea.'[30]

Dublin, Cork, Waterford, Wexford and Limerick, Ireland's main economic centres, were Norse collection points for onward slave shipments to Rouen and Muslim Iberia. Bristol shipped slaves to Dublin. Like Arab enclaves in east Africa, Norse Irish ports occupied little land, used hinterlands to source slaves and minted coins. Raids into northwest England also proved profitable. Amlaib, a Norse king in Dublin raided Britain in 871, returning with 200 shiploads of captives, 6,000 'Angles, Britons and Picts',[31] probably transhipped to Muslim Iberia. A Church Council at Meaux in 845 noted merchants moving slave columns through Christian cities 'into the hands of the faithless and our most brutal enemies...increasing the enemy strength,' preferring slaves sold within Christendom. A mid-10th-century Arab traveller noted many Europeans in Arab militias and harems.[32] The Norse were major suppliers. Iberian Muslims were proactive, sending diplomats to Scandinavia to organise it. In the *Laxdaela Saga*, an Icelandic chief visited a Swedish slave market and bought an aristocratic Irish girl from 'Gilli the Russian', said to be 'the richest man in the league of merchants.'[33]

Many Vikings settled Normandy and eastern England between 844 and 876, including Northumbria's Eoforwic in 866, renamed Jorvik. The East Angles in 869 and half of Mercia were conquered and settled by Danes. Danelaw's natural trade orientation was Scandinavia. Much of the West Saxon kingdom was also overrun in the 870s. In 871, Lundenwic was occupied. By 878, only part of England remained 'English'. Masters of the sea-lanes, Norsemen encircled the British Isles and sailed virtually unhindered on French rivers. Alfred the Great (r. 871–899) began to re-conquer occupied areas from his Somerset base. The 878 Treaty of Gudrun banned trade with Danes. Using Frisian mercenaries, Lundenwic, occupied for 15 years was recaptured in 886. For protection, the port was moved inside the old Roman walls from its beach market at Aldwych. Shallow ships were still pulled ashore and their cargoes sold. Alfred built a fleet of ships, unlike Frisian types and longer, faster, and steadier than Norse. In 896 they sunk 20 raiders. This shipbuilding ingenuity might have inspired Danish shipbuilding improvements.[34] A Norse noble visiting King Alfred at the war's height described his economic life as hunting walrus and receiving tribute from neighbouring Sammi; 'skins of beasts, the feathers of birds, whale bone and ship's rope made from walrus hide and seal skin...the highest in rank has to pay 15 marten skins, five reindeer skins, one bearskin and ten measures of feathers [eiderdown] and a jacket of bearskin or otter skin and two ship's ropes.'[35] Increased trade meant wealth creation and more powerful kingdoms. Ghent and Bruges appeared in the late-9th century and coins from Bruges suggest commercial importance, probably from cloth production.[36]

Alfred's son Edward (899–924) counterattacked the Norse in Mercia and Northumbria until 954. Chris Wickham thinks arguably 'these wars were only really fought for the increasingly rich trading entrepot of York [Jorvik] itself,'[37] but Norse settler numbers were small, 'not a mass peasant immigration.'[38] By Edward's death in 924, the English recovered everything south of the Humber. Harald Fairhair from the 890s brought some unity to the 27 Norse sub-kingdoms and settlements in Man, Shetland, Caithness and Sutherland, and got involved in Irish wars and on the Wirral, where Norse fleets from Dublin landed. At the Battle of Brunanburh in 937, Scottish, Celt and Norse forces were beaten by King Athelstan, who by 952 subdued Danes, Welsh, Cumbrian and Scottish kings. As British 'over-king' he encouraged a systematic survey of the Baltic and beyond, based on merchant feedback, encouraged Latin works translated into English and ordered that judges be literate. Anyone selling a fellow countryman as a slave had to pay a 'wergild', as if he had killed him, so slave exports declined. The main court for trade disputes was the Husting, a Viking word, inferring Norse traders remained and influenced its administration. Probably encouraged by Athelstan's success, Irish kings attacked Irish Norse ports in 968, taking jewels, foreign saddles, gold, silver, fine cloths, satin and silk clothes, indicative of wealth earned trading with Muslim Iberia, with access to east Mediterranean and Indian Ocean luxuries, because the Irish Sea linked Andalusia to Iceland and the Baltic. At the Loire's mouth, Nantes developed, but not into a major port, probably due to its hinterland's economic inertia, where feudalism's purpose, according to expert Marc Bloch, was 'the subordination of one individual to another'.[39] In ports, former serfs, villains and peasants by contrast, joined guilds, brotherhoods and councils, allocating revenues for road, gate and wall maintenance in free association.[40]

With growing stability, Lundenwic expanded trade with Ireland, Scandinavia and the continent; probably mainly wool to Flanders and wheat to Scandinavia, for fish, fur, amber, wine, honey, swords and silks. Northumbria's capital Jorvik, an inland port reached by shallow merchant 'knarrs', fatter versions of longships, was central in an expansive trade network, second only to Lundenwic in volumes. Its wharves were full of Baltic, Rhineland and Irish produce; amber, fur, skins, cattle, whalebone, pottery, whetstones, wine and corn. It was a much larger Norse port than Hedeby, Dublin or Trondheim, with a mixed population who, according to archaeological finds, wore silver disc broaches with carved animals, silver arm rings, and gold finger rings. Coins found include ones from the Caspian Sea, Bukhara and Samarkand of the 920s, where Swedish/Rus slave dealers were recorded in 922.[41]

Expelled from Dublin in 902, Norse settled the Isle of Man and Cheshire. Franks invited them to settle to protect inland regions, thus distancing themselves further from the coast. In the late-800s, Rollo, leader of a band who had plundered the Hebrides, England, Flanders and Paris, settled Rouen, and in 911 negotiated 'de facto' occupation into legal sovereignty with Charles the Simple, who formally recognised him. In return, he accepted Christianity and agreed to prevent other Vikings from entering the Seine to protect Paris. It was the foundation of 'Nordmanni', Normandy, with Rouen its capital. In the 920s and 930s its Jarl, Duke-equivalent, gained more land. Norman territory and power consolidated and trade grew with Scandinavia, England and Dublin. Towns like Alencon, Argentan, Dieppe, Falaise, St. Lo and Caen were established, the latter about 1025. Organising ability and military zeal made Normans a formidable new power and the duke's daughter married English King Ethelred.

Another motive for late-9th-century Norse migration was probably Norwegian centralisation under Harald Finehair (r. 872–930). Enemies fled to Shetland and Orkney, from whence they raided Norway, before Harald sailed there and killed them.[42] One of his sons was fostered in England and one, Erik Bloodaxe, became York's king, before Athelstan's reunification. They returned to play the Norwegian power game.[43] Norway exported timber, meat, hides, skin, furs and falcons. Norwegians also sailed across the Atlantic. Iceland was colonised from 870 to about 930 in various waves, 30–35,000 people, including Irish and Scottish slaves. Greenland was next in the 980s. With a warmer climate than today, farming flourished. By the 11th century, east coast North America was found, 'Stoneland', 'Woodland' and 'Vinland', probably Labrador, Newfoundland, Nova Scotia and Maine. Preserved cod was sent to Bergen after about 1000. Five American expeditions between 985 and 1011 were recorded in Icelandic sagas. Newfoundland's brief community failed, probably due to hostile tribes and lack of numbers, similar to some late-16th and early-17th century attempts.

A 20-year reign of terror was unleashed on the English coast from 980 by Norwegian and Danish kings, 200 years after the first raids. Designed to exert maximum tribute, the 'danegeld' escalated annually. Ethelred, the mis-translated 'Unready', 'un-raed', meaning lack of council or decision, a joke about indecisiveness,[44] was unlucky in being subjected to such aggressive, coordinated attacks. Planned counter-attacks were neutered by aristocratic in-fighting but under his auspices, the first London Bridge, built about 1000, was as much a barrier to Viking ships as a bridge, concentrating the port downstream from Lundenwic, triggering London's accelerated rise. The 991–1002 lists of its markets suggest Flemings were the most important foreign traders, with resident Frisians and Scandinavians. Cologne and Rouen's merchants regularly visited. Archaeology shows increased imported pottery from Normandy, Flanders, Paris and the Rhineland. Under Viking conqueror Knut (r. 1013–1037), more Danish merchants came. As trade grew, wooden wharves were built to berth larger vessels. Frisian cogs transported bulk cargoes like English wool to Flanders. Increased political stability, the growth of trade opportunities, successful resistance and lack of numbers meant raiding stopped. As they settled, as in eastern Europe and Normandy, they lost their own language within a generation or two.

In continental Europe there was no settled political order but an incoherent patchwork of laws, codes, local customs, Roman Law, Church Law and above all, violence and agricultural subsistence. Communication was restricted to the immediate vicinity. Only merchants were mobile and knowledgeable. No markets were created in 10th-century France, which stagnated. In 998 Emperor Otto III was introduced to an astrolabe, a star-measuring device well-known in classical times. Otto and his contemporaries looked on it with wonder. No surprise when Otto consulted holy hermits for advice, a tradition of western emperors since Theodosius II consulted Simon Stylites (388–460), an ascetic who lived on a 60-foot pillar, three feet in diameter,[45] on the basis that poverty and contemplation were synonymous with holiness and wisdom. Otto's chosen hermit was one Romuald, so holy that he lived in boggy salt-marsh beyond Ravenna, rarely washed and had turned green.[46] Visiting swamps for whatever holy reason was ill-advised as his father Otto II had died of "mal'aria", bad air, from those in Rome in 983 aged 28. He followed in 1002 aged 21, from the same condition from the same area. The word 'merchant' in surviving 9th-10th-century documents is rare, used for monastery and royal Court provisioning. Examples of lending are for trivial amounts. There was little security in inland travel and frequent references to brigandage. Any north European progress in the first 300 years of our period, despite the frequency of maritime raids, came from ports which connected the Black Sea, Constantinople, and the Abbasids to the Baltic, north Europe, and the Irish Sea to Iberia.

Chapter 4

The Muslim Mediterranean and Byzantine-Rus Black Sea

While northern Europe experimented with new hull designs, higher freeboards and stern post angles, and new ports interacted and expanded, much of southern Europe was inward-looking with little innovation, but much religious zeal. Mediterranean ports withered. Provence, Roman Gaul's richest province became its poorest. Between the late-600s' eclipse of Marseilles and Venice's rise, only gradual up to the 990s, there was no Mediterranean Dorestad equivalent.[1] In Iberia, Visigoth conversion from Arianism to Catholicism in 587 led to aggressive anti-Semitic policies. Sisebut's 613 edict started a recurring Iberian theme, that Jews had to convert or be expelled, precipitating an exodus to Gaul and North Africa. Successors outlawed Jewish rites. Converted Jews had to promise to kill any relapsing. Even converts, conversos, were declared traitors, their property confiscated and were enslaved in 694. Christians aiding Jews could lose 25% of their property and be excommunicated. Children were taken from parents and taxes increased. As Muslims swept through North Africa, in 698 they ignored Carthage's maritime wealth-creating past and potential, and built Tunis, better protected from the sea. In the circumstances, Iberian Jews viewed them as potential liberators. In 712, the capture of Visigoth capital Toledo gave them an Iberian state. From then on, continual Muslim raiding meant the 8th-century Mediterranean trade almost ceased. Instead, caravan routes linked Egypt to Morocco, taking Moroccan grain to Andalusia for pottery, textiles and metalwork. To Muslims the Atlantic was Bahr al-Zulamat, Sea of Perpetual Gloom, to be avoided, a reference to the *Koran*'s verse which likens unbelievers 'in the depth of a darkness in a vast, deep ocean...topped by black clouds.'[2] Unlike their Carthaginian predecessors they organised no voyages to west Africa or Iberian Atlantic coasts. Unlike Omani and Yemeni merchants' millennia-old maritime credentials, now also fellow Muslims, they refused to enter infidel lands,[3] except as raiders or conquerors.

Around 670, Burgundian Bishop Arculf went to Alexandria and found 'the commerce of the whole world', hyperbole no doubt, a surprise compared to Europe's poverty, but indicating it remained a major east-west nexus, albeit diminished from its second-century height. Al-Kindi (801–873) described Egypt as 'endowed by God by all kinds of commodities and advantages, the emporium for Mecca, Medina, Sana'a, Aden, Oman, India, Sri Lanka, China,' reflecting its eastern orientation. Ibn Khordadbeh in 845–46 described Jewish Radhanites 'speaking

Arabic, Persian, Greek, Frankish, Andalusian and Slavic', taking eunuchs, slave girls and boys, furs, and swords from Europe to Egypt, and from there on to India and China and returning, some to sell goods in Constantinople and some to Frankish kings, via Alexandria or Fustat.[4] The Red Sea-Mediterranean route had declined but was never abandoned,[5] and ancient Phoenician merchants' role in Egypt and Aden as east-west conduits since Pharaonic times demonstrates continuing activity after conversion to Judaism. Jews were also the main Mesopotamian conduits. Egyptian records show Jewish agents buying flax from small towns, shipping it west with copper, lead and olive oil from North Africa, dyes, madder, indigo, gold, timber, pepper, spices and pearls from the Indian Ocean. Eastern orientation and Mediterranean poverty meant that by 860 Alexandria's population dropped from a 600,000 peak to 100,000. The Pharos was neglected and ruined, while maritime-orientated Basra built similar structures.

The Frankish kingdom's 8th-century's rise was military in character, its nobility economically unproductive. Roads were unsafe and unrepaired, internal trade and town life diminished and tax gathering reduced. Charles Martel, the Hammer, effectively sealed Muslim presence south of the Pyrenees by victory in a skirmish at Poitiers in 733. He retook Avignon and advanced to Marseilles, whose duke had allied with them. Muslim conquest of Provence was thus prevented, although they raided Aquitaine in 733, captured Avignon in 737 and held Narbonne. That apart, Charles was virtually master of the south and west. Charles' son Pepin wrapped-up the rest, culminating in Narbonne's capture in 759. But Europe was now bottled-up by fierce Mediterranean Muslim raiding, in material and intellectual poverty. Pepin, the strongest military power, did a deal with the Lombard-threatened papacy. He deposed the slothful Merovingian king, seizing the Frankish throne with papal backing, for help against Lombards. The *Donation of Constantine*, forged before anointing Pepin in 754, conferred unlimited clerical and temporal power on popes over western Europe. Economic lethargy meant Jewish merchants were used. Abraham of Saragossa, protected by Louis the Pious, exempt from tolls, was allowed to buy foreign slaves to sell in Frankish lands, but in 846, Lyon's archbishop accused Jewish merchants of buying slaves in Provence and selling them in Cordoba,[6] possibly reflecting Church prejudice rather than fact.

Theodulf, bishop of Orleans' poem *Contra judices* about 798, emphasised the use of Arab gold coins in local and international exchange.[7] Charlemagne built a navy to defend the Rhone delta against Muslim raids but his empire was divided on his 814 death. The Mediterranean was not deemed a priority, even with Muslim ships raiding and attempting occupation of islands; Crete about 824–27, Sicily in 827, then the mainland, Brindisi in 838, Taranto in 839, looting Rome's suburbs in 846. A Venetian fleet sent to relieve Taranto was defeated. Marseilles was attacked in 838 and 842, Arles in 850 and a Muslim base established in the Camargue in the 860s. Bari and Otranto fell in the 840s, only regained in the 870s by Byzantine Emperor Basil I (876–886), who's growing power enabled him to more effectively protect Constantinople's Italian lands. But Syracuse fell in 878 and by 902 Muslims held most of Sicily. In the 890s they had La Garde-Freinet, near St. Tropez, from where they raided inland to Vienne. Emperor Otto II, Europe's most powerful monarch, never assembled the small force needed to expel them. It was retaken only in 972. The Balearics, parts of Sardinia, Corsica and some Aegean islands also fell in 902. Raiding provided opportunities to obtain slaves for North Africa. A late-9th-century pilgrim in Taranto saw 9,000 loaded onto Egypt-bound ships. Ibn Khaldun claimed 9th-century Muslims gained total Mediterranean control.'[8] By the early-10th century, Muslim merchants sailed seasonal convoys to Muslim-controlled lands. Timber was shipped from Iberia for shipbuilding. Of Provence, Robert Latouche writes, 'the wretchedness of its condition in Carolingian times can only be guessed at through a few sparse documents.'[9] Today's picturesque Provence hilltop villages were refuges of fearful, previously coastal populations. Tenth-century Islamic shipwrecks off Cannes, Marseilles and St. Tropez carrying Iberian amphorae, storage jars, millstones, bronze ingots, asphalt and lamps are evidence of raiding base provisioning, not trade.

Black Sea grain imports were no longer needed due to drastic depopulation accompanying Roman empire collapse. Procopius thought it best avoided.[10] Many Greeks still lived in Black Sea ports. Trebizond, terminus of eastern overland caravan routes, specialised in Asian luxuries. Rus merchants brought furs, hides, wax, honey and slaves to Constantinople. Its secret weapon against Muslim and Avar attack was 'Greek Fire'. This tube and air pump-ignited naphtha-based liquid blown at enemy ships was the Muslims' most-feared weapon.[11] Had Constantinople fallen in the 674 or 718 sieges, western Europe might have had to deal with a simultaneous two-pronged Muslim attack. Baghdad-based astronomer, geographer, and mathematician Al Marwazi (c. 770–874) thought Byzantines, 'a great nation… [with] extensive lands abounding in good things…gifted in crafts and skilful in the fabrication of articles, textiles, carpets and vessels', reporting revenues from customs collected from the merchants and ships from every region…and caravans [that] reach them by land,' which paid for its monuments, art and culture. Constantinople was known for 500 years as the 'Rome of the East,' 'the sublime porte.' It was an importer and entrepot for fur, silk, grain, olives and manufactured products, all shipped west. Nowhere in politically fragmenting western Europe approached its scale or splendour. After Constantinople's 670s–720s severe population decline, it recovered strongly in the 9th century.

In 809–10 Byzantine leading shipowners were wealthy enough that Emperor Nikephoros I forced them into a loan of 12 lbs. of gold at 16.67% interest, later fixed at between 4% and 6%. Despite few references to mercantile activity, Byzantine merchants and shippers generated wealth,[12] most from state-sponsored feeding of Constantinople, in short-haul shipments from Thrace and Anatolia, after Egypt's loss. But state-supported shipping and snobbery against trade discouraged entrepreneurship, creating 'an inward-looking, self-congratulatory ethos'.[13] Senators only involved themselves with land. Merchants were regarded as common. The Byzantine Code forbade gentlemen to trade, 'so that plebeians and merchants may more easily transact their affairs.'[14] Some spices from overland caravans to Trebizond, furs, eiderdown and slaves from Rus, and Indian Ocean goods via Egypt were imported. No products essential to the state could be exported. Merchants could not trade with Muslims, were heavily taxed, unable to accumulate capital, thus limited to coastal shipping, giving Italians, Greeks, Jews and Rus opportunities as intermediaries. Barriers to social advancement meant dependency on pro-active, foreign merchants, despite dislike of them.

Coins in Corinth and amphorae from Ganos in the Sea of Marmara reflect rising volumes from the 820s, as Constantinople revived.[15] A wreck off southwest Turkey dated to 880 had amphorae marked with the shippers' names. Wine was shipped to Crimea and glass from Thessalonica and Constantinople was exported. Apart from Greek traders at Trebizond, Crimea and Panticapaeum and contact with Rus, Byzantines never embraced the Black Sea, surrounded by threatening enemies. When Muslim unity collapsed in the late-9th and 10th centuries, Byzantines took back much of southern Italy, the upper Euphrates valley, Crete, Cyprus and by 969 Antioch, 971 Bulgaria and by 1018 all the Balkans, the wars paid for by its land tax. Antalya became an important Byzantine entrepot for trade with the Levant and Egypt.

Despite lessening maritime involvement, scholarship's momentum continued. Under Theophilus (829–42) embassies were sent to Baghdad to collect scientific works. Ancient Greek texts were copied and preserved,[16] but Theophilus had his wife's ship destroyed when it docked in Constantinople because it was beneath imperial dignity to be involved with trade. Patriarch Photios (858–67 and 877–86) was devoted to ancient Greek inheritance, Pagan and Christian, classical and medieval, scientific, legal and literary; in contrast to the west where secular education disappeared. Later denigrated as complex government run by effeminate, corrupt men obsessed with incomprehensible bureaucracy and ritual, 'byzantine' came to mean complex to the point of self-defeating, inflexible, characterised by intrigue, scheming, tortuous and devious. But between Byzantine achievements and western Europe's descent into poverty and ignorance, stripped of education and culture, was a chasm. Charlemagne's father had not had his son taught to read and write. The only place in western Europe to have high culture was Cordoba. Under Abd al-Rachman III, his Jewish counsellor Hasdai ibn Shaprut, supervised customs and foreign trade, wrote on religion, politics, music, nature and poetry. Cordoba was famed for textiles, leatherwork and jewellery, Jewish specialities. Tenth-century Rahman III and son Hakim (r. 961–976) built a 400,000-volume library, one of several in Iberia.

The Rus were so important to Constantinople and so ubiquitous on the Black Sea that some Arab geographers labelled it 'bahr-al-Rus'. Commercial treaties were made in 911, 912 and 944. Constantinople was a dream market; 500,000 people with churches, towers, wharves, warehouses, fortifications and palaces, reflecting power and permanence. Apart from silver, glass, silk and spices, trade agreements gave the Rus 'as much grain as they require' and merchants received 'supplies for six months and...when the Rus return homeward, they shall receive...whatever... is needed for the journey' trading 'without payment of taxes.' Constantinople was generous because Kyiv was commercially useful and first line of defence against steppe nomads, just 600 miles from the Black Sea. With Muslim stalemate, mutual toleration developed. Early-10th-century Patriarch Nicholas the Mystic wrote to a Muslim emir. 'It is necessary to live together in brotherhood; having different ways of life, rules of behaviour and religion does not mean [people]...be inimical toward one another.' Toleration and stability bred conditions for further commerce.

The Khazars adopted Judaism and neighbouring Volga Bulgars, Islam. It was therefore important for Constantinople to convert the Rus. Patriarch Photios (858–67) encouraged them to develop written forms of Slavonic and had the *Bible* translated. Vladimir (c. 956–1015) considered each religion. Islamic belief in fulfilling carnal desires with virgins after death appealed, but circumcision, prohibiting eating pork and drinking wine did not. 'Drinking is the joy of the Rus. We cannot exist without that pleasure.' Moreover, the Hagia Sofia's architecture and lavish services impressed. In 988 they accepted Orthodox Christianity.[17] Constantinople's architects built in Byzantine style, moulding Kyiv in Roman civilising tradition. Orthodox Christianity spread to Bulgars and Serbs. Papal insistence on the Latin *Bible* and services meant Catholicism became isolated in western Europe. Rus, Scandinavian, English and German mercenaries were formed into the Varangian Guard by Basil II in 988. But Constantinople's attitude to maritime trade was an invisible weakness. Like the Roman Empire after Marcus Aurelius and China most of the time, the need to defend extensive frontiers diverted focus inland. Its maritime mentality, already meagre, melted away. In the Mediterranean, despite a few 'highlights' described in this chapter, lack of 8th to 10th-century records reflect the paucity of commerce and capital.

Chapter 5

Italian Ports

Because Franks were ineffective against Mediterranean Muslim raiding, Italian ports tried to clear the seas to trade effectively. Established French ports like Marseilles and Arles withered, the latter's amphitheatre turned into a defence with 'a miserable clutch of dwellings...inside the arena.'[1] Italian maritime republics, Venice, Genoa, Pisa and Amalfi, fought and defeated Muslims, then competed with and fought each other for control of growing Mediterranean trade. Smaller maritime republics included Gaeta, Ancona, Trani and Noli in Italy and Ragusa on the Adriatic's east coast.

a) Amalfi

Naples had a huge harbour, but Amalfi on the Sorrentine peninsula on cliffs with a small beach below was a port from which southern Europe began to recover because it was difficult to attack. Such a location was only possible in hostile seas with small trading volumes. First mentioned in the early-6th century, it started trading its neighbour's grain, Sardinian salt, and slaves for Egyptian gold, with which it minted coins. Low-value, mass-consumption bulk cargoes were trades of the distant Roman past. The *Amalfi Laws* were a widely-used maritime code. It shared eastern trade with Gaeta, between Amalfi and Rome, in the 8th and 9th century and established Constantinople's first foreign merchant enclave. Its 850–1050 ascendancy was the Mediterranean's most dangerous time when trade volumes were still tiny. Its main street was a centre for southern Italian towns and merchants, but its peak population in about 1000 was only 70,000. In 812, Sicily's Byzantine governor asked Amalfi and Gaeta to help resist Muslim incursions there. When they beat a Muslim fleet off Ostia, a grateful Pope offered free-trade access for luxury goods from Sicily, Tunisia and Alexandria, but could not stop Sicily's invasion in 827. Amalfi's Pantaleoni family owned wharves and warehouses in Constantinople and had a 10th-century Fustat enclave whose Jewish merchants sold it pepper. By 1025 it had merchant enclaves in the Maghreb, Sicily, Egypt, the Levant and Venice. Impressive though it was, the contrast with complex high-volume long-haul Indian Ocean trade networks with this low-volume trade of small Mediterranean ports, where invasion and raiding were normal, is striking.

b) Venice

As the Roman empire disintegrated, the lagoons and salt marshes of the Po delta, remote from the fighting, offered safety to Italian towns sacked in 403 by Alaric and 452 by Attila. As refugees flocked in, Venice was formed in an extensive lagoon, like Amalfi, difficult to attack. In 548 it was wealthy enough for Justinian to seek its aid against Lombards. The 560s-570s Lombard invasion increased Venice's numbers. Fishing and seawater evaporating ponds for salt were its original industries. Absence of taxable land meant it relied on customs dues and imported food. Around 600 it started landfilling back to the mainland and later built smaller salt ponds for quicker evaporation and more efficient production. In 697 the Exarch of Ravenna, Constantinople's Italian representative, appointed a military commander, dux, duke or doge in Venetian, to guard the lagoon, but the Exarch fell in 751, ending Ravenna's role as Constantinople's entrepot. It was the impetus for Venice's growth.

It was one of the few Mediterranean ports where ancient maritime customs and laws were remembered, mainly because it was remote enough to retain independent thought. It ignored papal and Constantinople's orders not to ship timber, slaves and weapons to Muslim ports, unless it suited them, when needing Byzantine help suppressing pirates. It began to trade throughout the Adriatic despite Dalmatian pirates, which it gradually suppressed and established trade enclaves. Po delta marshes made it difficult to conquer by land, as Charlemagne discovered. Marseilles' and Arles' decline meant the Rhone route to the interior dried-up. Transalpine routes involving pack animals, not barges, meaning no bulk commodity trades, further impoverishing inland Europe. Venice concentrated on Byzantine, Levantine and Egyptian luxuries; silks, jewels, ivory, spices, gems, gold and saints' relics, sold to secular and ecclesiastical elites. Unlike most of western Europe, literacy was widespread. Larger 8th-9th-century churches strongly suggest trade-enrichment, even with small volumes.[2] Eighth-century Mediterranean trade did not reach North Sea levels because Venice was one of few active ports.[3]

Eighth-century maritime loans or credit are the first-known European *commenda* contracts, lending capital to merchants for commercial ventures, with acceptance of risk and specified division of profits. One partner advanced credit, the other accompanied the cargo, the *commenda* ending when the borrower returned the capital plus profit or minus loss. It involved agents warehousing cargo, acting as legal representatives, arbiters, port superintendents and custom tax farmers. Once hailed as a genius invention of Venetian merchants by Eurocentric historians, it was learnt from Egypt, its most lucrative trade partner.[4] As Braudel asks, 'How could the Italian merchants…have failed to note this convenient method of transferring a sum of money to distant parts, simply by a piece of paper?'[5] The Prophet's wife's caravan *commenda* had Mohammed travel as her agent. It was the usual way of organising long-haul trade to India, Southeast Asia and beyond; impossible without it. That European trade practices were borrowed is also suggested by vocabulary transfer; customs, doana in Italian, douane in French from Arabic, as was trade enclave, funduk in Arabic, fondaco in north Italy, funnaco in Sicily. The most prized goods reaching the Mediterranean were eastern silk, rice, sugar, ginger, musk, ambergris, cotton cloth, dyes, porcelain, paper and intellectual property; Indian numerals, Indian science, gunpowder and the compass for example. Venice and other north Italian ports plugged into and profited from existing Indian Ocean trade via Egypt, adopting its methods, techniques and business practices. Different *commenda* varieties became more common in the 840s,[6] but trade was still interrupted by Muslim raids. Islam, grafted onto the Indian Ocean-Mediterranean choke point, had different types of people; nomads and pastoralists in arid, inland areas and merchants and seafarers in thriving ports. The latter resumed their ancient role, linking the Mediterranean via Egypt, Yemen, Oman or the Levant via the Persian Gulf, to west coast India and beyond.[7]

By contrast, merchant caravans came across the Alps with horses, slaves, arms and woollen cloth, meeting Venice's and Amalfi's merchants in Pavia where they traded Byzantine goods. Customs posts in Alpine passes charged 10%, although English and Lombard merchants agreed about 1010–1020 that instead, every three years they would pay 50 lbs. of silver, two greyhounds with gold embossed collars, two shields, two swords, lances and fur coats, while Venice's doge would give the Lombard king 50 lbs. of Venetian deniers in tribute.[8] It demonstrates the trade's relative poverty. Chris Wickham thinks 9th-century Venice was more marginal to north Italy's economy than Dorestad for Frisia or Hamwic for Wessex.[9]

A routine 748 record of slave trading indicates it was well-established. Pope Zachary (741–752) recorded Venetian merchants in Rome 'buying a great number of slaves, both male and female…to transport to the pagans in Africa [which was] not right that those who had been washed in Christ's baptism should be slaves to pagans.' In 828 merchants smuggled St. Mark's body from Egypt to Venice. One account mentioned ten Venetian vessels in Alexandria at the time.[10] This surprisingly high number in a dangerous sea was because merchants were protected. Early-9th-century Ibn Sahnun explained, 'As to the Christian ships which come, whether they are far from port or nearby, it is not permitted to capture them if they are merchants known for their commercial relations with Muslims.'[11] In 829 Doge Justinian Partecipazio's will left real estate, bullion, cash, ornaments and 1,200 silver lbs. invested in foreign commerce. By contrast, contemporary Frankish documents reflect an exclusively agrarian world.[12]

But Venice faced multiple threats. In 836 an ineffective doge abdicated due to Dalmatian pirates. His successor reasonably successfully campaigned against them. In the 840s' treaty with Charlemagne's grandson Lothair, Venice pledged responsibility for Adriatic defence.[13] But between 827 and 902 Muslims took Sicily, raided further north and defeated Venetian fleets. In 887 a doge was killed in battle. In 899 Magyars, other central Asian steppe nomads, were finally defeated in Venice's lagoon. In the late-9th century, Venice subdued Istria when the northern Adriatic was called the Gulf of Venice. Voyages to Tyre for purple cloth, still made there, brought Phoenician glass making skills and artisans. Al-Muqadassi in 985 reported

Tyre's beads, bracelets and wheel-cut glass making,[14] although glass workshops were reported in Venice's lagoon's Torcello in the 7th century,[15] so this early influence was probably its glass industry's foundation. A wreck from about 1025 off Serce Limani, 12 miles north of Rhodes, held three tons of raw, broken and waste glass, millstones, 90 Byzantine wine amphorae, Levantine glassware, various ceramics for perishable foods and 64 spears and javelins. The ship had probably sailed from the Levant to a glass making centre, possibly Constantinople, but probably Venice, in which case, probably a Venetian ship.

Competition for salt production and distribution prompted Venice to destroy Comacchio's rival salt works in 932. Second-half 10th-century Venice paid Dalmatian pirates tribute to ensure free passage. The doge's powers were limited, preventing dynastic rule, but Venice was bedevilled by feuds until in 991 Doge Pietro Orseolo II stopped paying tribute and sent galleys to capture a pirate base. In 992 he sent warships for Constantinople's aid and was rewarded with reduced customs dues[16] and less bureaucracy in return for troop transport when needed and did a similar customs deal with the western emperor.[17] In 1000 he sailed the Dalmatian coast, punishing enemies and making treaties. Warehouses were opened, coastal frontiers extended, timber and food supplies accessed, and the Adriatic entrance secured. In 1002 he drove Muslim forces from Bari. The route to Egypt and Constantinople, the basis of its prosperity, was thus secured, a start to revitalisation. Trade immediately increased and he sent ambassadors to Islamic Mediterranean ports, especially Egypt, for easier trade access and lower duties. In 1002 Emperor Henry II addressed Orseolo as 'Doge of Venice and Dalmatia'. His leadership was the trigger needed. The millennium seems a symbolic start of Venice's future prosperity and southern European revival. Venice's future core policy was Adriatic domination, entirely commercial and maritime in character. Surrounded by richer east Mediterranean economies, it had more wealth-creating potential than north Europe.

c) Pisa and Genoa

Amalfi's and Venice's tentative success spurred Pisa and Genoa. Pisa's origins, according to Strabo, was associated with Pylos' King Nestor of Trojan War fame. Archaeology confirms a 5th-century BC Etruscan port and it had been a Roman naval base. Its importance was due to its location between Genoa and Rome, proximity to Corsica, Sardinia, Iberia and France and its grain-rich Tuscan hinterland. In 828 Pisan ships raided North Africa, assisted Salerno's defence against Muslim raids in 871, fought them in Corsica, and joined Emperor Otto II against them in Calabria and Sicily. After 950 it was increasingly active, funnelling Mediterranean goods including quality glazed Tunisian and Sicilian pottery into Tuscany while pressurising Muslim naval bases, sacking Palermo in 1064 and Palma de Mallorca in 1115.

Genoa, enclosed by mountains, produced wine, chestnuts, olive oil and herbs, but cut-off from Italian grain-producing regions, it needed wheat, meat and cheese imports. Not as remote as Venice and Amalfi, it was exposed to Muslim raids, the last in 934–935 by the Fatimid fleet, thus, not as comfortable with Muslim trade as other Italian republics. Self-governing from the 11th century, with Pisa, it defended Sardinia from Muslim onslaughts, but in 1066 they fought each other over it. Genoa was less advanced than Venice until the 1099 First Crusade gave it impetus. Islamic raiding delayed Mediterranean recovery, but when it stopped, trade volumes reached North Sea levels, then surpassed them. Egypt's trade with Italian ports kick-started it.

Chapter 6

Consequences of Indian Ocean Trade Acceleration

a) Mataram's Challenge to Srivijaya

Accelerating maritime trade stimulated choke point competition. After Srivijaya retreated from Java in the mid-9th century, local kings resumed control. King Sindok (r. 924–947) moved from Yogyakarta to Mataram, at the Brantas River mouth near today's Surabaya, draining land, settling farmers, growing rice, and was nearer the Moluccas for spice trade control. It attracted foreign ships, to Srivijaya's detriment, and independent missions were sent to China. Following Song China's 987 Southeast Asian missions to induce traders to China, Mataram's King Dharmavamsa aimed to replace Palembang as Southeast Asia's maritime hub, as Chinese demand grew.[1] Seducing formerly loyal west Java, he attacked and took Palembang in 990. Mataram was however, unprepared for the reaction. Part of Srivijaya's success lay in cultivating Chinese favour. Nine embassies had been sent between 960 and 988. Needing the Chinese market, Mataram sent one in 992. But under Chinese protection, Palembang was re-taken in 993. It sent an appreciative embassy in 1003, reporting a Buddhist temple built to pray for the emperor's longevity.

Srivijaya sent four more embassies up to 1018 and created unrest in Mataram, supporting rebel prince Wunawar, who in 1016 killed the royal family, except Airlangga, who escaped.[2] For over a decade Mataram ceased rivalry in nutmeg, mace and clove trades. A 1044–46 Tanjore inscription refers to these events in the gift of a Buddhist temple by the king of Kadaram, Kedah in Tamil, a Srivijayan sub-king, indicating friendly relations with Tamil India's Chola Dynasty and probably their neutrality during Mataram's punishment.[3] The Kaladi inscription from about 909 mentions Kling, (from east India), Aryans (northwest Indians), Sinhalese, Khmer, Champa and Mon traders and north Java's Cane inscription from around 1021 mentions Kling, Singhalese, Pandikiri, Tamils, Cham and Khmer, indicating many Indian traders and well-developed maritime trade networks. Airlangga rallied support in east Java and Bali, the Kahuripan kingdom with its Brantas river capital.

Srivijaya's choke point position between Yemen and China was strengthened by its benzoin, brazilwood, camphor, resins, cardamon, sandalwood, rhinoceros' horns and other forest products from different ports in an alliance of mutual interests and support, a federation of ports, a wealth-creating commercial network. One commentator likens it to a multi-national company with Palembang's maharajah as president, princes of adjacent areas, mainly relatives, as board directors or directors of subsidiaries,[4] structurally stronger than a single ruling family, especially as it was Buddhist and a Chinese ally.

b) Song China's Trade Encouragement

This dispute happened because of rising wealth due to Song dynasty trade encouragement. China's 750 population, about 50 million, doubled to 100 million in 1100.[5] Coastal Fujian outperformed with 286,000 households in 742, 654,000 in 980 and 1,537,000 in 1080.[6] Its Quanzhou region increased from 2.61 households per square kilometre in 742 to 16.71 in 1200, partly cause and partly result of increased trade and early-ripening rice introduced from early-10th-century Champa.[7] Some think these census figures are underestimates because 30% of south-easterners lived on ships and were omitted.[8]

To defend China from steppe nomads, the first Song emperor in 960, identifying maritime trade as a key revenue provider, issued regulations. He visited shipyards, established the 'Bureau of Licensed Trade' to buy foreign goods, sending four missions to Southeast Asia in 987 with gifts to lure 'foreign traders of the South Sea and those who went to foreign lands beyond the sea' to visit China, promising better facilities, protection against officials and easy import licenses.[9] Srivijaya immediately responded sending 16 missions with Southeast Asian and Arabian goods, including 13 frankincense grades, pepper, aromatics and medicines.[10] Chinese recorded Arab, Indian, Champa and Srivijayan missions comprising envoys with Islamic names. Those surnamed 'Pu', from Abu, from Champa settled southern Hainan,[11] spreading Islam from Southeast Asia to China. Early Song revenue was still mainly from improving agriculture, but increasingly from maritime trade, so much that in 1017, Palembang's maharajah wrote to China's emperor as 'the king of the ocean lands.' Fujian's coastal shipping, increasingly active at the end of T'ang, through the Five Dynasties period, accelerated. Cut-off from much of China by mountains, Fujian's maritime outlook led it to become China's leading economy, pre-eminent in shipbuilding, navigation and merchant endeavour. An 1137 document says most people with capital engaged in it, even small sums, making several hundred per cent profits.[12]

Chinese officials were not allowed to trade but those succeeding in promoting it, enhancing state revenues, were rewarded. This was not disguised tribute. The Song recognised that merchants were economically vital and in 989 Chinese were allowed to sail abroad for nine months, effectively meaning Southeast Asia,[13] although foreigners dominated. Some were descended from Arab or Persian Muslim merchants called 'Hokkiens' in Southeast Asia. *Commenda* contracts, joint-stock capital, joint-ownership of ships and goods, standard forms like modern charter parties for shipments were used,[14] partnerships grew and urbanisation increased as cities became commercial, some industrial. Customs rates were set to maximise revenue, lower rates on low-value goods, 20% on higher-value products. Increased volumes led to unprecedented economic growth and, as always, intellectual development and technological innovation; moveable print, improved seeds, water-powered mechanical clocks, the first paper money and gunpowder, invented about 850 was in the early-10th century, applied to flame throwers and fire arrows, by 1231 to bombs, grenades and rockets.

Ceramic, textile, wine and salt industries grew. Iron production increased to 125,000 tons a year in 1078, six-times that of 800,[15] used to improve ploughs, hammers, nails, chains and tools, enabled by using coke in blast furnaces, one smelter producing 14,000 tons of pig iron annually, compared to mid-17th-century England's total production of 20–40,000 tons. Massive expansion of cultivated lands, terracing and irrigation meant crop production tripled, including cotton, tea, hemp and sugar cane, refined in quantity from mid-11th-century Quanzhou, reflected in Wang Zhuo's 1154 *Classic of Sugar*, the first book on its technology. Paper was manufactured in huge quantities, due to increasing paper money, evolved from merchant receipts, documents, books and increasing literacy. Fujian became a leading centre of scholarship. Many Fujianese became provincial governors and high imperial officials. Fang Ta-Tsung recorded, 'every peasant, artisan and merchant teaches his sons how to read books.'[16] China led the world in productivity, innovation and technical capabilities. Iron export was banned as potential weaponry, but traded illegally.[17] Copper, cattle and horse export was also banned, encouraging smuggling in cattle, hides and horns. Hu Ch'uan noted in the 1150s, 'the government have not been able to make the prohibition effective.'[18] Internal trade and money circulation grew and credit instruments were widely used.

Apart from the double rice harvest, hemp, silk, cotton and lychees were intensely developed in 10th-century Fujian.[19] Kaifeng, the Song capital at the Grand Canal's northern end where it met the Yellow River, had 750,000–1,000,000 people, similar to Chang'an but more commercial, with ironworks and weapon manufacturing. Coastal traffic increased. Company partnerships and family businesses, bills of exchange and legal regulation of disputes were normal. There was unprecedented economic growth and in the 1070s-1080s, the highest level of copper coins at any time in Chinese history were produced.[20] Old attitudes to wealth creation expressed by 11th-century official Feng Shan; 'piling-up wealth is not a policy to be approved of' gradually disappeared.[21] Song trade stimulated the whole Indian Ocean and South China Seas. The 12th-century *Song Hui-yao* infers that from the 10th century, China also traded with Ma-yi, possibly Manila, with floral cloth, damask, white cotton cloth, rattan, palm leaf mats, aromatics, medicinal plants, timbers, wax, gold, silver and iron ingots. Butuan, an Indianised kingdom in north Mindanao, Philippines, appeared in Song texts from 1001, mentioning camphor, tortoiseshell, cloves, mother of pearl and aromatics. Cloves suggests a close relationship with Java and the Moluccas.[22] New Sumatran ports, Thi Nai (Quy Nho'n) in the Cham polity of Vijaya, the Viet's Van Don and Javan Japara, Tuban and Gresik appeared in the 11th and 12th centuries.[23]

The Grand Canal, serviced by feeder roads and sub-canals, enabled imports and food to reach central and north China. Chinese internal trade used rivers, lakes and canals of which 50,000 kilometres were built in the Song era, plied by specialised ships, many larger than Columbus' flagship,[24] some with paddle wheels carrying hundreds of people.[25] The northern threat needed a 1.25-million-man army and navy of vessels with crossbowmen for river, canal and sea, costing 75% of state revenue. Five-decked ships up to 700 tons with hundreds of crew were built at private and state shipyards. Improvements were made in keels, rudders, sails and navigation. Harbours were dredged. Maritime trade supervisorates at Guangzhou (971), Hangzhou (989), Ding-hao (992), Quanzhou (1087), Ban-qiao (1088), Hua-ting (Shanghai) (1113), Wenzhou (1131) and Jian-yin (1146),[26] signalled when they could officially trade overseas. Quanzhou's 1087 legalisation, prompted by smuggling in collusion with local officials, was enacted by Wang Anshan's 1070s-1080s reform administration.[27]

In addition to import duties, revenue was collected on the difference in purchase and subsequent sale prices. Government monopolised ivory, coral, rhinoceros horn crocodile skins and other luxury imports. However, a 1088 document referring to a southern Shantung town says 'when merchants who deal in overseas goods come…they all have frankincense, ivory, rhinoceros horn and such precious things. Although these things are prohibited [to private traders] it is quite impossible to prevent.'[28] Late 11th-century Li Hsun noted seafaring merchants value pearls, jade, rhinoceros horn, and tortoiseshell, inland merchants salt, iron and tea.[29] Imports were consumed widely. In rural fairs, frankincense, aloes and sandalwood were reported on sale.[30] As Fujian increasingly grew cash crops, many for export, it depended on grain imports, 'always concerned lest merchant ships [from Kuang-nan] may not arrive on time.'[31] China's main exports were silk, gold, silver, pewter, copper, tin, lead, lacquerware, semi-precious stones, paper, bamboo, lychees, pottery, tea and especially, porcelain.[32] The *Manual of the Lychee* explicitly refers to its export to 'Korea…Japan…the Ryukyu islands…Persia…merchants are trading ever more extensively in them.'[33] From Japan it imported sulphur for gunpowder, pearls, antler horn and weapons; from Southeast Asia, spices, pepper, aloes, sandalwood, tortoiseshell and rattan mats; from India, pepper and pearls; from the Levant, fruits and glassware; from the Gulf pearls and from the Mediterranean, coral. Imports of aromatics, with musk and ambergris as preservatives, spread to Japan. Song ships discharged them in Fukuoka, then called Hakata. Obsession with them in Kyoto's imperial court is described in early-11th-century's *The Tale of Genji*, whose members obsessed with mixing blends, competing to find the best.

Song ceramic and porcelain technical brilliance led to massive foreign demand, so kilns were built in or near Guangzhou, Quanzhou and Ningbo, shortening transport time, reducing damage and pilferage, enabling high-volume exports. Designs and styles were adapted for foreign taste. Bluish-white porcelain of Jingdezhen in Jiangxi province, China's most enduring and famous kiln, became a regular export, as northern kilns reduced exports, producing mainly for the imperial court. 'Once the shift south had occurred, no significant industry continued in northern China.'[34] Longquan's output was soon outstripped by the new kilns. The *Pingzhou Ke Tan* described 'several hundred people on big ships and over a hundred on the small...the products are mainly ceramics with sets besides sets, almost no gaps in between.' A technological peak was reached with these export-orientated kilns. North Sabah's 11th-century Tanjung Simpang wreck carried mainly Chinese brown-glazed pottery and bronze gongs. Artistry also flourished in silk and lacquerware.

In T'ang times, several officials recorded that many southerners could not speak Chinese, mainly remnants of Austronesian Yue seafarers. By the mid-1100s, the much denser population had been fully sinicised as migration south continued. Maritime trade fostered entrepreneurship in coastal regions. Ts'ai Hsiang observed 'even peasants, artisans and merchants all scheme away night and day in search of profit.' Late-11th-century Liu Yen wrote how men struggled to better themselves. Desire for wealth was considered natural and some emigrated to achieve it.[35] Su Tung-p'o said 'the entire province of Fujian makes its living by...seaborne commerce' from Korea, Japan, Champa and Southeast Asia. The *Songshi's (Song History)* chapter on Korea says most of the several hundred Chinese in its capital were Fujianese merchants. A 1076 decree stated some Fujianese in Champa served as officials.[36] Chin-chiang was recorded trading for ten years until 1049 when he became a monk, his wealth given to his partners.[37] Fo-lien, a Quanzhou Muslim, owned 80 ships and Quanzhou's Yang K'o amassed 200,000 strings of coins in ten years as a seagoing merchant. An 1138 stele records merchant Zhou Wei's one year-round voyage to Srivijaya returning 100% profit.[38] Wang yuan-mao, admired by Champa's king, returned after ten years with a million strings, continued trading and in 1178 one of his ships was absent for another ten years, returning with several thousand per cent profit.[39] Champa traders, some representing Arabs,[40] continued sending rhinoceros horn, ivory, timber, mats, textiles, aromatics, coconuts, camphor, pepper, cardamon, nutmeg, feathers, coral, frankincense, myrrh and glass.

In 1127 Jurchen nomads took Kaifeng, sacked Hangzhou and Ningbo and conquered north China, forcing Emperor Kao Tsung (1127–62) in 1135 to relocate the capital to Hangzhou, southern terminus of the Grand Canal. It quickly surpassed Kaifeng, emphasising the maritime contribution. Trade revenues doubled from late-11th to early-12th century and doubled again between the 1130s and 1150s. By the 1130s about a fifth of government income came from maritime trade taxes. An 1146 Song edict read, 'The profits of foreign trade contribute much to the national income...people of faraway countries are encouraged to come and abundantly circulate goods and wealth.'[41] Contrasting with paltry European volumes, the early-1100s Nanhai wreck contained 60–80,000 pottery goods, mainly porcelain and 6,000 coins. Twelfth-century conflict between Angkor and Champa probably arose from product-access and trade control, culminating in Angkor's invasion of Champa, to control increasingly wealthy ports, like Vijaya's Thi Mai.

c) The Rise of the Chola and Relations with China and Srivijaya

Tamil India's deep antiquity's 'Sangam' period, ending roughly in the 3rd century, known for its maritime trade-inspired prosperity and literary works, coincided with Red Sea dominance over the Persian Gulf as the main Mediterranean route and extensive Southeast Asian links, where a 2nd-3rd-century Tamil inscription is found at Vo-Canh, Vietnam. With Red Sea revival, connection with Tamil and Sri Lankan ports increased as natural calls for eastbound ships from Aden. Gulf ports supplied horses to their armies. From the mid-9th to 10th century, Chola kings conquered surrounding lands from Pandyas, Pallavas and Kalingas, capturing Madurai and Nagapattinam, culminating with Rajaraja the Great (r. 985–1018), who also conquered most of Sri Lanka and the Maldives, all ports between the Red Sea and Srivijaya.

The most important Kra Isthmus transit route was Kedah, where excavations have revealed a 1st-century jetty, iron smelting and monuments, an important transit port from antiquity, with Hindu and Buddhist temples, ship repair facilities and storehouses. Sailing from Mamallapuram during Pallavan ascendancy and Nagapattinam during Chola dominance, Indian trade guilds used various Kra Isthmus locations well before mid-9th-century inscriptions at Takua Pa, the best west coast Isthmus harbour, reveal the existence of the well-established Manigramam guild. Kedah Peak's Hindu temple's fire, its ruins still visible, aided navigation.[42]

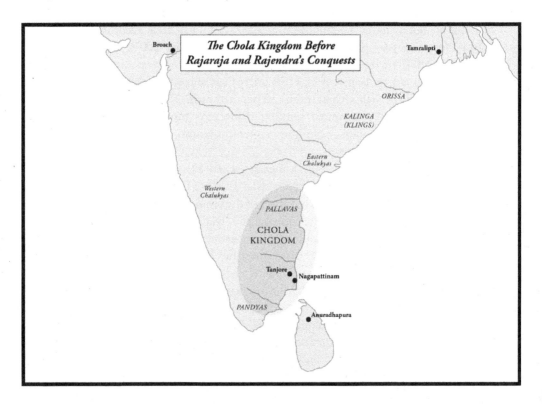

By about 1000 it was as important as Palembang, producing sandalwoods, aloe wood, ebony, camphor, ivory, rattan, lead and tin, the Kra Isthmus' preferred route. A stone slab at Songkla has a Tamil inscription indicating the direction of one overland route. Inscriptions suggest a Srivijayan official permanently lived in south India and that the Kedah choke point between the two was especially important in bilateral relations.[43] Rajaraja continued Pallavan policy to support trade guilds, the 'vanigrama', selling pepper, iron, areca nuts, spices, medicinal plants, jewellery, ivory, ebony, camphor and cloth, *Cholar Chelai*, and cloths from just-conquered Kalinga, to Srivijaya's and Kedah's traders. Although evidence is thin, Tamil merchants must have been frustrated at Srivijaya's choke point hold in this era of increasing commercial opportunities.

In 1005, Srivijaya told the Song Emperor that they had dedicated another temple to him and had a Buddhist monastery, the Chudamani Vihara, built in Nagapattinam, which seemingly gave thanks for Chola assistance to a Kedah king to regain his kingdom after internal revolt. Still standing until Jesuits destroyed it in 1867, a British observer in 1844 said it was 'the first object visible at sea.'[44] The inscription recording it refers to Srivijaya's ruler as 'King of Kedah' and 'Lord of the Srivijaya country,' indicating Srivijaya still ruled Kedah. Apparently simultaneously, Rajaraja donated a village's revenue to Chudamani Vihara's maintenance. These friendly Srivijaya-Chola gestures, 'temple diplomacy', were probably also diplomatic moves to maintain Srivijaya's privileged position without impeding Tamil guilds' China-bound ships. Tamil merchant enclaves had been in Guangzhou from at least the 3rd century. The Pallavas had seemingly previously attempted to outflank the loosely Srivijayan-held Kra Isthmus choke point at Takua Pa, but with ever richer Song trade, stakes were far higher. Traffic became heavier. Gold and silver Chola coins indicate greater prosperity than Pallavan lead and copper coins. In 1012, resuming 8th-century Pallavan embassies, Rajaraja sent a 52-envoy delegation to China via Kedah and Palembang, staying some months in each, with pearls, gems, aromatics and medicinal herb gifts, described in the *Songshi* and were recognised as a first-class tributary state. Good relations continued. Rajaraja and son Rajendra after 1014, continued to donate to Nagapattinam's Srivijayan monastery and new Hindu temple, as did Srivijaya.[45]

Temples had an important role in Tamil society as agents of social and economic cohesion, the 'institutional base for capital formation' and 'circulation of capital across various sections of society.'[46] Over half 9th-13th-century Tamil temple donations were from merchants, repaid with interest in food or service. Temples lent money to community members.[47] Merchants were honoured society members for enabling desirable imports, temple donations, empathy with local concerns and desire for religious merit.[48] Merchant guilds' exact relationship with government is obscure, but were supported. The Manigramam guild, mentioned in the Takua Pa inscription, concentrated on Southeast Asia, Ayyavole on west Asia. The Nanadesi, Nagarattar, Anjuvannam, and Valanijiya, specialised in other areas and products. They were increasingly important contributors of revenues to the Chola Court, dominating internal and external trade of south India and parts of Sri Lanka from the late-9th to the late-13th century.

The Khmer at Angkor expanded its frontiers into Laos, central Thailand and the northern Malay Peninsula. Buddhist Pagan united Burma, traded with China by land and sea, and had strong cultural and religious links to India. Its rulers also reached the border of Srivijaya's northern outposts. So Pagan, Angkor and Srivijayan frontiers quickly became adjacent at the Kra Isthmus, where Tamil traders had vital interests in free passage. The Khmer, like most Asian states, imported Indian cotton cloth. Angkor may have been trying to interfere in Kedah's affairs or bolster an alliance with Tamralipti, a copper port at the Ganges' mouth, which sent envoys to China in 1001, 1014 and 1016, when it was recognised as a second-class tributary state. Srivijaya continued sending envoys to China in 1016, 1017 and 1018. The Khmer sent Rajendra a gift, the war chariot with which its king had defeated his enemies. With gathering powers adjacent on the Kra Isthmus, was it offering an alliance because of Srivijayan threats? Did they feel threatened by Chola attempts to grab the Kra Isthmus? Did Kedah seek independence from Srivijaya? What part did Mataram's recent Srivijayan raids play? Historians have asked these questions and speculated. The evidence is fragmentary and ambiguous. But choke point issues and surging Chinese trade must have been key factors. Rajendra took Sri Lankan areas not already conquered. Polonnaruwa became its new capital. Its port, Trincomalee, faced east. By 1018, India's east coast to the Ganges, and its ports' valuable duties were subjugated; the height of Chola power.

Chola's Tamil culture, stretching to deep antiquity in literature, sculpture and music, arguably reached its zenith under Rajaraja. Stone and bronze sculptures were unsurpassed. His 216-foot tower in Tanjore built in 1010, was India's highest building, built with 28–40-ton granite blocks, topped by an 82-ton block, achieved by a 20-kilometre-long ramp, using geometry and elephants to push them into place, more stone moved than for Giza's pyramids. Rajendra built a replica at Cholapuram. They promoted maths and astronomy. Literacy, already high, rose to the world's highest levels, producing much new thinking. Irrigation involving tanks, reservoirs, dams, sluices, canals and wells were built. Their temples along the Kaveri River still stand. Madurai was their great cultural and commercial entrepot. Trade-inspired prosperity brought more luxury, artistic and cultural achievement, and more Shiva temples than any other Indian kingdom. Persian mathematician and astronomer Al-Biruni (973–1048) travelled throughout India, wrote its history and believed in a sea route around southern Africa, contradicting standard Ptolemaic belief.

Chola embassies were sent to China in 1020 and 1022. In 1023 the Chinese emperor advised Arab and Persian merchants to avoid the overland route to China, further stimulating Indian Ocean trade through Srivijaya, enhancing Chola revenue. There is no direct evidence of Ayyavole and Manigramam guilds' actions and ambitions but in the context of heightening tension, competing maritime powers and higher commercial stakes, it makes sense that they wanted better access to China via Srivijaya. Probably tensions regarding tight choke point control resulted in Rajendra's dramatic, apparently sudden 1025 attack on Palembang, Langkasuka, Jambi, Panai, Tambralinga, Kedah and eight other Srivijayan ports, returning with booty, thereafter, calling himself 'kadaram kondan', Kedah's conqueror. Added to the questions already asked must be, did Srivijaya perceive the Cholas as threatening their entrepot status and try to prevent or disrupt it and did Mataram's Airlangga (r. c. 1019–1049) encourage Rajendra?

He certainly took advantage, creating dams and canals on the Brantas; more land for rice cultivation. Productivity increased with two annual crops. He improved Hujing Galeh's harbour, today's Surabaya, as the Moluccan spice hub, ousting Srivijaya from influence in central Java and Bali and built Kambang Putih, inaugurated after his reign, attracting foreign merchants; Kling, Aryya, Singhala, Pandikira, Drawida, Champa, Khmer and Reman, meaning from all Asia.[49] Art, culture and religious tolerance flourished. Brantas warehouses stored rice, pepper, beans, fennel, salt and sugar.[50] Pepper and cotton from India, planted from the 9th century, by the 12th supplanted it as China's main pepper supplier. Bali and Java were China's main supplier of safflower dye.[51] It imported gold, silver, copper, ceramics, iron goods, lacquerware, silks and industrial raw materials for perfume, glassmaking and dyeing. Brantas delta and north Javan archaeological sites have yielded many T'ang and Song dynasty coins and ceramics, most numerous in the 12th and 13th centuries. Javanese pottery was greatly influenced by Chinese styles and techniques. The records are incomplete and obscure, but east Java's Kediri kingdom, an extension of Airlangga's Kahuripan kingdom, arose around 1042, lasting until 1205. It was considered one of the most prosperous and cultured. With a permanent army and navy, it secured the spice trade.

Rajendra's raid on 14 wealthy Srivijayan ports loosened its grip on its allies. Consequently, Tamil guilds established trading rights and Chola royal family members may have become viceroys in Kedah. Trade was seemingly disrupted temporarily, the Chinese emperor complaining, 'In recent years foreign shipping rarely came to Guangzhou.'[52] But in 1028 Srivijaya was back in business with a Chinese trade mission and by 1079 it donated a huge 600,000 gold pieces for repairing and maintaining a Guangzhou Taoist shrine. Only one Chola mission was sent after the raid, in 1033. An Ayyavole guild inscription of 1088 from Barus, west Sumatra, referring to tax on a camphor cargo, exported since antiquity, reflected continuing Chola trade and a flourishing social life. Ninth to eleventh century glass and ceramic finds suggests continuing Middle East trade.[53] Angkor reliefs and Javan statues from the 9th to 11th century show progressively more exotic fabrics, designs and patterns.[54] Lack of Chola missions to China, and probably Srivijayan misinformation, gave Chinese officials the impression that the Chola were Srivijayan vassals, corrected in 1077 when King Kulottunga sent a 72-merchant mission, gifts of glassware, camphor, brocades, rhinoceros horn, ivory, incense and spices, to promote Tamil trade, for which they received large amounts of copper. Srivijaya sent them in 1079 and 1088.

Srivijaya somehow made peace with the Cholas and in 1057 when Kedah revolted it was suppressed by a joint Chola-Srivijayan force. More surprisingly, in 1067 a Chola prince was sent to China as a Srivijayan ambassador, and three years later became Chola's king. A Chola force also apparently tried to assist a pretender to Kedah's throne, nominally a sub-kingdom of Srivijaya. A Chola inscription recorded their troops conquering much of the Kra Isthmus 'at the behest of the king who had asked them for help and to whom the country was returned,' whether on behalf of a pretender or rightful Srivijayan prince is unknown and disputed.[55] In 1078 Srivijaya sent two embassies to the Chola court at King Kulottunga's request, reaffirming the 1005 temple donations. Kulottunga also maintained friendly relations with Angkor and Pagan and was praised for abolishing tolls. These complex events, probably involving foreign support of ruling family factions, must be connected to Jambi's 1078 replacement of Palembang as Srivijaya's capital. Evidence is too patchy for certainty. Vizagapattanam (Visakhapatnam) was re-named Kulottungacolapattanam, indicating Kulottunga's trade support.[56] Srivijaya, despite the raids was, as after Mataram's attack, resilient. A 12th-century Chinese document reported, 'Chinese ships going to Ta-chih [Arabia] reach San-fo-chi [Srivijaya] repair their ships and exchange goods. Merchants from distant places congregate there. This country is therefore considered to be the most prosperous one,' and 'the most important port of call on the sea routes of the foreigners…all pass through it on their way to China.'

A 1055 Ayyavole inscription shows a certain arrogance; 'Famed throughout the world, adorned with many good qualities, truth, purity, good conduct, policy, condescension and prudence…born to be wanderers over many countries.' It mentions kingdoms in India, Persia, Nepal and commodities including precious stones, pearls, cloves, sandalwood, perfumes and spices, 'by selling which…they fill the emperor's treasury.'[57] Indians lived in south Chinese ports, Dhofar, Aden, Siraf and Fustat. Guilds were religiously tolerant. The Anjuvannam was 'a body of west Asian traders,' Jewish, Christian, Hindu and Muslim on the Malabar and Coromandel coasts and Java. A 12th-century Tamil text refers to Muslim Anuvannam traders in Nagapattinam cooperating with other guilds like the Manigramam. A Levantine Christian grant at Kottayam around 1220, bears signatures in Arabic, Hebrew and Pahlavi scripts. The Chola weakened from the mid-13th century, but there was no decrease in trade with Bengal or China and the Ayyavole and Manigramam were active, especially in southern Thailand and Burma, shown by a 13th-century Pagan temple inscription. In Sri Lanka between 1100 and 1300 over 15 Tamil inscriptions concern the Nanadesi guild. The 1244 Motupalli inscription of King Ganapati of the Kakatiya kingdom (north Andhra Pradesh) offered 'safety to [foreign] traders by sea'.[58] Marco Polo visited and 13th-14th-century Chinese pottery has been found nearby. Excavations at Manikapatnam in Orissa confirm Chinese trade increasing.[59]

Thus, widespread Tamil merchant penetration preceded and survived the Chola who seemingly tried to boost it by military expansion. Recent interpretations of guild inscriptions are that they were merchant appreciation for military protection.[60] Merchants donated to Buddhist temples and alms-houses and were held in high esteem. Although they were Hindu, they respected their hosts' beliefs.[61] Under Cholas, Hindu temples became larger, some associated with cultural, educational, and social services, a product of flourishing trade.[62] The Piranmalai inscription from 1300, running to several printed pages, gives the longest cargo list from rice, lentils, salt, nuts, pepper, turmeric and ginger to manufactured goods; various cotton textile types, forest products, animals, metals and high-value goods like musk, conch, coral and pearls, indicating burgeoning maritime trade.[63] A 13th-century Quanzhou inscription refers to a Shiva temple, indicating a large Tamil enclave and a 1358 Tamil inscription, also at Motupalli, assures fair treatment for merchants including Nanadesi, and reduced duties on gold, silver and sandalwood by local chief, Annopota Reddi.[64] All evidence suggests that despite rising and falling political powers, Indian Ocean merchant enclaves thrived, but Muslim continental invasion from north India with no interest in trade, started difficult centuries for Tamil merchants. Madurai was sacked by the Delhi Sultanate in 1311 and 1314.

Over six centuries, Srivijaya's only rebellions in her diverse territories were Indrapura, only briefly held in 802, 9th-century central Java, Mataram's 990 attack and Kedah's opaque 11th-century difficulties. Between 750 and 1000 Persian replaced Greek as the main Indian Ocean trade-language before Arabic took over. Due to Muslim conquest of Persia, many Zoroastrians/Parsis fled by sea and settled from Gujarat to Sri Lanka, seeking trade opportunities, avoiding continental Muslim destruction. Indian merchants from Bengal, Orissa, Gujarat and especially, Tamils, regularly traded with Southeast Asia. Despite China being a demand-driver, only from the 11th century did native Chinese merchants become important. This vast trade area is sometimes called the Maritime Silk Road, but the main cargoes were probably Indian cotton cloth, rice and porcelain. The Piranmalai inscription's long list shows the huge depth and variety, on which Indian Ocean maritime success was based, the product of India, Southeast Asia and China's inherent natural wealth, complimentary commodities, multiplicity of trader backgrounds and mutual toleration.

Chapter 7

Europe's Eleventh Century

In retrospect the millennium year is an easily understood dividing line in European history; when European, especially Mediterranean, progress accelerated. It was still sparsely populated, buildings mainly wooden, peasants poor. Cultural life was restricted to Courts and monasteries. But after 1000, with Norse and Muslim raids having largely ceased, populations rose, land was cleared, and agricultural production increased, enabling surpluses to be traded. The key to Europe's revival was control of sea-lanes. Maritime trade enabled wealth-creation, which financed military power. Greater control of territory around the Baltic and Mediterranean created more trade opportunities. Successful ports channelled wealth inland through Europe's rivers, except in France. The century was a watershed for Europe's Mediterranean trade.

a) The Mediterranean and Black Sea

Egypt, as conduit to the Indian Ocean, continued to drive Mediterranean trade. Amalfi, Pisa, Venice and Genoa became rich on trade due to Egypt's purchasing power. Gold currencies were only struck in regions in direct contact with it. The Fatimids conquered it in 969. As Shia Muslims, they aimed to continue to the Levant, then Baghdad, converting the Sunni world. The first two caliphs ran efficient administrations, assisted by Ya'qub Ibn Killis, an Iraqi Jew who moved to the Levant's Ramla, becoming its merchant representative, then Egypt. Having converted, as vizier he reorganised its finances until his death in 991, a merchant-organised state.[1] They conquered the Levant in the 990s. Third caliph Al-Hakim broke with toleration. In 1003 women were not allowed outside, even look outside. Shoemakers were banned from making women's outdoor shoes. Christians had to carry large crosses around their necks and Jews, bells. Churches and synagogues were demolished, dissenting officials executed. In 1012 Jerusalem's Church of the Holy Sepulchre was looted and dismantled.[2] In 1016 he announced he was God and tried to massacre Cairo's residents. His son ezZahar (1021–36) invited 2,500 debutantes to a palace reception and had them bricked-in to starve. EzZahar's son, al-Mustansir (1036–94) was also mad.[3] Despite intrigues, executions, assassinations and occasional bouts of religious insanity, churches including the Church of the Holy Sepulchre and synagogues were rebuilt and commercial life continued. Shias ruling a Sunni majority needed Jews and Copts. There was little interference in trade, which was conducted in relative tolerance, even liberality and freedom, enabling Jews to use family and partners, sometimes Muslim, in Aden, North Africa, Sicily, the Levant and Iberia to distribute Indian Ocean, Egyptian and Levantine products to the Muslim west and recovering Christian Europe. The Fatimids collected customs and taxes, but did not actively promote trade.[4] Egypt's increasing importance was aided by Abbasid and Gulf relative decline and trans-Saharan caravans' gold.

Detailed evidence of Jewish traders' activities, about 250,000 whole and fragmented business letters, contracts of marriage, divorce, employment, sales of houses and slave girls, in Arabic using Hebrew characters, were found deposited in the Geniza, Hebrew for depository, of Fustat's Ben Ezra synagogue.[5] Fustat was Egypt's capital until Fatimid-built Cairo two miles to the northeast. It had three synagogues, Cairo one. This sudden illumination of Jewish trade in Egypt was foreshadowed by evidence already discussed. Jews lived in about 75 Egyptian towns and villages, but only this synagogue yielded such documents, the usual practice, to deposit them after losing relevance if containing God's name, then bury them every few years.

By about 1000, Al-Qayrawan and al-Mahdiyah in Tunisia, termini of trans-Saharan gold routes were significant Jewish trade and cultural centres, similar to Amalfi, Pisa and Genoa, but without their political organisation. In the 1040s Libyan pirates harassed them and in the 1050s the Fatimids unleashed Berber hoards on al-Mahdiyah, devastating it. As a result, many Jewish merchants, already moving to Fustat and Alexandria from the early-10th century, accelerated their migration, adding to those coming from Mesopotamia. Fanatical Almohads from Northwest Africa then invaded and terrorised Tunisia. Repeated destruction of a once fertile, major Mediterranean grain exporter resulted in it needing Sicilian grain imports to feed itself thereafter, naturally organised by its Jewish merchants. Rebuilding the Ben Ezra synagogue about 1025, after al-Hakim's religious insanity, coincided with their arrival; not only merchants but scholars, dyers, glassmakers, silk weavers and other artisans. They became its most prominent members. Most Geniza documents were written by or to them.[6] No Jewish merchant from south France, north Italy, Thessalonica, or Constantinople left letters or is mentioned.[7] Only 36 letters and a few documents from Iberia remain, while Iberian iron, lead, copper, mercury and tin filled Egyptian markets, and many merchants were named al-Andalusi. It is therefore presumed they used a different synagogue.[8] The Ben Ezra synagogue followed Levantine liturgy, meaning its worshippers, the Geniza documents' authors, originated from there. There must have been grain exports to the Levant and Red Sea, as in antiquity, but no document shows involvement, nor in camels, horses, cattle, arms or timber from Cyprus, the Levant and Anatolia. This synagogue's Jews were thus only part of extensive Jewish merchant activity, other synagogues' documents not similarly preserved.

Shlomo Goitein who first reassembled and studied them, observes, 'one forgets that political boundaries existed,'[9] reminiscent of Braudel's 'capital laughed at frontiers.'[10] Early-11th-century Tunisia-born Joseph ben Samuel lived in Egypt and had a home in Palermo.[11] Mid-11th-century Jacob al-Andalusi, from Andalusia, also lived in Sicily, Tunisia and Egypt. Tunisian-born Nahray ben Nissim, active in Egypt between 1045 and 1096 dealt with over 120 types of goods, was a moneylender and money changer, returned to Tunisia and visited the Levant several times.[12] Some however, were sedentary and conducted business through correspondence and agents. Judah b. Moses Ibn Sighmar moved from Qayrawan to Fustat in 1048, was Tunisian Jews' merchant representative between 1055 and 1098 and letters from Mazara in Sicily and Alexandria say he was the representative. He used his slave as his overseas business agent.[13] 'Slave' may mislead. In the Middle East and north India, slavery was a means of recruiting for the army and bureaucracy. Merchants used them as apprentices and agents, who often took a profit share or shareholding. Egypt's main industrial crop was flax, 22 types mentioned, exported to Tunisia, Sicily and Iberia, exchanged for Iberian, Byzantine and Sicilian silk, Tunisian and Egyptian linen, Tunisian and Sicilian cotton and leather,[14] Tunisian olive oil, wax and soap, Levantine olive oil and dried fruits. Egypt also made and exported a mixed linen-cotton textile called fustian, from Fustat. Linseed oil as a flax by-product, used for lighting, was exported to the Levant and Aden. Iraqi raw silk was sent to Alexandria, although Persia was the main high-quality silk producer for the Mediterranean market;[15] textiles a major traded product. These goods demonstrate a sophisticated, comfortable life-style.

Merchant Jews had been mobile earlier. Tenth-century Ibrahim b. Ya'qub said a Seine fish reminded him of a Nile fish and in Mainz he found 'spices...pepper, imber, [ginger] cloves, nard, costus and galangal [blue ginger]',[16] but in the 11th century there were significantly more men, goods and money. Al-Hakim's decrees for Jew and Christian identification had been overturned and are not mentioned in Geniza letters, which avoid political comments.[17] Jews mingled freely with neighbours. Islamic laws obliging non-Muslims to pay double customs duties were not enforced.[18] Unlike Europe, where Jews were confined to a few occupations, Fustat's Jews were in all, including tax farming[19] and currency exchange, although they did not serve in the army except as physicians. Fustat was the 'monetary pivot of the Fatimid empire,'[20] a very different society to Europe's agricultural, feudal, hierarchical world with a few merchant-ruled ports.

Due to distance, agents often had considerable discretion in commercial transactions. A 1026 letter from Ahwaz in Persia enclosing fabrics, asked three Fustat-based Persian brothers to buy whatever they thought advantageous with the proceeds of the sale.[21] Another expressed confidence; 'a person like you needs no instructions.'[22] A letter from an al-Mahdiyah merchant to Fustat reported the market price for pepper was less than the writer was willing to accept, so he kept it until autumn convoys arrived, boosting demand. Prices rose and he sold to Iberian merchants. Then more ships arrived. Prices rose further and sold higher. He told his Fustat partner that he averaged the prices.[23] Sometimes instructions were precise. 'Please sell my saffron for five dinars on two months credit. [standard terms] If you do not find such a buyer, leave it until my arrival.'[24] All demonstrate mutual trust and friendship[25] often lasting a lifetime or several generations. Formal partnerships by contrast were of short duration for specific undertakings.

Fustat's craftsmen made porcelain, tools, tortoiseshell-embossed boxes and were prominent in gold and silversmithing, textile dyeing, pharmaceuticals and the ancient Phoenician craft, glassblowing, their skills spread centuries earlier. 'Jewish glass' was a familiar term in 7th-century France[26] for example, and Phoenician purple production echoes in the name Porphyrion, across the Bay of Acre.[27] Fustat's function was as entrepot for Asian spices, (pepper, cinnamon, ginger, cloves) aromatics, (aloes, camphor, ambergris, gums, frankincense, musk) dyes, (brazilwood, lacquer, indigo) jewels, (pearls, gems, turquoise, onyx, carnelian), paper from Baghdad and China, porcelain and cotton cloth for gold, silver, copper, textiles, paper and books. They dealt with Iberian metals, although this group's iron dealing was with Indian only, chemicals, Tunisian olive oil, Levantine dried fruit, Egyptian sugar and Egyptian and Yemeni alum. Egypt's link with Andalusia via North Africa enabled it to distribute Indian sandalwood, Southeast Asia's camphor and brazilwood for its valuable dye. In a 1085 letter, a Tunisian is reported selling brazilwood in the Levant at 150% profit to a 'Rum'.[28] Unlike Nahray ben Nissim's broad product range, Joseph Ibn 'Awkal specialised in luxury goods. He was sedentary, in his office/home or the Gem Bourse, but most prominent merchants travelled frequently in the Levant, Sicily, Tunisia, Aden and India.

Ibn Killis' policy of keeping peace with Byzantium continued. Seljuk Turks menaced both Byzantium and Fatimids. They defeated the Byzantines at Manzikert in 1071, migrating into Anatolia, and took Jerusalem from Egypt. Baghdad's cultural life revived, enabling Omar Khayyam (1048–1131) to write *The Rubaiyat*, musings on the fleetingness of life, enjoyment of nature's beauty and drinking wine. He also worked on algebra, geometric methods for solving cubic problems and astronomy, creating a solar calendar with an error of only one day in 5,000 years. Literacy continued to be widespread. Every mosque had a library attached. As late as Benjamin of Tudela's (1130–1173) journey, he was impressed with Baghdad's intellectual life, its 'philosophers, mathematicians and all the other sciences', but religious zealot influences were rising and intellectual life suffered.

Byzantium was Egypt's largest market. A 'Market of the Greeks' in Fustat is mentioned in 959. About 1035, in a fragrant wood boom, one wrote, 'they [Rum] did not leave a single piece ...when they departed.' A late-11th century merchant in Alexandria wrote to a Fustat colleague, 'Keep your pepper, cinnamon and ginger, for the Rum are keen only on them and all of them are about to leave for Fustat. They are only awaiting the arrival of two additional ships from Constantinople.'[29] A correspondent in Fustat was advised to hold his date-palm fibre until the Rum arrive from Damietta.[30] Rum, from 'Roman' is Arabic for both Byzantines and Italians, begging the question, were these Byzantine or Italian ships? Goitein specifically identifies Rum in this case as Byzantine without explanation. But in the late-11th century, with Venice in the ascendant, could it be that the latter makes more sense? Goitein shows that the best prices for pepper, alum, brazilwood and flax were expected from them.[31]

For example, a 1060 letter from Alexandria says that Rum merchants bought indigo and brazilwood at high prices and cannot distinguish good from inferior quality goods. A 1064 letter from Palermo explains that 'even' the Rum did not buy inferior black ginger, which had to be sold elsewhere at a loss,[32] seemingly indicating lower European standards, still not fully used to Indian Ocean product quality. Fustat's Jews used their ships in the Red Sea and Indian Ocean, but not in the Mediterranean, presumably because of unpredictable persecution. Besides, 'Rum' came to them. An early-11th-century Amalfi ship is reported bringing Sicilian and south Italian silk, honey and wine.[33] About 1050 a Rum ship brought coral from Tunisia to Fustat for export to India, a trade first recorded in the 1st century. This Italian ship trading between Muslim ports to Jewish traders, indicates Italian merchants' rising confidence. Al-Bakri (1014–1094) wrote mainly about trans-Saharan trade routes, but described a Muslim merchant ship's 45 stops between al-Mahdiyah and Alexandria. Jewish trade, long- or short-haul, was more direct, avoiding additional costs and delays.[34]

There was still some raiding. Tenth-century Pisa and Genoa had been frequently attacked, but fought back, establishing Sardinian bases to attack Majorcan pirates, and gained Tyrrhenian Sea control. After collaborative success, their interests began diverging, especially in Sardinia. Commercial rivalry increased. They still allied in 1015 to evict the emir of Sardinia and in 1016 attacked Sicily's remaining Muslim strongholds. In 1015, Genoa ousted Muslims from Corsica and in 1016–17 took most of Sardinia's coast. In 1051–52, fighting over the spoils, Pisa took Corsica from Genoa. In 1063 Pisa raided Palermo, the booty used to start grand buildings. Its cathedral used African marble and colourful Islamic ceramics to decorate churches and started pottery manufacturing, which eventually produced Renaissance majolica. A colourful, glazed bowl in San Piero a Grado's church facade near Pisa depicts a three-masted ship, typical of those trading between North Africa, Iberia and Sicily and a longer, faster two-masted ship in the days of south Mediterranean Muslim supremacy.[35] In 1077 Pope Gregory VII recognised Pisa's *Laws and Customs of the Sea*. In 1087 Pisa with Genoa raided al-Mahdiyah and obtained commercial privileges. In 1092 Urban II awarded Pisa supremacy over Corsica and Sardinia and Pisan ships helped Alfonso VI of Castile in Valencia.

Pisa and Genoa were governed by a few merchant families, especially the Doria and Spinola in Genoa and the Visconti and Alliata in Pisa, but as trade grew, new commercial men married into them, creating commercial oligarchies investing in longer-haul trade. Agents travelling with cargoes helped spread wealth. Genoese divided ship ownership into 64 easily-bought and sold shares, which when invested in more vessels spread risk, opportunity and exposure. Amalfi eventually could not compete with Venice, Genoa and Pisa when their hinterlands began manufacturing cloth and metal goods, pooling capital, linking-up to southern German towns, all new demand centres. Nevertheless, over 100 Amalfi merchants were killed in 996 by a mob reacting to a Fustat fire and rumoured Byzantine attack, a large number and losses equivalent to 84 lbs. of coined gold, a huge figure.[36]

While Italian ports led the fight-back at sea, non-trade related developments helped stability. One was the establishment of a Norman kingdom in south Italy and Sicily. The most credible origin is that Norman pilgrims returning from Jerusalem stopped at Salerno in southern Italy, when it was attacked by North African Muslims demanding tribute. While being collected, the pilgrims decided to retaliate and the raiders fled. In Normandy, word of military service opportunities spread and was enthusiastically met. Other sources have them arriving at the behest of various Italians against schismatic Byzantines, although there are more sources for the Salerno version.

In 1024 Normans fought with Lombards against Byzantines, captured Naples in 1029 and held Aversa as a fief in 1030. Between 1038 and 1040 another band under William of Hauteville in Sicily, fought with Byzantines against Muslims. In the early-1040s, they won lands around Melfi, were proclaimed dukes of Apulia and Calabria and in the 1050s successfully fought papal and imperial armies. By the 1060s, Norman power centres were Melfi under the Hautevilles and Aversa under the Drengots, while Sicily was invaded. Competition spurred territorial acquisition. In mainland Italy, advances were made in Byzantine Apulia and Calabria from the 1040s, Bari in 1071, Palermo 1072, Amalfi 1073 and Salerno 1077.

Meanwhile Byzantium was threatened by Seljuk Turks who took Baghdad and prepared invasion as the de Hautevilles prepared to dislodge southern Italy's and Sicily's Byzantine enclaves. Sicily had Greeks in the east, Latin Christians in the west and a mess of warring Muslim petty fiefdoms in the centre which Robert de Hauteville, known as Guiscard (Crafty), saw as a perfect conquest-opportunity. Further incentive was the Pope's gift of the empty title of Duke of Sicily to encourage campaigning against Muslims. In 1061 he captured Messina. Allying with one Muslim faction against another, he won battles and with Pisa's fleet, took Palermo in 1072, Syracuse 1086 and Noto in 1091 leading a kingdom of three religions and languages, enabling gradual knowledge-transfer from the Muslim world to Europe. The immediate significance was that Muslims could no longer raid further north and Sicily's flax became available to Europe. With less demand for Egyptian flax, its Indian Ocean products assumed greater interest for Italian merchants. Soon after Sicily's conquest, Roger, Robert's brother, landed at Malta and subdued Mdina.

In 1081 Robert led his army across the Adriatic to Durazzo (Durres) in Byzantine territory. Emperor Alexius Comnenus called for Venice's help in its defence because the old Roman Via Egnatia ran from it to Constantinople, Robert's ultimate target. Arguably the request was unnecessary because Norman power on both sides of the Adriatic threatened Venice's security too, but having just lost the 1071 Battle of Manzikert to Seljuk Turks, thus much of Anatolia, south Italy to the Normans, was defending the Danube against Pecheneg invasions and its naval strength had ceased, he obviously felt vulnerable. Venice put the Norman fleet to flight and captured Durazzo,[37] but gradually the Normans consolidated their Italian and

Sicilian conquests. In 1130 Roger was crowned King of Sicily and Naples. Careful not to return to weak, petty fiefdoms, bureaucracy was centralised and many castles built for the first time in stone. In Malta, Norman officials replaced Arabs. As a result, a strong central Mediterranean state was created.

Because of Venice's assistance, Alexius issued the *Golden Bull*, Venice's right to trade tax-free, customs-free in the Empire with an enclave and wharf by Constantinople's Golden Horn. He did not have to do it. It gave Venice a new market with huge competitive advantage enabling increased market-share and centuries of economic growth. St Mark's Basilica was built, its complex architecture and expensive decorations demonstrated Venice's new trade wealth, according to William of Apulia, 'rich in money, rich in men.' In Constantinople's orbit, commercial and secular in outlook, the papacy was naturally suspicious of Venice. Its commercial centre was the Rialto on the Grand Canal where bankers and merchants had offices, stalls, slave-auction yards, where cargoes were transhipped from ships to wharf or barge. Most Grand Canal houses were merchant homes with a dock to discharge cargoes into ground floor warehouses. Byzantine power increasingly depended on Venice's trade, money and navy. Lack of maritime ambition encouraged lethargy. Grain and wine prices were controlled and profits regulated. In the circumstances, the *Golden Bull* was tantamount to economic surrender.

In Iberia, Jews were influential in government, trade and intellectual circles. Reconquista, starting almost immediately after Islamic conquest, by 940 reached Porto and Barcelona. As Toledo fell to Castile in 1085, militant Moroccan Almoravids arrived, launching a conversion campaign. Militant Berber Almohads next tried to stem the Christian tide. Jews were driven out to Christian Iberia, Provence and Egypt. Christian Iberian kings, needing their support, employed them as tax-collectors, treasurers, bankers and physicians. They had prominent positions in trade and crafts. Nobles married Jewish women for financial support, similar to late-medieval and early-modern English nobles marrying wealthy merchants' daughters. But anti-Semitism was encouraged by the Church. Discrimination, never far below the surface, occasionally erupted.

Eleventh-century trade volume growth was impressive, given preceding centuries' paucity and remaining occasional raids. It spread wealth, culture and literacy inland. Venice encouraged economic development in its hinterland, in Lombardy and Tuscany, with Lucca's early-11th-century cloth manufacture and further inland through Alpine passes and rivers. Crops needed to feed these new centres encouraged agricultural surpluses. North Italian ports bewildered a German visitor because they sent boys not destined for Church careers to school.[38] Literacy was needed for business. By 1074 at the latest, Italian merchants were in Paris.[39]

b) North Europe

While Denmark unified in the early-8th century, it took longer for Norway and Sweden. The Norse diaspora had taken Saxons from Schleswig-Holstein into today's Saxony, Swedes (Rus) to the Black and Caspian Seas, Danes to England and Normandy and Norwegians to Scotland, Ireland and across the Atlantic. Migrating, trading and raiding, Scandinavia was volatile, energetic and unstable as its nobles fought for power. Kingdoms gradually emerged as trade created wealth and power. German merchants were in London around 1000. Some English priests preached against growing imported 'gold and lavish silk clothing' and 'luxury textiles embellished with gold.' Silk from archaeological excavations confirm increases.[40] Nevertheless, England's economy was still overwhelmingly agricultural with royal income mainly from landed estates and land tax.[41]

Inter-North Sea trade enabled an English-influenced Scandinavian Christianisation, especially Denmark. Bishoprics established in Hedeby, Ribe and Aarhus in the mid-900s spread over the region. The 1020s bishop of Roskilde was an Englishman.[42] Christianity spread by peaceful trade in Scandinavia, by war in eastern Europe by Charlemagne's successors. It mirrored Islam's spread in India, by peaceful trade on the coast, by war inland. Hedeby was destroyed in 1051 by Harald Hardrada, was sacked by east Europe's Wends and never rebuilt, but Harald brought the Orkneys back under control, began regular trade with Iceland, avoiding scurvy by taking Arctic cloudberries on his voyages.[43] Wend invasions were the most serious menace to Danish security and Baltic trade since Charlemagne. Nearby Schleswig had a deeper harbour and grew in size and importance from the 1070s. Lund, Scania's capital, the Swedish peninsula's southernmost region, was claimed to be London's equal, trading grain, fish, timber, hides, salt, fish glue, horses, bearskins, falcons, walrus hides, seal oil, honey, wax, malt, nuts, weapons and slaves for local and foreign markets.[44]

After Knut's reign in England, Edward the Confessor returned from his wife's Normandy home exile in 1037. Royal family intermarriages in originally Scandinavian polities in Normandy, England and Scandinavia led to the 1066 dynastic dispute and double invasion of England, one repelled, one successful. London, its richest city was key to subduing England and the City's support a necessity; a continuing theme. If English kings secured peace and stability, City merchants were content, but if these conditions were absent, threatening business, the result could be discontent and trouble. The Norman state in England deterred further invasions. England's trade-orientation was redirected south as Norse influence in the British Isles waned. In 1052 Diarmaid of Leinster seized Norse Dublin and in 1065 Thorfinn of Orkney died. Harald Hardrada's attempted invasion, defeated at Stamford Bridge before William the Conqueror's successful invasion, marks the Viking Age's last hurrah.

Without Norse predators, Dublin, Chester and Bristol began peaceful trading relationships. Norse achievements had however, been impressive. They founded ports from Ireland to the Basque country, became the ruling class in Russia and Ukraine, trading as far east as the Caspian Sea, Bukhara and Samarkand. From Normandy they established strong kingdoms in England and southern Italy. They had bases in Iceland, Greenland and briefly in North America. Tenth-century York linked the Arctic to Iberia, the Baltic to Baghdad, enabling the silver transfer that helped kick-start and lubricate north Europe's trade and economy.

North European ports began growing again. Dorestad and Quentovic did not survive Norse occupation. Their role was inherited by Bruges, founded by 9th-century Norse, its name thought to derive from *Brygge* meaning 'harbour' or 'mooring place', as does Bergen. It inherited trade with England and Scandinavia, protected by the Counts of Flanders. Many coins of Arnold II and Baldwin IV (956–1035) discovered in Denmark, Prussia and Russia demonstrate its commercial role.[45] The origin of Flemish cloth manufacture and trade is problematic. Quality Frisian cloths were sent as gifts by Charlemagne to Caliph Harun-al-Rashid from Frisian sheep. By the late-11th century, Flanders made superior cloth to England and France. How did Frisian become Flemish? The Germanic name Quentovic after Norse destruction, became Romance-speaking Etaples, meaning storehouse or staple, suggesting Romance-speaking Franks replaced Frisians, pushing them north, consistent with Charlemagne's eastward expansion and ethnic cleansing.

Woollen cloth had been made in England since at least Roman times, due to fleece fineness. Chedworth Roman villa had a fulling establishment and numerous Cotswold towns named Shipton or Shipston testify to the dominant industry, Shipston-on-Stour for example was an 8th-century sheep wash.[46] Flanders' 11th-century wool production was insufficient for its growing cloth industry thus England started regular exports. Production increased. English wool to Flanders and French Bay salt to the Baltic, became north Europe's two main trades. *The Domesday Book* (1086) records French and English merchant enclaves at Southampton, exporting wool and importing French wine. Ipswich and London also exported wool to Europe. As in Italy, hinterland manufacturing was stimulated, creating wealthy towns like Douai, Ghent and Ypres. Wool and cloth trading helped build medieval wealth along the Rhine in Mainz and Cologne, accessing inland markets. Further east, Hamburg and Lubeck, began to benefit.

For the first time since the Roman Empire, men with intelligence, energy, hard work and enterprise advanced from low-status by trade. Godric of Finchale, a late-11th/early-12th-century Northumbria-born peddler joined a merchant group, whose contacts, collective credit and defence, helped him become wealthy,[47] trading in Denmark, Flanders and Scotland, buying half one ship and a quarter of another. He was 'typical of many',[48] although not all were itinerant and some, including Jews, sourced produce for princes. In north Europe the necessity of cooperation, demonstrated in Godric's story, led to the growth of guilds. Forests were cleared, cultivable land widened, the population increased and new towns were founded but maritime trade practice was still inefficient. In London when a ship arrived, the king was given first choice of buying high-quality cargo, then London merchants, then Oxford's and Winchester's, then foreign. *The Domesday Book* (1086) recorded ships arriving or leaving Chester had to have 'the king's license' in lieu of which the king and earl was paid 40 shillings <u>per man</u> on board, an enormous penalty. Those with a license could sell cargo 'undisturbed' although the king's reeve could order those with marten pelts to let him inspect and buy first. The ship left after each on board paid the king and earl 4d,[49] again fairly onerous, inefficient practices. Nevertheless, fishbone evidence from middens indicates that from the early-11th century there was a notable shift from eating freshwater fish to saltwater, especially salted herring and dried cod, reflecting more and larger ships, more seafarers and growing towns.[50] Across the Channel, Frankish kings lived off their lands. Lacking educated professionals for administrative and judicial systems, civic obligations and justice gave way to personal dependence, homage and vassalage. Poor internal communications accentuated the trend.

Part II

Asia's Trade Accelerates: Europe's Trade Progresses

Chapter 8

The Western Indian Ocean

As the Red Sea route to the Mediterranean revived, Aden became the major Red Sea entrance port. Al-Muqaddasi described it as the 'ante-room of China, entrepot of Yemen, treasury of the west and the motherlode of trade wares.'[1] Despite its hot, unpleasant climate, its harbour was large, free of reefs, shoals or shallows, its winds and currents benign and adjacent waters rich in fish, whales, dugong and ambergris. Geniza documents show how Jewish merchant networks worked in Aden and Fustat, funnelling Indian Ocean produce from west coast Indian ports to the Mediterranean and its goods to India, exactly as their Phoenician ancestors had done. Many Geniza letters refer to recently deceased people with the words, 'may he rest in Eden', referencing *Ezekiel* 28.13, berating worldly Phoenician traders' origin.[2] The documents mention Yemeni ports other than Aden, Ghulafiqa and Zabid, Tunisian ports, Tunis, Susa, Al-Mahdiyah, Sfax and Tripoli, and Sicily's Messina and Mazara and west coast Indian and Sri Lankan ports. Fustat and Aden were the hubs holding this far-flung network together. The papers are only snapshots of business activities, but are deeply instructive because of their fortunate survival, indicating their well-established presence, predated by centuries.

Abraham Ben Yiju is one of Geniza's main 12th-century characters. From al-Mahdiyah in Tunisia, he left Fustat for Aden about 1120, meeting his mentor and business partner, Madmun ibn Bundar who was Nagid, or Chief Representative, of Aden's Jewish merchants, as his father Japheth Bundar had been, and Superintendent of Aden's customshouse, a key figure in Indian Ocean trade. Madmun was a close business associate of Aden's Muslim governor. The Red Sea canal was no longer useable, so the journey from Fustat followed the Nile to Qus to join a regular caravan to Aidhab, a busy Red Sea port until the 15th century, now ruined, where archaeologists have found much Chinese pottery.[3] From Aden he sailed to Mangalore, working there for 17 years, then Aden again for another three. Among Madmun's friends were Yusif ibn Abraham and Kalaf ibn Ishaq, who welcomed Ben Yiju into the group. Also active was Fustat's Abu Sa'id Halfon, merchant, scholar and patron of literature, originally from Damietta, who often travelled between Egypt, India, east Africa, the Levant, Morocco and Iberia on business,[4] Abu Zikri Sijilmasi, originally from Morocco, eventually becoming Fustat's Nagid, his brother-in-law, Mangalore shipowner Halfon ben Nethaniel in Iberia in 1128–30, then India in 1132–1134 and Andalusia, 1138–1139,[5] others manufacturing and trading Tunisian purple cloth. His nephew and son-in-law took clothing to sell in Aden, from where he went to Quilon.[6] Indeed, the documents indicate the importance of Indian textile and dye exports, especially indigo and lac for blue and red respectively.

They all demonstrate wide, cosmopolitan range of trading contacts and mobility. Despite Muslim law that non-Muslims pay double customs rates, they continued to pay the same. Aden's were higher than in the Mediterranean and rigorously enforced, but adjustments were made to accommodate market fluctuations because officials were also merchants. Sensibly, food imports were not taxed.[7] Ibn al-Mujawir said 70–80 ships a year transited Aden. Its protection was the seafront wall 'stretching…from mountain to mountain, with five gates' according to al-Muqaddasi.[8] Officials and merchants knew when to expect incoming ships due to predictable monsoon winds. Watchtowers monitored them and small ships met them. Crew, cargo and passenger lists were completed before discharge. Cargoes were inspected, counted and weighed at the Furda Gate customshouse, the duty calculated, mast, sails, rudder and anchor removed and returned on payment; a well-organised system.[9] The customshouse was Aden's economic heart. Nearby merchant houses' ground floors were storerooms. There were few complaints about lost or mishandled Indian goods.[10]

Shipbuilding was important to Aden's economy. Madmun mentioned launching at least two ships, including one for Sri Lanka. In a letter to Ben Yiju, extending greetings to three Hindus and a Muslim merchant, he asked for 'qunbar', coir, used to sew planks of hulls, or coconut husks for making it. In others, he requested Indian timber. 'Nur', the lime-fat compound used to coat hulls against teredo worm damage, was produced locally. Some timber was recycled.[11] Wreckage of Madmun's son, Halfons' ship on an Aden-Quilon voyage, collected from nearby beaches was identified by timbers and fittings. Property rights were enforced. After Halfon's wreck, the community court took possession of the estate for the widow, the rightful claimant, in an orderly system of potentially disputed property, central to Aden's attraction. All suggests an integrated, sophisticated maritime state.

Aden was the main, but not only entrepot. Joseph Lebdi left Fustat for India in 1099 and returned nearly two years later, not via Aden but Mirbat in southeast Arabia and Dahlak, a Red Sea island, apparently to avoid the 10% duty on cargo value that Aden required.[12] Dahlak was a rescue, supply and salvage base used by merchants not continuing up the Red Sea. Some documents suggest it was less well-regulated than Aden and perhaps that bribery could lower customs dues.[13] According to Samuel b. al-Majjani, the ruler made 'unreasonable demands' and 'took some of our possessions' including 'bales of cloth' after trying to flee, but actually appears to be strict rule-enforcement, not piracy, as he took nothing else. In contrast, the documents contain virtually no complaints about treatment or tax at Aden. Merchants obviously appreciated order and security compared with smaller ports. However, when the Ayyubids took-over in 1173, new Governor and self-proclaimed Caliph al-Malil al-Mu'izz Ismail (1179–1202) forced Jews to convert, had foreign merchants rounded up and excessive taxes imposed. When eventually executed by government troops, business returned to normal.[14]

Mangalore, a semi-autonomous northern Malabar coast port, had a hinterland rich in industrial crafts and spices. Ben Yiju acted as Madmun's agent or junior partner there, successfully trading and establishing a factory producing bronze trays, bowls, candlesticks, importing arsenic for which there was strong demand in Sri Lanka and Egyptian cotton, working with Muslim and Hindu partners. There were about 4,000 foreigners in Mangalore. The old port area is still called Bandar, port in Persian. Jewish merchants lived in other Indian ports. All were regulated by their own courts.[15] Ibn Battutah who visited Mangalore 200 years later, said it was usual for merchants from Aden and Persia to stop there. Southeast Asians seemingly preferred Calicut, founded in the 11th century, probably by Omanis, and Fondarina a little further south. Calicut's merchant community was larger, mainly from Southeast Asia, the Maldives, Yemen, Persia and Sri Lanka.

Ben Yiju was unusual in staying in Malabar, entrusting his slave Bomma, as already noted, more akin to apprenticeship, to visit Aden, once with goods worth 685 dinars, buying 93 dinars worth, the equivalent of 2.5 years wages of a mason.[16] Madmun's letters always contained a friendly greeting to Bomma, as a respected, trusted colleague.[17] Purchases included paper, rare in India where palm leaves were used, but plentiful in Aden, mats, cooking utensils, soap, clothes and sugar, which Egypt pioneered in the Mediterranean. Ben Yiju regularly visited Jurbattan, 100 miles south of Mangalore, Malabar's richest spice and pepper producing area, a major market where traders bought from producers,[18] all indicative of the volume of goods flowing through Aden.

Indian trade guilds are not mentioned in Geniza documents but the Anjuvannam and Manigramam are conspicuous in Malabar inscriptions. The late-9th-century Kollam copper plate records the grant of land and labourers to a Christian church and its maintenance to Anjuvannem and Manigraman.[19] The early-11th-century Kochi copper plates of Bhaskara Ravi Varman record the grant of the title Anjuvannam and trade privileges to Jew Joseph Rabban in Muyirikkdu. The 13th-century Kottayam plates also show continuing collaboration.[20]

Moroccan geographer and cartographer, al-Idrisi (1099–1166) at Roger II's Sicilian Court, noted that Hormuz specialised in growing date palm, sugar, cumin and indigo of 'incomparable quality,' all exported, that nearby Kis had cattle and sheep, vines and pearls, but one ruler attacked merchants, 'despoiling them of their goods and so weakened the country that the trade…turned from…Oman…to Aden.' Letters from Madmun to Ben Yiju and Khalaf b. Isaac to Cairo described a Kis raid on Aden in 1135, in which 15 ships and 700 men blockaded Aden's harbour for two months to ambush inbound ships. Presumably the news spread fast and kept ships away, damaging and changing merchant shipping itineraries.[21]

The underlying cause must have been, as al-Idrisi stated, Aden's increasing trade volumes and tax revenue. The siege was broken by two ships owned by Abu'l Qasim Ramisht of Siraf, a powerful, rich merchant and shipowner who traded as far as China. Aden and Mangalore's traders, including Madmun and Ben Yiju, often hired his ships for their cargoes. According to Ibn al-Athir (1160–1234), he gave funds to restore the Kaaba's cover at Mecca. Of all Aden-India ships in the documents, his are mentioned most. He probably lived in Aden, head of a family business. In a letter to Ben Yiju, Madmun mentioned three ships belonging to the family. An anonymous 12th-century annotator of Ibn Hawqal's geography described Ramisht's father as Siraf's richest merchant with a million gold dinars in cash, who lent capital to merchants on *commenda* basis. Ramisht's clerk told him that returning from China 20 years earlier, 'his merchandise was worth half a million dinars; if that is the wealth of his clerk, what will he himself be worth?'[22] Benjamin of Tudela noted around 1168 that Kis had about '500 Jewish residents where merchants from India, Persia and Yemen take their goods, such as silk, purple and flax, cotton, hemp and worked wool, lentils and spices,' but it had a bad reputation. Unlike Aden, it did not have a stable legal system. This incident was another rare example of conflict in Indian Ocean trade, another choke point issue during a time of strongly rising volumes.

Before Ben Yiju returned to Fustat, Roger II's army in 1153 ravaged Tunisia, 'Ifriqiya' in the documents. Ben Yiju's brother and nephew who lived there, were taken to Mazara in eastern Sicily, a busy port when Sicily was Muslim-controlled, linking it to North Africa and the Levant, but since eclipsed by Messina. Ben Yiju tracked them down and eventually got them to Fustat, where although he had numerous offers from rich merchants' sons to marry his daughter, he saved her for his nephew,[23] demonstrating their strong family attachments.

The letters describe situations understandable to modern commercial shipping; cargo claims, proofs of ownership, witness and settlement statements, contracts, orders to agents and commission agreements to source particular goods. They wrote to each other frequently about transaction progress, the market, whether instructions had been followed, juniors and agent's work quality, the importance of educating good trainees to maintain service quality, sustaining reputation. They constantly urge effort, diligence and care, praise market knowledge, intelligent action without detailed orders, acting on initiative, an appreciation of the right kind of character, of hard work and common sense. One wrote, 'In God's name, make haste. One like you really needs no instructions…there is no need for me to urge you on,' qualities demanded in today's commercial world. Markets change and merchants adapt. One scolds a junior, 'You had little to do in Fustat last year, whereas this year you are inundated on all sides. Much less work would suffice for someone like you.' Another, accused of not selling promptly to take advantage of pricing, defends himself, 'I am not the sort of man who needs to be told what to do.' Some merchants are professional, others have difficult characters and histories of broken partnerships, but all were keen to sustain future trade, with mutual trust, on-going relationships and market information. What is the market doing? When is my potential client going to move? When is the right time to buy or sell? Who in the market is reliable? Transactions are recorded and members vetted. Apart from indigo, lac, iron and pepper, other cargoes were sandalwood, aloes, fruits, vegetables, saffron, cardamom, turmeric, betel nuts, ginger, costus, sugar, perfumes, chewing gum made from pistachio and mastic trees in return for scrap copper, paper, arsenic and almonds.[24]

Sometimes goods didn't sell or fetched lower prices than expected. Some ships sank, although if close to shore, iron which formed most ships' part cargo, was often salvaged. Some perishable goods spoiled en route. One report tells of an attack of Indian pirates on a ship named *Gazelle*, necessitating jettisoning cargo for greater speed and manoeuvrability, losses born by all, although some was later salvaged.[25] The impression is of regular shipping, well-known, expected arrival times, organised by Yemen's Jewish communities sourcing local, Levantine, North African, Sicilian, Indian and Sri Lankan cargoes, cooperating with Muslim and Hindu merchants.

Benjamin of Tudela wrote with bitterness about Christian persecution but warmth towards Indian Ocean Muslims. The caliph of Baghdad for example, was 'an excellent man, trustworthy and kind-hearted towards everyone,' and found Jewish communities prospering, involved in growing, processing and trading pepper in Quilon, the ruler assuring security of their property, left in the open without guard. Sri Lanka had 2,300 Jewish settlers and a large Jewish community at Sohar was connected with Fustat, others with Indian trade guilds. Merchants 'from India import great quantities of spices and the inhabitants of the island live by what they gain in their capacity of brokers to both parties.' They brought rice and cotton from India, silk, porcelain and steel from China, slaves and ivory from east Africa via Fustat to Genoese and Venetian merchants and were granted their own funduq in Alexandria.

Despite Siraf's revival, the Persian Gulf route's decreasing importance relative to the Red Sea led to more interest in Sri Lanka. Aden's governor Bilal b. Jarir and Madmun partnered to load a large ship in Aden with most of its glass production. Craftsmen, including three goldsmiths scheduled to accompany the cargo, suggests other western Sri Lankan-bound cargoes. They also sent a large cargo of lac to Egypt, both examples of Jewish-Muslim maritime partnership.[26] Sri Lanka's 13th-century ruler Buvenekabahu's envoy to Fustat advertised its gems, pearls, elephants, various cotton cloths, timber, cinnamon and much else.

The first Geniza reference to Karim Red Sea convoys is from 1134. It used to be thought Karim were Arab merchants who displaced the Jewish network, karim from a Tamil word for business, 'karyam'.[27] Others thought it meant great, indicating wholesale merchants to distinguish from petty entrepreneurs.[28] Recent evidential interpretation is that they were merchants, irrespective of ethnicity, in Red Sea June-November sailing season convoys between Yemen and Egypt.[29] The documents indicate Jewish merchants' involvement.[30] Karim wealth helped build schools, hospitals and mosques in Alexandria, Cairo, Mecca and Jeddah.[31] Their more frequent references and apparent increasing importance accompanied increased state involvement in all trade, especially Italian-bound spices. A 15th-century Mamluk decree outlined the official responsible for overseas trade's duties. 'He will welcome the Karim merchants coming from the Yemen, seeking their goodwill, showing them courtesy, dealing with justly...likewise the merchants...

from the west, both Muslim and Frankish…for the profits…accruing from them are very great.'[32] When Mamluks were threatened by rebellion or Tamerlane, Karim merchants financed their victories, so were bound up with the regime.[33] Toleration continued. A 13th-century Indian bi-lingual Arab-Sanskrit mosque-endowment inscription by Hormuz-based shipowner Nuraddin Firuz, built with Hindu help, described him as a great merchant and 'righteous friends' with Gujarat's Hindu ruler.[34]

East Africa's over 30 ports, founded by Arabs and Persians were fortified. Kilwa's prosperity was tied to Sofala's gold exports. In 1154 al-Idrisi wrote, 'the residents of Zabag [Srivijaya] go to…Sofala and export iron from there, supplying to all the lands of India. No iron was comparable to theirs in quality and sharpness.' Competition may have caused the Mahdalis Yemeni merchant family to move to Kilwa around 1300, imposing themselves as rulers.[35] Today's Zanzibar Gujarati merchants' descendants speak the Kutchhi dialect.

Chapter 9

Europe's Twelfth Century

B y any measurable means, Europe's maritime trade lagged far behind Asian trade volumes and quality of traded goods, especially during Song acceleration and the stimulus it gave Indian Ocean trade. Perhaps the Europe-Asia gap was even wider than in the 7th century, but Europe had progressed. Viking and Muslim raiding ceased. Egypt's Jewish merchants continued to be the conduit for Indian Ocean goods with rising volumes. Thereafter, as Roger Bartlett explains, Europe's 'commercial expansion…took the form of a gigantic double pincer movement, hinged on Hamburg and Lubeck in the north and Genoa and Venice in the south,'[1] integrating its economy.

a) Mediterranean and Black Sea

Eleventh-century momentum gathered pace after 1100 assisted by an important non-trade development; the Crusades. Called in 1095 by Pope Urban II to unite Christian Europe under his authority, it aimed to recapture the Holy Land for Christendom. Triggered by Constantinople's Alexius's request for mercenaries to help check the Turkish tide sweeping into Anatolia after Manzikert, he did not anticipate, nor welcome this huge reaction. Commercial interests dominated north Italy's maritime republics, although many merchant family's commercial and religious imperatives were not mutually exclusive. Pisa and Genoa scented new possibilities. Genoese merchants set the pace, sailing in 1097 to support Crusaders, rewarded with a merchant enclave in Antioch. In 1099, Genoese Embriachi merchant family ships were dismantled at Jaffa to make siege engines for Jerusalem and in 1100 another fleet supported the new Kingdom of Jerusalem by conquering the coast, giving it maritime access. As Pisa's fleet sailed to the Levant, it occupied Byzantine Corfu and in 1099 it took Jaffa. Venice showed least urgency and coldest commercial motives. War was potentially bad for Egyptian spice business. Only after Jerusalem was captured in 1099 did a Venetian fleet sail, wintering in the Aegean first. More concerned with Pisan competition in Byzantine trade, they attacked its fleet returning from supplying Jerusalem and paroled its sailors, only on condition they did not trade with Byzantines. In 1100, Venice's fleet entered Jaffa, demanding free-trade rights throughout the Kingdom of Jerusalem, a church and a market in every town, a third of every town they helped capture and Tripoli. The desperate Crusaders agreed because most had returned to Europe. Thousands of Italian traders poured into Crusader states and the Black Sea, creating enclaves under their laws and home-appointed governors, from which imports and exports were organised. Genoa and Pisa contributed more to early Crusader successes and were similarly favoured. Acre's Genoese, Venetian and Pisan enclaves comprised 16, 11 and 7 acres respectively.[2]

Following the 1101 conquest of Caesarea the loot was divided. Each sailor received two pounds of pepper; good reward and indicative of further riches in larger ports.[3] In 1104 Genoa captured Acre, in 1110 Venice took Sidon and in 1118, Haifa. Pilgrims and Crusaders needed ships to get to the Levant. Encountering spices, sugar and other oriental products, they demanded them back home, increasing shipping demand. Italian merchant enclaves in Acre, Antioch, Tripoli, Beirut, Jaffa and Lattakia were crucial for Crusader survival, thus received favourable treaties and tax exemptions. Crusader victories may have affected Egyptian business. An 1103 letter from Fustat to Aden said the Sultan imprisoned Genoese and no goods were sold. 'It looks as if this recession will last long' and in 1133, 'this year business is at a standstill, for no one has come from the west and only a few Rum have arrived,'[4] but most trade continued independent of Crusading activity. Egypt's merchants depended on Europe's buyers.

Genoa and Pisa raided each other between 1119 and 1133 over growing southern French trade. Pisa conquered Amalfi in 1136, in decline under Norman rule, its maritime ambitions ended. Pisa by contrast was at its peak power, equal to Venice, its strength resented in Lucca, Massa, Volterra and Florence, all of whom wanted their own export port. To compete with Pisa and Genoa, Venice needed more ships, so combined various shipbuilders into a central complex, the Arsenal, with carpenters, sailmakers, armourers and other ship equipment providers, developing specialist ships for war and trade, standard designs and spare part stores.[5] Venice's military and merchant classes were not separate; nobles were merchants and merchants were nobles. Warships were designed with as much cargo space as possible and merchantmen had defensive capabilities.[6] Effectively, east Mediterranean trade was controlled by Italian ports. Byzantium was uncomfortable with Venice's dominant position, far exceeding what Alexius had expected. Successor John II Comnenus in 1118 tried revoking the *Golden Bull* to get equal competition. Expecting the privileges to be long-lasting, Venice had heavily invested in building the trade. Retaliating, it raided Byzantine Aegean and Adriatic lands, forcing John to restore and extend its privileges. Venice's naval and commercial power continued growing. Genoese oligarchy led to political factionalism, whereas Venetians accepted the doge's authority, the office changing hands between families like the Ziani, Tiepolo and Dandelos, who tended to dominate the most profitable trades.

The 1123 *Pactum Warmundi* between Venice and Jerusalem agreed an attack on Ascalon and Tyre in return for Venice receiving a trade enclave in every city in the kingdom of Jerusalem, a third of Ascalon and Tyre and self-administration; effectively mini-Venices. Tyre was captured and the agreement fulfilled. It eliminated the Fatimid fleet in 1128 and by 1140 Muslim maritime power had virtually ceased. Crusader states survived due to north Italian seaborne supplies and strong castles, but were inherently weak. Internal power struggles between Italian enclaves hardly helped. Christians clustered in cities, divorced from Muslims outside, readying for counter-attack. They were an occupation force, in constant war, constantly insecure, heavily-taxing caravans to Acre, Haifa, Tyre and Jaffa. Jihad was encouraged by Nureddin who spread the idea in an increasing number of madrassas.

Venice-Constantinople relations remained tense. Constantinople needed Venetian merchants, but hated them because of it. Venice played the protector well. In 1148 for example, despite deteriorating relations with Byzantium, they combined against renewed Norman attack in western Greece. But an 1155 Byzantine counter-attack on southern Italy took Bari, Trani and Ancona, risking control of the Adriatic entrance. Venice quickly came to terms with the Normans, forcing Constantinople's withdrawal. Venice demonstrated with crystal clarity its strategic priority. As already recorded, Roger II, controlling Italy south of Rome, in 1130 commissioned a world geography from Moroccan cartographer al-Idrisi. Drawing on Muslim merchant knowledge in Africa and the Indian Ocean, he created the most accurate pre-modern world map, demonstrating Norman curiosity and Messina's importance for Muslim-Christian interaction. Commanding trade routes through the Mediterranean's central choke point, it attracted Pisan and Genoese merchants. Ibn Jubayr called Messina 'the mart of the merchant infidels, the focus of ships from the world over.'

Roger was a great patron of art, architecture, culture and tolerated other faiths and inter-marriage. Ibn Jubayr noted 'the Normans tolerated and patronised a few Arab families in exchange for knowledge.' He was also ambitiously expansionist especially against Byzantium. He took Corfu in 1148 and attacked Corinth, Athens and Thebes, the Byzantine silk manufacturing centre, seizing bales of damasks, brocades and Jewish workmen for Palermo's royal silk factory. Anxious Emperor Manuel Comnenus renewed Venice's trade privileges after it helped expel Normans from Greece and Corfu. Roger briefly seized almost every important North African port between Tripoli and Bougie, referred to in the previous chapter with its impact on Ben Yiju's family, and sold Sicilian grain to Tunisia. North African expansion was abandoned on his 1154 death, turning to north Italy as its main market.

Genoa needed Sicilian grain, salted pork, wool, lambskins and cotton, the basis for Genoa's textile industry. In this new Mediterranean, goods were distributed to Europe without Muslim raids. Cargo volumes rose. North Italian traders in Northwest African ports imported west African gold and North African leather, wool, ceramics and grain. In 1152 and 1160 Genoa negotiated commercial treaties with Bougie (Bejaia) and Ceuta and traded with Moroccan ports. Genoese documents of 1155–1164 describe its largest trade with Alexandria, the Levant and Sicily, followed by south France, Constantinople and North Africa.[7] In 1182, 29% of Genoa's trade was with Ceuta, 37% with North Africa as a whole,[8] with funduqs in Tunis, Bougie and al-Mahdiyah, organised by family companies.

Venetian wealth and power irritated Constantinople, which repeatedly tried to replace it with rivals Pisa and Genoa under less favourable terms, Manuel

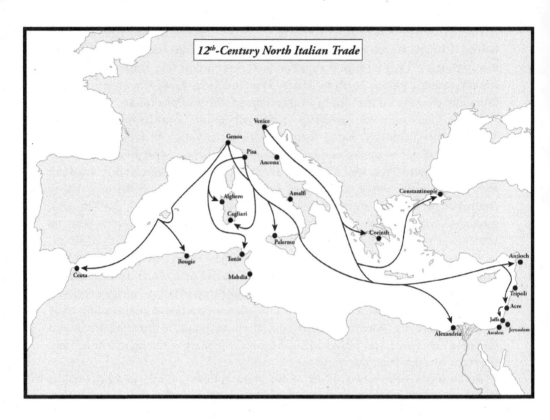

12th-Century North Italian Trade

Comnenus with Genoa in 1169 and Pisa in 1170, reducing tariffs from 10% to 4% while Venetians still had exemption. Of the 80,000 Latins in Constantinople, the palace secretariat complained that Venetians had become 'so insolent in…[their] wealth and prosperity as to hold the imperial power in scorn.' Manuel, confident after capturing the Dalmatian coast from Hungary, engineered a coup. In 1171 Genoa's Constantinople enclave was destroyed. The emperor immediately blamed Venice, arrested all Venetians, confiscated their goods, and made trade agreements with Genoa and Pisa. Venice was enraged. Only two years before, the emperor had guaranteed Venetian security, encouraging its merchants to inject more capital into trade. Simultaneously, Venice hosted a meeting between the pope and Emperor Frederick Barbarossa, who's self-proclaimed aim was 'to restore the Roman Empire, its ancient greatness and splendour,' inimical to both papacy and Venice. In the resulting treaty, Venice secured free passage for its merchants and exemption from imperial tolls, in return for the same for imperial subjects 'as far as Venice but no further', acknowledging Venice's Adriatic supremacy.

Venetian trader Romano Mairano started in the 1140s from Constantinople's Venetian enclave, first trading with Greek ports, then Alexandria and began ship ownership. By 1158 he supplied 50,000 lbs. of iron to the Knights Templars and built Venice's largest ship. Byzantine confiscation of Venetian traders' goods in Constantinople in 1171 forced him to rebuild with Ziani family assistance, starting with timber to Alexandria, for pepper and alum.[9] Genoa-based Solomon of Salerno and wife, bought spices and dyes in Egypt in 1156 and traded with Majorca, Spain and Sicily.[10] Genoa's elite invested in his ventures, including timber for the Fatimid fleet. He was also at the mercy of politics and war. Friendship with Sicily's king and its wheat and cotton trade had to be abandoned as Emperor Frederick Barbarossa forced Genoa to join his army against Sicily while the Levant was cut-off in a Genoa-Jerusalem quarrel. This entrepreneur also survived to trade with North Africa, especially Bougie.[11]

Of 400 surviving Venetian trade contracts, half deal with Constantinople, seventy-one with Egypt, then the Kingdom of Jerusalem.[12] But tension with Constantinople was constant, as imperial policy flip-flopped. After Manuel's death in 1180, Latins were favoured but Andronikos Comnenos engineered a massacre of mainly Genoese and Pisan merchants in 1182, the stupid action of a weak man, resentful of Norman attacks and being beholden to former Venetian subjects. If Byzantium had not lost control of their maritime commerce, he would not have been in this position. Nicetas Choniates complained, 'the accursed Latins...lust after our possessions and would like to destroy our race...between them there is a wide gulf of hatred. Our outlook is completely different and our paths grow in opposite directions.' Yet in 1186 the emperor not only promised to defend Venetian territories but undertook a shipbuilding programme under Venetian control, an extraordinary concession that put Byzantine naval control in unpopular foreign hands. Byzantium was weak, but did it have to go this far?

The papacy condemned trade in war materials to North Africa, but Venetians and Genoese ignored it. Merchants took commercial, intellectual and artistic risks and put wealth creation ahead of dogma. So did many small traders elsewhere. In 1161, a Genoese merchant carried silk and linen to Bougie 'to sell as best he can, to invest [the proceeds] in wax or alum, whichever seems best...or...gold' and send them promptly.[13] Furthermore, many 12th-15th century treaties between Catalan, Majorcan, Italian, French and Tunisian rulers conferred equality and explicit protection to Christian and Muslim merchants in each other's ports. Muslim merchants received loans from Christians. Leasing Christian ships to Muslims was a right specifically agreed in some treaties, even joint ownership, demonstrating stable, tolerant trade.[14] Two 1201 letters from an Arab correspondent of Pisan merchants after political incidents forcing them to leave Tunis without goods or settling debts also reveal close cooperation in attempting satisfactory settlement; that the customshouse keep the assets until return, when 'you will be treated with every regard and honour as has been customary.'[15]

From the 12th century, Muslims increasingly used Christian shipping, perhaps due to differential taxation or Andalusian emigration under Reconquista pressure, depriving Muslim merchants of Iberian connections.[16] An example of differential taxation, albeit from 1329, is Cagliari's import/export duties; Muslims and Jews 8% import/4% export, Italians 3.33%/1.66%, Catalans and French 2%/1%, Sardinians 1.66%/1.66%.[17] Even in Crusader states Muslim and Christian merchants cooperated. Iberian Ibn Jubayr noted Muslim caravans passed through Christian territory to Christian ports and 'in Muslim territory, [no]…Christian merchant is forbidden entrance or…molested.' Both paid taxes. 'Reciprocity prevails…warriors are engaged in their wars, while the people are at ease.'[18]

As European spice demand and shipments increased, Egypt's Fatimids seemed to take a keener interest, in 1118 sending their ships and soldiers to Yemen after a pirate attack, an apparent attempt to protect taxable imports. They also taxed timber and iron imports, used to fight Seljuks and Crusaders. In 1154 Pisa concluded an Egyptian treaty giving it a Fustat funduq, complimenting Alexandria's. Egypt fell to Saladin in 1174 adding to domination of the Levant and Yemen. He removed Pisa's Fustat funduq for unclear reasons. Sugar and paper continued as Fustat's two main industries and its Jews continued specialising in glass, textile dyeing, pharmaceuticals, gold and silversmithing. Tolerance towards Jews was maintained and low taxes encouraged trade. After Reynard of Chatillon's Red Sea raids, Saladin thought it threatened merchant activities in Yemen, especially Aden's Karimis and the Mecca pilgrim route. He built a fleet to block Levantine ports, Crusader states' lifeline, to bleed them of supplies and cultivated relations with Italian port-republics to obtain war supplies. After crushing Crusaders at Hattin in 1187 and taking Jerusalem, they still retained Tyre and defeated a Muslim fleet in 1190. But Crusader states were too weak for sustainability. Meanwhile German, French, Catalonian and English merchants also established Alexandrian funduqs.

Benjamin of Tudela recorded about 400 Tyre-based families as glass makers and shipowners. William of Tyre (1130–1185) who became its archbishop in 1175 boasted of its fine sand and exquisite glass vessels made from it, 'carried to far distant places…which surpass all products of the kind.'[19] Geniza documents record glassware from Antioch, Tyre and Beirut, the latter, holders of a secret recipe for red glass. Crusader Marquise de Monferrato brought Levantine glassmakers to Piedmont, the forerunners of the Altarese glassmaking community known as the Universita d'Altare. Venice's glassmaker guild members in 1224 had virtually all Semitic names. Venice's Rialto was a glass-trading hub, manufactured on the island of Giudecca, Jew Town, reportedly 1,300 family heads in 1152, and growing strongly.

A ten-year war between Pisa and Genoa erupted in 1165, again over the southern French market and Sicily where both cities had trade privileges. In 1192 Pisa took Messina. In 1204 Genoa took Syracuse, key ports at the centre of Mediterranean trade. In 1199 Pisa also fought Venice, blocking Brindisi, which ended in defeat. In 1206 Pisa gave up Adriatic expansion, allying with Venice against Genoa.

As the Reconquista progressed, Aragon, a kingdom since 1035, continued conquering. Its port of Barcelona was in 1160, according to Benjamin of Tudela, 'small and beautiful,' containing merchants from Genoa, Pisa, Sicily, Alexandria, the Levant, Africa and Greece; Jews, Muslims and Christians. Crusader ships from England and the Netherlands conquered Lisbon en route to the Levant in 1147. Tortosa and Almeria were captured by Genoese in 1147–1149 in return for promise of a third of the city and the Balearics were occupied by Pisa. Genoese merchants thereafter were in Almeria, Malaga, Cadiz, Seville and Lisbon selling cloth bought at Champagne fairs for sugar, fruit and African gold and by the century's end had negotiated treaties giving ships safe passage and fixed tariffs. Twelfth-century trade became more complex, sophisticated and richer in commodities. Dispute resolutions were developed for poor cargo quality on arrival, non-payments, business failures, and *commenda* disputes. A shipper in an 1191–92 Genoese document promised 'securitas'. It is debatable whether at this early date it meant safety or insurance, but later it definitely meant insurance.[20]

Henry II, crowned king of Sicily in 1194, was determined to destroy Byzantium and, like Barbarossa, reunite a Roman empire. Venice, from being a Byzantine vassal was transformed into a drug to which Byzantium was addicted. Weakened internally and facing many external threats, the addict had handed her defence to its former vassal. Trade volumes accelerated, mainly controlled by north Italian and Jewish merchants. More Europeans got a taste for luxury items from the east. In Sardinia around 1183 Ibn Jubayr recorded 80 Muslim slaves for sale; a sign of successful Christian fight-back. Yet Muslims occupied Anatolia, southern Iberia and successfully retaliated in the Levant. Nevertheless, despite politico-religious confrontation and virtually continuous war, extensive Muslim-Christian merchant trade cooperation enabled gradually richer economies and better qualities of life.

b) Atlantic Europe

England's Norman monarchy needed London's trade-generated revenue. Its confident merchants wanted to be self-governing. On William II's death, his brother Henry I (1100–1136), needing their support to maintain his grip on power, gave them the right to collect taxes and elect a sheriff. Foreign and provincial merchants were only allowed to stay 40 days and foreigners only to deal through local intermediaries. By the early-1100s, London's population was about 18,000, still well-short of Roman London's 45,000. The waterfront wall was demolished for rising ship calls. A fire about 1136 destroyed much of the timber-built port and bridge giving it opportunity for renewal. Stone warehouses were built. Ships no longer waited to sell cargoes but immediately stored them, enabling increased cargo capacity. Before 1000, ships probably carried a maximum of 20 tons. By 1000 it was nearer 60 and in the late-1100s, 100,[21] real progress even if from small volumes. Trade-growth served a growing population, favourably affecting its hinterland's economy. Wool exports to Flanders, already regular, increased to supply cloth manufacturing growth from Flanders to Cologne. Bruges' River Zwijn was opened up by a 1134 storm enabling ships to discharge in town but immediately started silting. It imported Portuguese figs, dates, raisins, almonds and honey, Italian wine, spices and sugar, Baltic herring, grain, cheese, bacon, fur, textiles, skins, wax, metals and English wool for multiple destinations. Spanish trade led to Robert of Ketton's translation of Al-Khwarizmi's work on algebra, *Algorithmi*, Europe's major text on it until the 16th century.

In 1130, William Count of Poitiers, Duke of Guyenne seized La Rochelle, a small coastal village, granting it extensive privileges to attract merchants. After adding Anjou and Maine to the Norman realm, England's Henry II (r. 1154–1183) on marriage to Duke William's daughter, Eleanor in 1154, added Aquitaine, enabling La Rochelle's further development for regular wine shipments to England.[22] A marriage alliance with Saxony's Henry the Lion's daughter established good relations with German Baltic towns, a daughter to Alfonso of Castile did the same, his son to Brittany's heir ensured safe south-bound sea-passages and the Count of Flanders allied. A period of peace ensued. Bruges, with new walls, canals, a wool and cloth market in the 1130s, hosted an English merchant enclave. Traffic was frequent. In 1127 news of the murder of Flanders' Charles the Good reached London within two days,[23] as wool exports grew, essential to Flanders' economy. Ghent, at the rivers Scheldt and Leie confluence, developed quickly into about 80 hectares (198 acres) in the early-12th century. By the mid-12th century, municipal councils founded schools for burghers' children, north Europe's first lay schools since the Roman Empire. By the 1180s at the latest, 'cloth of Ypres' and 'cloth of Arras' were sold in the Mediterranean and Levant.

In England, 120 new towns were established, many centrally-planned specifically for trade. Richard I (r. 1189–99) founded Portsmouth and John (r. 1199–1216) Liverpool, for example. Not all were ports but most were on key trade routes. A century after conquest, Norman England had a sphere of influence from Iberia to Scandinavia, including important manufacturing towns in Flanders and north Germany. Oslo and Bergen were linked to Iceland and Greenland colonies. By 1200 Denmark also developed maritime strength with its new port, Copenhagen, while Sweden expanded into Finland.[24]

Lubeck, formerly an Abodrit royal centre, had a large merchant enclave but was sacked by other Slavs in 1138. Occupied by Germans thereafter, Count Adolf rebuilt near its old port which was destroyed in the 1147 Wendish Crusade. Henry the Lion took it, merchants returned and it prospered from 1159.[25] Its merchants spread through the Baltic. England's east coast Boston and Lynn mainly traded with Norway. In *Sverris Saga* in 1186 a Norwegian king explained the relative merits of Bergen's foreign merchants. 'We...thank the Englishmen who have brought hither linen and flax, wax and cauldrons and the men of the Orkneys, Shetland and the Faroes and of Iceland who have brought here such things as to make the land richer, which we cannot do without. But there are Germans who have come here... taking away butter and dried fish, of which the export must impoverish the land, and bringing only wine.' This references the Hansa, originating about 1159 when Lubeck and Hamburg merchants agreed to build a canal between them to ship salt, mined nearby at Luneburg, triggered by the silting of the Limfjord, former Baltic entrance, as ships otherwise had to sail around Jutland. Norway's complaint was pertinent, showing it depended on grain imports, an exploitable weakness by Hansa merchants, demonstrated to full effect in the next century.

Because the Church forbade meat consumption half the year, the preservation, trade and transport of herring, a plentiful Baltic food for millennia, tightly pressed 830–840 to a barrel, was very important. Having to be salted within 24 hours of catching, the canal cut sailing times. The barrels were inspected, sealed and stamped, part of a commercial infrastructure distributing them throughout Europe by Hansa merchants also dealing in grain, timber and amber, shipped in 'cogs', probably first appearing in 10th-century Frisia. Baltic oak-built cogs had a mast, square-rigged sail, flat-bottoms and stern-mounted central rudders instead of side-mounted steering oars. In the 13th century, decks were added. With larger carrying-capacity, higher hulls, and therefore better for both cargo and fighting than low, Viking-type long ships, they dominated growing maritime trade relatively quickly.

Visby on Gotland had a German merchant enclave trading with Novgorod for Russian furs, wax and Byzantine goods. Christian lands were created by Teutonic 'Knights of the Sword'. After Jerusalem's reconquest, these originally Acre-based knights, became Riga-based infidel-fighting mercenaries, ethnically cleansing pagans and eliminating the oldest Indo-European language, Old Prussian, in Crusades. Into the void, tens of thousands of mainly German peasant-colonists with iron ploughs that Slavs lacked, flooded-in, building towns and castles, draining marshes, cutting-down forests, planting crops and opening trade routes. Some were Flemings and Frisians, who like the Dutch, were drainage experts. From the 1160s Lubeck and Hamburg's Hansa settled Wismar, Stettin, Rostock, Riga, Reval (Tallin) and Danzig, trading fish, salt and cloth, opening up Pomeranian and Wend hinterlands, newly-settled by German, Christian farmers, outlets for agricultural surpluses. They farmed more efficiently, increasing food supply, especially grains like rye, bringing south Baltic ports full of German merchants, mainly from Lubeck, into western Europe's trade.[26] A bishopric was established in Riga in 1186, not long after its founding. In this way, German farmers, artisans and merchants settled vast areas of Livonia, Finland, Pomerania and Silesia, settled under 'margraves' or border counts, known in English as 'marches', ruled from castles. Immigration swelled Riga's population to around 2–3,000 by the 1230s, a port for trade and crusading.[27] Flemings emigrated as far as Vienna, Constantinople and South Wales. From a small overpopulated land threatened by the sea, industrious migrants, described by Gerard of Wales in 1188 as 'a people skilled at working in wool, experienced in trade and ready to face any effort or danger at land or sea in the pursuit of gain,' spread and settled.

By the late-12th century, Hansa ports included Cologne, Danzig, Reval, Riga, Bremen and Visby, at the mouths of major rivers from the Rhine to the Vistula, capturing growing north European and Baltic trade. Its lynchpin was Lubeck, its four main overseas trade enclaves, *kontors*, Bruges, Bergen, Novgorod and London. Trade in salt, textiles, furs, herrings, amber, honey, spices, copper, wine, grain, timber, masts, hemp, pitch, flax and tar for shipbuilding, collectively known as naval stores, wood for herring barrels, potash for glass making and iron, boosted economic activity and growth. The Hansa also trained pilots, built lighthouses, dredged channels and ensured quality control. Lubeck and Hamburg's merchants uniquely had the location, vision, expertise and capital to increase north European and Baltic trades. Its English members, 'Easterlings' from where the word 'sterling' originates, meaning 'of assured value,' were London-based. Each merchant group's aim was to obtain privileges in other cities; in short, a diverse, loose association. Over the next centuries, the number of cities involved varied from around 60 to 200, depending on the source's assessment of their degree of attachment. It had no treaties, statutes, chairman, representative authority or means to punish disobedient members, except exclusion. But it was formidable.

Sweden exported iron and copper, Finland and Muscovy furs, leather, timber, pitch, hemp, wax and flax. Novgorod controlled trade on the River Volga. A city republic with only a few thousand inhabitants, its kremlin and five-domed cathedral from the 1040s and its merchant church from 1207, attest to wealth derived from these exports. Bergen concentrated on dried cod, London and Boston on wool and cloth, Flanders and Brabant on high-quality cloth through Bruges. Viborg exported timber and tar while Danzig, Elbing and Konigsberg were the main Pomeranian grain ports. Traded goods reached inland and those from north European ports met those from the south at Champagne's fairs.

London's merchant self-government with its own mayor, gave impetus for growth. By 1203 an eighth of national revenue was collected there.[28] Its wooden bridge, destroyed by fire, was replaced by a massive stone bridge lasting over 600 years, a symbol of prosperity and confidence. Late-12th century William Fitz Stephen, writing just before the bridge was built, said London was 'amongst the noblest and celebrated cities of the world…possessing …abundant wealth, extensive commerce, great grandeur and magnificence…to this city from every nation…merchants bring their commodities by sea.'[29] Nobles bought luxury goods including spices, incense, palm oil, gems, silk, fur and weapons. London manufactured decorative iron work and pewterware using English tin and lead. Bristol dominated Gascony's wine trade and in 1172 Henry III gave its merchants rights to live and trade in Dublin. Chester traded with Gascony and Ireland. Newcastle exported coal to London. The Cinque Ports commanded the Channel ensuring trade security. A century earlier in 1098 Anselm, Archbishop of Canterbury arrived in Rome to discover popes had been condemning lay investiture since 1078, information deprivation impossible 100 years later.[30] As in the Mediterranean, the 12th century was crucial for northern Europe's growth and communication, driven by ports and maritime trade.

Chapter 10

Europe's Thirteenth Century

Thirteenth century Europe built upon the previous two centuries' successes with significant trade expansion allied to agricultural productivity, population growth which by 1300 was three-times that of 950, and money supply increase. It is sometimes described as a 'commercial revolution.' Maritime trade made major ports and rulers of maritime regions wealthy. Streets were broadened, town squares created, painters, sculptors and architects patronised and inland transport improved. Trade's influence spread inland and by 1300, Europe had an urban and manufacturing belt from southern England to northern Italy. Robert Bartlett concludes, 'the unity of the medieval west was, in part, a trader's unity.'[1] Disastrous for Byzantines, the century was otherwise important in Europe's recovery.

a) Mediterranean and Black Sea

The 1204 Fourth Crusade's target was Egypt. It needed naval transport and agreed with Venice a massive contract for 200 new, large ships, a major investment, to carry 4,500 knights and 30,000 soldiers, for 80,000 francs and a share of captured territory. As part consideration, Pope Innocent reaffirmed a dispensation to export non-strategic goods to Egypt.[2] Motives for what followed are controversial. For some historians attacking Egypt, Venice's wealthiest trade partner, was a conflict of interests, the last thing Doge Dandolo wanted. For others, they separated commerce from politics. Surviving Venetian commercial documents from 1150 to 1250 show Egyptian destinations only 11% of Venice's total,[3] although destination does not necessarily reflect value. Venice's problem was that the assembled Crusaders were two-thirds smaller than contracted for. The solution found was that Venice's people lent the Crusade 3,400 marks, equivalent to nine tons of silver, in return for retaking Zara (Zadar), on Dalmatia's coast, recently fallen to Hungary. Venice's whole raison d'etre depended on Adriatic control and it was taking great financial risk in bailing out the Crusade, the only means of preserving it, to finance a foreign army with very poor credit. But booty from Zara still fell short, although an enemy was weakened and Venice's security increased.[4] Incredibly to some, although there had been talk in Venice for some time, to bail out Venice and a Crusade whose target was Egypt, Doge Dandolo persuaded enough Crusaders to capture Constantinople and enthrone a compliant claimant instead. Venice's prize was Black Sea trade dominance.

The emperor had sold off anchors, sails and rigging of the few remaining ships in the empty dockyard since his equally weak brother had gifted Byzantine shipbuilding to Venice 16 years before. He fled with gold, jewels and women, leaving his wife and children. The Crusaders landed at Galata's trading enclaves, and marched to the centre. Geoffrey de Villehardouin wrote, 'All those who had never seen Constantinople gazed very intently on the city, never having imagined there could be so fine a place in all the world.' It made the Rialto look ordinary,[5] an international city with goods from multiple eastern markets, an architectural jewel of wealth, taste and distinction, the last repository of the Roman world. It didn't matter. With the treasury empty, three days and nights of murder, rape, looting and destruction followed. Thousands died. Images and icons were smashed, manuscripts burnt, bronze treasures and statues melted and silk hangings torn down.

Venetians by contrast, had orders to purposely loot art for Venice. Constantinople was stripped and raped. Its puppet on the throne, it took Corfu, most Aegean islands, bought Crete, and proclaimed itself 'lord of a quarter and one half [quarter] of the Empire of Romania,' the right to trade, free of controls and taxes, under her own law over the whole empire. Genoa and Pisa were excluded. A chain of bases to Constantinople was established; Crete's main port, Candia, Negroponte in Euboea, Modon the 'receptacle and special nest of all our galleys, ships and vessels', Coron, 'the two eyes of the republic' and Lepanto commanding the Gulf of Corinth, the bases and basis of her maritime supremacy, important because her long, narrow galleys for high-value cargo needed rowing crews of over 100. All needed food, water and frequent port calls. Dalmatia's coast's, 725 islands and innumerable inlets, ideal for piracy, as Venice knew, needed bases at Korcula, Budva, Kotor, Split, Zara, Fiume and Pula to maintain control. Ragusa (Dubrovnik) was nominally incorporated and became important, trading mainly with Ancona. It based its constitution on Venice's and imported Italian artists and craftsmen. Its merchants were active at hundreds of Balkan trade enclaves, Constantinople, even England. It outlawed slave trading and torture and encouraged education; a pure merchant city-state port.

The Fourth Crusade transformed Venice into a multi-based power. Trebizond-based Comneni proclaimed their own empire. Nicaea and Epirus were other alternate centres. Fragmented, the empire weakened. The Egyptian attack was cancelled and Venice's Egyptian commercial interests preserved. Southern European famines had given Venice a sense of vulnerability so Black Sea grain revived antiquity's shipments from the old Greek colony of Tana on the Don. Convoys of eight to ten escorted galleys sailed there annually. Caffa, the ancient Greek Crimean port of Theodosia (Feodosiya), handled grain, fish, salt, furs and slaves. After 4th-century Hun destruction, it had reduced to village-size, but after 1204 re-emerged into the maritime world and flourished. At Trebizond, Genoese who allied with the Comneni, exported silk, furs, metals, spices and luxury goods for western glass, textiles and other manufactures. It had docks, warehouses, workshops, shipping companies, a bazaar and lodgings for overland caravans. Greeks had dominated

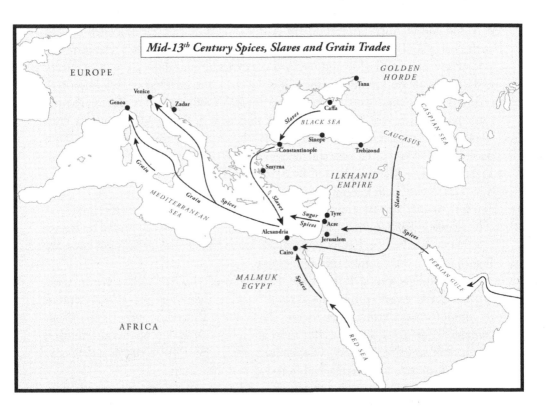

Mid-13th Century Spices, Slaves and Grain Trades

it since its foundation. Even in valleys south of Trebizond in the 15th century, 90% of people spoke Greek. In 1920 it was still around 75%.[6] Some Arab maps called the Black Sea 'bahr al-Tarabazunda'.[7] The Black Sea became the hub of an economic network stretching from China to Barcelona, from Tabriz to Novgorod. Caffa in the north and Trebizond in the south, were energised by Greek, Armenian and Levantine merchant enclaves. To Italian city states, it was *il mare maggiore* the Great Sea, rivalling Egypt and the Levant for eastern products.

Venetian trade was state-organised, controlling routes, departure times, quantity, product type and appointing consuls in its colonies. Financiers and merchants in politically powerful positions invested heavily in overseas trade but anyone with surplus capital including widows, craftsmen and clerics invested, whereas Genoese investments tended to be more from rich merchant families.[8] Both used public debt rather than tax to fund investment in infrastructure and defence, even before 1200, and citizens lent money in return for interest-bearing shares. Forced loans were introduced in Venice and Florence but Genoa continued the individual or family approach. Most Venetian investors funded multiple merchants in different areas to spread risk and merchants raised funds from several investors.[9] Successful merchants often became investors, including its 5,000 Jews. Codified law systems, impartial judges, permanent courts and judicial enforcement developed and helped good governance. Profits were widely distributed and helped mould Venetian character, cohesion and identity. From the 11th century, the doge's power had been limited with checks and balances of overlapping councils and magistrates, ensuring the rule of law. State officials could be fined for dereliction of duty. To prevent rivalry or factionalism, no family was allowed more than one member on any important board. The business of government was trade. Venetian nobility dominated the most profitable routes, leaving grain, salt and wine to lesser merchants. In both Venice and Genoa, government was run as a business, with different models, both pooling capital and using permanent agents in overseas enclaves. In contrast, south France's Aigues-Mortes, planned by Saint Louis between 1226 and 1270, was a minor trade port, built mainly to consolidate the crown's hold over the Rhone valley and for crusader embarkation. Nor did trade flow up the Rhone as substantially as it had done in Roman times, although Lyon's annual fairs were attended by Italian merchants. For France, Lyon's importance lay as the centre for Church councils. France remained predominantly agricultural.

The Mamluks, ruling Egypt from 1250, showed similar indifference to trade as their predecessors, except the shrewd Saladin. Economic power was centred in interior cities; Cairo, Aleppo and Damascus. Egyptian ports operated no commercial or naval shipping. But as in antiquity and earlier medieval centuries, Egypt was strategically and commercially vital. The Fifth Crusade (1218–21) attacked Damietta but overreached in trying to attack Cairo.

Sicily was the central Mediterranean conduit for trade, making it with state monopoly of grain exports to Tunisia, woollen and linen goods, timber, butter, cheese and fruits, western Europe's wealthiest kingdom. Its ports were Naples, Bari, Gaeta and Salerno, home to Europe's oldest medical school. The Messina Straits were the direct route to Pisa and Genoa. Emperor Frederick II Hohenstaufen, grandson of Roger II of Sicily, was perhaps the most vigorous and intelligent of western emperors. Naturally therefore, he was often at war with the papacy and excommunicated four-times. He spoke six languages, was an avid patron of the arts, literature and poetry and had a thirst for knowledge. He enlisted Muslims in his army and bodyguard, employed Sicily's Jews to translate Greek and Arabic works, corresponded with scholars on scientific subjects, instituted a civil service and founded Naples University in 1224 to train it. Paris university trained churchmen, whereas Naples' charter explicitly stated its aim was to train intelligent men for imperial service, not theologians, symbolising the start of Europe's Renaissance, gradual re-learning, much brought from Muslim Iberia, nurtured in Sicily by Roger and Frederick. Commercial advance, as always, was accompanied by intellectual, cultural and artistic progress. In 1229 Frederick negotiated the return of Jerusalem to Latin Christians. But the papacy, which logically should have welcomed this bloodless victory, allied with Venice and Genoa in 1238 against him and Pisa. Their 1241 joint raid sunk 25 Genoese ships and took 1,000 people including several bishops and took two cardinals prisoner. The pope invaded Frederick's lands and invited the prince of Anjou to evict his son from Sicily after his 1250 death.

A sixth crusade against Egypt in 1249–50 repeated the disaster of the fifth. Venice kept trading with it, probably its most profitable market, spices and sugar, exchanged for Lombard, Florentine and Flemish cloth. By 1250 the Mediterranean and Black Sea were Latin lakes. Dinars were replaced by Italian gold florins and ducats, illustrating Florence and Venice's economic dominance. Louis IX's crusade against Tunis achieved nothing.

The speed of Iberian Reconquista varied regionally. Its greatest gains were in the 13th century.[10] Increasingly zealous and intolerant Islamic Berber sects weakened themselves by persecuting Jews. As Castile's advance stalled, Aragon conquered and united Catalonia and Valencia in 1304. Barcelona grew and was the birthplace of the *Llibre del Consolat*, the maritime code which regulated Mediterranean trade as far as the Levant. Pedro II (r. 1196–1213) dreamed of a *regne dins el mar*, a kingdom in the sea.[11] Trade was protected by 100–150-oared galleys equipped with battering rams, catapults and crossbowmen. They regularly clashed with Muslims especially around the Balearic Islands and Minorca, won late in the century. Hohenstaufen Sicily was given to the Angevins by the pope in 1266, the so-called Sicilian Vespers. Sicily appealed to Aragon, who took over. The resulting 20-year war with France ended with them keeping the mainland. Aragon got Sicily, Malta and Gozo where their galleys regularly traded. Some ships still went in convoy, protection against piracy, still problematic despite naval supremacy of Italian and Catalan merchants' fast galley patrols.

Genoa, excluded from the northern Black Sea, focused more on the western Mediterranean, Iberian and North African ports. It developed Ibiza into the largest regional salt producer and trader. Barcelona competed with north Italians for Mediterranean trade mastery in wheat, woollens, salt, fur and North African slaves, gaining access to Tunis, Alexandria and Tlemcen, a new port and trans-Saharan gold terminus from the 1200s. While Muslims still had both sides of the Gibraltar Straits, its waters were controlled by Genoese and Aragon-Catalonia. Cadiz's capture in 1262 gave them a superb harbour, control of the Gibraltar Straits and access out of the Mediterranean. As Portuguese took the Algarve, Genoese merchants in Lisbon helped them develop a navy and merchant contacts in the Mediterranean and northern Europe. Genoa's later strong merchant presence in Iberia started decisively in the 13th century.

In 1261 Genoa supported exiled Michael VIII Paleologos of Nicaea to become Emperor in Constantinople. In return, Genoese were given privileges formerly held by Venice; access to Black Sea grain, slaves, wax and fur. But Michael knew that Venice was inherently stronger. It was best to play them off. In 1268 he permitted them an enclave in the Galata suburb rather than Constantinople's docks. Genoa never excluded Venice from Black Sea trade, but after 1261 became its dominant power in Sinope, Trebizond, Sevstopolis, Licostorno, Maurocastro and Caffa where Mongols allowed their trade enclaves. Venice's strength remained at Tana and Sudak.

Pisa's heyday was around 1100–1150, but continued prospering until defeat by Genoa at the 1284 battle of Meloria. Meanwhile in 1298 Genoa defeated Venice off

Korcula, after which the poet Rustichello, sharing a prison with Venetian prisoner Marco Polo, wrote his story. It became known as *Il Milione* after its supposed million lies. He had travelled east in 1275 so unlike his father and uncle's earlier expeditions, he avoided Genoese-dominated Constantinople. Returning through the Black Sea, he wrote briefly, 'there are so many who...sail [it]...Venetians, Genoese, Pisans and many others...constantly making this voyage that everybody knows what is to be found.'[12] In short, it was common knowledge, too well-known to be included in the sensationalist story.

Literacy was widespread in ports. Trade made it necessary. The more complex the trade, the more international, the greater the skills needed. Traders' families sent their sons to tutors. In the 12th and 13th centuries, many north Italian towns and Ghent created the new lay public school. By the early-14th century in Florence, according to Giovanni Villani, resident merchant and historian, 8–10,000 boys and girls learned to read, close to universal literacy.[13] 'Whoever is slow in writing his records cannot live long without damage and error,' said a 13th-century Genoese merchant.[14] Arithmetic's revival started in ports. The *Liber Abbaci* of Leonardo Fibonacci of Pisa, a merchant's son in Bougie, North Africa, rejecting the abacus for Indian numerals, used commercial transactions as examples for his mathematical problems.[15]

Many merchants completed their education at Bologna University, many in commercial and maritime law. Pisa's code probably dates from before the 12th century.[16] An impressive achievement of 13th-century Italian merchants was the transformation of accounting, developing into a full double-entry system in the early-14th century. They were knowledgeable about foreign customs, measurements, merchandise and languages, the latter often learnt from foreign wives in long residences abroad. In Italian ports more was written in connection with business than with any other activity, most thrown away when no longer relevant. Genoa ordered notaries to deposit all minutes in municipal archives, most of which concerned trade. Only 150 13th-century minute books remain, under 1% of those written. Portolans, descriptions of ports and their approaches survive from the 13th century, but must have existed earlier.[17] Merchant entrepreneurship, knowledge of markets, plants, minerals, products and processes was responsible for the diffusion of many technical innovations, raising living standards. Merchants published commercial encyclopaedias. The oldest, from Pisa in 1278, listed goods available in different markets, their qualities, how to identify them, their cost including transport, taxes, weight, coin conversion and models of commercial contracts. The best was probably Florence-based Pegolotti's *Pratica della Mercatura* (*The Practice of Commerce*) from about 1310, containing calculations of interest, discounts, and several chemical and metallurgical processes.[18] Increasingly, as in ancient ports, dry calculations gave way to literature. Florence's spice merchant Dante Alighieri (1265–1321) wrote the greatest medieval poem[19] and Boccaccio (1313–1375), the age's greatest prose writer, son of a Florence-based Bardi banker, wrote stories in which merchants were discriminated against by knights and the Church, but were at the forefront of social change.

Venice practiced what it learned in North African funduqs. From 1228, German, Polish and Bohemian merchants had to live and deposit their goods in the *Fondaco dei Tedeschi*, a state-run and surveiled enclave opposite the Rialto, where they sold their hardware, fustians etc. for Venetian goods; pepper, cloth, cotton, wool, silk, spices, pearls, sugar and gold generating considerable revenues as it excluded them from protected, long-haul maritime trade. Venice's heart of business, information, banking, markets and financial services was the Rialto. From the mid-12th century private banking developed and became increasingly specialised. The Consoli dei Mercanti heard commercial disputes. The Giustizia Vecchia controlled trade in food, market and guild regulation, weights, measures and price controls, all aiding trust necessary in undertaking risk.[20] Nearby Campo San Bartolome was Europe's spice centre. Venetian glassmaking spread to southern Germany. To aid commercial development, north and central Italian city-states organised road and bridge building.[21]

Despite war, competition stimulated economic activity, enterprise and growth. Wool, cotton and silk imports stimulated north Italy's many textile-making towns. Venice prospered and the Grand Canal was lined with palazzo. Churches became taller and more lavish. In 1264 the Piazzetta was paved and a new Rialto bridge built. Venice's gold ducat from 1284 based on Florence's florin, symbolised Europe's economic renaissance. Pisa's 1284 defeat at Meloria eliminated her as a major maritime power. Corsican claims were dropped and part of Sardinia given to Genoa. Venice dominated the east Mediterranean and Venice-Genoa jointly the Black Sea. In 1290 Genoa destroyed Porto Pisano, Pisa's port, shortly after which the river Arno changed course, preventing ships from reaching it. Genoa took-over. Its trade share judged by customs dues, quadrupled between 1274 and 1293.[22] Wars consumed huge resources. During the second Genoese-Venetian War (1294–99) in 1295, Genoa put an exceptional 165 galleys and 35,000 men to sea, but fleets of 40–50 galleys were common. Permanent naval bases were therefore required.

In the Levant, Acre's merchant enclaves' rival merchants fought in full view of Muslims. In Genoese-Pisan conflict, Genoese merchants evacuated to previously Venetian dominated Tyre. The permanent loss of Acre in 1291, delayed by internal Muslim power struggles was followed by Sidon and Beirut. Coming after the sack of Baghdad (Chapter 13) it further undermined Gulf-Levant caravans. Venice reinforced its valuable Egyptian focus. Genoa concentrated on Aegean, west Mediterranean and Black Sea bulk cargoes, their trade revenues seven-times Constantinople's.[23] Incredibly, Emperor Andronikos II (1261–1332), fighting a losing battle against Turks and Bulgars on his land frontiers, had his 80-ship navy dismantled, surrendering any vestiges of naval control to Genoa and Venice, who needed Byzantine survival.

Castilian merino sheep imported from 12th-century North Africa, had by the 13th, developed into great migratory flocks, formed into a national association in 1273, the Mesta, dominating Castile's economy, the wool exported mainly by Barcelona's merchants. Florence's luxury cloth was made from imported English,

Castilian and Burgundian wool. Silk, cotton, alum and dyes were imported via Venice and Genoa from Anatolia and the Levant. Silk imitation, 'damask', originally from Damascus, was manufactured in Lucca, and improved in Bologna, Florence, Venice and Genoa. Some Lucca workers moved to Venice. Various cloth types were distributed throughout Europe and the Mediterranean; wool, linen, cotton, silk, velvets, damasks and cloth of gold, made finer by embroidery, London's speciality, or by adding fine fur and skins. Paper was initially imported from Egypt. As demand grew for record-keeping and correspondence, it was also made in Italy and spread to France and Germany.

The 13th century saw advances in ship technology. A port book covered the Mediterranean by 1250, charts were more accurate, the mariner compass and central rudders used, the latter a Basque invention. They shipped Basque iron to Genoa; 45,000 tons in 1293.[24] Bigger ships sailed in winter by 1270 and in the 1290s, Venice's Arsenal was enlarged. In 1277 two Genoese ships reached London for the first time with sugar, spices, ceramics, silk and alum and a Majorcan in 1281. Already importing Castile's wool, Genoese wanted finer, more expensive English wool, so that north Italian cloth could compete with Flanders' cloth. Genoese Benedetto Zaccaria, a wool, cloth and dye merchant found a large alum deposit near Phocaea in Anatolia. In 1274, in return for naval assistance to Constantinople, he obtained a fief to it and equipped its factories with huge vats protected by a fort, shipping the cargoes from Phocaea to Mediterranean ports, then England and Bruges in 1278 in the new Genoa-London-Bruges convoys.[25] His family raised production to almost 700 tons by 1330 out of a total 1,800-ton Mediterranean production, a huge market share.[26] Europe's strongest monarch, France's Philip the Fair (1285–1314) entrusted his finances to Florentine merchant Musciatto Guido and his fledgling navy to Genoa's Zaccaria.[27]

In 1293, the Muslim Gibraltar Straits' naval force was defeated by a joint Castilian-Genoese fleet, enabling more regular sailings to north Europe, including Catalan, Portuguese and Castilian ports en route. Genoese merchants were stronger in the west Mediterranean and Bruges, Venetians in Egypt and Antwerp. Venice's dominant position in eastern goods meant Genoa's merchants had to be more innovative. Genoa minted gold coins in the early-1200s, Florence following in 1250, Venice only in 1284. Genoa pioneered financial innovations and commercial Iberian connections. The first voyages to Bruges and London were Genoese. In 1270 Genoese reached the Canaries. In 1291 its Vivaldi brothers ambitiously attempted to reach India via the Atlantic, for pepper and spices that Venice imported from Egypt and dominated. Last sighted near the Canaries, they were however, never seen again. Neither Venice nor Genoa could monopolise rapidly increasing cargo varieties and volumes but energetically and entrepreneurially took advantage of widening trading opportunities in this economic revolution. Chronicler Galvano Fiamma (1283–1344) contrasted end-century luxurious clothes and food with the frugality at the start.[28]

b) Atlantic Europe

Atlantic Europe's 13th-century was equally crucial. Lubeck was the engine of growth, colonisation and trade. Its merchant families settled Pomerania's coast from the 1160s, as German farmer-settlers transformed lands from the Gulf of Finland to Transylvania from thick woodlands into productive farmland, from Pagan Slavic to German Christian, obliterating Wendish and Prussian Slavic languages. In these inland regions, labour was scarce and thus mobility was restricted, tied to the land or forcibly removed with their moveable property and livestock to new areas; the origin of east Europe's serfdom.[29] Stettin, Wismar, Stralsund and Rostock were all founded with Lubeck law and German oligarchies. Robert Bartlett thinks 'Rostock's charter was like a starting gun',[30] transforming the country into grain-growing farms, small towns with churches and markets. Riga, Reval and Danzig developed as their hinterlands opened up, in Danzig's case using the River Vistula, connecting several agricultural regions for grain and timber export. When early-13th-century Danzig got city rights, it also adopted Lubeck law. Maritime commercial words slipped from German into Polish, ballst to ballast, kogge to kogga, pfund (pound) to punt.

Core Hanseatic ports, Lubeck, Hamburg, Bremen and Cologne, had privileges in Bruges, London, Bergen and Novgorod. The Hansa dominated Baltic grain, especially rye to western Europe, potash, hemp, flax, timber for barrel making, Novgorod's reindeer products, whale blubber, walrus ivory, Arctic squirrel and fox furs, leathers, skins, wax and cod. Iceland's cod was also fished by Basques. Unlike herring, cod was salted, dried and stacked in ships. Most salt came from the Loire estuary, Noirmoutier island, Bourgneuf and the Isle de Re.[31] Iron and copper came from Sweden. Baltic imports were high-quality Flemish and Brabant cloth, spices, salt and wines, all via Lubeck.

In the early-1200s a French fleet tried to capture Bruges and reported finding 'wealth beyond all…hopes, brought in by ships from all parts of the world,' highlighting silver, copper, tin, iron, cloth, hides, wool, cotton, potash, timber, coal and Chinese goods, demonstrating widening, deepening trade, a point lost on French kings, who in 1224 took La Rochelle and closed it to English shipping. The alternative, Bordeaux was a less attractive port, far from open sea in the Gironde estuary with difficult-to-navigate sandbanks. Locals were not natural seafarers. Trade was developed by ships and merchants from England, the Netherlands, Brittany and Bayonne, sourcing wine via the Garonne as far as Toulouse and Albi. With La Rochelle competition removed, wine exports quickly increased and potash, dyes and alum exports for the cloth industry developed, doubling Bordeaux's size during the century.[32] Gascon wine to England became a regular, large, well-developed trade, supplanting Rouen and Rhineland wines, peaking in the 1280s-1330s.[33] So much was it England's core trade that the tun, a 252-gallon barrel, became the standard measurement for ship's cargo. The unit changed; the term remained.

Flanders' cloth industry needed English wool. Bruges, Ghent, Ypres and Douai were wealthy clothmaking towns because of it, enabling them to pay the Count of

Flanders for the independence needed to continue it, often torn between his feudal obligations to France's king and support for wealth-creating clothmaking towns. When Henry II's sons rebelled, in 1173 the Earl of Leicester led a Flemish army into eastern England 'to destroy King Henry…and to have his wool, which we long for.'[34] In 1208 King John (r. 1204–1215) got Flemish towns' and merchants' loyalty. Flemish nobles, bribed by French king Philip Augustus, supported France. This was the start of enduring themes; French ambition and tactics in Flanders and its urban-rural divide. In Anglo-French war, Ghent, Bruges, Lille, St Omer, Douai and Ypres swore allegiance in return for trade privileges,[35] enshrined in the 1236 England-Flanders settlement. Exports grew, mainly handled by Flemish merchants with English perpetual safe conducts and reciprocal Flemish arrangements for English merchants.[36]

Unlike inland Paris, merchants were important in London's development because of its port. City government was the Lord Mayor and a council elected from merchant guilds. Each guild had a hall, meeting together at the Guildhall. Typical mayors were John of Gisors (1246 and 1253–59), a major wine importer who had his own wharf, Adam de Basing (1251–52), a prominent Draper (cloth merchant) and Andrew Bukerel of Bucklersbury (1231–37) who exported hides and wool and imported wine.[37] Meat-eating restrictions meant Fishmongers increased in importance. In 1313 they were third, after Woolmongers and Drapers, exporting wool.[38] Mercers dealt specifically in foreign cloth; silks, velvets and cloth of gold. In 1206 sugar first appeared in an English king's accounts with almonds, cinnamon, nutmeg, ginger and other spices, so we must assume 13th-century penetration to noble consumers. None of this suggests English kings saw maritime trade as an engine of growth to be nurtured; a later development. For example, the 1206 expedition to France relied on commandeered merchantmen. John wrote to Southampton's constable, 'detain for service all vessels fit for passage that are able to carry eight or more horses. Man them with able seamen at our cost…remember to enrol the names of the owners…if any ship be laden with merchandise…cause it immediately to be unloaded and taken into our service.'[39]

Magna Carta (1215), the result of baronial rebellion against King John, an attempt to limit royal powers, was backed by London merchants, always attempting to protect and govern themselves. William Hardell, London's Mayor helped draft it, his influence seen in clause 10 about repayment of borrowings to Jews after death, clause 13 ensuring the City had its 'ancient liberties and free customs' which other cities and ports should assume, clause 35 ensuring the standard measure for cloth and for ale and corn 'throughout the kingdom' was 'the London Quarter', clause 42 espousing 'the public interest' with merchants' interests[40] and clause 41 ensuring merchant freedom to travel to, from, and throughout England, free from tolls.

The English Parliament also flexed its young muscles. Convened by Henry III in 1244 to rubber-stamp a tax, it established a 12-man committee to consider it; establishing the precedent as a deliberating body with powers to grant or deny taxation. In 1255 London refused to pay a tax and Mayor Thomas Fitzthomas told Henry III, 'so long as unto us you will be a good lord, we will be faithful and duteous unto you,' but supported Simon de Montfort's 1263–65 revolt. The City was never cowed by the Crown, especially as London's 13th-century export share increased from a seventh to a third. In the revolt, Henry III's opponents seized wool in English ports, assuring Margaret Countess of Flanders that it was in protective safe custody. She however, seemingly over-reacted, although crucial documents are missing, seizing English goods and merchants.[41] After winning the 1265 Battle of Evesham, Henry reversed the barons' measures, proclaiming safety for all foreign merchants. Safe conducts were issued and property restored, but in 1270, Margaret re-arrested all English merchants. Flemish merchants in England were arrested in retaliation. Probably Henry then attempted to negotiate directly with the towns, while embargoing wool exports to Flanders. Seemingly this was widely ignored.[42] Edward I returning from Crusade reported no shortages in Flanders. Nevertheless, the prospect of a long total ban meant agreement was reached in 1274, but Margaret did not honour it and Flemings were banned from trading in England, and wool export to Flanders.[43] Still refusing, some town burgesses agreed to settle the main debts, Margaret reluctantly the balance in 1278. The dispute ended, but Flemish merchants never recovered their former ascendancy in the trade. Wool growers found other buyers, some Hansa, but mainly Italians.

Florentines, first mentioned in 1224 were the largest Italian group in England, although Italian merchants had been resident for years. The Bucointes and the Bukerels probably originated from 13th-century Italians. Pegolotti's price list from around 1318 reflected earlier buying practices, listing 194 English monasteries who sold them wool, also bought from nobles and small producers at fairs,[44] encouraged by Crown charters, allowing producers to deal with foreign buyers and sellers of spice, wax, dried fish, etc., drawing merchants throughout Europe for an annual four-week event. Flemish merchant withdrawal helped English merchants, especially in Southampton and Sandwich, but Italians were the immediate beneficiaries.

Flanders' importance to England grew as wool exports increased through the century to 32,743 sacks in 1273.[45] The most long-lasting outcome of the Flanders dispute was the 1275 'Great Custom', permanent tax on wool exports of 7s 6d per sack, negotiated with English merchants in return for opening more Flanders trade. It was collected at ports before loading, enabling loan repayments to lenders to the Crown, who were the Riccardi between 1275 and 1294. In 1275 England's leading wool export port was Boston with 9,623 sacks, then London with 7,020, Hull 3,415, Southampton 2,883, Lynn 1,350, Newcastle 873, Chichester 536, Ipswich 376, Sandwich 320, others with lesser quantities.[46] One sack contained the wool of 180 to 250 sheep and filled one wagon. It was often loaded as backhaul on ships discharging Gascon wine. Discharged in Bruges, north Europe's major port, it was then divided and transported to its destination. Bristol became busier. A new deep channel was cut through the marshes providing a deeper quay and water was piped to it from springs outside. Cotswold woollen cloth was exported and Gascon, Bordeaux and Iberian wines imported.

Rising wool imports meant that by the 1290s Ghent's population reached 60,000, Bruges and Ypres 50 kilometres away, probably 30,000 each. Bruges also produced cloth. As in north Italy, manufacturing spread inland, aided by road and bridge improvements on the Thames, Ouse, Rhine, Elbe and Danube. At Bristol, a new harbour was created in the 1240s. In Flanders and Brabant, towns and rulers cooperated to make canals or canalise rivers. Woollen cloth producing Zoutleeuw in Brabant owed its 13th-century prosperity to a late-12th-century road from Bruges to Cologne. The small river Gete was made navigable to Antwerp. Lighthouses were erected at Calais. St Omar, Ypres and Bruges built a canal to sail 600-tonners inland from the new port of Gravelines. An account covering 122 days in the winter of 1296–97 showed 3,250 barges and 87 vessels paying tolls on arrival at Ypres from Nieuwpoort.[47] Ghent built the Lieve Canal in 1259 to join it to the canalised Zwijn at Damme, built in 1180, giving Bruges' silting harbour access to deeper water. There were no such ports in north France, no appreciation of the benefits of maritime trade, despite the tantalising glimpse of Bruges' wealth. Southern French ports were also weak compared with north Italian ports, so trade, wealth, industry and culture did not flow inland. Paris, western Europe's largest city, was a consumer, dependent on the French Court, trading and manufacturing little compared to London, Bruges, Cologne, Lubeck or Ghent.

An example of how maritime trade spread wealth inland and how French kings could destroy it is perfectly illustrated by Champagne's fairs, ruled by the counts of Brie and Champagne, connecting Europe's northern and southern ports. Hansa merchants came from Flanders and Germany with cloth, manufactured goods, fur, leather and silver from central Europe. Italian, mainly Genoese, came with spices, silks, brocades and porcelain, buying cloth for north Italian manufacturing and dyeing towns. Originating as local agricultural fairs, the first documented in 1114, Troyes' was said to originate in Roman times.[48] Under the counts' guidance, they became Europe's main market, attracting French, Spanish, Portuguese, English, even Levantine, Cretan and Cypriot merchants, so a full range of traded foods, cloths, alum and dyes in high volume were involved. Troyes and Provins established textile production. Pegolotti noted Champagne's linens were marketed through Europe to Constantinople and mentioned in Italy in 1230 and in Acre from 1248.

Six fairs lasting six weeks or more were spread throughout the year in Troyes, Provins, Bar-sur-Aube and Lagny, specific days allocated to different products, making it an almost permanent market in goods and currency exchange, an innovation giving the region huge advantages over other medieval fairs. Their pre-eminence from about 1180, grew in volume and specialisations. The counts organised accommodation, huge warehouses, still standing in Provins, and canals from the Seine to Troyes; innovative, creative, sensible infrastructure. Prompted by seizures of goods en route by rapacious nobles, they negotiated treaties with neighbours guaranteeing safe conduct, in 1209 with France, in 1220 with Burgundy, in 1232 with Boulogne and by mid-century with Italians. 'Guards of the Fair' policed them, heard complaints, enforced contracts, imposed penalties and collected fines.[49] They gave employment in hostels providing food and lodging, to notaries, agents and porters. The counts received rents for halls, stables and houses leased to merchants, collected fees for licences and held a monopoly over flour mills and other ventures.

A Provins mint since the 10th century made its coinage eastern France's, and by the 1170s central Italy's dominant currency.[50] Troyes' weight standard became the international 'troy weight' which moved north to London with goods. The counts levied tolls at low rates, but high volumes made them and the area wealthy. Short-term credits were made and recorded, extended from one fair to another and from the early-1200s, cheques were cashed in Italy from Italian merchants in Champagne. This money market, credit, bookkeeping and banking function was Champagne's greatest contribution to Europe's growing economy.

But from 1284, because the daughter of the last count married the French king's son, Philip IV annexed it. Taking for granted the valuable revenue-stream, he increased tolls and taxes, leading to an almost immediate, precipitous drop in volume and revenue. Effectively, he encouraged trade to go elsewhere. Revenue received was spent in Paris rather than Troyes or Provins and on war to annex Flanders, English wool's main market. The fairs, so carefully nurtured, declined swiftly into purely local markets, their place taken partly by Lyon and Cologne, but mainly Bruges, already busy with Flemish cloth, English wool, Rhine and Bordeaux wines, French Bay salt, Spanish iron, Baltic fish and furs and Iberian dyes. Difficulties in Champagne and increased sophistication of long-distance credit motivated Genoa in 1297 to regularise the Bruges-London voyages begun in 1277 in larger ships, resulting in Bruges' greater importance with Italian merchants living there. Damme on its river, was silting, so Sluys opened in 1290. Genoese brought Phocaean alum from Chios, needed to manufacture Flanders' cloths, spices and silks, returning with English wool and English and Flemish cloth and silver.

In 1294 Philip used a feudal pretext to confiscate Gascony from Edward resulting in the 1294–1297 Gascon War, precipitating forced loans from English growers and an agreement with a merchant assembly to increase tax to 20 shillings per sack and 40 shillings per last of hides.[51] France declared war on Flanders in 1297. Flemish merchants were excluded and raw wool and un-dyed cloth export barred. English wool exports dropped from over 30,000 sacks between 1290 and 1294 to between 15,000 and 21,000 sacks in 1294–1297.[52] Italian firms had been cementing their position in wool. Lucca's Riccardi from the 1240s, who financed Edward I's (r. 1272–1307) Welsh conquests, Piacenza's Scotti, Florence's Bardi from 1267, Cerchi from 1268, the leading 1270s exporter, and Frescobaldi and Falconieri from 1272 who all had greater liquidity, buying in advance for their own clothmaking industries, loaning in return for export licenses to Italy, Holland, Zeeland and Brabant, excluding Flanders.[53] With relatively cheap credit, they moved easily from wool, cloth, silk, spices, etc. to money itself. Edward sent 305 ships with 9,000 troops to France in 1297. Because Flanders depended on English wool, supply interruptions caused unemployment and starvation. English chronicler Heminburgh said it was 'well-nigh empty because the people cannot have the wools of England.'[54] France's kings ended the century having destroyed trade prosperity in La Rochelle, Champagne and Flanders.

Iberia's 13th-century Reconquista's major gains; Cordoba in 1236, Murcia in 1241 and Seville in 1248 meant previous north Iberian ports exports, iron, horses, wine, wax, furs and hides were supplemented by southern products, more wines, dried fruits, olives, olive oil, dyes, salt, mercury and wool, shipped to Bordeaux and especially Southampton, London and Bruges. Spanish volumes thus outstripped Portuguese, shipped mainly in Basque ships by merchants with a long fishing tradition, a hinterland of iron, wines and wool and abundant timber for shipbuilding, diligently replanted, with resin and pitch for caulking.[55] Regular, frequent, and well-established Iberian trade led Southampton granting Castile's merchants residence for seven years in 1263. They had no such privileges at Winchelsea, yet at least 12 Castilian ships called in 1266–67. In 1285 Juan de Mundenard, probably the agent of a family firm, settled and became a town burgess.

By the early-1300s, frequent Genoese north-bound fleets were joined by those from Barcelona and Majorca, with goods formerly traded via Champagne. Seville and Lisbon were important ports of call. Italian merchants dealt with all Iberian ports. Iberians also ventured south. Portugal's deep-sea fishermen developed a knowledge of Atlantic winds, weather and currents. Soon after 1250, Cape Verde was rediscovered. Skills lost over a thousand years were gradually re-learnt.

Trade volumes to Iceland and Greenland were relatively minor. Greenland sold fish, walrus ivory, walrus hide rope and oil. Iceland sold fish. In 1262 it agreed subjugation to Norway's crown. In return for Iceland paying taxes, Norway sent minimum six ships annually. By the mid-14th century, demand increased that to 10–20.[56] The Hansa dominated Norway's trade. In 1284 they restricted Bergen's imports of grain, flour, malt and vegetables for winter, so Bergen banned foreigners from buying butter, furs and fish if not importing rye, malt and flour. The resulting Hansa blockade caused famine, forcing Bergen to pay 2,000 marks 'compensation'[57] and grant them the same rights as locals. This was the basis for Bergen's *kontor*, a double row of long, two-storied wooden sheds next to the water; warehouses below, living quarters above, behind locked gates, a secretive world with initiation rites, no outsiders allowed in,[58] each merchant trading for himself. The Hansa dominated Baltic grain and herring, Atlantic cod from Iceland, timber, pitch, tar and cloth from Flanders and England. As profit margins were low, monopoly control was considered necessary. That involved bullying trade partners, especially Norway.

They were granted their first English charter in 1260 by Henry, well-used to dealing with Italians. The Hansa's Steelyard base, like other Hansa *kontors*, except Bruges' which was open, was a walled enclave, an 18 by 10 metre building with ground floor warehouse and upper floor administration dating from 1282. In Jewry near the Guildhall, Jewish traders lent money with interest, an essential banking service, until 16,500 were expelled in 1290. Thirteenth-century London grew as a market for wealthy consuming classes with expensive town houses. The impact on surrounding counties grew with increased need for supplies. Seals for authenticating documents appear in the 13th-century archaeological record, mainly English, Frisian and German. In summary, 13th-century North Europe increased trade volumes and made more Iberian and regular Mediterranean maritime connections.

Chapter 11

Accelerating Song Maritime Trade Boom

Increasing volumes and velocity of Chinese trade described in Chapter 6 continued and accelerated. From the 12th-century, junks up to 600 tons, built at private shipyards in Fuzhou, Mingzhou, Zhangzhou and Quanzhou with floating rudders, waterproof hulls and 60-man crews, typically had four masts, though some had 12, with bamboo matting sails. They covered 300 miles a day with following monsoon winds.[1] Large fleets sailed through the Malacca Straits, no longer transiting the Kra Isthmus, with silk, tea, lacquerware, porcelain, rice, grain, salt, iron and steel, reflected in the huge increase in Jiangxi, Zhenjiang and Fujian porcelain in south India, Sri Lanka, Middle East, Siam's Satingpra in the north Malay Peninsula, Kra Isthmus ports and Angkor. Some went to Aden and east Africa. Chinese traders settled in Champa, Kra Isthmus entrepots, north Sumatra and Nagapattinam.

Al-Idrisi's 1154 *Tabula Rogeriana* mentioned Song junks in Aden laden with pepper, aloes, tortoiseshell, ivory, ebony, rattan, porcelain and leather saddles although they are not mentioned in the Geniza papers. Al-Idrisi noted Hangzhou's glassware and thought Quanzhou's silk the best. The contemporary Tanjung Simpang shipwreck from north Sabah, had been heavily looted when discovered, but Chinese ceramics and three to four-kilogram bronze gongs, were found. They traded with Kyushu's ports where Chinese merchants lived, but in 1151 after a samurai attack, 1,600 Chinese merchant families fled. Chinese ships also called at Honshu's ports, mainly for north Japan's furs and gold. The Ise Taira, a powerful military Court family, built a trade empire in western Japan from 1159 to 1180. Chinese trade guilds developed. Ports and merchant wealth eclipsed land-derived wealth.

By 1178 China concluded it no longer needed Srivijayan merchants and their embassies were banned. Chinese merchant associations became more sophisticated with increased capital. A *Song Digest* passage for 1201 reads 'people combine to pool their recourses and accept a common set of rules...[usually for] ten years... each year the group will meet to work out its profits...leaving the capital sum invested as before.'[2] Europe did not see similar organisations until England's 1555 joint-stock Muscovy Company and compared with multi-masted Song ships, its were single-masted. Increasing wealth encouraged social mobility. Luxuries like pepper were widely consumed. The *San-shang Gazetteer* of 1174–1189 recorded that fashionable, foreign-influenced clothing 'is no longer the pure simplicity of former times.'[3]

With northern China controlled by Jurchen, the emperor needed overseas trade to finance and defend the state, explaining, 'The profits from maritime commerce are very great, properly managed. They can amount to millions [of strings of coins]. Is this not better than taxing the people?' A canal navy of crossbowmen and exploding projectile-hurling machines was developed to repel Jurchens. Finance minister Zhang Yi explained, 'Our defences today are the [Yangtse] river and the sea, so our weakness in mounted troops is no concern.' Defence forces grew from 11 squadrons and 3,000 men in 1174 to 20 squadrons and 52,000 men in 1237, controlling the China Sea from Fujian to Japan and Korea and patrolling its main rivers. Increased revenues improved harbours, widened canals, built warehouses and coastal navigation beacons every ten miles. Specialised ships continued to be developed. Abandoning their superior stance to other cultures, Chinese scholars studied Arabic and Indian navigation, made their own star and sea charts and invented the floating mariner's compass.

By 1200 Hangzhou was the world's largest city, probably nearly two million people, 40-times London's size. Fujian's Quanzhou was second, generating maritime dues of half a million strings of coins around 980, a million in 1100 and two million about 1150.[4] It imported rice, grain, pepper, nutmeg, cardamon, balsam, myrrh and sandalwood, distributing them inland via canals and rivers, produced silk for export and had foreign merchant enclaves, mosques, and a foreigners' cemetery from the 1160s.[5] Radiating from Quanzhou, Anhai and Yuegang, further from official supervision, allowed freer, more adventurous trade while Guangdong and Zhejiang province also increased volumes. Quanzhou had mosques and Hindu temples in its self-governing merchant enclaves. The 1225 *Zhu-Fan-Zhi*, (*Records of Foreign Peoples*) was written by Quanzhou's ex-Inspector of maritime trade. 'In his watchful kindness to the foreign barbarians our government has established at Guangzhou and Quanzhou Special Inspectorates of maritime trade and whenever any…foreign traders have difficulties or wish to lay a complaint they must go to [it].'

Attitudes to wealth creation evolved. Thirteenth-century traveller Li Chih-yen approved of profit as unavoidable to make a living but not 'in disregard of human fellow feeling', like undue profit for necessities like grain. Increased trade transformed Fujian from a subsistence economy to one exporting oranges, lichee, sugar, cotton, manufactured stoneware and porcelain with proactive Chinese merchants. Jewish merchants from Persia and India lived at Kaifeng, Hangzhou and other ports. Excavated graves of foreign traders include Husayn Ibn Muhammad Khalati's, from Khalat, Armenia in 1171, Najib Muzhiral Din in 1351 from Siraf and numerous 13th-century Indians with lingams, Shiva, Vishnu and Hanuman, the *Ramayana's* monkey god, motifs. Quanzhou's Kaiyuan Temple was an important focus of Indian culture.[6] While Hinduism in Fujian eventually disappeared and Islam was marginalised, the monkey god, 'monkey magic', became deeply etched into popular culture, and remains.[7]

These large Indian merchant enclaves in China show that Chola political decline did not affect 12th-13th-century Ayyavole and Manigramam guilds' trading. A

1281 bi-lingual Tamil-Chinese inscription reports a Shiva statue dedication in a Quanzhou Hindu temple and in 1267 Chinese merchants built a three-story Chinese pagoda at Nagapattinam.[8] Of the over 1,800 Chinese coins found there, some from the 2nd century, most are from 1265–1267, during its construction, reflecting intense direct trade. The Song initiated and presided over this commercial maritime revolution. They no longer self-indulgently wanted luxury goods, no longer a passive recipient. Hence the encouragement of silk and porcelain production and export, shipyards and relaxed import controls.

Chapter 12

Effects of Song and Yuan Maritime Trade on Indian Ocean Trade

The 1178 news that Srivijayan embassies were no longer permitted in Hangzhou was a deadly blow to centuries of prosperity, already declining because of direct Song trade to Indian Ocean ports. North Sumatran ports no longer needed Palembang or Jambi as entrepots and severed ties. Srivijaya's declining revenues could not pay the Orang Laut, the navy's backbone, who turned to piracy. Thirteenth-century Tambralinga seems to have gained control over Kedah and Langkasuka. Sri Lanka's Galle, the Song ships' first port of call after transiting the Malacca Straits, revived and Dondra and Weligama developed as trade volumes rose. China increased imports of gems, pearls, incenses, dates, sandalwood, sugar and spices direct from the Gulf, India, Sri Lanka and Southeast Asia. They in turn, consumed Chinese goods including large volumes of low-value bulk products.

Srivijaya may have already been economically surpassed by Java. Chinese historian Chou kiu-fei in 1178 thought, 'Of all the rich foreign countries that trade precious commodities, no one is greater than the kingdom of Ta-che [Arabs], the second is Chopo [Java] and the third is Sanfotsi [Srivijaya],'[1] of which he said 'the walls of the capital are made with bricks...the king...is seated in a boat...protected from the sun by a silk parasol and his guards have gold pikes...the inhabitants live either disseminated around the city or on the river in floating houses covered with bamboos. They don't pay taxes. They are skilled fighters on shore or on boats...they don't use copper coins but...silver...there is in the city a Buddha statue called the Mountain of Gold. Each new king before being enthroned casts a new gold statue of his effigy to replace the old one...if a vessel passes in front of Sanfotsi without calling, all the local boats sail to attack according to a planned tactic...and this is the reason why the port has become an important port.'

An early-12th-century Chinese record precedes this text. 'If a merchant ship passes without entering [their harbour] their boats go forth to make a combined attack and all are ready to die. This is the reason why this country is a great shipping centre.'[2] Zhao Ruguo, (1170–1231) Quanzhou's Superintendent of Maritime Trade, who wrote the 1225 *Zhu-fan-Zhi* after talking with foreign traders and consulting earlier documents, described Srivijaya as 'an important thoroughfare for the traffic of foreign nations, the produce of all other countries is intercepted and kept in store there for the trade of foreign ships.' Ships trying to avoid taxes passing Srivijayan ports, he said were attacked.[3] Al-Idrisi at Roger II's mid-12th-century

Sicilian Court however, thought the Chinese admired Srivijaya's 'equity, their good behaviour, the agreeable nature of their customs and their good business acumen.'[4] Force and intimidation were not normal Indian Ocean trade characteristics. Only Chinese texts infer Srivijayan coercion and since they were written by officials familiar with earlier records, but not direct observation, this coercion must be questioned especially as other Chinese records infer no coercion but its supreme importance en route to China.

Without Chinese support, Srivijaya's various polities competed, as tempted to do after the Chola attack. This time the multi-port empire disintegrated. Java's rice-based economy supported a large population and was nearer the Moluccas, who's trade it continued to control, assisting it to become one of Southeast Asia's wealthiest areas. The *Zhu-Fan-Zhi* stressed Omani-Yemeni wealth. 'Of all the wealthy foreign lands [with]…precious and varied goods, none surpasses the realm of Arabs' and Kediri in central and east Java which also controlled parts of Palua, Sumba, Bali, Timor, western Borneo, Sulawesi and one of the lesser Sunda islands. Actually, it was slightly out of date, as in 1222 a successful rebellion had replaced Kediri with the Singhasari kingdom. It is understandable. It was a confusing time of political intrigue, warfare, sub-kingdoms, divisions and reunification caused by Srivijaya's demise, and incorporates material from Chou kiu-fei's 1178 document,[5] but trade continued.[6] In northeast Sumatra, Kota Cina flourished from the 11th to 13th century based on Indian, Sri Lankan and Middle East trade. It apparently belonged to what China called Arru, which the *Zhu-fan-Zhi* says was formerly a Srivijayan dependency, 'but following a battle it set up a king of its own,' indicating Srivijayan political troubles.

Javanese potters produced exact copies of popular Chinese shapes which continued into the 14th and 15th centuries. Siam conquered the Kra Isthmus in 1273. Singhasari sacked Jambi in 1275 and conquered Malayu in 1286. The rise of other Southeast Asian ports created more demand for silk, ceramics, ironware, copperware and food.[7] Huge volumes of Chinese everyday pottery, high-quality elite porcelain and silks were exported. Chinese trade acceleration positively affected the Viet who offered tribute including gold, huge pearls, aromatic woods and textiles. Its port Van Don thrived in the 12th and 13th centuries on China-Southeast Asian trade.[8]

Chinese kilns specialised; basins, storage jars, bowls, dishes or bottles, directed at the export market. The Nanhai wreck from about the 1270s, contained over 70,000 blue and white porcelain exports. Temasek, the future Singapore, of which nothing is previously known, emerged as one of these new export markets, with a merchant enclave.[9] Chinese food and drink were also exported. Langkasuka imported rice and wine; Tambralinga, rice, wine, sugar and salt; Jambi rice, wine, sugar and wheat.[10] Sugar cane was grown in Java, refined in China and shipped back to Southeast Asia. Chinese rice wine was also considered superior to Southeast Asian spirits. Despite Java being a major rice-producer, by the early-13th century, glutinous rice and wine were two of Fujian's largest exports. Lychee, grown in

Quanzhou, Fujian, Zhangzhou and Xinghua provinces and dried bananas from Fujian and Guangdong were exported from Song times. In 1257 over 19,000 ships were registered in Mingzhou, Wenzhou and Taizhou, and over 7,000 operated on Fujian's coast.[11]

Mongol Genghis Khan's grandson, Kublai Khan, from 1257 attacked Song China. His ruthlessness meant Sichuan and Hebei provinces took centuries to recover. Chengzhou's entire population was slaughtered, a million more at Nanjing. He captured ships and built more. By 1268 he had four fleets. The Song resisted fiercely, but when Pu Shougeng, Quanzhou's Muslim Superintendent of Maritime Trade redirected revenue to Kublai Khan, it spelled the end. By 1279 they had Hangzhou. The modest three-masted, 24 by 9-metre Quanzhou wreck of 1277 had 13 cabins, 12 watertight bulkheads and a cargo of incense, pepper, cowrie shells, ambergris, frankincense, tortoiseshell, cinnabar, animals, coconuts, precious woods and ceramics. It was possibly scuttled as Mongols overwhelmed Quanzhou.[12] Wooden tags indicate pickled vegetables were also exported, the first evidence for 'wet food' exports from China to southeast Asia in sealed containers.

Mongols maintained Chinese institutions, taking the dynastic name Yuan, but remained aloof from their subjects and culture, encouraging Chinese xenophobia. Kublai Khan seemingly viewed the ocean as an extension of the steppe. He coveted Japan's gold and pearls, and in Mongol 'continual conquest' ethos, attacked. Tsushima and other islands were devastated. Some survivors turned to piracy, attacking Korea's coast and encouraging Japanese militarisation under Kamakura's Shoguns. In 1284 and the 1310s, the Yuan apparently tried to revert to tribute, but it had no effect. In the 1290s, 21 edicts on foreign trade dealt with penalties for evading taxes, smuggling, arming merchants and banned iron, gold, silver and copper export. In 1326 the emperor denounced tribute as a waste of resources.[13] Trade momentum increased. Maritime duties were reduced from 10% to 4%, relying on Muslim merchants and officials in southern ports, often in joint-ventures with Mongol royalty, combining government ships with merchant expertise, the profits shared 7:3.[14] Muslims operated many ships and foreign merchants from Champa and Malabar with large Muslim populations were encouraged.[15] Kublai Khan sent missions to India's Malabar and Coromandel coast and Sri Lanka. Yuan official, Yang Tingbi, led several, travelling on private ships, indicating state support of merchants.[16] Sumatran, Sri Lankan and south Indian merchant enclaves were strengthened. Over 200,000 ships navigated the Yangtse each year and inland Grand Canal ports thrived.

Yuan overseas trade volumes surpassed that of the Song. Marco Polo said Quanzhou's harbour was the world's greatest, its pottery the 'most beautiful vessels and plates of porcelain in great quantity, more beautiful than…in any other city… are carried…throughout the world,' in four-masted 60-cabin ships with watertight bulkheads and 200–300 crew. He noted numerous Indian ships discharging pepper there.[17] Chinese shipbuilding increased although some merchants contracted ships from Siam and Borneo where shipbuilding costs were 40–70% lower.[18]

Kayalpattinam was a Pandya port dating from the 1st century. Polo called it Cail, 'the great and noble city' where 'great business [is] done,' important in the Hormuz, Kis and Aden horse trade, bred in Oman's mountains, that dated back to the 6th century BC and boomed from the 11th. Many commented that few horses survived more than a year in India, including Marco Polo, necessitating continual shipments. His first chapter on India was almost entirely about shipbuilding. When he passed the Malacca Straits in the 1290s, he stopped in north Sumatra's Samudera Pasai, controlled by Indian merchants. He noted east coast India's Motupalli exported muslins and diamonds. Its king protected merchants with a fixed duty and safety guarantee. A 1323 wreck from South Korea's Sinan coast contained 18,000 pieces of Chinese pottery including 2,900 pieces of celadon-ware, eight million Chinese copper coins, probably Japan-bound,[19] over 1,000 pieces of three-metre red sandalwood, a Southeast Asian luxury re-export and over 500 other objects, demonstrating vigorous regional trade, with China the key player where foreign merchants lived tax-free, especially Indians, Polo stressing it was 'frequented by all ships of India…[bringing] spicery and all other kinds of costly wares.'

Polo described trade and personal consumption levels undreamed of in Europe; annual iron production of 125,000 tons, not reached in Europe until the 18th century, annual salt production of 30,000 tons in a single province. Quanzhou had nearly a million people and took three days to walk around. He compared Alexandria's trade as 'trifling', commenting that for every pepper ship in Alexandria, a hundred were at Quanzhou, later claiming the ratio nearer 1:10. 'It has 12 principal gates and at each…are cities larger than Venice or Padua,' a place of trade, pleasure, carnival and excess. Of the Yangtse he wrote, 'this river goes so far through so many regions and there are so many cities on its banks that the total volume and value of the traffic exceeds all the rivers of the Christians put together plus their seas.' Polo thought Hangzhou 'the biggest city I have ever seen on the face of the earth.' Even in inland Beijing, in each suburb were 'many fine hostels…for merchants…on business in great numbers…because it affords a profitable market.'[20]

Tangier-based judge Ibn Battutah in 1343–1344 visited Quanzhou and thought it the world's greatest port, 'a huge and important city…its harbour is among the biggest in the world or rather is the biggest. I have seen about a hundred big junks there and innumerable little ones.'[21] Some merchants 'own [many] ships on which their factors are sent to foreign countries. There are no people in the world that are wealthier than the Chinese.' He described gardens on Yuan vessels, growing vegetables, ginger and herbs, multiple decks, private toilets, stewards, lifeboats and private cabins where he took female slaves, which he noted were cheap in China. Ships' bamboo sails 'are never lowered but they turn them accordingly in the direction of the wind' and rowers are 'covered with a roof during battle' to protect them. 'A ship carries a compliment of 1,000 men, 600 of which are sailors and 400 men-at-arms, including archers, men with shields and…men who throw naphtha. Each vessel is accompanied by three smaller ones,' built at Quanzhou and Guangzhou.[22] These were the Chinese ships dominating Indian Ocean trade.

Nowhere compared with China in agricultural productivity, industrial technology, commercial organisation, urbanisation and living standards when it dominated China Sea-Indian Ocean maritime trade. The over 300 Jingdezhen kilns increased, were licenced, regulated and taxed, its porcelain exported in huge volumes, including new blue, red, light green and multicoloured glazes, highly prized in the Middle East, Europe and North Africa. Some incorporated new motifs, especially Islamic, for export which Ibn Battutah recognised from Tangier. By 1350, Quanzhou had at least six mosques and a Shiva temple. While Chinese merchants had taken over much Srivijayan Indian Ocean trade, Indian, Arab and Persian enclaves in Chinese ports show it was a vast, vibrant multinational, Song-inspired trade zone which continued and expanded under the Yuan.

Srivijaya's demise meant Java's Singhasari became Southeast Asia's most powerful kingdom, which rebuffed Kublai Khan's tribute demand. In 1293 a 1,000-ship Yuan armada attempted punishment, precipitating internal rivalry. Vijaya supported the Mongols and defeated Singhasari, only to turn on his allies, forcing them to flee. These dramatic events signalled the rise of the Java-centred, Hindu Majapahit empire ruled from Trowulan, another attempt to create a Srivijaya-type Java-based polity. It ruled its immediate surroundings, east Java and Bali directly, outlying territories more loosely, a mixture of marriage alliances and force. The federation claimed 98 tributaries from Sumatra to New Guinea including the Kra Isthmus, southern Thailand, Philippines, Brunei and East Timor, controlling the maritime

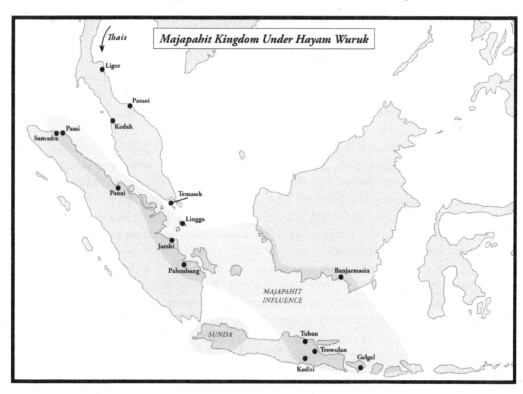

choke points of Southeast Asia, including Temasek. Its exported camphor, aloes, cloves, sandalwood, nutmeg, cardamom, ivory, gold and tin, lasting 200 years, its peak in 1350–1389 during the reign of Hayam Wuruk.

Trowulan, over a hundred square kilometres,[23] was fed water by a five-hectare (12.35 acres) reservoir and had a network of roads and canals for efficient transportation and irrigation. Industrial districts had specialised goldsmiths, ironsmiths and potters. Foreign traders had separate quarters. Archaeologists have found gold-plated kris, (Javan daggers) jewels, and diamond-encrusted bronze crowns, supporting Friar Odoric of Pordenone's 1318–1330 stories, that Java's king had a grand, luxurious palace with gold and silver-coated stairs and walls. The 1365 *Nagarakretagama*, a eulogy to Hayam Wuruk, depicts a sophisticated court with refined art and literature.

Chapter 13

Crusades, Blame Games and the Mongols' Maritime Significance

B orn of Pope Urban's (1088–99) desire to supplant the emperor as Europe's leader, the Crusades channelled religious bigotry into holy war for land and loot. The huge response was partly due to Europe's fear of encirclement. William of Malmsbury described the world divided into Asia, Africa and Europe, all formerly Christian, only part of Europe remaining. 'This little portion of the world...is pressed...by warlike Turks and Saracens; for 300 years they have held Spain and the Balearic Islands and...live in hope of devouring the rest.' Crusades have been blamed for subsequent introverted Muslim thought, rejecting western commercial maritime-led advances. 'Modernism became alien.'[1] This is unjustified. Odious dictators Saddam Hussein and Muammar Gaddafi, calling western enemies new Crusaders, attempted a con-trick to hide corruption, cronyism, economic incompetence and failure. We must not fall for it. Crusades, launched to save eastern Christendom, failed to save the Levant, Anatolia, southeast Europe up to the Danube and the momentum continued with Cyprus in 1570. In other words, Crusaders lost, Muslims won. What really accounts for Muslim introversion?

A 10th-century Muslim world geography described Mesopotamia 'near the centre of the world', 'the most populous country of Islam', 'a haunt of merchants and a place of great riches,' and Baghdad 'the most prosperous town in the world.' Baghdad declined after Harun-al-Rashid but was still wealthy and civilised.[2] Many 11th-century fires, famines, floods, religious conflicts and an 1117 earthquake left part, according to Ibn Jubayr in 1184, 'an effaced ruin', although in other parts there were cotton, silk, mat, glass and ointment manufacturing and markets.[3] Losing commercial importance it retained a cultural legacy, a literate population, libraries and a university. However, religious authorities' asserted control, limiting then extinguishing curiosity, knowledge-pursuit and the burgeoning intellectual revolution described in Chapter Two, with schools only teaching theology, just as Europe's growing ports introduced challenging new ideas, debate, competition and curiosity, within organised, law-abiding frameworks, allowing calculated risks for financial gain, while China's maritime growth spurred technical and artistic innovations.

Abbasid and Baghdad's decline is key to subsequent Muslim history. It turned in on itself. A continental, ultra-religious version took control. Braudel says it became 'the prisoner of its own success, the comfortable conviction of being at the centre of the world, of having found all the right answers and not needing to look for any others.'[4] While Marco Polo was curious about peoples, customs and places he visited, Ibn Battutah was only at home in his 'Dar-al-Islam', its customs, laws, people and daily life. In unfamiliar lands with alien customs, he became depressed. In China, 'whenever I left my lodging. I saw many offensive things which distressed me so much that I tended to stay at home…When I saw Muslims, it was as though I had met my family.'[5] This was the weakness Braudel and others highlighted, lack of curiosity and intellectual pursuit, the opposite of early Baghdad's falsafa scholars and travellers. More problems followed.

Since Qin and Han times, Xiongnu (Hun) and Jurchen steppe nomads threatened China and Europe. Unable to create surpluses or sustainable politico-economic systems, plundering, then exploiting resulted in impoverished lands. Genghis Khan's 13th-century Mongol nomads, in similar tradition, conquered most of Eurasia, double the Roman Empire's size, his 'greatest joy', 'to conquer one's enemies, to pursue them, to seize their property, to see their families in tears, to ride their horses and to possess their daughters and wives.'[6] Chroniclers' figures of those killed run into millions. Even with exaggeration, the slaughter was unprecedented.[7] Estimates suggest 18 million between 1211 and 1223.[8] Many parts of Eurasia never recovered and became semi-desert. A hundred years later, a Persian wrote, 'as a result of… Mongols and the general massacre of the people…if for a thousand years…no evil befalls the country yet it will not be possible to repair the damage.'[9] And so it was. Genghis saw the steppe as central and superior, adjacent sedentary civilizations, peripheral, China, a treasure house to plunder.[10] Expansion continued after his 1227 death. North China, outside Song control, fell in 1230. After taking Kaifeng, they considered killing all northern Chinese to make pasture for Mongol herds, but finally decided to tax them, although the next census showed 30 million less people.[11] William of Rubruck in 1253 travelling in Eurasia recorded south of Lake Balkhash numerous destroyed villages enabling Mongols to feed their animals.[12] In the west, Genghis's sons ravaged Poland, Hungary, Bohemia and Muscovy. Kyiv fell in 1240 and in 1254 they attacked Persia. They lost interest in Europe about 1250, not wealthy, nor worth the effort to conquer.[13] In 1258 they targeted Baghdad. The religiously-preoccupied caliph had neglected its defences. Between 800,000 and two million were killed,[14] and 500 years of accumulated Abbasid treasure taken. Manuscripts were dumped into the Tigris, which turned black with the ink.[15] Persian Gulf ports declined, the exception Hormuz, surviving by moving to an adjacent island. Further Mongol expansion west was stopped by Egypt's Mamluks at Ayn Jalut in the Levant in 1260, making these originally Eurasian slave soldiers the main Islamic power until the Ottomans.

Crusader states, approached by both sides for alliance, had opted for cautious neutrality, agreeing that Mamluk forces could march through unmolested. It was pragmatic as they were not rich. They inherited sugar production and export with sugar factories at Acre, Tyre and most ports. Almost all Europe's 12th-13th-century sugar consumption were their exports.[16] Local silk, linen, Jewish glass and purple dye were also still exported. Greater revenues came from Asian re-exports; spices, cinnamon, cardamon cloves, mace, musk, nutmeg, indigo, ivory, silk, porcelain, etc., brought by Muslim merchants, who were treated with commercial courtesy. Part of Acre's Great Mosque, converted into a church, was reserved for them.

Genoese enclaves were in Acre, Tyre, Jaffa, Beirut, Tripoli, Lattakieh and Antioch, Venetians in the larger ports, Pisans in Tyre, Acre, Tripoli, Botrun, Lattakieh and Antioch and Amalfians in Acre and Lattakieh. Steady streams of soldiers, pilgrims and diplomats, passengers gave shipowners useful additional revenue. Unlike Jaffa's open roadstead, Acre's safe harbour was the busiest Crusader port for Damascus' factories and Yemeni merchants. Lattakieh in the north at the Orontes river mouth was convenient for small ships for Antioch and Aleppo. But the king's 10% customs tolls were sold to vassals, Church and Military Orders. Crusader state revenue was thus inadequate. They were only viable if living peacefully. Muslims witnessed violent merchant rivalry in Acre in 1266, disunity and weakness,[17] when Genoese ships retreated to Tyre after inter-enclave fighting. Furthermore, Italians supplied Muslims with timber and metal, essential war materials. Occasional raids into Muslim lands for plunder to shore up state finances, encouraged counter-attack. In short, Crusader states were unsustainable, constantly secured and saved by maritime power. But in 1268 Antioch was taken, Jerusalem and Lattakieh in 1287, Acre in 1291, Tyre, Sidon and Beirut quickly followed.

When Mongol terror was replaced by four relatively settled Khanates; the Golden Horde, Persia's Ilkhan, Turkestan and China, there was a window of Christian opportunity to convert one. Mongols were religiously tolerant. In 1282 the Ilkhan khan, a convert from Nestorian Christianity to Islam, was overthrown. Arghun, his successor had mainly Nestorian Christian and Jewish friends, although he favoured Buddhism. He sent an embassy west, headed by a Nestorian, who met all rulers at Constantinople, Rome, Genoa, Paris and Edward I in Bordeaux. While warmly received by each, his goal, alliance against Mamluks, their common enemy, was ignored. Other Mongol embassies came for the same mission, all in vain. If they had allied and attacked, Mamluks would have been defeated, Acre would have survived longer and the Ilkhanate possibly opened to Christian conversion. Instead Mamluks continued for 300 years, razed every port from Sinai to Iskenderun, erasing Levantine maritime vitality. Within four years of Arghun's death, the Ilkhans became Muslim.[18] So Islam, which had shunned the falsafa movement, received repeated continental influences; Turkic Seljuks, Mamluks, Mongols, Mughals, finally Turkic Ottomans.

This was the real problem for the Muslim world. In contrast, Muslim Iberian learning, scholarship, and creativity was influenced by Jewish advisors, scholars, artisans and traders. North African Muslim failure to pro-actively trade with non-believers was also crucial. As Reconquista progressed, North African religious fanatics influenced its Islam. So Islam in general became influenced by a continental-inspired mental straitjacket and static Koranic interpretation. By the 15th-century, Muslim cartographers largely contented themselves with recycling old world images derived from great pioneers of 10th-11th-century mapmaking.[19] They were therefore ill-equipped for a modern maritime world. Crusades damaged Muslim-Christian relations in Egypt and the Levant, although merchants cooperated. But Saladin's humanity and nobility was replaced by Mamluk intolerance. Steven Runciman's conclusion, 'an intolerant faith is incapable of progress,'[20] is surely correct. The process started with Abbasid decline, the falsafa movement's end, continuing with multiple continental influences.

Open, tolerant Muslim Indian Ocean traders continued, but lacked mainstream political authority. Christian Europe experienced the liberating effects of wealth-creating maritime trade and early tolerant, curious Baghdad based Muslim scholars, Toledo-based Muslim, Christian and Jewish translators of Greek philosophical and scientific works and Muslim writers and philosophers between 1150 and 1275; the vanguard of Europe's intellectual recovery. But Turk, Mamluk and Mughal mentality was continental, indifferent to trade. The geographical maritime-continental divide is again demonstrated. Economically Europe revitalised itself, led by maritime trade. Increasingly, European port-led economic enterprise met Islamic economic lethargy and religious militancy. Crusades stimulated Venice, Genoa and Pisa's growth and increased shipping demand. They united Europe in common purpose, a catalyst, helping reintegrate, expand horizons with tastes in spices, sugar, silk, porcelain and brocades for which they needed to sell Europe's produce, which helped stimulate cloth production[21] and merchant-driven ports.

The effect of Mongol conquest of Eurasia was devastation of Mesopotamia, northern India and China, but unlike 2nd-5th century steppe nomad invasions, they did not devastate Europe, allowing recovery and regeneration. Mongol control of central Asia, the Khanates, *pax mongolica*, made land routes more secure. Pegolotti indicated the Crimea-Beijing route as 'perfectly safe by day and night,'[22] encouraging Venetian and Genoese merchants to investigate trade possibilities in Asian goods overland from Black Sea ports, further enlarging European horizons, by-passing Islam's barrier. Marco Polo's father and uncle explored commercial possibilities for Venice via Crimea's Sudak, its initial contact point for Mongol China. They left Venice in 1260, returned, left again in 1271 with Marco, who returned in 1295, sent by Kublai with a Yuan princess to the Persian Ilkhan, significantly by sea from Fujian to Persia, even at *pax mongolica*'s height, because sea-travel was always safer, then the Black Sea to Venice. Not mentioned in Yuan records, Polo was one of hundreds of European merchants, compared to the thousands of Arabs, Persians, Indians and Southeast Asians who went by sea. Mongols therefore were agents of change, encouraging western catch-up, while Persia and Mesopotamia, previously maritime-inspired areas, were scarred for centuries.

An unexpected *pax mongolica* consequence was another boost for Europe. Roger Bacon was credited with discovering gunpowder in 1267. The recipe was well-known and widely published in China. His description seemingly described Chinese firecrackers. His friend William of Rubruck returned from China in 1256–57, one of many. Great Song technical advances were probably gifted/diffused to

Europe.[23] The first metal-barrelled gun emerged in China in the 1250s-1270s, the first cannon about 1288, Europe's first in 1326 in Florence and 1327 in England. Illustrations show a bench-mounted arrow-firing cannon with no evidence of earlier European development, but centuries of Chinese.[24] Other developments, paper and sugar making diffused slightly earlier, courtesy of the Crusades. Mongol civil war made the land route to China unsafe from about 1344.[25] China was cut off again from Europe. A maritime way had to be found, but only after Europe's recovery from the Black Death, another Mongol bequest.

Chapter 14

Perspective and Reflection.
Asia-Europe Maritime Trade to the
Mid-14th Century

Aceelerating, constructive, prosperous long-distance Indian Ocean maritime trade contrasted with lower but growing European volumes, at first led by north Europe, then overtaken by Mediterranean volumes. Europe's timber, furs and slaves were comparable with east Africa, which attracted maritime Omanis and Yemenis since at least the 3rd millennium BC. Unlike them and maritime Persians who tenaciously sailed to China, accessing all ports between, the main Mediterranean Muslim imperative was anti-Christian raids and conquest. They were religiously and culturally hostile with no maritime heritage, failing to participate in any technological advance. North African agriculture declined. After taking Sicily in the 9th century, Muslims could have traded its grain for timber for shipbuilding which they lacked, but instead used it as a base for mainland raids, which led to the Norman arrival. In the Islamic Mediterranean, Fustat's Jews filled the maritime trade vacuum, using ancient connections, while Iberia's Jews helped develop its flourishing civilisation. Unlike Carthaginians who had sailed to west Africa for gold and skins, Mediterranean Muslims used overland Saharan routes. Thus, while east African ports imported Gujarati cotton, even Chinese silk, west Africa's coast was neglected; a telling contrast between the eastern and western Islamic bloc, maritime, and continental visions. Even so, as <u>political</u> elites pursued war, abundant evidence shows Christian-Muslim <u>merchant</u> cooperation in North Africa and the Levant. Mohammed asserted 'the ink of the scholars is more precious than the blood of the martyrs,' wisdom ignored by continental-influenced Muslims who preferred the *Koran*'s hostile verses against unbelievers. Indeed, Islam and Christianity were interpreted by their adherents' geographical and cultural outlooks.

In many ways this period's Indian Ocean characterisation as a golden age is correct. It had been a rich, varied maritime area since antiquity, the India-Gulf trade always especially voluminous, and India had continually attracted Omanis and Yemenis to settle, but it was not an Arab or Muslim golden age as some claim. China was the largest demand driver and consumer. Islamic fundamentalism outside maritime areas was inimical to tolerant, profitable trade. It was one thing for the Prophet's religion to convert Arabs in what was at least, partly an uprising of Arab nationalism, but another to convert non-Arabs. The Persian conquest was bloody, won by scores of battles despite fierce resistance, including Caliph Umar's

644 assassination by a Persian slave. Most Persians did not convert until the 9th century, settling as Parsis or Christians in Indian and Sri Lankan ports for trade opportunities.

Al-Biruni (973–1048) explained, 'India is full of riches and as its people are mainly infidels and idolaters, it is right by order of God for us to conquer them,' which inflicted huge damage on regions and people, especially in previously prosperous northwest India. The first Muslim massacres were between 710 and 713 in Sind in the Indus Valley. It had only just recovered from Huns. Raids extended to Gujarat and Rajasthan in 725. Hindu temples were sacked and demolished in north Indian pilgrim cities. Unlike Jews or Christians, Hindus were not 'people of the book' and were killed or enslaved. Mahmud of Ghazni from 1000 conquered much of northern India, plundering the holy city of Mathura in 1018, Kannauj in 1019, massacring its people. Buddhists were slaughtered, temples, monasteries, libraries, art and writings destroyed, killing Buddhism in the land of its birth. In 1025, 50,000 were killed defending a Gujarati Shiva temple, the campaign yielding about six and a half ton of gold.[1] Northwest India was reduced to poverty and misery.

Mahmud's successors continued. Between 1175 and 1206 Muhammad of Ghur ravaged northwest India with repeated massacres and began the Delhi Sultanate in 1192, capturing most of northern India. Muhammad Bakhtiyar Khalji captured Bihar, destroyed Nalanda University, burnt its library, killed its scholars in 1202, and conquered Bengal. In 1309 Ala-ud-din launched the conquest of southern India. Of the Delhi Sultanate's Muhammad Tughluq who wanted to annex southern India, Ibn Battutah wrote, 'of all men [he is] the most addicted to the making of gifts and the shedding of blood. His gate is never without some poor man enriched or some living man executed'[2] and 'was far too free in shedding blood'.[3] He killed idolaters, doctrinally impure subjects, scholars who questioned policies and callously evicted Delhi's whole population without possessions.[4] Millions were massacred. In Tughluq's employ, Ibn Battutah got himself assigned to a Chinese embassy, but travelling south into the chaotic interior was repeatedly attacked by bandits, captured and almost killed. Southern India's Vijayanagar empire, incorporating Chola lands, consolidated resistance against Muslim conquest. Trade continued, but fewer merchant guild inscriptions suggests weakened structures, operations and power in the face of northern Muslim militancy. The *Koran* proclaims 'Let there be no compulsion in religion' and 'Believers, make war on the infidels who dwell around you.' Maritime Indian Ocean Muslims chose the former, North African and continental Muslims, the latter, because those were their cultural and geographic dynamics.

Continental Muslims were attracted to India for gold accumulated in temples, slaves and conversion, maritime Muslims for trade and progressive scientific and mathematical discoveries, in a sophisticated economy, with manufactured products, regulated production, credit, safe roads, supervised markets, low tariffs, plentiful capital, good ports and a long tradition of maritime culture and infrastructure.

Wantonly destructive Islamic conquest contrasts with Indian Ocean and Chinese ports' mixed Hindu, Muslim, Christian, Jewish and Chinese merchants and Tamil and Gujarati entrepreneurship. Growing volumes favourably affected Viet, Cham, Burmese, Javan and Malay ports. Siraf and southern Gulf ports also continued maritime vigour. Islam continued to spread peacefully to Southeast Asia. Pirates aside, Indian Ocean trade back to antiquity had largely been peaceful with little antipathy to merchants' religion. There is another strong geographical imperative; the vast Indian Ocean's huge coast and the smaller Mediterranean, Atlantic Europe and North Sea, full of contestable choke points.

While religious and cultural hostility surrounding and threatening Europe was the origin of counter-attack, Reconquista and Crusades, jihad in reverse, the key to Europe's successful resurgence was competition; between northern European ports, between north Italian ports, between merchants with privileges and those without, between salt producers in Lubeck, Bourgneuf Bay and Portugal, Rhineland, Gascon and Iberian winemakers, between English and Spanish wool, English, Swedish and Iberian metals, Lubeck's North Sea herrings and Bergen's cod from Iceland, even between Hanseatic ports themselves as trade volumes and opportunities grew. Competition was fierce because trade was increasingly lucrative. Hence, Europe's first commercial wars since antiquity, between Carthage, Greece and Rome for Mediterranean trade route control. North Italian ports fought each other for trade, especially the Black Sea entrance, then on Baltic trade control and its entrance. It gave European trade a toughness and violence absent from Indian Ocean trade before the Portuguese.

European universities taught classical manuscripts and learning transferred from Messina, Constantinople, and Iberia. Peter Abelard in mid-12th century Paris University espoused his philosophical principles. 'Careful and frequent questioning is the basic key to wisdom' and 'by doubting we come to questioning and by questioning we come to perceive the truth.' Such classical-inspired freethinking aroused ecclesiastical suspicions. Bernard of Clairvaux accused him of heresy. Into this Paris in 1137, Eleanor of Aquitaine arrived after marriage to the future Louis VII. Aquitaine was still tolerant of other customs and beliefs. Recovered from Muslim and Viking raids, it sent wine to England and imported jewels, damascene metalwork and spices from Muslim, Jewish and its own merchants in Iberia. Jewish merchants settled a Bordeaux hill, still known as 'le mont judaique.'[5] They and Santiago de Compostela pilgrims returned with new ideas in music, medicine, astronomy, architecture and maths, much inspired by Jewish communities. The tolerant, optimistic mid-12th-century Aquitaine, with new towns and replanted vineyards, contrasted unfavourably for Eleanor with religiously-obsessed Paris, where Abelard's freethought was considered dangerous or heretical, where dour clerics denounced Lucca's new silks as 'worms' excrement'.[6] Eleanor's curiosity made her repeatedly unpopular with the Church. Paris had a university, but freethought was not encouraged. It was suspicious of new ideas, strange people and spices she used.[7] Continental Europe received classical and Arabic writings, but did not all naturally embrace it.

Marco Polo's late 13th-century and Ibn Battutah's 1320s–1350s description of Indian Ocean trade are instructive. Ibn Battutah said in the Maldives, 'when a vessel arrives...small boats go out to it', the merchants hosted and housed.[8] Its coir was exported to India, China and Yemen and was, he thought, better than hemp. 'Indian and Yemeni ships are sewn together with them.' Cowrie shells were sold to Bengalis for 'rice in abundance'. Yemenis used them as ships' ballast. To Aden came 'great vessels from Cambay, Quilon, Calicut, Fandaraina, al Shaliyat, Mangalore, Fakanur, Hinawr, Goa and other places.' Egyptian and Indian merchants still lived there. 'The merchants of Aden...have enormous wealth with...vast capital.'[9] From Yemen, 'thoroughbred horses are exported to India.'[10] In Mangalore 'merchants from Fars and Yemen disembark and pepper and ginger are exceedingly abundant'. Its 4,000 Muslims often clashed with each other, the Sultan making peace 'on account of his need of the merchants.' Jurfattan's Sultan had a large fleet trading with Oman, Yemen and Persia. He controlled Dahfattan, 'with many orchards, coco palms, pepper trees, areca palms, betel plants' and bananas. The early-14th-century Galle trilingual slab written in Chinese, Persian and Tamil indicates that merchants frequented Galle and Dondra, where Ibn Battutah also went. He described Colombo as Sri Lanka's greatest port.

At the Persian Gulf entrance, Ibn Battutah explained opposite Hormuz 'is New Hormuz...an island whose [port]...Jarawan...a fine large city with magnificent bazaars...from which the wares of India are exported to the two Iraqs, Fars and Khurasan.'[11] Essentially, he meant nearly all India-Persia trade was channelled through it. It always had done so. New Hormuz was created when old Hormuz, sacked in 1302 by Mongols, moved to Jerun (Jarawan). Twelfth-century Al-Idrisi had written that Hormuz was 'rich and commercial' and 'the great market of Fars.' Marco Polo said it had taken much of Siraf's trade in cotton, cloth, pearls, dried fruits, spices, porcelain, ivory and horses. An eastern saying was 'Were the world a ring, Hormuz would be the jewel in it,' yet it did not have its own water supply and needed food imports. Polo described other Omani ports. Dhofar's 'great traffic... [to] India...merchants take hence great numbers of Arab horses...making great profits thereby.' Wang Dayuan's 1349 *Record of Overseas Countries and People* described two to three-decked ships carrying several hundred. He noted Qalhat also exported horses and imported grain, although it subsequently declined after an earthquake. Ibn Battutah described its 'fine markets'. Oman and Persia's choke point position at the Gulf's entrance was a continuing theme after Baghdad, Basra and Siraf declined.

Marco Polo thought Indians 'the best merchants in the world and most truthful,' and that Chinese ships carried up to 6,000 baskets of pepper in up to 13 holds, carrying ten smaller boats, crews of 250–300 with 60 merchant cabins. Ibn Battutah noted Quilon's Hindu ruler's mainly Muslim and expatriate Chinese merchants. He was impressed with Sri Lankan rubies, sapphires, topaz, other gems, spices, cotton, cloth and fine leather. He praised Cambay's buildings, noting 'the majority of its inhabitants are foreign merchants...who are always building...fine mansions and magnificent mosques,'[12] and although most were privately owned, noted the Sultan of Delhi's vessels sailing from Cambay to Oman and Yemen.[13] Indian merchants, 'banians' from Cambay, regularly went to Egypt. 'On the Sea of China, travelling is done in Chinese ships only.'[14] Thirteen with up to 12 split bamboo sails were there when he arrived. He noted most of Mangalore's merchants were from Fars and Yemen and that pepper and ginger were plentiful.[15] Marco Polo did not mention Calicut, but Ibn Battutah described it as 'one of the chief ports of Malabar.' Its name derives from calico, its fine hand-woven cloth, so-named by Europeans from the original Malayalam 'Kozhikode'. It attracted Javan, Sri Lankan, Maldivian, Yemeni, Persians and Chinese. With a large harbour, it quickly became south India's most important port. Jews were active in Cochin's spice market in 'Jew Town' where all spices, especially pepper, were traded. Ibn Battuttah described Quilon as 'one of the finest towns' and most Chinese merchants resident, some of whom were probably Muslim. 'Its Hindu ruler is tolerant of all faiths.'[16] Indian teak-built dhows averaged 300–600 tons some up to 800, compared to Magellan's 120 tons. Their descriptions highlight western Indian Ocean ports' importance, diversity, their trade and traders' vigour.

One caveat to the peaceful nature of Indian Ocean trade was piracy, attracted by the richness of trade. The Geniza documents suggest endemic Red Sea piracy. Twelfth-century Kis near Hormuz, was a semi-pirate state raiding as far as Aden, east Africa and west coast India. Marco Polo described 20–30 pirate vessels in a cordon of hundreds of miles. Kerala's backwaters were ideal for hiding. Wang Dayuan said some Temasek residents attacked returning merchant ships from India in the 1320s. Ibn Battutah sailed on a Red Sea ship with 50 archers and 50 soldiers as protection, the usual practice, and was a victim off west coast India. Chinese vessels had to be heavily armed. Ibn Battutah said they carried 1,000 men, including 400 archers and other soldiers.[17] Piracy apart, what is striking however, is the seemingly unchanged peaceful, hospitable tradition of Indian Ocean ports.

Ibn Battutah described east Africa's Kilwa as 'one of the most beautiful and best-constructed towns.' When the Portuguese arrived 150 years later, they were impressed that they were similar in quality to Portugal's. Its people dressed in gold-covered silk and cotton cloths, women in gold chains and bangles on arms and legs with earrings of precious stones. Archaeologists have found large warehouses, a customs house with imported Chinese and Middle Eastern porcelain and glass. Islamic pottery quality declined. Chinese celadon and blue and white pottery was more numerous.

Ibn Battutah gave only one example of conflict between ports and it was not over trade. Following a family quarrel, the sultan of Goa's son, invited Quilon's sultan to seize Goa, promising to accept Islam. He attacked and temporarily took it.[18] But this was an isolated example. The real divisions were not Islamic-Christian, Islamic-Hindu, Catholic-Orthodox, Shia-Sunni, but maritime-inspired verses continentally-influenced, areas tending to encourage openness, individuality, creativity, toleration, wealth creation, intellectual progress and culture against societies enforcing hierarchy, rigidity, uniform belief, usually associated with violence, cruelty and ignorance.

Fourteenth-century Cairo's 600,000 population was far larger than western Europe's largest city. Tamerlane's sack of Aleppo and Damascus had a similar effect on Egypt and the Levant as Mongol destruction on Baghdad; their commercial and intellectual vigour declined as European textiles gradually supplanted local ones. Mediterranean trade wealth however, meant Genoa, Pisa, Venice and Florence competed fiercely for it, but Baltic and North Sea bulk, low-value goods meant less profits and onus on control of both supply and demand areas, which the Hansa perfected. Necessary Norwegian grain imports were blocked when it tried to reduce Hansa privileges in 1284–85 and England had to grant Hansa representatives exemption from most taxes and the right to their own judges. English sheep farming, commercially directed at export helped create mentalities leading to investment, creating social mobility. Hull's 14th-century de la Pole merchant family became Earls of Suffolk within a generation. While they were exceptional, gentry families exploited wool's economic potential without worrying that trade was socially demeaning, as French nobles believed.

Europe's growing population was fed by Baltic and Black Sea grain. Their ports became consumers. Improvements in textile quality, variety, colour and design is shown in contemporary paintings. Marine insurance, banking and accountancy were practiced in its ports, spreading inland. Credit and debit entries, posted in different leger sections, alphabetically indexed accounts, every entry listed in various legers, cross-referenced were produced and double-entry bookkeeping developed in early-14th-century Genoa.[19] Ragusan Benedetto Cotrugli's 1458 *On Commerce and the Perfect Merchant* advised merchants to keep a leger, journal and memorandum and either 'get instruction' or an 'expert young bookkeeper. Otherwise, your commerce will be chaos.'[20] He thought merchants helped poor people have better lives and customs dues enriched the state.[21] Medieval Europe advanced economically and culturally by road and river transport improvement, harnessing wind and water power, for purely economic motives, started in maritime-inspired areas. European per capita income probably doubled from 1000 to 1500, driven from its ports.

Despite impressive resurgence, a comparison between Europe and China in the early-1400s in terms of maritime commerce and skills was sobering, at least for Europeans. Nanjing was the world's largest city, a centre of learning that had an 11,000-volume encyclopaedia of knowledge.[22] England's Henry V had six books, three on loan from a nunnery. The Chinese 1393 census recorded 10.65 million households and 60.5 million people. Portugal had about a million, England five million. Asia's population was five-times that of western Europe. North Italian, Baltic and North Sea ports were busy and Venice especially was a centre of art, culture and endeavour, but were small compared to Chinese ports. Venetian canals were insignificant compared to the Grand Canal, over a thousand miles long, linking Nanjing to Beijing in the north and Hangzhou in the south, crossed by exquisite bridges. Italy's River Po and Germany's Rhine were arguably Europe's most used rivers but Marco Polo explained 'the multitude of vessels that invest the [Yangtse]…is so great that no one…would believe it. The quantity of merchandise carried up and down is past all belief…it is so big that it seems to be a sea rather than a river.'

Whereas European cities were mired in filth, Chinese cities collected ordure to use as fertiliser in outlying fields.[23] Chinese junks were five-times larger than Columbus' *Santa Maria*. Henry V crossed to France in 1415 with 5,000 men. The contemporary Yongle Emperor's army was over a million. Despite Europe's port-led advance, France and Castile remained predominantly agricultural, conservative and technically backward. Compared with Europe's manufacturing, trading and intellectual advances, Asia still appeared in a different league in almost every sphere; maritime, demographic, cultural, technical, intellectual, organisational, military or political.

In 1350 the gap between Asian and European volumes of maritime trade was if anything greater than in the 8th century. Srivijayan maritime power had been replaced by the weaker Majapahit, but with China's pro-active trade so vigorous, it was unclear that this was detrimental. Europe's trade steadily increased in the Baltic, Black Sea and especially the Mediterranean as Europe's population grew, but the massive Song and Yuan scale-up of China-India-Aden trade, meant it remained far behind. The negatives were that Mongols had devastated Eurasia, Mesopotamia, Persia, northern India and northern China. Important Gulf ports were now limited to the south. Islam's heartland had become introverted. The Yuan had reignited Chinese xenophobia, so far with unclear effects. A European positive was that Mongols did not devastate Europe and Italian merchants used *pax mongolica* to reach China. No Asians made the reverse trade journey. Returning Europeans brought back developing cannon technology. Furthermore, trade competition caused constant European war, in which weapon technology, could with inquisitive western minds, be improved, such as improving armour of which China remained unaware. Although these were important potential Asian negatives and European positives, no actual harm had been done to Asian maritime trade volumes. This further means that most of the millennium maritime trade revolution that swung maritime power toward Europe, happened after 1350! How? A precondition was that as a colder climate and the Black Death hit Europe's economy, unlike similar circumstances surrounding the Roman Empire's decline and fall, Europe's growing economy, from multiple, competing maritime centres, was more resilient and after a few difficult decades, continued to grow.

Part III

Asia's Own Goals: Europe's Catch-Up

Chapter 15

The Ming Revolution and its Maritime Consequences

Unprecedented volumes of Indian Ocean and China Seas maritime trade, not only elite products, but rice, wine, salt, lychee, pickled vegetables and ceramics, benefited more people over a wide area. Huge Chinese demand and ability to supply long-haul destinations in volume meant that China affected trade and political stability far beyond. As volumes rose, more Asian ports became involved as supply and demand centres and Chinese enclaves in Champa, Siam, Cambodia, Java and India grew.

While Confucian theory had been a constant background to government since the 6th century BC, it coexisted with Buddhist, Taoist and practical thinking. The T'ang Empire from its start had contained Turks, Uighers, Persians, Arabs and Hindus. Chinese curiosity was however, tempered by Confucian suspicion of foreigners. 'These two emotions battled each other like waves in a turbulent sea, shifting without warning.'[1] During the Song Dynasty, Confucian views were displayed, but merchants and shipowners vigorously traded abroad. The Yuan continued Song trade policies for revenue, but also taxed peasants heavily and discriminated against Chinese. In 1352 the Yellow River inundated vast areas, leading to famine. Europe's 1348 Black Death originated in Eurasia and plague also affected China. Blatant corruption triggered rebellions which united into civil war and the Yuan were ousted. The new native Ming Dynasty, ruling from 1368, took extreme action. They took Confucian teachings literally. Foreign travel, Confucius thought, interfered with important family obligations. Trade necessitated travel. He wrote, 'while his parents are alive, the son may not take a distant voyage abroad. If he has to take such a voyage, the destination must be known. The mind of the superior man dwells on righteousness, the mind of the little man dwells on profit.' Farming and government service were considered virtuous professions but merchants, ranked below artisans, were forbidden to wear the finest silk. First Ming Emperor Hongwu's (1368–98) vision of China was completely Confucian and he banned foreign travel and private foreign trade in 1372, effectively forcing it into a tribute system structure, registering and checking tribute-bearing missions in Guangzhou <u>only</u> who were then escorted to Nanjing, given gifts and returned.[2] Other ports were bypassed. Forts were built to ensure conformity and prevent smuggling, criminalising every Fujian merchant or seafarer.

This revolutionary act was a disaster for Chinese ports which depended on trade in foods, manufactured goods, especially ceramic exports. After centuries developing the world's finest, most sought-after porcelain and celadon, its manufacturing faced potential ruin. Some aspirational merchants became cash crop producers of sugar, tea, indigo, fruit and cotton. Cobalt imports had been needed to produce Yuan blue for ceramics, but the export potential of ceramics themselves was the major problem. Some potters had already moved to Vietnam during the Mongol invasion, some moving on to Sukhothai in Thailand. Thai tradition has high-ranking officials arriving in 1283 and 500 potters in King Ram Khamhaeng's reign (1292–1299). Striking similarities in technique, design and sudden quality improvement demonstrate the shot-in-the-arm received. China no longer enjoyed ceramic and porcelain monopoly but it was still immense. Banning private foreign trade slashed manufacturers' export market and income, further encouraging foreign production. Many, especially from Longquan kilns, and merchants facing ruin, moved to Palembang, Ayutthaya, Sukhothai, Malacca, Manila, Ryukyu Islands, Bantam, Brunei and Phnom Penh; creating or strengthening Southeast Asian 'Chinatowns'.

Fujian's mountains isolated it from the rest of China. It did not grow enough grain to feed itself. It depended on the sea and its ports. Its merchants shipped grain coastwise from the Yangtse and Pearl River deltas, giving it some cover for newly illegal foreign trade.[3] Shipwrecks demonstrate the gradual shift to Viet and Thai ceramic exports, the vigour of regional trade and continuing demand for Chinese or similar porcelain. The 'Turiang' wreck, probably from the 1340s–1350s, heading for Borneo or Sulawesi, carried Sukhothai, Vietnamese and Yuan celadon, iron ore and fish. It shows Thai and Vietnamese pottery already exporting in volume, directly competing with Yuan China's. The 'Nanyang' wreck from about 1380, ten miles from Malaysia's Tioman Island, had nearly 10,000 Thai celadon pieces.

Because of high foreign demand and a long coast, local officials colluded with merchants in ports other than Guangzhou, flouting the ban. The 'Longquan' wreck from around 1400 was loaded with high-quality Chinese celadon and some Thai ceramics. It probably held over 100,000 pieces; high-volume smuggling! The 28 metre-long, seven metre-wide 'Royal Nanhai' wreck off west Malaysia's Kuantan from about 1460 contained over 20,000 pieces of fine Chinese, Viet and Thai celadon and porcelain including some blue and white pottery in a secret compartment, thought to be rare pieces from 1372 to 1440 following the ban, some ivory and tin. The 'Xuande' wreck, thirty miles from Tioman island, is probably from 100 years later and has the same Chinese-Thai mix. Some from Emperor Xuande's 1425–35 reign indicates a similar trade in antique ceramics. Seemingly deliberate overproduction was <u>intended</u> for smuggling. Nor was contraband the only option. Some from coastal communities joined Japanese pirates, active since the failed Yuan invasion. In 1385 a fleet-commander in south China argued, 'the Japanese...should be opposed on the sea'[4] and in 1417 a returning ambassador had to fight a Japanese-Fujianese pirate fleet.

After 1372 there were no more huge Chinese trade fleets. Although Muslim traders had already influenced some western Indian and Southeast Asian communities, the Chinese commercial vacuum meant many Gujarati Muslim merchants accelerated

Islam's spread. Furthermore, Quanzhou, lavishly described by Marco Polo, ringed by a 20-foot wall of brick and glazed tiles, with its Malays, Persians, Indians, Italians and other merchants, its mosques, Buddhist temples, Orthodox, Nestorian and Catholic churches declined, never regaining its former greatness. Yuegang on the Jiulong River near Amoy (Xiamen), became the main smuggling centre. As for lost customs revenues, control of salt production contributed up to 80% of government revenue from over 200 salt deposits;[5] a dangerous over-dependence.

Banning Chinese foreign trade also had profound implications in Southeast Asia. A major theme in Malay-Indonesian history was the interaction of maritime Malays who created Srivijaya's trade empire and Javanese of Singhasari and Majapahit (1222–1451), rice-based economies. After driving out Kublai Khan's Mongol navy in 1292, the Majapahit empire had gradually taken over Srivijayan lands plus Brunei, Pahang, Makassar, the Bandas and Moluccas. Under Hayam Wuruk (1350–89), Majapahit's agricultural base, enriched by expanding trade, exerted its power in south Sumatra. When Hongwu came to power in 1368, Palembang's ruler Paramesvara was subservient to it, but nevertheless sent a mission to China, as it had previously. In 1377 Hongwu recognised it as a tribute state, ignoring Javanese de-facto overlordship.

Angry at Hongwu's recognition of Palembang, Hayam had Chinese envoys sent to confer the honour killed and Palembang punished. Paramesvara fled to the Malacca Straits. Hongwu then implicitly recognised Hayam's sovereignty. Problems triggered by the ban and granting tributary status escalated. Palembang slipped from Majapahit control as Fujianese and Guangdong's merchants, escaping the trade-ban, settled there, just as Islam's spread and new Sumatran enclaves also weakened it. By Hongwu's death, Palembang was ruled by a Chinese community, formerly some of China's most productive subjects, who had been turned from legitimate traders into smugglers. After Hayam's death, civil war ensued and it was unable to keep control of its territories as Siam increasingly penetrated the Malay Peninsula. Meanwhile, Paramesvara set up a new Palembang-like trade hub, first at Bintan in the Riau Archipelago, then Temasek, killing its Siamese-backed ruler, finally fleeing Siam's revenge to Malacca, which his enterprise soon made into the major Southeast Asian entrepot, inevitably further weakening Majapahit.

Hongwu had little idea of the profound consequences inside and outside China. His goal was to re-establish his idea of how Emperor-centric tribute worked. Song and Yuan's wealth creation was considered undesirable. The only overseas goods allowed by Hongwu and successors were those officially classed as tribute. In 1380 he executed his chancellor, hundreds of officials and their families for alleged involvement in intrigues with foreigners and illicit foreign trade; a total of 100,000 during his reign. Tribute missions were restricted to Cambodia, Siam, Korea and the Ryukyu Islands' Okinawa, which also became a smuggling centre in spices, porcelain, food, weapons, silk, Indian clothes, Japanese swords, deer hides, glass, ivory, ebony, perfumes and tin. During the war bringing the Ming to power, many canals, including the Grand Canal, had been damaged. The ban's raison d'etre was that China could supply itself. Ships were therefore needed for coastal supply but with the Grand Canal finally repaired and thousands of barges built, in 1415 coastal grain shipping was also abolished!

Despite the private foreign trade ban, one of the Yongle Emperor's (r. 1402–1424) first orders was to double the size of the Longjian shipyards near Nanjing, spread over several square miles with seven large dry docks for the largest wooden ships ever built. These he sent in six huge fleets (1405–07, 1407–09, 1409–11, 1412–14, 1417–19, 1421–22) of around 250 ships, over 60 of which were 440 feet long and 80 feet wide, according to contemporaries, ten-times bigger than Europe's largest, supported by water tankers, transporters for cavalry, grain, pigs, animal feed and patrol boats. An excavated 36-foot-long rudder post, even suggests a 500-foot hull! They had up to 13 watertight compartments and nine masts, the smallest at 180 x 68 feet, about the size of Nelson's flagship, HMS *Victory*.[6] Europeans were mainly using single-masted cogs. China had built multi-masted ships for centuries. European technology had improved but could not compete with this. Under imperial eunuch Zheng He, the voyages lasted two years each, following roughly the same route as Song and Yuan traders, each fleet manned by about 27,000 men, to India and, on the last three, the Gulf and east Africa.

One commentator concluded that these voyages were trade-inspired explorations.[7] Nothing is further from the truth. The Indian Ocean had been continuously and increasingly traded for millennia. The Chinese had aggressively dominated it for 300 years. Its geography was well-known. This was neither exploration nor trade. The Yongle Emperor simply decided that his greatness deserved tribute from further afield, so the fleet was sent with troops and cavalry 'to display his soldiers in strange lands…to make manifold the wealth and power' of Ming China. Despite impressive entrepreneurship in Chinese ports, the Ming stifled their potential. On inscriptions commemorating the voyages, the purpose was made clear; to enforce the tribute system and confine trade within it. 'Barbarian kings who resisted transformation and were not respectful were captured and bandit soldiers… exterminated. Because of this, the sea lanes became pure and peaceful and foreign peoples could rely upon them and pursue their occupations in safety.'[8] In return for tribute, Jingdezhen pottery was given as presents, so output increased. In 1433 the Court ordered 443,500 pieces, well after the last voyage. It is assumed they continued overproducing for smuggling.

The first three voyages went first to the Hindu kingdom of Champa, Chinese ally and entrepot. The Yongle Emperor needed it against Annam. Champa's King Jaya Simhavarman V (1400–1441), almost constantly at war with Annam, welcomed Ming assistance. Next was Malacca, claiming Srivijaya's legacy, China's old friend, a rival entrepot to Samudera Pasai and Aceh in north Sumatra. Imperial eunuch Yin Qing had been sent the previous year to offer a crown and mantle of protector in return for tribute. Sri Lanka was next, then up the Malabar coast to Quilon, Calicut and Cochin. Calicut was first described by Ma Huan, accompanying Zheng He as 'the Great Country of the Western Ocean'. Its Hindu ruler was the 'Raja

Samudera' or 'Sea King', whose Muslim merchants traded from the Red Sea to the South China Sea,[9] aided by Indian-built, five-masted, triple-planked ships with watertight bulkheads.

The voyages certainly demonstrated military superiority. Returning from the first voyage in 1405, Zheng He destroyed Palembang's fleet, killing 500 and taking back its leader for execution. On the third, Sri Lanka's Ravigama's king, queen and whole Court were taken to China and held for five years for plundering embassies neighbouring countries had sent to China.[10] In the fourth, a campaign was launched against a Sumatran pretender. The fleet split at Cannanore, a Malabar pepper port, to send ships to Hormuz and on the fifth (1417–19) to Aden, Somalia, Brava and Malindi, where camels, ostriches, leopards, zebras, lions, rhinos, elephants and giraffes were presented, for silks and porcelain. Another squadron split in north Sumatra to visit Cambodia, Bengal, the Maldives and Seychelles. A Tamil bell found in New Zealand whose inscription reads, 'Mohideen Baksh's ship's bell', dated tentatively between 1400 and 1500 may have been from a ship co-opted by Zheng He. Five copper coins from Kilwa found on Australia's Northern Territory's Marchinbar Islands, two from the 10th and three from the 14th century,[11] also demonstrate Tamil maritime expertise.

Zheng He's fleet overawed most polities without the need for force. In return for submission, local rulers received recognition with seals of office, official robes, silks and a Chinese calendar. Rebels of recognised rulers were punished. Luxury products were exchanged. News must have spread along the heavily-used Indian Ocean sea-lanes, ensuring suitably submissive rulers to concede that the emperor was indeed supreme ruler under heaven. Building these vast fleets of huge ships, projecting Ming power for so long without major losses, without supply bases, keeping an army of 500 cavalry healthy at sea for 20-month round voyages was an unrivalled logistical achievement. Compare Venice's need for frequent bases for galleys, the Portuguese fleets' over 50% death rate from scurvy 80 years later or the two-thirds death rates of the first English expeditions to the Moluccas in the 1580s. These were demonstrations of power to important Indian Ocean polities for tribute to satisfy the imperial ego. The cost of the fleets, housing, entertaining and indulging rulers of about 20 countries for many years made it a massive loss-making enterprise and internal criticism increased.

Paramesvara knew the 'trade as tribute' charade and value of control over the Malacca Straits. Using inherited regional trade-knowledge, Zheng He's protection, Chinese expatriate merchants and superb location he made Malacca, Southeast Asia's main port connecting China and the Indian Ocean. His choices of Bintan and Temasek were equally good choke point locations, but too influenced by Siam. Malacca also had tin mines nearby. In 1409 Zheng He bestowed symbols of office on Paramesvara demonstrating legitimacy and tribute-status to China. Siam, which had formerly claimed Malacca was warned off. Malacca's 6% cargo value customs dues and 3% for resident Arabs and Indians were lower than Islam's standard 10%. Chinese paid nothing except 'presents' representing 1–2%, the sums independently assessed by five Kling and five other merchant communities. In addition, the facilities were excellent. Ma Huan described its godowns (warehouses) for storing species with pepper held in state store rooms, sold at a fixed price. A legal structure was established where an official oversaw business disputes, regulated cargo sales in auctions according to well-known, accepted rules. With Paramesvara and many officials owning and chartering ships and engaged in trade, great care was taken to maintain good relations with China.

Like his Palembang forefathers, he made three tribute visits between 1411 and 1419. Paramesvara was given imperial robes, gold, belts, horses, saddles, jade, silk and gold, silver and copper coins. He married a Muslim from the port of Samudera Pasai and converted, taking the name Iskandar Shah. Whether or not conversion was genuine, it was good for business. Since many merchants were Muslim, negotiations, commercial dispute adjudication and diplomatic alliances were conducted in a known, acceptable Islamic framework. Malacca was thus instrumental in Southeast Asian Islamisation. Earlier Buddhist and Hindu networks had worked in similar ways, giving trust and confidence.

To return to the voyages, they should be seen in the context of the emperor's attempted conquest of Annam, extension of the Great Wall, the capital's relocation to Beijing, the Forbidden City's construction from 1404 to the 1420s, necessitating extending the Grand Canal and five campaigns against the Mongol menace. Each were massive, expensive undertakings. After Hongwu expelled the Yuan, they were far from a spent force. Indeed, Tamerlane conquered Persia, Baghdad <u>again</u>, northern India, massacring Delhi's population in 1398, Damascus in 1401 where a 70,000-skull mound was erected, as far as the Volga. As he prepared to reconquer China, he died in 1405.

These undertakings put great strain on the Chinese state. Forests in China and Annam were denuded to build the Forbidden City, Zheng He's fleet and Grand Canal grain barges. Imperial finances suffered. A third campaign against the Mongols and a catastrophic fire which destroyed the newly-completed Forbidden City in 1421 triggered the voyages' suspension. Emperor Xuande sent a final voyage (1431–33) for the same motives as the Yongle Emperor.[12] Given Indian Ocean maritime trade wealth, the voyages were wasteful opportunity losses, recognised by later Manchu historians who summarised, 'the goods and treasures…that he acquired were too many to be accounted for, yet they did not make up for the wasteful expenditure.' To prevent a return to the practice, ships' records and drawings were destroyed. Wrapping itself in a Confucian blanket, China's intellectual dynamism dribbled away, maritime dynamism transferred to illegal ventures and the Indian Ocean power vacuum caused by official Chinese withdrawal, continued to be filled with Muslims.

Korea, heavily influenced by China, Confucianism and Buddhism was aristocratic with strict class boundaries and also anti-trade. Its culturally isolated nobility thought it inconceivable that anything of value could be obtained anywhere except China. On condition that imports be first offered to the throne, King Sejong in the 1430s opened some ports to traders from Tsushima. So many ships arrived that he limited them to 50 annually. Sulphur, herbs, silver, copper, lead and dyes were exchanged for cotton cloth, hemp cloth, hides, ginseng, porcelain and Buddhist books, but this limited commercial intercourse threatened to increase and was suppressed in the 1490s. Under Tsushima's daimyo's pressure, it re-opened for 25 ships in 1512 and Ryukyu Island ships brought 'tribute', aromatics, sugar, buffalo horn and other Southeast Asian goods, but Koreans were prevented from going abroad except to China.[13] Effectively China and Korea were officially closed for business.

Chapter 16

The Needham Question

From about 1400, China failed to match the pace of its previous technological advance and progress elsewhere, especially Europe. There has been much debate why China relinquished its technical lead over Europe. In historical circles it is known as the 'Needham Question'. The question was asked before him, but his studies of Chinese science highlighted it. Commentators have cited Chinese bureaucracy siphoning talent from merchants, overpopulation negating the 'need to devise machines to spare human labour',[1] eastern cultures' respect for traditional opinions, the rise of European universities and the Renaissance. Comparative religious and philosophical ideas, cultures and experiences have been explored. They are all dead ends. Isolation from maritime trade is overwhelmingly the main reason. It was the wrong policy at <u>any</u> time. Closing horizons starkly contrasts to increasing European maritime endeavour and widening horizons. Maritime trade, smuggling and piracy were of less concern to Beijing, far from south China than the Mongol threat. Concentration on domestic infrastructure contributed to a relatively prosperous early-Ming period in central China, especially along the Grand Canal. But neglect of foreign trade became China's overwhelming weakness. With increasingly dynamic maritime culture in T'ang, Song and Yuan dynasties, China's creative intellect flourished. Under the Ming, knowledge-pursuit for its own sake disappeared. Hongwu threw away China's technological and scientific advantages, marched in the wrong direction, and sent China backward.

Needham almost answered his question, describing the middle and late-Ming's introspection coinciding with a decline in many branches of science and technology. Patricia Risso writes of the 1500s, 'China was not experiencing economic growth or technological innovation comparable to the Song era and therefore did not stimulate Indian Ocean trade navigation and shipbuilding as it had in the past.'[2] But that puts the cart before the horse. Timothy Brook persuasively explains that the Hondius globe in Vermeer's painting *The Geographer* contains a cartouche asking those embarking on '<u>frequent</u> expeditions…to all parts of the world' to report new information which he calls a 'feedback mechanism'. Seventeenth-century Europeans constantly revised their maps. Chinese geographers did not trust foreign maps and had no feedback. Brook concludes, 'The outside world remained outside…outside was where the world should stay.'[3] Without mariners going to foreign lands and bringing back new ideas and information, intellectual life narrowed and ossified; Hongwu's disastrous legacy. The Forbidden City symbolised China's might at the very time it chose to turn inward. It stressed harmony. The Gate of the Supreme

Harmony led to the Hall of Supreme Harmony to the Hall of Central Harmony to the Hall of Preserving Harmony. Two of Xuande's ships were called *Pure Harmony* and *Lasting Tranquility*.[4] But without foreign trade, harmony became torpor. The exam to enter China's bureaucracy was intellectually difficult, but rewarded conformity, caution, tradition and conservatism.

Adam Smith satisfactorily analysed China's problem. 'A more extensive foreign trade…could scarce fail to…improve very much the productive powers of its manufacturing industry. By a more extensive navigation, the Chinese would naturally learn the art of using and constructing themselves all the different machines made use of in other countries, as well as the other improvements of art and industry which are practiced in different parts of the world.' They already had a distinguished history of that. Hongwu threw it away.

In 1425 China conferred a seal of office on Palembang's Chinese ruler, but quickly lost interest. The ban on private trade was reaffirmed and those involved considered pirates, the penalty for which was execution. In 1436 building seagoing ships was banned. In 1437 Okinawa's king asked for new Court costumes, because the seas were dangerous and he didn't know when he could come again. No wonder, because China's navy was under half the size 20 years earlier, a few years later, a tiny fraction of it. Thailand and Vietnam filled the gap in the ceramic market, especially Thai celadon and Vietnamese blue and white. In 1471 Champa, China's erstwhile ally, was annexed by Annam. In 1500 a decree made building ships with more than two masts a capital offence, one in 1525 forbade the building of any ocean-going ship and destruction of existing ones. For a time, learning foreign languages was banned. Official tribute relations with Japan were supposed to be conducted through Ningbo in Zhenjiang, with the Philippines through Fuzhou and with Southwest Asia through Guangzhou. Their frequency and size were restricted, the Japanese for example, once every ten years, in two ships with 300 men.

Whatever the official restrictions, bribing officials was common. Wei Juan, Guangzhou's eunuch Superintendent of merchant ships for tribute, got rich from bribes to ignore private trade.[5] From the mid-15th century, despite ever more restrictive laws, there was a spurt of private shipbuilding. Zhang Xie's 1618 *Dong Xi Yang Kao* (*A Study of the Eastern and Western Oceans*) said that from 1465 to 1505 rich Chinese families had large ships and foreign ships arrived to trade. Chinese and Arab traders are shown in temple paintings in Tirunelveli in Tamil Nadu. In the 1530s Fujian and Zhenjiang nobles and rich merchants organised smuggling and excavations in Tamil Nadu and Kerala found substantial 16th-17th-century Chinese porcelain,[6] blue and white-ware being a voluminous smuggled export. However, piracy, ignored in the 1380s, grew far worse. By its height in the 1550s, 20 Chinese ports were taken, Hangzhou plundered in 1556, peasants massacred and 1,000 boats filled with booty. Following a Fujian official's request, trade was allowed under government license from 1567.[7] In 1589 Emperor Wanli granted permission for 88 ships annually, increased to 137 in 1597,[8] many to India where cargoes of Indian cotton cloths and European goods were bought.

Chapter 17

Mediterranean and Black Sea: Fourteenth and Fifteenth Centuries

These years demonstrate:

1) North Italian industries exported to the Black Sea and North Europe.
2) Black Sea grain, fish, fur and slave exports increased for west Europe's manufactured imports, especially cloth.
3) Regular Mediterranean-North Europe round voyages. Volumes increased.
4) Catalonia emerged as a merchant-driven state with its main port Barcelona.
5) A temporary reversal in volumes after the Black Death (1348–50)
6) Sugar was planted in Mediterranean islands, manufactured and shipped, aided by Black Sea-sourced slave labour.
7) Following Ottoman conquest of Constantinople (1453), Black Sea closure and subsequent east Mediterranean jihad, trade volumes swiftly declined.

Venice's great merchant galleys, introduced in the 1290s, required 200 crew, mainly rowers, for only 50 tons of cargo.[1] By 1400 galleys were three-times larger with two main masts, a smaller stern mast but similar crew size, reducing shipping costs. Sails increased manoeuvrability. Armaments decreased vulnerability to piracy. State-owned galley convoys were developed, but most of Venice's merchant fleet and all Genoa's and Barcelona's were large bulk carriers, more efficient and cheaper to run. Galleys carried high-value goods like spices, pepper, ginger, pearls, silk, wine, woollen cloth and silver. Bulkers carried cheaper goods; grain, salt, timber, wax, honey, furs and dried fruit. Genoa's fleet was smaller than Venice's, but had larger ships because of bulk specialisation, three-times larger than the largest Hanseatic cogs. By the late-14th century, Genoa had 1,000-tonners and by the 15th, 2,000-tonners, not exceeded until the 18th century, enabling 25% freight reductions in the 14th century, more thereafter.[2]

After Mongol invasion, stable Eurasian Mongol polities like the Golden Horde and the Ilkhans encouraged *pax mongolica* trade. Scores of languages were again heard in Black Sea ports. Tana and Sudak were bases for Golden Horde trade, through which the Polo family and many others ventured to China, demonstrated by a 1342 Nanking tombstone for Caterina Ilione, daughter of Domenico, a prominent Genoese merchant.[3] Wars between the Golden Horde and Ilkhans produced Mongol, Circassian, Russian and other Eurasian slaves for flourishing slave markets in Alexandria, Venetian Tana, and after 1261 Genoese Caffa. Venetians and Genoese provided ships to transport them. Mongol disdain of peasants and ability to quickly, quietly cross the steppe, led to annual slave-hunts into Poland and Muscovy, the basis of Crimea's Khanate's economy. Slavery had uniquely died out in western Europe in the 11th and 12th centuries, but opening Black Sea hinterland supply complimented Alexandrian demand for girls for harems and boys with central Asian horseback fighting skills, for soldiers to fight Mongols and Crusaders. Mamluk slave soldiers had a strong professional élan. The promise of eventual freedom ensured loyalty. When freed, they attained high command. They were crucial against Mongols at Ayn Jalut in 1260. Slavery crept back in southern Europe for use in salt mines and Ibizan, Cretan and Cypriot sugar plantations, by Genoese in Phocaea's alum mines and as galley-slaves, although Venice used paid, free oarsmen.

Antiquity's trade pattern, Black Sea, Egyptian and Sicilian grain, feeding Mediterranean cities, repeated itself as population levels recovered. Venice's grain imports from Sicily and Apulia were increasingly supplemented from Anatolia and the Black Sea. After 1261, Genoa imported annually over 30,000 tons of wheat.[4] Mongol-Italian trade was occasionally interrupted by conflict. Italian enclaves were vulnerable. In 1308 the Khan of the Golden Horde attacked Caffa, ostensibly due to kidnapped Mongol children sold into slavery. After several months the Genoese fired it, escaping by ship. The real reason may have been previous Genoese support for Ilkhans against the eventually victorious Golden Horde. Trade in kidnapped Mongol children may have occurred or been an excuse. A small incident led to war between Khan Jani Beg and Venice and Genoa in the 1340s. Mongols had more conflicts with Genoa than Venice.[5] Genoese arrogance was resented and denounced from several Black Sea areas. Venice was only interested in bases, Tana, Trebizond and Sudak, safe harbours to access local markets. Genoese bases with more autonomy pursued aggressive territorial expansion, initially aiming to exclude Venice from the Black Sea entirely. Venice had had time to attain strong positions and greater trade volumes. Genoa, as a late-comer, felt it had to protect its newly won trade gains, if necessary, by violence.

A huge variety of cloths were manufactured in Europe and the Black Sea was a strong market. A Latin-Cuman-Persian vocabulary, grammar and phrase book, the 1303 *Codex Cumanicus* for Italian merchants, listed European linens starting with Champagne's and Rheims' as the best.[6] The Golden Horde charged 3% on Italian Black Sea colonies' import and export values, later raised to 5% for Venetian trade bases and Crimea's governor took a land tax. When in an altercation, a Venetian killed a Mongol noble and requests to return him were ignored, the resulting war led to Tana's bombardment and Caffa's siege in 1343, in which plague decimated Mongol armies. A ship carrying plague, sailed to Europe, also spreading overland via caravans, resulting in the Black Death. Genoese Caffa paid tribute to the Golden Horde. Venetian ambassador Jacopo Cornaro's mission there between 1360 and 1362, during civil war, shows Venice's focus on good relations reducing the tax to 4%,

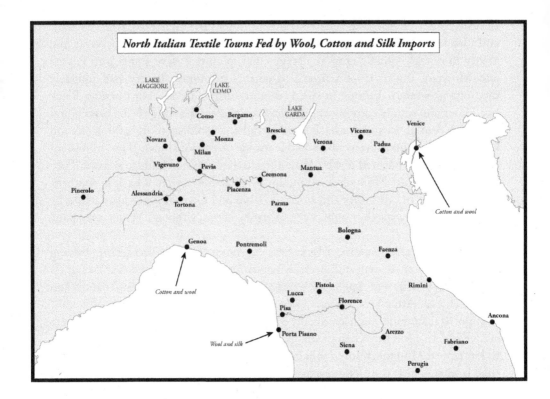

North Italian Textile Towns Fed by Wool, Cotton and Silk Imports

another in 1369 to 3%.[7] In the 1380s, Genoa took control of much Crimean coast but did not challenge the Golden Horde. In addition to grain, Castilian traveller-writer Pero Tafur in 1437, wrote of River Don fish, 'especially great quantities of sturgeon', shipped to Castile and Flanders, their caviar to Greece and Anatolia.

As the Byzantine emperor pawned the crown jewels, gold, and silver, Venice's and Genoa's Black Sea trade prospered. Venice embellished its already rich architecture. Commercial prosperity coincided with mutual Christian-Islamic toleration. Ibn Battutah said he took a large Genoese ship to Anatolia which 'treated us honourably and took no passage money from us,'[8] but the Mediterranean was not entirely secure. He noted that the emir of Yazmir, 'continually engaged in a jihad' sending war galleys near Constantinople to seize prisoners and booty, and 'after spending it…he would go out again to the jihad.' A firm Byzantine response finally ended his raids and he 'died a martyr's death.'[9] The Mediterranean and Black Sea never quite subsumed religious tensions. Recidivist Muslim nobles sometimes raided, yet merchants of different faiths cooperated and partnered. Historian-philosopher Ibn-Khaldun (1332–1406) wrote optimistically, 'businesses owned by responsible and organised merchants shall eventually surpass those owned by wealthy rulers.' It wasn't a majority view.

Genoa's manufacturing depended on raw silk imports from Sicily, Spain and the east and Elba's iron. Majorcans, Catalans, and Venetians followed Genoa's pioneering convoys to Bruges and London. Genoa's six docks specialised in different cargo types, at the head of which customshouses levied duties, volumes peaking in the early-1300s.[10] It welcomed outsiders. Residents living there over three months a year could own land and enter partnerships,[11] although a few entrepreneurial families dominated; Doria, Grimaldi, Giustiniani and Adorno,[12] but Jews, French, Catalan and Flemish merchants participated and Genoa never enforced anti-Jewish regulations. It seemingly drafted the first insurance policy in 1343.

The earliest depiction of Mediterranean two-masted ships was in 3rd-millennium BC Crete. The earliest after Roman collapse, with square and lateen sails, was from a 1353 Catalan contract, quickly becoming common, the earliest of a three-masted ship from a 1406 manuscript. Catalans and Genoese were in the forefront of advancing shipbuilding design in the 1300s-1400s[13] but could only dream of technologies involved in huge Chinese multi-masted vessels or the demand needed to fill them.

Black Sea importance meant its entrance was strategic. War in 1350–55 was over Venetian access. In 1352 Genoa was granted more land at Galata and the right to exclude others from Sea of Azov trade. Venice persuaded the emperor to give them Tenedos island controlling the Dardanelles entrance. Genoa deposed him and installed another who gave Tenedos to them, emperors mere puppets. After the war, Venice lost Tenedos and Dalmatia and recognised Genoa's rights in Cyprus, especially in sugar, but remained dominant in the Levant and Egypt.

North Italian ports' hinterlands made woollen, cotton, silk, linen and fustian cloths. There was mining around Vicenza, arms and armour manufacturing in Brescia plus glass, spectacles, pottery, soap and paper industries that spurred south German ones. Florence supplanted Flanders as the main English wool buyer. In the 1330s, 30,000 people, a third of its population, depended on the cloth industry, producing an annual income equal to the kings of France and England combined.[14] Europe's main silk-weaving and export centre was Lucca but spread throughout north Italy. Venice attracted 300 of its silk artisans. One in Bologna invented the water-powered silk-throwing machine enabling four workers to do that of hundreds. Venetian merchants imported raw silks from Persia, the Levant, Greece and south Italy, exporting finished and semi-finished products, dominating Levant markets in silks and woollens. By the 1450s, Venice, Bologna and Florence dominated in silk.[15] Venice also imported Sicilian cotton, English and Iberian cloth, supporting superior cloth-production and finishing. Italian majolica, from Majorca, the key distribution point of Valencian and Andalusian glazed earthenware that it copied, was itself later copied and manufactured in France and the Netherlands.[16]

It was a familiar pattern. Merchants imported; manufacturers imitated, also true of cotton whose production spread to south Germany, Egypt, Sicily, Cyprus, Crete, Apulia, Calabria and Malta. Similarly, with Venice's 13th-century glass making relocated to Murano, it was transformed with new technology and Levantine alkaline ash into glass, crystal, mirror, spectacles and beads for European export and mosque lamps for Muslim markets, which some estimate 20% of the total,[17] the Levant's glass industry totally eclipsed.[18] Venice's strength increasingly came from chemical, glass, metal and paper processing and manufacturing luxuries, by-products of maritime trade.[19]

Venice shipped central European copper to the Levant and Mamluk Egypt to make coins and sugar vats. It was also entrepot for pepper and ginger, roughly in a 5:2 ratio,[20] spices, aloes, balm, camphor, madder, mastic, sandalwood, porcelain, coral, lacquer, etc. It had Europe's best ships, most accurate navigators and most successful merchants. Skilled workmen and doctors were encouraged to settle with a two-year tax exemption. In 1335 the state paid a full-time salary to 12 surgeons who, with other doctors, had to attend yearly anatomy courses. Public health was a state priority and in 1368 state medical schools were established. By 1400 it was respected for its wealth, architectural beauty and justice system, protecting rich and poor. Women uniquely retained legal control over dowries and some invested in spice and silk trades. In 1349, its most profitable galley routes were brought under state control. While heavily regimented, it was Europe's richest, safest, well-ordered, most beautiful city.

Venice's maritime bases were also productive. Dalmatia produced salt, Crete wheat, oil, cheese and wine, Cyprus, cotton, salt and sugar, all exported. Introduced from India, sugar was produced in Egypt from about 700, introduced to the Levant and exported mainly to Venice. Fustat had 63 refineries in 1324. In the 12th century, production began in Andalusia, Crete and Cyprus, where the sugar mill was invented. Crete and Cyprus' plantations, worked by Black Sea-sourced slaves made Venice's Cornaro family its richest. Venice became Europe's refining and distribution centre, selling it in conical, variously-graded loaves and syrup. An expensive European luxury, Marco Polo had been impressed by the amount grown in Fujian. Crete and Cyprus produced malmsey, produced from late-harvested grapes, semi-sun dried, making it sweeter with high alcohol. Venetian-owned, its galleys took malmsey to northern Europe where it was popular.

Ragusa, under Venice from 1204, both aristocratic republics, gained de facto independence in 1358 and expanded shipbuilding. Under Venetian control it had been limited to Aegean and Balkan exports of silver and lead. After independence, it traded between Sicily and the Black Sea in wax, hides, cattle, horses, honey, cheese, saltpetre, glass, paper and luxury goods. With Ottoman protection and good western relations, it thrived with over 120 small ships.

An estimated quarter of Europe's population died in the Black Death. Port populations collapsed even more, Genoa by about 50%, Venice about 60%. General demand collapsed. Florence's Bardi and Peruzzi banks failed. It and other trading cities were rent with conflict. Marseilles faded and Catalans sent fewer ships to England. Labour shortages increased slave demand. Slaves became more numerous in Florentine, Genoese and Venetian households. By 1400 most well-off Tuscan households had at least one, imported and documented on bills of lading and duty paid on them,[21] many 12–18-year-old non-Christian girls. Merchants and manufacturers noted with apparent pride, births and baptisms of children by them. Despite plague reoccurrences, population levels gradually recovered, and with it demand, although in crowded ports, it took almost a century. It is significant that Venice's Arsenal was not expanded until 1473, nor Genoa's port facilities until 1461,[22] suggesting a major pause in trade volumes. Venice's Black Sea galley convoys declined from eight to ten ships to two to three. Genoa's population dropped more.[23] Between Justinian's reign (527–565) and the Black Death there were no reports of plague due to 7th-century trade collapse. Its reappearance was due to previously blocked maritime and overland Asian trade routes re-opening.

War between Genoa and Venice broke out again after Genoa seized Chioggia in 1379 in the Adriatic but Venice reversed the situation in 1380, destroying Genoa's fleet. Rising trade volumes allowed them to indulge in battles even during years of depressed demand. As long as the east was the main wealth source, Venice was geographically better suited with Adriatic control and better contacts with German merchants led it to overtake Genoa. By 1400, it had 3,300 ships and 36,000 seamen.[24] Private ships conformed to state specifications. Standard spares enabled quick conversion into warships when needed. Participation in Venetian international trade was limited to patricians. Young ones worked on convoys, building up capital, like early-15th century Andrea Barbarigo.[25] Six main convoys, about 500 ships, each bound for different directions, arranged months ahead, sailed on pre-determined routes, making regular speed for accurate arrival dates. After leaving Venice they divided at Modon, one for the Black Sea, Alexandria, Tripoli, Ibiza, Sicily, Italy and southern France, the other to England and Flanders. A core of investors, patrons, and captains, tended to specialise in specific routes.[26] Some travelled and some, like mid-15th century Guglielmo Querini, ran his Mediterranean-wide business by correspondence.[27] Low insurance rates reflected state convoy safety. Cargo variety was wide but high-value luxuries like spices and silks were favoured. Private ships transported grain or oil.

Venice occupied Corfu at the Adriatic entrance in 1386, Argos and Nauplion in 1388, Durazzo and Scutari in 1396, and it recovered the Dalmatian coast by 1409, an expanded overseas empire, its *Stato da Mar*,[28] and large hinterland territories; Padua, Vicenza, Verona as far as Lake Garda, southern Dalmatia, most of the Cyclades and Dodecanese islands. But land concentration was dangerous for a maritime nation. Raffaino de Caresini (1314–90), Venice's Grand Chancellor asserted, 'It is Venice's concern to cultivate the sea, where honour and riches are abundant and to leave the land alone, which repeatedly has brought her scandal and error.'[29] Furthermore, state-control changed Venice from a low-tax into a high-tax economy, to pay for the 16,000 Arsenal workers and civil servants.[30] Such success meant it needed peace. Doge Mocenigo in 1423 tried to prevent the succession of a war candidate, warning of catastrophic wealth loss, whereas with peace 'you will find you are the masters of the gold of Christendom.'[31] Pepper, spices, cotton, grain, wine and salt were transported inland by 40,000 horses annually. Braudel calculates an average 40% return on foreign trade, enabling constantly embellished city buildings with paved streets, stone bridges and clean canals.

After the Chioggia war (1378–81) Genoa concentrated more on the west Mediterranean, and North Africa, including Tlemcen, a gold and slave port of 40,000 people. Late-14th century Genoa's population was about 100,000, Lubeck's 25,000,[32] demonstrating that despite north Europe's growing trade, Mediterranean wealth and volumes were still superior, especially as Aragon-Catalonia emerged, absorbing Majorca in 1343, which transhipped African and Iberian goods. Its wool and salt were mainly handled by Jews and Muslims. Venetian, Genoese and Catalan ships called en route. Genoese in Portugal's service in 1341 explored the Canaries for them, also claimed by Castile, although neither exploited it for a century. Genoese were also first to reach the Azores, the 1339 Genoese Dulcert map showing three islands in roughly the correct positions and Madeira on slightly later maps.

Catalan merchants took advantage of Genoese-Venetian-Pisan rivalry to become competitors in North Africa, Alexandria, the Levant and Bruges. Their base was Catalan iron ore and textiles to Sicily and Africa. Its merchant-influenced constitution was based on contract between ruler and ruled with allocation of powers, obligations and liberties, reflected in governmental institutions. A non-authoritarian federation, each territory represented by a three-year term viceroy, had its own parliament, laws and institutions, voting royal subsidies independently.[33] The Bank of Barcelona was probably Europe's first public bank. In Barcelona's *Casa de Contratacion*, built in 1382, Catalan merchants met Italians, Muslims, other Iberians, Flemings, French, Jews and Greeks, trading spices, dyes, metals and many miscellaneous products, reflecting an increasingly wealthy society. Italian merchants there bought from Spanish and Majorcans using Spanish ships, but were not allowed to buy from other Italians.[34] Unlike Tuscany's hundreds of towns and villages, Barcelona's hinterland was a vast area of noble-dominated rural peasants.

At Valencia between February 1395 and March 1398 at least 300 ships called. Import certificates show 559 ship calls in 1488 and 420 in 1494,[35] impressive for a middling port. It specialised in sugar, silks, raisins, rice, saffron, almonds, wool and textiles, sent to north Europe in Genoese ships. Lacking capital, its merchants were not as influential as north Italians or Barcelonians, which dominated insurance and finance. It imported agricultural produce from Sardinia and Sicily, gold, leather, silk and spices from Granada and North Africa, exchanged for its cloth. In contrast, Marseilles never became commercially important. Importing Sicilian, Sardinian and Italian food and North African ceramics, its merchants' commercial acumen was inferior to north Italians and Rhone trade suffered from the Champagne fairs' collapse.

Francisco Datini was a self-made, prosperous merchant from Prato near Florence. His surviving 84 account books and 126,000 letters to and from his European agents are extremely instructive. From armour-dealing in 1372, by his 1410 death he embraced virtually every commodity, mainly concerning textiles. One of many textile firms with a network from Barcelona to Bruges, Lisbon and Sicily, his was not one of the largest.[36] One 1380 letter shows the relative security of galley fleets, instructing, 'if many galleys are sailing, send without insurance,'[37] but in war years schedules were kept by self-defence. The Mannini brothers in 1392 wrote, 'we have chartered…one third of a ship…accompanied by 50 good men furnished with arms and cross-bows…it will be in Southampton on the 8th November.'[38] Insurance premiums were generally low, 3.5–5%, although malmsey to Sluys was nearer 8%[39] often 12–15% was considered reasonable.[40] Risks were plentiful; war, plague, famine, insurrection, competition, sinkings, product deterioration and piracy. Datini's success was due to caution, vigilance, adaptability and patient accumulation of small profits. Thirteenth-century messages were sent twice a day from north Italian ports to Champagne fairs. In the 14th, Venice had a regular postal service to Bruges which took seven days. Fear of plague outbreaks from the Black Sea was ever-present. Datini told his wife that one in 1394 prevented a planned slave import for her.[41] His household had many, treating them much like servants and children, part of *la famiglia*, freeing them in his will. Political events were seen through the prism of repercussions on trade; truces or resumptions of war, death of princes or popes. Arrival of galley fleets made prices fall, with delays they rose, with news of shipwrecks they soared.[42] The need for diligence and training promising sons of agents and apprentices are similar in tone to Geniza letters.

Unlike the Bardi, Peruzzi, Acciaiuoli and Orlandini, Datini never lent to princes, financed wars or favoured particular Italian factions. The greater any company involvement in politics, the more likely a spectacular demise. He took risks, expanding in troubled times, with hostile rulers attacking, sinking and plundering, but spread those risks, bought in advance, credit only given to other merchants and trading companies. Prato was a clothmaking town, using English, Spanish and neighbouring wool. He bought wool from Tuscan firms in London who bought from monasteries or farmers[43] importing it, woad and indigo dyes and English cloth, dyed in various colours, considered good value with only 2% export duties compared with 33% on wool,[44] all through his Pisa branch, often in the bi-annual Venetian galley fleets from Sluys, London and Southampton. The process of buying and shipping wool, clothmaking and selling returned Datini and other Tuscan cloth makers under 9%, although some of his companies returned more.[45] Datini also imported iron, wax, alum, sandalwood, resin, dyes, furs and slaves from the Black Sea, wool, lambskins, fine leather and Toledo swords from Iberia, leather, wax and ivory from North Africa, and sugar, spices and camphor from the Levant.

Castile fought Reconquista long after Catalonia-Aragon. The Church enjoyed a privileged, powerful, stultifying position. Society was orientated towards war.[46] Its nobility's ideals were plunder and booty, riches won by force of arms especially against Muslims, not by trade or labour. Unlike Aragon, Castile's Crown had no obligation to call regular Cortes meetings. Nobility and clergy were exempt from tax, so towns bore the brunt. Commercial vigour was stunted. There was no outlet for dissent and discussion. Need for Jewish support lessened with Reconquista success. In 1391 there were many pogroms with 4,000 massacred in Seville. Jews were forced to convert or die, live in separate areas, prohibited from practicing medicine, commerce or holding public office. New Christians, conversos, outwardly observing Christianity, but Judaism in secret, became an issue.

Faced by similar pressures, Sicily's former ubiquitous Jewish trading communities, active in Geniza letters, gradually dispersed to north Italian ports where increasing trade volumes and opportunities appeared irresistible. Encouragement for foreign skilled workers to settle in Venice did not include Jews, but they came anyway, quickly prospering. With rising debts to them, in 1395 they were expelled, allowed to return for 15 days only, wear distinguishing marks, yellow circles on breasts or yellow caps and forbidden to hold property, until rules were gradually relaxed, but over the centuries, similar policies reappeared and Venetian Jews' fortunes fluctuated.

Weakened by plague deaths, Mongol Tamerlane's 1380–1390 conquests in central Asia, Mesopotamia, Persia, Armenia, Georgia and the Levant, were followed by Delhi's plunder in 1400. His victory over Ottomans at Ankara in 1402 gave Constantinople 50 more years to ship its heritage west. His sack of Tyre, Ephesus, Smyrna and Phocaea, slaughtering all inhabitants, resulting in the usual piles of skulls, destroyed trade. On his death his 'empire' disintegrated. Disruptions increased slave-supply; demand already stimulated by the Black Death. Pero Tafur in 1437 described Caffa 'as large as Seville or larger with twice as many inhabitants…all the nations of the world' and thought, 'they sell more slaves…than anywhere else in the world.' Ibn Battutah thought its bay held about 200 'ships of war and trading vessels, large and small…one of the most notable harbours in the world' and 'I have seen none equal it, except…Quilon and Calicut in India…Sudak…and Zaitun [Quanzhou] in China.'

At Trebizond, Genoese loaded pearls from the Gulf and India, furs from the north, Indian and Sri Lankan gems, pepper, ginger, Moluccan nutmeg and cloves. In return wine, cloths, and other manufactured goods were sold, profitable trade despite the circuitous route of eastern goods. Throughout however, the Red Sea remained the main Indian Ocean conduit as sea transport was cheaper. Pero Tafur described the Black Sea's 'spices, gold, pearls and precious stones…above all…furs.' Muscovy's Siberian expansion increased volumes and qualities, making Venice's fur guild rich.

Florence conquered Pisa in 1406. Emulating Venetian fleets, Florence ran its own galleys from there from the 1430s to Alexandria, England and Flanders with high-value luxuries.[47] In the eastern Mediterranean, Venice's gold ducat was the standard currency, demonstrating dominance. Giacomo Badoer's accounts from Constantinople (1436–1440) show him receiving wool and silk textiles from Venice, exchanged for wax, pepper, spices and Byzantine silk. His agent network in Black Sea ports, Crete, Beirut and Alexandria, traded wine, linen, oil, pork, metals, wheat and slaves, benefitting from trade agreements, reduced customs and tariffs and Senate support in commercial disputes.[48] Consuls also assisted merchants. Biagio Dolfin in Alexandria (1418–1420) for example, intervened over spice-sale litigation, relic exports, convoy departure times, debts and confiscations and young Venetian

Giovanni Foscari in London and Bruges in the 1460s, lacking a correspondent network, relied on the Bruges' consul as guarantor and intermediary.[49]

Alexandrian living standards had peaked in the 13th century. Under Ayyubid rule, central Asian Mamluk slave soldiers fighting Crusaders and Mongols, made one of them ruler in 1250. The militarised Mamluk state hindered economic development and commercial vitality as it lacked maritime expertise. The government owned land and bought products to consume or sell to Italian merchants. Corruption followed. The canal connecting Alexandria to the Nile was neglected, irrigation suffered, villages were abandoned, agricultural and industrial production declined, but Genoa's and Venice's Alexandrian funduqs still flourished. Alexandria's Venetian consul was a patrician, his 12-man council lower status. Crete's Jews seemingly played an important role, although there is no evidence of contact with local Arab-speaking Jews.[50] Pepper, sugar from Fustat's refineries, flax, Egypt's largest export since antiquity, were sent to Europe but merchants were forced to loan money and productivity declined. Of 66 sugar refineries active in Fustat in 1324, only 19 operated in the early-1400s. In 1429 Sultan Barsbay established a government pepper monopoly in Alexandria and in 1434 banned contracts between Karim and Venetians, later expanding the monopoly to other goods.[51] A commentator in 1438 thought Cairo an eighth of what it once was. By the 1450s, two-thirds of Alexandria was in ruins, the only commercial activity, foreign shipping.

Byzantines settled in Venice and some churches became Orthodox. Venice did not have Dante, Petrarch, Boccaccio, Bruni, Mirandola, Brunelleschi or Donatello and were not financially or navigationally as innovative as Genoa, but they were practical, pre-eminent in printing and book-binding, essential to the spread of ideas.[52] Florence's banking wealth was developed from Venetian and Genoese maritime trade. Ragusa's Benedict Kotrulic about 1400 wrote *Mercante Perfetto* about book-keeping, accounting and merchants' values; moral virtue, culture, honesty, sensitivity to local interests and laws. Inspired by its Roman past and Greek learning, republican Florence began identifying with republican Rome and Athens, reviving critical, secular methods. Fifteenth-century Black Sea grain exports increased to Mediterranean ports, even to the former breadbasket, wheat-impoverished Tunis. Florentine gold florins were standard throughout Europe and banking houses had London and Bruges branches.

With Trebizond and Nicaea independent and Byzantium under Latin occupation, it was further weakened. After the Seljuk Sultanate of Rum expired in 1305, a small Islamic Turk emirate led by Osman Gazi emerged. They became known as Osmans, Othmans and finally Ottomans. Attacking all, they expanded in Anatolia and the Balkans, sometimes with Byzantine blessing when fending-off Serbs and Bulgars, reducing Byzantine lands to the area around Constantinople and expanded in southeast Europe. From the 1390s they built a fleet. Venice and Genoa coped until in 1452 Mehmet II demanded every ship transiting the Bosporus be inspected at the Rumeli Hisar fortress. A Venetian galley evading it was sunk. When Ottomans finally took Constantinople in 1453, the usual looting was allowed, but a special decree ordered that no shipwright was to be harmed.[53] Mehmet had his own naval ambitions; military not commercial. The Grand Vizier told Constantinople's Venetian envoy, 'You can tell the Doge that he can leave off marrying the sea. It's our turn now,' referencing a ceremony initiated by Doge Orseolo of his and Venice's marriage to the sea, symbolising its income source, not religious conquest.[54] Venice failed to anticipate Constantinople's 1453 fall, distracted by its extensive north Italian territories, drawing recourses away from trade that funded it.

Before and at Constantinople's fall, waves of émigré scholars arrived in Rome, Venice and Florence. For over 200 years scholars had shown interest in Greek scientific and philosophical enquiry, brought from Byzantium and the Islamic world. Arabic numerals became quite common in 14th-century Europe. Scholars studied astronomy, maths and medicine in Barcelona, especially Euclid's geometry and Galen and Hippocrates' medicine, but the pre-conquest outpour from Constantinople was very influential. It even affected the papacy. Nicholas V in 1446 founded the Vatican library and commissioned translations of Greek literature, although he was exceptional. Pius II (1458–1464) showed the usual prejudice, remarking that every Venetian was a slave to 'the sordid occupation of trade.' Other minds were slowly opening however, as Lorenzo Valla revealed the *Donation of Constantine* a forgery. Venice attracted more Byzantine refugees than other cities and Padua University, in Venetian territory, which specialised in medicine, in 1463 established a chair in Greek. Convoys to northern Europe took these ideas to Flanders. Dutch scholar Erasmus learned Greek in Venice and Thomas Linacre, who studied medicine at Padua, founded London's Royal College of Physicians. Gutenberg started a printing press in 1454. By 1500, 25 German printing firms in Venice made it the 15th-century information distribution centre with more books printed than any other city.

After Constantinople's fall, Mediterranean trade faced severe setbacks. Mehmet II styled himself 'Sovereign of the Two Seas', the Black Sea and Mediterranean and wanted 'one empire, one faith, one sovereignty of the world.' In 1475 Crimea's Khanate accepted suzerainty. The Balkans up to Belgrade and the Danube estuary were already Ottoman. Trebizond surrendered in 1461, Tana and Caffa in 1479. Italians were expelled and Mediterranean-bound grain cargoes ceased. Carrying the torch of militant Islam, Ottomans saw Venice's empire as ripe for Islamic conquest, not a complementary wealth-creating trade opportunity. The turbulent 1450s-1460s damaged Venice's merchants. Giovani Marcova for example, who worked in London from 1417, married a Londoner, returned in 1438, invested in ventures to Egypt and Constantinople, prospering at first, but declined in the troubled years and was almost bankrupt on his 1458 death.[55] In 1469 an 80,000-strong Ottoman army and huge fleet was unleashed. In 1470 Negroponte in Euboea fell. All males over eight years old were killed, others enslaved. Otranto at the Adriatic's mouth was captured in 1480.

South German merchants shifted focus from Venice to Antwerp, in the 1480s-1490s, Europe's new printing, spice and sugar redistribution hub. Ottomans used Black Sea meat, wheat, salt and slaves to provision Constantinople, not the Christian Mediterranean. Slave-trading increased, the tax on slave sales accounting for 29% of Ottoman tax revenue.[56] Slave supply to Chios' and Crete's sugar estates ended, endangering production. Almost deserted in 1453, newly-named Istanbul grew to perhaps 700,000 in the 16th century, again Europe's largest city.[57]

Mehmet's successor temporarily made peace. But proclaiming a return to Islamic law, he summoned those 'who wish to join the sacred conquest, engage in the pleasure of raiding and jihad and who desire booty and plunder.' Venice also faced a coalition of European powers. Furthermore, Venice's dominant pepper and spice trade came under severe attack. (Chapter 21) In 1497 membership of the brokers guild was limited to Venetian citizens, although in 1507 a Board of Trade tried to rationalise commercial policies, attract foreign merchants and facilitate long-haul trade.[58] In 1499 Lepanto, a vital Venetian base on the Gulf of Corinth was taken, Modon in 1500, by which time Mediterranean trade volumes were in full retreat. Venice's galley routes unravelled, the last to the Black Sea in 1452, to North Africa, Lisbon, Flanders and England in 1533.[59]

Chapter 18

Atlantic Europe:
Fourteenth and Fifteenth Centuries

These years demonstrate:

1. Iberian ports increased importance as Italian and Catalan ships called en route to north Europe. Iberian merchants had significant enclaves in Bruges and London.
2. England changed from a wool to a cloth exporter, driven by war with France in defending Flanders, its major export outlet. Consequently, its cloth challenged Flemish cloths in Europe's markets. Its other major concerns were Baltic and Castilian trade. From the 1320s English merchants became more mobile, pro-active and ambitious.
3. Baltic economic activity spread in Pomerania, Poland and Livonia. The Hansa, a 12th-century trade enabler and engine of growth, a 13th-century bully, became a brake, blocking Dutch, English and Scandinavian competition, even some of its affiliated ports. Denmark's continuing aim, to control the Sound, fuelled conflict as trade volumes rose.
4. Bruges' dominance was challenged by a number of Scheldt estuary ports and largely replaced by Antwerp after 1480.

Twelfth and thirteenth centuries' main northern European trades, English wool to Flanders, wheat to Scandinavia and Gascony, Bourgneuf Bay salt to north Europe, Norwegian dried cod, Lubeck's salted herring and Gascon wine to northern Europe became more complex in the 14th century. Polish and Pomeranian grain supplanted English in northern Europe, shipped by Hansa merchants in Baltic-built ships. Rhineland wines competed with Iberian and Gascon. Swedish metals partly replaced Iberian. Italian merchants and financiers worked in London, Bruges and Iberian ports. Genoese ships brought Anatolian alum to Sluys, Zeeland's port connecting Damme to Bruges, Ghent and England. Venice was slow to follow Genoese ships to Bruges, Southampton and London, but by 1314 sent regular convoys. Iberian ports commercially enhanced the route. Genoese merchants had settled in Lisbon, Seville, La Corunna and Malaga. Further north, Venetians favoured El Ferrol and Nantes while Genoese used smaller Breton ports.

Hundreds of early-14th-century mainly Bayonne-built ships carried thousands of casks of wine annually to England; an efficient high-volume, low-cost, low freight rate operation. After discharge in English ports, ships loaded wool for Bruges or Italy. A Florentine merchant noted the cheapest way was in a just-discharged wine ship to Gascony, then overland to Aigues Mortes, then shipped to Porto Pisano,[1] many organised by the Bardi or Peruzzi. Genoese changed from galleys to bulk carriers by about 1340 but conservative Venetians kept galleys until the 15th century. Castile exported copper, fruit, iron, wines, fish and merino wool to Bruges and England. Financial innovation, international cashless payments, credit, bills of exchange, used in Champagne by Genoese, were further developed in northern Europe's ports.[2]

Rich northern Europeans' taste for food and wine spiced with pepper, cloves, nutmeg, cinnamon and ginger increased. Spices were also used medicinally. Elites ate rice, olive oil, oranges and lemons from Castile, originally introduced from 10th-century India, grapes, raisins and dried figs from Greece and sugar from Cyprus and Crete. Foreign merchants stayed in Bruges at special hotels. Since the 1250s, one run by the Van der Beurse family gave its name to the adjacent Place de la Bourse, where Italians concentrated.[3] The Bourse opened there in 1309, the world's first stock exchange. Bruges' hinterland manufactured woollen cloth, linens, tapestries, carpets, brass, pewter, armour, swords and books; 'the industrial heartland of medieval Europe.'[4] Cloth trades were supervised by local agents, similar to Champagne's 'Guards of the Fair', Bruges-appointed brokers and weighers with responsibility for honest exchange.[5] Port dues were mutually negotiated.[6] Merchants self-organised in 16 'nations'; five Iberians, Bruges' largest foreign community, (Catalans, Aragonese, Castilians, Navarrese, Portuguese), seven Italian cities, Biscayans, Germans, English and Scots, each living near their consulate, officially recognised and protected from property seizures.

Crop failures in 1315 and 1316 led to famine. A tenth of Ypres' and Tournai's population, major cloth manufacturing cities, died in four months in 1317. Grain prices rose so much, it became economic to ship it from the Mediterranean. A Genoese galley, usually specialising in luxuries, was chartered from North Africa to England.[7] There is no record of what must have been the exceptional freight rate.

Foreign merchants carried two-thirds of England's wool exports, with more capital, ships and insurance. Nevertheless, during troubles with Margaret of Flanders from 1265, (see page 95) English merchants had a not inconsiderable £10,000 of goods confiscated. When wool exports were only allowed under special licences between 1271 and 1276, 450 English merchants applied. Their 1273 applications covered 35% of the trade.[8] But most could not compete with the Frescobaldi, Bardi and Peruzzi, who loaned the Crown money in return for wool export licenses. Lucca's merchants had financed Edward I's Welsh conquest, Florence's Frescobaldi Edward II's Scottish war.[9] Italians dominated north European finance. In the early-1300s Florence's third largest company had 15 branches, employing 41 factors. Genoese also took wool to Italy but few lived in England, most buying on their ships' arrival.[10] The king negotiated the *Carta Mercatoria* with foreign merchants in 1303, additional wool duties and import taxes. They were passed on, raising English prices, including on imported cloth, encouraging English cloth manufacture. English customs revenues were six to seven-times those 70 years earlier, but still insufficient to pay for war.

After reduced English wool exports in the 1294–97 Gascon War, they boomed back. The 34,608 sacks of 1300–01 reached 46,382 in 1304–05. Some had been delayed from the previous year, but 41,412 for 1305–06 and 41,574 for 1306–07 confirm the increase,[11] many from west coast ports; Bristol, Exeter and Barnstaple. Philip renewed hostilities with Flanders. Its count was imprisoned and a governor installed; attempted annexation. Bruges led the resistance and defeated them. Unsurprisingly, difficulties continued. Following England's 1294 Brabant alliance, exports were mainly through Antwerp. For reasons now obscure, Flanders supported Scotland in war against England, seemingly illogical given English commercial power and shared interests. English retaliation led to merchant arrests in Flanders and tit-for-tat in England.[12]

Gradually for English national security and merchant advantage, the idea of a staple, a fixed place through which wool exports were directed by an English merchant monopoly gained traction. It was easily-taxed and the monopoly could make royal loans with the security of guaranteed exports, lessening the need for Frescobaldi, Bardi, Peruzzi or other foreign loans. For English merchants, staples excluded foreign merchants and squeezed higher prices from buyers. Moreover,

The Netherlands' Maritime Provinces. Flanders, Brabant, Zeeland and Holland

foreign ports competed to become the staple for revenues and knock-on trade generated. The 'Company of the Staple' was in Antwerp in 1313, Calais in 1314, and various cities to 1326 when staples were established only in English cities; denying foreign merchants access to wool producers.

Philip had insufficient resources to attack both Gascony and Flanders, while Edward II intermittently fought Scots and barons. Louis X (1314–16) and Philip V (1316–22) continued the push to Flanders, taking Bethune, Douai and Lille, towns probably then speaking a Flemish-Frisian language, spreading French cultural influence, but dealing major blows to economic prosperity. In 1326 the French fleet sailed from the Mediterranean to the Channel, threatening England with invasion, while French troops were in Scotland. In 1331 with Flemish political uncertainty, Edward III invited its cloth workers to settle in England. French privateers terrorised the Channel and Bay of Biscay, targeting English merchant ships. In 1336 Philip arrested all English merchants in Flanders and abolished Flemish town and craft guild privileges, triggering revolt. In 1337 Edward retaliated, banning wool exports and cloth imports to and from Flanders, halting Ypres, Bruges and Ghent's wool trade, but continued supplying Brabant provided it did not pass it to Flanders, where starving hordes of weavers roved the land, while French ships raided English ports.

Thus, the Hundred Years War, actually 116 of war and interruptions, was not, as often depicted, an Anglo-French dynastic dispute, but English defence of her two main trades; wool to Flanders and wine from Bordeaux to London, Bristol and Dublin, which tied the Angevin empire together, and whose customs duties on wine exports in Bordeaux were worth more than England's Crown estates. Only in 1337 when Philip again declared Gascony forfeit did Edward claim the French throne, a decent claim had not the French dredged-up ancient law preventing succession through the female line in 1328. Edward could have claimed it then, had it been a main concern. Attacking Flanders attacked England's wool export destination, its largest income source, on which much of southern England's agricultural lands, market towns, merchants, traders and shipowners depended. Flanders cloth industry depended on English wool; unhealthy over-dependence for both. The Lord Chancellor in Parliament sat on a woolsack symbolising what in 1297, the barons stated was half England's value. The 1353 Ordinance of the Staple called it 'the sovereign merchandise and jewel of this realm of England.'[13] Edward's queen, Philippa of Hainault, was William Count of Hainault, Holland and Zeeland's daughter. Flanders and England were economically and politically interdependent. Independence from France was vital for both. England had to retaliate. English merchants supported special taxes voted to fight the menace. Their future depended on it.

To finance war, Edward III used wool exports, supported by English merchants, an assembly of whom, led by Hull's William de la Pole and London's Reginald Conduit in 1337 accepted the need to double the duty to 40 shillings per sack, agreed by the House of Commons in 1341.[14] Two convoys carrying 30,000 sacks were assembled from east and south coast ports and discharged, some at Middelburg, most at Dordrecht, more than a monopoly, a virtual department of state,[15] given national interests at stake. In 1339 all port customs except London were assigned to de la Pole as repayment for loans. The Acciaiuoli, Albertini and Buonaccorsi also made loans in 1337.[16]

Early-14th century England's Gascon lands had been reduced to a narrow strip from Blaye, south of La Rochelle, to Bayonne. Booming wine exports encouraged other goods; dairy products, dyes and salt. In 1318, 232 Gascon wine ships discharged in English ports, about 20–25% of its exports, most of which went to north France and Bruges, and from there to the Baltic.[17] From the 1320s, a noticeable trend was English, especially London merchants taking over from Gascons.[18] Gascony depended on English grain, wool and leather and had few ties with French lands. It spoke an Occitan language, *langue d'oc*, rather than *lange d'oil*, spoken north of Bordeaux, as different linguistically and culturally as Catalonia, Normandy or Paris.[19] Plantagenet English kings regarded it as integral to their domains and of great economic value. Henri de Waleys was mayor of Bordeaux and London. Appeals could be made in England against decisions made in Gascony.[20] For France, Gascony's conquest was a logical step in territorial growth, irrespective of cultural and linguistic differences. Three hundred years of improved farming had turned forests into fields and vineyards, in landlubbing French eyes, a potential valuable taxation-resource.

In Flanders in 1338, Ghent elected Jacob van Artevelde who took control of Bruges and Ypres. France's puppet count fled in 1339 and towns were ruled as a kind of republic,[21] prioritising commercial values. Edward allowed wool export again and in 1343 the staple was in Bruges, probably the main destination from 1340. More Flemish weavers, fearing more French heavy-handed interference, migrated to England, resulting in growing English cloth-production. France coveted Gascony and Flanders without understanding trade dynamics, learning no lessons from Champagne.

Anglo-Castile trade peaked in the 1320s-1330s. At Sandwich in 1325, 18 out of 76 arriving ships were Spanish but since many recorded were local fishing boats their trade-share must have been well above 25%.[22] They were also at Exmouth, Exeter, Fowey, Bristol, especially Southampton and London, where there was a small, settled enclave. England was an attractive market with well-ordered legal and administrative systems. Sandwich, at the Wantsum Channel's head, connected to the Thames estuary and thus London, was one of England's foremost ports from the 11th century, still important in the 14th, before silting up in the 15th. Castilian leather imports declined and as England's cloth industry grew, tallow, greases, oils, soaps and dye imports for it increased. Prospects appeared bright. Gascon merchants had close ties with Castile's north coast ports. Before the war, France and England sought Castile's military favour, for France to use its ships, for England its neutrality.[23] France diplomatically triumphed with a pre-war treaty which meant Castile's merchants were technically alien enemies in England and their ships and goods were arrested until 1338. Its merchants sought safe conduct passes and royal protection. Edward tried to treat them fairly. Despite losses from piracy, which medieval governments couldn't control, Spanish merchants again became active in English ports, even Boston, where there is no record of them previously, and Bordeaux.[24]

Philip invaded Gascony in 1337. Wine exports collapsed 75%. In the next hundred years, in times of truce they rebounded, in intense war and Black Death they fell, but never reached even half pre-1337 levels as vineyards and wine stores were destroyed and sea-lanes became insecure. Freights and prices increased, fluctuating depending on security. Gascon merchants, active early in the century, reducing from the 1320s were almost totally absent by the 1340s and less wine reached European markets, most going to London, Hull, Bristol or Southampton.[25]

Edward established himself at Antwerp as champion of local independence against French expansion. French privateers burnt many south coast ports, while in 1340, 200 French ships and 60,000 troops, preparing to invade England from Sluys were destroyed by English ships, although French privateers continued attacking south coast ports. Flanders and Gascony, the wool and wine trade, were central to Edward's thinking, telling the pope's envoy that he would surrender claims to the French crown, if Philip granted him Aquitaine as in Henry II's day, in full sovereignty. France's position on female inheritance was proved farcical when Philip supported a woman claimant to the Duchy of Brittany in 1341. Edward needed it friendly for English ships' safety en route to Bordeaux, Portugal and Castile, so invaded Normandy to ensure his candidate prevailed, taking Gascony, Brittany and Normandy and marched to Flanders. At Crecy in 1346, adjacent to Flanders, its count died and the French army lost to English longbows. Meanwhile Bardi and Peruzzi loans to Edward over-extended them. They lent more than their capital and used depositors' money. Edward's inability to repay on time, collapsed them in 1345.[26] Edward relied on wool export duties and English merchant loans.

About 1340 Europe's population reached about 80 million. In the Black Death from 1348, Bruges' 35–40,000 population halved, not reaching similar levels for a century. Wine demand dwindled further but the buoyancy of English wool exports show how quickly Europe's economy recovered,[27] although they declined in the 1370s due to civil strife in Flanders and Florence,[28] partly compensated for by Holland's new cloth industry from the late-1300s. Italy's direct wool shipments were under 20% of total exports.

The count of Flanders' son restored his authority there, Ghent submitting in 1349, wool exports stopping in 1348, the staple moving to Middelburg, home staples again in 1352 to support non-staple monopoly merchants, then Bruges between 1359 and 1362. In the First Treaty of London (1358), France surrendered Gascony, Limousin, Poitou and adjacent regions' sovereignty. England dropped claims to the French throne, but demanded Anjou, Maine, Normandy, Calais and Brittany's overlordship. The 1360 Treaty of Brétigny assigned Calais and some outlying villages, the 'Pale of Calais', to England. The English Company of the Staple at Calais was established in 1363 to make it pay for itself. Edward used wool to keep Flemish clothmaking towns allies against France thereby raising money faster. Calais was governed by 26 merchants, one mayor for the town, one for the staple. By 1372 it was a Parliamentary borough, England's wool gateway to Flanders, almost half the population connected with wool. This 'brightest jewel in the English crown' accounted for a third of English revenue, although Flemish merchants found it difficult to access in wartime. In the difficult year 1384, only 83 sacks were discharged, most sent to Middelburg.[29] Wool was taxed at about 33% and cloth 2%,[30] increasing Flemish cloth prices, invigorating English merchants, lowering wool exports, increasing English cloth production and exports, helped by Flemish cloth workers' exodus to England. The war also stimulated shipbuilding, arms-manufacturing, metal-working and mining. A growing English identity was reflected in Edward's Statute of Pleading in which English was declared the language of Parliament and the courts.

London's 12th-century trade guilds became increasingly affluent and influential. Mercers, Fishmongers, Merchant Tailors, Vintners and Skinners built 14th-century halls, some rebuilt in the 15th, with new halls for Drapers, Goldsmiths, Grocers and Clothiers. The Guildhall was rebuilt from 1411. Trade guilds did not restrict themselves to one commodity. London's wool exports were dominated by Grocers and Fishmongers, the biggest individual exporter, Grocer Nicholas Brembre with 1,432 sacks and six others with 230–540 sacks,[31] the most successful Fishmonger John Curteys with 677. Vintners and Drapers were also represented. The Calais staple discouraged foreign merchants. The Hansa withdrew in the late-1360s, but Italians continued. Bristol, located between Iceland and the Mediterranean, became important for cod, Gascon and Castilian wine and Portuguese sherry imports. In 1379 over 20,000 sacks of English wool were imported into Flanders, but its civil war meant they fell sharply.

Castile's English imports increased in the 1350s and for the first time, many English merchants were active in north Spain, following their increased activity in Gascony from the 1320s, selling the increasing varieties of English cloths, expertly finished and dyed in many colours, red and green predominating,[32] helped by Castile's dye imports. Unlike Hansa merchants, Castile's did not try to exclude English. While the Hansa dealt directly with English wool producers, English merchants were blocked in Hansa markets. Castile was therefore an ideal cloth market, bigger than other Iberian kingdoms, easily accessible, no Hansa equivalent restricting foreign merchants, only a small local cloth industry, a wealthy nobility and large towns with rich Italian merchants; in short, demand for all cloth types. During Castile's 1360s civil war, the king was friendly with England, enabling profitable, complimentary trade. That ended in 1369. Usurper Henry II owed his throne to French support and was hostile to English merchants. With embargoes, mutual ship seizures, bankruptcies and high taxes, trade plummeted for over a decade, conducted instead through Bruges and probably Portuguese ports.

The Black Death hit Norway's small trade to Iceland. In 1347, it sent 20 ships, in 1349 just one and none in 1350 and 1355. It increased later, then declined to

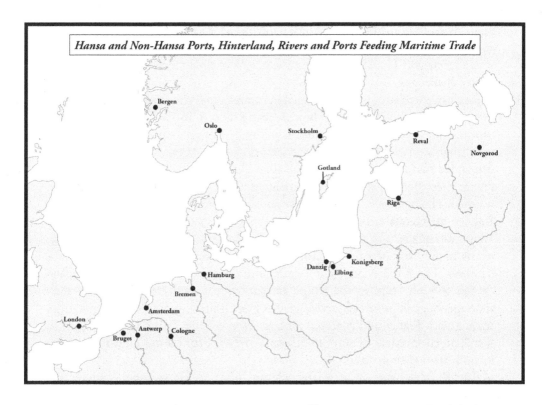

Hansa and Non-Hansa Ports, Hinterland, Rivers and Ports Feeding Maritime Trade

almost nothing partly due to the Hansa's sack of Bergen in 1393–94. English ships, first recorded in Iceland in 1412, seemed to have saved their situation. Greenland fared worse and after 1448–49 no ships arrived for nine years. English ships visiting Iceland rapidly increased from Hull, Lynn, from 1424 from Bristol and from the 1440s Devon, Cornwall and Welsh ports, taking woollen cloth, linen, beer, wine and wheat flour. Hansa hostility to them diminished interaction.[33]

After Bruges, Antwerp was north Europe's second port. Amsterdam originated in the late-12th century near a River Amstel dam connected to the Rhine. Its traders, Frisian descendants, were adventurous, one of their ships recorded confiscated in Lubeck in 1248. In 1323 Count William III of Holland set a toll on beer exports, the contacts for which were the basis of other trades. Hansa merchants dominated Baltic, North Sea and Channel ports, monopolising many Baltic trades, especially Pomeranian, Prussian, Polish and Livonian grain. By the late-1300s, 75% came from Danzig. Its Great Mill from the 1330s also made possible large-scale flour exports. Timber, leather, furs, herrings and honey were also exported for French Bay salt, English and Flemish cloth. Amsterdam objected to Lubeck's discriminating policies and English merchants were increasingly irritated at being denied Baltic access. The 1370 Treaty of Stralsund gave the Hansa Sound control and a Scania monopoly, from when it enjoyed its golden century. Almost 700 ships visited Lubeck in 1368,[34] 250 fully-laden from Scania, its annual trade about 70,000 barrels.[35] The Hansa dominated Novgorod's furs, Baltic and Norwegian timber, Baltic naval stores and grain, Swedish iron, Scania's herrings, Bergen's cod, English and Netherlands' cloth and France's and Portugal's salt and wine. Of Bergen's 14,000 population, 3,000 were Germans.[36] The Hansa were at the height of their powers. Such domination invites challenges.

English merchants, disadvantaged at home and the Baltic, pressured the government to obtain parity.[37] They had some success. In 1377 the Royal Council investigating Hansa 'abuses', found it guilty of raising Baltic goods' prices, but with English merchants restored to parity, prices rose anyway. The Royal Council demanded that English merchants be allowed to trade freely in Hansa areas. The Hansa rejected it and embargoed England until the London *kontor* had its charters restored. Hansa merchants in Scania and Norway were ordered not to protect English merchants against murder and robbery if negotiations failed to end in Hansa advantage. The 1380 settlement restored Hansa privileges on condition no harm was suffered by English traders. Nevertheless, they continued to be harassed. The 1382 Navigation Act requiring cargoes exported from England carried only on 'ships of the King's allegiance', was ineffective because of their shortage. English privateers, active against French ships, started attacking neutrals trading with France and captured a Hansa fleet off the Zwijn. Danzig's English merchant enclave had to move to Stralsund, which with Elbing, grew but in 1388 it confiscated their goods.

English merchants were finally allowed back in Danzig, but without the privileges of London's *kontor*. At Elbing, Danzig and Stralsund they were still not allowed to trade outside towns, with other foreigners or hire Hansa ships. In 1405, the Hansa conceded parity with English merchants in the Baltic and its merchants in England but Lubeck embargoed Baltic goods from English merchants and prohibited commerce. Persistent English merchants found that Prussia, Pomerania and Livonia <u>wanted</u> English cloth and that the Hansa was an impediment. Access enabled them to buy Baltic timber and when harvests were poor, grain. It was desperately dangerous. In 1406 the Hansa caught 96 English fishermen and threw them overboard, hands and feet bound. Between 1406 and 1427 London's annual Baltic cloth exports averaged 6,000 pieces, 1438–59, 10,000 and 1479–82, 13,500 and continued rising.[38] Some exchange happened in Flanders, but most first half 15th-century Baltic exports were direct. This increasingly successful struggle for English merchant-access was backed by the Crown. As with its defence of English trading interests against France, mercantile interests governed England's Baltic policy.

Some Hansa ports discovered that Lubeck's dictats were not in their interest. Reval, Riga and Danzig were supposed to ship through Lubeck, whereas their own interest lay in escaping its grip. Lubeck's discrimination against Dutch merchants pitted Antwerp and Amsterdam against Hanseatic Bruges. Dutch and English merchant struggles for Baltic access threatened Hansa's Baltic domination, while eastern Baltic Hansa ports pursued their interests. Denmark attempted to take back Sound control but the Hansa reduced Danish and Swedish merchant fleets to impotence and destroyed Norway's. In London, conflict increased between the Hansa and English merchants.

Castilian and Portuguese trade was more open. Gilbert Maghfeld, without trade guild affiliation for example, imported iron from Bayonne and Bilbao for grain and cloth, expanding into wine, beaver pelts, saffron, liquorice, woad, wax, linen, copper, millstones, green ginger and Spanish asses,[39] epitomising widening opportunities, selling them throughout England. But there were political risks. He died in debt, due to Richard II's (r. 1377–1399) cash demands for an Irish expedition. A 1392 charter party between an English master and Seville-based Italian merchants allocated four weeks loading at Seville, four days discharge at Southampton and twenty-five days at London, indicating a three to four-month round voyage.[40] Customs officer and poet Geoffrey Chaucer,[41] wrote the late-1300s *The Canterbury Tales* depicting a cross-section of English society, including a merchant in a Flemish beaver hat and a shipman who knew all Gotland's to Finsterer's harbours, all Brittany's and Spain's creeks and how to 'reckone wel his tydes'. Early-1400s Southampton built northern Europe's first two-masted ships, still well behind Mediterranean endeavours,[42] but all showed growing northern European and Atlantic European trade volumes and English merchant tenacity.

Meanwhile, in the interrupted Hundred Years War, France rallied under Charles V (1360–1380), defeating an English fleet off La Rochelle in 1372 and overwhelming Flanders in 1382. Bordeaux' wine exports further slumped. Another

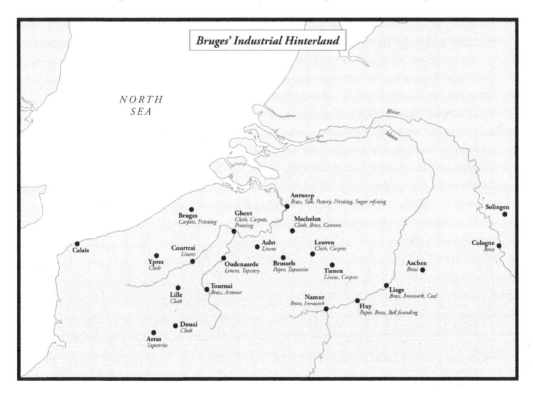

invasion threat was seen-off but wool exports were disrupted. Annual customs revenues fell from £46,000 to £26,000 by 1403 while Calais cost £17,000 to run and defend. France gave Gascony to Charles VI's son and invaded, while privateers roamed the Channel attacking English ports. Despite this, Anglo-Castile trade recovered in the 1380s-1390s.

John Duke of Burgundy (1404–19) and Count of Flanders, who controlled the Netherlands, suggested his daughter marry Henry IV's son, offered four Flanders' towns and assistance against France. The alliance revitalised England. New king Henry V invaded Normandy. Anglo-Castile trade was temporarily upset as Harfleur, made famous in Shakespeare's *Henry V,* which he besieged and took, had Castilian trade privileges. Thereafter victory at Agincourt (1415), near Crecy, was overwhelming. John's 'wealthy and cultured civilisation',[43] was not centred in Burgundy but Bruges, Ghent, Brussels, Amsterdam, Amiens and Arras, where art and learning went hand-in-hand with commerce.[44] Weaving gold thread into huge wall tapestries was Arras' speciality, Burgundian an adjective for lavish dress and conspicuous consumption. Local peculiarities were respected, contrasting to uniformity demanded by French kings.[45] Castilian Pero Tafur who travelled extensively between 1436 and 1439, wrote of Bruges in 1438 that 'the goddess of luxury has great power there…this town has everything…oranges and lemons from Castile…wine from Greece…spices from Alexandria…furs from the Black Sea' and 'the number of ships sailing from…Bruges exceeds 700 a day.'[46] Durer came to buy paints, including lapis lazuli dye from Afghanistan. Tafur contrasted it with Venice where only Venetians operated, while at Bruges all Europe's merchants traded. Despite Tafur's telling Venetian contrast, it was later known, because of its canals, as the Venice of the north, attracting sculptors, musicians and artists; Jan Van Eyck (1390–1441), whose 1432 Ghent cathedral masterfully created layers of light with oil paint, Petrus Christus (1410–1475), Gerard David, Rogier van der Weyden (1400–1464) and Hans Memling, (c. 1430–1494) who pioneered European secular art, portraits, still-life, every-day scenes and landscapes.

French territorial ambitions in Gascony and Flanders, constant dangers to English trade, meant Henry started subduing France, region by region, first Normandy, en route to Gascony and Iberia. Philip of Burgundy (1419–67) continued supporting England, encouraging his Dutch subjects to trade freely with it. He suggested dividing France between them. In the Treaty of Troyes, Henry married the French King's daughter in exchange for a promise that he became heir to the throne, only for him to die in 1422, aged 35, just before French King Charles. Before that, Henry had written to the Hansa, complaining about lack of parity in Danzig, Stralsund and Elbing, continuing Crown support for English merchants. The Hansa threatened, then negotiated but in 1435, they closed the Steelyard, the Hansa's London base and moved to Bruges, another attempted embargo. Other Hansa ports however, broke ranks and after two years, parity was granted. The Hansa got their charters back in return for an English return to Danzig, Stralsund and Elbing, with tax exemptions imposed the previous century. Seemingly on the cusp of a meaningful breakthrough, merchant tenacity leading the way, they again barred English ships from the Baltic, Norway and Iceland.

Trade with Castile had resumed. The number of English safe conducts and Spanish guarantees probably reflect regular contact with merchants knowing each other well.[47] Philip's 1435 switch of allegiance, recognising Charles VII as French king, sealed England's fate and, as he should have foreseen, Burgundy's, taken by France in 1477. Ineffectual English King Henry VI lost Bordeaux in 1451. His weakness and financial problems reopened wounds from when Henry of Lancaster had usurped Richard II in 1399. England slipped into civil war; the War of the Roses, intermittently from 1455 to 1487, which did lasting damage to proactive English merchants and shipping.

Nevertheless, Anglo-Castilian trade rose strongly, leading to a 1467 treaty ensuring mutual lower customs duties and Spanish merchants able to lease English houses without host supervision. Sweet Andalusian wine, fruits, olives, oil and dye imports for cloth increased. Cloth to Castile rose from 2–4% to 14–15% of total exports compared to the Hansa increase from 10–11% to 25–27%, its two main markets and safe conducts were no longer needed.[48] An annual average of 30 mainly Basque ships arrived in London in the 1490s.[49] Gascon wines were imported but in foreign ships.[50] Parliamentary Acts in 1485 and 1488 requiring their import in English ships show the value of this former 'nursery of seamen', the Acts' ineffectiveness and civil war damage to English merchants and shipping.

During the Hundred Years War, the turnaround from wool to cloth export was dramatic. Increased wool duties to finance war triggered it, although the rise of Dutch cloth-making using English wool suggests the advantage was not overwhelming. In 1310, 35,509 sacks of wool were exported and negligible cloth with foreign cloth equivalent to 3,302 sacks imported. By the 1390s wool exports dropped to around 19,000 sacks and cloth exports increased to 37,000,[51] 60,000 in 1447, and reached 130,000 of rich variety by the 1540s, accounting for 92% of export value against wool's 8%. Flanders imported Castile's wool as replacement, although a fraction of former English volumes and of lesser quality until 16th-century improvements. In 1300 England was a colonial economy exporting raw materials, importing finished goods. By 1450, it exported mainly manufactured cloth. Metal-working also grew. By the 15th century there were 100 London pewter workers, spreading to other cities and 150 London goldsmiths. Iron-working guilds rose from three in 1300 to 14 by 1422. The first cast iron cannon was made in 1509. Even with Gascony's wine trade collapse, up to 6,000 merchants still went there to buy it,[52] despite consumption dropping.

Had he lived, Henry V would have been unable to hold France, a large country able to recover from repeated English victories. France's economic future rested on agricultural exploitation. Its economic weaknesses was lack of populous ports and merchants lacking royal support. England, free of continental feudal and dynastic entanglements, bedevilling it since 1066, used strengths that France lacked, her maritime outlook, royal support of merchants, ports and trade. Rather than trying to rule great swathes of France, trade-generated wealth was a more realistic economic base, her route to prosperity and identity, forged in apparent defeat. It was enunciated in the anonymous *Libelle of Englyshe Polycye*, a verse treatise on English trade written sometime after 1436, identifying England's future as its merchant interests, to govern the surrounding seas with a strong navy protecting its trade, the Calais wool staple and potential imports. These it listed; Zeeland's salted fish, Ireland's otter skins, Portugal's oil, wine, figs, raisins, honey and fine leather, Castile's figs, raisins wine, hides, liquorice, oil, grain, soap, wax, wool, iron, saffron, honey, mercury, nuts, tallow and dates, Prussian bacon, bow-strings and beer, Danzig's iron, copper, steel, timber, bows, tar, pitch, flax, skins, furs, canvas, beer, meat and wax.[53] It was a vision of national interest in which maritime trade was the key and the Dover Straits choke point control as especially necessary.[54] It was very influential, if not immediately, printed in Richard Hakluyt's *Principal Navigations* (1598), owned by Elizabeth's Treasurer William Cecil, used by John Selden for his *Mare Clausum* (1635) and owned by Samuel Pepys.

Trade growth was also significant in Parliament's importance. Early-15th-century customs duties, accounting for over half royal revenues, were a prerogative, but tax had to be raised with Parliament's assent. The Assembly of Merchants was consulted frequently. Loans from the Company of the Staple's wool trade monopoly were necessary. Merchants' interests were integral with the war. Wealthy merchants bought land. Laurence Ludlow the greatest early-14th-century wool merchant and Crown financier bought Stokesay Castle, a beautiful, still-surviving fortified manor house. The Drapers' Sir John de Pulteney, four-times London's mayor, became Earl of Bath. Unlike France and Castile, English merchant and landed interests fused. Wool and cloth export profits were charitably gifted to English cathedrals and lavish churches in wool-producing regions, East Anglia, the Cotswolds and west country, and increasingly Oxford and Cambridge colleges.

By about 1400 the Hansa exported 100,000 casks of herring in 250-ton cogs. However, during the 14th century, herrings gradually migrated from the Baltic to the North Sea, making English Yarmouth and Dutch Brielle attractive new herring ports for Europe's merchants. Setubal's related salt trade also increased. Because of increasing Baltic trade volumes, Danish, Swedish, Dutch and English competition, and new Baltic ports, the Hansa had huge control problems. Dutch merchants shipped cloth and manufactured goods to Riga and Danzig, returning with grain, timber, metals, furs and naval stores, settling in Baltic ports, circumventing Hansa, advancing credit, and stimulating local shipbuilding, especially in Danzig, whose shipyards received Dutch orders. Scandinavia bitterly resented Hansa trade dominance. Denmark's kings, controlling Sweden and Norway since 1397, favoured Dutch and English traders and in 1429 imposed tolls on ships passing the Sound. The Hansa war machine defeated the Danes and secured exemption. During the 1438–1441 war between Hansa and Dutch, Baltic access was again at stake. Yet the Hansa remained extremely powerful, especially in Norway. In the 1440s, Bergen's Hansa killed its bishop and the king's representative, but received only a small fine.[55]

Elsewhere Hansa power did weaken. By 1475–1476, 25% of Danzig's shipping was in Dutch ships and Prussia refused to join the Hansa's Dutch blockade, but Denmark and grain-deficient Norway were powerless. Baltic goods had to be shipped through Lubeck and Netherlands' cloth via Bruges, in Hansa ships. At the century's end, Denmark again attempted control of the Sound and favoured the Dutch, but Hansa forces with Swedish allies, forced Denmark's king into exile.

Danzig, ruled since 1308 by Teutonic Knights, in 1454 asked the Polish king to oust them and became part of Royal Prussia in 1466, separate from Ducal Prussia. Royal Prussia's Danzig, Elbing and Thorn, gave it political ideology and culture based on ideas of freedom and liberty, different from the values Prussia is usually associated.[56] Commercially dynamic, its government was based on municipal liberties, protected by Poland. Ducal Prussia's 1520s peasants' war was fiercely suppressed and serfdom continued. It juxtaposes again neighbours with opposing maritime and continental traditions, rooted in geographical imperatives. By 1534 Charles V's secretary noted that from a large village Danzig had become 'the most powerful and wealthy city in the Baltic Sea.'[57]

Bristol continued growing. William Canynges, five-times mayor, twice MP, owned ten ships and employed 800 seamen, later rebuilding a church; typical merchant philanthropy. After 1453, Bristol lost access to Gascon and Bordeaux wines, but increased Irish hides, linen and Iberian imports. Prominent 1430s–1450s Bristol merchant Robert Sturmy, typically traded with Ireland and Gascony, importing dyes, fruits and paper. In the 1440s he developed Pisan contacts and his ships sent wool, while transporting pilgrims to Jerusalem and Santiago de Compostela. He prospered.[58] These Mediterranean ventures exceeded northern Europe's contemporary shipping horizons; the adjacent continent, Iberia, Iceland and the Baltic. But in 1457, with partner John Heyton, he planned a three-ship Mediterranean expedition with tin, lead, wool and cloth. The main aim was to load alum, essential for cloth production, Bristol being surrounded by Cotswolds and west country cloth-producing regions. Since the Ottoman capture of mines and taking Constantinople in 1453, supply had fallen and prices increased but were only available from Genoese merchants at Chios, the maritime end of caravan routes across Anatolian alum-mining regions.[59] Sailing in winter to avoid hostile galleys,[60] Sturmy knew exactly where he was going and why. He was financed by many Bristol merchants, former Henry VI favourite James Stourton, a major west country landowner in burgeoning clothmaking areas, probably the Earl of Worcester, possibly even Richard Duke of York.[61]

He sold the wool in Pisa, called at Naples and loaded 137.9 tons of alum in Chios, enough for 34,000 cloths, almost equivalent of England's annual import;[62] seemingly attempting to replace Genoa as alum importer. Alum accounted for 17% of his cargo <u>value</u>, spices, gunpowder, turpentine and cotton, 14.21%, sweet wine 21%, rich cloths and jewels 19%, were the most prominent.[63] All were normal Genoese cargoes to England. Effectively it was an audacious take-over bid. Genoa learnt of his massive Chios purchases. Realising that if successful, it would damage their shipping to northern Europe, enticing other English competitors, it commissioned Lesbos-based freebooter Guiliano Gattilusio to eliminate them. Two ships were captured, Sturmy was killed, only Stourton's ship escaping. In retaliation, all Genoese merchants in all English ports were imprisoned, their assets seized and tried before King and Council, which awarded compensation. English ships appear to have called at Chios regularly thereafter and merchants were resident by 1479,[64] but nothing on Sturmy's scale. It was almost a century before English ships ventured to Anatolia, although Anglo-Iberian trade led to occasional trade with Morocco from the 1470s, and by the 1500s at least one Canaries sugar estate was owned by an English merchant.[65]

In 1475 the Hansa prevented Bristol's merchants from buying Icelandic cod. Its fishermen therefore sailed further west. In 1481 two of them, Croft and Jay, found cod in the Grand Banks off Labrador in unprecedented density. In 1490, Iceland offered to rescind the cod ban. Croft and Jay were not interested. Trans-Atlantic fisheries added to Bristol's trade with Ireland, Gascony and Iberia, making it England's second port. English merchants and financiers owned fleets of up to 100 vessels. La Rochelle's fisheries, the Isle de Re saltworks, wine and merchant-led local government helped make it France's main port. [66] Its fishermen sailed west with salt, returned with salted cod and its merchants exported wine, cheaper than Gascon or Spanish, vital in encouraging seafaring, navigation and exploration.

Genoese Giovanni Caboto, anglicised to John Cabot, knowing Bristol's fishermen had sighted land from the Grand Banks, sailed in 1497 in Henry VII's service to find a route to Asia. Instead, he found Newfoundland, Cape Breton Island, perhaps also Maine, claiming the area for England. Portuguese, Bretons, Basques, French, Hansa, Dutch and English fished the Grand Banks, encouraging seafaring, navigation and exploration. In 1508, 10% of fish sold in Portugal's ports, Douro and Minho, was Newfoundland salt-cod.[67] Aviero's salt, considered Portugal's best, made it a salt-cod centre. For 200 years, 60% of fish consumed in Europe was cod, enriching Bristol, St Malo, Nantes, Bordeaux, Bayonne and La Rochelle.

London's share of England's maritime trade value in 1200 was about 17%, in 1400, 36% of a greater volume and by the 1470s, 61% of an even greater volume. In cloth export London had about 13% in 1350, 40% in 1430 and 61% in 1500,[68] helped by Bruges, Antwerp and Calais' proximity and Crown support, making London increasingly wealthy with Italian luxuries in great demand. Italians controlled about 25% of English trade and banking but Florence's galleys stopped in 1480. Dominic Mancini in 1480 described London's 'huge warehouses for imports and numerous cranes of remarkable size to unload merchandise from the ships...In one street minerals, wines, honey, pitch, wax, flax, robes, thread, grain, fish and other rather sordid goods,' in another, cloths only, and in a third 'gold and silver cups, dyed stuffs, various silks, carpets, tapestry and much other exotic merchandise.' Increasing volumes paid for harbour investments. A Venetian envoy to London about 1497 thought England, Europe's richest country as the Strand hosted 52 goldsmiths, more than Italian cities,[69] probably reflecting relative Italian decline.

During the Wars of the Roses the Hansa took advantage with foreign merchants probably controlling 40–47% of London's overseas trade value.[70] Over 6% of its population was born overseas, mainly Netherlands' artisans, merchants and commercial firms' apprentices. In 1461 Edward IV, (r. 1461–70 and 1471–1483) prohibited foreigners exporting wool and was popular in the City. Hanseatic goods were seized in 1468 and the Steelyard destroyed in 1469, but Edward had to negotiate with them to help regain the throne in 1471. Hansa assistance to Henry VII (r. 1485–1509) also resulted in confirmation of Hanseatic privileges, less customs dues than English merchants, but elsewhere they faced competition. Non-affiliated Antwerp grew and Baltic ports evaded restrictions. More English exports were wrested into English merchant hands, but despite native merchant desire to overturn foreign privileges, there was by necessity more cooperation in credit, joint ventures, employment of foreigners and intermarriage.[71] In 1480–81, 224 vessels were recorded in London, 40% of them English, over half from London.[72] The Steelyard's *Maria* made six round-trips that year plus ships from Hamburg and Danzig with timber, fur, pitch, tar and fish, for cloth, pewter and candles.

Henry VII's overriding aim was increasing customs revenue[73] and tried assisting English merchants by reducing foreigners advantages. Treaties with Denmark and Florence helped. Acts were passed forbidding unfinished cloth exports by foreigners' (1487) to encourage weaving and finishing (1498), prohibiting silk imports (1504) in foreign vessels, but did not interfere in Hansa's English privileges. In 1496 England and the Netherlands signed, 'Intercursus Magnus', providing favourable commercial conditions for English merchants in Antwerp, recognising English and Dutch fishermen's freedom, and use of either country's ports in emergency.

Lisbon was Iberia's largest city. Its merchants were in Pisa, Valencia, Seville, Bilbao, Bristol, Southampton, London and Bruges. It welcomed traders from those ports, Genoa, Barcelona, Bordeaux, Danzig and Reval. The River Tagus' adjacent regions were Portugal's most fertile, producing grain, vegetables, fruit, wine, olive oil and honey for export. Twenty Portuguese vessels in London in 1480–81 discharged oranges, sugar, cork, woad, alum, grain, dates, raisins, paper, iron, oil and wine. They brought Setubal's and French Bay salt to Bristol, as England's fishery growth outpaced its saltworks. Atlantic shipping, although less valuable than Mediterranean, was growing fast, while Venetian shipbuilding declined, reflecting stagnating east Mediterranean and no Black Sea trade. Venetian ships reduced London visits, tending to discharge in Southampton and Flanders.[74] North Europe's horizons widened quickly and vessel sizes increased. Portuguese 'caravels' developed into larger 'carracks' with two or three masts, square and triangular sails, and a stern rudder. Genoese recognised their use for bulk cargoes and built large ones. Catalans and Venetians followed. Improved maps, rutters, portolan charts, and compasses all assisted in expanding trade.

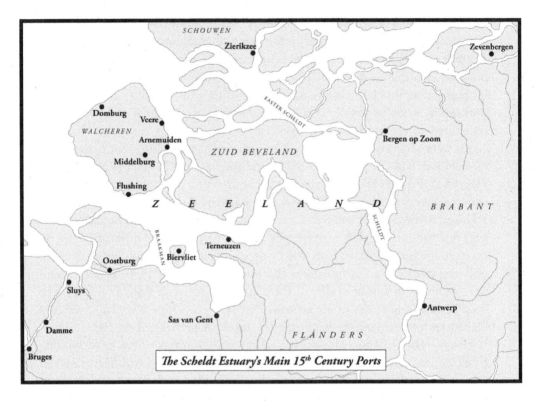

The Scheldt Estuary's Main 15th Century Ports

As Bruges' harbour and River Zwijn silted-up, after 1400 some ships discharged at Walcheren Island's outports in the Scheldt estuary at Flushing, Veere, Sluys, Middelburg, Bergen op Zoom and especially Arnemuiden, which had ample space for large ships and 29 piers to tranship cargo to and from other Scheldt ports. Around 1450 only 14 vessels a year anchored there, but 345 by 1550,[75] discharging salt, wine, fruits, cork, oil, timber, flax, hemp, tar and pitch. These autonomous, adjacent, competing ports were mutually dependent in shipping services; storage, accommodation, repair, agency, provisioning and pilotage, serving the same hinterland.[76] Bruges and Ghent frequently revolted against high Hapsburg taxes, hindering development. Silting and need of transhipment outports also strangled potential. Antwerp's harbour was larger than Bruges, was free of stifling Hansa restrictions and Hapsburg taxes, so quickly, about 1480 replaced Bruges as north Europe's largest port, trade and financial centre, Portuguese spice and sugar hub, (see page 174) and English cloth recipient, a third of its imports. The Fuggers and Welsers moved there. Ruled by Counts of Brabant, it behaved more like a free city. Ghent's and Bruges' cloth industry also moved north.

*   *   *

An important development of these two centuries, especially in the context of this book's overall story was the rise of tenacious, pro-active English merchants from the

1320s in Gascon trade and 1350s in Iberian and Baltic trade. Increasingly Dutch and Hansa dominated Baltic trade. But the Wars of the Roses badly affected English control of its shipping. Sound Tolls show no English ships until 1504.[77] English woollen cloth's price advantage, product variety, quality and colour range, over 12 types in over 20 shades was sold in the early-1400s in the Baltic, Mediterranean and Iberia, including to its royalty.[78] Brabant's and Dutch producers saw them as threats. With War of the Roses weakness from the 1450s Crown-supported merchant activity lost traction and they resisted English dyed and finished cloth imports to protect their finishing industry. Dependence on Antwerp for so much of England's cloth exports thus became a weakness.

After chapters on 14th-15th century European maritime trade, a Mediterranean-Atlantic volume and value comparison should be made. Peter Spufford found the evidence patchy and problematic, but fair comparison in Lubeck and Genoa between 1379 and 1384. He concluded Genoese trade perhaps five or six-times greater, Venice's similar to Genoa's,[79] and Mediterranean trade ten-times greater than the Baltic.[80] After the Chioggia War (1378–81), Genoa's was second to Venice's, especially to the Levant. Lubeck's late-14th-century population was about 25,000, Genoa's and Venice's about 100,000 each. Bruges' figures are also problematic but after Antwerp became north Europe's main port in the 1480s, volumes and values escalated.[81] He thinks exact 15th-century comparisons unsafe, but in its second half, Atlantic volumes and values obviously grew and Mediterranean problems meant its volumes shrank. (Chapter 23)

Chapter 19

The Indian Ocean and China Sea After Zheng He and Before the Portuguese

Before Zheng He's last voyage in 1433, Malacca was already strong and populous with policies designed to capture maximum trade volumes. Its rise undermined rival ports such as north Java's Grise, further weakening the Majapahit empire. Portuguese Indian official Tome Pires counted 84 languages spoken at Malacca, and described 61 merchant communities, from Cairo, Mecca, Aden, Kilwa, Malindi, Hormuz, Champa, China, Timor, Philippines, Brunei, Java, the Maldives, Bandas, Moluccas, various Indians, Sinhalese, Siamese, Malays, Khmers and 'Rumes', probably Italians from late-Yuan China, ethnic or religious communities; Jews, Mappilas, Gujaratis, Fujianese and Armenians. The government offered warehouses and elephants to carry cargo and the king assigned each merchant a 'nayre' to protect and serve him,' a 'chatim' clerk to keep his accounts and look after his affairs and a broker, probably originally Palembang practices.

Given the family link, we must question the 1178 and 1225 Chinese accounts of Srivijayan coercion to force passing shipping into its harbour. As suggested by other accounts, perhaps it would have been commercially perverse <u>not</u> to call there. Chinese government mentality saw coercion as natural and perhaps wrongly assumed it, more logical given Indian Ocean trade's hospitable nature and the praise received from foreign traders, <u>unless</u> there was a brief period when Song dominance forced desperate measures, but there is no evidence for it.

Malacca's most important merchants were Hindus and Jains from Gujarat, about 1,000 resident and 4–5,000 visiting annually. Cargo volumes were so great and diverse, they were divided by origin; the Middle East, India and Sri Lanka; Siam, Cambodia, Ryukyu and China; Sumatra; and the rest of Southeast Asia, each overseen by a 'shabandar' originally a Persian word for 'ruler of the harbour'. Pires documented 30 Indian cloth types, tin, silk, porcelain, sandalwood and spices and identified Cambay's large ships as most significant with smaller ships from lesser Gujarati ports. He concluded, 'Malacca cannot live without Cambay, nor Cambay without Malacca, if they are to be rich and prosperous.' Cambay 'stretches out two arms, [one]...toward Aden...the other toward Malacca;' the Indian Ocean's most important ports.[1] To sustain its population, Malacca imported rice from Pegu, Java, Siam and Bengal.

Cambay was Gujarat's pre-eminent port despite the estuary silting and fast tidal bores. Muslim-ruled, its long-haul trade was dominated by Hindus,[2] exporting multi-coloured cloth to Africa, the Red Sea and Southeast Asia, importing spices, silk, gold, silver, mercury, copper, glass beads and weapons. Gujarati joined Arabic as an Indian Ocean trade language with Tamil and Bengali in the Bay of Bengal. Chinese merchant withdrawal aided their rise. A Florentine in 1510 wrote self-deprecatingly, 'we believe ourselves to be the most astute men…the people here [Gujarat] surpass us in everything…they can do better calculations by memory than we can do with the pen…they are superior to us in countless things, save with sword in hand, which they cannot resist.' Pires said, 'they are men who understand merchandise…the business of trade is a science.' He suggested Portuguese factors go to Cambay to train, echoing Marco Polo who thought Indians 'the best merchants in the world.'

Further south, Calicut, to which Ma Huan devoted 10% of *Yingya Shenglan* (*Triumphant Visions of the Ocean's Shores*) had prospered with revival of Red Sea trade and was well-administered by the Samudra Rajas. Samudra, sea or ocean in Sanskrit, reflected Calicut's maritime trade dependency. Foreigners were encouraged to settle with land grants and trade privileges in self-governing enclaves. It had been Zheng He's western Indian Ocean operational base. He and Ma Huan were Muslims. Calicut had over 20 mosques, about 30,000 Muslims, plus Mappilas, Hindus and Jains. Its envoys had precedence when paying tribute in China, which Ma Huan described as a three-month process, silks and porcelains for camphor, pearls and gems. Ma Huan lavished praise on its people; honest, trustworthy, smart and distinguished. He noted pepper and coconut plantations, wheat imports and various rice types. In 1516 Portuguese clerk, factor, shipbuilding overseer and interpreter, Duarte Barbosa noted its Muslim merchants trading 'pepper, ginger, cinnamon, cardamoms, myrobalans, tamarinds, canafistula, precious stones…seed pearls, musk, ambergris, rhubarb, aloes-wood, cotton cloths, porcelain,' and much else to Alexandria and Cairo. Goa was the main horse import port from Persia and Arabia.

Two-thirds of pepper was from the Malabar coast, the rest from Southeast Asia, Sri Lankan cinnamon, Banda Islands' nutmeg and mace and Moluccan cloves were low-volume, high-value cargoes, distributed from Malacca. Pires estimated annual mace production as 100 tons, 1,200 each of nutmeg and cloves, only 5% reaching Europe. Far more rice, salt, textiles, porcelain, metals, silk, horses, timber, carpets, mangrove poles, perfume, jewellery, gold and silver were shipped. Early-16th-century traders taking pepper from Malacca to China made huge profits. In Calicut, mace cost 12–15-times, nutmeg 30-times Banda Islands production costs.[3]

Calicut, Cochin, Cannanore and Quilon were semi-independent within the Hindu Vijayanagar kingdom. It encompassed 300 east and west coast ports. Its capital, a vital inland trade hub, had a 60-mile ring of seven-fold walls around it. Their kings called themselves 'Lord of the eastern and western oceans'. Established in 1336, it was the culmination of southern India's resistance to Islamic invasions. Efficiently administered, its wealth-creating ports perpetuated problem-solving Tamil culture; water-management, irrigation, literature, art, music and architecture.

Deva Raya II ruled from 1424, quelling independent lords, including Calicut's and Quilon's rajas, invaded Sri Lanka, and became overlord of Burmese kings at Pegu and Tenasserim after Zheng He's visits. One early-1500s inscription read, a 'king should improve the harbours of his country and so encourage its commerce that horses, elephants, precious gems, sandalwood, pearls and other articles are freely imported,' welcoming foreign merchants with 'dwellings in the city…daily audience, presents…allowing decent profits.'[4] About 1500 its capital had 500,000 people, the world's second largest city after Beijing, twice Paris' size. Army and administration were open to all. It welcomed Muslim merchants, while resisting their northern, intolerant co-religionists.

Southeast Asian Islamisation, encouraged by the Ming ban continued. Visiting Java and Sumatra between 1512 and 1515, Pires said most east coast Sumatran kings were Muslim, most west coast Sumatra's and Java's were not. Muslim traders spread Islam peacefully; those escaping Hindu lower castes or wanting to make trading in a Muslim world easier, converting from convenience; practical men, willing to interact and trade with anyone at decent prices. Armenian Christians, Jews, Muslims and Hindus did business, in stark contrast to early-1400s Ahmad Shah who routinely slaughtered non-Muslims in Islam's southward march. Delhi's Sikander Lodi (r. 1489–1517) destroyed Hindu temples, turned them into madrassas, discriminated against non-Muslims and burned a Hindu holy man for saying 'Islam and Hindu

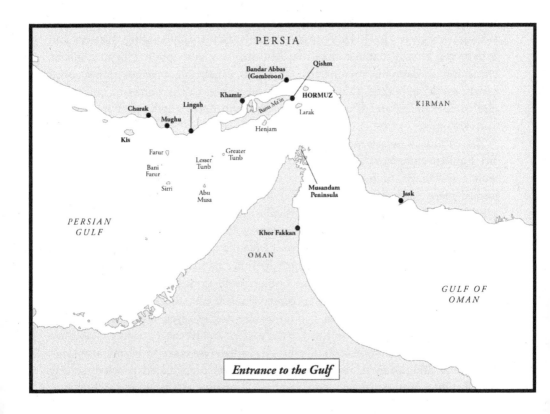

Entrance to the Gulf

Dharma are both equally acceptable to God if followed with a sincere heart.'[5] Descended from both Genghis and Tamerlane, Babur swept across the steppe, reconquered Kabul in 1504 and Delhi in 1526, creating the Mughal, from Mongol, empire. Mass slaughter and towers of skulls resulted. Central Asian steppe-nomad brutality had, like the Ottomans, found Islam's intolerant strand a perfect bedfellow.

Hormuz continued as the India-Persia entrepot. Ma Huan recorded that 'foreign ships from every place and foreign merchants travelling by land come...to attend the market and trade, hence the people...are rich.' Their dress was 'handsome, distinctive, elegant.' Pires said Hormuz was 'the key to Persia', and its king's wealth derived from customs dues on an exhaustive list of cargoes including horses, seed pearls, saltpetre, sulphur, silk, 'black pepper, cloves, cinnamon, ginger...other spices and drugs...greatly in demand in...Persia and Arabia ...[and] much rice.' Duarte Barbosa in 1518 explained how well-dressed and fed its people were, with the wealthy having mainland country houses. Aden was so rich, according to Ma Huan, that Muslim women wore four pairs of gold earrings inlaid with gems, strings of pearls, bracelets, armbands and rings on fingers and toes.

East African ports continued their network role. Lamu specialised in mangrove poles used in the timber-deficient Middle East. Mogadishu's merchants, Ma Huan explained, continued long-haul ambergris and frankincense trade, benefitting from Red Sea proximity. Duarte Barbosa described Malindi's Muslim inhabitants as 'great barterers who dealt in cloth, gold, ivory and divers other wares with...the great kingdom of Cambay.' Sofala, not on his itinerary, was Great Zimbabwe's gold export port from the 10th century. From the 11th to the 15th century, it produced as much as ten tons a year, at first via Kilwa but later directly with India for cloth including Calicut's bright coloured 'kambaya', Chinese and Persian porcelain, cowrie shells, Levantine glassware and silk worn by its rulers. From about 1200 it was southern Africa's most powerful country, the core of wider trade in ivory, salt, copper and iron, but was abandoned about 1450. Mombasa, Kilwa, Mogadishu, Aden, Hormuz, Calicut and Malacca were completely dependent on maritime trade.

China's 1491 census population of 60 million was, due to tax-dodging or forced labour avoidance, probably underestimated by up to 40 million.[6] Europe's was roughly 50 million. China's huge, mainly self-sufficient economy consumed half spice production, aromatics, silver and horses. India, Persia and Ottomans also consumed huge amounts of spice. In 1488 Korean official Ch'oe Pu, shipwrecked on China's coast, allowed to return in 1492, reported 'all the treasures of the land and sea...thin silks, gauzes, gold, silver, jewels, crafts, arts and great and rich merchants,' especially in the south where canals connected towns and 'even village children, ferrymen and sailors can read,' indicating internal stability. Japan sent copper, horses, sulphur, swords and fans to China as tribute and used coins minted in China from Japanese copper. China's trade ban increased the importance of Ryukyu Island's Chuzan Kingdom. A bell cast in 1458 said its ships were 'a bridge between 10,000 nations.'[7] Pires noted their merchants' honesty and that they sold Japanese veneered boxes, fans, paper, silk and swords. Between 1432 and 1570 at least 44 official missions were sent from the capital Naha to Siam, Annam, Patam, Malacca and Sunda, and they traded with Borneo, Sumatra, Luzon, Korea, Japan and China; entrepots in waters vacated by China.

The Indian Ocean and China Sea had the world's richest trading opportunities. There was no need to round the Cape to the Atlantic, although the Chinese would have been technically able well before mid-century Ahmad ibn-Majid did so and sailed into the Mediterranean. It was not worth repeating, as the Red Sea route was shorter.[8] Gujarati and Malabar ports had no long-range political ambitions, no navies. Malacca was commercially, not militarily powerful. Its sultan wrote to Okinawa's king in 1468, 'we have learned that to master the blue ocean, people must engage in commerce and trade, even if their countries are barren...life... [was never] so affluent in preceding generations.' They never thought to forcefully capture the world's richest trades. There was no need. Such ideas were forming in an unexpected place.

Chapter 20

Portugal's Ambition

Portugal's 15th-century main exports were fish, wine, olive oil, fruit, cork and hides to Flanders, England, the Mediterranean and Morocco, its imports wheat, cloth, iron, and timber from Europe and gold from Morocco. Lisbon had about 40,000 people, Oporto 8,000, other ports only 500–3,000, but had strong maritime traditions. Portugal's Reconquista had been conducted by land and sea. In 1317 King Denys conquered the Algarve in a galley fleet headed by Genoese Admiral Emanuele Pessagno, endorsed by the pope as Crusade.[1] Red Sea access, denied to Europeans since Muslim conquest, meant ideas of what lay beyond were limited to a few travellers' accounts and Prester John fables of an eastern Christian king. Odoric of Pordenone, sent east by the papacy in 1318 returned with descriptions of pepper forests. Niccolo de Conti (1393–1469) seeking absolution for converting to Islam while traveling in the Indian Ocean, granted in return for recounting his experiences to papal secretary Poggio Bracciolini, an inquisitive Renaissance man preparing a world encyclopaedia, confirmed seeing Sri Lankan cinnamon trees, Sumatran camphor fields and told of nutmeg, clove and mace islands. He said Calicut was 'eight miles in circumference, a noble emporium... abounding in pepper, lac, ginger, a larger kind of cinnamon;' 'a great maritime city.' He and Pero Tafur (1410–1489) described Chinese multi-sailed ships. Florentine geographer Paolo Toscanelli (1397–1482) wrote what sounds like a recycled Marco Polo story. 'The number of seagoing merchants in China is so great that in a single port they outnumber all...other merchants of the world...westerners should seek a route there...because great wealth awaits us from its gold and silver...gems and spices [and] for...China's learned sages and philosophers.' This was China before the ban.

Portugal's King John achieved independence in 1385 with English assistance. In 1415 he sent three sons to capture Ceuta, a rich North African caravan terminus for trans-Saharan gold-for-salt trade, which had spread Islam in central and west Africa and supplied two-thirds of Europe's gold. John proudly declared that he 'washed his hands in infidel blood.' While plundering, they found Chinese silks and Indian muslins embroidered with silk. 'Our poor homes look like pig sties in comparison,' wrote a chronicler.[2] Portuguese Ceuta did not continue as a gold terminus. Trade and traders move when threatened. John's son Henry, fascinated with Africa and Prester John, amassed at his Sagres, Algarve base, some of the liveliest intellectuals, Jewish and Arab cartographers, Genoese and Venetian navigators, Europe's largest collection of navigational maps and had ships built to sail south, leading a 19th-century historian to entitle him 'the Navigator'. Because of trans-Saharan routes, he knew by sailing south, gold could be found. Commercial and religious motives fused. Europe's first three-masted ship, 'caravels' then 'carracks' were developed at Sagres, with stern rudder and lateen sail; small, fast, shallow, ideal for pioneering. Continuous adjustments were made in sails, rigging and hulls as knowledge of Atlantic conditions improved. They first sailed west against the winds, letting westerlies blow them back, the 15th-16th century maritime revolution effectively a 'discovery of the world wind system.'[3] Maritime skills, technology and knowledge were discovered purposefully.

Having re-discovered the Azores in 1427, settlement began in 1439 and produced woad, exported to Flemish cloth workshops. In 1418–19 Madeira was discovered. Occupied from 1425, it produced dyes, wheat and vines. Sugar was introduced from the 1430s with Genoese capital. Henry licensed traders for 20% of the profit and in 1452 became a partner in Madeira's first sugar mill. West African slaves were imported from the 1440s and settlers attracted from Portugal, Genoa, Flanders, Germany, and Tuscany. The first sugar cargo arrived in Bristol in 1456, in Bruges in 1468. Demand boomed just as Cyprus', Crete's, and Algarve's sugar exports were threatened by Ottoman Black Sea closure.

From the 1440s west African voyages paid for themselves with gold, ivory, melegueta pepper and slave imports, for cloth, trinkets and horses. A chronicler in 1445 reported over 200 slaves auctioned at Lagos in Portugal. West African wars produced many. Ibn Battutah had, in 1354, noted strings of young slave women driven north, the death toll far greater than the later trans-Atlantic trade.[4] Portugal, adjacent to the Muslim world, accepted slavery. Negro and Berber domestic slaves were common in Lisbon. By Henry's death in 1460, Portuguese took 30,000 a year to Madeira when Cape Verde was settled, and sugar and slaves introduced to uninhabited Sao Tome after discovery in 1471. A west African trade monopoly was awarded from 1469 to 1475 to Fernao Gomes, who profited and discovered 2,000 miles of coast.[5]

Constantinople's fall in 1453 and Athens in 1456, triggered papal bulls encouraging and legitimising Muslim enslavement as missionary activity. Africa thus became Madeira's alternative slave source. *Romanus Pontifex* (1455) praised Henry as Christ's soldier who would round the Cape and find Prester John.[6] In 1457 Lisbon's mint issued gold cruzados (crusades) from west African gold. The Congo was reached by 1480, encouraged by regular papal bulls, giving them the Guinea coast and jurisdiction 'all the way to the Indias.' In 1482 a fort was built at Sao Jorge da Mina on the Gold Coast to protect gold shipments, Portugal's largest income source, but it became dependent on Genoese bankers.

Dynastic Portugal-Castile war (1474–1479) was mainly land-based but some Castilian privateers took it to Portugal's new sugar islands, Guinea coast bases, and took the Canaries. Portugal retained the Azores, Madeira and the Cape Verde Islands. The Canaries were ideal staging-posts for future trans-Atlantic voyages, less demanding than rounding the Cape to India in distance, navigation and financing.

By the early-1480s, 60–70 ships a year loaded Madeira's sugar, about a third for Antwerp, overtaking Venice as Europe's sugar-refining hub. The rest was shipped to Lisbon, Venice, Genoa, London, Bristol, Constantinople and Chios. In 1484, production started in the Canaries. By 1500 Madeira's production was six-times that of Cyprus, which uncompetitive, relied on timber, wheat and malmsey wine exports. Lisbon did not become Europe's commercial capital. Europe's economic gravity had already shifted north. Antwerp was 'as much the successor of Venice as Bruges,'[7] especially as Europe's sugar distribution hub.

John II's 1481 accession to Portugal's throne ignited a burst of energy. He executed detractors of the aggressive southern policy and improved trade ties with ally England. He reserved for the Crown, gold, slaves, spices and ivory imports and export of horses, carpets, textiles, copper, lead, brass, utensils, beads and bracelets. Private traders could import by buying licenses for less valuable parrots, seals, monkeys and cotton. The Crown subsequently leased import rights of slaves and ivory, but always monopolised gold.[8] In practice it was impossible to stop private trade. Monopoly in melegueta pepper was awarded to Duarte Brandao, otherwise Sir Edward Brampton, a Jewish merchant on Portugal's and England's royal council.[9] As concentration shifted from Sagres to Lisbon, John frequently visited the 'Casa da Mina', his palace warehouse complex, incorporating customs departments, royal mint, arsenal and the India House. Francois I of France derogatorily called him *le roi épicier*, spice-seller and grocer king, typical of French kings' inability to understand trade's benefits. In 1487 John sent Pedro de Covilhão to India. His reports of the trade volumes in cinnamon, cassia, pepper and spices may have been instrumental in Lisbon rejecting Genoese opportunistic sugar trader Christopher Columbus' offer to sail across the Atlantic to India. He was one of many Genoese bankers, traders, masters, pilots and map makers living in Lisbon. They anyway thought his estimate of the world's size absurd. Columbus hawked his idea to Castile, France and England, eventually finding favour in Castile after Grenada's conquest in 1492.

The pope encouraged John's Indian Ocean plans, telling him to take the Ottomans 'in the rear.' Dias rounded the Cape in 1487, reconnoitring east Africa. When Columbus returned from the Americas, the Portuguese were sure he had not reached Asia, but to protect their interests, in the 1494 Treaty of Tordesillas, Portugal agreed not to compete in the west Atlantic. The dividing line, 370 leagues west of the Azores, left them a free hand in Africa, Asia and Brazil, which they may have sighted before officially discovered in 1500, as John fought for a line further west than originally suggested. The pope's legitimacy to decree this global carve-up of 'such islands and lands…as you have discovered or are about to discover' was widely criticised. As Francois I told the Spanish ambassador, 'to pass by and eye, is no title of possession.'[10] Henry VII ignored it too, granting Genoese John Cabot a trade monopoly in lands discovered for the English Crown.

The potential use of immobile cannon at sea was problematic. Pioneered by England at the 1340 Battle of Sluys, 15th-century Venetians installed bombards in war galleys and England designed ships armed with cannon. At Sagres, technology like recoil-absorbing runners was developed. Gold, sugar and slave income doubled Portuguese Crown revenue between 1480 and 1500, transforming Lisbon into a buzzing commercial city, with sugar, spices, slaves, lemons, almonds, sardines, tuna, cod, ivory, dyed cloth and exotic birds. It was at the cutting edge of shipbuilding, navigation, mapmaking and cosmology, with anchor, cannon, armour and arms workshops and after Spain's 1492 Jewish expulsion, more mapmakers, entrepreneurs, mathematicians and astronomers.

Part IV

Connecting Worlds:
Fifteenth To Mid-Seventeenth Century

Chapter 21

A Portuguese Maritime 'Empire'?

A small European country attempting an audacious Indian Ocean commercial take-over is a dramatic story, but any impression that it was the main player is to see Indian Ocean trade through a narrow Portuguese lens. Its gunnery and Reconquista mentality changed the largely peaceful nature of trade, diffused trade hubs and increased trade-volumes, but they never dominated. Imposing themselves on an already rich maritime trading world, they briefly extracted profit, but were one of many traders in a Gujarati, Tamil, Persian, Arab, Chinese and Austronesian world; a newcomer. Their target, spices, was a small volume trade among many. The key to success for any Indian Ocean port had been infrastructure; services, facilities, fair-treatment, hospitality, low customs duties, law and order. Trade officials welcomed merchants of any religion or ethnicity. There has always been shared camaraderie among shipping professionals. Whether Hindu, Muslim, Jew or Christian, they shared common outlooks. Portuguese arrival however, was a dramatic turning point introducing intolerance and violence to Indian Ocean trade and cheaper pepper to Europe.

Prior to Portuguese involvement, Indian pepper growers were paid one or two grams of silver a kilo, rising to 10–15 grams in Alexandria, 14–18 in Venice, and 20–30 by the time it reached London.[1] Despite intelligence gathering, little about Indian Ocean pricing or its toleration, that much of Calicut's Hindu ruler's trade was in Muslim merchant hands was known when converso Vasco de Gama sailed to India.[2] Buckling before Castile's intolerance, in 1496 Manuel expelled Jews and Muslims, some of whom had just fled Spain. Jewish businesses were seized and leased to Florentines, who funded de Gama. His knightly Order of Santiago excluded Jews, Muslims, heathens, money changers, merchants, employees, craftsmen or anyone 'unworthy of our knightly order.' Buying and selling was acceptable only if it weakened the infidel. India's maritime economy was more advanced and productive than Europe's. Portugal's sole lead, in naval warfare, was however, crucial.

Mombasa had overtaken Kilwa and Zanzibar as east Africa's largest port with Malindi as rival. None had defences, because commercial rivalry did not involve war. They were Muslim with strong links to Oman and India. The first Portuguese ashore in 1498, asked what they were doing, answered, 'we come in search of Christians and spices.' A Gujarati navigated de Gama to Calicut. The Portuguese were impressed. The square mile palace area was surrounded with lacquered walls. Muslim traders and shipowners dominated its commerce. Some owned up to 50 ships. The Hindu ruler, Samudra Raja, corrupted by Portuguese to 'Zamorin', wore a bracelet with a large diamond, a pearl necklace, an emerald, rubies, and spat into a gold cup. His trade representatives reportedly laughed at Portuguese trade goods; cloth, bells, sugar, honey and beads. One remarked, 'The poorest merchant from Mecca or any…part of India would give more.' Instead, they had to exchange silver tableware for spices and gems. Without a local navigator, they took almost three months re-crossing the Arabian Sea, returning to Lisbon with less than half the crew and two ships lost, but enough spices to more than pay for the voyage, useful intelligence that there was no strong Indian Ocean maritime power and a letter from the Zamorin to Manuel offering cinnamon, cloves, ginger, pepper and precious stones for 'gold, silver, coral and scarlet cloth.'

The ultimate goal was audacious, given they had only just rounded the Cape, knowledge of the region's geography and politics was hazy and the vast distance from Portugal, whose population was only a million; to take the spice trade from Venice, replace it at Lisbon, and market it to north Europe through Antwerp, link-up with Prester John, assault the 'citadel of the infidels,' Mecca and establish trade bases at Kilwa and Sofala, missed on the first voyage. In 1499, Manuel entitled himself 'Lord of the Conquest, Navigation and Commerce of Ethiopia, Arabia, Persia and India;' quite a mission statement.[3]

Pedro Alvarez Cabral, the second expedition's leader with 13 ships, only six of which reached India, told the Zamorin that he should expel Muslims and sell only through Portuguese. He replied he could not 'expel 4,000 households…who have lived in Calicut as natives…and who had contributed great profit to the kingdom.'[4] A 70-man trade enclave was established. A spice-laden Muslim ship leaving for the Red Sea, spices ultimately Venice-bound, was seized and in retaliation, the Portuguese compound was attacked with 53 killed. Portuguese cannon bombarded Calicut, forcing the Zamorin to flee, while Cabral seized ten more ships. Cochin, Calicut's competitor, allowed them to load spices and establish a fort on an easily-defended island. Calicut's great days were over and many merchants left. A Venetian banker depressingly noted, the 'King of Portugal could call himself the king of money' because he thought Venice's price was 60–100 times that in Calicut due to duties, customs and bribes paid through the Red Sea. The Cape route was longer and riskier but the savings huge. Cabral returned to Lisbon in 1501 with 700 tons of pepper, other cargoes including cinnamon, partly bought, partly seized. Already in 1501 Manuel taunted Venice's ambassador, 'from now on you should send your ships to carry spice from here'. Venetian spice trader, Girolamo Priuli wrote, 'I can clearly see the ruin…of Venice, because without the [spice] trade the city will lose its money, the source of Venice's glory and reputation.' It was natural for Venetians, under Ottoman attack and seeing Black Sea and Egyptian trades disappear, to be depressed. Lisbon, 2,000 miles nearer north European ports, safe from Ottoman attack and overland charges, offered spices far cheaper. Lisbon's first ships with spices arrived at Antwerp in 1501. From 1503 they were large and regular. With Venice's commercial reputation threatened, the Fuggers established a Lisbon branch in 1503. In 1510 Venice surrendered its mainland territories.

De Gama's second expedition in 1502–03 was not only a 'Casa da India', royal venture, with 13 of its 25 ships merchant-owned. A large Calicut-owned ship was seized, its goods and pilot transferred to the Portuguese, who torched it including its passengers. Calicut was again bombarded and its palace plundered. Portuguese writers wrote triumphantly in Reconquista terms about killing Muslims and controlling 'trade in precious stones, pearls and spices.'[5] A 'cartaz' system was developed, a variation of a Mamluk system, ship passports carried on pain of seizure, plunder and sinking, containing ship identification, list of arms, intended route and forbidden cargo; spices, weapons, iron, timber, coir, sulphur and saltpetre, to the Red Sea.[6] The fee was modest, but ships had to call at Portuguese-controlled ports where 6% duty was payable, a deliberate attempt to constrain navigational freedom on a large, complex market. Blocking Persian Gulf and Red Sea choke point entrances was crucial to stop spices reaching Venice. De Gama left in 1503 with two fragile trade posts at Cannanore and Cochin, whose ships were allowed to trade. The expedition returned with 1,700 tons of pepper, similar to Venice's former annual imports.

Francisco Almeida's 1505 expedition of 21 ships and 1,500 men, aimed not just to load spices and return but to stay three years as viceroy, a permanent presence with coastal forts in east Africa, India, Persian Gulf and Red Sea entrances. Kilwa initially agreed to be Portugal's vassal, paying annual gold tribute but failed to follow through so Portugal replaced the sultan with a puppet and a 150-man fort. Mombasa's merchants lived in well-built stone houses full of rich cloths and carpets, which were looted and burned. Sofala, mindful of Kilwa and Mombasa's fate, allowed a fort but then rebelled, which was quashed and an acceptable replacement sheikh from local merchants appointed.

Egyptian and Ottoman revenues were threatened as much as Venice's. The Ottomans thus built a Red Sea fleet and were defeated in 1509 off Diu, southern Gujarat. Alfonso Albuquerque, the next expedition leader wrote to his king in 1510 that he wanted Goa as an easily-defendable port half-way up India's west coast, trading with Arabia, Persia, Sri Lanka, China, east Africa and other Indian ports. Its hinterland had grain, textiles, silks, spices, diamonds, rubies and pearls. It imported rice, horses, slaves, silver, coral and gold for local goldsmiths, with a 4–6% customs duty and shipbuilding of equal quality to Portugal.[7] It was captured in 1510. Malindi, Hoja, Lamu, Brava, Socotra, Muscat and Hormuz were subdued. Killing, burning, cutting off hands, ears and noses was considered routine, no worse than Hansa reprisals on Baltic competitors, Ottoman Mediterranean warfare and nothing compared with Eurasian nomads' towers of skulls or Mughal conquests, resulting in famines in which millions died. But it was shockingly new in the Indian Ocean. Goa became capital of Portugal's *Estado da India*, so-named from the 1560s, headed by Viceroy Albuquerque (1509–1515). He aimed to make it a Christian and Hindu city, thus Muslims were killed, except good-looking women,[8] married to Portuguese men, given land, a house, horse and animals. From 1509 Lisbon merchants settled in Cambay and married locals.

In 1510 pepper and spice trading was opened to Portuguese competition, the fleet financed by Florence's Serringi. Gold remained a royal monopoly. By 1513 Calicut was under control, Goa's fort was strong, Oman's coast raided, Muscat destroyed, Socotra and Hormuz captured and forts built at Hormuz, the Musandam Peninsula, Bukha, Khasab, Limah and Dibba. The island of Socotra was however, too far to prevent ships entering the Red Sea. It was time to attempt to secure that too, Aden as always, its key. Italian Ludovico di Vartherma described Aden as the rendezvous for all ships from India, east Africa and Persia and was impressed by traffic supervision, recording each ship's origin, cargo and timetables and that no ship sailed without paying port dues.[9] Portugal's 1513 attack on it however, failed, but in these early years, Indians were still in shock at its rapid establishment of power. A fleet from Goa cruising around the entrance attacking ships leaving Calicut, was effective. Control of Colombo in 1519 maintained Sri Lankan indirect control through indigenous rulers. The Coromandel coast's Meliapur (Sao Tome) was established to ship south Indian cotton cloth to Southeast Asia; sensible diversification, more voluminous than spices. The effects of blockading the Red Sea on Egypt and Venice was disastrous. Already in 1504, Venetian galleys at Alexandria and Beirut found no spices. In 1515 Venice bought them in Lisbon. Mamluk Egypt, heavily dependent on taxing pepper en route, was fatally weakened and conquered by Ottomans in 1516–17.

Portugal cast its eyes further east, Albuquerque wrote, 'if there were another navigable route, yet all would resort to…[Malacca where]…they would find every different sort of drug and spice…in the world.' Pires wrote, 'no trading port as large as Malacca is known, nor anywhere they deal in such fine and highly prized merchandise.' Malacca was 'made for merchandise…for a thousand leagues on every hand must come to Malacca…whoever is the Lord of Malacca has his hand on the throat of Venice.' It was captured in 1511 although the Sultan, from Bintan in 1521 and Sumatra in 1526, resisted.

But the Portuguese gained little as Muslim traders moved to Johor, Makassar, Pahang, Patani, Bantam and especially north Sumatra's Aceh. Portugal had insufficient ships to block every sea passage. Aceh's traders sailed well south of Sri Lanka to Aden without calling at Gujarati ports. Additionally Malacca was not especially secure, being dependent on rice imports and in danger of attack by Johor and Aceh, receiving Ottoman military equipment.

Albuquerque's original plan to oppose Muslims everywhere was abandoned because he needed Gujarati sailors and pilots, explaining to King Manuel in 1514, their merchants 'have…great trade and the Hindu kings are very closely connected to them, owing to the yearly profit they derive…and…the principal Hindu merchants…rely entirely on Muslim shipping'[10] Muslims were allowed to trade at Malacca due to competing entrepots' success. Early crusading fervour was increasingly subservient to commercial realism, but initial Portuguese actions stimulated militant Islam, formerly unknown. Militant Aceh and Java's Demak conquered neighbouring Hindu kingdoms and attacked Malacca.[11] Meanwhile

Malacca's original sultan's resistance died with him and his son Alaúd-din, established a Johor River base and made peace.

Arriving on Molucca's main island, Neira in 1511, the Portuguese only built a fort in 1529. Spain's Charles V employed Magellan to sail to the Bandas and Moluccas. In contrast to Portugal's organised, strategic, multiple-entry to the Indian Ocean and China Seas, they arrived at Tidore in 1521, loaded cloves, cinnamon and mace, claimed the Moluccas and Philippines, then ignored both, only establishing a base on Cebu in 1565 and Manila in 1570, where they found around 150 Chinese. Ternate, long-time rivals of Tidore, welcomed the Portuguese, but as all islands fell to them, brutal governors achieved a hitherto unthinkable alliance of previously competing islands.

Recognised by Portuguese as the land of Prester John, the Coptic Christian kingdom of Ethiopia became an Ottoman target in the battle for Red Sea control. Having conquered Yemen in 1515 and Egypt in 1516–17, both weakened by the drastic fall in pepper revenue, it began establishing Red Sea strength and in 1528 invaded. Fearing it would link up with hostile Mombasa, the Portuguese destroyed it and forced the Ottomans out in 1541, but within two years the latter occupied Massawa, Ethiopia's Red Sea port and Aden in 1547. Despite Ottoman naval officer and cartographer Piri Re's urging, Sultan Sulayman indulged himself in familiar land-war with Persia, the Balkans, Hungary and later in destructive Mediterranean wars.

Exploratory Portuguese Bay of Bengal ventures with Kling merchants resulted in regular trips from Goa to Chittagong, Pegu and Pulicat in the 1520s. By the 1540s two ships were involved, initially owned or hired by the Crown, later by private traders. In 1535 Portuguese traders got permission to anchor ships at Macao, a formerly uninhabited peninsula, which the Chinese could isolate if necessary, and in 1552 built storage sheds in return for clearing the Pearl River of 'pirates' and an annual tribute, conceded partly to reduce Fujian's illegal trade. The Portuguese sold Chinese silk, Indian cottons and spices to Japan via its Nagasaki enclave from 1543, in return for silver, copper and lacquerware, shipped to China for porcelain. The Japanese created an artificial island, Dejima to limit their influence. It was the most profitable part of Portugal's Asian empire and Fujian's traders cooperated with them.

Japanese had always been suspicious of foreigners. Tenth-century Chinese were limited to one ship every three years and Japanese trader trips abroad were discouraged. In the 12th century 1,600 Chinese families in Hakata traded porcelain, tea, copper coins and books for gold, pearls and lacquer boxes,[12] but the Ming ban encouraged Japan's isolationist tendencies. Tome Pires recognised, 'the king…is not given to trading, nor are his subjects…they have no junks, nor are they seafaring men.' Portuguese opportunistically acted as middle-men, exporting Japan's newly-discovered silver to China and India, and because of civil war, slaves for Indian cloth, European clocks, glass, wine, deer skins and swords.

A continuing Portuguese problem was how to eliminate Gujarati competition at Diu and Cambay and stop spices reaching Venice via the Red Sea. Part of the

Gujarat Sultanate, independent of Delhi since about 1400, Diu's relative isolation and the policies of its ruler, Malik Ayaz's, attracted many merchants, especially Turks. Malik himself was a great trader and shipowner.[13] Weakened by Mughals, in 1534 the Sultan gave Portugal a small port and fishing village, Bassein and Bombay which had a deep-water harbour to which merchants sailing to and from the Red Sea were bound to buy cartazes and pay duty. In 1535, fleeing Mughal advance, he allowed Portugal to build a fort in Diu in return for military support. In 1559 Daman in the Gulf of Cambay was also acquired.

Much trade was unaffected by Portugal's presence. Early 16th-century Pulicat was the Coromandel coast's main port followed by Nagapattinam. After the 1550s Masulipatnam, nominally Golconda's port, overtook them, linking with Southeast Asia's Pasai and Kedah and Bengal's Chatgaon, seemingly due to Persian merchant influence. Two 16th-century Pasai sultans were probably Persian. Late-16th century Persian merchants also influenced Golconda's Court which took a close interest in Masulipatnam.[14] It exported iron, textiles and gems to Aceh and imported benzoin, camphor, pepper and silk.

Indian Ocean ports competed, offering hospitality, infrastructure, security and legal remedy. Portugal's *Estado da India* by contrast administered trade, military posts and naval forces. Headquartered in Lisbon, but run from Goa, it aimed to force control of trade by cartazes, 'a vast protection racket' from Portuguese-created and sponsored violence.[15] By the 1550s, Portugal had 54 forts from Sofala to Macao with Goa central. Its success was due to determination, perseverance, naval superiority and inter-Asian rivalry, exploited by Portugal; between Calicut and Cochin, Mombasa and Malindi, Ternate and Tidore, three Sinhalese kingdoms, Gujarat and Mughals.

As early as 1506, spices produced 27% of Portugal's royal revenue, by 1518, 39%.[16] In the 1520s with half Portugal's revenue coming from re-exports, in 1527 Venice offered to buy Portugal's spice monopoly.[17] Despite restricting Red Sea shipping in the early years, not wishing to aggravate Persians, needed against Ottomans, they instead used Hormuz to heavily tax trade. Thus, spice reappeared in Venice in the 1530s. Portugal faced too many serious problems for ultimate success. The Indian Ocean was so huge, the Portuguese needed more ships and men. About 2,400 mainly young men left in the 16th century. Few returned. By 1600 less than 10,000 able-bodied Europeans and Eurasians served from Mozambique to Macao at any one time. At its height, Portugal had no more than 300 ocean-going ships, impressive for a small country but insufficient for a worldwide empire.[18]

It meant Portuguese were never able to maintain complete control. Furthermore, cartaz centralisation was impossible. Albuquerque for example, gave Cannanore's captain 100 blank ones for distribution. Red Sea cartazes were issued for merchants supporting Portuguese, politically or financially. Goa relied on Gujarati food so allowed ships to sail to Mecca for the Haj. Even if it had taken Aden, in 1534 Ottoman expansion reached Basra, thus Gulf-Mediterranean caravan routes carried pepper via Aleppo to the Levant, then Venice, which built warehouses, customshouses and roads at Split on Dalmatia's coast. Shallow galleys were built for Split-Venice voyages, the crew transferring to sail back. Many Portuguese officials were corrupt and employed locals as agents. Others turned pirate and preyed on Portuguese ships.[19] Lacking men and ships to mount effective annual Red Sea blockades, in 1569 they abandoned it, paving the way for full Red Sea revival. Furthermore, as ever, merchants were mobile.

Calicut was never fully subdued, its fleet inflicting intermittent damage. Portugal's fort at Chaliyam was important for naval supremacy, but this 'pistol at the Zamorin's throat' was captured in 1571. Cambay was little affected by Portuguese. In 1570, Vincent Le Blanc wrote, 'Trade is very faithfully carried out there…retailers… furnish the merchants with dwelling houses…you are provided with women of all ages for your use…all strangers live with the same freedom and liberty as the natives, making open profession of their own religions.'[20] After Hormuz was taken, most merchants moved to Basra or Banda Abbas, which revived, as did Mocha, Jeddah, Cairo and Aleppo. Teixeira described Hormuz's thriving Persian, Portuguese, Armenian, Georgian, Nestorian, Indian and 150 Jewish merchant houses before Portuguese conquest, 'whereupon it began to decline by reason of the oppression and violence of the Portuguese captain and his officers.'

Mughal Sultan Akbar (1556–1605) in 1572 captured Gujarat and visited the Gulf of Cambay in 1573, the first time he had seen the sea, and captured coastal Bengal in 1576. He was uninterested in foreign traders. Mughal mindset was land-based. Prestige depended on land-control. The sea was alien, where power and glory were absent. Numerous Mughal aphorisms made the point; 'merchants who travel by sea are like silly worms clinging to logs,' 'wars by sea are merchants' affairs and of no concern to the prestige of kings', 'God had allotted that unstable element for their big rule.'[21] In this, they were like Ottomans and Safavids, other land-based, self-reliant Asian economies. Subservient peasants were taxed up to half their produce, although Akbar was tolerant of Hindus. Merchants were free to trade, but not encouraged. Officials rotated every three years so maritime expertise was not acquired. With 80% of Mughal imports bullion, Europeans were only charged 3.5% duty on goods and 2% on bullion.[22] Mughals continued conquest south and east. In 1565 Vijayanagara was defeated and its capital destroyed, detrimental for Portuguese who depended on its Hormuz horse trade for its army, velvets and satins for the Court. The familiar pattern of land-based powers damaging superior maritime trade-inspired civilisations was repeated. Vijayanagara managed to survive until 1646. In 1551–52 Ottomans sacked Muscat and besieged Hormuz, Muscat again in 1581. Mombasa was supportive, so the Portuguese took it and built Fort Jesus, paid for by a 6% customs duty.

Portuguese inability to close the Red Sea, meant by the 1560s, Venice imported as much pepper from Alexandria as in the 1490s. Thus, despite the huge quantities shipped to Lisbon, 80% pepper,[23] by mid-century it again flowed through the Red Sea to Egypt and Venice. In 1497 Europeans consumed under two million pounds of pepper annually. By the 1560s six to seven million, an estimated two-thirds via the Red Sea, only a third via the Cape.[24]

In European maritime tradition, each Portuguese sailor had a *caixa*, a crate, size depending on rank, filled with spices, which would establish him for life if he returned to Lisbon. Many 14th-15th century foreign merchants had lived there, but 16th-century Lisbon was one of Europe's great cities with shipbuilding, banking, merchants and mansions. A mid-century observer wrote of merchants in 'Rua Nova dos Mercadores', Merchants' New Street, from all parts of the world.[25] Despite Lisbon's rise, spices did not lead to economic transformation. The Crown was too strong and spent its new-found wealth lavishly. Portuguese merchants became extensions of foreign ones. In 1565, Augsburg trader Konrad Rott and Milanese trader Rovalesca, bought the exclusive European spice distribution at a fixed price. But with Venice resupplied, it was not a monopoly! They were bankrupted by falling prices.

Many traders left Diu after Portuguese capture and it declined, even though Hindu and Jain merchants and bankers remained. Sofala and Hormuz also declined as Muslim traders moved. Cambay silted-up and declined, replaced by Surat, which by 1600 was India's greatest port with Hindus, Jains, Armenians, Jews, Persians, Turks and Portuguese. The Malacca-Cambay connection that impressed Pires was replaced by Aceh-Surat. Portuguese concentrated trade on their ports, especially Goa, which prospered, but Gujarati ports still controlled ten-times that of the Estado, a gap which widened. When challenged it declined. Cochin became Portugal's pepper port but its Raja had no control over pepper-growing areas or routes to ports and traders evaded Portuguese fleets. Like Hansa Baltic rivals, they used smaller, freer ports. East Africa demonstrated the same pattern where Pate and other ports around Lamu developed. Moreover, Gujarat's traders started arming their ships. Portuguese patrols outside Colombo could not control cinnamon export. Most Bay of Bengal trade was conducted by Klings and Persians. In short, it was impossible to impose the cartaz on the vast Indian Ocean with inadequate political and financial power. The Estado was vastly outnumbered, always short of allies, alienating almost everyone. Their directly controlled ports were scattered from Madagascar to Japan. In Goa, Portuguese traders were outnumbered, especially by Gujaratis. Tidore's and Amboyna's forts spread influence thinly. Most Asian trade was carried in Asian ships.

There were other mid-century changes. Portuguese private traders became regional traders in Indian ports, especially supplying cloth to Southeast Asia. As early as Albuquerque's viceroyship, Portuguese intra-Asian private trade was larger and more lucrative than between Goa and Lisbon. Much more cloves, nutmeg and mace were shipped to India and Hormuz than Portugal. While much Lisbon-Goa trade profited the Crown, intra-Asian trade profited thousands of private traders outside the Estado. The Coromandel coast's Miquel Ferreira had a merchant fleet.[26] Crown weakness showed repeatedly. In 1523, 1524 and 1536 Ternate cloves were loaded on private ships because traders paid more than the Crown factor. Crown

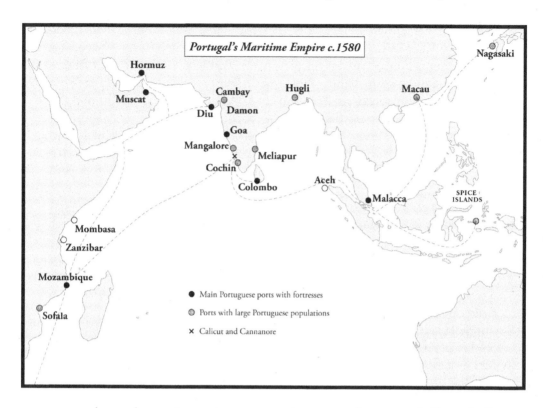

monopoly on cloves, ginger, cinnamon, mace, nutmeg, lacquer and silk gradually eroded. In 1539 clove and nutmeg trading was declared free, except 33.3% to Crown factors at cost price. In 1570 private Portuguese traders were allowed to load Portugal-bound spices at most Indian ports, Hindus at Cochin, Muslims still excluded. In 1575 Ternate was lost. Portuguese had to buy spices in Malacca. The Crown withdrew from intra-Asian trade except Goa-Banda Islands, which survived until the 1580s. In 1585 Omanis swept down the Swahili coast, capturing 20 Portuguese ships and vast booty.

More voluminous trades than spices were rice, salt, cloth, pickled and dried fish, palm wine, fragrant woods and metal wares. In the 1570s, Gujarat's customs revenue was three-times higher than Portuguese Asian revenue.[27] Around 1600, Hormuz hosted only 17% Portuguese and 10% Indo-Portuguese and Indian Christians. Only about 30% of traded mace went to Lisbon, most to China, Southeast Asia, India, Persia, Ottomans and Arabia. The growing trade was Indian cloth to Southeast Asia.

Calculations of Portugal's spice trade profitability vary depending on whether costs of forts, loss of ships and protection are included and what freight rates applied, but a 100–200% return seems to be accepted, variable at different times and although cheaper than overland routes, more ships were lost and more cargo damaged via the Cape. Of all ships sailing from Portugal for the Indian Ocean between 1500 and 1634, 28% were lost at sea,[28] and only 470 returned; less than four a year. Perhaps an average of seven a year sailed from Portugal, each 1,000 tons or so. Many stayed in the Indian Ocean. Portuguese imports as a percentage of European consumption also fluctuated with Portuguese successes and failures and Venetian-Ottoman conflicts. Southeast Asian production increased between four and twelve times between 1514 and 1554.[29] West coast Indian production also increased, due to increasing demand, rising populations and living standards. But as production rose, Portugal's purchases flatlined, declining from 25% to 10% of production.[30] First half-16th-century Portuguese spice imports were about 1,475 tons, declining to about 1,160 in the second half, while 16th century European consumption doubled.

Southeast Asia's maritime hubs continued competing; Aceh, Pasai, Johor and Malacca. Aceh attacked Johor in 1564. Johor felt strong enough to break its Portuguese alliance and besieged Malacca in 1584. The Portuguese counter-attacked, sacking Johor Lama in 1587, but the Sultan moved to a different Johor River location and joined Aceh in another Malacca attack in 1616. Aceh's Islamic fervour made it disruptive, threatening Jambi and Palembang, its slave raids on Kedah and Terengganu, peaking in the early-1600s.

The broad picture is a half century of Portuguese success followed by half a century of Asian trade rearrangement by merchants avoiding Portuguese control. As European spice demand doubled between 1550 and 1600, Portugal responsible for popularity and availability, had insufficient recourses to control it against fierce competition. In Asia, Patricia Risso harshly concludes, 'Portugal made little long-lasting impact beyond stimulating the local markets,'[31] the amount of trade redirected on their ships, small compared to overall Asian trade. Ironically, Spain inadvertently stimulated it more, by new American foods; corn, peanuts and sweet potatoes, contributing to significant population rises in parts of Asia, boosting demand.

Crucially South America also provided silver. Since antiquity, Europe-Asian trade had been based on European bullion export. Discovery of silver in central Europe in the 1460s assisted.[32] West African gold made Portuguese trade in India possible. Japanese silver discoveries in the early-1500s also provided lubrication, shipped to China by illegal Chinese traders and Portuguese. After China lifted the trade ban in 1567, it remained for Japan. Mid-century silver from the Americas was shipped in huge volumes. Adam Smith persuasively argued that the discovery of America and rounding the Cape to Asia were the two most important events in history, crucial that they were almost simultaneous. Without American silver, Portugal's Asian trade opportunities would have been frustrated. Despite this, the Crown faced growing liquidity problems.

The Ottoman-Portugal contrast was highlighted by an anonymous Ottoman 1580s mapmaker. 'It is...strange...that a group of unclean unbelievers have become strong...voyaging from the west to the east, braving the violence of the winds and calamities of the seas, whereas the Ottoman empire which...situated half the distance in comparison...has not made an attempt to conquer [India despite] voyages there yield countless benefits [returning] desirable objects and articles of luxury.'[33] Phrasing like 'violence of the winds and calamities of the seas,' confessed his Turk landlubbing identity. They had little interest in the Indian Ocean, even though they controlled Yemen and Aden after 1538. They were losing interest in the Mediterranean too, their priority to control and tax land and turned to war with Hungary and Persia from whom they seized Georgia and Azerbaijan between 1576 and 1590.

Portugal also developed Brazil, initially to prevent French brazilwood traders from settling. Virtually virgin territory, with no towns and few natives, wiped-out due to low resistance to western diseases, 90–95% of its 1530 exports was brazilwood, a highly-prized dye for Europe's textile industry, very profitable with little investment. With the Azores deforested, Sao Tome small, a colder climate constraining sugar production in northern latitudes, Brazil's forests were by contrast seemingly limitless, fuel to produce large sugar volumes with west African slave-labour available. Its first sugar mill was established in 1530. By 1570 there were 60, by 1583, 130, by 1610, 240,[34] making it Europe's richest colony. Planters' tables were covered with silver and porcelain. Women wore jewels and precious fabrics. One Portuguese sugar planter ate his meals listening to an orchestra of 30 beautiful female slaves.[35]

Brazil's first sugar shipment to Lisbon undercut Madeira's prices, which concentrated instead on wine exports. By 1550, Brazil produced over 2,200 tons a year. Manufactured goods, textiles, horses and trinkets were exchanged in the Congo and increasingly Angola after Luanda's foundation in 1575 for about 10–15,000 slaves a year,[36] shipped to Brazil. In Asia, Portugal concentrated on low-volume, high-priced spices, in Brazil high-volume, low-priced sugar, brazilwood and timber. Unlike the Crown's initial Indian Ocean role, it took a back seat, selling territories to entrepreneurs, success probably dependent on this policy. Sugar's European popularity was 'largely a Portuguese achievement,'[37] Brazil a more successful venture, which by 1600 was the world's leading sugar producer. Portugal's empire consisted of coasts, harbours and fortified ports and in Brazil, sugar plantations. Spain's empire was vast lands it could not use, develop, administer, defend or supply, of mines and ranches. Apart from bullion convoys and limited inter-colonial trade, it turned its back on the sea, its main towns inland.

Portugal's role in the Jewish diaspora should not be forgotten. Dominant in Portuguese trade when its Inquisition was created in 1536, they either converted or emigrated to the Netherlands, France, England, north Italy, Sicily, Crete, Ottoman lands and Spanish America. 'Portuguese' became synonymous with converso, or 'New Christian'. In 1548 Livorno invited Jews and conversos to settle. By 1553 about 150 families lived in Ancona, trading in the eastern Mediterranean. They were important in Brazil's sugar production and export when the Dutch took over much Portuguese territory in the 1620s. (Chapter 30) From there they spread to the Caribbean which is described in subsequent chapters.

Chapter 22

The Netherlands, England and the Baltic

I n northern Europe the Reformation freed intellects with more open, rational beliefs, appealing to educated, trading, free-thinking merchants and artisans. In eastern grain lands however, there was no free movement, nor freethought. As western European grain demand rose, Polish, Hungarian and Bohemian nobles turned free peasants into estate-serfs, while the Inquisition and French nobility kept southern Europe Catholic, except for Protestant pockets, notably La Rochelle. Antwerp was north Europe's great port from about 1480 to 1560, assisted by the flight of Mediterranean capital and expertise. Financiers like the Fuggers, Weslers, Hochstetters and Affaitade had agents there. In 1531, it built a new Bourse. Galleries surrounded a courtyard with an upper floor for art, the model for London's Royal Exchange and Amsterdam's Bourse (Beurs).[1] On its walls was carved, 'for the use of merchants of all nations and tongues.'[2] In the 1540s, commodity prices and exchange rates, information previously between merchants, were published, reflecting a more voluminous, transparent market, increasing certainty in business decisions.[3]

The Netherlands' 17 provinces included today's Holland, Belgium, Luxembourg and some adjacent French and German lands. Within it, Flanders and Brabant had been north Europe's wealthiest provinces since the 12th century. Castile's merino wool exports, mainly from Bilbao, gradually replaced English wool. In 1500 almost half England's revenue was from taxes on foreign trade. Henry VIII's (1509–1547) two main ministers were contrasts. Cardinal Wolsey, 'the most disappointing man who ever held great power in England',[4] never grasped trade's importance, made no attempt to exploit it, made enemies of Spain and France and spent the reserves. Thomas Cromwell after 1533 by contrast, encouraged trade. The Merchant Adventurers were the main company selling cloth in Antwerp, with 3–4,000 English merchants concentrated around its residence. It occupied the same privileged position in cloth as the Company of Staplers had done for nearly 200 years in wool, but different as at Calais they were removed from most English merchants at Antwerp, from which Merchant Adventurers claimed descent.[5] The 1540 Navigation Act confined foreigners' privileges to those using English ships, encouraging them to England. The break with Rome ended English merchant prosperity in Spain. The end of Venice's fleets further encouraged English dependence on Antwerp. In Geoffrey Elton's words, 'English trade put nearly all its eggs in the Antwerp basket', although Cromwell, close with the Merchant Adventurers, had far-reaching plans to exploit England's position as main cloth supplier to dependent Antwerp, intending to transfer the staple to London, selling at home to all-comers.[6] His fall meant the plans were abandoned and purposeful government lost. During Henry's reign however, coastal maps were made, dockyards established at Deptford, Woolwich and Chatham and in 1546 a Navy Board and Trinity House were established, responsible for lighthouses and coastal buoys.

The Merchant Adventurers and growing Antwerp dependency helped London increase its cloth export-share from under 50% in 1500 to nearly 90% of export value in the 1540s.[7] Exports of 50,000 lengths a year in the 1480s rose to 133,000 by 1550, the boom ending in 1552. There were 300–400 Merchant Adventurers and were managed by 40–50. Merchants made their own decisions, but shipped jointly. It oversaw general principles and protected merchants against interlopers. The organisation was not adventurous, as the name suggests, but conducted a safe, secure trade in a mature market, the shortest sea route from London, enjoying Antwerp's judicial immunities and tax reliefs, similar to the Hansa in England, making 20–25% profits. Many imports also came via Antwerp; Spanish iron, oil and soap, Netherlands' linens, south German fustians, Gascon and Iberian wine, pepper, ginger and sugar. Antwerp dependency was accentuated with the 1558 loss of Calais and Hansa resistance to English merchants in the Baltic. Early Tudor monarchs could not get concessions equivalent to the Steelyard's, despite 25% of cloth exports, all finished and dyed, going to the Baltic, for which demand increased.[8] Merchant Adventurer strength destroyed rivals at Southampton, previously the main Italian and Spanish trade port.

Antwerp handled 75% of Netherland's exports, 250,000 tons annually, four-times London's, serviced by outports, Middelburg, Arnemuiden, Bergen op Zoom and Sluys, where ships were lightened and goods transhipped, 345 in Arnemuiden in 1550.[9] Antwerp also dominated Portugal's sugar and spices and Castile's wool imports. By the 1550s, half Castile's exports, including silver and other colonial produce, went there.

After closure of the Black Sea, some east European grain exports switched to the Baltic, increasing competition. The 1397 Kalmar Union united Scandinavia under Denmark, but Hansa prosperity depended on weak kings. Swedes however, were also nationalistic and ambitious. The Hansa won a 1509–1512 Hansa-Denmark war. Denmark got theoretical leverage when Christian II (r. 1514–1523) used his Hapsburg wife's connections to get the Sound blockade relaxed. But his vision of Sound trade control, favouring the Dutch, whose sovereign was also a Hapsburg, was unacceptable to the Hansa, who encouraged a Swedish uprising while invading Denmark, forcing Christian into exile. But his successor, Frederick II (r. 1524–33) and Sweden's Gustav I (r. 1523–60) allowed foreigners Baltic access. Even kings owing their thrones to Lubeck, refused to be mere puppets.

Lubeck blocked the Sound again in 1532–34 but Danzig depended on Dutch shipping and refused support. Its choice was reliance on regulated, expensive Hansa ships and ports or free-trade prosperity, meaning mainly Dutch merchants, although English merchants were still tenaciously trying. Nor could Lubeck contain Riga and Reval (Tallin). Even Hamburg secretly came to terms with the Dutch in 1534.

Hansa cohesion eroded and were defeated by Sweden and Denmark in 1535. By this time, Dutch reliance on Baltic trade, especially Polish, Prussian and Livonian grain, was so great that interruption could lead to famine and social disruption. Denmark closed the Sound to Dutch ships in 1542, but Charles V got them exempted from Sound Tolls at the 1544 Peace of Speyer. From seeming triumph in 1524 when Christian II had been evicted and Sweden detached from Danish union, the Hansa was losing control and Sweden became a potential competitor. Moreover, Muscovy coveted a Baltic port. With Europe's largest commercial fleet, Amsterdam's merchants concentrated on the Baltic, lived there, especially Danzig, its main grain port, semi-autonomous within the Polish kingdom, in Dutch-style buildings of imported bricks, organising trade-agreements, advancing credit, stimulating trade and local shipbuilding.

The Hansa exclusively used the Lubeck-Hamburg canal. Dutch merchants used the longer, cheaper route through the Danish Sound. Between 1500 and the 1560s, Baltic trade to north Europe grew six-fold with Danzig, Riga and Reval especially benefiting, the latter for timber, hemp and tar. Elbing and Konigsberg grew more modestly, also benefiting from Hansa decline. The Sound Toll recorded under 1,000 ships annually between 1500 and 1540 but by the 1560s nearly 3,380, about 40% Dutch, and by 1590 over 5,000. Other studies estimate the Dutch fleet more than quadrupled between 1500 and 1567.[10] The Hansa could not control this huge increase as each Baltic region and port pursued its own interests.

Charles V taxed the Netherlands heavily, but was born there, spoke Flemish, and helped get exemption from Sound Tolls in 1544, even if some subjects were heretics. But successor Philip II didn't understand his wealthiest territory or its independent people whose dykes, dams, canals and drains were governed by local boards. He centralised them with French-speaking bureaucrats in Brussels and increased taxes for wars unrelated to them. Moreover, the seven northern provinces, Holland, Zeeland, Gelderland, Overijssel, Friesland, Utrecht and Groningen, previously poor cousins of urbanised Flanders and Brabant, albeit also with major rivers flowing deep into Europe, were Protestant, the southern provinces divided. The northern provinces concentrated on Baltic grain, timber, honey, pitch, tar, copper, iron, salted herring and Bergen's salted cod, buying directly from producers. They took textiles, salt, wine and sometimes were inter-Baltic carriers. The best hydraulic engineers, they reclaimed land from the sea, innovatively rotating crops, enabling higher production. A richer, freer peasantry concentrated on meat, milk, butter and cheese production, vegetables and industrial produce like hops, flax and hemp. Uniquely, they used a dense network of interlinked canals moving people, industrial and agricultural produce cheaply. Specialisation enhanced productivity in rural and urban economies. But Philip equated Protestantism with rebellion and responded with the Inquisition, a futile attempt to impose religious belief on free-thinkers, damaging for wealth-creating Netherlands' trade and England's dependence on it.

Philip attacked north Europe's economic heart, shaking Antwerp's prosperity. William, Prince of Orange (1553–84), Philip's 1560 Governor-General

(Stadtholder) told the Council of State that he remained Catholic, but did not approve Catholicism's imposition on others and became leader of the resistance. In 1568 Philip sent the Duke of Alva to suppress it, instructing him, 'the towns must be punished for their rebelliousness with the loss of their privileges, everyone must be made to live in constant fear.' Alva, 'Butcher of Flanders', followed these counter-productive orders, but by 1572, most of Holland and Zeeland was independent. These were not passive Castilian peasants but a confident emerging nation, typified by its successful ports, industrious merchants and artisans. In the 1560s, Holland alone had 1,800 seagoing ships including 400 new herring 'buss', used for fishing and on-board herring processing, the earliest fish factory ship.

Meanwhile in England, Henry VIII's wars led to debt and coinage debasement to half its previous value. Sir Thomas Gresham (1519–79), son of a leading Mercer and Lord Mayor of London, was the Mercer representative in Antwerp and in 1551 the Crown's financial agent, a time when large debts were owed to Antwerp's bankers. England's credit was low, trade and industry demoralised and commercial relations dislocated. Familiar with Antwerp, its Bourse, new streets, houses and squares reflecting new prosperity, anxious about England's dependency, Gresham financed and in 1566 laid the first stone of London's Royal Exchange. His remedy for the financial crisis in Edward's, Mary's and Elizabeth's first years was to use the Merchant Adventurers to loan money in return for cloth monopoly shipments to the Netherlands and Germany. That meant suppressing the Hansa, for centuries prominent in English trade, bringing most Baltic produce, taking cloth to Bruges and Antwerp, about 20,000 pieces in 1509–10, 44,000 in 1549. In 1547 Henry had negotiated with Hansa merchants to supply masts, cordage, pitch and flax, but its privileges were suspended in 1552 to force all cloth export, through the Merchant Adventurers. Briefly restored in 1554 by Mary, they were, following Gresham's advice, restricted by her and revoked by Elizabeth in 1558. In 1555 the Merchant Adventurers persuaded the City to exclude Hansa merchants from Blackwell Hall, where cloth was sold, while making large loans to the government. Thus the Hansa lost control of English Baltic exports, over 20,000 pieces, previously only 40% controlled by English merchants. After the 1570 Peace of Speyer, Elizabeth further reduced Hansa privileges. Once again, with royal support of English merchants, albeit a privileged group, the Hansa crumbled.

In 1557, cloth export duty, 2s 9d for foreigners, 1s 2d for English and 1s for Hansa merchants was made 14s 6d for foreigners, 6s 8d for English and Hansa. That displaced the Company of Staplers from their fiscal and commercial pre-eminence.[11] However, vesting so much power with the Merchant Adventurers had disadvantages. As Northumberland wrote to Cecil in 1552, government and trading 'are of two natures' and while apparently advantageous to government it 'must be weighed with other consequences.'[12] The Netherlands' cloth industry, weakened by having to rely on local and Spanish wool, restricted English cloth to unfinished imports in order to bolster its own finishing industry, weakening English finishing and dyeing, where much of the value lay. Several English statutes since 1487 stipulated it should be finished before export, but licences were granted to circumvent them. The Merchant Adventurers' narrow remit meant it abetted foreign rather than the national interest, yet became England's main agency of trade tax, loaning the government money, essentially the Bank of England's role after 1694, thus part of the government's financial organisation. Policy was not governed by economic theory but desperate need for cash as Elizabeth sold much Crown land.

Abandoning Antwerp in 1564, due to the Dutch Revolt, the Merchant Adventurers set-up in Emden, en route to Cologne and Frankfurt, then Hamburg on a 10-year lease and was granted privileges; a serious breach of Hansa monopoly. Lease renewal was denied under pressure from other Hansa ports. They instead used Stade, attempting to prevent other English merchants trading in Germany. Historian George Unwin concluded the triumph of excluding the Hansa, establishing monopoly trading companies (Chapters 24 and 25) were at England's commercial expense, leading to depression, although some cloth was carried by merchants outside the monopoly to Dutch and German ports, especially Amsterdam. Undoubtedly correct that monopoly was inefficient and favoured a few privileged merchants over the hard-working entrepreneurial majority, it is difficult to envisage what else Gresham could have advised in the circumstances. The fault was in subsequent decades, letting monopoly become a convenient revenue-raising prop, extendable to many industries. (Chapters 27 and 28)

England's active 1350s–1450s shipping suffered after the War of the Roses. The 1560 investigation into defence resources found only 50,000 tons of English-owned ships, only a few over 100 tons. It depended on Antwerp. War with France in 1562 and its privateers worsened the situation. The 1560s were probably English merchant shipping's nadir. In 1562, 1,192 Dutch ships entered the Baltic, only 51 English.[13] First-half 16th-century Sound Toll registers note only two over 100 tons.[14] In 1572, England had only 14 ships over 200 tons. But with Antwerp destabilised, English merchants explored Mediterranean and African trade opportunities, heralding shipbuilding expansion. Between 1571 and 1576, over 51 ships over 100 tons were built and in 1577 England had at least 130, in 1582 about 177, many of which were London-owned with a significant Baltic trade share, 30% in 1567, 50% in 1576.[15] Two other significant mid-century English developments were first, no meat was to be eaten on Wednesdays, Fridays and Saturdays, fuelling fisheries, some fish exported. Second, Newcastle's coal shipments, 35,300 tons in 1549–50 increased to 140,700 tons in 1597–98.[16]

Baltic grain export growth to satisfy Europe's growing population meant Danzig's 166 ship calls in 1530 rose to 699 by 1583. Sound Toll registers show Hansa and Dutch competing until mid-century, then Hansa numbers crashing. Some ships entered in ballast, as salt, herring, cloth and wine imports did not grow as fast, although as Polish-Lithuanian land-owners became wealthy, they also demanded spices, quality textiles, sugar and manufactured goods. Poland's whole economy was directed at Danzig. Its merchants bought the harvest and sold it there to foreign buyers, almost 8,000 tons in 1562. In the north Baltic, Sweden's Gustav I founded Helsinki in 1550 for Finland's natural resources, rivalling Hansa's Reval. Timber to build growing ship numbers, increased north Baltic volumes, leading to competition between Poland, Muscovy and Sweden for control of Riga, Reval and Narva and inland routes to grain and timber-producing hinterlands, breaking Hansa control there too.

English cloth exports increased 150% between 1500 and 1550, then declined in the mid-century crisis Gresham addressed. Needing new markets, apart from the Mediterranean and west Africa, the idea of finding shorter routes to Asia had its roots in Seville's merchant enclave, the only Englishmen who knew what was happening in the Americas. One, Robert Thorne, an early propagandist for overseas expansion, after Magellan's 1525 discovery of the eponymous Straits to Asia, thought England might try via the Arctic. He died disappointed in 1532, but the idea fermented[17] until Hugh Willoughby and Richard Chancellor in 1553 attempted a northeast passage, financed by 240 London merchants,[18] because it was, 'inconvenient that...commodities of England, especially cloth, should so depend upon the Low Countries and Spain.'[19] Chancellor carried Edward VI's letter extolling trade's mutual economic benefits and capacity to form friendships, a strategy Elizabeth later employed. Chancellor did not find Asia but direct access to Muscovy's products, previously only available from Baltic ports, cordage, tallow, whale blubber, wax, flax, hemp, walrus teeth, timber and numerous furs; Arctic squirrel, hare, marten, ermine, sable, beaver, wolf, bear and lynx. Ivan III had expanded east to source furs and west to Novgorod and in 1492 adopted the title 'sovereign of all Russia' and with the Byzantine empire gone, Czar (Caesar), turning Muscovy's 15,000 square kilometres into 600,000. Ivan IV continued expansion and grasped Chancellor's offer, promising English merchant trade privileges and sought western technical help. England's joint-stock Muscovy Company was formed in 1555.

Ivan wanted a Livonian port. Muscovy had earlier probed west, but its 1558 conquest of Narva led Ivan's enemies to name him 'the Terrible.'[20] Sweden annexed northern Livonia including Reval and established a staple at Viborg. Poland took Riga and Courland. Denmark took Lithuania. Wars for control of Riga, Reval, Narva and their hinterlands between varying coalitions of Muscovy, Sweden, Denmark, Lubeck and Poland-Lithuania continued to 1583. Essentially, ports nominally under the Polish-Lithuanian Commonwealth formed in 1569, were taken by aggressive new powers, Sweden and Muscovy. The latter also fought for a Crimean outlet, whose Tatars looted and burned Moscow in 1571, before defeat in 1572.

Muscovy's control of Narva meant diverting its exports from Swedish Reval, whose 98 shipments of flax, hemp, wax, tallow, hides, furs and skins passing the Sound in 1566 declined to 76 in 1567 and 59 in 1568. By the mid-1560s, 95% of Baltic tallow and 81% of Baltic hides came from Muscovite Narva, which thrived. Muscovy and Poland-Lithuania had the best grain lands, but Poland-Lithuania was weak, decentralised, and lacked a strong army. The Peace of Stettin allowed Danes to levy Sound Tolls and in 1574 Frederick II (1559–88) built Elsinore castle, famous as the setting for Shakespeare's *Hamlet*, overlooking the Sound, to help ensure payment. By 1577 most of Livonia, except Riga and Reval, was controlled by Ivan,[21] but Sweden recaptured Narva in 1581. Reval revived and Narva's exports declined. Muscovy founded Archangel, as her alternate, inferior 'window on the west' in 1584, close to where Chancellor had landed, her main export port, including about 200,000 furs a year. Even spices, silk and pepper from overland routes were loaded on English ships in Archangel.

In the early-1600s during Muscovy's political turmoil, it lost Novgorod to Sweden and Smolensk to Poland, but never forgot controlling Narva. It recovered economically by exploiting Siberia's furs, especially sable, where some peasants moved to escape slave raiding. Moving further east they reached the Bering Sea by 1648.[22] When a Russian reached Beijing in 1617, the Ming considered him an unimportant tribute-bearer. In 1652 the Czar sent an ambassador to report on China's trade possibilities. In contrast, they discovered huge potential. Archangel's viability, despite only open in summer, emphasised the need for a Baltic port. Meanwhile, sparsely-populated Sweden wanted to develop a more substantial North Sea port, its only outlet, Alvsborg. The south and west coasts of modern Sweden were Danish-controlled and Denmark hoped to recover the rest, capturing Alvsborg in 1563, only returning it after the Nordic Seven Years War (1563–1570) for a substantial ransom.

Meanwhile in 1577 Danzig attacked Elbing whose 1590s imports consisted of over 40% English cloth. The monopoly Eastland Company's formation in 1579 eliminated inter-English Baltic competition. Its 65 members' debts were checked and convoy sailing times specified. Like the Merchant Adventurers, it was 'regulated', not joint-stock, the model for distant trade with more commercial risk. Between 1579 and 1600 cloth exports to the Baltic increased four-fold, mainly in English ships, 80–90% of England's Baltic exports, as Holland and Zeeland fought most intensely against Spain.[23] England concentrated on Elbing, Prussia's main export port, rather than Hanseatic Danzig, which wanted to free its restrictions. Dutch vessels returned strongly in the 1590s but English ships had established a foothold. Would Baltic cloth exports have risen so much without the monopoly company? Some Ipswich clothiers refused admittance, sent a factor who brought back orders which were exported in return for hemp, flax and potash. When the Eastland Company proceeded against them, they tried to show the untapped demand that monopoly missed and free trade found. Frustrated, thereafter Suffolk's cloth trade steadily declined.[24]

Granting monopolies for a price, a royal prerogative to protect struggling or new industries, was considered appropriate to counter the prevalence of privateering and Hansa hostility, even though monopoly tended to raise prices. Industrial monopolies however, coal, soap, salt, starch, iron, leather, books, wine, fruit, playing cards, obtainable only with courtier influence, had become more revenue-raising than economic regulation.[25] Unpopular, they multiplied so much that Parliament's 1601 list of those granted since the last, led one MP to ask, 'Is not bread there?' Elizabeth was forced to revoke many. Continuing grievances about them helped mould English 17th-century economic thought. The 1580s-90s economic depression, especially cloth exports to the Netherlands, caused hardship in manufacturing areas. Raleigh in 1593 said Newcastle's merchants 'lay still from fear' as 'our trade decays every day.'[26] Cecil was aware of Merchant Adventurer monopoly disadvantages and after 1586 thought all restrictions accumulating since 1564 should be removed, including Steelyard restoration and cloth export opened to all English merchants,[27] but entrenched interests prevailed. Selling monopolies raised money for a desperate Crown.

In the Netherlands, the 1579 Union of Utrecht declared the northern provinces independent, each sovereign, raising their own taxes. The States General could act only with unanimous agreement. In practice, Amsterdam dominated. Two de facto states, the Spanish Netherlands and the Dutch Republic squared off. Spanish troops conquered Antwerp in 1585, adding it to Ghent and Bruges. The Dutch closed the Scheldt, severing Antwerp from the sea. Repression and economic collapse led to the exodus of about 150,000 people, 10% of Flanders' and Brabant's population, to the Dutch Republic including merchants, bankers, Jews with capital, workers in textile, printing, publishing and sugar refining. Antwerp which had 80% of pre-revolt exports against Amsterdam's 4%,[28] declined immediately. Its population halved to 42,000 between 1583 and 1589 with similar declines in Bruges and Ghent, while Middelburg's and Leiden's population by 1609 trebled,[29] a new focus for lighter, brighter 'New Draperies'. Thirty thousand settled in Amsterdam, quickly transformed into north Europe's most important port, centre of international payments, grain futures contracts, marine insurance, commodity price and exchange rate information. Antwerp merchant Jacques de la Faille, moving there in 1594 said, 'Here is Antwerp itself changed into Amsterdam', but in addition, Amsterdam had many shipowners.

Leuven University weakened as the Inquisition curtailed free thought. In the northern provinces, universities were founded in Leiden (1575), Franeker (1585), Harderwijk (1600), Groningen (1614) and Utrecht (1634), attracting foreign students and academics. Publishers flourished as religious, philosophical and scientific tracts were printed and exported. The Dutch Republic became Europe's leading commercial and industrial power, taking 70% of English cloth for finishing, dyeing and continental distribution. Baltic ports took 11%, finished and dyed, then the Levant, France and Russia, 80% controlled by London merchants.

England's dangerous reliance on Antwerp's convenient proximity for imports and exports ended. It had to diversify. Its intense Baltic and Mediterranean commercial drive accelerated.[30] Immigrants from Brabant and Flanders, encouraged by Cecil, set up East Anglia's 'New Draperies', lighter cloths for southern Europe, as Spanish and Italian cloth industries declined. By 1590 immigrant artisans comprised perhaps a third of Norwich's population.[31] They and Italian-origin artisans from the 1560s contributed to a growing economy. Dutch ports replaced Antwerp's Baltic and Ottoman exports. England's exports to the east Mediterranean increased but after 1598, its Baltic exports declined due to Dutch competition and cheaper Silesian cloth. Most English 16th-century Baltic trade was conducted via London, but Hull inherited York's former trade, as Ouse navigation in large ships was impossible. Newcastle, Ipswich, Lynn and Yarmouth were also involved. Two of Whitby's ships are recorded paying the Sound Toll. It had a fishing fleet and exported herring and butter, both requiring imported salt.

Late 15th-century Prussian grain exports, about 22,000 tons, quadrupled to 88,000 in the late-16th, catapulting in 1618–19 to about 220,000, 80% through Danzig, plus timber, fur, tar, hemp, ash for glass making, wax and amber,[32] averaging about 1,500 annual ship-calls, up from 699 in 1583. The Dutch shipped grain to Lisbon, even Venice in the 1590s, as famine ravaged southern Europe, denied Black Sea grain, exchanged for Mediterranean produce demanded in the Baltic. War with Spain, far from hindering Dutch economic expansion, inspired it. The skills influx, Calvinist certainty, ship and commodity-trading mentality made them resist Spanish oppression and expand trade. Groups of investors built, owned, chartered and freighted ships. Often the master was part-owner, directly involved in the cargo sale. A mid-17th century writer claimed 99% were operated in these 'rederijj'.[33] Needing Baltic grain and fish, the Dutch controlled an increasing share. Growing sugar volumes supported 22 refineries by 1622, initially fuelled by local peat, increasingly by Newcastle coal. Raleigh thought the Dutch wanted to control 'the whole trade and shipping of Christendom.' New warehouses, town halls and merchant houses on newly dug canals were built.

Because of increasing Baltic volumes, Lubeck still maintained some intra-Baltic routes but little long-haul trade. Hamburg which allowed Protestants from Antwerp and Portuguese conversos to settle, rapidly outgrew it. Amsterdam and London grew faster than both. While fighting Spain, the confident Dutch traded with it. In 1584, 93 Dutch ships left Spanish ports for the Baltic against 51 Hansa ships but in 1585 Philip embargoed Dutch ships. The Hansa benefited, but Spain struggled to provision itself and lifted the embargo in 1594, when the Dutch sent 101 ships, 169 in 1595. Embargoed again in 1598, another mistake, the Dutch were incentivised to seek <u>direct</u> access to Spain's colonial goods. Meanwhile industries grew; brewing, shipbuilding, sailcloth, fishing, ropes, barrels, salt refining and cloth manufacture. The Dutch also dominated whaling, Muscovy's Archangel trade and North Sea herrings, 'the mother of all commerce.' In England in 1598 the Steelyard closed and by 1600, the Hansa only had 3–4% of English trade.[34] European commercial and naval expansion meant Baltic timber, hemp, Swedish copper and iron were increasingly needed, exchanged for wine, salt and cloth.

The Dutch pulled ahead in the 1590s because of more and better ships as English merchants were excluded from Iberian ports. Holland's 1,800 ships of the 1560s increased to about 9,000 by 1580, astonishing growth, fuelled further around 1595, after years of experimenting, by fluytschips, (fluyts) purely commercial vessels. Pine not oak-built, simply-rigged, lighter, longer, with flatter keels ideal for shallow Baltic ports and without gun platforms, they carried more cargo and had lower building and maintenance costs and smaller crews. Protection costs were eliminated, enabling lower freight rates, helping Dutch cloth exports to the Baltic, where over 400-tonners were used, some adapted for long mast trees. Ships in dangerous Mediterranean trades were more heavily built, also in standard design and size, mass-produced with timber cut to standard dimensions with saws powered by windmills, increasing shipbuilding capacity. As Charles Boxer writes, Dutch success was because of the 'remarkable economic development of the two maritime provinces of Holland and Zeeland, the agricultural wealth of the remaining five provinces being of scant importance by comparison.'[35] They tightened their grip on cloth, sugar, and spice exports to Poland, Russia and Ducal Prussia, with almost 80% of Baltic trade at English and Hansa expense, 70–80% of Baltic grain exports in Dutch ships, feeding over half a million people, a major technical, logistical and commercial accomplishment, enabling more specialised production and efficient maritime trade, which Jan de Vries thinks was the main source of productivity growth before the Industrial Revolution,[36] although estimated agricultural output between 1510 and 1650 also increased by 150%.[37]

Emigrants to Holland and Zeeland had relatives and business associates throughout Europe from the Baltic to the Levant, stimulating trade especially in Amsterdam. In 1596 its town council boasted, 'this country in merchant marine and shipbuilding is so much more advanced than the kingdoms of France and England that is scarcely possible to make a comparison.'[38] The fluyt design gave impetus to Copenhagen, Stockholm, Danzig and Riga shipyards, where Dutch merchants established linseed oil and saw mills. Inspired, Riga's merchants invested in tanneries, foundries and shipbuilding. The Dutch offered Europe's lowest freight rates and largest merchant marine, a third lower than English in peacetime.[39] Northeast Baltic competition between Narva and Reval continued but despite increasing overall volumes, Narva's were lower than their 1560s zenith, despite squirrel pelts peaking at 177,000 and 13,000 other furs in 1605.[40]

Increasing Sound dues emboldened Denmark to attempt political hegemony. It again attacked Sweden, banned Dutch shipping to it and raised the Sound dues. Sweden's Gustavus Adolphus made some gains in Muscovy, but lost Alvsborg. The Dutch allied with the Hansa and Sweden to quell Denmark's ambitions. Having inspired Sweden's rise, Dutch merchants entrenched themselves in its trade and industry from the 1580s, importing copper and iron from Stockholm to Amsterdam, to build the arms and ammunitions industry needed to counter Spain. The struggle for Baltic trade was not settled. Every country and region fought for what it considered its share, switching alliances when greater threats appeared. The Dutch, formerly poor neighbours of the rich southern provinces, were supreme in agriculture, fishing and industry, based on windmill power. Its new, efficient ships enabled trade domination. All were products of the entrepreneurship of problem-solving ports with Amsterdam pre-eminent, linking the Baltic to Iberia.

Chapter 23

Sixteenth-Century Mediterranean Setbacks

Reversing previous centuries of Mediterranean trade resurgence based on Egypt and north Italian ports, the 16th-century Mediterranean's tone was set at each end, Castile and the Ottoman empire by religious bigotry, not trade. Castile's merino wool exported to European markets made it wealthy, but Reconquista ideology skewed its path in a different direction from Portugal and Catalonia-Aragon. Like the Portuguese, military-religious orders involved in Reconquista imbued them with holy intent. But unlike Portugal which turned to the sea, power and prestige in Castile derived from land and booty from war, not trade or manual labour. Sheep migration from summer pastures in the north to winter pastures in the south and back was Castile's rhythm of life. Ports bore the brunt of taxation and had no political influence, which rested with the 'Mesta', the powerful association of sheep holders, controlled by about 25 of the largest landowners. The nobility and Church were tax-exempt. Commercial life increasingly suffered.

Aragon by contrast, and main port Barcelona, despite the Black Death and subsequent plague outbreaks, was the third-largest Levant spice trader. Its banks lent commercially. Valencia had a maritime commercial law. The maritime insurance principle of General Average was contained in the 1494 Law Code. General Average divides damages in maritime accidents, encapsulating the compromises involved in maritime society. In 1488 a notary recorded 740 chartering contracts and tax records and 559 calls at Valencia, still 420 in 1494,[1] declining but not collapsing. However, since Castilian Alfonso the Magnanimous inherited Aragon in 1416, his military and naval concentration and heavy taxation weakened the economy and sapped Catalan merchant energy, gradually replaced by Genoese who dominated Barcelona's trade and took-over Naples' finances. When Ferdinand of Aragon, Sicily, Naples and Sardinia and Isabella of Castile united kingdoms in 1469, agricultural, conservative Castilian values predominated, setting the tone for subsequent expansion. In the late-15th century Aragon collapsed in social revolution.[2] Had it not suffered recurring plague outbreaks, or inheritance by Alfonso, then Spanish 'union', really a take-over, might have had more of a Catalan, maritime merchant-quality. Castilian officials replaced Aragonese in Mediterranean lands. Catalan cloth exports to Sicily and Sardinia declined as Genoese textiles flooded her market, while Ragusan merchants shipped in Sicilian wheat and salt.

Muslim Granada exported silk, leather, arms, ceramics, jewellery, fruits, nuts, olives and almonds, the resulting wealth enabling it to delay conquest. With Ottoman east Mediterranean advance, Ferdinand was keen to eliminate Islam's bridgehead. Thus Castile finally entered Muslim Gibraltar in 1462 and Granada in 1492. There had been a small Jewish exodus after the 1391 massacre. Subsequent proselytising fervour and the Inquisition, established in 1478, targeted moriscos and conversos, suspected of adhering to Islam and Judaism respectively. In 1492 after Grenada was taken, Jews, and in 1502 all non-Christians, were expelled, another continental 'own goal' with huge economic cost, hollowing-out Spain from the start. Jews were also excluded from Aragonese Sicily in 1492. Senior bankers and officials reported the economic damage resulting from losing their economic activity,[3] but in vain.

In Christian eyes, 'Reconquista' was taking back unjustly conquered lands. But North Africa had also been Christian. The royal secretary wrote, 'it looks as if God wishes to give your Highnesses these African kingdoms.' Melilla was taken in 1497 and between 1505 and 1510 a fleet from Malaga captured Mers el Kebir, Oran, Mostaganem, Tlemcen, Tenes and the Penon, a small island off Algiers. Charles V hoped to make it a Catalan shipping centre, forcing Venetian galleys to call there. Doubling customs dues in 1516 scuppered that. Venice instead concentrated on Oran. But crusading moved <u>not</u> to North Africa where threats still existed, but the Americas. Failing to follow through in North Africa, Braudel thinks they sacrificed security at home 'to the mirage of Italy and the comparatively easy gains in America...one of the great missed opportunities in history.'[4]

Hundreds of thousands of Jews and Muslims fled to North Africa, Portugal, Navarre, existing Italian communities and Ottoman lands. Expelled Muslims in Tunisia preyed on merchant ships. Greeks, Albanians and Calabrians joined. These so-called Barbary Corsairs' leader Hayrettin, nicknamed Barbarossa, ferried Spanish refugees and captured ships, cargoes and thousands of people for enslavement. Raiding Minorca in 1514, he said his vengeance would not cease 'until I have killed the last one of you and enslaved your women, your daughters and your children.'[5] The Bey of Tunis provided him and his brother with his harbour for 20% of the plunder. In 1516 he captured Algiers, asked to be part of the Ottoman Empire and was appointed emir.

As already related, late-15th-century Europe's estimated 3.5 million lbs. of annual spice and pepper imports through Venice,[6] collapsed with Portuguese shipments via the Cape, with only partial recovery from the 1530s. Hvar, at the Adriatic entrance revolted against Venice in 1510. Venice increasingly declined. Its maritime priorities weakened. Its 13th-century law blocking investment in land, to channel it into trade, was revoked. Nobles invested in estates and villas instead. That gave Jewish traders an opening. They had been expelled in 1497, then let back in a government-controlled ghetto in 1516, a second in 1541. Using their Levantine contacts, they were important traders, scientists, physicians, money lenders, gold and silversmiths, glassware manufacturers and jewellers. Increasingly, foreign merchants including Dutch, Armenians and Greeks came to live and trade in 16th-century Venice. None had formal residential enclosures, but lived in similar areas. In 1515, in religious frenzy stirred-up by a Franciscan monk, Ragusa also expelled its Jews. They blocked Apulian grain export, so had to be allowed back.[7] Genoa expelled Jews in 1516 but they returned.

Ottoman aggression against Venice and Christians continued. In 1512 Rhodes' Knights Hospitaller captured eight grain ships from Egypt to Istanbul, causing 50% price rises. In 1517 the Ottomans took Egypt, the Levant, North Africa, and the Hijaz including Mecca and Medina. Genoese Admiral Doria recovered Coron and repulsed 60 Ottoman galleys but Hayrettin took 25 Venetian islands. For the first time in centuries, Muslims sought Mediterranean military control. Maritime trade suffered. Even in peaceful periods, the threat of piracy and enslavement was ever-present.

Ottoman Black Sea slave raiding increased in the 16th through to the mid-17th century.[8] Marched back in chains, many died en route, the ill or wounded killed. With 10% frontier tax paid, they were sold in Caffa's slave market to Greek, Jewish, Armenian and Ottoman merchants. Caffa's mid-16th century 16,000 population imported Turkish cotton cloth, European woollen cloth, fish, wine, arak, hemp, flax, nuts and olives. It sold an estimated 10–20,000 slaves annually in the 1570s, 30,000 in 1648 according to a French officer, 70% of whom were shipped to Constantinople; beautiful women for the sultan's harem, strong men for palace service and army, the rest for galleys.[9] Since mortality was high, a continuous supply was needed. In 1521 the Crimean Khan, according to a later source 'took…from Muscovy so great a multituide of captives as would scarcely be considered credible; they say the number exceeded 800,000, part of which he sold in Caffa to the Ottomans and part he slew.'[10]

Without official Black Sea grain, Italian cities paid higher prices than Istanbul's command economy, so Ottoman officials assisted illegal trade. Muslim merchants were active in Venice from well before 1453. Turbaned figures appear in contemporary Venetian paintings. Partnerships with them were illegal, but occurred. Despite frequent war, Istanbul-Venice trade was constant,[11] and recognising it in 1621 Venice established a *Fondaco dei Turchi* for Ottoman merchants; who were Turks, Jews, Armenians and Greeks. In Genoa, 54% of 16th-century imports was food, 42% timber and only 4% luxury products.[12] As in antiquity, Mediterranean maritime trade was overwhelmingly driven by food demand, with grain prices volatile.

Charles V saw himself as Christendom's secular head, Charlemagne's heir, giving the world 'one pastor and one flock.'[13] Humanist scholars left Spain, others were rounded up by the Inquisition, fuelled by denunciations to achieve Catholic orthodoxy by torture, banning books, prohibiting study abroad, confiscating property and burning. Ottomans allowed expelled Jews to settle. The sultan joked, 'the Spanish king impoverishes his country and enriches our own'. Those who went to Portugal and Navarre, a former haven for Europe's Jews, were also persecuted, leading to a second wave to Antwerp where they masqueraded as Portuguese merchants. One, Joseph Nasi (1524–1579), from a converso merchant family in Lisbon, moved in 1537 to Antwerp, then Italy, and in 1554 to Istanbul, becoming a counsellor and diplomat for Selim II. After negotiating peace with Poland, he was granted extensive trading concessions, had agents in Lviv and scores of branches in eastern Europe. Some Jewish, previously Khazar converts, were already resident. So successful did his network become, that in Buda, east Europe's main centre, a third of Jews were Sephardic.[14] In Tlemcen, Algiers and Fez, Jews were artisans, traders and financiers of caravans of gold and ivory. Whether rich or poor, all were aspiring. Chios had 500 when Benjamin of Tudela had visited. When more arrived, they traded local cheeses, wine, marble, silk and mastic resin. In 1586 Venice had 1,424 Jews, Amsterdam perhaps 2,000, but Istanbul and Salonica had 160,000,[15] with substantial communities in Smyrna, Thessaloniki, Adrianople, Caffa, Sudak, Olbia, Tana, Cairo, Damascus; mainly busy ports.

Aggressive Ottoman expansion continued. While laying siege to Vienna in 1529, Barbary pirates raided Valencia's coast, seizing merchant ships. The Mediterranean had not been this dangerous since the 9th century, but because of subsequent trade-growth, there was more to lose in the 16th. Spain, Naples, Sicily, Sardinia and Balearics fought Ottomans and Barbary allies. Mediterranean peace ended. Toledo's archbishop, a rare cleric who understood maritime trade's importance, wrote to Charles, 'unless this disaster is reversed, we will lose the commerce of the Mediterranean from Gibraltar to the east.'[16] In 1533 Hayrettin became an Ottoman admiral, rapidly expanding to 70 galleys, burning Imperial galleys in Naples and enslaving villages. Charles' fleet retaliated, taking Tunis in 1534, burning the Ottoman fleet. They built another 200 vessels. Hayrettin attacked Minorca, taking 1,800 slaves, sacked Venetian islands in Greece, and ravaged southern Crete. In 1541 Spain lost 148 ships, 15 galleys, 8,000 men and 300 nobles in a failed attack against Algiers. France, at war with Charles, hosted Heyrettin's fleet in Toulon in 1543, which for years raided the Spanish and Italian coast, enslaving thousands, damaging trade and infrastructure. In the 1560s the west Mediterranean was infested with pirates, mainly from Algiers. Genoa's grain stocks ran low, prices rose and ships from Provence and Corsica dared not sail to provision it. A 1561 Marseilles document noted 100 North African ships prowling the coast, adding, 'it is raining Christians in Algiers.'[17] Charles quadrupled Castile's tax-yield, whose trade and industry withered. Spain's apparent great imperial age was one of insidious weakness and insecurity due to failure to follow through in North Africa and reform at home, heralding its 17th-century catastrophe. Castile's trade with Flanders and Aragon's with the Mediterranean shrunk.

In the 1550s, Venice's staple trades in nationalised galleys were replaced by private ships.[18] Galley convoys ended in 1567. Under threat from Portugal's Indian Ocean spice venture, its merchants were jealous and confused. Patrician merchants, heavily invested in galleys and Levant trade lost out to non-patricians, including Jews, who were expelled again in 1550, but soon back, Venice reluctantly dependent on them. By 1600, they controlled a third of its trade. Some went to Bologna, Milan and Naples. A secret diaspora mechanism seems to have centred on the Universita d'Altare in Piedmont, established during the Crusades when Marquise

Monferrato settled Levantine glassmakers there, Venetian glass' main competitor. Another Sephardic family, the Dagrua were recorded at Savona, Altare's port, importing soda for glassmaking in 1480 and shipping glass to Nice in 1487.[19] They used Savona, not Genoa, because of Genoa's Spanish vassal status, which in 1567, expelled its Jews. Its glassware deteriorated, then disappeared. Savona became a haven for Sephardic conversos who went to the Netherlands and England.[20] They became prominent in red coral exports to India. Some settled in Yemen and Goa, joining ancient Jewish settlements in Kerala, the trade's conduits.[21]

Driven from its Aegean bases, retreating from Ottoman aggression, Venice was torn between appeasement and resistance. They made peace in 1567, but hearing of Ottoman preparation for renewed attacks, prepared to resist. In Spain, moriscos were a potential fifth-column, appealing to Istanbul for years. Rules prohibiting Moorish dress had not been enforced. In 1566–67 Philip II decreed that Arabic could no longer be spoken. Veils and public baths were banned. They revolted. As the Ottoman fleet roamed the Mediterranean, the situation appeared serious enough in 1570 for Philip to order the Balearic Islands' evacuation, although it was not enforced.

Only Ottomans and Hapsburgs were capable of continuing intense war, in Spain's case, inside its own borders! The Ottomans had over two million square kilometres with 22 million people, three-times Hapsburg inhabitants. The morisco revolt collapsed, but Ottomans captured Cyprus, a source of Venice's grain, salt, wine, sugar and cotton. Famagusta's siege cost Ottomans 60,000 elite troops.[22] At the 1570 Battle of Lepanto, following Famagusta's fall, the 200-ship Christian fleet, including over 100 Venetian, defeated the Turks, who lost 180 ships and 20,000 men. Added to Cypriot casualties, it meant 80,000 lost. Supply was not inexhaustible. The battle was considered decisive because it held off Ottoman conquest, preventing Islamic roll-up of the Mediterranean and eastern Europe.

Elliot calls it a 'deceptive triumph.'[23] Europe rejoiced but an Ottoman bureaucrat explained to Venice's ambassador, 'in wresting Cyprus from you, we have cut off an arm. In defeating our fleet, you have shaved off our beard. An arm once cut off will not grow again, but a shorn beard grows back all the better.'[24] It was not just bravado. Ottoman aggression continued. Spain's capture of Tunis lasted only a year. In a sonnet to Philip II, poet Hernando de Acuna looked forward to when there would be one shepherd, one flock, 'one monarch, one empire and one sword'.[25] Would he have known about Mehmet's similar aim to rule 'one empire, one faith, one sovereignty for the world'? Both believed enforced religious unity realistic. Not withstanding recapturing some Indian spice volumes via the Red Sea, Venice's power withered, while artists and architects illustrated its proud maritime history culminating in Lepanto, the Venetian myth developing as it declined.[26] After Lepanto, Venice's debated whether to implement the 1571 Jewish expulsion order. One argued against, that Jewish weapon-making craftsmen 'expelled by the King of Spain' had strengthened the Turks.[27] The Mediterranean was still infested with pirates and in the 1580s–1590s Marseilles discussed ransoming its prisoners held in Algiers, which was totally dependent on piracy, often re-selling stolen goods in Livorno, Spain's navy seemingly ineffective.

Venice's decline led to interference with rivals. It destroyed Trieste's saltworks in 1578 and sent galleys to Ragusa to prevent grain ships from supplying it, attempted tariff war against Ancona to force Adriatic traffic through Venice,[28] because Ancona and Ragusa took advantage of Venice's difficulties to ship iron from Trieste to Italy and textiles, wool and wine from Apulia to Dalmatia.[29] Ancona imported silk, cotton and spices for soap, oil, Apulian wine and Florentine and north European textiles with Ragusan Greek, Turk, Jewish and local merchants. The Jews had strong links with Ancona's 1,770 Jewish households, under papal protection from 1523 until 1555, enclosed in a tiny ghetto. In 1556, papal protection was withdrawn, 25 were burned alive and 26 condemned to the galleys. Ancona inevitably lost trade. The Duke of Ferrara protected Florence's conversos until Church pressure in 1581 resulted in arrest. Three were burned in Rome in 1583.

Ragusa imported Sicilian wheat and shipped it to Spain for wool, salt and colonial products.[30] Its revenues multiplied during major Ottoman-Christian conflicts, quadrupling in 1537–40, perhaps six or seven times in 1570–1573, mainly Ottoman trade at Venice's expense,[31] with increasing ship-sizes. About 1540–44 it had 132 ships totalling 24,320 tons, in 1560–70, 180 totalling 56,000 tons and in 1570–85, 170 of 52,800 tons, coinciding with Croatian literary 'cultural effervescence'.[32] By 1599 however, its fleet declined to only 112 of 37,929 tons, effectively sidelined by Ottoman instillation of Arab pirates at Ulcinj, south of Kotor in 1571, and by English, Dutch and French competition.

Fanatical religious war, far more detrimental than previous Mediterranean commercial war, diminished trade, filling Algiers' and Tripoli's slave markets. Between 1609 and 1614, 300–400,000 hard-working moriscos, descendants of baptised Moors, artisans and farmers were driven out of Spain, two-thirds of whom died of starvation in North Africa. Mediterranean wealth-creating trade and industry suffered. Economic power dribbled away as north Europe's trade consolidated.

Chapter 24

The World Market: French, English and Dutch

In the 1490s and early-1500s Castile conquered Caribbean islands, in the 1520s Mexico, in the 1530s Peru, in the 1560s Costa Rica, giving Castilians a 'messianic nationalism', earning hatred from other Europeans.[1] It borrowed the Catalan-Aragon Mediterranean model of viceroys and councils, staffed by elderly, status-conscious officials.[2] Native Americans became vassals. Cortes' philosophy was 'without settlement there is no good conquest and if the land is not conquered, the people will not be converted. Therefore, the maxim of the conqueror must be to settle.'[3] Castile treated the Americas as a God-given income source, without need for work or investment, exploitable for the Church and itself. Business-minded Aragon was excluded. The union of crowns was personal. Both kept their own laws, institutions, languages and commercial connections. Alongside Jewish expulsion, another weakness was created at birth. Granting American trade monopoly to Seville, 60 miles up the Guadalquivir, it ignored Cadiz and Barcelona. Seville's merchants were incorporated into a guild, enmeshed with royal bankers, officials of the *Casa de la Contratacion* (Council of Trade) modelled on the *Casa da India*. With monopoly, inefficiency was baked in; smuggling became endemic.[4]

England and France never accepted the Castile-Portugal New World carve-up. Despite Francois I's *roi épicier* insult, his interest was sparked by Portugal's change of fortune and Lisbon's rise. In 1534, he sent St. Malo's Jacques Cartier to locate 'certain islands and countries, where they say great quantities of gold are to be found.' They discovered Quebec, on which he based his claims to the whole area. On subsequent voyages he reached Montreal and took St. Pierre and Miquelon islands in 1535, whose flags depict maritime Breton, Basque and Norman heritages.

Gold was found on Hispaniola in 1500, extracted with local slave-labour. Columbus having traded sugar from Madeira to Genoa, saw potential and planted sugar-cane. Cattle-raising provided hide exports. Guatemala exported indigo, cacao and hides, Venezuela, pearls, dyes and emeralds. African slaves were first shipped to work Hispaniola's gold mines in 1510, a Flemish and Genoese monopoly. By the 1550s Hispaniola had 100 sugar factories, 70% of its exports, but when gold ran out, colonists moved on and sugar-production plummeted. By 1600, only 11 were left. Sugar was also planted in Cuba, Jamaica and Mexico, but only about 240,000 16th-century Castilians from around Seville emigrated.[5] The lure of silver and gold, not entrepreneurship drove them, the aim to make money, buy an estate with a prestigious title, disincentivised to trade by heavy excise duties, the Crown the only buyer. Before 1525, between 23 and 27 tons of gold was shipped to Spain, mainly Aztec loot. Gold exports peaked in the 1550s with registered annual exports of over 4.2 tons. Silver was far more consequential. Discovery of silver mines at Potosi in Peru in 1545 and Mexico's Zacatecas in 1546 triggered large-scale exploitation by forced labour by 1560. Potosi became America's largest city with around 120,000 people in the 1570s. Collected at Vera Cruz, it was shipped to Havana, an annual 19 tons in the 1540s, 103 in the 1560s, 123 in the 1570s and 298 in the 1590s.[6] One annual convoy, averaging 60–70 ships,[7] sailed to Seville, two after the 1560s. A third originated from Mexico, two-thirds from Peru.[8] By the late-16th century an average annual 150–200 ships were involved, double the number and size of the 1520s, a four-fold capacity increase. Argentina, literally 'Silverland', shipped silver from Buenos Aires to Castile in the 1590s, but thereafter declined. Much was not officially recorded and massive fraud at every stage defrauded Madrid, yet the 'quinta', a fifth of officially-recorded production, provided it with 20–25% of its revenues. Spanish American silver exports were 80–90% of all its exports to Seville around 1600.[9]

French agricultural recourses and centralising government of landed values meant overseas trade was relatively unimportant in its economy. Its ports developed independently. Protestantism flourished there, especially independent-minded La Rochelle. Trashing delusional Iberian world-ownership claims. French ships first attacked Spanish ships and ports. Columbus' third voyage evaded a French privateer and in 1523 Dieppe merchant John d'Anjo captured a Spanish galleon packed with gold, jewels and sugar. A short-lived Huguenot settlement was built on St. Kitts in 1538. England's break with Rome brought English merchants in Spain to the Inquisition's attention. With forfeitures and imprisonments, they were increasingly insecure, especially when in 1545 Robert Reneger seized a treasure ship.[10] William Hawkins sailed to west Africa and Brazil in the 1530s, for ivory, gold, pepper, brazilwood and other dyes. But French adventurers set the pace, capturing Cartagena in 1543, Santiago de Cuba in 1553, Havana in 1555, Cartagena again in 1559, when France and Spain agreed the Treaty of Cateau-Cambrésis, in which fighting west of the Azores, south of the Tropic of Cancer would not cause European war; 'no peace beyond the line.'[11]

La Rochelle was France's biggest Newfoundland cod-fishing port, trading cod liver oil, salted and dried-cod, mid-century exporting about 5,000 barrels of wine to England, Flanders and other French ports, salt to England, the Netherlands and the Baltic, wheat and flour from her hinterland to Iberia for wool and alum. Her traders financed their own voyages and acted as bankers. They tried colonising Brazil and Florida but were expelled by Portuguese and Spanish respectively. During France's Wars of Religion, (1562–98) Elizabeth supplied besieged La Rochelle with arms, money and sailors. She encouraged English privateers to attack Spanish ships en route to Flanders and follow Huguenot ships raiding Castile's Caribbean. Its landlocked capital and government was oblivious to merchants' and colonists' needs. In 1549 Santo Domingo asked Charles to licence Flemish ships to maintain supplies, cloth, paper, cutlery, cheese, butter, wine, foods and slaves, to its never very numerous colonists, but was ignored. Huguenot, English and soon Dutch ships obliged. Unwilling to modify its universal claim it was unable to prevent others trading and settling.

European expansion meant huge leaps in geographical knowledge, consolidated by Gerardus Mercator (1512–1594), born near Antwerp. In 1538 he produced the first world map showing the Americas and Asia. Arrested and imprisoned by the Inquisition, he fled to Duisburg, whose duke made him Court cosmographer and in 1569 he published a more accurate one. His friend Abraham Ortelius produced the first atlas in 1570, demonstrating maritime Europe's curiosity. Although jumping chronologically, it is worth noting that when Sir Thomas Roe presented atlases to the Mughal Court in the 1600s, they were returned after four days, again demonstrating maritime-continental differences. Despite its glittering Court, Mughal India declined because it lacked curiosity about the maritime world and technological advances.

In 1551 and 1552 Thomas Wyndham led expeditions to Morocco and in 1553 to Benin for gold and pepper. Plymouth merchant John Hawkins traded with the Canaries. Following his father's enterprising west African venture, in 1562 took English cloth and 300 slaves to Hispaniola's colonists, where he loaded hides, ginger and sugar. Three voyages, the second in 1564–65, invested in by Elizabeth, were profitable. The third in 1566 was intercepted by a Spanish fleet. Much cargo and many ships were lost.[12] Most English voyages up to 1640 did not trade slaves,[13] but whatever the cargo, in Castile's eyes, Hawkins was a smuggler. Inability to colonise in larger numbers, to share with Aragon and unwillingness to allow trade with others when unable to adequately supply colonists was unrealistic. In 1564 Philip licensed privateers to destroy a Huguenot settlement in Florida and broke the promise that surrender would spare their lives. Incensed, in 1568 French privateers found five Spanish bullion ships heading to pay the Duke of Alva's troops. Running for shelter to England, they were arrested and confiscated. English property in Spain and the Netherlands was seized in retaliation and all trade frozen for five years, previously two of England's main cloth markets while Philip began contemplating invasion.

Two significant non-commercial events in the 1570s–1580s helped shape maritime rivalry in world markets. First, childless Portuguese King Sebastian, absolutist, religious, disconnected from merchants, aiming to continue Reconquista and conquer Morocco, was killed there, with most Portuguese nobles in battle in 1578. Castile's relations had seldom been friendly. Its 1383 invasion had been repulsed by their English trade allies' longbows in 1385. Portugal attempted take-over from 1474 to 1479. The 1580 Spanish invasion forced a union. Spain promised non-interference in Portugal's affairs and protection of her Indian Ocean and Brazil trade empire. Even if promises were kept, it was detrimental for Portugal. Her lucrative spice and sugar re-exports to England and Holland ceased as Lisbon was closed to English ships, further incentivising north Europe's merchants to expand horizons worldwide, while Portugal had to follow Spain's religious myopia. Portuguese religious attitudes in the Indian Ocean had become more relaxed. Spain however, sent Jesuits and the Inquisition. Having expelled its most economically productive subjects, many to Holland and England, to their benefit and its loss, it invited worldwide competition. After 1580 many Portuguese conversos, incentivised by Peru's silver, emigrated to Spanish America as shopkeepers or merchants, commercially overwhelming it.

Portugal's trade empire and Castile's Americas and Philippines were commercially potentially symbiotic. The Philippines sat between the huge Chinese market, Malacca and the Moluccas. But Manila's rulers were outnumbered over ten-times by Chinese traders; 'sangleye', from trade in Amoy's dialect.[14] Spanish colonials feared them and despite occasional massacres, they kept arriving for economic potential. Castile and Portugal never economically cooperated. As Castile promised, their colonies were administered differently, one from Lisbon and Goa, the other from Castile, the Philippines from Acapulco. Spain fought wars everywhere, which Portugal was drawn into. Administrative divisions therefore worked against them. Potential cooperation of the Philippines with Malacca, Goa and Macao to establish Iberian eastern trading hegemony never emerged because insular Madrid dictated the rules.

It was clear to some that the Atlantic had replaced the Mediterranean as most important, politically, militarily and economically. In 1585, Cardinal Granvelle urged Philip to move his government to Lisbon to learn about the new Atlantic world and its maritime routes to the Indian Ocean, the Americas and to be nearer its north European enemies. Philip however, returned to Castile's heartland. Instead of an opportunity for reorientation and reform, Portugal's annexation was a wasted opportunity for Spain and a disaster for Portugal. Between 1580 and 1640, 360,000 people left Portugal for Brazil and Africa, a huge exodus for a small country. Catalonia, Aragon, Navarre and Castile had not been integrated, while Portugal, sparsely-populated and maritime-inclined was different from pastoral regions. 'One monarch, one empire, one sword' was fiction. Spain was divided and dysfunctional. It could not reform itself. The attempt to make the River Tagus navigable to Toledo in the 1580s was abandoned. Theologians, not engineers, were summoned to consider building a canal linking the Manzanares and Tagus, but decided that if God intended the rivers to be navigable, he would have made them so. Seville never built a bridge over the Guadalquivir, nor tackled silting.

Failure to improve infrastructure for economic benefit contrasts with China's 7th-century Grand Canal, 11th-century London Bridge and maritime Europe's 13th-century transport infrastructure improvements. Spain remained backward, uninterested in science or technology. Inertia defined it. Castilian estate owners showed no interest in irrigation or improvements. Agricultural production languished. The economy stagnated. A fatalist attitude pervaded. Moriscos' 1609 expulsion, further negatively affected landed estates and towns. Castilian contempt for commerce and manual labour and hunger for titles led ambitious men to the Church, Court or New World. Refusal to construct a modern state out of independent medieval polities and address the rapidly changing world would prove fatal. France too remained backward and agricultural.

'Privateering', a word first used in 17th-century Europe, was licensed opportunistic attacks on enemy ships, endemic in the 16th-century Mediterranean and used in the Atlantic because of Spain's exclusionism. Hawkins and cousin Francis Drake committed spectacular depredations in the late-1560s and 1570s. Drake's three voyages to Panama were financed by London merchants. En route he released embargoed ships in Vigo and raided Santo Domingo and Cartagena. In 1577, charged by Elizabeth to repeat Magellan's circumnavigation, he captured a Brazil-bound Portuguese ship, with woollens, linens, velvets, silks and wines. Learning southern Atlantic sailing conditions from the pilot, he reached the Moluccas and America's west coast, returning with treasure, cloves and nutmeg. A grateful Elizabeth removed £50,000 to pay off the national debt, but it still repaid its investors 50-times. Inspired, English privateering started in earnest. Stories of rich opportunities galvanised London merchants. In 1580 Drake brought back 100 tons of silver and 100 lbs. of gold. In 1586 Cavendish accomplished another circumnavigation, returning with Spanish booty, ostentatiously in damask and gold sails; a great recruiting advert for adventurous foreign trade and adding navigational and geographic knowledge.

They were the most successful privateers, but between 1585 and 1604 over 200, many financed by London and Bristol merchant syndicates, gentry and nobility, risked scurvy, dysentery, typhus or battle to return annually £100,000–200,000 in gold, silver, dyes, spices and sugar. Some found trading with Spanish colonies, starved of provisions, just as profitable with less risk.[15] Philip declared all English ships and goods in Iberian ports confiscated in 1585. Almost immediately a squadron under Raleigh's brother captured Iberia's fishing fleet.[16] Portugal was never again a dominant force in Newfoundland fishing. Early Portuguese fishing bases were re-named in English.[17]

At its height, plunder accounted for 10–15% of imports, mostly by merchant syndicates, a means of war but also deliberate attempts to seize Spanish and Portuguese colonial goods and find new markets, encouraged as strategic policy and economic enterprise. Seized sugar triggered sugar refineries. By 1595 London had seven. Richard Hakluyt's 1589 *The Principal Navigation* and several more editions, enunciated England's main commercial policy. 'Our chief desire is…ample vent for our woollen cloth, the natural commodity of this realm'. Walter Raleigh, England's leading advocate of North American colonisation argued the way to humiliate Spain was not 'pinching and picking' in the Netherlands but crippling its Caribbean money flow, its 'sinews of war'.[18] He concluded, 'He that commands the sea, commands the trade, and he that is lord of the trade of the world is lord of the wealth of the world and consequently the world itself.'

The second non-commercial event affecting trade was the 1588 Spanish Armada's failure. English privateers had detained vessels sailing from Poland to Spain with naval stores. Poland protested and suggested Spain occupy Ireland and the Isle of White.[19] Spain's war with the Dutch was partly thwarted by Elizabeth's support, providing 1,000 cavalry, 6,350 infantry and subsidies for Flushing, Brill and Ostend until post-war repayment. Drake's 23-ship merchant-backed,[20] raid on Cadiz where 60 ships prepared invasion delayed the Armada by a year. He destroyed 24 ships, food and stores. Off Sagres he captured and sunk incoming Mediterranean and Azores ships, including one with £140,000, which he brought to Plymouth.[21] As Philip prepared to invade, navy treasurer Hawkins, knowledgeable about Spanish maritime fragility, led improvements in English ships' handling, speed and manoeuvrability, organised a census of all merchant ships, masters, mariners and men whose work was maritime related.[22] The City was asked for 15 ships and 5,000 men. They counter-offered 30 ships and 10,000 men! Indeed, national defence did not depend only on 34 naval vessels, ten under 100 tons. Many of the 163 private ships involved had privateering experience. Thirty were 200–400 tonners with 40 guns and 23 were paid for by ports.[23]

Superior ships, guns, tactics, preparation and City private enterprise destroyed the Armada's integrity. Bad weather finished it off. Its failure had huge psychological impact, crystalising an English sense of identity, self-confidence felt in Shakespeare's (1564–1616) uplifting prose, unrivalled creativity and strong stories, especially *Henry V*, echoing defiance against seemingly overwhelming odds. It emboldened England. Between 1589 and 1591 English privateers captured 300 Spanish non-naval ships worth about £400,000, which continued until the war's end in 1604.[24] It also empowered Dutch resistance. They sacked Pernambuco in 1595 and Puerto Rico in 1598, taking their fight to the Indian Ocean. It sent news of a new naval power to the world. Many English and Dutch anxieties about Spanish power evaporated. Spanish self-confidence was shaken. Economic power again significantly shifted to northern Europe. It was unclear to Spain that it had lost the Atlantic battle against Protestant sea-powers, defaulting for the third time, nor to all Dutch and English for whom the Spanish-Portuguese empire still appeared formidable.

Philip should have seen the Armada's failure as the end of any realistic chance of defeating the Dutch. He was not a realist. In 1600 a Spanish critic blamed New World gold and silver for so mesmerising Spain 'that it has given up trading with its neighbours', that national productivity should increase, not lucky bullion inflow.[25] Unlike England, Castile's merchant values were held by an impotent, unconnected minority. Its docile American labour force, silver and land-focused Reconquista tradition meant colonists sought vassals to provide seigneurial income and life-style in city control centres.[26] Spain's far-flung overseas empire was ironically land-obsessed, but fought Dutch and English, commercially-astute, maritime powers.

Portugal's Asian bases were ruthlessly attacked by Dutch, some of whom had worked on Portuguese ships. Jan Huyghen van Linschoten's 1596 *Itinerario* revealed maps, charts, descriptions, each port's commodity prices, market information, traders' languages, the best provisioning ports, wind patterns and highlighted the few Molucca-based Portuguese; effectively a guide to take the spice trade! Dutch merchants rounded the Cape to the Moluccas, the Magellan Straits to Japan, and sent three expeditions in the 1590s to find a northeast passage via Archangel. Excitement about spices was fuelled by extravagant claims. The *Itinerario* listed curative powers; 'nutmegs fortify the brain and sharpen the memory, warm the stomach and expel winds…give a clean breath…stop diarrhoea and cure stomach upsets.' 'Cinnamon warms, opens and tones up the intestines.' Others claimed spices cured plague and the 'bloody flux'.[27] Cloves were supposed to be good for ear-ache, pepper for colds, mixed spices for trapped wind and even assist 'the forces of Venus.' Medicinal and Viagra-like powers, which makes the food taste better? No wonder spices were popular.

The Moluccas were the source of cloves, the Banda Islands of nutmeg and mace; a group of over 100 isolated islands in an area half the size of Europe. Its rulers were weak. The Portuguese since 1574 had hardly been there, preferring their Malacca base. Ten pounds of nutmeg sold for less than a penny in the Bandas, were worth about £2.50 in London,[28] ten pounds of mace less than 5d, sold for £16,[29] profits easily offsetting the considerable costs of building and equipping large fleets, fighting Portuguese, establishing and running fortified settlements. In 1591 the Levant Company sent three ships to the Malacca Straits.

In 1598–99 a 22-ship expedition from five Dutch trading companies made a 400% profit. Their first voyages were better-planned than the English and more aggressive than the Portuguese.[30] Finding prices in Bantam, Java's Sunda Strait port, too high they bombarded it. At Madura, the local prince, in hospitable Indian Ocean tradition, sailed out ships in welcome. They were blown out of the water.[31] Emboldened with initial success, in 1599 they raised pepper prices to the English from three to eight shillings a pound. It was the shock English merchants needed. In 1600 a group encouraged and financed by the Levant Company petitioned the Queen. The Company of Merchants of London Trading to Asia, subsequently the East India Company (EIC), was given a 15-year monopoly with South and Southeast Asia trade. Such long-haul trade tied up capital for a long time, involved more valuable cargo, large, expensive ships and permanent trade stations, factories, where their factors operated. Greater outlays involved greater risks. The joint stock company, pioneered by the Muscovy Company, was a proven way to accumulate capital and spread risk. Elizabeth had maritime trade, taking over from privateering, at the centre of policy to strengthen the realm. Meanwhile Dutch companies targeting Asia mushroomed, with 14 fleets totalling 65 ships sailing in 1601.

James Lancaster had traded with Portugal until the 1580 Spanish-Portuguese union. He headed an EIC expedition with a cargo of lead, iron and cloth, arriving at Aceh in 1602. Elizabeth had written the sultan a flattering, standardised letter denouncing Spanish-Portuguese arrogance in claiming world domination. It declared that no nation was self-sufficient, and 'out of the abundance of fruit, which some region[s] enjoyeth, the necessity or want of others should be supplied' and thus, 'several and far remote countries' should become friends 'by their interchange

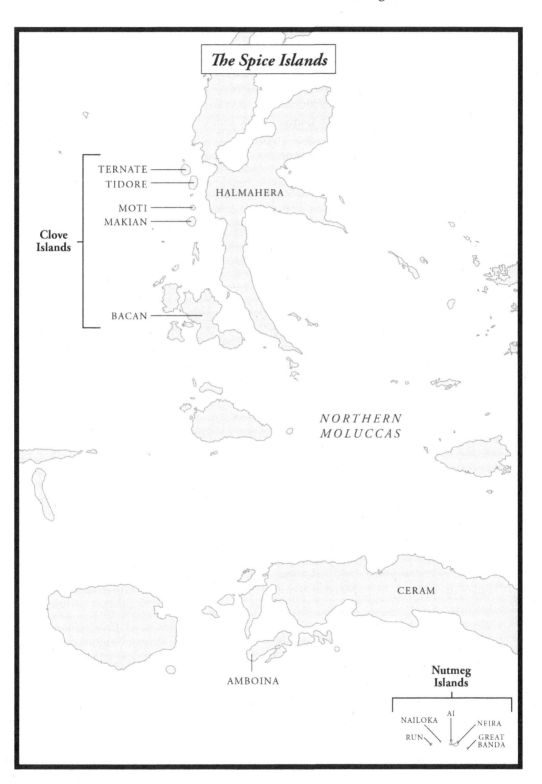

The Spice Islands

TERNATE

TIDORE

HALMAHERA

MOTI

MAKIAN

Clove Islands

BACAN

NORTHERN MOLUCCAS

CERAM

AMBOINA

Nutmeg Islands

NAILOKA   AI   NEIRA

RUN   GREAT BANDA

of commodities.' 'Trade…breeds intercourse and exchange of merchandise, love and friendship betwixt all men,' she wrote.[32] The sultan knew about the Armada and as Portuguese Malacca's competitor, was keen to make an alliance. Although pepper prices were five-times higher than expected, they did not conduct Dutch-style bombardment, but left diplomatically, disabling a Dutch ship loaded with calicoes and batiques, headed for Bantam to exchange them for cloves and nutmeg and establish a factory. Bantam was originally Hindu from India's Coromandel coast,[33] but conquered by Islamic Demak in 1526. A Kling and a Chinese were on its council and Chinese brokers, interpreters and weighers were used. One ship sailed for the Moluccas and loaded 230 sacks of spices for England. The EIC's first venture was a resounding success. They found few Portuguese, more friends and allies, discovered that Indian cotton was popular in Java, and discharged £1 million worth of spices in London, although half the crew was lost and they did not achieve permanent contact with the Moluccas, giving the Dutch two years to consolidate.

Eight competing Dutch companies tended to raise spice prices at their source. Suggestions that they merge preceded EIC formation, only achieved in 1602 into the Vereenigde Oost-indische Compagnie, the Dutch East India Company (VOC). Unlike the EIC, capital was not raised for a specific voyage but 21 years, which later turned into permanent capital, giving it greater resources. Ruled by eight directors from Amsterdam, one each from eight other ports and one rotating, their headquarters was on Amsterdam's inner canal, the Herengracht, so were known as the Heren XVII. The EIC was backed by over 100 London merchants, but the VOC had eight-times the capital, an unprecedented concentration of economic and military power, as 50–70% was <u>military</u> spending.[34] They aimed to build fortresses to take over Portuguese trade. Johor's Sultan welcomed them and in 1603 jointly attacked the *Santa Catarina* sailing for Macao. The cargo raised 3.5 million florins, equivalent to half the VOC's capital,[35] firing imaginations even further. In the next ten years, 14 expeditions, 65 even-larger ships compared with the EIC's 12, were sent. Like the EIC, it had authority to establish military bases, build and own ships, and negotiate with foreign rulers.

The confident Dutch happily invested. Unlike the EIC, it had the right to make war and peace and hold overseas territories, a 'state within a state' or a semi-detached empire.[36] Merchants' interests were state interests, its expeditions instructed to 'attack the Spanish and Portuguese wherever you find them.' It has thus been described as 'less a…trading firm than…a syndicate for piracy aimed at Portuguese power in Asia, dominated by government interests but drawing its funding from investors rather than taxpayers.'[37] The VOC arrived, like the Portuguese, state-sponsored predatory traders, cannon blazing. English merchants, by necessity and temperament, sought allies. The VOC captured Ternate in 1603 and Portuguese forts on Amboina and Tidore in 1605. In 1606 the Portuguese repulsed a joint Johor-VOC attack on Malacca. A ten-galleon fleet sent to assist was destroyed by the Dutch off Gibraltar in 1607. Malacca weakened. Johor, Aceh and Bantam became stronger rival entrepots. Portuguese, Dutch and English efforts in Indian Ocean trade focused almost exclusively on spices. Despite the hostility of the Estada and VOC, Europeans needed to collaborate and cooperate with Asian merchants and powers in this vast area, relying on local finance, navigational and market knowledge.

Bankrupt Spain needed a Spanish-Netherlands truce. Having banned Dutch vessels from Iberian ports, making Baltic naval stores supply more difficult, it again lifted the embargo. Whatever Spain did, its inherent weakness strengthened and emboldened the Dutch. They were displacing Portuguese as Europe's dominant Asian traders while choking Antwerp. Amsterdam thus grew apace, the focus for sugar, tea and tobacco distribution. The Dutch owned almost 50% of Europe's ships, three-times that of the English. From winning their long-term Baltic struggle, they ruthlessly burst into Asia. Shipping and trading wealth paid for a standing army of 70,000 and subsidised allies to fight Spain. Furthermore, Dutch marine insurance and trade with Brazil increased in the 1590s, collaborating with Portuguese conversos, so by 1621 the Dutch had 50–65% of the Brazil-Europe trade.[38]

In 1595, Portuguese slave trader Pedro Gomes Reinal, in addition to his Angola-Brazil traffic, signed a Spanish American supply contract and in the next five years, transported to Spanish America 80,500, pushing the 16th-century total to 150,000, excluding another 50,000 to Brazil.[39] From 1599 to 1608, 200 Dutch ships sailed to west Africa for gold, slaves, ivory, rubber, hides, gum Arabic, wax, ambergris, redwood and sugar. The English imported similar commodities including gold. London merchant John Davies previously financing privateers concentred on redwood shipments for dye from about 1607, which led to the joint-stock Guinea Company in 1618.[40] When Richard Johnson in 1620 was offered slaves, he said that English did not engage in it, which was mainly true. The Guinea Company charter made no mention of it. Hawkins' early venture was an exception. Slaves shipped to Barbados in the 1640s were from interlopers and Dutch.[41]

Cabot had claimed North America for England in 1496 but there was no serious attempt to settle until Sir Humphrey Gilbert's expedition in 1583, by which time France had a St. Lawrence base. Greater privateering profits held back English settlement. Sir Francis Walsingham, Elizabeth's Secretary of State tried to show its advantages. Hakluyt and other propagandists for assertive Protestantism, thought trade and settlement would check Catholic Spain and aimed to exploit timber, pitch, tar and plant tobacco, hemp, flax, dyes, vines and mulberry trees. But it was difficult to settle under threat of Spanish, privateers, Caribs, North American natives, disease and starvation. North of Florida, Spain's insignificant strength removed one potential threat. The first Dutch settlements were on Guyana's Essequibo River and Brazil's Amazon in the 1590s.

When France emerged from religious wars, the Duc de Sully in the late-1590s reaffirmed France's long-standing direction, opposing trade and colonies, insisting that 'ploughing and grazing are the nipples of France;' its ability to feed itself. Originally Protestant Henry IV, however, gave licences to companies to trade in Canada. Emigrants tended to be enterprising French Protestants, Huguenots, who traded fur and fish with the English. The 1602 Edict of Nantes designated La Rochelle one of three cities where Protestantism was permitted. In 1605, France's first settlement was Port Royal on the Bay of Fundy followed in 1608 by Quebec City by Samuel Champlain, probably from a Huguenot mariner family. He had a fur trade monopoly with Dugua, a Huguenot trader. Henry demanded that 'New France' start above 40 degrees north, away from Spanish interference, without realising eastern seaboard climates at such latitudes make growing vines and wheat impossible. After 1610, Regent Marie de Medici showed no interest in New France. Dugua was denied access to court and Port Royal declined.

Chapter 25

English and Dutch Entry into the Mediterranean

The Caribbean, Arctic, west African and Brazilian coasts were familiar to English and Dutch seamen before they really got to know the Mediterranean in the 1560s–1570s, when they sailed there directly. To growing energy, expertise, confidence, the need to lessen England's Antwerp-dependence and find new markets for cloth were added two main demand factors. The 1570–73 Venice-Ottoman war triggered demand for war supplies. Livorno's registers noted three English ships in 1572–73, nine in 1574, two in 1575's incomplete record, three in 1576, five in 1578, nine in 1579, two in 1580, 13 in 1581, culminating in 16 in 1592–93, all carrying lead and tin. They also called at Sicily, Naples, Malta and the Levant with similar cargoes; gunpowder, saltpetre, iron, copper, cloth, canvas, iron balls for shot, mast trees and coal. A 1580 Venetian decree said that before the Ottoman war, five to six Venetian ships took raisins and wines to England, returning with 'woollen cloth, tin and other goods' but after, 'foreign' ships replaced them. Venetian ships still sailed to northern Europe until the century's end, but northern European ships began to take over north-south shipping,[1] and consequently, some inter-Mediterranean routes.

English merchants exploring potential new cloth markets led. Since Sturmy's 1457–58 expedition, English merchants had become stronger, Venetians and Genoese weaker and Ottomans very receptive. From the 1550s, English merchants sold cloth in Morocco for sugar, 85% of Moroccan imports, supplemented with almonds, aniseed and gold.[2] From about 1575 factors were established in Livorno and Venice, dealing directly with Ottoman-based merchants. Richard Hakluyt gave credit to London-based Sir Edward Osborne and Richard Staper's visits, after which the sultan wrote to Elizabeth, inviting merchants. He was interested in English tin for bronze cannon. Istanbul's French ambassador noted English bronze and scrap steel for guns, London's Spanish ambassador told Philip II in 1579 of an English ship sending 20,000 crowns-worth of bar tin and lead. An English cargo at Milos in 1605 contained 700 barrels of gunpowder, many guns and swords.[3] Allowing each other's ships safe conduct, England gained favoured nation status and after 1578, Ottoman duties reduced from 5–10% to 3%. Smyrna became its main port where Greek merchants, strong from antiquity, Ragusans, Armenians and Sephardic Jews exported local cotton and regional products, attracting French, English, Dutch and Venetian traders who had large warehouses by the harbour on Street of the Franks.

Elizabeth's 1579 introductory letter to Murad III stressed their common Spanish enemy. The Turkey Company, established in 1580 by 12 rich, influential merchants, was re-named the Levant Company in 1581. With safe conduct and privileges, restricted to 20 members with Elizabeth a leading shareholder from the £40,000 of bullion captured in 1579, it was granted seven years exclusivity to trade east Mediterranean markets, dependent on providing customs revenues of £500 a year. In 1581 it returned 300%. The monopoly angered independent merchants. Colthurst and Company said they had traded there for 14 years, with less risks than Spanish trade, having just lost their ship *Dolphin* to Spanish, while their *Eagle* was discharging tin, lead and cloth in Venice. The Crown continued to grant charters but much, perhaps most trade was done by interlopers.[4] In 1592 the Levant Company absorbed the Venice Company; sugar, almonds, aniseed and gold imports for cloth. That year the estimated profit on currants was £11,500. Government customs meant it doubly profited. A parson noted the disadvantage in 1586. 'When every nation was permitted to bring-in her own commodities, foreign wares were far better, cheaper and more plentifully to be had,' highlighting currants six and sugar seven-times more expensive.[5] In 1600 the Levant Company license was renewed again for 15 years on payment of a semi-annual £2,000.

The Barbary Company (1585) with similar merchant investors, probably modelled on the Levant Company charter, concentrated on North Africa. The Muscovy and Eastland Companies, already discussed, and the Africa Company (1588) were part of the same commercial thrust. By the 1580s, English traders had networks in the southern and eastern Mediterranean with factories in Istanbul, Tripoli and Aleppo, termini of Persian Gulf caravan routes. By the early-1600s English merchants in Chios, Smyrna and Patras competed with Venetians and French, despite Barbary pirates, buying silk, dyes, malmsey, muscadet, alum, wine, currants, cotton, carpets, pepper and spices. Braudel thinks that when north Europeans entered, Mediterranean merchants inevitably declined due to timber deficiency after Levantine, Sicilian and Italian deforestation. Sixteenth-century Seville and Venice had already imported north European timber, increasing shipbuilding costs.[6] While Braudel's point is sound, Ottoman-Castilian religious zealotry surely was the key to Mediterranean merchant decline.

The Levant Company was England's most profitable official overseas venture, despite Istanbul embassy costs, Levantine and Alexandrian consuls and interloping. Before 1600 it bought goods mainly with bullion. Thereafter it found English cloth competitive with Venice's,[7] which declined, partly due to English New Draperies, but mostly Mediterranean instability. In the early-1600s the Levant Company carried 6% of English cloth exports, lead, tin, munitions, grain, salted fish and silver, and by 1602 had 6% of spice, silk, carpet and currant imports. In the 1580s it operated about 20 ships, convoying to the Levant, Alexandria, Cyprus, Chios, Zante and even Algiers. Its *Edward Bonaventure* comparable with medium-rank warships, fought against the Armada. Between 1583 and 1591, agents travelled from the Levant to the Indian Ocean as far as Sumatra, hatching the idea of an East India Company. By 1600 the Levant Company had about 30 mainly 150–300 tonners, some up to 500 tons with heavy cast iron cannon, on which English manufacturing had a virtual monopoly until about 1600. Their perseverance, honesty, low cloth prices, organisational skill and ship quality reaped rewards.[8]

The second demand factor was a deepening food crisis. Mediterranean climate and geography as factors in inter-Mediterranean trade in foodstuffs was highlighted in this series' previous volume.[9] Braudel also explains that only 46% of Italy, 39.1% of Spain, 34.1% of Portugal and 18.6% of Greece were cultivated, North Africa even less.[10] Frequent small inter-Mediterranean grain shipments were far more voluminous, but less well-known than pepper and spice re-exports. Sixteenth-century famines and epidemics were common due to unreliable harvests. There was a Castile-Andalusian famine in 1521, known in Portugal as the 'Year of Hunger', in Andalusia again in 1525, Tuscany in 1540 and the Papal States in 1583.[11] Urban famines were even more frequent. Florence had 111 between 1375 and 1791 against only 16 very good harvests. In famines, ships were often seized. Venice had permanent grain regulations and in 1408, 1539 and 1607, banned grain export. If its food supply was endangered, no Adriatic wheat cargo was safe.[12] Early-16th century Portugal, concentrating on profitable orchards, olives and vines for export, imported north European grain. Flanders and England exported to Venice in 1527, Rome in 1530, Genoa mid-century and Andalusia in the 1550s-1580s. Ottoman shipments to Livorno in Ragusan and Ottoman ships stopped after 1555 as it too suffered shortages and banned exports[13] as Istanbul was hit by famine and plague.

As Genoa and Venice declined, Tuscany's Grand Duke Cosimo I improved Livorno's harbour in 1574 and dug a canal to the River Arno, enabling regular intercourse with Pisa and Florence. His successor surrounded it with walls and in 1593 welcomed 'merchants of all nations' including Jews and Muslims to trade duty free. Livorno was quickly transformed into a significant Mediterranean port and beacon of enlightenment. Mediterranean food supply got worse after consecutive bad harvests from 1586 to 1590. In 1590–91 Tuscany's Grand Duke sent agents to Danzig, Lubeck, Holland, France and England with orders rumoured to be worth a million ducats. As a result, 40 Dutch, English and Hansa ships arrived. Venice's Danzig agent Marco Ottobon, sent five shipments and in 1593, Livorno recorded about 16,000 tons of wheat and rye, half ordered by the Grand Duke and half by 18 merchants from Lucca, Bologna and Florence.[14] Dutch ships also shipped Sicily's grain to north Italy.

Only a week from Gibraltar, Livorno profited handsomely. Ships backhauled with alum, completing with Iberian salt to north Europe. Venice further away, imported for herself but missed out on greater distribution. The risks were Spanish embargoes, Barbary pirates and cargo deterioration. One of Ottobon's five vessels were lost and one discharged instead in Lisbon as the grain was about to spoil. The grain crisis alleviated itself in the 1600s with renewed Mediterranean self-sufficiency, but English ships had found new cloth markets and Dutch, occasional visitors before 1585, found Mediterranean markets second only to the Baltic in importance by 1605.[15] After the grain emergency, Hansa ships were no longer competitive.

Charles V had borrowed from Genoese merchants from 1528 but after the 1557 bankruptcy, German bankers replaced them. Despite Genoa's maritime decline, Philip II turned to its bankers again after 1570, the start of the Ottoman war. They made loans in return for promises of repayment in silver as soon as it arrived from the Americas. Genoa replaced Antwerp as Europe's main banking centre, paid with American silver, the clearing house for payments, controlled by the Grimaldi, Lomellini, Spinola and other families. Other Italian towns were involved, but Genoese controlled Philip's finances. Silver was discharged in Seville, re-shipped from Barcelona to Genoa in hundreds of ships, a vast bullion traffic, insured at only 1.5%, indicating few accidents.[16] This silver circulated throughout Europe, fertilising its economy.

Overcommitted on all fronts and winning in none, Philip annulled all agreements with the Genoese in 1576 causing huge losses. They in turn, blocked gold payments to Flanders. Unpaid soldiers went on deadly, costly rampages in Antwerp, further contributing to its decline. Philip U-turned in 1577. Attempted reliance on Castile's merchants had failed, having insufficient capital and unable to circumvent Genoa's bills of exchange and gold embargo. In subsequent quarrels each time Castile defaulted, it lost. Philip declined to set up a state bank in 1582. He was hopelessly out of his depth in international finance, losses always borne by Castile's already overburdened taxpayers. Volumes increased after the 1580s; the great age of Genoese finance following the brief one of the German Fuggers and preceding Amsterdam, continuing until at least 1627, when in another payment suspension, Olivares promoted Portuguese conversos as moneylenders and in 1630 agreed with England to divert silver to London in exchange for resuming Spanish trade. Genoa retained importance for a couple more decades, but Amsterdam's Portuguese conversos and Dutch merchants quickly overtook it in financial services.

Braudel stresses Mediterranean continuing prosperity until 1620–1650,[17] pointing to Genoa's continuing financial importance and Venice's wealth, its port volumes steady until 1625. But foreign ships had made great inroads at their expense. Venice's galley convoys were long gone, her remaining fleet declining, textile industries uncompetitive, especially as government regulations required them to be carried on Venetian ships, output halving from 1600 to the 1650s, Levant trade, a former strength, was increasingly in foreign hands, spices with Dutch and English merchants. Decreasing revenue led to higher customs dues, encouraging smuggling and reliance on foreign traders. Genoa's shift from shipowning and trading to Spanish finance meant most ships there were foreign, mainly Ragusan and Dutch. England's merchants seeking markets for cloth, lead and tin and Dutch merchants with Baltic grain, herring and cod replaced Mediterranean traders. Venice's trade dynamic deflated because of Ottoman aggression, Iberian religious intolerance and lost spice and sugar distribution. Its exclusionist mentality was no longer fit for purpose. By 1600 Dutch, English and Jewish traders were everywhere in the Mediterranean.

Chapter 26

The New World: Castile's and Spanish American Trade Perspectives

In 1521, Cortes overthrew the Aztecs in Mexico. A decade later Pizzaro conquered the Inca. The two Spanish viceregal cities became inland Mexico City and Lima with its port, Callao. As soon as conquest was complete there was exchange; Mexican flour to Havana, Yucatan wax and honey to Veracruz. Pacific coast trade between Mexico, Panama, Nicaragua and Peru was little more than peddling supplies at first.[1] Timber from the Atlantic side of the Panama isthmus and cordage, nails, anchors, pitch and tar sent from Seville was carried to the Pacific.[2] By 1529, five ships owned by Pizzaro and other officials traded between Panama and Nicaragua,[3] providing timber, mast trees, pitch, fibres for cordage and food. Early restrictions reserving shipping and trade for officials were relaxed. Settlers built, traded and enslaved workers and crew without restraint,[4] although the priority was still exploration. Many Mexican conquistadores, disappointed at not finding gold or silver returned to Spain, the Caribbean or continued to Peru. In 1536, Cortes lacking Spanish funds, tried to profit by supplying horses, arms, saddles, wheat and sugar from his Mexican estates to Panama and Peru, but difficulties beset the ventures; perishables spoiling en route, the Inca civil war, rotting ship timbers and constant repairs. From 1538 the Crown complained that Peruvian gold and silver arrived in Seville without proof that it was properly assayed or taxes paid. What did they expect? As Cortes' companion, Bernal Diaz del Castillo said, 'We came here to serve God and the King, and also to get rich'. A New Castile feudal aristocracy lived in urban luxury, exploiting huge tracts of land and commodities, especially precious metals.

From mid-century, Mexican shipbuilding concentrated in Tehuantepec, trade in Huatulco, administered by viceregal appointees, from where passengers, mules, horses, sheep, pigs, cattle, beans, tallow, quince, sugar and other foodstuffs were shipped after a long, slow journey from Mexico City. Mules died, perishable cargo spoiled, royal officials were slow in paying but meticulous in meddling and much time was spent repairing ships. Cortes' family accounts show 20% profits on his ships between 1553 and 1556, but did not include depreciation and repair costs, thus actually probably loss making.[5]

Nevertheless, from the 1550s a few small ships sailed regularly between Mexico and Peru. In 1578–89 Drake captured some of them, the larger ones Peruvian-owned, as they needed Mexican supplies to supplement Seville's slow deliveries.

Most traders travelled with their goods, as factors were unreliable.[6] Provincial governors sold licences needed to trade, settle, secure debt repayment, claim deceased relatives' estates, and establish factories. Peru's prices were higher than Mexico, due to distance from Spain and difficulties importing via Panama.[7] Licensing for shipbuilding was freed up between 1535 and 1560, but all cargoes and passengers were registered. No one could leave the province in which they were registered without a governor's license and no one could go to Peru without Madrid's royal license! All who had, were officially expelled. In 1544 the Crown ordered officials to return them, leading to, according to the historian of this Mexico-Peru trade, 'official blindness in exchange for cash.'[8]

In 1539 Mexican Viceroy, Antonio de Mendoza established a register system for the Pacific coast. Its preamble complained that some ships' masters were not filing registers, shipping forbidden products and that vessels, cargoes and passengers had to be registered before justices. Evasion continued.[9] Rules were continuously tightened up to the 1580s when merchants had to get a license before buying, then a license to export, effectively rationing Peru. Its merchants were also subject to regulations on sale of goods. Obviously, rules were flouted. Many goods were landed at small ports without officials or ones where they were too poorly paid to expect enforcement. When declared, values were routinely lowered considerably. Bureaucracy was rigid, fragile and inefficient. Ports lacked commercial, cosmopolitan identity.

Mexico's development started earlier, so its surpluses of horses, arms, clothes, shoes, hats, dyes, slaves, furniture, etc. were shipped from Spain via Panama. Peru developed farming, ranching and manufacturing. Sugar production began in the 1550s although in 1561 it cost 2.5-times more than Caribbean sugar via Mexico.[10] Peru mainly exported silver. From 1567 mercury was shipped to Mexico as a royal monopoly, used to refine lower grades of silver ore. Large Peruvian surpluses were stored in leather bags, which rotted, the mercury lost. In the 1590s mercury entered a Mexican Crown-controlled stock, instead of sending it to Spain, allowing Spanish mercury to be sold in Europe, which could have partly alleviated foreign import dependence.

Developing Ming maritime policy must now be briefly explained as background to the Manila-Acapulco galleon trade. China's lack of a navy meant it couldn't prevent illegal trade. The 1525 Court order to destroy all private seagoing ships couldn't be enforced. When another northern threat emerged, it was unable to use customs revenue, or even collect tax in the south, so land-tax doubled, rebellions and famine ensued. Beijing was distant with little effective control in Fujian. Japanese tribute was allowed only every decade, so Macao-based Portuguese imported Japanese silver, but illegal trade continued. Fujianese never forgot how to build and sail ships. Port officials were bribed to ignore 'fishing boats' sailing with silk and porcelain even though, after 1551, they were not even permitted to go to sea. Fujian had famous porcelain kilns, lychee, tea, sugar cane, flax, mulberries for silkworms and it made and dyed silks, especially blue from cultivated indigo and various reds from other plants. Exchange was impossible to eradicate! Beijing blamed maritime instability on 'wokou' Japanese 'dwarf pirates'. Some were Japanese, some from the Ryukyu Islands, but many were Chinese illegal traders, who had fleets in Amoy (Xiamen), Guangzhou, Fuzhou, Yuegang and the Ryukyu Islands, where silk sold for ten-times the Chinese price and porcelain, sugar and musk were in demand. In 1547, Dutch traders set up on Wu Island, near Yuegang. Fujian's governor sent soldiers to drive them out and continued to execute smugglers and sink boats. Portuguese Macao traded with Nagasaki, Manila and Bantam. Chinese merchants formed fortified towns against government forces. In 1567, finally recognising they were outgunned and outmanned, Beijing reversed policy. They permitted restricted trade, except to Japan because Kyushu's daimyo had colluded in keeping illegal trade alive and some Japanese and Fujian 'pirates' had attacked China's south coast in the 1550s.

Previous emperors produced currency chaos, alternating between paper and coins, with each new emperor declaring his predecessors' coins worthless, destroying trust. By the 1570s taxes paid in silver encouraged Portuguese supply from Japan. From 1573 Spanish Manila sent galleons with silk, damasks, satins, porcelain, lacquered wares, iron and copper goods to Acapulco. Japan's silver was perhaps a third of world output. South American production was so large it quickly became 80–85% of it! Despite Madrid's aim to ship most home to finance its wars, from 1581 two galleons sailed annually between Acapulco and Manila, exchanging silver for Asian goods. Chinese silver demand attracted American silver, either via Manila or via European merchants. Spanish Americans thought silk and porcelain cheap and China paid twice Europe's silver price, a huge incentive for evasion, 'smuggling on a grand scale'.[11] This attracted other goods like Indian cotton goods for Manila for silver to India. An estimated eight-times the declared amount of Acapulco's silver export was illegal! Chinese merchants flooded into Manila, where a special area, the Parian, was created for them in 1580. Yuegang especially sent many junks with silk, porcelain, iron, sugar, flour, chestnuts, oranges, poultry, gems, lacquerware, etc., but were vulnerable to Dutch predators approaching Manila. About 20 a year arrived in the 1580s, over 30 by 1600 and by 1603 Manila's Chinese population reached 25,000. The suspicious Spanish massacred all but 500, who returned to China.[12]

American crops including chili peppers were introduced to Fujian, influencing Sichuan cuisine, tobacco, maize and sweet potatoes, saving many lives in Fujian's 1594 famine. They helped Asian population growth, contributing to general demand and trade growth. American turkeys became fashionable pets in China.[13] Because of silver and illegal trade on two continents, China, self-isolating for two centuries, was brought into the global maritime exchange networks, albeit reluctantly. As China's population reached 150 million, its products overwhelmed Acapulco's official restrictions via wholesale smuggling and fraud, both highly lucrative. Trade shifted quickly away from Huatulco, which Cavendish finished off in 1587. Prices in Chinese goods were so attractive that in 1580, 1581 and 1582 direct shipments from Manila to Callao were made. As soon as Philip II heard, he forbade them and told the viceroy not to allow Manila's cargoes to be bought with silver. Under Peruvian pressure he reluctantly permitted some goods to be transhipped from Acapulco for a while, then reimposed the ban. Mexico ignored it and was rebuked in 1587. In 1590 Peru's viceroy sent a ship to Manila, excusing himself to Philip that its galleons had not arrived and Peru was short of iron and copper for silver mining. Manila's authorities seized the ship, probably on Philip's orders. Banned cargoes were listed as legal imports, as bribery increased. Philip, short of money, in 1590 increased taxes and seized all discharged bullion in Castile. His agent gave promissory notes but merchants were not reassured. In 1591 he permitted reshipment of goods not needed in Mexico. Peru's problem, summarised in its viceroy's report, explained its merchants trading with Spain were ruined due to the difficulty of actually securing shipments or the long periods waiting for capital returns, whereas those trading locally or with Mexico enjoyed quick turnover and steady prosperity.[14] Atlantic-based privateers targeting ships heading for Veracruz increased the problem. In contrast, Chinese goods were cheap, abundant and easy to sell. Supply was regular, more profitable, distances were shorter and privateers infrequent.

Chinese silks were cheap enough, even for locals. They sold for a ninth of Spanish textile prices in Peru with Mexican cloth in-between.[15] Seville's lucrative monopolies were ruined. In 1594 Viceroy Cañete wrote to Philip about merchant complaints of multiple Spanish and Panamanian taxes, inconvenience and lack of security. Buying goods in Mexico 'avoids all the expense and risk of going to Spain. This year and last a dozen ships have sailed to Mexico, leaving this colony swept clean of silver.'[16] By the 1590s Peru's main merchants bought Manila galleons' cargoes at Acapulco, re-shipping it before Mexican merchants could react. Cañete said most privately-exported silver went to Mexico and they taxed Chinese goods at higher rates in Callao, substantially increasing revenue. In the 1590s, Mexico-Peru trade value including reshipments from Manila galleons was two to three million pesos, in 1602 about five million, an extraordinary 12 million in 1597, contrasting with the 150–200,000 in the 1560s–1570s, with colonial products only perhaps 10% of the total, much less in 1597.[17]

Philip's aim had been to prevent Peru developing textile and wine production, to protect Spanish exports. When Cañete reported it was full of people born there without Spanish ties, was self-sufficient in food, wine, sugar and textiles and that Acapulco's shipments supplied silks, linens, etc., he concluded Manila's trade had to stop and Peru's silver buy only Spanish goods. In 1591, a limited trade in Chinese goods between Mexico and Peru was allowed, but Manila was restricted to two Acapulco-bound 300-tonners and 250,000 pesos for two years, then banned. It had no effect. Cañete was reluctant to enforce it; officials and merchants resisted. His successor tried harder but was unable to stop it. Merchants and officials smuggled hand-in-hand, the biggest loophole, the Inquisition's claim that its cargo should not be inspected. Many Chinese goods entered this way.[18] Profits were too large, bribes too tempting. Volumes increased. A Spanish American saying was that 'laws were like spider's web; they catch small offenders but not the big ones'[19] In Lima's 'Calle de Mercaderes' (Merchants Street) luxuries were sold in dozens of shops. In 1602 Peru's viceroy told Philip III that 'people live most luxuriously. All wear silk and of the most fine and costly quality...[with women's gala dresses] so excessive that in no other kingdom...are found such.'[20]

A 1604 decree limited the two vessels to 200 tons and Mexico-Peru trade to three 300-tonners with no bullion.[21] All restrictions failed. From the 1620s Venezuela shipped large cacao shipments to Mexico, on which there were no restrictions. But in 1631 all Mexico-Peru trade was banned, pressured by resentful Spanish merchants, a final bid to curb Acapulco-Manila trade draining silver to China.[22] It didn't work. Considering Chinese goods were also officially restricted, obtained by Chinese smuggling syndicates, two massive egos on opposite sides of the world, vainly attempting to restrict maritime trade, was self-destructively bizarre. The Spanish ban was as counter-productive as China's had been. Seventeenth-century Spanish bullion receipts declined, dwarfed by huge, growing unofficial bullion to Europe, variously estimated at 208–325 tons a year, to Asia, perhaps a century total of 15–16,000 tons.[23] In 1677 an Irish friar in Mexico City noted 'men and women are excessive in their apparel, using more silks than stuffs and cloths' with 'millions worth of gold, silver, pearls and jewels'.[24] Spain did not invest its windfall on infrastructure but war, impoverishing itself. Maritime-orientated regions' merchants were enriched.

Chapter 27

Dutch Ascent v Stuart Neglect:
Europe and the Americas

When James VI of Scotland succeeded Elizabeth in 1603, he announced himself as 'an old experienced king, needing no lessons,' but his Scottish experience misled him. He should have been familiar with traditional support for English merchants, the navy, privateering and sympathetic to Hakluyt's and Raleigh's American vision as a supplier of England's needs and future cloth market. He missed the growing realisation that England depended on maritime trade far more than other nations except the Dutch, England's merchant fleet growth over 40 years for pro-active Baltic, Mediterranean and Asian trade, trebling coal volumes over 30 years, quadrupling over 40, the growth of deep-sea Atlantic fisheries, 200 in Newfoundland which had employed only 30 in 1574; a new maritime world. Dutch growth was even more dynamic.

Medieval England's commercial fortunes had often been invested in land, blurring distinctions between urban-commercial and country-agrarian, different from France and Spain where trade was beneath gentlemen's dignity. English wealthy medieval merchants had virtually equal social status with gentry. William Russell, 15th-century MP for Weymouth, shipowner and wine merchant, was grandfather of the first Earl of Bedford. Hull's de la Pole merchant family became Earls of Suffolk. Younger sons of landed country families often entered merchant companies as apprentices and older ones married city heiresses.[1] This peculiarly English social mobility brought vitality to commercial life, unknown in Spain, France, China, Mughal India or indeed Scotland and an important policy influence. The trend accelerated as England's main export, cloth, found new late-16th-century markets. Elizabeth had backed merchants. James' and Charles' biggest failure was to ignore them, deliberately antagonising City and Parliamentary interests.

The 1604 peace James made with Spain effectively stopped privateering and was probably fiscally sound, but in it he accepted English merchant exclusion from Spanish America. He later told Spain about Raleigh's 1617 South American-bound fleet and in 1618 executed him, an appalling act of appeasement. Despite Parliament's hostility to industrial monopolies, on which Elizabeth recanted in 1601, probably under Cecil's advice as he disliked them, James sold more and by 1621 there were allegedly 700, affecting everyone, increasing prices, doubling coal prices when Newcastle burgesses acquired its supply to London,[2] limiting output, raising prices, lowering standards. A 1604 Commons committee described cordage monopoly as 'a strong and shameful monopoly'.[3] There were protests against monopoly glass manufacture in 1614 and gold and silver thread manufacture in 1618. In 1624 Parliament declared monopolies against England's fundamental laws, but were increasingly used.[4] From 1604 customs revenue was collected by business syndicates, 'farmers', who paid the Crown annual rent for collecting it, another loathed, inefficient monopoly benefitting financiers who made royal loans, anticipating collection. One economic historian summarised early Stuart public finance as 'no better than a racket.'[5] The Muscovy Company was managed by only 15 directors and one Russian agent. Venice's ambassador in 1622 reported London's monopoly companies 'declining owing to the charges laid upon them…they are compelled to disburse great sums to their favourites, the lords of the Council and other ministers.' London's merchants resented royal meddling.

In contrast, from the 1590s the Dutch made astonishing economic progress. The Bank of Amsterdam's (1609) major depositors were Spanish Netherlands immigrants. The Bourse, (1611) modelled on Antwerp's, to trade stocks and commodities, the VOC, Leiden's New Draperies and the Lending Bank (1614) were established. As Baltic grain, timber, iron, guns, spices, sugar and fishing had switched from Antwerp to Amsterdam, so did refining and finishing industries. English cloth and German linen were finished, English barley brewed, Brazilian sugar boiled and refined, Baltic timber converted into ships and barrels. In a few decades the Dutch cornered the most profitable economic activities, dominating markets. Its merchants travelled around England, France and the Baltic, buying goods in advance at discounts, enabling them to be sold abroad at lower prices than domestically.[6] It dominated commercial shipping. In London in 1601 Dutch ships outnumbered English 360:207.[7] A 1610 Dutch merchant's estate revealed shares in 22 ships from 1/16th to 1/32nd.[8] Crucially, its interest rates were 4% compared to England's 10%. The 1609 Truce with Spain meant the Dutch focused on commercial maritime expansion. The 1615 English pamphlet *The Trade's Increase* lamented its loss to the Dutch, especially in the Baltic. Twice the number of early-17th-century ships entered the Baltic than in the 1560s, but many Dutch ships sailed there from England until the 1621 resumption of Spanish-Dutch war.[9]

London's cloth exports were 100,000 pieces in 1600, by 1614, 127,000.[10] The Merchant Adventurers had never had it so good. Proximity of London's City and Court ensured trade interests were heard. But England's foreign trade over-depended on exporting undressed, undyed, woollen cloth to north Europe, perhaps 90%.[11] Eastland merchant Cockayne's 1613 suggestion to James to ban undyed cloth export in favour of dyed and award him the monopoly was reviewed by a 1614 report which concluded that 50–100% more export value could be expected and more employment,[12] that 30,000 Suffolk dyed cloths were exported to 'Eastland, Russia, Spain, Barbary, France, Turkey and other places' in blues, greens, azures, violets and other colours.[13] Alum had been discovered in Yorkshire. The EIC supplied dyes. A 16th-century Dutch schedule estimated dyeing was worth 47%

of profits.[14] All were excellent reasons, but English dyed cloth had been effectively shut out of the Netherlands after the War of the Roses.

Sixteenth-century difficulties for Baltic and Spanish trade, dyed cloth markets, meant over-reliance on the Netherlands. Its cloth interests protected their declining industry by rejecting English finished cloth, encouraging instead undyed cloth to bolster its industry. The Merchant Adventurers with no stake in cloth quality, accepted it. Behind protective barriers, Antwerp's industry reached high standards, while English high quality declined.[15] Following Cockayne's initiative, the Dutch banned English cloth imports. It may have been a well-thought-out, wealth-creating plan or a Court plot, swapping one monopolist group for another,[16] a get-rich-quick ruse, such was James' Court. The new King's Merchant Adventurers replaced the Merchant Adventurers in 1614 but lacked ships for Baltic export and capital, resulting in 500 bankruptcies, reduced wages, unemployment, riots and emigration. James persisted for three years before restoring the old company.

Cloth exports to north Europe collapsed from 120,000 in 1606 to 45,000 pieces by 1640.[17] Leiden's protection of its New Draperies was effective. With northern markets closed or unpromising, the Mediterranean offered the best hope of compensation and both countries merchants deployed major efforts. To compound problems, poor English harvests necessitated Baltic imports. Parliament criticised the Merchant Adventurers' monopoly, 75% of it benefitting less than 40 people, it was said,[18] and in 1624 gave freedom to outsiders to export cloth, but Charles gave monopoly back in 1634. The Greenland Company resented the soap-boilers monopoly, the EIC, as saltpetre importers, the gunpowder monopoly. Economic slump showed up a rigid economy, manipulated by royal prerogative, ill-suited to compete with adaptable low-cost Dutch merchants. The joint-stock Guinea Company, granted west African monopoly in 1618, imported hides, wax and ambergris unprofitably, more successfully in redwood. Taken over by Nicholas Crispe in 1625, it reorientated towards gold but was only partially successful due to growing Dutch dominance and lack of English naval protection.

James neglected the navy, for him a source of patronage, appointing men of social status instead of experience. Lesser offices were sold, ships disintegrated, everyone bribed and was bribed, and sailors died of bad food and conditions. In 1612 Barbary pirates inflicted £40,000 damage on the Newfoundland fishing fleet and caused continual interruptions in coastal shipping. In the Mediterranean, seamen were regularly enslaved.[19] Between 1616 and 1642 Barbary pirates captured 400 English ships and nearly 7,000 men, many from English waters.[20] Despite this, merchants braved the Mediterranean, selling New Draperies because traditional European markets had been captured or closed despite England having lower labour costs than Dutch and its own wool. Estimates of 130 ships lost annually in the Mediterranean between 1625 and 1628, a third over 100 tons, an extraordinarily high number, should be robustly questioned. John Newberry's 1583 letter claimed ships sailing in pairs could outsail and outgun enemy galleys and the trade was as safe as former London-Antwerp sailings.[21]

A 1615 Order in Council required Mediterranean goods brought to England only in English ships, a 1624 Order excluded the Dutch from American trade,[22] and in 1633, a similar order to 1615, was applied to the Baltic, the value of that trade doubling from 1622 to 1669,[23] but lack of means of enforcement meant they were useless. Between 1610 and 1619, 25% of ships sailing from England were Dutch. The percentage grew. First-half 17th-century Dutch ships passing the Sound outnumbered English ships by roughly 13:1.[24] In 1621 preacher Thomas Scott compared the industrious Dutch, their canals, windmills and liberty with England's idle nobles, hunting, hawking, dancing and drinking, while England decayed.[25]

Caribbean trade in 1600 was dominated by Dutch and English merchants. Spain was even less able to supply her colonies than before. While Portugal had audaciously attempted a take-over of the largest, most entrenched maritime trade network, Spain was unable to adequately supply a few thousand colonists, its goods sent from Seville, too few or too expensive compared to Dutch or English, who were classified as smugglers and met with brutality. Venice's ambassador to England in 1604 reported two English ships captured. They 'cut off hands, feet, nose and ears of the crew and smeared them with honey and tied them to trees to be tortured by flies and other beasts.' Another anti-smuggling attempt involved forcefully removing Hispaniola's population to around Santo Domingo. Not allowed to bring their cattle, a third died. Inability to supply their colonies and self-defeating countermeasures defeated the whole purpose of having them. They preferred evangelising Florida's natives. Not effectively colonising allowed Dutch, French and English entry.

Many English were keen settlers with economic and/or religious motives, encouraged by some as potential new markets for cloth and sources of timber, tar and hemp for which England had relied on the Baltic. Tobacco, brought to England by Raleigh, was planted in Virginia in 1613 for export. In 1619 it sent 20,000 lbs., 500,000 by 1627 and 1.3 million in 1637, creating labour demand. Maryland started in 1622. By the 1680s output became 28 million lbs.[26] Competition came from the Dutch in Venezuela and later Curaçao. Agricultural experiments were aspirational ideas of improvement and trade. Despite James' 1604 *A Counterblast to Tobacco*, describing smoking as 'loathsome to the eye, hateful to the nose, harmful to the brain,' hardly a poster for emigration and planting, it became popular. He also wrote on witches and flirted with Jean Bodin's ideas of absolute monarchy. Sir Anthony Weldon described him as 'the wisest fool in Christendom, meaning…wise in small things but a fool in weighty affairs.' Unlike Elizabeth, he was lazy, wilful, self-indulgent, irresponsible and corrupt, especially after Cecil's death in 1612.

North American settlements, 'plantations', modelled on Irish plantations of people, often sponsored by merchants, aimed to create societies in which enterprise could create wealth and enrich the state. For James, granting patent monopolies raised money. Virginia was bought by the South Virginia Company, later known as the London Company, which established Chesapeake Bay's Jamestown in 1607 and the North Virginia Company, later known as the Plymouth Company, from where they originated. Trading companies as colonisation's agents, unlike Spanish conquistadors and bureaucrats, demonstrate commercial aims; determination to combine personal profit and national advantage. Thinking Jamestown would fail, as Sagadahoc (1607), Wessagusset Bay (1622–23) and Cape Ann (1624) had, Spain did not attack. It nearly did fail. In its 1609–10 winter, 'the starving time', dogs, cats, rats, mice, shoe leather, even the dead were eaten, confirmed when a 2013 Smithsonian team found crude butchering on a 14-year old's skull. In 1622 Indians attacked it and killed about 350, after which, the revenue from tobacco exports saved it. Salem's first colonists also struggled against disease and starvation.

The Windward and Leeward Islands also presented opportunities. The first settlers on St Lucia and Grenada were chased off by native Caribs. In 1623 gentleman yeoman Thomas Warner landed on St. Christopher (St. Kitts), a fertile, 65-square mile, centrally-located island with fresh water and salt deposits, to grow tobacco. A French ship also arrived and despite Anglo-French political rivalry, the settlers allied against Caribs. From there, the 50-square mile island of Nevis was settled in 1628, quickly becoming profitable from tobacco exports, nicknamed 'Queen of the Caribees'.

Barbados' settlement showed enterprising north European Protestantism in microcosm. Visited by Spanish about 1500, it was then neglected. William and Philip Courten were English sons of a Dutch emigrant trader during the Duke of Alva's oppressive rule. William married a Dutch trader's daughter and developed connections in Europe, Greenland, Asia and the Caribbean and owned ships. In 1625 one of their captains found Barbados. The Courtens got a Crown patent to establish a settlement, the first 50 arriving in 1627. They also backed a Dutch settlement in Guiana growing tobacco, corn, cassava, ginger, indigo, sweet potatoes, bananas and other fruits. Arawaks taught growing techniques in return for land.[27] They concentrated on tobacco, inspired by Virginia's success. By 1628 St. Kitts and Barbados sent back 100,000 lbs. a year.

Dutch demand for salt grew with massive growth in herring exports. At Punta del Araya, Venezuela, huge salt pans were found and Dutch ships arrived in 1599. Up to 1608, 768 Dutch ships sailed there, one in ten loaded, the rest in ballast.[28] The Spanish routed a fleet in 1605, killing 400, mutilating others. The Dutch returned with armed ships. The 1609 Truce with Spain opened Setubal's salt pans, but after 1621, war resumed and they returned. The Spanish blockaded it, although other Caribbean sources were developed. The Dutch matched Spanish brutality, massacring 1,200 and selling 100 women and children to Barbary pirates after a raid on La Margarita in 1623.

The Dutch and English, having failed to find a northeast passage to the Moluccas, tried the northwest. The Dutch instead discovered Manhattan Island in 1609, bought it from natives for 60 guilders worth of trinkets and invested another 20,000 in New Amsterdam in 1625, sending back over 7,500 high-value beaver furs, bartered for more trinkets, to be felt for waterproof hats. It irritated James who claimed the whole American coast because of Cabot's discovery. By 1630, its population was only 300, but by 1655, 2,000–3,500, including Germans, Swedes, Finns and Huguenots. The Dutch ambassador told James they had regular trade 'and keep factors there, continually resident.' He was probably also aggrieved at New Sweden on the Delaware River.

Castile and England colonised differently. Castile's was theoretically closely regulated, based on native tribute and services, bullion mining and export. England's was by motivated religious groups or merchant companies. Plymouth, Connecticut and Rhode Island had no royal charter, were self-governing and self-motivated. England sanctioned projects providing refuge for religious minorities, often very entrepreneurial. Castile prevented Jews, Moors and heretics to migrate[29] and regulated authorised colonists. Institutions were imposed. Much energy was spent jockeying for rank in deference to the Crown.[30] In 1631 the Marquis of Castro Fuerle bemoaned Castile's labour shortage, 'because of constant recruiting for service in America, the Netherlands, Italy, the garrisons and the fleet…the kingdom is very short of men.' Restricting the Americas for Castile meant Valencia and Catalonia prevented colonial recruitment.

In English colonies, most institutions evolved from below, grounded in ideas of representation.[31] The Virginia Assembly first met in 1619. Also in 1619 the Bermuda Company sent Nathaniel Butler to Bermuda with instructions to summon an assembly promptly, as 'every man will more willingly obey laws to which he has yielded his consent.'[32] Voting was normal in joint stock companies and there was a natural predisposition to create representative bodies based on Parliament, representing traditional English liberties. By 1640, eight such assemblies operated.

English colonies' salvation came from innovative efforts to cultivate and export profitable crops. They kept close to the coast, whereas early evidence of gold made Spanish settlers range into the interior. Unlike Castile's colonies, England's labour came from English indentured service, constituting 75–85% of Chesapeake's settlers. Private ownership was crucial to success. Profit was strong motivation whether for Virginia's tobacco planters or pious New Englanders.[33] In 1624, Charles dissolved the Virginia Company, imposing direct royal rule for 'one uniform course of government' a dangerously continental, authoritarian, non-commercial notion. Elsewhere, much as Charles desired royal control, he had no enforcement means. Corporate or individual proprietors were in control. Lacking precious metals, other accessible local commodities or local labour, private enterprise and hard work were preconditions of eventual success.[34]

In 1627 Spain ordered all Caribbean non-Spanish expelled and took some islands. They missed Nevis but in 1629 St. Kitts surrendered. Its tobacco plantations were destroyed. Some settlers were sent home, some enslaved, but many returned and started daughter settlements in Montserrat and Antigua. Spanish actions thus just spread French, Dutch and English further. In the 1624–29 Anglo-Spanish war, England probably lost over 300 ships, including more than 100 over 100 tons, a large loss for a small fleet.[35] Barbados lay away from Spain's galleon route, so avoided Spanish and Carib threats, but not famine when tobacco prices slumped. The Earl of Warwick's 1629 Providence Island Company attempted colonisation, midway between Jamaica and Costa Rica, close to the Spanish route from Vera Cruz to Havana, as a Puritan colony. Centrally controlled from London with colonists as tenants without security of tenure and half the profits going to investors, they had no incentive to experiment. It failed and instead became, with Tortuga, on Hispaniola's north coast, and Jamaica, privateering hubs. According to Sir Thomas Gage in 1637 'the greatest fear that possessed the Spanish in this voyage was the island of Providence,'[36] but in 1641 the Spanish took it.

Unlike Virginia, Massachusetts' soil could not support its growing population and became dependent on fishing and trade with England and the Caribbean. In 1625 a Whitby shipbuilder built a 500-tonner for the New England Company.[37] Discovery of alum nearby, saw the port, its population and fleet rise further. In the 1630s–40s as many dissenting religious groups emerged, Whitby's George Fox established the Society of Friends, the Quakers, an example of free minds with new ideas, becoming an important economic force. Newcastle coal, increasingly shipped to London, encouraged northeast English ports. At first dependant on English imports, by the 1630s Massachusetts sold timber to the Caribbean and fish to Iberia, whose wine and oil were sent to England with English manufactures back to Massachusetts. By 1642 it had 16,000 settlers, mainly East Anglian and Lincolnshire Congregationalists, believers in education. A college was endowed in 1636, to which John Harvard left his library two years later. By 1660, 60% of adult men and 30% of women were literate.[38] After Laud became Archbishop of Canterbury, many puritan clergy emigrated. Between 1629 and 1640, about 80,000 left for New England and Caribbean islands, many in family groups, inspired by clergymen. Some were merchants with London and Bristol relationships. Up to 70–80% were rural poor, indentured servants suffering the 1630s economic depression, inflation, and bad harvests, serving four to five years in return for passage, board and lodging.[39]

Establishing colonies was risky but economic hardship, anti-puritan religious policy, incompetent governance and promises of great returns from Virginia's tobacco encouraged it. Ports in Salem, Connecticut and Rhode Island diversified into fishing, fur and timber trading. From the austere north to the tropical south, English settlements developed differently, thus ideally interdependent. Having developed independently, with much risk, Charles tried to subordinate colonies, but their financing depended on merchants. Industrialists, merchants and grain growers wanted freer trade, no monopolies and a strong navy to protect trade, fishing and colonisation. The Dutch facilitated trade and wealth creation; the Stuarts hindered it.

Newfoundland's trade was triangular. Cod was shipped to the Mediterranean, Canaries, and Iberia which sent bullion, cork, olive oil, wine and fruit to England and Holland which sent labour and supplies to Newfoundland. It was known as the sack trade, derived from 'vino de sacca', exported wine. England's Iberian trade thus grew,[40] especially from west coast ports like Bristol. Most were Dutch and French ships taking fish to the Mediterranean, Spain, Portugal, France and England before 1640, but London wine merchant Kirke, Berkeley and Co. started in 1627 and in the 1627–29 war with France, obtained letters of marque to privateer against French Canada, taking several ships. It started sack trading in the 1630s, by which time 300–500 ships annually fished off Newfoundland.[41] David Kirke and family settled in Ferryland, Newfoundland, founded in the 1620s, where he also traded St. Lawrence and Hudson Bay furs for fish. Berkeley traded with Virginia, Bermuda, Greenland and New England. Both were typical City merchants pursuing North American commerce. Charles gave them a Newfoundland shipping monopoly in 1637, with a 5% tax on fish caught by foreign vessels, discouraging the Dutch.[42] By 1640 they were major fish producers, linked to fish brokers in west coast ports, which sold to Spain. Ships were heavily armed. A charter party clause addressed the cost of gunpowder, 'spent…in defence', reflecting French hostility. Returns, about 15–30%, were never consistent. Losses and fluctuating insurance rates encouraged traditional ship ownership division. Most of its vessels were London-based but by the late-1640s, Kirke operated Ferryland-based ships and traded with Boston.[43]

Finding no gold in Jamaica, Spanish settlers moved on. By mid-century its natives were extinct, its economy moribund. English privateers settled there for pre-emptive attacks on Spanish ships and colonies. They became known as buccaneers from *viande boucanée*, smoked meat, on-board food sold with tobacco, sugar and hides.[44] Dutch also settled on three Windward Islands, Curacao in 1634, Aruba and Bonaire off the Venezuelan coast, and on St. Martin in 1631, St. Eustatius in 1636, and Saba in the 1640s.

By the 1640s, England had more people in the Caribbean than others and more than mainland America until the 1660s. It was much more economically important. From 1640 to 1649 Virginia's tobacco exports boomed from 1.4 million lbs. to 15 million, much re-exported from England.[45] Increasing Caribbean production meant prices crashed from 20 to 40 shillings in James' reign, to just a few pence by 1630, a penny a few years later, driving Caribbean tobacco from the market before 1650. Virginia's was still profitable and production increased. But Barbados' early-1630s 'starving time'[46] was exacerbated by a seven-times population growth between 1635 and 1639.[47] Cotton was attempted as a replacement. More capital intensive and more difficult to grow, they nevertheless succeeded with help from Dutch in Brazil and by the late-1630s marketed it in England, hitherto dependent on Cypriot and Levantine cotton. Meanwhile Portuguese Brazil's sugar plantations grew, despite war with the Dutch.

In 1642, expelled Dutch planters from Brazil took sugar, even more demanding than cotton to grow and process, first to Barbados, then other islands. It became the main crop, produced cheaper than in Brazil. Caribbean agriculture's reorganisation, the Sugar Revolution, needed more land, labour, capital, expertise and equipment. Barbados' first successful sugar planter, Henry Drax sent his sugar to Bridgetown, shipped in Dutch ships to Amsterdam, London and Hamburg. As in the

Mediterranean, west Africa and Brazil, sugar production meant slave labour. As production expanded, so did demand for slaves.

By 1645, 40% of Barbados' agriculture was plantation sugar. With Brazilian production and export disrupted, (Chapter 30) prices soared and Barbados transformed from starving time to boom time. Sugar growers became rich. It no longer fed itself, thus trade with North America from the 1640s became vital for both areas. A Virginian ox bought for £5 was worth £25 in Barbados. Dependency on New England food nurtured its shipbuilding. By the late-1640s, Rhode Island bred horses for Barbados. Samuel Winthrop of Massachusetts in 1647 carried wine from Madeira to Barbados, considered living on St. Kitts, but decided Barbados a better bet. William Vassal, a founder member of the Massachusetts Bay Company also relocated to Barbados and traded between the two,[48] but Dutch ships carried its cargoes.

Barbados' success encouraged emigration. Thomas Kendall, a wealthy London merchant with Caribbean trading experience and brother-in-law Thomas Modyford, son of an Exeter merchant, sent two ships in 1647. They planned shipping English goods to the Canaries and Cape Verde Islands, exchange them for horses to sell in Barbados and establish a plantation in Antigua. Richard Ligon noted Bridgetown in 1647 home to around 1,500 merchants, artisans, servants and slaves, 'boats plying to and fro as numerous as I have seen below the bridge at London,' estimating 100 a year. Modyford bought a half-share of a 200-acre sugar estate. Ligon described how a couple of voyages between England and Barbados could triple an investment, enough for a down payment on an estate. One of 200 acres could produce a crop worth £7,000.[49] This was a land of opportunity for those with energy, industry, foresight and determination, but with an unhealthy climate. European and tropical diseases, until the early-19th century caused about a third of all whites to die within three years of arrival. For those who survived and bought estates, wealth accumulation was rapid. Some indentured servants became overseers, some even became wealthy plantation owners.

Chapter 28

Dutch Ascent v Stuart Neglect: EIC v VOC

T he VOC reached Calicut in 1604 and allied with it against the Portuguese but couldn't take Goa. Surat and Cambay were termini of land routes to north and central India and hajj embarkation ports. As Cambay silted up, Surat's late-1500s merchants made it Gujarat's main port, with Cambay retaining its industries. In 1612 the EIC received Mughal permission to trade at Surat, the VOC five years later. Both quickly extended trade inland. In 1610 the Raja of Vellore, controlling the Coromandel coast's Pulicat, gave the VOC a quasi-monopoly over its trade. Realising his mistake, in 1614 he invited the EIC. The VOC gained Jaffna from the Portuguese for its cinnamon exports. Cotton cloth weaving centres were India-wide. In 1611, the VOC established a factory at Golconda's Masulipatnam, to supply cloth to Bantam, Ayutthaya, Patani on the Malay Peninsula and Hirado in Japan, where the cooler climate appeared promising for English cloth sales, for silver with which to buy spices, a perfect triangular trade. But it made little headway. With more resources and ships, the VOC were already there.

In 1607–08 an EIC commander reminded Red Sea Ottoman governors that Levant Company merchants already traded with Ottoman Mediterranean ports. The Persian Safavids, continental-minded, originating from northwest Persia, competed with Ottomans for Mesopotamia, Armenia and Kurdistan. Shah Abbas (r. 1588–1629) however, was more aware of international trade and made overtures to Dutch, English and French. In 1611, he asked the EIC to help attack Portuguese Hormuz, and offered silk for bullion at Jask, which weakened Hormuz. In 1620, EIC ships broke a Portuguese blockade[1] and in 1622 agreed to attack Hormuz if the Shah paid half the costs, they receive exemptions from customs duties and half those collected from other merchants. Hormuz was destroyed. Portuguese trade was diverted to Muscat and Basra and the EIC given permission in 1623 to settle at Gombroon, now Banda Abbas, little more than an anchorage compared with Hormuz. But the VOC arrived, supplanted them with more cash and spices compared with the EIC's tin and cloth. The EIC insisted the VOC should pay them customs duties as agreed with Shah Abbas, but they refused. The market was small, just silk, traded through Isfahan's Armenian merchants, the wealth generated still seen in Isfahan's architecture. VOC recourses enabled the 1631 Persia-VOC free-trade treaty. In 1637 they bought over three-times that of the EIC.[2]

Henry Middleton, Bantam's EIC representative thought 'if this frothy nation [the Dutch] may have the trade of the Indies to themselves, their pride and insolence will be intolerable.' EIC attempts to build factories on Tidore, Ternate and the

Banda's Run were frustrated by the already ensconced Dutch. In 1607 an English expedition was sent with £17,600 of gold and £3,000 worth of goods. Cloves bought for £3,000 could be sold in London for £36,000. In 1608 Middleton bought spices from a Javanese vessel in Sulawesi and he soon had a factor in Makassar. The combined profit of the EIC's first two voyages was 95%, the third and fifth 234%, averaging 95% over eight years. Its 15-year charter was extended indefinitely, but more ships were needed. In 1609 the VOC sent a fleet to the Bandas 'to win them... by treaty or force.' The 1610 EIC mission, conscious of its weaker position vis-a-vis the VOC, aimed to woo native Banda traders, alienated by VOC aggression. Many ports were visited en route to search for potential cloth markets to 'drive a trade without the transportation of money.' England had adapted her cloth for Mediterranean and Levant markets, but wool was unsuited to the tropics.

Jan Pieterszoon Coen was from Hoorn, an aggressive VOC port. Its 17th-century buildings, warehouses and *Peperstraat* near the harbour are still there. Disciplined and motivated, Coen ruthlessly executed his aggressive philosophy; 'Trade in Asia should be conducted and maintained under the protection and with the aid of our weapons...wielded with the profits gained by trade. So, trade cannot be maintained without war or war without trade.' His second trip in 1612 was as chief merchant.

Banda Islands' chiefs preferred the EIC, whose factor John Jourdain pleaded for more ships; 'the people will live and die with the English, for now all the Bandanese hath open wars with the Hollanders.'[3] A chief explained that the English 'hath done no hurt to any of our religion, or doth seek to overthrow our law...but only peace and friendship doth seek trade without violence' and asked for arms to destroy Neira's VOC fort. The EIC complained of VOC warlike behaviour and an Anglo-Dutch conference discussed the differences from 1613 to 1619. The English had got there first but the Dutch built buildings first. While they talked, Coen sent back huge cargoes of spices. The VOC Council ruthlessly instructed, 'something must be done against the enemies; the inhabitants of Banda must be subjected, their leaders must be killed or driven out of the land and if necessary, the country must be turned into a desert by uprooting the trees and shrubs.' Meanwhile, having taken Ai, the EIC took the last remaining tiny island of Run, yielding 330,000 lbs. of nutmeg and mace a year, but was blockaded by Coen. Its desperate people and refugees from other islands, in the hope of protection, conferred sovereignty on James, King of England, Scotland, France, Ireland, Run and Ai. One wit thought these miniscule islands would yield more profit than Scotland.

Coen seized Jakarta, 50 miles east of Bantam in 1619. It became the Dutch equivalent of Malacca, but 375 miles south, nearer the Moluccas. The locals objected. Typically ruthless, he burnt it and built Batavia, adjacent to the Sunda Strait. Its rice-growing hinterland was something Malacca lacked. Constant warfare with Bantam was, the EIC factor said, because the VOC intended 'to kill all trade there',[4] which they did, as its Chinese traders moved to Batavia. Under VOC direction, Java and Sumatra replaced India's Malabar coast as the world's main pepper supplier.

The 1619 Anglo-Dutch Conference agreement was that the VOC and EIC stop fighting, return captured ships, release prisoners, the EIC get a third of Moluccan trade and both should cooperate to expel Spain and Portugal from Asia. It was too generous to the EIC, its failing strength not fully appreciated. Coen ignored it and took Run from the EIC. When the Bandas revolted in 1621, Coen killed, enslaved and deported its people. Many died en route, replaced with Dutch planters, African and Bengali slaves and Japanese mercenaries.

Spices became increasingly profitable for the VOC. Coen depopulated Banda by cutting off inbound rice shipments in 1620–21. Clove imports to Holland peaked in the 1620s as the VOC burned stores in Asia and Amsterdam to lift prices and profits. In 1622 they unsuccessfully attacked Macao, occupied Mauritius, tried capturing Portuguese convoys in the Mozambique Channel, built Fort Zeelandia on Taiwan in 1624 as a Macao equivalent, where Chinese merchants were attracted by abundant deer, their hides in demand in Japan, and occupied part of Sri Lanka to rival Portuguese Goa. Like Portuguese private traders, the VOC recognised regional trade opportunities. Coen in 1619 wrote, 'piece goods from Gujarat we can barter for pepper and gold on the east coast of Sumatra; rials and cottons from Coromandel for pepper in Bantam, sandalwood, pepper and rials...for Chinese goods and Chinese gold...silver from Japan with Chinese goods; piece goods from the Coromandel coast in exchange for spices....one thing leads to another.'[5] Indeed, intra-Asian trade became its most lucrative activity, its profits according to VOC directors in 1648 'the soul of the company...if the soul decays, the entire body would be destroyed.'[6] Europe's annual 1620's spice consumption, around five million lbs. of pepper and a million of cloves, nutmeg and mace,[7] was puny in terms of Asian trade volumes.

In 1620 an EIC commander took the Cape of Good Hope, but James ignored the claim and it remained no-man's land until VOC take-over in 1652. Until 1621, the EIC operated from its governor's home with only six permanent staff, although its warehouse, 30–40 ships from Deptford and Blackwall with wet and dry docks, timber yards, foundry, cordage works, bakery and saltings made it one of London's largest employers. But it struggled against VOC resources and James' indifference. Amboyna with 280 square miles of clove plantations was the Molucca's largest island. In 1623 the VOC executed 18 Englishmen, 'the Amboyna massacre,' triggering seizure of Dutch ships in the Channel in 1626. In 1633 the EIC ordered their Bantam merchants to reoccupy Run, but the VOC had destroyed the nutmeg trees and killed or enslaved the population. EIC ships sailing east fell by two-thirds, overheads and employees were slashed. In 1639 it sold its ships and shipyards, reflecting Dutch spice superiority and James' and Charles' economic torpor. From then on, the EIC chartered ships from shipowners for consecutive voyages. With Bantam's sultan unwilling to accept Indian cloth as a currency, an EIC factory was established at Jambi.[8] Makassar became popular with foreign traders as a spice entrepot, where seafaring Bugis and Malays sold them to all-comers, including EIC representatives.

The EIC concentrated instead on Surat's indigo, initially the most valuable export and calicoes, establishing a factory at Masulipatnam in Golconda to supply Bantam. Varied soils and thousands of years of cotton domestication had produced many regional cloth varieties. Indian cotton cloths, the world's first manufactured product, traded for millennia, became its most voluminous traded commodity. Spice-obsessed Portuguese had shipped little back, selling instead in Southeast Asia. The VOC followed suit where they had weakened the EIC. Thus in 1623 the EIC took the risk to aggressively market them in Europe; 'the use [of calicoes] is not generally known…[sales] must be forced and trial made into all ports.'[9] EIC European sales were its only success, importing 221,000 pieces in 1625, compared with the VOC's 12,000 or so,[10] some re-exported to the Mediterranean. Persian silks by contrast were barely profitable.

A 1630s Gujarati famine devastated weaving districts, so the EIC concentrated on Coromandel cloth, got Mughal permission to establish factories in Bengal and imported pepper from Jambi, its main supplier.[11] In 1639 Golconda's Sultan visited Masulipatnam, including VOC and EIC enclaves, noting EIC poverty compared with the VOC.[12] Other English merchants however, looked enviously at EIC monopoly. Four non-EIC ships arrived in Canton in 1637. Charles granted licences, contrary to EIC monopoly, for other expeditions including the Assada Company to Madagascar to grow crops and as an inter-Asian trade base.[13] Charles' trade policy veered between shambolic and non-existent.

Golconda's king granted the EIC preferential trading conditions at Masulipatnam, for painted chintz cotton exports to Southeast Asia. They were invited into Madrasapattinam village (Madras), and allowed to build a factory and Fort St. George in 1639. A source of hope for the beleaguered EIC, artisans flocked there, lured by increased calico weaving and chintz painting. It prospered for 14 years until a famine. The VOC were in Bengal after the 1632 Mughal expulsion of the Portuguese. One historian thinks high Mughal officials in Bengal and Bihar after Hugli's capture in 1632, carried on 'pragmatic merchant-like policy' vis-à-vis Portuguese,[14] citing Shaista Khan, who took Chatgaon from Arakan in northwest Burma and cornered the wax market around Agra, one of many Mughal officials getting rich by trade. Another interpretation is they exploited their privileged political appointments. Bengal's main trades were slaves and rice, in which the VOC were interested from the 1620s, but were often frustrated by Arakan regulation and control.

As the Japan-China trade had been lucrative for Portugal, the VOC targeted it more aggressively than the EIC. The Shogun, the real power behind Japan's revered, powerless emperor, perceived Christianity as a threat to stability, the hard-won peace and centralisation of Nobunaga, Hideyoshi and Tokugawa Ieyasu. By demanding powerful daimyo's attendance at Court, their former wealth-creating trading activities were checked. Overseas trade directed through Nagasaki had come under Hideyoshi's control in 1587. Taxes on it bolstered revenues. Once the Toyotomi clan was defeated in 1615, the only perceived challenge was Christianity, which had grown with Spanish-Portuguese missionary activity. EIC and VOC traders reinforced Japanese suspicions, emphasising that they separated religion and trade. The need to negate Christianity's threat and complete centralised control resulted in *sakoku* or exclusion. A series of edicts from 1633 to 1651 restricted trade and enforced control, especially 1635's *sakoku-rei*. The Japanese were to be kept inside Japan, lest they be tainted with foreign ideas, Europeans kept out, both on pain of death, Catholicism and missionaries forbidden and trade with the Portuguese cut. Only the VOC were allowed in Dejima, a tiny 236 by 82 pace, man-made island in Nagasaki. Trade with China was conducted via the Ryukyu Islands, consistent with conducting trade with Korea via Tsushima and with Ainu via Matsumae. Merchants had to obtain special trade licences and only specific vessels were permitted. Like all bans, they were flouted. The Shimazu family, Lords of Satsuma, continued smuggling with agents in China, but the ban prevented deeper economic development.[15]

Chapter 29

Anglo-Dutch Intellectual, Scientific and Cultural Advances and Exchanges

Late-16th and 17th century European maritime culture was mainly Anglo-Dutch with smaller hubs in Danish, German, Swedish and Mediterranean ports. Livorno replaced Venice for the same reason that Hamburg overtook Lubeck; tolerance of diversity. Intellectual, scientific, philosophical and artistic accomplishments were, not coincidentally Anglo-Dutch affairs, often colluding at the time of greatest maritime endeavour, despite Asian rivalry. Long-haul Asian and American trade stimulated commercial problem-solving that went hand-in-hand with intellectual stimulus in literature, art, philosophy and science, starkly contrasting with ossified thought in France, Spain and central Europe, which accelerated serfdom's harsh conditions.

Unrestrained intellectual enquiry from naturalists, medical practitioners, mathematicians and inventors began the realisation that 'earth, air, fire, water' no longer adequately explained the world. They corresponded, swapped information, specimens and ideas. A 1570 version of Euclid emphasised maths as useful for business. Elizabeth's chief minister Cecil directed funds at mining and metallurgy. Vernacular writing and inquisitiveness accompanied maritime expansion, with English translations of the *Bible* and Homer. Francis Bacon (1561–1626) encapsulated it, demanding investigation by planned procedure and scientific methodology, for 'inventions which shall overcome...and subdue our needs and miseries,' a practical, progressive programme, a 'medicine' to arrest decline.[1] This started the movement to 'improve'; practical invention. He also promoted colonies, simple law, opposed feudal privileges and religious persecution, identifying England with classical Athens. His namesake Roger Bacon (c. 1220–1294) had explored mathematics, optics, astronomy and alchemy as European attitudes to knowledge adjusted with widening horizons, but looked for answers in Muslim lands, writing to the pope to establish an encyclopaedia of knowledge. Seventeenth-century self-confidence to progress by experiment replaced deference to ancient knowledge. An early product was William Gilbert who in 1636 calculated that some stars were over 20,000-times larger than the sun, leading him to ponder human significance.

Literature's variety and quantity accompanied maritime energy and scientific thought. Edmund Spencer's (1552–99) *Faerie Queene* captured England's mood. Christopher Marlowe (1564–1593), its foremost dramatist, wrote *Tamburlaine* and *Doctor Faustus*; foreign characters. He influenced Shakespeare who re-used many ideas in enduring human themes that Ben Jonson (1572–1637), known for satirical plays and lyric poems, rightly declared, 'was not of an age, but for all time.' Comedies, tragedies, love stories and histories, transcending time and culture, summarised emotions in simple, elegant verse that entered the English language; sea-change, vanished into thin air, refuse to budge an inch, the game's afoot, tongue-tied, tower of strength, slept not one wink, stood on ceremony, lived in a fool's paradise, cruel to be kind, too much of a good thing, eaten me out of house and home, there's the rub, pride of place, one fell swoop, insisted on fair play and many more. His characters, especially poignant, complex ones, *Hamlet, King Lear* and *Macbeth*, are unequalled in any other literature, illuminating human emotional range; pride, envy, greed, loyalty, treachery, self-doubt, prejudice, madness, whimsy, ambition, the difficulties of family, giving future moral and political philosophers a rich seed-bed of thought-provoking material. Is there a 'divinity that shapes our ends, rough hew them how we will'?[2] *Othello*, a Moor, could not have been written with such sympathy in Spain, nor indeed any other country. *The Merchant of Venice* begins as an apparently stereotypical Jewish hate-figure with asides about hatred of Christians, his audience perhaps reminded of Marlowe's dastardly *The Jew of Malta*, written nearly ten years earlier, then elicits sympathy. 'If you prick us do we not bleed? If you tickle us do, we not laugh? If you poison us, do we not die?' It is impossible to envisage such philosophical questions about tolerance and diversity elsewhere. Nor were they written for a cultural elite. 'The Theatre' at Shoreditch was supplemented by the 'Rose' in 1587, modified for an audience 20% larger just five years later, the 'Swan' in 1596, and the 'Globe' in 1599, testament to London's dynamism,[3] totalling 17 in 1629 compared with only one in Paris, as London handled 80% of English trade,[4] Paris indifferent to it.

Shakespeare's Spanish contemporary Cervantes (1547–1616) had *Don Quixote* (1605) tilting at windmills, interpreted as attacking the Church, Inquisition, or outright nihilism, while Lopes de Vega's (1562–1635) *Fuenteovejuna* criticised government oppression, both in sharp contrast with the vitality and optimism of contemporary English literature, depicted in *Henry V* as a 'happy band of brothers.' John Webster (1580–1634) wrote more macabre and disturbing tragedies with women his main characters in *The Duchess of Malfi* and *The White Devil*, impossible in Spain, although his cynicism may have reflected England's lost purpose after Elizabeth. Similarly, Hobbes' translation of Thucydides' *History* in 1629, capturing Athenian dynamism and Spartan immobility, must have triggered Anglo-Dutch political comparisons.

John Donne (1572–1631) was a prolific metaphysical poet, his poems and sonnets noted for their strong sensual, sometimes erotic style. His satires dealt with legal corruption, pompous courtiers and mediocre poets, but also true religion, arguing that it was better to carefully examine one's religious convictions than blindly follow established tradition, an important development, thinking for oneself, reflected in his shift to more personal poetry. His quotes, 'No man is an island' and 'Any man's death diminishes me, because I am involved in mankind,' are early expressions of humanity, only possible in a nation connecting with others in productive trade, with new people, cultures and products in a necessarily tolerant way, expressed in geographical metaphors.

The Dutch Republic's commercial rise was also accompanied by free enquiry. In the 1580s, intellectual debate centred on ideas developed at Leiden University, whether a state needs a uniting religion and religious toleration. Toleration won. Rene Descartes, (1596–1650) sometimes called the father of modern philosophy, wrote his major works during his stay there (1628–1649). In 1621 he enthused, 'is there another country where you can enjoy such perfect liberty?' 'What place on earth could one chose where all the commodities and all the curiosities one could wish for were as easy to find in this city?'[5] Best known for his philosophical quote, 'I think therefore I am,' he changed the way of thinking from 'what is true' to 'of what can I be certain' and was key in replacing revelatory religious truth and Church doctrine with individual judgement through reason. His influence on algebra and analytical geometry was crucial to discovering calculus, later developed by Newton. He used geometry in optics, laws of refraction and reflection, and mentored Christian Huygens (1629–1695), astronomer, physicist and mathematician. Amsterdam's growth became a magnet for Sephardic Jewish merchants. The converso exodus from Portugal after 1580 provided an economic boost, to Portugal's detriment. By the 1630s Jews controlled an estimated 6–8% of Dutch trade, 15–20% of Amsterdam's,[6] especially with Iberia including half Brazil's sugar trade and contributed to 21 sugar refineries built in the Twelve Years Truce. Between 1609 and 1620 the number of Sephardic accounts at the Amsterdam Exchange Bank rose from 24 to 114.[7]

Dutch surveyor and embankment engineer Cornelius Vermuyden, summoned by James I in 1621 when the Thames overflowed, in 1626 drained Lincolnshire's Isle of Axeholme, settling in England, later reclaiming the Great Fen for the Earl of Bedford after the Civil War.[8] The most famous Dutch hydraulic engineer, Jan Leeghwater (1575–1650), added huge areas of land to the republic. England improved agriculture with Dutch techniques and new Dutch crops; turnips, cabbages, cauliflowers, carrots, parsnips and peas to market gardens around London.

Grotius (1583–1645) wrote *Mare Liberum* in 1610 at VOC behest on international law, inventing the idea of freedom of the seas, arguing that liberty, order and virtue were best preserved under consultative government reserved for those with wealth, education and leisure. His son Pieter de Groot explained, 'What constitutes the wealth of the republic? The opulence of its trade…what is the source of that trade? Good government. For nothing is more attractive for the whole world than freedom of conscience and security of possessions.' In contrast, early-16th century Spanish contacts with foreign intellectual centres did not lead to 17th-century science and technology because from the 1550s its students were forbidden to attend foreign universities to avoid contagious heresy and between 1625 and 1634 no licenses were granted for printing novels and plays.[9]

Anglo-Dutch scientific enquiry went hand-in-hand with great art. The Stadtholder in the 1620s-1630s patronised artists and architects. Wealthy merchants followed suit. Following extravagant Flemish Catholic painter Rubens (1577–1640), religious painting declined and a diversity of secular subjects arose; landscapes with animals, church towers, windmills, some in winter with frozen canals, cloud formations and resulting lights cast on land. Seascapes with warships or Indiamen were favourite topics, the republic dependent on them. In still life, popular subjects were flowers, fruit and dead game. Scientists often posed with their instruments and the objects of their study, most famously in Rembrandt's *Anatomy Lesson of Dr. Nicolaes Tulp* (1632). Portraits and family groups were popular with servants dressed almost indistinguishably from the family served. Many were painted at home, the living room, kitchen, in the study reading a letter, playing cards, taking a music lesson, drinking from a translucent glass, pondering over charts and maps, reflecting a widening world, a woman weighing silver, lubricating increasing trade volumes. No more naked cherubs and angels, but reflections of widening trade contacts and the wealth it brought; Chinese porcelain, silks, Turkish carpets and beaver felt hats.[10]

Foreigners were impressed with the quantity of Dutch art, over 1.3 million pictures painted between 1640 and 1660, meaning low prices and accessibility. The artists were not always popular at the time. Vermeer, Hals and even Rembrandt in his last years struggled to earn a living. *The Night Watch, Storm on the Sea of Galilee* and self-portraits however, became instantly recognisable classics, as did Vermeer's *Girl with a Pearl Earring*, yet he was considered an artistic artisan, not important enough to warrant an inscribed gravestone. Dutch architecture reached new heights in town halls, storehouses and merchant houses, still standing by Amsterdam's canals. Although Flemish art influenced German art, the latter still portrayed demons and goblins, a world of superstitious ignorance.

English and Dutch cultural and religious similarities fostered bonds in other fields. Dutch and Flemish artists were well-established at the English Court before the Civil War. Rubens painted in England, most notably the ceiling at the Banqueting Hall in Inigo Jones's (1573–1652) Palace of Whitehall. After a career in the theatre designing moveable scenery, Jones was the first architect employing classical symmetry and proportion in building designs, seen at Covent Garden, the first internationally celebrated. Other Dutch painters had strong English links like group and portrait painter, Gerard van Honthorst (1592–1656), Jan Lievens (1607–1674), Adriaen Hanneman (1603–1671) who painted portraits of the exiled British Court in the style of Anthony Van Dyke (1599–1641), a Court painter in England, Peter Lely (1618–80), George Geldorp (c. 1580–1665), who painted for the Cecils and Balthazar Gerbier (1592–1663), mathematician, architect and painter, commissioned by the Duke of Buckingham.

In England, as much charitable money was given between 1600 and 1640 as in the previous century, a quarter from merchants,[11] not to friars, monasteries, churches, prayers or chants for dead souls. Catholics cherished poor, holy hermits and charity for the moral betterment of donors, Protestants for the social and economic improvement of recipients, believing there was no virtue in poverty, a social evil and dangerous for the soul. Apprenticeship and training schemes increased, especially merchant-sponsored.[12]

Chapter 30

"All the wars carried on in Europe have been mixed up together and become one"

While exciting commercial opportunities were seized world-wide, Spain restricted its subjects, spent its silver and tax revenue on huge military commitments in the Netherlands and a large Mediterranean galley fleet to protect Naples and keep Ottomans and Barbary allies at bay. Failure to re-capture the Dutch provinces after 50 years and repeated defaults on her debts led to the Twelve Years Truce of 1609. When negotiating it, the main issue was Dutch insistence on the right to trade with Spain, Asia and the Caribbean, a problem fudged by an exemption of countries 'that chose to grant permission'; meaning if colonists willingly accepted Dutch goods for their silver, sugar, tobacco, ginger, indigo, hides and cacao. Spain did not accept that the Truce was an admission of defeat. For everyone else it was. Spanish nationalists thought it betrayal, angry at reputational loss. Portuguese and Spanish ships were even insured on the Amsterdam market. After 50 years of war, the Truce could have ushered in peace, but did not apply outside Europe, allowing Dutch expansion, attacking Portuguese spice traders just south of the Philippines with apparent impunity. The Armada had failed spectacularly. The Scheldt was closed. Antwerp wasted away. People already talked of Spanish decline. It imported European manufactured goods, naval stores, grain and weapons, mainly in Dutch ships, draining it of silver and gold.

It badly needed political and economic reform. The 1596 default was followed by another in 1607. By 1598, interest payments took 40% of its revenue and in 1618, eve of The Thirty Years War, 50%. If France regained stability, Spain would have extra problems. Apparently inexhaustible Peruvian and Mexican silver, giving Philip confidence to fight on all fronts, was spent frighteningly easily, but 75% of Spanish revenue came from taxes on Castile, Naples and Milan. Yet xenophobia and religious purity still ruled heads. From 1621 chief minister Olivares decided on aggression. His mentor Zuniga was more cautious, noting in 1619 that 'whoever looks at the matter carefully…must be impressed by the great strength of those [Dutch] provinces by both land and sea, their strong geographical position, ringed by the sea and great rivers…that state is at the very height of its greatness, while ours is in disarray' and 'to promise ourselves we can conquer the Dutch is to seek the impossible, to delude ourselves.'[1] Olivares however, wrote to Philip III, 'You are the main support and defence of the Catholic religion; for this reason, you have to renew the war with the Dutch and with other enemies of the Church,' although he did realise that 'to attack the commerce of the enemy is…to cripple him.'

Embargoes hurt Spain more than the Dutch, and were circumvented via Bordeaux, Nantes, Dieppe, Bayonne and La Rochelle.[2] During the Truce, Dutch ships traded directly with Spain. Dutch trade with La Rochelle was mainly salt, barley and wine for herrings, cheese and Baltic products. Before 1600, Dutch entrepreneurs at Nantes, the Loire wine export port, used inferior wines to make brandy and taught Nantes' residents how to make brandy barrels, the same design as herring barrels. The Truce's end meant the Dutch again needed an entrepot as cover for Spanish trade, although a few traded direct, masquerading as Hansa or Scandinavians. Bilbao's merchants had strong ties with La Rochelle and had been in Nantes from the mid-16th century dealing in wool and textiles.[3] As the Nantes-Holland brandy trade took off, Nantes' Dutch merchants, including Sephardic Jews offered an alternative entrepot for Spanish trade, especially during French naval action against La Rochelle in 1621–22 and 1627–28, demonstrating Calvinist and Sephardic entrepreneurship, regional expertise and the reach and depth of Dutch trade, financing and investment. The Nantes-Holland brandy and silver trade boomed between 1621 and 1648, when Spain embargoed Dutch ships.

The Dutch sold arms to Spain for silver, weakening its merchants and welcomed Portuguese Jews and European labour. Throughout the Thirty Years War, its population grew, attracting wealthy, talented, educated, Jewish, Huguenot, Scot and German merchants, complimenting and strengthening the state. Values were not imposed. Their commercial rise was <u>created</u> by merchants, industrialists and entrepreneurs, enabling it to finance a 70,000-strong army, a formidable navy, subsidise allies, build and maintain fortresses, protect arms manufacturing, textiles, diamond cutting, herring distribution and cheese export. Sugar refineries handled 250 ships a year from Brazil alone.

Gustavus Adolphus summed up the Thirty Years War in this chapter's title. He was thinking of the European theatre, but Dutch battles with Spanish-Portuguese were fought world-wide, mainly against Portuguese ports, more vulnerable to maritime attack than Spanish viceroyalties. There are many interpretations of the war, triggered in 1618 by dispute over the Emperor's election and Defenestration of Prague. From maritime trade's viewpoint, it saw the zenith of Dutch trade in the Baltic, northern Europe, France, Iberia, Mediterranean, Caribbean, North America and Asia, benefitting from England's torpor under James and Charles. The Dutch had ambitious, focussed leadership at home, mirrored abroad by the VOC's Coen and Van Diemen. However, because the traditional 1618–1648 dates emphasize the German-focused phase, the war is usually told from a German perspective as a humiliation. The story goes like this; Frederick Barbarossa (1122–1190) and Frederick II Hohenstaufen (1194–1250) attempted to make the Holy Roman Empire a coherent political force but were thwarted by the papacy. This time, Germany was again prevented from uniting by foreign powers fostering division between her independent territories, precipitating death and disaster. The Peace of Westphalia (1648) enshrined enforced disunity. It is a landlocked, self-pitying, German-centric view, that it even caused massive German depopulation.

John Pike's soon to be published book on this 'gothic myth' will deconstruct the lie. Peter H. Wilson has wisely written 'The Thirty Years War was an extremely complex event. The problems of interpretation derive from attempts to simplify it by over emphasising one fact to the detriment of others.'[4] It is impossible in this story not to emphasise maritime trade and impossible to understand without this perspective in the Baltic and growing Brazilian sugar and Asian spice imports. The five main European political struggles were control of the Netherlands and Dutch independence, control of Baltic ports and hinterlands, of Germany, of Italy and French-Spanish political rivalry. Maritime trade issues dominate the first two.

The Holy Roman Empire was internally chaotic with hundreds of political entities. As Voltaire famously said in the 18th century, it was neither holy, Roman, nor an empire. It never had been. After Charlemagne's unity of constant war, it became a pretend-empire, an artificial grouping of autonomous and semi-autonomous feudal principalities, often at war with each other, and like France and Spain, without maritime inspiration. Hapsburg issues within it ignited an inflammable mix of European disputes, but in maritime trade's context, the Dutch fought Spain and Portugal world-wide and Swedes and Danes fought all-comers for Baltic control. The war clearly juxtaposed the continental and maritime dynamic. The conflict was not caused by burgeoning maritime trade, but would not have followed the course it did without it as a major factor, as Baltic port revenues were key targets for Denmark, the Empire and Sweden. Portugal's maritime empire was the key Dutch target, having already captured the main Spice Islands in 1605. Many late-17th and 18th-century European wars were fought globally, driven by commercial imperatives. The First World War was ironically confined to a smaller geographic area because Germany lacked world-wide trading interests of 17th-century Spain, Portugal and Dutch Republic. Charles Boxer persuasively says it 'deserves to be called the First World War rather than the holocaust of 1914–1918.'[5]

By 1621 the VOC produced 10% of Dutch GDP with just 2% of its merchant fleet. Holland and Zeeland's merchant elite had large shareholdings and were thus disproportionately powerful in political and strategic decision making. The Dutch also believed in attacking Spanish-Portuguese in the Americas. The driving force behind the Dutch West India Company (WIC), formed in 1621, with over seven million guilders capital, compared to the VOC's initial 6.5 million,[6] was William Usselinx, a Calvinist refugee from Antwerp, who thought the Americas potentially the most valuable export market. Of many possible targets, Brazil's sugar industry appeared most profitable. Most Spanish Caribbean sugar industries had faltered. But Portugal's Brazilian sugar plantations and exports were firmly established. Santos was captured in 1623. In 1625 Olivares sent a Spanish-Portuguese fleet to Bahia to recapture it, but Dutch merchants including Jews, entrenched themselves. Amongst them was Rodrigo Fernandes' family. They had left Porto for Amsterdam in 1618 when the Inquisition arrested, imprisoned and burnt Jews. There he traded woad and tobacco. His son Isaac concentrated on Brazil. Three other sons, Jacob, Arao and Moises migrated there, owned two small plantations and a sugar mill.

Moises was Dutch Brazil's most prominent tax farmer, buying a large plantation with a partner.[7]

* * *

Denmark and Sweden had fought the 1560s Livonian wars and Kalmar War in 1611–13. Denmark's main economic asset was the Sound Toll. Sweden's Charles IX (r. 1604–11) attracted Dutch merchants to a fish and fur trade station on Hisingen Island opposite Jutland with 20 years of tax exemptions and low customs rates. Dutch planners and engineers were contracted to drain its marshes and build what became Gothenburg. Like other Dutch ports, Amsterdam, Batavia and Manhattan, it was populated by Dutch merchants and immigrants and governed by Dutch laws. Denmark, anxious about Sweden's growing power, saw Gothenburg as a potential threat, a good reason in Denmark's eyes to put the Swedes back in their place.

They attacked in 1611 and took the Alvsborg and Gullbergat fortresses. In the 1613 peace treaty, Denmark's control, through Norway of Lapland was confirmed and a high ransom paid for restoring Swedish forts, although a major concession was Swedish exemption from Sound Tolls. Dutch investments began transforming Sweden's economy. Dutch loans paid the indemnity, repaid in copper to Amsterdam, which replaced Lubeck as the staple copper market. Dutch arms dealers like the De Geer-Trip partnership manufactured arms, bought them from England and Germany and encouraged Sweden to create its own arms industry, especially cannon using its copper and iron, with Dutch capital, techniques and industrial expertise; a key element in Gustavus' innovative military tactics and battlefield success in the 1620s.

Thereafter Baltic trade boomed with an average 2,000 Sound Toll passages a year, the revenue building a large financial reserve for Danish King Christian IV, who also sought lucrative tolls and harbour dues in ports along the adjacent north German coast. In 1621 he took Lubeck and surrounded Hamburg and Bremen, wanting control of the whole coast. But these ports were jealously independent and Christian had competition.

Nurtured by the Dutch as a counterweight to Denmark since the late-1500s, Sweden was becoming the Baltic's most dynamic economy and efficient military state, the Dutch its main market for its metals, arms, timber, pitch and tar. From importing under 10% of Sweden's exports between 1610 and 1620, it rose to 64% in the 1650s; cannon, cannon balls, arms, pikes, armour, spades, horseshoes, etc. Sweden was Europe's leading iron producer. Its 16th-century iron bars, exported via Danzig, from the 1620s went directly to Holland in Dutch ships, underwritten by Dutch capital. Exports rose from 3,000 tons a year in the late-1620s to 11,000 in 1640, 18,000 in 1650, around 40% to Holland. 'Copper', wrote Oxenstierna, Sweden's chief minister, 'is the noblest commodity which the Swedish Crown produces… wherein a great part of the Crown's welfare stands.' It produced 1,250 to 1,900 tons a year in the 1620s, increasing to 3,000 tons by 1650, 50% of Europe's production.

Gustavus Adolphus also established shipbuilding with Dutch technical expertise. Sweden was transformed in his reign (1611–1632), under Oxenstierna's intelligent eye with Dutch capital, technical, commercial and trade knowledge, turning its mineral wealth into manufactured iron and copper goods, giving Gustavus the revenue to fulfil his territorial ambitions. It became a powerful Hapsburg enemy and alternative iron source to Spain's. De Geer, De Besche and other Dutch merchants established a network of Swedish iron making plants around Leufsta and Osterby and De Geer brought workers, establishing the Walloon iron works.

This economic boost allowed Gustavus in 1621 to seize Riga, the wealthiest east Baltic port with 30,000 people and substantial harbour dues from grain, hemp, flax, masts, timber, pitch and tar exports. Riga and its Livonian hinterland further boosted Sweden's economy. Muscovy had wanted Livonia ever since Ivan the Terrible's brief control of Narva, but was politically convulsed. Fearing a potential Polish-Hapsburg alliance, Gustavus invaded the Polish-Prussian coast in 1626 at Pillau and quickly fanned out, enabling control of tolls at Elbing and Memel (Klaipeda). Swedish occupation of Elbing ruined its economy and high duties damaged the Eastland Company, which tried to open in Danzig, even though the Hapsburgs aimed to subjugate it.[8] The Truce of Altmark in 1629 ended the Polish-Swedish war. Sweden got most of Livonia and it collected tolls at Pillau and Memel, and separately, part of Danzig's and Libau's.

Olivares, aiming to destroy Dutch commercial power, needed to attack its source, their Baltic trade. So, he also needed control of the southern Baltic coast, to close the Sound to Dutch shipping and attack Dutch ships entering and leaving Dutch ports. Only Imperial general Wallenstein apparently shared this strategic insight. Olivares wanted a Hapsburg Baltic fleet from an Imperial-controlled Baltic coast, protecting Danzig, which handled 1,500 ships a year, carrying Poland-Lithuania's annual 200,000 tons of grain exports. But there were cultural obstacles. Aristocratic wealth derived from growing and selling grain through Danzig. Their main focus was thus land-acquisition from Russia or Ottomans, not Baltic control. Polish noble Mikolaj Rey had explained in 1567. 'We Poles have never…needed anything from anyone else…every day many other countries…work as hard as peasants for us, offering all their produce in return for food…we Poles with little effort…enjoy the fruits of their valuable labour.' Ducal Prussia's nobility, owing fealty to the Polish crown, despite its ports, also had a landlocked outlook. Moreover, Castile's land-based, military outlook meant Olivares was opposed at Court, the admiral refused commands, the fleet was inefficient and ineffective, controlled by conservative aristocrats, their ships and tactics hardly changed since 1588.

Thus, the wealth created by Baltic trade, which beguiled 15th-16th-century English and Dutch merchants and caused 16th-century Russian-Swedish-Danish rivalry, suddenly, belatedly, became a Hapsburg target. Olivares wrote in 1624, 'we must bend our efforts in turning the Spanish into merchants', encouraging them to invest capital into trading companies,[9] but the militant crusading society dominated by Church and aristocracy, increasingly technically backward, discriminated against entrepreneurs. Merchant societies do not persecute or expel their best entrepreneurs and wealth creators, in this case Jews, conversos and moriscos, or stifle ideas by fear and oppression; the Inquisition. Spain did <u>all</u>. Egotistical mentality also impeded reform. As Montesclaros, President of the Council of Finance said, 'Lack of money is serious but it is far more important to preserve reputation.' Spain's main objectives, Catholicism, Hapsburg dynastic interests, retention of the southern Netherlands, defeat of the Dutch republic and exclusion of foreigners from the Americas remained unchanged; all far beyond Spanish resources.[10] For Spanish unity, Olivares wanted it 'composed to the style and laws of Castile,'[11] doubling down on its weakness. A leading minister opined 'novelties are absolutely bad when they run counter to the established state and government.' Opponents of reform in the Cortes said 'novelties have always brought great difficulties and inconveniences in their train.'[12]

Then there were the military problems. The strategy required Swedish defeat. Wallenstein wrote in 1625 of his military success on land, 'but the sea remains free to Denmark, Sweden, England and the Dutch. The war would have to be financed with Indian gold and silver for 30 years or so before any advantage would come of it.' A Baltic fleet had to be built and the Dutch ousted if long-term Imperial victory was possible. A 1628 Olivares memo plotted, 'if we join hands with the Emperor at sea, we will be able to interrupt the commerce of all heretic powers of the north who have allied themselves...with the rebels...we will not dissolve the league until the arms of the Empire and Spain dominate the Baltic.' Theoretically true, it was totally unrealistic. Oxenstierna's aim had been Baltic trade-domination, specifically toll and harbour dues collection. He wrote in 1651 without hindsight of 'the exceedingly rare and precious harbours, mainly in the Baltic and the North Sea and the Kattegat, asking only its exploitation to benefit and avail the inhabitants of Sweden.'

Imperial forces first attacked and defeated Danish forces in Germany, marched into Holstein and Jutland, but not on Danish islands, including Copenhagen due to Denmark's navy and absence of an Imperial one. Wallenstein recognised the opportunity. 'There are 28 ports in Pomerania. We must fortify them all.' They captured Wismar in 1627, a good start for Olivares' vision. He also created privateer squadrons to attack Dutch shipping. In 1621 he wrote, 'the English and Dutch have made themselves masters of the sea and of commerce to the extent that they are able to jeer at all our power on land...his majesty must have a substantial fleet in the waters of Flanders...there exist only two appropriate ports, Dunkirk and Ostend...[the aim] tightening our stranglehold upon all the commerce which is their substance, until we can break it.' Spending on naval matters jumped 300% between 1621 and 1627, albeit from a low base and they had early success. Privateers in 1625 captured 150 herring ships, 20 escorts and 1,400 sailors.[13] From 1627 to 1634 over 2,500 Dutch merchant ships were lost. They bore the extra cost of naval patrols, increased insurance and ship defence systems. Olivares also tried to close the Rhine by digging canals to block Dutch traffic, although not successful. He damaged Dutch trade, but not enough to win and could not <u>create</u> Spanish trade.

Spanish Admiral Gabriel de Roy attempted to build an Imperial Baltic capability at Wismar. Olivares' master-plan, the only way the Dutch could possibly be beaten however, was scuppered by diversion of resources to the largely irrelevant, costly war in Mantua, part of the battle for Italy, distracting from the Swedish threat. He also thought the Imperial army had defeated Denmark. But Christian's navy deployed troops along the Baltic coast and destroyed nascent imperial naval facilities. While imperial forces were diverted, Jutland and Holstein were retaken, enabling a favourable peace treaty. Taking his eye off the Swedish threat by the Mantuan diversion, Olivares effectively lost the war and doomed Spain. There were other problems of policy implementation that weakened the Imperial-Spanish hand. Wallenstein was supportive of the general economic thrust of Olivares' Baltic policy but wanted to maximise harbour dues, tolls and economic activity in his territory, so released seized Dutch vessels.

The imperial army's failure to take Stralsund at the Oder's mouth in 1628 was a turning point. To Protestant Europe, the war had seemed a worrying imperial cake-walk. In Germany, no emperor since Frederick Barbarossa had been as powerful as Ferdinand II. Half of Germany was occupied, the other half intimidated to comply with Imperial dictats. But the red mist of that continental urge for uniformity descended. Ferdinand issued the Edict of Restitution outlawing Calvinism, something only achievable with overwhelming force. At a stroke, he alienated neutral powers and wealthy cities, especially Baltic ports and dismissed Wallenstein, the only man who had the remotest chance of implementing Olivares' Baltic policy. Olivares was furious. 'Both majesties' he wrote in 1630 'would gain far more by turning their armies against the Dutch.' 'They [the Emperor's advisors] believe the situation to be what they would like it to be and think about re-catholicisation and not about recruitment.' True, but Olivares had already compromised his Baltic and anti-Dutch policy by his Mantuan venture and could never imitate Dutch entrepreneurship in Spain.

Four weeks after Wallenstein's dismissal, Gustavus landed in Pomerania, like his seaborne Livonian and Polish invasions, logistical and strategic triumphs, an attempt to surround the Baltic. After consolidation, he marched south to the Oder and Stettin, the logistical base for the rest of the war. The Edict of Restitution enabled him to cloak his Baltic economic ambitions by appearing as champion of the Protestant north, which allied with him. After victory at Breitfield, Sweden collected customs and tolls at Riga, Danzig, Stralsund, Rostock, Stettin, Memel and Pillau, giving captured territories to Protestant princes, in return for their logistic and military power.

To make matters worse, Piet Hein from Delft, the WIC's Bahia fleet leader, in 1628 captured or destroyed 26 merchant ships, seized silver ships at Matanzas and brought back an astonishing 117,000 lbs. of silver, 66 lbs. of pearls, two million hides and substantial amounts of silk, musk, amber and other rarities, yielding as much profit as the previous 13 years, during which it had taken 547 Spanish and Portuguese ships.[14] Shareholders received a 50% dividend, officers and men a 17-month bonus, 1% for the directors and Piet Hein. It was a disaster for Spain, whose armies and bankers awaited payment.

In 1630 the WIC retook Recife, Pernambuco's capital, with almost twice as many sugar mills as Bahia. This time no fleet was sent as Mantua absorbed recourses, even though Spain had promised to defend Portugal's empire. The Dutch used Piet Hein's treasure fleet dividend to conquer 1,000 miles of northeast Brazil and Portugal's sugar and slave trade, spearheaded by Amsterdam's Portuguese-speaking Jews, significant WIC shareholders, traders, sugar refiners and financiers and a third of Dutch settlers. Resident director Prince Maurice of Nassau noted the need for reliable slave supply, attacking El Mina in 1637 and Luanda in 1640, and expanded Dutch Brazilian territories into Bahia. Spanish ships failed to make any impression, fuelling more Portuguese bitterness against Madrid. The WIC also occupied Curacao in 1634, another neglected Spanish colony with the Caribbean's best natural harbour, supplying Spanish colonies. Dutch ships took Brazil's sugar to Amsterdam's 40 refineries by 1650, the world's undisputed sugar capital.

After Sweden's invasion of Pomerania, Gustavus was killed in 1632 and momentum lost. Defeat in 1634 at Nordlingen changed the military balance and the imperial army re-occupied Swedish-controlled regions. With Saxony and Brandenburg changing sides, France decided to intervene directly instead of subsidising imperial enemies. Cardinal Richelieu, (French Secretary of State 1616–1642) was clear-sighted and ruthless. But in terms of maritime trade policy, he inherited French Catholic indifference and concentration on eastward expansion by land. He was fascinated by Genoa's success, 'which only has rocks to share,' yet one of Italy's richest cities, and Holland, 'which produced nothing but butter and cheese, yet provided every nation in Europe with the majority of what they required,'[15] failing to draw the logical conclusions. He certainly intended to sell as much to foreigners as possible and buy as little as possible from them, but this was unremarkable. Sir Thomas Smith's 1549 *Discourse of the Common Weal of this Realm of England* expressed similar sentiments. Bills proclaiming foreigners could not load anything except salt were issued, but with a small merchant class and few ships, were unenforceable.

Richelieu encouraged the expedition to St. Kitts in 1627 where the English also had a small settlement and exempted it from tobacco duties. In 1633 he sent Champlain back to Canada with 200 Catholic peasants and priests to convert natives, hardly a commercial imperative. Population growth was thus much slower than in English colonies further south and settlement limited to the St. Lawrence River valley. He did much more damage to trade by violating the Edict of Nantes, attacking and taking Huguenot cities in 1627–1629, which encouraged migration to the Dutch Republic, England and the Americas, persecuting its merchants, entrepreneurs and mariners thereafter. In the 1627–1628 La Rochelle siege, Dutch cargoes were confiscated by the French navy, reinforcing Dutch concentration on

Nantes. Richelieu also took the fur trade monopoly from Champlain and Dugua and gave it to Catholics. Nevertheless, Champlain managed to develop trade with Rouen merchants, but religious discrimination hindered potential. France's St. Kitts colony could not survive without Dutch merchant aid and when the Spanish chased them off in 1629, Dutch from St. Martin helped re-settle them, by which time Virginian tobacco was dominant. They gradually followed Barbados in sugar production.

Nantes boomed, especially after the La Rochelle siege, trading with Spain under French or neutral flags. Despite Dunkirk privateers, Nantes' wine and brandy trades were not unduly affected. In 1631 Dutch merchants sent 235 stills to Nantes; investment in production and export.[16] Wine and brandy investors also owned breweries, refineries, distilleries, herring and whaling ships. Diversification spread risk in uncertain, hostile times. Hiding behind regular Nantes-Bilbao trade, Nantes was probably Europe's main entrepot for Spanish silver.[17] Never especially friendly to merchants, in 1632 the French Royal Council decreed restrictions on capital removal by foreigners on death were lifted and in 1635 that Dutch merchants' commercial privileges became identical to French. What was Richelieu up to? Had he seen the commercial light? Timing suggests otherwise. Until 1635 he kept France out of war, subsidising the Dutch. These were bribes to keep them sweet, especially with heavy fighting in the Netherlands and the Spanish navy creating headaches for Dutch trade.[18]

France colonised Martinique and Guadeloupe in 1635, which had 8,000 white settlers by 1664. It was not immediately strategically significant, except as another Spanish loss. These were early years for Caribbean and North American colony development. Barbados had about 2,000 people in 1630, 6,000 in 1636, and 10,000 in 1640. A fifth of those leaving London in the mid-1630s headed there.[19] English attempts were also made to colonise St. Lucia, Hispaniola, Trinidad, Tobago and Surinam, but were all wiped out by Caribs, disease and starvation. Dutch vessels loaded French colonies' tobacco and discharged it in Amsterdam, so even though France had 14 sugar islands, the Dutch profited most. France's mid-century Caribbean population was about 7,000, mainly from Normandy and Brittany, and 12,000 slaves.

* * *

From 1629 to 1636, Portugal catastrophically lost an estimated 155 ships and cargoes in Indian Ocean battles. When Anthony Van Diemen became VOC Governor General in 1636, Goa was blockaded every year. He thought 'daily experience' proved 'the Company's trade in Asia cannot subsist without territorial conquests.' The VOC were aware of anti-Portuguese sentiment, caused by Jesuits in Sri Lanka and in 1638 joined the Sinhalese king in Kandy to conquer them. The Sinhalese however, found they had swapped one invader for another. The VOC's first cinnamon cargo sold in Amsterdam at twice the purchase price. The

VOC brought Tamil slaves to work cinnamon and tobacco farms, organised from Pulicat. Portuguese were expelled from Java and the Malay Peninsula and by 1636, eliminated as serious rivals. Batavia's VOC merchants were active from Mauritius to Amboyna, Dejima to Taiwan's Fort Zeelandia.

One of the VOC's most profitable trades was Japanese silver and copper bars to India, where they were made into coins, for Indian cottons and opium for Southeast Asia, both at significant mark-ups, reducing the need to export bullion. This led Van Diemen to establish trading posts in Siam, Annam, Tonkin and Cambodia where ray-skins for samurai sword handles, buffalo and deer hides could be exported to Japan where they fetched high prices, and rice and benzoin used in medicine, perfume and incense to Batavia. Portuguese, Japanese, Chinese, Cham, Malay, Vietnamese and Javanese merchants were already there, but VOC involvement was immediately significant, in 1640 exporting 75,530 deer skins to Japan from Cambodia alone. These factories were extremely profitable.[20] But the death of Cambodia's king in 1640 ushered in dynastic rivalry. The new king allowed Portuguese to ship cargoes to Japan on Cambodian-based Chinese merchant's junks. The VOC reserved the right to seize them. Two worlds collided; land and rice-based absolute monarchy, against the VOC, the most powerful, ruthless, trading entity yet known.

Cambodian kings viewed all traders in Cambodia as subjects. If the VOC made trouble with other traders for non-Cambodian reasons they would be expelled. Disputes between merchant groups had to be avoided. The VOC agent, threatened with death, thought Cambodia had further export potential, mainly to Japan, from which the Portuguese were excluded after 1639. When in 1641 the VOC captured Malacca, many Portuguese fled to Cambodia, becoming with Chinese, the largest foreign trading community. Meanwhile, in bloody dynastic disputes in 1641, a usurper-king converted to Islam, the obvious allies, Muslim Malays and Chams. The VOC seized a Chinese ship carrying Portuguese goods to Japan in the Mekong. The king ordered the VOC to pay reparations. When they failed to do so, most Dutch in Cambodia were killed. Van Diemen tried blockading the Mekong, Cambodia's foreign trade entrance, the affair only settled after van Diemen's death in 1645.

He was Governor General during the years of maximum damage to Portuguese interests, Malacca's conquest in 1644, repeated sieges of Goa, the establishment of the spice monopoly, the conquest of parts of Sri Lanka, the expansion of cinnamon production and export and increasing Japanese trade. Furthermore, he delivered an astonishing dividend record to shareholders, from 12.5% to 15% in 1639, 35% in 1640, 40% in 1641 and 50% in 1642. He established a Latin school at Batavia, required trading posts to give descriptions of lands, military potential, government, customs, religions and trade and encouraged officials to write scholarly works about the countries with which they were familiar, including pioneering studies of 1630s–40s Siam.[21] He sent four voyages of discovery to the northeast Pacific and Australia under Abel Tasman which however, produced no trade, gold or silver.

*   *   *

In Europe, the 1639 French destruction of Pasajes dockyard and capture of Spanish troop-ships to Flanders made Olivares send a fleet. Defeat at the Battle of the Downs ended his naval dreams and Spanish ambitions. Portugal's flagship was sunk, Spain's escaped in a battle fought exclusively for Spanish interests. In 1640, the Dutch also defeated a Spanish fleet off Pernambuco in Brazil. Catalonia rebelled due to oppressive taxation and forced billeting of troops. Portugal, whose empire Spain could not protect, was asked for extra taxes to quell it. Before 1607, 70% of Portugal's trade revenue and 50% of government revenue derived from spices, lost because Olivares had not considered Asia, his focus to recover Spanish reputation in Europe. He never grasped the latent opportunity in linking the hard-won Portuguese trading empire and windfall Spanish empire of gold-diggers more purposefully, reinforcing Manila and using its forces to protect the spice trade. Spanish silver propped up Hapsburg power, emphasising Empire and Catholicism, while van Diemen seized Portuguese Asia, factory by factory, ship by ship, producing record dividends. By 1640, Brazilian sugar was overtaking spice in terms of revenue generation, but the Dutch had taken much of that. So, Portugal too rebelled against Castile. Olivares' Baltic company had already failed due to capital shortage, lack of business culture and basic freedoms. His tenure of power, writes J.H. Elliot, 'saw the final alienation of Spain's native business community from its king and the final defeat of native commercial enterprise.'[22]

Around the Baltic after Nordlingen, Sweden re-consolidated. The Dutch blockaded Spanish Flanders and attacked Dunkirk privateers. Nevertheless, in 1635 they lost 124 herring busses and 975 fishermen. Sweden was back on the offensive by the late-1630s. In 1637 Christian IV attempted a Danish comeback, banning weapons shipped through the Sound, targeting Sweden's cannon exports to Holland. In 1638 he allied with Spain, instituting inspections of cargoes and ships, especially Sweden's and raised the Sound Toll 40% between 1638 and 1643, on some cargoes 300%! Sweden had to retaliate. A joint Swedish-Dutch fleet destroyed the Danish in 1644. Danish Sound monopoly was over. Oxenstierna's economic reforms encouraged Baltic trade, especially Muscovy's. Novgorod customs receipts increased by 154% between 1644 and 1656, a 244% increase on those of 1631, dramatic increases in southwest Baltic port dues and new commodities from central Russia, including potash to Narva.[23] Stuart lack of interest in England's Baltic merchants led to their replacement by Dutch.

Catalonian and Portuguese rebellion meant Spain finally had to attempt a general peace, which meant recognising the independence of the re-named United Provinces and end an 80-year conflict. The Dutch, grown rich on the back of war, agreed a truce in 1641. Portugal's empire had crumbled. Under WIC attack in Brazil and west Africa, the partial loss of Sri Lanka from 1638 to 1641, Cochin and other Indian ports except Goa, her loss of Nagasaki, the 1641 capture of Malacca, the richest customs revenue sources for the Estado were severe blows. It ended Portugal's Asian trade network. Only isolated Macao, Goa and the Lesser Sunda Islands remained after Omanis took Muscat in 1650. The revenue contribution to Portugal was tiny. Portuguese merchants were still trading regionally from Makassar, Phnom Penh and Timor. Portugal decided to concentrate on regaining Brazil and west African supply bases. The WIC had not taken over completely and unlike Asian bases, Portuguese had deeply colonised it inland. Only 10% of Recife's inhabitants were Dutch. Furthermore, while the WIC had taken El Mina, they failed to take Luanda, from where slaves were shipped, for sugar, manioc, tobacco, hides and rum. The war destroyed sugar estates, raised costs, reduced volumes and restricted credit, collapsing Dutch sugar production, which for a few years had dominated European markets, giving Caribbean sugar its export opportunity. By the late-1640s Dutch Brazil's economic raison d'etre disappeared. It was of far greater value to Portugal.

Swedish armies roamed Hapsburg lands. France attacked the Spanish Netherlands, taking Arras, Luxembourg and Gravelines. Mazarin who succeeded Richelieu, offered to withdraw from Catalonia and Roussillon if Spain ceded the Spanish Netherlands, 'an impregnable bulwark for the city of Paris', French frontiers extended to Holland and the Rhine. The Dutch feared swapping a Spanish enemy for a greater French enemy. Nevertheless, in 1646 they jointly took the Dunkirk privateer base. Dutch fear of French success drove them to make a separate peace with Spain.

In Nantes, commercial activity still depended on Dutch merchants dealing along the Quay de la Fosse, still called 'Place de la Holland'. After Richelieu's and Louis XIII's death in 1642 and 1643, resenting Dutch trade monopoly, Nantes' municipality introduced a tax on foreign merchants and restricted Dutch traders from dealing directly with wine producers.[24] While noble landowners needed Dutch merchants to buy the harvest, Nantes' zealous taxation and friction led to the wine and brandy trade declining in the late-1640s.

Sweden still controlled customs dues in ports on major German rivers especially Stettin, Stralsund, Mecklenburg, Wismar, Bremen and Verden. Dutch influence in Stockholm was still strong and in 1648 the Trips were authorised by the Swedish Tar Company to become sole tar supplier to Amsterdam from Swedish ports in Livonia and Courland, its origin mainly within Russia. Swedish copper's main destination was also Amsterdam.

The war's clear winners were France, Sweden and the Dutch, the latter two strengthened by trade and industry. It could not have been won by Hapsburgs because they failed to control sea-lanes and maritime trade, whose explosive rise enflamed existing rivalries. Bankruptcy ensued again in 1647. Cadiz replaced Seville as the port for America, but controlled by foreign merchants. Illusions of power drained away. Spain's administration and government stagnated in a fast-changing world. Genoa's links with Spain meant it declined quickly. Olivares' attempt to turn the Spanish into merchants was a pipe-dream. Attempted control of the Baltic coast was ended by Wallenstein's dismissal and Swedish invasion. Dutch defeat may have been possible by more concentration on arming Dunkirk privateers. Richelieu and Mazarin were capable, but their zeal for religious uniformity were destructive. The lessons of the Edict of Restitution were not learnt. The Spanish-Dutch element of the war ended with decisive naval engagements, the Downs and Pernambuco. The war signalled the rising power of maritime trade and industry. After the war, Colbert in France recognised it, but few continentals learnt lessons. Oxenstierna and Queen Christina saw education as necessary for a modern state. Uppsala University was founded to train men to run Sweden's Baltic empire. Protestant victory was based on maritime superiority and potency.

The war catapulted the Dutch into maritime trade domination in almost every part of the world, 1648–1652 the height of their commercial power. They had 75% of Baltic grain shipments, 50–70% of Baltic timber, 30–35% of Spanish metals and 75% of French and Portuguese salt. Over 50% of Baltic cloth imports were made or finished in Holland. It was Europe's largest spice, sugar and porcelain importer and distributer.[25] Its fisheries were of more economic importance than the WIC. Moreover, it had invested in and developed Danzig's industries, influencing how it developed, did the same for Sweden's hitherto untapped potential and similarly with Nantes' brandy industry. In 1618, little suggested that Sweden would remain anything but a regional power competing for Livonian ports. In nurturing it as a counterweight to Denmark, the Dutch helped create Sweden's dynamic economy, breaking the Empire's counter-reformationary, continental, authoritarian potential, and keeping Russia from recapturing a Baltic port.

Burgeoning Asian trade opportunities, after VOC's 1641 conquest of Malacca, benefitted regional ports; Aceh, Johore, Batavia, Manila, Ayutthaya, Pattani, Phnom Penh, Macau, Nagasaki, Goa, Hoi-Ann, Palembang, Saigon, Cochin, Colombo, Galle, Hormuz and Makassar. Makassar was closer to the Moluccas, where state ships sent rice surpluses. Its rulers guaranteed merchant safety and autonomy. Outstanding leaders, Karaeng Matoaya of Tallo (1593–1610) and Pattingalloang of Gowa borrowed Chinese and European knowledge and shipbuilding techniques. With Aceh and Malacca, it was the only pre-colonial Southeast Asian state to have gold coinage. It adopted Islam in 1604, but ancient toleration continued. Indeed, when the VOC demanded Portuguese exclusion, Sultan Alauddin declined, declaring 'God made the land and the sea. The land he divided among men and the sea he gave in common. It has never been heard that anyone should be forbidden to sail the seas.'[26] Grotius was thrown back in their faces! At its height, mid-century, Makassar's population was about 100,000. English, French, Indian, Danes, Javanese and Malays traded there. Bajau boat-living people, partly Makassar-based, traded or plundered over a wide area, taking women, selling stolen goods and ships; part-trader, part-raider. Bugis were another commercially aggressive Makassar-based trading boat-people, embodying ancient seafaring traditions,[27] described in this series' first book. An Indian merchant became a leading Makassar-based trader and financier with Aceh and Golcondan ports sending their agents. Francisco Vieira de Figueiredo, one of 3,000 Portuguese who settled there after Malacca's fall, sent his ships to China, Sumatra, Batavia and the Philippines with his own and third-party cargo. When the VOC took it in 1668–69, he moved to Timor.

Gujarati, Tamil and Chinese merchants were still active at Bantam in Sumatra's pepper trade to China. Chinese at Jambi took pepper to Batavia to sell, but the

VOC lacked the capacity to carry all its trade, so it tended to be licenced to Chinese merchants in Sumatra and Java. The VOC concentrated on Coromandel cloth exports. In the Philippines the Spanish did not trade, but Asian ships and merchants continued there. Interlocking trade interests became more complex as resident merchants in trade hubs, native or foreign, were increasingly important. 'Banian', Portuguese for Indian trader, became the word used for Indian agents acting for European merchants, many of whom became rich.

In the early-1650s the VOC's profitable Surat factory traded cloves, nutmeg, mace, tea, Japanese silver and copper and Chinese porcelain and had outposts at Ahmadabad, Baroda, Broach and Agra. Gujarati cotton piece goods were shipped to Southeast Asia, but Europeans did not dominate. Slaves, sold as an alternative to starvation in Indian famines, were also shipped to Batavia, over 26,000 between 1621 and 1665, organised from Pulicat.

The VOC's Van Goens, sent to Sri Lanka and India in 1653–54 to audit trading posts, became suspicious of private employee trade reducing VOC profits in regional triangle trade developed at Surat's initiative. Spices, cotton and tin sent to Mocha for silver and coffee, were taken to Basra and sold at a good profit, but he found the fixed-price contracts low, raised them, and still found willing buyers, improving profits by over a third, previously pocketed by the VOC's chief Surat factor, who returned to the Netherlands in 1655 with a hefty fortune.[28] Insistence on company monopoly was to become a serious structural VOC weakness, but it was still ascendant among Europeans. He enthused to the Heren XVII of Sri Lanka's and India's vast potential, far greater than Southeast Asia. In 1656 the Portuguese in Colombo surrendered. Van Goens wanted to make it, as its Governor General from 1658 to 1672, the strategic hub of an Asian maritime empire. He expelled Portuguese from Tuticorin, Jaffnapattinam and the Malabar coast, encouraged Dutch settlers and plantation owners, extending Sri Lankan geographic control, and argued for relaxing monopolistic trade within the Indian Ocean.

Cochin, Portugal's first Indian ally, fell in 1663. Surat's pepper price doubled as traders anticipated a Molucca-Banda-style stranglehold with further VOC breakthroughs. But they never managed the same control over pepper, grown widely in India, Java and Sumatra. Cinnamon, cloves, nutmeg and mace were the VOC specialities, the profits from Molucca and Banda spices far higher, perhaps 17-times the price in Europe and 14 in India. The VOC had fewer west coast Indian ports so they did not participate as much in cotton textiles, tea and opium trades. Cape Town was taken in 1652 as a crucial stage for voyages to and from Asia.

In 1658 Portugal lost Nagapattinam to the VOC but relocated to Porto Novo further north, and traded with Aceh, Malacca, Pegu, Goa and Manila. The Portuguese and Dutch imported coercion and violence into Indian Ocean trade networks but they didn't hijack them. The VOC tried to reserve east coast India to Java textile trades for itself, but locals competed effectively. Competition between locals, Dutch, English and Indian traders stimulated textile exports, increasing an estimated 233% between 1620 and 1655.

Part V

Maritime Trade To Centre Stage: An Emerging Modern World

Chapter 31

The Peace of Westphalia

The emperor's 1620s victories were, by later defeats, thwarted. The various treaties of Westphalia (1648) asserted German states' sovereign and Protestant religious rights. The price of their liberty was military impotence of a potential German empire, which drove many 19th and 20th-century German nationalists in their desire for German union. A dispassionate view of Westphalia is that statesmanship and pragmatism trumped religious zealotry. The Holy Roman Empire's power was diminished. Over 3,000 independent political entities, held together by a Diet and laws, operated only by consensus. The emperor's prestige remained, but his army and finances were small compared to polities like Brandenburg, catapulted into prominence with 30,000 square kilometres of western Pomerania, much unproductive, because France wanted to counterbalance Swedish power. In many areas, different religious denominations co-existed. If not, it was relatively easy to go to an area where one's faith was in the majority. Diversity worked. Attempted imperial Catholic domination had not. Westphalia allowed peaceful coexistence. It was also an important milestone on the road where the state was not seen as a monarch's domain, but a political entity deploying its resources for national ends. Trade strengthened the state. Dutch, Sweden and Elizabethan England had proved it. Surely the private realm of the monarch and dynastic obsession had to adapt or die? France tested that proposition over the next 150 years.

Crucially, Westphalia encouraged trade, abolishing ad hoc 'contributions' forced on occupied land and tolls on rivers, designed to hinder Dutch trade, especially on the Rhine, whose navigation was to be free and unhindered, benefiting Dutch merchants who needed efficient delivery to and from Europe's interior. While Swedes and Dutch won exemptions, Sound tolls were radically reduced with Sweden exempt, an important stage in the direction of freer trade. In Asia however, the Dutch accelerated Portugal's protectionist model.

Despite being the longest running peace process in Europe, involving thousands of diplomats, from 1641 to 1654, Westphalia did not solve all European issues. War between Spain and France continued for another 12 years, despite Spain's desperate condition, as she believed the Dutch peace and French Fronde rebellions improved her chances of avoiding humiliation. Humbled, she was not ready to accept total defeat, especially to Portugal, which gradually recovered Brazil, sugar and slave trades from the Dutch, virtually done by 1648, confirmed in 1654, freeing resources for continuing war with Spain, whose armies it defeated in 1663 and

1665. However, it lost Malacca in 1641 and Colombo in 1656 to the VOC and Muscat to Oman in 1650, which took control of east African trade. The VOC took Makassar in 1668 to re-establish clove, nutmeg, mace and cinnamon monopoly. Spain only recognised Portugal's independence in 1668. Portugal's success in Brazil reduced WIC's territories to Curacao, Surinam, Saba, St. Martin, St. Eustatius and Luanda. The islands were useful trade stations, essential in the Dutch network, but as England and France planted tobacco, sugar, indigo and other useful export crops, these tiny islands were of little value, unless they could dominate trade without plantations. It became a key problem.

Westphalia also did not solve the problem of sustainable power balance in the Baltic's busy shipping market. Russia was denied a Baltic outlet and it was only a matter of time before Sweden again tried to take Scania while its Pomeranian coast was coveted by north German states. In theory, with Jutland and Scania in Danish control, it controlled the Sound choke point, but in practice the Dutch had sailed through and defeated Denmark in 1645. There were other unresolved issues. English bitterness to the Dutch Republic owed much to Coen's earlier ruthlessness in Asia, despite close personal friendships and increasing scientific cooperation at home. The Mediterranean, for long the driver of European trade and wealth creation was, as Venetians had feared, sidelined by the Cape route and Ottoman blockade of Egypt, Persian Gulf and overland alternatives. Their damaging religious fundamentalism and Barbary corsair allies' depredations helped make north Europe the new focal point of economic development.

The war, so often told as a landlocked story, proved the importance of navies; Gustavus' in the Baltic, the Dutch worldwide, both following Portugal. One battleship containing 20 cannons, similar firepower to a 25,000-man army, appearing unexpectedly, could quickly reduce a port to surrender and capture its trade. Above all, with Dutch and Swedes the main winners, Westphalia confirmed the overriding importance of maritime trades' explosive growth and ability to enrich, whether or not Ottomans, Castile, France or Holy Roman Emperors recognised it.

Chapter 32

The English Commonwealth
and the Dutch Republic

Frenemy is a modern American pop-culture word describing people who are part-enemies, part-friends. It describes 17th-century English-Dutch relations rather well. England and the newly officially named, United Provinces were locked in a friendly religious and cultural embrace, born of a common enemy, geographical proximity, similar culture and values, but earlier fierce commercial rivalry in the Moluccas and Bandas. Weak English leadership led to loss of competitive power everywhere. Having humbled Spain, the Dutch were Europe's leading commercial, industrial and financial power. Its strong navy defended its commerce, enabling higher living standards than elsewhere. The cost of the navy, chain of barrier forts, army and loss of Brazil was financed through public loans, a permanent debt held by its citizens. Unlike the Spanish, it could never be repudiated, resulting in heavy taxation, albeit on incomes much higher than the rest of Europe. It dominated European and Europe's Asian and Caribbean trade.

In 1642 at the start of the English Civil War, the navy offered its services to Parliament, which unlike the King, paid well, punctually and appointed leaders with seafaring skill. War depressed England's already weak economy. The Dutch even controlled much English coastal shipping. Its merchant and naval fleet was over double England's. Up to 20% of Dutch males were at sea at any one time.[1] Most Baltic shipbuilding materials came in Dutch fluyts. Dutch fishing fleets dominated the North Sea, its whalers, the Arctic. In short, they were Europe's dominant shipping and trading power, despite losing Brazil. Spice, sugar and tobacco trades converged on Amsterdam, where by 1660 there were 50 sugar refineries. It was Europe's main entrepot through which food, raw materials and finished products arrived and manufactured or processed goods exported. Sugar refining, manufacturing, tobacco processing, diamond cutting, other finishing and craft industries thrived, many large-scale, using windmill power, including shipbuilding in Zaandam. Wind-power, long-used to drain waterlogged land, with the economy of water transport, produced Europe's most advanced economy.

In taverns and coffee shops, market intelligence about freight, insurance, agency, ship arrivals and shipping services were exchanged. They were complimented by a Corn Exchange. Warehouses stored products, bought when prices were low. Brewing and brickmaking needed coal imports from Newcastle and Sunderland, although most northeast England's coal shipments, nearly 200,000 tons around 1600 growing to nearly 700,000 by 1700, were for London.[2] Cloth production, about 50,000 pieces a year in 1600, increased to about 130,000 by 1660, those Mediterranean-bound, mainly replacing Italian products. The Dutch still controlled finishing and marketing of English cloth exports. They led Europe in manufacturing, printing and agriculture.

As spice demand weakened, that for silk and porcelain increased. Jingdezhen's best quality items were rarely exported, but even their inferior pottery was better than the best European. In 1640 an Englishman in Amsterdam noted 'any house of indifferent quality was well-supplied with Chinese porcelain.'[3] Just as earlier Chinese potters adapted their styles and products for Middle East markets, they now did so for Europe. Blue and white delftware imitated it. A quarter of Delft's labour force worked in ceramics, used throughout Europe.[4] Delft's delftware and Leiden's linens, silks and cottons were alone worth almost half England's overseas trade.[5] John Evelyn in 1641 wrote of Amsterdam's 'innumerable assemblies of ships and vessels...the most-busy concourse of mortal man, now upon the face of the whole earth and the most addicted to commerce.'[6]

From 1640 Parliament began to rectify matters, even as Civil War from 1642 weakened English merchants worldwide. An Act prohibited dissolving Parliament without its consent, all prerogative revenue collection was declared illegal, prerogative courts were abolished, victims of Charles' personal government were released, as he lost control of London. From 1641 for the first time, taxation fell on gentry, on customs from trade, manufacturing and consumption, which worked in favour of merchants and industrialists. The Excise was payable on a range of goods; beer, cider, spirits, meat, salt, alum, hops and many imported goods. Parliament's 1642 Book of Rates outlined a protection policy against Dutch merchants and in 1645 it prohibited whale product imports except in Greenland Company ships. It abolished industrial monopolies, but not the right of merchants to form privileged trading companies. The Levant Company followed the Greenland Company's example, in 1648 petitioning Parliament to prohibit Ottoman imports 'from Holland and other places, but directly from their places of growth.' Baltic traders added their voice to growing calls for protection. In 1654 men recalled this 'Long Parliament' as a 'trading Parliament'.[7] But Civil War cut American and Caribbean colonies from English dependency, necessitating trade with the Dutch, who supplied slaves, made loans to planters transitioning to sugar and established a strong foothold in Chesapeake's tobacco trade.

Charles was tried and executed in 1649, logical and necessary, and the English military-fiscal state reformed on meritocratic Dutch lines, so that English merchants could compete. The republic's assessment was realistic. 'It is no wonder that these Dutchmen should thrive...Their statesmen are all merchants...they understand the course of trade and they do everything to further its interests.'[8] Cloth, still England's main export, gave relatively little ship employment compared with Dutch fishing and Baltic bulk trades. The Dutch kept the Scheldt closed, clearly breaching

Grotius's *Mare Liberum*, ensuring Antwerp's suppression as competitor. Spanish embargoes were lifted. With insurance and freight rates down to pre-war levels and low interest rates, the Dutch unleashed their full accumulated, competitive power and swamped English traders in its American colonies, Spanish America, the Mediterranean, Iberia, the Levant and Baltic, where the Muscovy Company lost its privileges in 1649.

In England, without royal interference and indifference, a new, vigorous tone was set. Slingsby Bethel, a Council of Trade member espoused the republic's philosophy; 'nothing makes countries rich but trade and nothing increaseth trade but freedom.'[9] Pieter de la Court further explained, 'All republics thrive and flourish more in arts, manufacture, traffick [trade], populousness and strength...where there is liberty there will be riches and people.'[10] Benjamin Worsley after two years in Amsterdam became Secretary to the Council of Trade, advising the government to make 'merchandise and trading and the encouragement of it, the Great Interest of State,'[11] policies promoting national prosperity, including colonies as one economic system. Mazarin's English resident told him that England's rulers toiled for the public as if for themselves, living without ostentation.[12] The Levant Company claimed that French privateers encouraged by Royalists in 1649 captured 5,000 tons of ships worth £600,000 and 480 guns.[13] England's merchants and trade needed protection.

In 1650, Parliament imposed a 15% surcharge on customs duties to pay for convoys, 'the first explicit acknowledgement by any English government of a duty to protect merchantmen outside home waters,'[14] the first in the Mediterranean in 1651. With Dutch ships given Sound Toll discounts from 1649, the already abysmal 1650 Dutch-English Baltic ratio of 13:1 worsened in 1651 to 50:1.[15] Furthermore, a 1650 Spanish treaty gave Dutch ships advantages. English ships were driven from Spanish and Mediterranean markets with English merchants using cheaper Dutch ships.[16] To the English navy's shaky morale, disastrous finances, many enemies and 39 warships of 1649,[17] an astonishing 147 were added by 1654, built or captured.[18] As republican England built its navy, in 1651 the Dutch voted to increase its fleet from 150 to 226, clear intimidation, as Admirals Blake and Penn imposed England's naval will where merchant interests demanded. Expanded navies created strong demand for timber, iron bars, tar, pitch and hemp; Baltic and Norwegian trades. Between 1649 and 1660, 216 ships were added to the navy, half newbuilds, half prizes.[19]

England's new trade policy was encapsulated by the 1651 Navigation Act, which banned foreign ships from bringing goods from outside Europe to England or its colonies, reserved for ships built, owned and manned by English or colonial ships, or ships from the country of origin. It was designed to ensure that colonial products were first imported into England before re-export. Fish imports and exports and all coastal trade were reserved for English ships. In effect, it excluded efficient Dutch ships from carrying fish, American, Asian and Baltic goods to England and attempted to re-impose commercial control in its American colonies, lost during Civil War.[20] In 1651, 126 Dutch ships were brought to English ports to be tried in Admiralty courts. English justification was 'sovereignty', enunciated in 1631 by John Selden's *Mare Clausum*, rebutting Grotius' *Mare Liberum*, upholding the ancient concept of territorial waters of undefined limits, rejecting arguments that neutrals were entitled to trade with anyone. The Plantation Act forbade colonies trading with foreigners, so 24 Dutch ships were seized in Barbados in 1651–52. The 1652 Tariff Act levied a 1s 5d per hundredweight duty on English colonial and 35s 10d on foreign sugar, merchants and MPs determined to counter Dutch trade hegemony. Because the Dutch exported little of its own manufacture or produce to England, they were intended to damage them, to England's merchants' advantage and led to the First Anglo-Dutch War (1652–1654). Republican England directly challenged the Thirty Years War's most decisive victor. Knowing the risks, its Grand Pensionary anxiously wrote, 'The English are about to attack a mountain of gold, we are about to attack a mountain of iron.'[21]

England was partly belligerent due to earlier perceived slights. Seen as ungrateful for Elizabeth's aid against Spain, they had grown stronger, caught most North Sea herring, had driven the fledgling EIC out of Southeast Asia, perpetrated the cowardly Amboyna massacre, propagated Grotius's free trade doctrine where it suited, but forcefully monopolised where possible and replaced English merchants in Iberian trade. They supplied England's American colonies during the Civil War from their New Amsterdam base. The greater their grip on trade, the greater the resentment. Just as the Channel was the focus of Hundred Years War battles, Sluys, Crecy and Agincourt, with English resurgence, the Channel and North Sea choke point now became the scene of battles for the next century and a half.

In 1653, England drove the Dutch back, cutting them off from Baltic grain. Prices soared beyond the reach of many. Dutch ally Denmark kept the Sound closed to English shipping, ceasing her Baltic trade. After Dutch victory at the Battle of Livorno in 1653, they controlled the Mediterranean entrance. They captured three ships off Jask in Persia, blocking navigation at the Hormuz choke point,[22] while the VOC reigned supreme in the east. With Dutch forces concentrated against England, Portugal more easily recaptured Brazil. The 1654 Anglo-Portuguese Treaty allowed English merchants to trade with Brazil, Bengal and west Africa on more favourable terms than Portuguese, with liberty of conscience. In 1660 there were 60 English merchant companies in Lisbon, only two in Spain. In place of James' and Charles' feeble pro-Spanish foreign policy, post-1649 governments promoted England's merchant interests, who once again began to think ambitiously global. At the war's end, the English were 'perfectly lords and masters of the narrow seas', and no Dutch merchantman could show itself in the Channel.[23] England had captured over 1,000 Dutch merchant ships, some estimates 1,500, more than England's whole merchant fleet, because fluyts were not armed. England lost only about 250, enabling English merchant shipping to rapidly increase into a well-balanced fleet with defensible <u>and</u> efficient unarmed ships.[24]

Republican England's fight-back was decisive. Cromwell as Lord Protector from 1653 added more warships, built or captured, 14 of which carried more guns than the best Dutch, improved organisation and discipline. He sent an expedition to help New Englanders capture Dutch settlements in North America. With peace in 1654, they instead captured Nova Scotia.[25] The Dutch had to acknowledge the Navigation Act. But the war's conclusion did not rectify England's deteriorated overseas trade position, except where England was consumer, so Cromwell offered Sweden assistance to free the Sound and thus Baltic access. A treaty with Denmark allowed English ships to pass on the same terms as the Dutch. One with Portugal gave English merchants reparation for losses, freedom from the Inquisition, and liberty to trade with her colonies.[26] Nothing so sensible was forthcoming from Spain. Algiers came to terms, but Tunis was hostile, so Blake bombarded it.[27]

Spain was exhausted, bankrupt and unable to obtain credit. Its warehouses in Vera Cruz were stocked with over-priced goods sent years before, which no one bought. A Caribbean war against Spain could, Cromwell thought, be profitable in the short-term, strategically beneficial in the long-term, and satisfy religious animosities. Barbados already showed Caribbean potential. Two-thirds of England's sugar imports were re-exported to Europe. Barbados was the most densely populated and intensively cultivated area in the English-speaking world. Its 40–50,000 white inhabitants, the same as Virginia and Massachusetts combined, were an important market for English manufactured goods and New England's pork, beef, butter, timber, ironmongery and livestock, traded for sugar, molasses, cotton and a new product, rum, swelling customs revenues. Its planter-elite consumed conspicuously. Its richest planter, James Drax worked 700 acres. Early-1650s sugar exports of 5,000 tons, rose to 8,000 in 1654, although prices declined as Brazil's production resumed.

An influx of Dutch and Sephardic Jews expelled from Brazil, introduced fresh expertise into the Caribbean. Many more concentrated on Curacao. Despite various Spanish American expulsion orders, some Jews still lived there. A 1640s anti-Semitic campaign culminated when 13 were burnt at the stake in 1649. They found religious and trading freedom in the Caribbean and North America. Small Sephardic communities were established in New Amsterdam and in 1658 in Newport, mostly from Brazil via the Caribbean.

As indentured labour contracts expired, many sought their fortunes in less populated Caribbean islands. Cromwell thought they needed larger labour forces. As a result, prisons were emptied and prisoners of war from failed Scottish and Irish rebellions (1649–51) shipped over, ensuring fledgling colony workforces. After Drogheda Cromwell wrote, 'Every tenth man of the soldiers killed and the rest shipped to Barbados.' England had more people in the Caribbean, but Dutch were still the main carriers.

Cromwell was, however, more ambitious. The 'Western Design' to capture and settle Spanish colonies was the first official English colonisation beyond Ireland, the first time English colonies were targeted by government rather than merchant groups or religious dissenters, for their economic potential in the national interest and the first time England organised trans-Atlantic military operations. Cromwell's aims were Cuba, Hispaniola and central America. Eventually, instructions were just to take Spanish territory. Although defeated at Santo Domingo, Jamaica was taken in 1655 by Admiral William Penn and the enlarged navy. It was the combined size of all other English islands, 25-times bigger than Barbados, the first large island lost to Spain. Most Spanish had moved on, seeking gold. A few sugar mills were left but the main activity of its 2,500 people was hunting wild cattle and pigs, selling meat to passing ships and exporting their hides to make shoes, boots, protective clothing, saddles, bags, harnesses, pumps, bellows and belts for driving machines, vital for Peru and Mexico's silver mining, but a wasted opportunity for an island with such agricultural potential.

Cromwell thought it poor reward compared to his vision. With all colonies needing larger populations, he encouraged settlers and planters, in 1655 pardoning criminals on condition they emigrated. In 1656, 400 women from London brothels were shipped to Barbados so that 'by their breeding they should replenish the white population.' Irish slaves costing Bristol merchants £4.10s were sold for £35 in Barbados and 50,000 from Munster were shipped over the next five years.[28] Cromwell's recognition of Caribbean importance was shown by James Drax's knighthood in 1657. Jamaica gradually replaced Curacao as Spanish America's main entrepot, geographically better located, giving Boston and Rhode Island merchants advantages over Dutch. However, mainly Spanish Netherlands' privateers took an estimated 1,000–1,800 English merchant ships, unlike the Anglo-Dutch War, not equalled by English captures.[29]

Spanish Caribbean attacks encouraged English self-protection. Buccaneers operating from Providence Island and Tortuga made hit-and-run raids on Spanish settlements. With threatened invasion, Jamaica's Governor D'Oyley invited them to Port Royal, its population still small. In 1656–57 Admiral Blake blockaded Spain, capturing a ship carrying two million pesos, preventing it from repaying loans. The ten million pesos hidden in Tenerife, where Blake sank 16 Spanish vessels, was also not collected, and further silver ships were taken.

* * *

Between 1611 and 1620 the EIC sent 55 ships to Asia, 46 in the 1620s, 35 in the 1630s but only about 20 in the 1640s-50s. Early profits declined, reflected in decreasing investments. Ejected from the Moluccas, it imported Persian silk, Indian cotton and pepper, despite declining prices. Mughal conquests in the 1630s caused famines. A million died in Gujarat, including 17 out of 21 EIC Surat factors, where trade collapsed. At Masulipatnam trade steadily increased and new factories at Sind and Basra were established but Surat's outposts at Broach, Baroda, Cambay and Ahmadabad were withdrawn in the 1630s and the EIC's 18 London employees took pay cuts in 1635 and 1639.[30] Gombroom survived only on its share of customs revenues. In 1643 the EIC suspended shipbuilding and sold Deptford and Blackwall in 1654, the latter to Henry Johnson who, for the next 30 years, ran the largest Indiaman shipbuilders. As William Courten challenged EIC monopoly, the Council of State insisted that EIC and competitors merge into a new joint-stock company. In 1653 voyages resumed, but it soon ran out of money. By 1656 it was on its knees. Bantam's EIC factor received no ships for three or four years. The VOC filled the void. The EIC had no fortified Goa or Batavia. Madras held promise but famine destroyed many years work. A Golconda-Mughal war led to a search for new markets in Bengal and Burma. In Persia, VOC outnumbered EIC ships 4:1, and kept expanding, taking Cape Colony in 1652, settling it with Dutch farmers, 'boers'. In 1656 they took Colombo, occupied much of Sri Lanka, captured Quilon from Portugal in 1658 and increased trade with Siam and Cambodia. In 1657 the EIC board decided to liquidate. Run, their share in Banda Abbas customs and their Indian rights was put up for sale, the asking price only £14,000.

Alarmed, Cromwell made a new charter which, like the VOC, raised a permanent working capital and traded on the London Stock Exchange. It was given authority to settle and fortify overseas territories on the lines of Portuguese Bombay, Dutch Cape and the new English St. Helena, their stop-off point to and from the Indian Ocean. Within a month, over £750,000 was raised and within six months, 13 ships sailed east, rebuilding not in VOC-dominated Moluccas and Bandas, but India for cotton cloth and saltpetre, the ingredient for gunpowder, in which Madras had invested heavily. In 1657, under Mughal permit, it built factories on the Ganges' tributary, the Hugli, buying and exporting huge quantities of cotton cloth from village handlooms; hundreds of thousands of weavers, dyers and washers, the world's foremost industry in quality and quantity. The EIC were back, weaker than the VOC, but with new direction, energy and governance. With wide variety of cloth types, colours and patterns, the EIC increased marketing. Surplus pepper, sugar and cloth imports were re-exported to northern Europe and the Mediterranean. It chartered 300–500-tonners with assurances of employment. Some EIC directors were members of owning groups.

*   *   *

Dutch Sephardic Jews were an important element in Dutch global commercial success. There was an extensive Sephardic diaspora in Ottoman ports. In 1593 the Medici Grand Duke of Tuscany had declared Pisa and Livorno free ports, goods held customs-free before re-export, granted Jews protection with Jewish law applied in intra-Sephardic disputes. Venice had blown hot and cold, tolerating them, expelling then, tolerating them again in two ghettoes. Native Venetians resented them for their superior Levantine contacts and Venice's decline. Livorno therefore attracted the majority. Venice's and Livorno's treatment of Jews was a familiar contemporary topic.

After Antwerp's decline, many moved to Amsterdam. In 1607 the first Amsterdam synagogue was founded by James Lopez da Costa. He chartered a ship with rye, wheat and beans to Corfu and Venice in a deal with Venice's Jews. The Da Costa's had branches in Spain, Portugal, England, Russia, Venice, Genoa, Antwerp and

Lyon.[31] Hamburg recognised them in 1612 and allowed public worship in 1650, but Amsterdam was most favoured because of earlier toleration and greater commercial opportunities. They were active in Nantes, Bordeaux, Bayonne, Toulouse, Lyon, Montpellier, La Rochelle and Rouen, helping innovate, create and control trades, had helped establish the WIC in 1621, were active in Brazil in the 1630s and 1640s, started communities in Curacao, Surinam, Barbados, Martinique and the Leeward Islands. Wherever they went, they quickly rose to prominence in trade and finance, helping establish banks, exchanges, shipbuilding, minting, manufacturing, arms, sciences, literature and music. In 1622, Christian IV of Denmark invited Amsterdam's Jews to settle Gluckstadt. Competition for Sephardic favour in forward-thinking, flexible, tolerant ports reflected growing realisation of maritime trade's capacity to generate wealth and strength. In the early-1650s, about 4,000 Sephardic refugees from Brazil fled to Holland, the English and Dutch Caribbean and from there to New Amsterdam. Free of Spanish dependence, Genoa allowed Jewish residence in 1659, a victory for secular, commercial interests over the Spanish Church.

In England, many had lived as Portuguese or naturalised English. Roderigo Lopez had been Queen Elizabeth's physician. Shakespeare's *Merchant of Venice* was the first literature portraying Jews more sympathetically. Some came to London in the 1630s as Portuguese traders led by Antonio Fernandez Carvajal. By 1643 he had a house-warehouse complex in Leadenhall Street, trading his ships in Asia, the Caribbean and Brazil, with agents throughout Europe. Debate about possible re-introduction intensified in the 1640s and 1650s. Menasseh ben Israel's appeal for readmission stressed 'merchandising is…the proper profession of the nation of the Jews' and 'there riseth an infallible profit, commodity and gain to all those Princes in whose lands they do dwell.'[32] Recognising the commercial advantage, Cromwell made another important decision. Expulsion was rescinded. Under Cromwell's protection, a synagogue and a burial ground was built.[33]

* * *

Cromwell pointed the way in other areas. After Jamaica's capture, he investigated the possibility of a Mediterranean entrance base. In the Anglo-Dutch war, the Dutch controlled it. Cromwell's spy Montague reported the obvious place was strongly fortified Gibraltar. Other possibilities were Spanish Ceuta or Portuguese Tangier. Cromwell favoured Gibraltar which would 'enable us…with six nimble frigates…to do the Spanish more harm than by a fleet.'[34] A ship sent to investigate cutting the isthmus to the mainland however, was captured.[35] The visionary idea was not forgotten. Another choke point was secured in 1658 with English troops fighting under Huguenot Turenne in the Spanish Netherlands, winning the Battle of the Dunes, giving Dunkirk to England, a commercial bridgehead. A hundred years after the loss of Calais, England again had a toe-hold on the other side of the Channel. Thurloe thought it 'a bridle to the Dutch'. In the Baltic in 1656, Cromwell secured access to Swedish ports on equal terms with the Dutch, avoiding the military alliance Sweden wanted. He refused to help Venice against the Ottomans because English capital there was vulnerable.

Revolutions typically unleash energy, but compared to the later French and Russian ones, English energy was channelled purposefully for national interest, contrasting with Louis XIV's *l'etat, c'est moi*. Financing this energetic re-boot was crucial. Permanent taxes from 1645 made state borrowing possible. From the 1650s repayments were made sequentially, making the Commonwealth the first reasonably creditworthy English government. Thus, its fiscal innovations survived it, with Navigation Acts, Caribbean policy, strong navy at sea for several years in distant waters with offensive capability, toleration and the new EIC, the foundations of national direction for well over a century, aggressive assertion of English trading interests, a proforma of what was possible with stable, purposeful government. Parliamentary committees oversaw army, navy, church and foreign trade far more efficiently. A civil service arose and City merchants served on committees for finance, trade and colonies.

In 1639 Barbary pirates captured and enslaved English sailors in the Channel. Venice's ambassador in 1640 reported 'England...has become a nation useless to the rest of the world and consequently of no consideration.'[36] As Blake bombarded Tunis in 1655 and Penn won Jamaica, a message was sent that England was no longer to be messed with. Privateers were cleared from Algiers to Dunkirk and English merchants protected. Growing trade and efficient administration increased customs yields from £140,000 in 1643 to £502,000 by 1658. For all the many domestic disputes of the Republic and Protectorate, they were united in trade protection. England was suddenly powerful. European states sought Cromwell's help.

In 1640 woollen cloth still accounted for 80% of all English exports. Republican government and Cromwell's initiatives changed everything, something he could not have realised when he died. John Dryden (1631–1700) said he made the English lion roar. Milton described him as 'our chief of men,' for his leadership in war and peace, his faith, fortitude and in saving free conscience, all of which were valid reasons, but Milton died in 1674, and could not have fully realised his long-term economic legacy in paving the way for England to become Europe's entrepot for colonial and Asian goods, hidden by Dutch commercial dominance and his 1658 death. When monarchy was re-established in 1660, many lessons had been, or should have been, learned. It was impossible to re-impose direct 'divine right' authoritarian rule. Compromise was necessary. The talented, reform-minded civil service was too useful to discard. Laudian and Presbyterian intolerance was set aside in a legacy of toleration, even for Catholics, dissenters and Jews, the latter two vital in a reinvigorated post-Restoration merchant economy. The Interregnum saw the acquisition of Jamaica, St. Helena, Surinam, Dunkirk, Nova Scotia and New Brunswick in a foreign policy dominated by national economic interests.

Chapter 33

Ming, Manchu and the
Last Asian Maritime Power

With Chinese trade permitted from 1567, distant Beijing's aims were still not aligned with maritime traders, even though effective management could have filled its treasury with customs revenue. The Ming could not reconcile dislike of dealing with foreigners with their need for silver, the supply of which was in the hands of Portuguese and illegal Fujian shipowners/merchants. Many had impressive organisations. One of the biggest, trading in Japan, Manila, Macao, Taiwan, Annam and Ryukyu Islands, was controlled by Li Dan, known to all as Captain China. After centuries of Japanese civil war ended, many unemployed soldiers turned to the growing smuggling fleets. One employee was Zheng Zhilong, Nicholas Iquan to Europeans, as he lived in Macao and converted to Christianity. Son of a Chinese father and Japanese mother, he accompanied Macao's ships to Japan in the silver for porcelain trade and there worked for Li Dan, shipping Chinese goods to Manila, Okinawa, Ayutthaya, Taiwan and the VOC, who could not penetrate China directly. With the VOC, he captured Manila-bound ships and cargoes and owned 20–30 ships carrying people from Fujian to Taiwan during droughts and revolts. After his main rival died, all competing merchant groups were incorporated.

The Ming referred to him as Lord of the Straits, Master of the Seas.[1] Reputed to be China's richest man from a 40% cargo tax, his villa's three miles of walls enclosed gardens, lakes, fountains, a zoo and art pavilions. During the 1620s, Macao, Manila, Yuegang, Xiamen (Amoy), Taiwan and Kyushu expanded trade with Europeans. A new system of trade permits allowed Li Dan and Nicholas to build their maritime empire from Taiwan. After Li Dan's death, as the strongest maritime power, he tried excluding Portuguese and VOC from the lucrative Japan-China trade but in 1628 did a three-year deal with the VOC, supplying raw silk, sugar and textiles for pepper. The VOC coveted Macao, attacking in 1601, 1604 and 1622 but failed. As an alternative, Taiwan inhabited by native Austronesians and used by Iquan, seemed an attractive option, so the VOC built a trade-base, Fort Zeelandia.

Between 1604 and 1635, 355 ships sailed from Japan to Southeast Asia[2] and in the 1620s a Japanese enclave at Ayutthaya was established, already hosting Chinese, resident since the 13th century and Portuguese, Javanese, Malays, Makassars and Pegu's merchants, Siam's Japan trade, the most valuable.[3] In 1629 its king reintroduced royal monopoly over foreign trade.[4] As the Shogun restricted

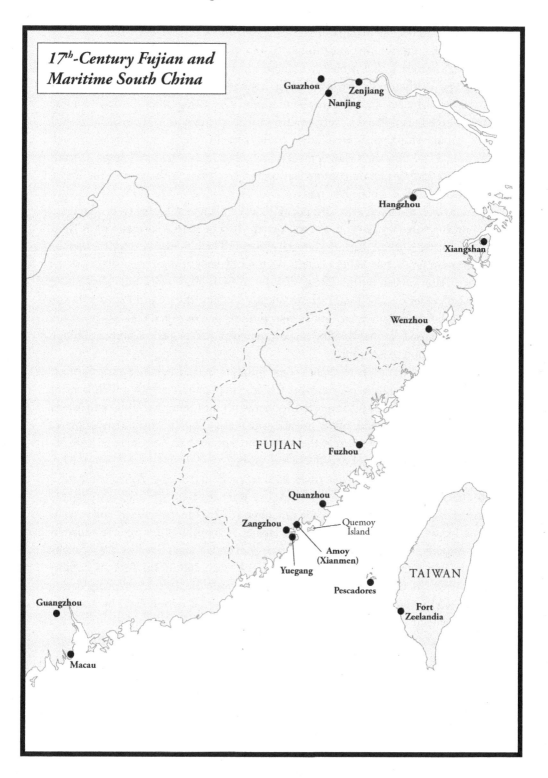

17th-Century Fujian and Maritime South China

Guazhou

Zenjiang
Nanjing

Hangzhou

Xiangshan

Wenzhou

FUJIAN   Fuzhou

Quanzhou

Zangzhou   Quemoy Island

Amoy (Xianmen)

Yuegang

Pescadores   TAIWAN

Guangzhou   Fort Zeelandia

Macau

trade in the 1630s, Siam's Japan trade decreased, but increased with China, mainly porcelain and silk for rice and timber. Siam's officials were mainly Gujarati and Chinese, chartering Siam-based, Chinese-owned ships, trading with Chinese smugglers. With private trade officially banned, it was hidden. Excess official tribute was labelled 'ballast on tribute ships.' Departing ships loaded Chinese goods, also labelled 'ballast', more valuable than the tribute.[5] The official annual three tribute ships, with auxiliaries, could actually mean ten cargoes in each direction, 3,000 tons each way. A royal monopoly administered by foreign officials and tribute hiding private commercial trade,[6] was about as bizarre as the illegal Acapulco-Manila-China silver trade.

Meanwhile, the latest northern non-Chinese to threaten China were Manchus. Renouncing tributary status to the weakened Ming in 1616, they attacked in 1618. In 1619, leader Nurhaci, declared himself emperor. The Chinese silver price dropped to European levels, but Ming tax rolls were set by weight, compromising national defence. After breaching the Great Wall in 1629–1630, Ming China slipped out of control, beset by rebellion. Infrastructure, including the Grand Canal, fell into disrepair. Some Fujianese left for Taiwan to farm rice or sugar. Chinese porcelain exports collapsed. In the 1650s Japanese porcelain developed, exported through Dutch and Chinese networks.

China's pepper imports tended to come from Jambi via Bantam, Sumatra's west-bound pepper through Aceh. Bantam's Chinese merchants competed with Batavia. Jambi's Chinese merchants imported Indian cloth into Sumatra. VOC employees, unable to officially trade, often privately financed Chinese merchants, some of whom moved to Batavia, while the VOC concentrated on Coromandel cloth to Southeast Asia and pepper and spices to Europe.[7]

The VOC thought Iquan's trade empire their major east Asian competitor and attacked his Xiamen base in 1633, but were defeated. In 1641 they agreed commercial terms again. Meanwhile in China, 1639 tax increases were followed by floods, locusts and epidemics. The 1639 Japanese exclusion of Portuguese ended its silver imports. Macao became a backwater. Korea was conquered by the Manchu in 1636, and retreated from outside contact. Korean culture ossified; its nobility uninterested in change. In 1644 the Manchu took Beijing. Iquan, considering himself a Ming advisor, sensibly suggested financing Fujian's defence by maritime trade; 'open-up the sea lanes, stimulate trade in each port in order to satisfy… material needs', the surplus reinvested in a war effort.[8] Iquan stood to profit most, but was common sense. Sweet potato imports had saved Fujian from starvation in 1594 without Ming involvement. An active maritime policy would give them back authority and power, but it fell on deaf ears. Perhaps it was too late anyway. The Manchus continued to march south. In 1644 the emperor killed his family and himself. Nanjing fell in 1645, Fuzhou in 1646. Iquan knew the Ming were finished, but his son Coxinga fought on, winning and losing land battles in the 1640s–1650s, a thorn in the Manchu side, ignoring their offer of pardon.

He turned his father's decentralised trade network into an integrated, well-administered, centrally-commanded organisation with five companies and two trade fleets. Each company had two branches, dealing with inland and maritime trade. Over 80% of junks trading from Nagasaki to Southeast Asia belonged to it. Others paid a toll. It dominated the Japan-China trade; silk, ceramics, gold, copper, silver, sulphur and spice re-exports. In the 1650s it was an estimated five-times more profitable than the VOC in east Asia, equivalent to about 10% of Manchu government revenue.[9] He had shipbuilding in Xiamen and by 1655, 250,000 well-equipped soldiers and 2,300 ships. A Manchu assault on Xiamen in 1656 was easily repelled. The VOC thought him 'the man who can spit in our faces in eastern waters.' Had the VOC offered the Manchu assistance against Coxinga in return for a Macao-like trade enclave, they may have agreed. The VOC, wanting to trade in the immediate future however, needed a friendly Coxinga. The Manchu also courted him, writing to him, 'even with the pacification of the coastal region, we would still require the competent organisations of defences…would you not seem the ideal candidate?…you may repel or destroy pirates at your discretion. You may retain the responsibility for inspecting and taxing maritime cargo…you shall achieve the pacification of the seas.'[10] He ignored them, explaining to his father, now in Manchu custody, 'the coastal area has long been in our possession. The profits from the eastern and western trade are well-enough for our own survival and expansion…why should I not enjoy this autonomy and subjugate myself to others?'

This was a reasonable commercial position. But dangerously, he envisaged rolling back the Manchu. His 90,000 men, 200 warships and 90 supply ships advancing on Nanjing was defeated at the Grand Canal's entrance in 1659. To finish Coxinga, the Manchu had to deny him repair facilities and provisions. They took typical heavy-handed action. Orders from 1661 to 1665 banned coastal trade, the penalty immediate execution. Those reporting it inherited confiscated property. All ships were ordered burned. The coast from Beijing to Guangzhou was evacuated for 30 miles inland. Farmers and fishermen were given days to leave before soldiers destroyed everything within the no-man's-land;[11] a scorched earth policy inflicted on China's coastal population. In this 'Frontier Shift', formerly prosperous ports and villages were burnt. Forts were built along the evacuation line. Hundreds of thousands became refugees. Coxinga's refusal to work with Manchu in a sensible maritime policy as his father advocated might have been justifiable. But his land-based military actions led to another disaster for China's ports.[12] Coxinga evacuated homeless refugees to Taiwan, swelling its Chinese population to over 100,000, while he retained Xiamen and Quernoy, supplied from Taiwan. The five-company system resumed soon after the 'Frontier Shift'. A Manchu officer reported, 'some merchants who monopolise the supply of products, bribe officials and soldiers guarding the coast and trade with the Zheng family [Coxinga] secretly. Consequently, the profits on the sea are manipulated solely by the Zhengs and their wealth and supplies become more and more abundant'.[13] Taiwan became Southeast Asia's most important Chinese entrepot.

Macao avoided evacuation by bribes. The VOC aimed to take it again. Coxinga used his Taiwan base, which had undeveloped arable land and shipbuilding potential, to attack Manchu-controlled areas. He evicted Fort Zeelandia's about 1,000 people in 1662, reorganised farming and provisioning under efficient bureaucracy, rejected Chinese conquest, and demanded tribute from Manila, which anxious about its Chinese traders' loyalty, expelled all non-Christian Chinese, who fled inland or to Taiwan.

On his death in 1662, the Manchu put former Coxinga men in charge of a Manchu fleet. His successor Zheng Jing, ruled as king of Taiwan, still dominating the expanding trade empire under the five-company system. After 1668, the Manchu felt secure enough to relax coastal prohibitions as Taiwan stopped being an important issue. Even so, it took time for China's coast to recover. A secretary of Zhenjiang's governor wrote in 1672, 'land without people is worthless and people without wealth is valueless...poverty affecting the whole population is unprecedented.' In contrast, a letter to a Manchu negotiator in 1667 said Taiwan 'has become an independent glory out of..[Manchu] territory. We have food storage enough for several decades and the barbarians...are complying with us. All goods are circulating smoothly and our people live...strongly and healthily.'[14] In 1670, Bantam's EIC resident signed a trade deal, granted the right to establish a factory, buy silk, copper, sugar and deerskins for gunpowder, guns and iron. As Zheng Jing consolidated, he reconsidered taking the Philippines, realising its strategic trade value, a plan which may have succeeded against so few Spanish, further weakened and demoralised by continual European defeat, Portuguese independence and a potential Chinese-Japanese fifth-column.

Governor Antonio de Morga had conceded in 1609, 'without the Sangleys, the city cannot... maintain itself because they are masters of all trades and good workers who labour for moderate wages.'[15] Zheng Jing missed the opportunity, although trade in silk, porcelain, gunpowder, iron, steel, mercury, copper, flour, etc., developed peacefully, mutually beneficially. This could have been the way things continued; a strong, stable, 'maritime China' in Taiwan, trading with all-comers. But in 1673, anti-Manchu rebellions broke out in Guangdong, Fujian and Yunnan. Fatefully Zheng Jing was sucked in. The 1,800 soldier-colonists in Taiwan were ordered to Fujian for support, leading to an immediate crop-yield fall. In 1674, he recaptured some ports including Xiamen, which reopened for free trade. The EIC, Annam and Siam sent trade envoys. In 1676 he nearly reached Guangzhou.

While expanding, problems were contained, but when losing ground, morale eroded and provisions diminished; a vicious circle. By 1677 most major ports were lost and his military collapsed. In 1680, just as the EIC established an office, the Manchu took Xiamen.[16] Taiwan's food crisis descended into famine in 1682 and 1683. The Manchu assisted by the VOC, sent a fleet to Taiwan, which was incorporated into the empire. The VOC were, as reward, allowed to trade in Fujian. Northern problems still dominated government thinking, especially Mongols and Tibetans. In 1685 the Kangxi emperor drafted the *Taxation Rule for Sea Trade* allowing it <u>only</u> at Guangzhou within the traditional imperial tribute convention, administered by 'hong' merchants, despite Xiamen's superior commercial services. Fujianese bought these posts, collecting customs duties. Zheng Jing's mainland invasion, abandoning plans to conquer inadequately defended Manila, jeopardising Taiwan's trade and farming base, were tragic mistakes. Continuing the 1660s–1670s two China's, the maritime Taiwan-centred commercial company would have rivalled and complimented the VOC and EIC with healthy competition.

Japan's Shogun, already anxious about silver export, banned it in 1668. From then on, Japanese knowledge about the world was only obtained in Nagasaki. By 1683 over 100 ships from China arrived there and was seen as too dangerous, so its Chinese residents were, like the VOC, forced to live in a restricted area. With the EIC expelled from Bantam in 1684, it traded in China directly. The damage done by the Ming was not repairable by Manchus, who inherited a similar anti-trade bias. New regulations covering ship and crew size, export prohibitions and proper conduct of alien tribute-bearers were enacted. Private foreign trade continued to be banned. Officials, as usual, evaded regulations, labelling all outbound cargo, 'ballast'. The dynamism of the Iquan-Coxinga-Zheng Jing maritime empire, and crucially Chinese maritime power, finally disappeared. Most Asian powers looked inland. The oldest, most active, richest maritime area had been repeatedly compromised by landed, continental despoilers; Gutians, Jurchens, Huns, Mongols, Ming and Manchu. Japan and Korea also turned inward. Mughal preoccupation with taxing peasants and making war on Hindu kingdoms in the name of religious uniformity, limited their horizon. Neither had credible maritime naval power to counter western incursion. Lost opportunities were directly due to continental invasions or mind-set. Abandonment of Taiwan's trade empire for the chimera of continental conquest was the final Asian watershed mistake. Most intra-Asian trade was still arranged and shipped by Asian traders and ships, although VOC Moluccan spice monopoly virtually ended Javanese, and after 1668, Makassan ports and shipping. Crucially there was no longer any significant Asian military maritime power.

Chapter 34

European Competition: The 1660s and 1670s

After the 1660 restoration, core English economic policy remained unchanged; increase wealth by maritime trade; the Dutch both example and rival. Parliament's expanded role, less royal interference, landed classes contributing tax, generally lower than elsewhere, created a new dynamic. The economy expanded. In 1660, the Council for Trade and the Plantations was established and the Navigation Act strengthened; the declared aim, 'the increase in shipping,' and from 1660 to 1663 many foreign-built ships were purchased, followed by an English shipbuilding recovery, with new designs, so merchant shipping grew fast.[1] Foreign-built ships were registered to clarify ownership.[2] Differential duties were imposed ensuring Caribbean planters shipped semi-processed muscovado, maximising shipping demand and encouraging refining industries in English ports. Duties on re-exported goods were refunded, to be competitive in Europe.

The programme for national enrichment aimed to make London, not Amsterdam, Europe's leading entrepot.[3] It meant expanding and developing Navigation Acts, especially about American trades. Josiah Child's *A New Discourse of Trade* described it as 'one of the choicest and most prudent acts that ever was made in England' in the ability to own ships, control trade and train seamen. 'Without the Navigation Act, you should see 40 Dutch ships at our plantations for one English.'[4] Some Dutch were driven out of England's Baltic trade, the average annual number passing the Sound after 1660, nearly double that before 1650. Adam Smith later thought them 'perhaps the wisest of all commercial regulations of England.' Manufactured goods were sent to the colonies, including brass, copper, ironware, silk, linen, glass, pottery, paper and woollen cloth. English ships sailed fully-laden both ways. Volumes of sugar, cotton, indigo, ginger, dyewoods, pepper and Indian cottons rose.

A few large timber merchants handled Norwegian timber imports through factors there, often family members or former apprentices, using chartered and partly-owned ships. The trading pattern was often northeast England's coal to London, Holland, or lesser amounts to Hamburg or Copenhagen, then ballast to Norway to load timber for England, then coal again. Charter parties usually allowed 6–10 days to load, making four or five round voyages a year possible from March to December.[5]

By 1660, shipbuilding and maritime trade were the leading activities of New England's ports, which owned about 200 ships. Recognised early as a source for naval masts, the first shipment was in 1634 and were supplied regularly in the First Anglo-Dutch War and thereafter.[6] Its imports were mainly English, except wine from the Canaries. Tobacco was shipped to Holland by Massachusetts' merchants, returning with European goods to New England. Navigation Acts were not enforceable in Massachusetts' Courts which backed their own merchants, declaring it was not subject to 'the laws of England any more than we live in England', but took advantage of them when it suited, to drive out competition. The Navigation Act 'system' was therefore imperfect and smuggling widespread in sugar, molasses, rum, bullion, wine and fur. Dutch, English and French merchants carried Spanish silver and Portuguese sugar to Amsterdam, London and La Rochelle respectively.

In 1660 England had well-established Newfoundland fisheries, almost 25,000 people around Chesapeake Bay growing and exporting tobacco, over 35,000 in New England, providing Caribbean colonies with fish, horses and timber and about 80,000 in the Caribbean with sugar plantations, some lingering tobacco, indigo and cotton. These trades constituted only 4% of England's overseas trade, but all believed it would grow.[7] Barbados supplied two-thirds of England's sugar. Hundreds of windmills powered its machinery and entrepreneurs hired labour, contrasting with Brazil's sharecroppers who sent their cane to landowners' mills for limited amounts of refined sugar. Charles saw Jamaica as 'the naval of the West Indies,' a base from which to observe Spain, 'beyond the line.' The Western Design showed colonies were essential to England's economic well-being. Charles pursued a similar commercial policy, partly because he hoped more tariff-revenue would reduce dependency on Parliament. England with a quarter of France's population could, he thought, only be 'considerable by our trade and power by sea,'[8] a lesson of the Interregnum, the vision shared by James Duke of York, Prince Rupert, and Edward Hyde, who invested in colonial land, privateering, slave trading and colonial companies.

Increasingly confident colonies gave opportunities. Robert Livingston spent his adolescence among Scottish traders in Rotterdam. Arriving in Albany in 1674, partnering with fellow Scot James Graham, they became major fur traders, using contacts gained from Livingston's secretaryship of the Board of Indian Affairs.[9] The Earl of Sandwich's 1671 *Comments upon New England* predicted in 20 years it would be 'mighty rich and powerful and not at all careful of their dependence upon old England.'[10] The French threat from Canada, merchant ties and ability to flout the Navigation Act with Caribbean islands made this unduly pessimistic.

Lee's 1667 *London Directory* listed 1,829 active overseas merchants, most living close to the Royal Exchange, the Customs House and 21 Legal Quays between London Bridge and the Tower.[11] Pepys used the Royal Exchange to hire ships for the navy and insure ships. Meanwhile the Merchant Adventurers, Levant and Eastland Companies declined. Less capital intensive than long-haul trades and with a stronger navy, private merchants conducted these trades. American colonial goods helped transition England to a more diversified economy with greater export variety, with America needing English imports. Hakluyt's and Raleigh's policies had triumphed.[12]

The Netherlands was at the height of its power under Grand Pensionary Johan de Witt (r. 1653–1672). He noted in 1671 that grain and Baltic trades were the 'source and root of the most notable commerce and navigation of these lands.' An estimated 75% of capital on Amsterdam's 1666 Bourse was engaged in Baltic trade.[13] Fishing and ancillary trades employed about 450,000 people compared with 200,000 in agriculture, 650,000 in other industries, with Rotterdam and Enkhuizen the main fishing centres and Amsterdam, the whaling hub. The VOC were wealthy and powerful, expanding in India and Sri Lanka, dominant in cinnamon supply. The WIC dominated trade in west Africa and the Caribbean. New Amsterdam took New Sweden in 1655, the enlarged territory developing otter, mink and beaver pelt trading, expanding to Fort Orange (Albany), where the Hudson became too shallow to navigate. It had thriving Dutch towns, English communities and Jews from Brazil. The Dutch had maritime dominance virtually worldwide. Leiden was Europe's largest industrial concentration. In 1670, Venice's Senate concluded that the only way to revive their textile industry was to import Dutch equipment. Portugal, resuming her English alliance that Spanish union ruined, was transformed from Reconquista zealotry. In 1662, she pragmatically gave Dutch merchants the same trading rights in her Brazilian and African colonies as English, concentrating on resisting futile Spanish attempts to retain union.

In 1661 Charles married Portugal's Catherine of Braganza. Spain thought it better to ally with the Dutch, their interests identical in not allowing France to absorb the Spanish Netherlands. Part of Catherine's dowry was Tangier, Portuguese since 1471, a base near the Mediterranean entrance, but unable to control it. Run-down and virtually empty, partly due to difficult Berber neighbours and an exposed anchorage, its small port had 1,200–2,000 soldiers and Dutch, Portuguese, North African and Jewish merchants trading with Turks and Armenians from Smyrna. The other part of her dowry was Bombay with a secret clause in which England agreed to defend Portugal's other Indian settlements from the VOC. Charles sold it to the EIC in 1668 for ten pounds of gold a year. Despite its deep harbour, it had negligible trade due to a limited hinterland. Surat with a 200–400,000 population had replaced Cambay as Gujarat's premier port and business hub, so most European business was done there in undefended factories; the VOC the largest with 50–60 people. Having silted up, ships trans-shipped into lighters 10–12 miles away. It was linked by roads to manufacturing centres; Bharuch, Cambay, Ahmedabad. The EIC bought Gujarati saltpetre, in which Europe was deficient. Figures are only available from 1664 when 589 tons was shipped to London. Annual 1670s imports were 632 tons, and in the 1680s, 733 tons.[14]

Surat's traders included huge magnates with vast capital for which credit notes, 'hundis', were used for large transactions. Mir Jumla, a Persian trader of the 1640s had his own ships carrying third-party cargoes from the Red Sea and Persian Gulf to the Maldives and Southeast Asia, exchanging cloth for spices.[15] Muslim, Hindu and Jain families spread investments into shipping, tax-farming, money-lending, banking and trading. Europeans wrote in awe of Surat's Jain merchant, Virji Vora

(c. 1590–1670), head of a family business with branches throughout India, the Gulf, Red Sea, and Southeast Asia. Reputedly the world's richest man, worth about eight million rupees, he lent money to Mughal nobles and the EIC alike and was shipowner and trader in indigo, pepper, Mediterranean coral and cloves.[16]

Surat was governed by Mughal soldier-officials, operating semi-independently from Delhi, an insecure business environment, although customs duties were only about 5%. Their exaction of money, jewels and presents was a business cost. Property seizures caused financial harm and reputational damage if they endangered the ability to honour obligations. Fear of Mughal exactions meant concealment and secrecy. Jains and Vaishnavist Hindu traders lived frugally. Many religious sub-sects became intermediaries to the EIC and VOC. Some cultivated Mughal patrons, keeping representatives at their Surat and Delhi durbars, offering tribute for favours, religious toleration and a safe business environment.[17] The EIC did the same, regarding gifts as bribes, immediate return favours, rather than an elaborate game of placating egos, financing military campaigns and meeting the cost of expensive lifestyles. Vora and other merchants normally bankrolled local governors and nobles and was influential enough with the governor that he prevented local traders from dealing with the EIC for a time. Present giving and loans were major income sources for Mughal nobles. In return some merchants collected land revenue, customs and occasionally were policy advisors.[18] The crucial difference with emerging European maritime economies however, was that rulers <u>and</u> public invested in Venice, Genoa, Amsterdam and London's maritime ventures. Indian merchants placated a ruling elite uninterested in it, and thus were unable to create publicly funded companies.

Nevertheless, Mughals while not encouraging trade, needing gold and silver, did not unduly hinder it. Toleration, started by Akbar continued, accepted by Hindus. The Coromandel coast also had great merchants. Kasi Veeranna sent ships to Southeast Asia from Pulicat and Madras. Tranquebar supplied cotton cloths to European companies and direct markets and had agents in all main Southeast Asian ports. Tamil Muslim merchants, (Chulias from Chola) competed and complimented Europeans. Sufis also formed a network. Spreading since the 11th century from Persia to Indian and Chinese ports, Ibn Battutah had remarked on them in Cambay, Calicut, Quilon and Guangzhou. Traders had many social and religious backgrounds; Brahmins, Hindus, Jains, Shia, Sunni, Parsis, Arwi, Armenians, Turks, Arabs and Europeans, congregating for trust and security in markets liable to rapid, unexpected fluctuations.[19]

All changed with Aurangzeb (r. 1658–1707) who thought toleration and his father Jahan's personal philosophy un-Islamic. In 1657, in wars between four brothers over succession which Aurangzeb won, Surat was plundered for funds by Murad, the youngest. Another's head was presented to his imprisoned father, another cut in pieces. An iron-willed, devout, selfless bigot, he was disastrous for India. Toleration was abandoned and sharia law instituted. He dismissed Hindu clerks and Court musicians, ordered Hindu temples destroyed, re-imposed punitive taxes on non-Muslims, outlawed winemaking and Diwali. The Sikh Guru was tortured and beheaded for not converting. Widespread war resulted. Hindu powers, especially Marathas under Shivaji (1627–80) descended from mountain forts with Mongol-like speed and from the sea in fast ships, attacking Mughal armies and ships.

Political breakdown caused commercial chaos. Marathas plundered Surat in 1664 and 1670. Vora was one of many who suffered with houses and warehouses demolished and his grandson murdered. In 1669 Jains and Hindus were targeted by a Surat judge who forcibly converted several wealthy Hindu, circumcised a Hindu scribe, and threatened to destroy local temples.[20] Eight thousand shut their shops, left en-masse for Bharuch and entertained offers from Ahmedabad's governor that they settle under his protection. After two months, an edict assured them of safety and religious tolerance. Some returned.[21] But many of Surat's Hindu and Jain merchants moved to Bombay. Although not maritime, another once strong Asian power was self-harming.

*   *   *

Having been granted a monopoly in 1660 of English west African trade, the 'Company of Royal Adventurers Trading to Africa' targeted Gambia River gold, hitherto dealt with by private traders, after the Guinea Company's near failure. Half its £400,000 revenue came from gold, a quarter each from ivory and slaves,[22] but was unable to satisfy soaring Caribbean slave demand, despite shipping 3,000 to Barbados in 1663's first seven months. Dutch merchants were pre-eminent in slaving. The Second Anglo-Dutch War (1665–67) was encouraged by the Royal Adventurer's head, James Duke of York, to challenge Dutch dominance, specifically WIC west African trading posts. All merchant interests supported war, including the EIC, angry that the VOC professed *Mare Liberum* in India, while enforcing monopoly elsewhere in Asia. The Levant Company wanted to intercept the valuable annual Dutch Smyrna convoy. Dutch and English merchant stimulus had expanded Smyrna's population to about 80,000; Turks, Greeks, Armenians, Jews and Levantines. Many factors married Greeks.[23] The convoy was a valuable target. Pepys thought the country 'mad for war.' 'What we want,' said the Duke of Albemarle in 1664 'is more of the trade that the Dutch now have.' War was triggered by England's seizure of Dutch west African slave stations and New Amsterdam in 1664, which Charles thought 'a place of great importance to trade and a very good town.'[24]

The Leeward Islands' Governor noted in 1664, 'the King of France pursues his interest in the Indies very high…with the power of shipping and men,' predicting that with Spanish power withering, 'the dispute will be whether the king of England or France shall be the monarch of the West Indies.' The war included the recapture of Run in 1665, albeit denuded of nutmeg trees. But most fighting was in the Atlantic. After De Ruyter's' 1665 failed attack on Barbados, England launched an offensive, Charles said, 'to root the Dutch out of all places in the West Indies…especially Curacao.'[25] Former Barbados planter Thomas Modyford, from

1664 Jamaican Governor, unleashed the buccaneers and by 1665 most Dutch settlements were in English hands. In 1666 France entered the war supporting the Dutch, reversing English victories, devastating Antigua, the English part of St. Kitts, capturing Montserrat. Nevis escaped and prospered. England was once again excluded from the Baltic by Holland's Danish allies and suffered the Great Plague (1665) and Great Fire (1666), while the Dutch recaptured Surinam and most west African posts, ruining the 'Company of Royal Adventurers', which hardly traded after 1665. The navy, Cromwell's pride, poorly equipped, inadequately manned and unimaginatively led, was humiliated. In 1667, Dutch ships sailed up the Medway to Chatham where the English fleet, stranded for lack of money, was partly burnt and the *Royal Charles* flagship towed away. Holland spent double England's expenditure, mobilising tax revenues better, its state-borrowing superior to Charles' high-interest, short-term royal loans, as Parliament didn't fully trust him. Dutch ships were superior and lighter. Pepys wrote, 'In all things, in wisdom, courage, force and success the Dutch have the best of us and do end the war with victory'. Charles backtracked. 'Don't fight the Dutch. Imitate them.'

The 1667 Peace of Breda restored pre-war territories except New Amsterdam remained with England, renamed New York, exchanged for Run and Surinam, which because of sugar, many thought a better deal, but New York's acquisition closed a Navigation Act loophole. Surinam replaced lost north Brazil's sugar lands. Brazil's plantation owners returned to Amsterdam or, like Isaac Navarro to Curacao, brother Arao to Surinam then Barbados, the closest island, which took many Jewish refugees from Brazil. By 1689, 54 families lived on Bridgetown's Jew Street.[26] Others set up in Guiana, between Venezuela and Brazil. By 1684 there were 222 Jewish households in Surinam, 28.6% of its European residents.[27]

Livorno had become the main 17th-century Mediterranean port with commodity price lists printed in 1627, exchange rates in 1663, which became a regular bi-weekly publication. Its Jewish merchants were not directly involved with the Americas but imported sugar, indigo, coffee and timber into the Mediterranean and exported coral to India for diamonds. From the 1660s, coral to India became increasingly an EIC trade. In a few decades London became the world market for rough diamonds.

Having unwisely sold Dunkirk to Louis XIV in 1662, needlessly weakening England's position, Charles gave him Nova Scotia in 1668, something Pepys thought Cromwell would never have done, due to its recourses, especially coal and copper.[28] The weakened English navy and fast recovering Dutch trade meant Navigation Laws had to be relaxed, allowing Dutch ships to import European products. Pepys reported, 'Everybody do nowadays reflect upon Oliver and commend him.'[29] Sir Josiah Child in 1669 thought the English would have lost the bulk trades if not for about 200 fluyts 'taken in the late Dutch war'. Another in 1670 commented, 'no English ship hath been built for the timber trade since the Rump first made the Act of Navigation,'[30] presumably meaning shipping demand was met by fluyts captured in two wars. The Leewards, St. Kitts, Nevis, Montserrat and Antigua were slowly developed, despite occasional Carib raids. Already in 1660, Bristol Quaker Jonas Langford set up Antiguan sugar estates there and within five years sent 1,000 tons to London, significant even if dwarfed by Barbados. Caribbean opportunities gave merchants renewed vigour.

Rapid London rebuilding after the Great Fire ended the masons' building monopoly, unleashing new energy. The Royal Exchange, the heart of London's commercial life, was completed in 1669 and the Guildhall by 1671. Defeat made Charles ponder the merits of Cromwell's administration and decided government by committee better than deference to a noble.[31] A distinction between English merchant ships and warships was clear before the 1660s. The first Livorno convoy in 1651 was escorted by warships. Except for Indiamen, it was no longer assumed that merchantmen could defend themselves. They thus became increasingly competitive, especially the Dutch who built larger ships with the same crew as smaller ships. Amsterdam's maritime and commercial infrastructure supported them. In 1668 Sir William Temple, England's ambassador there wrote, 'In this city…is the famous Bank, which is the greatest treasure…known around the world. The security of the Bank lies not only in the effects that are in it, but in the credit of the whole town or state of Amsterdam, whose stock and revenue is equal to that of some kingdoms.'[32]

English Caribbean islands' sugar produced 4.5% customs revenue, about £300,000 annually. Some, like St. Lucia failed because of disease and Carib attacks between 1663 and 1666, but Barbados boomed. By 1668, it produced 85% of England's sugar imports, its per capita income far higher than England or New England,[33] whose furs were quickly depleted. In 1670, the Hudson's Bay Company was formed to deal with it. Cotton and tobacco were grown on Barbados' poorer soils and there were small ginger and indigo operations but sugar accounted for 90% of its export value. Success was not achieved without risk; epidemics, heavy rains, hurricanes, plagues, drought, the huge cost of equipment, servants, slaves, land and livestock, as sugar prices fell.[34] Nevertheless a 1671 visitor noted, 'the island appears flourishing and the people…live splendidly.' From the early-1660s, 35–65 vessels a year with timber and provisions from Boston, Salem and Newport discharged in Bridgetown.

Modyford wrote enthusiastically to London about Jamaica's excellent harbours, healthy climate, building material availability and soil fertility. He brought 700 sugar planters from Barbados and persuaded Charles to waive English customs duties until sugar was established. In 1663, Jamaica's 18 sugar works produced a lighter, finer-grained sugar than Barbados, but its main export remained hides, its main crops cotton, indigo and cacao until the 1670s. Enduring Spanish threats however, meant buccaneering was as necessary as planting. Modyford complained in 1667, 'the Spanish look upon us as intruders' and they 'would soon turn us out of our plantations…it must be by force alone that can cut in sunder that un-neighbourly maxim of their government to deny all access to strangers.' Without a strong navy Modyford continued to use its over 1,000 buccaneers, selling their prizes in New England, Bermuda and Jamaica.[35] Henry Morgan, indentured servant turned buccaneer, pre-emptively raided Puerto del Principe. Spain's treasure fleet's base on the Panama isthmus, Puerto Bello's warehouse could house 25 million pesos, twice Charles's annual income.[36] With Spanish fleets less frequent, Modyford attacked it, capturing 25,000 Spanish dollars, because the Spanish 'had full intention to attempt this island…they still hold the same minds…it is very unequal that we should… be restrained while they are at liberty to act as they please upon us.'[37] Morgan cruised off Venezuela. Another fleet lay off Havana and the Yucatan peninsula. In 1669 Lake Maracaibo settlements were raided and a Spanish fleet defeated. At the 1670 Treaty of Madrid, Spain abandoned claims to Jamaica and the Cayman Islands. Privateering therefore diminished as more settlers concentrated on sugar production. Ireland became the Caribbean's great provisioner, English ships loading barrelled beef, pork, butter and cheese en route.

The Dutch lost the battle for Caribbean territory, except Curacao, but continued successfully trading. Jamaican Governor Lynch, replacing Modyford in 1671, knew 'the Dutch can sell European goods 30% cheaper than we, and will pay dearer for American goods.' They continued to supply French, Spanish and English colonists. Jamaica increased sugar production and its capital Port Royal became an entrepot for Caribbean trade, especially slaves. The 57 plantations of 1671 grew to 246 by 1684. Barbados still produced more sugar, but its soil was becoming exhausted. Many emigrated to Virginia, the Carolinas and other islands.

Another Royal African Company (RAC) was founded in 1672. Unlike the first, it mainly traded slaves, 40% of its income from other goods. In 1674 it agreed to supply 5,600 slaves annually to the Caribbean, Virginia and Spanish colonies via Port Royal. With increased sugar production and indentured servant-supply reduced, English islands' slave demand increased. In the 1680s, Barbados took about 5,000 a year, an estimated 90–100,000 between 1672 and 1689. The RAC could not satisfy demand. Even at its highest involvement, interlopers supplied 25% of arrivals.[38] By 1675 Barbados had 32,000 negroes and 21,000 whites, about half of which were free, the ratio of slaves to whites never as high as other islands. It imported timber from the 1680s from other islands and the Carolinas, even Newcastle coal. Historians have calculated English shipping tonnage differently but none dispute its huge rise from 1660 to 1688, at least double, employing perhaps 10–20% of non-agricultural workers.[39] Treaties of 1648, 1659, 1667 and 1670 placed Spain's trade, mainly slaves to its colonies, with the United Provinces and France.

Brazil's sugar shipments to Portugal were probably Europe's largest long-haul trade, its main sugar source until 1700, employing more ships than between Spain and its colonies, probably rivalling it in cargo value.[40] Unlike England, Portugal had no refineries. Brazil refined it, shipping it in armed convoys due to Barbary corsairs, many in Dutch and English ships. Sugar supported Portugal's economy in taxes, duties and re-exports. Brazil continued to export brazilwood and timber, its whaling fleet supplied oil, illuminating sugar mills. It imported wine, olive oil, flour, salt and cod. Portuguese Guinea exported gold, ivory, gums, resins, melegueta pepper to Portugal and Angolan slaves were shipped to Bahia, paid for with Brazil-grown tobacco. In 1673 Brazil and the Caribbean produced 50,000 tons of sugar. By 1700 it rose to 80,000, requiring more slaves.[41]

* * *

George Downing (1623–84) was a product of this widening, mobile, Anglo-Dutch, trans-Atlantic world. Son of a Dublin barrister and sister of a Massachusetts Bay Governor, brought up in Salem, he graduated from Harvard, visited the Caribbean, became Scoutmaster General of Commonwealth forces in Scotland, official resident at The Hague before the First Anglo-Dutch War, mediated between Portugal and Holland over Brazil, between Sweden and Denmark and defended English Baltic traders' interests against the Dutch. An MP since 1660, speaking confidently on financial and commercial matters, he helped the 1660 Navigation Act and 1663 Staple Act through Parliament and was one of the loudest voices for war in 1665, explaining that the Dutch say 'we shall wholly destroy the English in the East Indies, we are the masters of Guinea, we shall ruin the English trade in the Caribbean Islands and western parts [and wish to] ruin all the English shipping there,' and 'it is mare liberum in the British seas but mare clausum on the coast of Africa and in the East Indies.'[42]

Sent to Holland before the Third Anglo-Dutch War to replace pro-Dutch Sir William Temple, these two embody the English dual view of the Dutch; frenemy indeed, in Downing's case, reluctant admiration and jealousy. He explained, 'the herring trade is the cause of the salt trade, and the herring and salt trade are the cause of this country's having...wholly the trade of the Baltic Sea,' contrasting English ships ballasting into the Baltic, 'which makes freight backward from thence to be double of what it would be.' Few men did more to translate collective private interests into practical national policy.[43] Herrings were their 'mother of all trades', 1,500 ships catching, salting, packing and exporting to France and England, where they sold cheaper than those caught by English vessels. Whaling closely followed with about 40,000 barrels of blubber. The Dutch fleet, equivalent to all other Europeans together until 1669, comprised 600,000 tons and 48,000 sailors. Like Downing, Pieter de la Court thought smoked and salted fish and allied trades were worth half of all its trade.[44]

The Dutch always aimed for monopoly, but could not force strong powers; Persia, China and Japan to comply. However, nutmeg was secure. Illicit clove trading in Makassar was stopped by Dutch conquest in 1668. The sultan had to agree to a VOC export-import monopoly. The VOC sold pepper, cloves, nutmeg, mace and cinnamon in Amsterdam, Surat, Masulipatnam, Hugli, Banda Abbas, Mocha and the Mediterranean, accelerating Venice's decline. Japan banned silver exports in 1668. The VOC adapted, buying copper and lacquerware with Indian cotton, Bengal raw silk and Chinese porcelain. All European companies were increasingly attracted by Indian Ocean trade, especially India itself. The VOC's Masulipatnam base concentrated on patterned textiles to Southeast Asia. They increased their presence in Pulicat and in 1690, Nagapattinam. The EIC concentrated on Madras.

The EIC opened up intra-Indian Ocean trade to employees in 1674, realistic as they accepted the risk of contracting tropical diseases in return for a chance of enrichment without subterfuge. The EIC stopped shipping Indian cotton cloth to

Bantam, concentrating on exports to England. A new agreement with Bantam's sultan ensured west Sumatran pepper supply, which he controlled. VOC victory in Makassar and inroads in Banjarmasin's pepper areas increased Dutch options. But European pepper prices fell and capital needed for ships and stock grew faster than the trade's value. Portuguese, VOC and EIC only got a fraction of Indian Ocean trade. Gujaratis, Mappilas, Tamils, Omanis, Austronesians, Armenians and Jews carried most, although English and Dutch merchants dominated trade with Europe.

* * *

France's ascent to leading European power after 1648 led to dreams of competing worldwide. Louis XIV's substantial revenue from heavily taxed peasants supported the traditional policy of eastward expansion. Food was mainly grown for subsistence, there was little industry, no arms production or metal industries. Lyon's silk industry served only the rich. Moneymaking focused on office-holding, not commerce or industry. During the Thirty Years War, tax take tripled, leading to peasant rebellions. Louis' finance minister, Jean-Baptiste Colbert explained, 'The art of taxation consists in so plucking the goose as to obtain the largest amount of feathers with the least amount of hissing;' taxpayers were plucked, not economically incentivised.

When Philip IV of Spain died in 1665, Louis attacked the Netherlands, forcing Spain to acknowledge Portugal's independence. He aimed to weaken the nobility and Huguenots, take the Netherlands, so that the United Provinces and Rhineland would be at his mercy. Colbert, like Olivares and Interregnum England, identified the Dutch as the economic threat. Dutch merchants in French Atlantic ports, controlled salt, wine and brandy exports, spices, cloth, grain, herring, timber, tar, sugar and tobacco imports. Lower interest rates ensured dominance over much French trade. To increase French power, Colbert needed to reduce Dutch trade and for French companies to ship their own cargoes, to supplant the Dutch in west Africa and the Caribbean and control slave supply to Spanish colonies, the same aim as England's in Jamaica.

Thus, in a radical departure from agricultural dependence, between 1664 and 1674 Colbert attempted to create centrally-directed commerce and industry based on overseas colonies as raw material sources and as a captive market for French manufactured goods, shipped in French ships, protected by a strong navy, to make France self-sufficient, no longer beholden to Dutch merchants. He erected high protective tariffs and formed joint-stock companies for the Caribbean, Asia, west Africa, Levant and Baltic, reducing foreign imports and increasing exports in French ships. He initiated road and canal-building programmes like the Canal du Midi, constructed shipyards, harbours, arsenals, copied England's Navigation Act, excluding foreign ships in 1673. He regulated guilds to improve manufacturing quality, founded glass factories in 1665 to limit Venetian glass imports, banned in 1672, encouraged cloth weavers, like the 50 accompanying Jose Van Robus to

Abbeville in 1665 and Venetian lacemakers to settle and founded Gobelins' tapestry works.

Huge resources went into luxuries like silk, lace, tapestry, embroidery and linen making, a small part of Europe's textile industry, but potentially profitable exports. High import duties on Italian silk helped France overtake Italy as Europe's fashion leader, promoted through *Mercure Galant*, published from 1672, circulated in Europe, including novel fashion advertisements.[45] Nearly two-thirds of Colbert's many regulations concerned textiles. When Strasbourg was occupied in 1685, it was given four months for its people to stop wearing German for French clothes.[46] He established manufacturing in Languedoc, so Marseilles could export cloth to the Levant, competing with English cloth. Part of his legacy was that fashion and luxury goods averaged half French registered 18th-century exports, Lyon silks alone 12–14%.[47]

Detesting idleness, vagabonds were sent to the galleys. He tried bringing intellectual and artistic life under state control, nationalising the *Académie des Sciences* (1666), similar to the English Royal Society, but state sponsored, less vigorous, less meticulous. Opera production was given to a one-person monopoly. The *Comedie Francaise* was state funded, controlled, and regulated, subverting French intellectual independence. An observatory was built in Montparnasse, copied by Charles at Greenwich, and he financed a scientific expedition to French Guiana. Far-sighted, he had oak trees planted in 1670 to provide masts for a 19th-century fleet.[48]

There were obvious fundamental flaws. Like Olivares' companies, unlike Dutch and English, they were not merchant driven, nor accompanied by freedom of thought. The king and officials were the main shareholders. Colbert scorned weak merchants as little men with 'little private interests', because he saw the bigger picture, France's long-term interests without any concept in which 'little private interests' could be harnessed for France. He wrote to his West Indies Company directors, 'we should raise ourselves above our private interests to seek the general good,' as if Dutch and English merchants were not patriotic. He addressed English and Dutch commercial competition, projecting French power in the Caribbean and Asia, but with certainty of expensive war. The Asian company insisted on colonising Madagascar. Merchants just wanted a stop en route to India, but by 1670 Madagascar had absorbed so much money and material, without return, that it was sidelined and factories established in India. Merchants realised the importance of textiles, but the company concentrated on spices until the mid-1670s, so its Indian debts mounted and in 1680–82 it was opened up, only monopolising transport and warehousing.

The state took the initiative because outside independent-minded ports, there was insufficient commercial knowledge, expertise or backing. Harnessing Huguenot expertise, as Cromwell did with Jews, was to Louis, unthinkable. River navigation continued to be choked by private tolls. Bureaucracy increased. Like Olivares, he could not reform taxation, collected by a chaotic system of private syndicates, 'tax farmers' whose unfair, inefficient methods did not deliver the necessary revenue from a well-populated, largely fertile country. Its peasants and workers were always close to subsistence. France had about 22 million compared to just under five million in England, two million in Ireland, about 1.2 million in Scotland and 0.3 million in Wales.[49] Colbert's companies imported raw materials tax-free. Imported manufactured goods were taxed and exports subsidised. They therefore never made money. Attempting to create trade by central direction and rigid regulation discouraged initiative. Most remained in Dutch hands. However, despite shipbuilding subsidies and buying foreign ships, he reduced the public debt and the Dutch were weakened.

Barbados converted to sugar by 1650, but almost 20% of early-1670s Martinique's cultivation was still tobacco. Before the 1667 Peace of Breda, French from Tortuga began settling western Hispaniola as wild cattle hunters and buccaneers, later as planters, driven by Colbert's belief in colonies. The largest Caribbean island's mainly fertile 26,000 square kilometres was over double Jamaica's size. Colonists tripled in the 1660s and 111 sugar plantations in 1671 increased to 172 by 1685, slaves from 6,382 to 10,343.[50] Productivity doubled, but still lagged English islands. Sugar shipped to France in French ships rose sharply, encouraged by Colbert's favourable 1665 tariffs with refineries built in Dunkirk, Nantes, Bordeaux, La Rochelle, Marseilles and Orleans. After 1670 no foreign refined sugar entered France. Subsidised refined sugar was exported. The French consumed less than English.[51] French Caribbean colonies were supplied with stores, flour, wood, cod and slaves by New England's merchants for molasses for making rum. Hispaniola held the greatest potential.

France prided itself that French Canada was a perfect microcosm of itself with a similar class structure. Although Huguenots arrived first, further emigration was Catholic, still only 4,000 by 1667. Colbert sent fresh emigrants and troops, and by 1714, it had 19,000, still far less than the 200,000 English from Maine to Virginia. He established colonies in Reunion in 1664 and bases in Chandernagore, near Calcutta in 1673 and Pondicherry, south of Madras in 1674. They supplied pepper, although most still came to Amsterdam and London. Manuals on business practice, published from the late-16th century appeared more regularly in French, like Jacques Savary's 1675 *Le Parfait Negociant*.[52]

The change in French foreign commercial policy, especially sugar production and centrally-directed trade was dangerous. When finances were healthy, Colbert built 120 warships by the early-1670s, more than the Dutch and English combined, forcing England to concentrate on another Catholic absolutist state, closer and potentially stronger than Spain. War with the United Provinces (1672–78) merged Colbert's aim to damage the Dutch and Louis' desire to become Europe's main power by the traditional aim, absorbing Flanders. The policy assumed future expansion, Dutch defeat, liberation from its economic dominance, with French companies replacing Dutch ones. But Colbert's monopoly companies all failed.

Nevertheless, the sugar revolution encouraged more pro-active merchants in its ports. French historian Paul Butel notes Caribbean convoys arriving in La Rochelle and Nantes, spurred luxury trade with Cadiz. Some of Colbert's duty advantages enabled French traders in 1686 to have 40% of Europe's shipments to Spanish America via Cadiz, 3.5-times Genoa's and three-times England's[53] and Rouen's Ansincq company started buying Basque whale oil instead of Dutch. France was Spain's main manufactured goods supplier. England was Portugal's and Brazil's. Despite the failure of his monopoly companies, Butel says private merchants gained trade with Spain and the Levant.[54] In the overall picture of Europe's strongly growing trade however, these were relatively small gains. Nevertheless, merchant shipping increased impressively. A list of ships over 100 tons prepared for him in 1664 show Le Havre had 75, St Malo 48, Rouen 26, Marseilles 21, Bayonne 19, La Rochelle 18, Honfleur 14, Nantes 12, Bordeaux 11, other ports under 10. Comparable figures four year later were St Malo 117, Le Havre 114, Dieppe 96, La Rochelle 93, Nantes 84, Bayonne 61, Dunkirk 59, Marseilles 47; a 75% increase, reflecting new Caribbean, Canadian and African trades.[55]

While Colbert introduced flawed monopoly companies, Interregnum England had abolished industrial monopolies as commercial monopolies lost ground to private traders and Parliamentary hostility. The Greenland Company, Merchant Adventurers and Eastland Company were opened up. Colbert competed aggressively, but with yesterday's tools! After his replacement, parts of his policy were kept and parts ignored. Imports of some goods were limited to specific ports, quality regulations strengthened and innovation discouraged.

Using bullion to pay for EIC purchases offended European financial orthodoxy, but Sir Josiah Child argued that 80% of its imports were re-exported, the returns on which were over triple bullion's value, some of which bought African gold. In 1663, EIC bullionist enemies were defeated in a legal case but damages were awarded to interlopers 'wronged' by the EIC on the grounds that it had not been established by Act of Parliament.[56] Nevertheless, it grew impressively. Even the RAC's nominal capital quadrupled while French companies failed. Unlike France, the English landed class accepted paying a fair share of taxation; after 1663, 10%. Customs tax farming, resumed in 1662, was abandoned in 1671. This fiscal policy revolution necessitated a vastly expanded customs service,[57] a reform not attempted in France, where tax fell inefficiently, mainly on the non-privileged. In Holland it fell heavier on industry. In every case, England strengthened its finances, freed its merchants and balanced its social classes more efficiently than France.

As French naval growth and Louis' ambitions made clear, France was England's real enemy. But Charles and a ministerial Cabal governing without Parliament, switched alliance to Louis against the Dutch. Charles and Louis agreed that after victory, England could take key Channel positions, even though he had sold Dunkirk. Parliament was deeply suspicious of his French alliance as a threat to liberty and Protestantism. Forgetting Interregnum lessons, Charles was now supplicant to the 'Roi Soleil'. Simultaneous to attempted English blockade of the

Dutch, the French crossed the Rhine, which they countered by opening the dykes, flooding the country. The Dutch called 1672 'Rampjaar', 'Disaster Year'; a French army roamed the country and Amsterdam's Exchange crashed. The Dutch Golden Age's end was not immediately discernible. Charles failed to blockade Amsterdam from Baltic grain or intercept the Smyrna convoy, because Parliament withheld funds. Furthermore, Dutch privateers captured 700–800 English ships.[58] This Third Anglo-Dutch War, (1672–1674) part of the Franco-Dutch War (1672–1678), was very unpopular in England.

If Louis had captured the Spanish Netherlands, it threatened England far more than Spain had. The Dutch needed it as a buffer against France, the greater threat. English ships were again denied Baltic entry and were attacked by Channel, Mediterranean and Caribbean privateers. Sir William Coventry encapsulated why the French were the greater threat by its growing naval threat compared to the Dutch commercial threat. 'Since the Act of Navigation we have grown upon them, not they upon us; they have only gained upon the nutmeg trade since the Amboina business, but in all other parts of trade we grow upon them.'[59] Indeed, the WIC went bankrupt in 1674. It was reconstituted but increasingly lacklustre performance led to dissolution in 1730. Amsterdam was enormous, but other European ports, London, Hamburg, Bremen, Stockholm and Copenhagen were growing.

In England, Parliament denied Charles a 1674 war budget and passed the Test Act to exclude Catholics from public office. England lost St. Helena and New York and an EIC squadron was defeated off Masulipatnam. Charles was forced to drop the French alliance and conclude peace with the Dutch, who suffering from French attack, were generous in the peace treaty. England got back New York, St. Helena and £1 million. Dutch occupation of Surinam was confirmed but it was clear that dynamic private English Atlantic trade was gaining on them. With more American territory, England had potential for more trade, which encouraged domestic industry.

The Dutch were weakened nationally. Charles was weakened personally. England again lacked a coherent foreign policy, despite alignment of interests with the Dutch against France. William of Orange, now Stadtholder, with influential English assistance, flooded England with tens of thousands of pamphlets accusing Charles of conspiracy with Louis to turn England Catholic. Unable to pass the Test Act's provisions, James resigned as Lord High Admiral. Shaftesbury began to think of ousting the Stuarts. Danby, convinced that an Anglo-Dutch partnership was vital for English interests, arranged the marriage of James' daughter to William of Orange in 1677. From the war's 1674 end and the 1678 Franco-Dutch peace, England managed significant trade gains in Baltic and Iberian markets. Some were lost after 1678 but its Baltic trade was treble pre-war levels. Inbound Portuguese salt was retained, eliminating inbound ballasting.[60] Iberia was England's best cloth market, supplemented by lead, tin, brass, ironware, beaver hats and Newfoundland cod for imports of wine, iron, fruit, olive oil, cochineal, indigo, logwood and silver. Pepys thought English total Dutch wars' losses, maximum 500 ships,[61] but Dutch losses enormous, enabling reconstruction of the English merchant fleet with Dutch fluyts. Between 1664 and 1686, ships clearing London went from 43 to 114 for North America, from 45 to 138 for the Caribbean, from 26 to 111 for Norway and from 22 to 65 for the Baltic,[62] the greatest increase in trans-Atlantic and Norwegian timber trades. Increased cloth exports to the Levant was not matched by back-haul volumes, but raw silk grew,[63] which was also sold at Livorno en route.

In the 1678 Treaty of Nijmegen. France gained 15 Spanish Netherlands' towns, adding them to the 1668 gains, diminishing the Dutch buffer, but Ghent was restored. France drastically cut tariffs as Dutch resumed their role as main provider of France's manufactured goods. Both countries were exhausted with debt, but the Dutch survived Europe's strongest army and navy, prevented French continental hegemony, only possible because of its still dominant maritime trade. France's Indian and Madagascar bases were small. Marseilles' Levant trade was static, although French Caribbean trade grew as Martinique's and Guadeloupe's planters increased production.

Chapter 35

European Competition: The 1680s and 1690s

Ominously, the VOC empire began turning territorial. From 1675, Java's Mataram's king, beset by rebellion, sought assistance in return for territory and opium monopoly at low fixed prices. In 1684 he sold the VOC his pepper crop at VOC-dictated price, expelled EIC factors and closed ports to foreigners. Mataram's 1703 succession dispute allowed the VOC to place its chosen prince on the throne. This meant it controlled the best ports and most lucrative trades, a sixth of Java directly, the rest indirectly through vassals, allowing leverage against Aceh. The English moved pepper purchases to Bencoolen on Sumatra.

Unlike the EIC, the VOC banned employees from trading privately, encouraging 'smuggling', mostly Bengal's opium to Southeast Asia, using VOC ships and often its capital, perhaps as large as official VOC shipments, and in 1676, several times VOC volumes.[1] Director Jacob Verburg started a company in his wife's name with two VOC shareholders, nephews-in-law whose position allowed them to warehouse private goods and board incoming ships to buy private cargo below market value. Off Bantam they were discharged into small boats before harbour entry, preventing confiscation.[2] Intra-Asian trade, the foundation of eventual European success, demonstrated Asia's vigorous interdependent maritime economy before European penetration. VOC private trade prohibition handed EIC employees crucial advantages. At Banda Abbas in 1683 VOC ships and Persian forces blockaded an EIC Bombay force sent to recover customs arrears, estimated at £450,000,[3] but the VOC found trade increasingly problematic and agreements with the Shah difficult to enforce.

Because of Aurangzeb's religious intolerance, Indian resistance and Surat's merchant exodus, by 1688 Bombay grew into a military, naval, trading and banking centre with local merchant enclaves and a 60,000 population, despite distance from textile producers. Aggressive anti-Hindu policy and almost constant war in the Deccan and Afghanistan against Marathas, Rajputs, Sikhs and Golconda occupied Aurangzeb's last 25 years. In 1688 Maratha leader Sambhaji was tortured and dismembered joint by joint, limb by limb. Two million died in famine and plague following Deccan war in 1702–03.

Like Bombay, Madras also had disadvantages. Ships had to lie off the bar, trans-shipping cargo and passengers in heavy surf. Its hinterland had fewer, inferior weavers than Bengal or Gujarat, but its reputation for security, religious toleration and harmony attracted them, planters, moneylenders and merchants, who were allowed to use traditional arbitration by caste elders, and English settlers including wives. The EIC bought pepper, indigo, saltpetre and bright cotton calicoes with bullion. Decorated, their colour permanent, washable and lighter than linen or 'new drapery' woollens, cotton and calicoes accelerated the trend to lighter textiles. Demand quickly developed throughout Europe. Printed cottons were used as upholstery, cushions, napkins, bed hangings, sheets, tablecloths and handkerchiefs. Pepys decorated his wife's study with chintzes but did not wear them, although many did. It added to re-exports through Amsterdam and Hamburg, alarming Europe's textile industries. In the Indian cotton and silk craze, a consumer society was born, especially in England. The royal family displayed EIC gifts, copied by aristocrats and commercial elites. Chintzes mimicking expensive satins, silks and taffetas were affordable by the middle class. By the late-1690s, cotton cloth accounted for two-thirds of EIC imports, and was also used to clothe slaves. Madurai's Great Shiva Temple demonstrates the wealth English trade brought to Tamil lands.

Ahmedabad had a large industry of spinners, weavers and finishers. The EIC and VOC sent agents to provincial commercial centres and their trade grew. The EIC became the largest, wealthiest company in the English-speaking world. The 221,500 cloth pieces imported in 1627 declined in Charles I's reign, averaged 199,000 between 1663 and 1670, then broke through with 578,000 in the 1670s, 760,000 in the 1680s, equivalent to 14 yards per head of population and 707,000 in the 1690s, giving the world Indian clothing words, chintz, calico, dungaree, khaki, pyjama, sash and shawl.[4] Peak import, 1,760,315 pieces in 1684 was not approached for another 80 years.[5] Between 1660 and 1683 its imports expanded 14.4% annually.[6] Its share price, £100 in 1657 declined to £70 in 1665, but was £245 by 1677, and by 1683 it fluctuated between £360 and £500.[7] It accounted for virtually half England's trade by value, generating envy, hostility and interlopers. Its growth mirrored the vigorous, dynamic Atlantic, but its two monopoly companies, the RAC and Hudson's Bay, played little part. Batavia's increasingly moribund VOC was overtaken by an invigorated EIC.

The EIC, deliberately, proudly less aggressive than the VOC, followed Sir Thomas Roe, who steering England's first merchants in India between 1615 and 1619, warned against 'the error of the Dutch who seek plantations…by sword', counselling 'if you will profit, seek it at sea and in quiet trade…it is an error to affect garrisons and land wars in India.' It remained faithful to this wisdom, declaring in 1677, 'our business is trade, not war,' a deliberate rejection of Coen's doctrine; 'trade cannot be maintained without war, nor war without trade.' In 1679, EIC directors, 'averse to all kinds of war in India', thought it imprudent 'to contend with those great and mighty princes which might seem to obstruct our trade and ruin us.' However, EIC Governor and influential political economist Sir Josiah Child, earlier involved in a Jamaican plantation,[8] employed aggressive, buccaneering tactics in Siam in 1683 when an EIC delegation demanded its king buy £30,000 worth of goods from their Ayutthaya factory and dismiss his main trader. Siam retaliated, excluding all foreigners except Dutch. Despite this, in 1685 Child told EIC Surat factors, 'we are now in such a posture in India that we need not sneak or put up

[with] palpable injuries from any nation' and in 1686 decided the EIC's position was 'a sovereign state of India.'

Aurangzeb's war machine was too strong, but Child believed the EIC could only operate effectively from secure settlements, proposing to fortify Bombay and Madras and take a Bengal base by force. Despite Maratha help during the 1686–1689 war, Aurangzeb blockaded Bombay, its plantations were devastated and Surat's factory closed. Annual EIC imports plummeted from £800,000 in 1684 to £80,000 in 1691.⁹ The conflict potentially helped France, but its textile industries clamoured for protection, there was growing criticism of bullion export and its Indian company's financial situation worsened. Peace was concluded on Mughal terms. The EIC paid an indemnity, but its trading rights were restored. Needing EIC silver, Aurangzeb asked them back to Bengal, where they started to build Calcutta on the Hugli. A VOC factory and Armenian merchants also relocated there and thrived.¹⁰ In 1696 permission to fortify it, Bombay and Madras was given. Calcutta became the key to the Ganges, India's richest region, although in 1700, Madras had the largest private fleet trading from the Red Sea to south China. Inland, Aurangzeb waged relentless, futile war.

* * *

English Caribbean-based merchants lived luxuriously, served by livery-clad black servants. Craftsmen's wages were three-times higher than in England. Nevertheless, they felt vulnerable 'in the Spanish bowels.'¹¹ Jamaican buccaneers established dominance, raiding Puerto Bello again in 1680, continuing to Ecuador, Peru, and Chile, while Spanish raided loggers' camps and captured the Bahamas' New Providence. Soon a bigger Royal Navy provided effective defence. Their regular post-1685 visits heralded buccaneering's decline. Jamaica's Port Royal, the Caribbean's' most heavily defended port, became settled. Its English, Spanish, Portuguese, Dutch and Jewish merchants supplied slaves to Havana, Puerto Bello and Cartagena in exchange for silver, which bought New England's timber, fish, livestock, etc., enabling purchase of British manufactured goods and Mexican chocolate. Jamaica's 246 sugar works in 1684 heralded another sugar transformation 30 years after Barbados.

Quaker William Penn, son of the great admiral, founded Pennsylvania. Its capital Philadelphia had busy shipyards and a rich agricultural hinterland. Quakers were disciplined merchants and soon established trade in farm products for Caribbean sugar and rum. In the 1680s, Jamaica's slave and manufactured goods sales meant London received about £100,000 a year of bullion, almost as much as Virginian tobacco.¹² By 1690 a fifth of Barbados' exports went to New England.¹³ The Carolinas shipped corn, peas, timber, cattle and hogs to Barbados, deer skins to England, by 1700 annually 50,000. Philadelphia's trade with fellow Quakers in London, Bristol and Barbados helped increase its population to 1,800–2,000 by 1700. In Spain, the Guadalquivir silted up, and from the 1670s, Cadiz began replacing Seville as the Spanish American entrepot, transfer official in 1717, but dominated by foreign merchants.

France continued to pressure the United Provinces, taking Strasbourg in 1681, William's family's seat at Orange in south France in 1682 and Luxembourg in 1684. In 1687 it banned Dutch herring imports unless preserved in French salt and doubled Dutch import duties, making cloth sales impossible. Its biggest market for herring and whale exports dramatically dropped. As 300 Dutch ships arrived in Bordeaux and Nantes to ship the wine harvest, Louis impounded them, but Dutch discomfort did not benefit France. Merchant-driven England with strong American and Caribbean trade growth and revived EIC trade enjoyed surging customs revenue. Crown debts reduced. While France's Caribbean sugar islands progressed, Dutch lack of them became a weakness as volumes boomed. English per capita sugar consumption quintupled between 1650 and 1700. In the 1690s, England imported 23,000 tons a year, its most important commodity, supporting shipping and shipbuilding as London's recorded trade trebled from 1660 to 1700. Growing maritime volumes encouraged efficiencies; standard containers, faster loading/discharging, reduction of arms, crew sizes, insurance and more direct routes. Freight rates fluctuated because of wars, but the trend was down, tobacco, the best documented, about 3d in the 1620s to about 1d in the 1670s–80s, but 2.5d at the war's height.[14] Although cheaper tobacco and sugar prices counted most in reducing prices in England, increasingly efficient shipping greatly helped.

Improvements in French trade were wasted. Arrogant, vain, capricious, overambitious and incompetent, Louis spent 75% of revenue on war for small territorial gains, huge amounts on Versailles, while anti-Huguenot actions damaged entrepreneurship and trade. In 1685 new restrictions were imposed. Their pilots were fined if they escorted ships in or out of French ports. French ships were banned from leaving unless two-thirds of the crew were Catholic. Ex-Huguenot captains could sail only if they left their family behind. Confident that France could not compromise Catholic uniformity, purity and absolute monarchy, he revoked the Edict of Nantes, which had granted Huguenot toleration, a coup 'intended to amaze and confound.' His belief, 'One Faith, One Law, One King' was depressingly familiar. Colbert had encouraged immigration of skilled workers. Now emigrants poured out on a far larger scale, including half of Picardy's Huguenots, a third from Orange and Dauphine, a quarter from Normandy to Bordeaux. The 175,000–200,000 people was not significant compared to France's population. But they were tax-paying artisans in wool, linen, velvet and silk, jewellers, watch and clockmakers, printers, paper makers, glass and metalworkers, navigators and shipbuilders, over-contributors to its promising overseas trade, lost to France, benefiting their new host cities; Geneva, Lausanne, Zurich, Rotterdam, Amsterdam, London and English American colonies invigorating their trade, industry and finance. Silk workers set up in Spitalfields. French Canada's beaver furs made hats in London and Gobelins factory workers moved there. The linen industry in Ipswich and Lisburn, Ireland was invigorated by them. Between 1680 and 1700, 40,000 Huguenots settled in London, 35,000 in the United Provinces. Many resident Dutch and English merchants left too, because of revived anti-Dutch policies in wine and salt trades.

With American and Indian exports to England accelerating, more were re-exported to Europe. Of little commercial value before 1660, by 1689 re-exports were a third of all exports. Maritime trade's significance to England's economy had increased for centuries in volume and extent but in the 1660s–1680s it took off. Increasing customs revenues allowed Charles to govern without Parliament after 1679, another Stuart absolutist attempt, supplicant to the despised Louis. In the 1670s New Hampshire was made a royal colony. In 1681 New York, a proprietary colony of James Duke of York, was denied permission to summon an assembly. The Special Court of Assize petitioned him against arbitrary tax burdens as 'contrary to the laws, rights, liberties and privileges of the subject', unlike flourishing neighbour colonies. He backed down.[15] But Livery Companies lost their charters. The City lost its charter in 1683 and was governed by royal officials. Parliament met only five times between 1679 and 1688; just 171 days. American colonies were governed on the Spanish viceregal model. In 1685 the Dominion of New England was established, uniting separate colonies under a Governor General, without legislative assembly. The Carolinas were assigned to eight English nobles. Bermuda's private charter was recalled. The struggle for English liberty and religion, intimate with merchant freedom, was trans-Atlantic. Traders became increasingly vocal against their 'slavery'; meaning arbitrary behaviour of Crown appointees. Antagonising England's merchants, especially London's, had never worked. Most felt increasingly threatened by undermining City independence, Parliament and colonial governments.

Catholic James became king in 1685. Holland's William and his Stuart wife Mary were expected to inherit England's throne on James' death, the reluctant assumption that a Catholic interval was a necessary evil, but that all would normalise thereafter. James II, lacking tact, moderation or common sense, alienated the country by attempting to repeal the Test Act, introduce pro-French Catholics, Irish and Scots into the army, universities, courts and government, seen as the prelude to the imposition of popery, 'the handmaiden of arbitrary government.'[16] In much changed times this was even more provocative than his father. The trigger for a challenge was his wife's delivery of a healthy baby boy. The prospect of perpetual Catholic monarchs, despotism, threatened England's constitution and liberty.

Louis reintroduced discriminatory tariffs on Dutch goods in 1687 and talked of a Rhineland invasion, seemingly the prelude to Anglo-French Catholic alliance in Europe, Asia and the Caribbean. Dutch ships in French ports were arrested. If Antwerp fell, he would force the Scheldt and Antwerp open, spelling potential Dutch ruin. Amsterdam's instinctively anti-Orangist republican merchants rallied behind William who was forced into a dangerous invasion of England to expel James. Jonathan Israel thinks it 'reasonably certain' that had Louis not resumed his *guerre du commerce* against the Dutch, William would not have been forced into this gamble.[17] For William, waiting on events was not a viable option. If invasion failed, it would cause what it tried to prevent, an alliance of the two largest European navies and largest army against them; Dutch national destruction. English contacts encouraged officers, troops and public opinion for support. Dutch trade, shipping and fisheries had already been badly damaged. Brandenburg was asked to defend the Rhine and Dutch borders, while William gathered a huge armada. It is extraordinary testament to James' stupidity that William, the ruler of a bitter trade rival, even if a 'frenemy', fighting England for 38 years in three wars, intervened as a liberator. His *Declaration* described a three-year Catholic revolution in the English socio-political order, which William came to restore with a 'free and lawful Parliament assembled as soon as possible.' It was well-received, including by England's most talented soldier, John Churchill, his brigade and James' other daughter, Anne.

James' ineptitude was aided by Louis' 'blundering arrogance', contemptuous of Dutch 'cheesemonger' merchants.[18] James fled to Versailles. Its Court's verdict was, 'when you listen to him, you realise why he is here.'[19] This 'Glorious Revolution', called by contemporaries the Happy Revolution,[20] ensured English monarchs governed only with Parliamentary approval; a consensual power-base. The state was more important than monarchs, who symbolically transformed Charles' Greenwich Palace into a hospital for seafarers, emphasising England's new direction. American colonies ousted their viceroys and reinstated representative governments. Their interests were aligned with City, Parliament, merchants and Crown. Charles I's American ambition, 'one uniform course of government' failed. As 1688 reaffirmed representation on both sides of the Atlantic, businesses confidently invested in trans-Atlantic trade. America's population doubled every 20 years after the 1680s, expanding into the interior, attracting new migrants, creating a huge market. Politics became more participatory, the economy more diversified. 'None of these creative developments could have happened had James and his heirs remained in control.'[21] Only after 1688 did English governments assume without question that 'trade must be the principal interest of England,' as Slingsby Bethel had vainly tried to convince Charles in 1680.[22] The RAC lost its monopoly in 1689. In 1698 African trade was opened on payment of 10% duty on exports, and fully opened in 1712.[23]

In Spanish America, unlike Spain, by mid-century merchants married landowners, but the aim was always conquest and control. In English America, independent governments in diverse environments fostered trade, stability, tolerance and prosperity. Spanish America was shaped by Spanish attitudes and assumptions, sceptical of innovation, authoritarian, ordered, a culture of obligation and hierarchy. English America was, with some caveats, innovative, libertarian, sensitive to individual conscience, liberty and rights. Slingsby Bethel thought Spanish decline was due to failure to grasp the relationship between people, prosperity and liberty, emphasising Dutch and English 'industry and ingenuity...justice, good laws and liberty.'[24] Encouraging commerce was central to England's national interest especially with its American colonies. As Josiah Child said, far from depopulating the country, plantations augmented its strength.[25] Spain, inadequately provisioning its colonies, banning American west coast trade encouraged illegal coastal and trans-Pacific trade and discouraged local enterprise. In 1683–84 Pepys went to Spain and puzzled, 'men of the sword are put into most employments at sea without knowing anything of their business...never were a people so overrun with fools.'[26]

Despite neutering the French threat, Dutch economic growth slowed. Booming sugar refining in 1650 slowed because of English Navigation Acts, Dutch lack of large sugar islands and increasing English refining. A third of Dutch refineries closed. Sugar imports from Asia and Surinam grew, partly compensating, but England's sugar imports, 80,000 tons in 1658, grew to 188,000 in 1683, to 240,000 in the 1690s.[27] After 1688 the VOC consistently lost money in Asian trade. Despite rising volumes, running costs of distant territories rose three-times quicker than revenues.[28] The Heren XVII, originally aggressive merchants, gentrified. Merchants, excluded from the Amsterdam Chamber after 1690, became a hereditary elite, investing in bonds, not maritime trade,[29] similar to events preceding Venice's decline. England became the dominant naval power, undercut Dutch insurance rates and blocked Baltic naval supplies to France via Dutch merchants. To protect manufacturers, France banned painted, dyed or stained calico imports, as did England after 1700, which should have given the VOC advantages, but centralised and gentrified, they missed the opportunity. The EIC marketed other cloth qualities.[30]

Between 1660 and 1688 only six Parliaments met for 22 sessions averaging under ten weeks each, producing 564 statutes. After 1688 annual sessions averaged 20 weeks and between 1689 and 1727, 2,510 Acts were passed, the average annual number increasing from 19 to 66.[31] Parliament was permanent, regular and vital. William could not, and did not, try to act without it, immediately securing a City loan to fight France, whose privateers attacked returning Mediterranean and Caribbean convoys, which according to a Lancaster merchant in 1689 'quite put a stop to the commerce by sea betwixt London and this county.'[32]

Post-Colbert policy was to attack English trade-generated wealth, but Colbert emphasised its creation and preservation, even if by flawed methods, but after his death the Court was indifferent to trade and industry and hostile to the navy. England won set-piece battles, but St Malo's, Ostend's, and Dunkirk's privateers took, it was claimed, 1,500 ships worth £3 million between 1688 and 1699. In 1693, the English 400-ship Smyrna convoy was attacked and 92 captured or destroyed, although in 1695 the Levant Company said no further losses were suffered due to convoy excellence.[33] St Malo's ships took over 1,200 prizes and ransoms out of a Nine Years War (1688–97) total of 4,000 according to Admiralty estimates, although some were repeatedly taken and ransomed. Merchants themselves claimed the figure, part of arguments for improved protection, too high,[34] probably nearer 3,500,[35] still ruinous losses, and not only around Europe. In 1694 France captured 30 Leeward Island-bound ships, destroyed over 50 Jamaican sugar works and took 2,000 slaves, whilst Nova Scotia was overrun and Newfoundland settlements ravaged.

* * *

Were Navigation Acts, as most thought, or increasing English competitiveness responsible for English trade take-off? Nuala Zahedieh persuasively argues that England lacked means to enforce the Acts and credit for surging trade should instead go to efficiencies in finance, manufacturing, shipping and distribution, especially in London. Its customs service was diligent, but if merchants had not been efficient, regulations could have been circumvented. Despite low risk of evasion and weak enforcement, there was widespread compliance. If English prices had been higher, the legislation would have been ignored.[36] For 500 years English merchants had shown ingenuity and courage, but the 1382 Navigation Act was ineffective because England lacked ships. The Republic's and Cromwell's support unleashed commercial energy and inventiveness. The Act must however, have had some affect. In 1660, the Dutch besieged Charles with offers of friendship and hope of repeal, giving him superb Italian and Dutch paintings, Roman antiquities and a yacht. It is perfectly possible, indeed probable, that the Act, the Republic's navy, and increasing efficiency accounted for 1660s–1690 trade acceleration, continually reinforced by further Navigation Act strengthening.

Ralph Davis' meticulous research on four 17th and early-18th-century ships' not especially efficient trading history may not be representative, but show the importance of market knowledge. Their owners and masters changed loadports after each voyage, rather than repeating it, thus they could not build local relations to ensure well-paying cargoes and quick turnround times to catch the right seasonal wind.[37] Trans-Atlantic trade growth and predictability must have increased efficiency. Then as now, shipping investors expected gain, but returns fluctuated depending on delays, freight market conditions, weather, accidents and repair costs. They tolerated low returns for occasional exceptional gains.

London's population rose from about 400,000 in 1650 to 575,000 in 1700. Amsterdam had 150,000. London's share of England's population increased from 7% to 11%, and 70% of England's urban population.[38] In an aspirational city of opportunity, a commercial, legal, financial and industrial hub, trans-Atlantic trades made the major contribution. From 1660 to 1700, London's imports increased 25%, exports about 33%, but Atlantic tonnage from 1660 to 1680 doubled. By 1700 trans-Atlantic trade and shipping accounted for nearly 20% of London's imports and 15% of exports, most growth before 1689.[39] Navigation Acts provided the framework but if merchants and shipowners had not responded, it would have remained wishful thinking.[40] They did so in a rapidly expanding market. New England's, Chesapeake's and Caribbean's 140,000 people in 1660, increased with the Carolinas and Pennsylvania, to around 400,000 in 1700.

Zahedieh focuses on the 159 largest merchants, out of about 1,500, whose Atlantic activities were recorded in the City's 1686 Port Book. Apart from the RAC and Hudson Bay Company, all trans-Atlantic trade was competitive. In the 1680s, private slave trading was at least 50% of the RAC's, because despite supposed monopoly, it could not meet demand, nor enforce monopoly.[41] Interlopers operated with lower costs without the expense of starting and protecting trade posts. Low

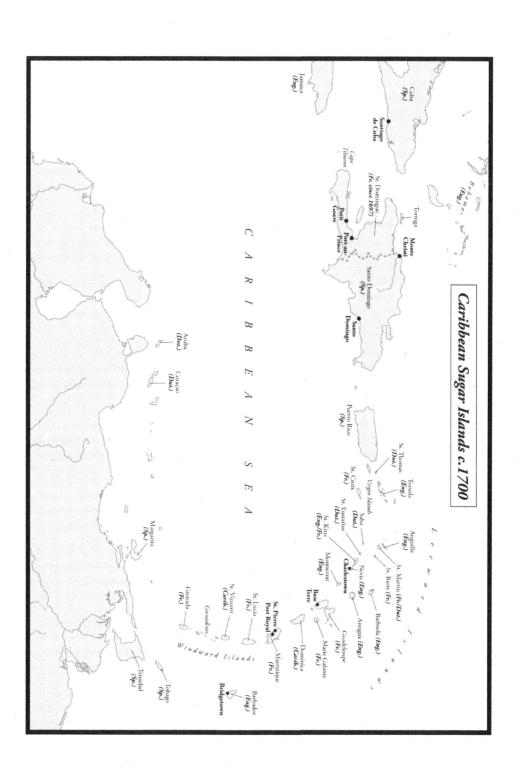

Caribbean Sugar Islands c.1700

Jamaica
(Eng.)

Cuba
(Sp.)

Bahamas
(Eng.)

Santiago
de Cuba

Cape
Tiburon

St. Domingue
(Fr. since 1697)

Tortuga

Monte
Christi

Petit
Goave

Port-au-
Prince

Santo Domingo
(Sp.)

Santo
Domingo

Puerto Rico
(Sp.)

St. Thomas
(Dut.)

St. Croix
(Fr.)

Virgin Islands

Tortola
(Eng.)

Saba
(Dut.)

St. Eustatius
(Dut.)

St. Kitts
(Eng./Fr.)

Nevis (Eng.)

Charlestown

Montserrat
(Eng.)

Anguilla
(Eng.)

St. Martin (Fr./Dut.)

St. Barts (Fr.)

Barbuda (Eng.)

Antigua (Eng.)

Basse
Terre

Guadeloupe
(Fr.)

Marie Galante
(Fr.)

Dominica
(Carib.)

St. Pierre
Port Royal

Martinique
(Fr.)

St. Lucia
(Fr.)

St. Vincent
(Carib.)

Grenadines

Grenada
(Fr.)

Tobago
(Sp.)

Barbados
(Eng.)

Bridgetown

Trinidad
(Sp.)

Margarita
(Sp.)

Curaçao
(Dut.)

Aruba
(Dut.)

Windward Islands

Leeward Islands

C A R I B B E A N   S E A

slave prices encouraged more cultivation. Most large trans-Atlantic traders had been apprenticed to merchants, learning about charter parties, bills of lading, invoices, contracts, bills of exchange, insurance policies, weights and measures and other business details.[42] This private trade dynamic, in which English merchants challenged monopolies even before Civil War, contrasts with Seville's monopoly, dependent on complex, mutually reinforcing state interests governing shipments to and from its colonies, impervious to reform,[43] and French failed monopolies.

As the Geniza letters demonstrated, private merchants cherished their reputation for business integrity. A 1687 arbitration showed it working in practice. Bought in advance, a muscovado sugar cargo's quality on arrival was so low that the buyer refused delivery. In the interests of preserving a long-term relationship and his own reputation for 'square dealing' the buyer made a 'fair proposal' to pay a shilling over the best price offered in the market. In other words, buyer and seller took losses to preserve reputation and continue business,[44] an example of compromise and tolerance. In long-haul trade, risk increased. Because of it, agents were not given rigid instructions, but told to 'carefully, diligently and faithfully employ [themselves] according to the best and utmost of [their] power, knowledge and experience.' One wrote to a Caribbean agent, 'You know at this distance I cannot well judge of things';[45] more Geniza echoes! Groups of merchants in similar trades met at specific taverns and coffee shops to exchange information. Many networks were reinforced by family or shared religious beliefs. Jews, Quakers, Baptists, Huguenots and others in London and the colonies enabled commercial trust over long distances and time lags, gaining competitive edge. Quakers kept their word as a point of the honour of God's truth. Persecution from 1660 to 1668 encouraged tight-knit, disciplined groups with regular meetings in counties, colonies and an AGM in London, sending directives against business imprudence and the importance of trust.

English Sephardic networks became increasingly important in the 1680s. One of Zahedieh's London merchants, Anthony Gomezsera, arrived in 1665 from Bayonne. His business partners were from Amsterdam, Bordeaux and Portugal. His Jamaican correspondent Abraham Perera lived there since 1669, before that, Barbados and England, and before that France, Flanders and Amsterdam. Willingness to move as economic opportunities presented themselves defines merchant values. In 1687 the EIC took over shipping Mediterranean coral to India with Sephardic intermediaries including one of the ubiquitous da Costas, financed by Brazilian gold to Portugal, arranged in London and Amsterdam by a group of merchants also involving a Da Costa.[46] George Ravenscroft, son of an English shipowner trading Venetian glassware, was engaged by the Glass Sellers Company to research English glassmaking and hired Jewish glassmakers from the Universita d'Altaire, the Altarese glassmakers. Consequently, it seems Giacomo da Costa brought the use of lead oxide for crystal glass production to England, which Ravenscroft patented.[47] By the 1680s many Jewish traders in London, Barbados, Jamaica, Surinam and New York were involved in glassmaking. Expelled from Brazil, Benjamin da Costa established Martinique's sugar industry in 1655 but was expelled in 1685. Some tried in Louisiana and St. Eustatius, a tiny Dutch Caribbean Island.[48]

Venice's decline accelerated, but in 1685–86 it became more aggressive towards Ottomans, capturing Nafplion and Herceg Novi in 1687. Venice's main issue was no longer protection of Levant trade, already lost to English, Dutch and French, but protection of Dalmatia. However, Venice's maritime trade had become a sideshow.

Jewish and dissenter merchants operated in similar ways to Indian Ocean religious, family and ethnic groups. Thirty-two of Zahedieh's merchants had family or co-religionist links in the colonies and two-thirds spent time there. By 1686, trans-Atlantic trade consumed over half London's shipping capacity, but only 16% by value; mainly a function of distance.[49] Zahedieh thinks English ships were used, not because of Navigation Acts, but because they suited Atlantic conditions and were built in England competitively.[50] Trans-Atlantic shipping demand created a 'nursery of seamen' for war, an estimated 6,300 sailors in the Atlantic merchant fleet, more on the docks, as traders competed to achieve efficiency. England's 1615 Virginian-Maryland tobacco imports, 50,000 lbs., rose to 15 million in the late 1660s, 28 million in the mid-1680s and 38 million by 1700, about a third re-exported.[51] The government taxed it heavily as prices halved from the 1640s to 1680s. From the EIC and Levant Company came spices, silks and fine fabrics, two-thirds by value of colonial imports. Asian trade employed only 5% of tonnage; 60% was employed in Europe, 35% in the Atlantic. London's plantation imports doubled between 1660 and 1700, accounting for 20% of London's inward trade and 33% of its re-exports to Europe.[52] 'Sack trade' volumes increased. Improving agriculture allowed English grain export. Newcastle coal exports grew as new industries moved away from charcoal.

English shipbuilders built cheaply operated ships, fluyt replacements, especially in Sunderland, Newcastle, South Shields, Stockton and Whitby, with Norwegian and Baltic timber.[53] Ambrose Crowley's London ironworks, mainly making ships' fittings, moved to Sunderland in 1682 with many craftsmen, although the EIC still depended on Thames-built ships. Swedish iron bar was increasingly demanded. From 1620's exports of 6,500 tons, 17,000 in 1650, it reached 30,000 tons in 1700. England was dependent, unable to expand its iron output beyond about 10,000 tons until the 18th-century's second quarter. New England's shipbuilding increased. Timber, tar and pitch was available and iron started to be worked, supplying its coastal, Caribbean and fishery needs, some English advocating it. By 1686 half the ships trading between England and New England were American-owned and probably American-built.[54] Sir Henry Johnson, Blackwall's shipyard owner and largest ship investor, owned parts of 38 ships, mainly East Indiamen, only one over 1/8th.[55] As always, ship-ownership division raised capital more easily, limited risk, enabled family, business partners, potential ships' stores suppliers and former masters to become part owners. It was safer than land-based partnerships, regulated by maritime law, administered by the Admiralty High Court, ship-shares easily transferable by bills of sale without reference to other part owners.[56]

In 1686 traded sugar value exceeded tobacco four-fold. Slave demand therefore accelerated. Bristol sugar merchant John Carey thought African trade, 'the best traffick the kingdom hath' giving 'so vast an employment to our people both by sea and land' and by their labour 'tobacco, cotton, ginger and indigo are raised, which being bulky commodities employ greater numbers of our ships.'[57] Sugar stimulated England's economy as sugar refining required substantial capital. Dyes like indigo and logwood, cotton, cocoa, ginger, lime juice, drugs, gums, hardwoods for furniture, all entered London from the Americas,[58] gold and silver bullion through plunder, smuggling or trade. Irish barrelled, salted food, wine, spirits, indentured servants and manufactured goods including cloth were shipped back. Colonies as markets for English cloth, an original aim, became reality as exports grew faster than tobacco and sugar imports, generating significant customs revenue. It would have been impossible to displace Dutch traders, if not for London merchants' efficiencies. Trans-Atlantic trade was thus vital in encouraging skills, information and capital, reflected in falling interest rates, which by 1700 allowed London to rival and soon overtake Amsterdam.[59] In 1700, the Dutch still led in tonnage employed in inter-European trade, but England led in trans-Atlantic trade, hugely stimulating shipbuilding, a dramatic turnaround since 1650.

Navigation Act enforcement rested largely on the customs service and excise officers at home, the army and navy abroad. There were seemingly few infringements in England but American colonies were serial smugglers with French and Dutch Caribbean islands, because it carried minimal risk. Ireland's governors also disregarded it if reward outweighed risk. When an English naval force arrived in Barbados in 1656, they found the harbour full of Dutch ships. Many subsequent governors attempted to enforce them, often to the detriment of their popularity. Codrington, England's Barbados representative, persuaded planters that money raised would be spent improving schools, hospitals, fortifications and wharfs, but later built a warehouse and wharf to land non-RAC slaves.[60] On arrival as Lieutenant Governor of the Leewards in 1700, everyone traded illegally, officials supplementing their income by 'winking' at it.[61] Others complied, believing it damaged the Dutch. By 1690, 20% of Barbados's exports went to New England, whose merchants however, profited more by trade with French islands, whose molasses was cheaper, as they were banned from making rum, to protect France's brandy industry and Caribbean salt was exchanged for salted-cod; slave food.

* * *

Apart from sugar and tobacco, England also imported coffee, tea and chocolate. Coffee, originally cultivated in Ethiopia in the early-1st millennium, introduced to Yemen, was shipped from Mocha. Mid-16th century Levantine traders introduced it to Istanbul and Cairo, where there were many coffee shops. It arrived in Amsterdam in 1610, England in 1645, and became fashionable. Amsterdam's coffee shops influenced London's, the first opening in 1652. Catherine of Braganza drank tea in Lisbon, known there for a century and popularised it with the wealthy. Amsterdam dominated cacao trading but not tea and coffee.

Edward Lloyd's coffee shop, first mentioned in 1688, hosted marine insurers, shipowners and insurance brokers. In the 1660s–70s Amsterdam insured most ships but London steadily increased. Fire insurance dates from after the Great Fire. Statistical mathematics developed by Graunt, Petty and the Royal Society made life insurance possible, enabling provision for dependents after death without buying land.[62] John's Coffee House was the main meeting place for merchants, shipowners and captains. At the Jerusalem and Jamaica taverns, Levant and Caribbean traders gathered. Admiralty ship auctions moved from Broad Street's Castle Tavern after the Great Fire to Cornhill's 'Ship and Castle' until 1688. Hains changed its name to the Marine Coffee House in 1676. Coffee, tea and chocolate were served at Garraway's, the Virginia Wine House, Antwerp Tavern and Sun Tavern. After leaving the Royal Exchange, merchants and brokers went to each one looking for buyers, sellers, ships, space in ships, or in Jonathan's, share prices. Newspapers, periodicals, customs entry forms, auction notices, flysheets with price lists, exchange rates, interest rates, stock prices, announcements, information on charters, ship availability and cargo sales were available, aiding information flow. Coffee invigorated congregating merchants, financiers, stockbrokers and shipbrokers, a short walk from London's 21 Legal Quays between London Bridge and the Tower of London where cargoes were discharged, with the latest news from foreign markets.[63]

The number of London quays and wharfs increased 30% in the 1670s–1680s, similarly in Bristol. Increasing warehousing and ships contributed to London's growth. In 1686 the over 300 ships clearing London for America needed provisions for over 9,000 men for two or three months, larger than the population of all but six or seven English towns. Demands made on fishmongers, brewers, butchers and bakers stimulated food production and commercialisation. Those ships carried nearly 600 commodities needed for life and work; glass, furniture, furnishings, alcohol, tombstones, etc., stimulating the economy.[64]

From 1692, Lloyd provided lists of ship arrivals and departures, marine casualties, and other information in *Lloyds News*. By 1716 there were seven weekly or twice-weekly business newspapers providing information about prices, ships, cargoes and exchange rates. The Stock Exchange was incorporated after 1688. London was catching Amsterdam as premier financial, insurance and shipping centre. By the time *Lloyds News* was renamed *Lloyds List* in 1734, it had overtaken it.

The 1697 Treaty of Ryswick ending the Nine Years War made France restore all invaded territory, renounce Spanish Netherlands' claims, recognise William's heirs as England's kings, allowed Dutch forces in frontier forts and cancelled its import duties. St. Domingue was ceded to France, although it produced little sugar. Louis viewed Ryswick and previous treaties as temporary. In 1700 troops re-entered the Spanish Netherlands, expelling Dutch from frontier forts. Taxation to which the clergy and nobility were exempt, continued to punish merchants, industry and peasants. In Spain, Catalan and peasant revolts dominated the 1680s–1690s.

Encouraged by monopoly-disapproving Whigs, English interlopers violated EIC monopoly. In 1693 it offered £700,000 to Parliament to continue exclusivity. Rival merchants bid two million and a new company was formed. But it lacked forts, factories, networks of suppliers, agents and financiers. The EIC invested in the new company, becoming its largest shareholder. About 1700 a merger was mooted. They complimented each other, uniting in 1702, the mechanisms finally agreed in 1708. In 1700 it accounted for 10% of Britain's public revenue, shipping 1.5 million cloth bolts annually, 83% of the value of its imports. Spices were yesterday's profitable cargo. Cotton cloth was king, 90% from India, mainly shipped from Surat, Bombay and Madras, prompting English spinners and weavers to petition Parliament for relief, but Josiah Child in the House of Lords, killed off bills to ban its import. In 1701 a Chief Justice thought royal grants and charters restraining trade were 'contrary to the liberty of the subject,' thus void. In 1702 Parliament declared 'trade ought to be free and not restrained.'[65]

In 1694 Whigs and influential trans-Atlantic merchants persuaded Parliament to create the Bank of England, modelled on the Bank of Amsterdam. Loans were guaranteed by Parliament. Those with capital quickly appreciated the difference between a king's word and national debt as investment security,[66] described by contemporaries as 'Dutch finance', lent at 8%. Dutch investors piled in to high, safe returns. Surplus Dutch capital boosted English credit. England was the world's only monarchy with a legislatively governed national bank. Its society intertwined noble, maritime, merchant, manufacturing and financial wealth. Parliamentary monarchy encouraged and protected maritime trade. After 1695, the Stationers Company's monopoly on printing ended. When the Board of Trade was recreated in 1695 it contained the EIC's Josiah Child, banker Gilbert Heathcote, economist Davenant, but also Wren, Newton and Locke, not merchant puppets but intelligent, independent-minded men.[67] By 1700 London was the fulcrum of an Atlantic economy and accelerating global trade, which Davenant and King thought the fastest expanding wealth source. Even in France, protests against monopoly suggest trade's increased value. A 1701 Nantes' trade deputy was not alone suggesting monopolies were 'prejudicial to trade'.[68]

Chapter 36

Second-half 17th Century European Maritime Trade, Culture, Philosophy and Science

Three Anglo-Dutch Wars from England's need to challenge Dutch maritime supremacy occurred in a continuing atmosphere of cooperation in arts and scientific enquiry. The volume, variety and balance of scientific advances shifted more to England after the 1650s, just as its trade reinvigorated. Between 1649 and 1658 in Wadham College Oxford, Christopher Wren, Robert Boyle and other maths and science enthusiasts performed 'inquisitive experiments.' Formal meetings developed into the Royal Society in 1660. Five years later it began publishing 'philosophical transactions,' its motto *Nullius in verba*, 'take no ones' word for it.' Wren studied astronomy, cosmology, physics, optics, muscles, agriculture, ballistics, refraction, magnetism, mechanics and architecture. His wide expertise helped exchanges of ideas between other scientists. He observed, measured, dissected, built models, invented and improved instruments, including microscopes and telescopes and designed a 'weather clock' recording temperature, humidity, rainfall and barometric pressure.

The Royal Society's first official biographer Thomas Sprat, praised Dutch scientific ingenuity and inventiveness, which he thought was due to toleration. In this developing intellectual climate, John Milton's (1608–1674) *Areopagitica*, defending free-speech and freedom of the press, called for 'the liberty to know, to utter and to argue freely according to conscience, above all liberties.' His *Eikonoklastes* (1649) defended republican principles, responding to Charles' self-serving *Eikon Basilike*. In 1659 *A Treatise on Civil Power* attacked the idea of a state-dominated Church and in 1672, *Of True Religion* argued for toleration, due to the importance of conscience. The Levellers went further and thought all men should vote as they were by nature, free and equal under God; a momentous transition, even if not widely shared.

A 1659 House of Commons petition and debate on 73 political prisoners 'sold into slavery in Barbados' in 1654 give insights into views on embryonic 'human rights'. Petitioners asked 'by what authority…[against] the free people of England' gave 'merchants [the right to] deal in slaves and the souls of men?'[1] The Carolinas granted to eight courtiers, thought in 1669 that native Americans' 'idolatry, ignorance, or mistake gives no right to expel or use them ill.' Settlers however, subverted their good intentions.[2]

Thomas Hobbes' (1588–1679) *Leviathan* made him the father of modern political philosophy. He addressed the problem of social and political order, how people can live in peace and avoid civil conflict, much influenced by the practical problem of 1650s-England, the only viable solution under Lord Protector Cromwell. He concluded, in order to avoid chaos, 'the life of man, solitary, poor, nasty, brutish and short,' people must agree a 'social contract' under a sovereign authority. Abuses of power were the price of peace. Questions posed opened up debate. Who determines what individual rights are? Who enforces them and who exercises political powers? Machiavelli had secularised questions of political power, emphasising its harsh realities. Hobbes stressed individual right, natural equality of all men, that all legitimate political power must be representative and consensual. People must be free to do what the law does not specifically forbid. His arguments with clerics, mathematicians, scientists and philosophers opened new ways of thinking about what bound society together and where sovereign power lay, hitherto accepted unthinkingly through scripture and tradition. This intellectual revolution accompanied the political revolution, removing a king acting against national interest in an age of vigorous maritime trade, frustrating English merchants unable to fully participate due to royal ineptitude. Hobbes insisted that theological disputes should be separate from politics, that human judgement was unreliable, needing guidance from developing science, 'the knowledge of consequences.' Hobbes set the terms of politico-theological debate enfolding in maritime Europe. John Locke accepted them, but came to a different conclusion.

John Bunyan's (1628–88) *Pilgrims Progress,* for years the most popular book in English, was the precursor of the novel by Daniel Defoe. William Harvey's rediscovery of blood circulation pumped by the heart, published in 1628 only became prominent after 1640. Christopher Hill notes that before 1640, Bacon was a 'voice crying in the wilderness [but] by 1660 his was the dominant intellectual influence.'[3] The first organised movement for national education took place, many schools were established and English prose improved.[4] Mathematics was fashionable. Cromwell's brother-in-law, John Wilkins of Wadham College Oxford wrote *Mathematical Magic* (1648), 'profitable knowledge of those chargeable adventures of draining mines, coalpits etc.'[5] Most new crops that became important were started experimentally in the Interregnum. After 1662 the Royal Society suggested improvements. At its behest, the Treasury appointed the first Inspector General of Exports and Imports in 1696 to collect trade statistics.[6] There was a related growing preoccupation with the poor, which Gregory King thought over 1.3 million out of England's 5.5 million population, a waste of human energy. These ideas were brewing before the Interregnum, as in the 1649 proposals for social order and economic reform to stimulate employment for national welfare.[7] Josiah Child's 1665 *Brief Observations* expressed his concern to better employ them for the national and their good, noting 'wherever wages are high…it is an infallible evidence of the riches of the country and when low, its poverty.' Charles Davenant wrote similarly in 1698. Carey, sugar and madeira merchant, and Firmin, linen manufacturer, founded educational institutions for the poor.[8]

Descartes lived and published in the United Provinces. Thomas Hobbes had his books published there until his return to England. John Locke, also forced to take refuge there in 1683, returned to England in 1688. Leibniz in Hanover had to exercise self-censorship but Locke had no such problems in post-1688 England. His *Two Treatise of Government* (1689) emphasised reason, not historical precedence and demolished Divine Right. Basing his thoughts on Hobbes's 'social contract', Locke's political writing, dating from his enforced United Provinces' sojourn advocated government for and by consent of men of property, its governing body's purpose to protect individual rights, especially property and protection from foreign enemies. It became the intellectual cornerstone of subsequent political thought. Voltaire thought, 'Never, perhaps has a wiser, more methodical mind, a more precise logician existed than Mr. Locke.' Divine Right monarchs seized property, levied arbitrary taxes and imprisoned those who disagreed with them. Locke stood for government ensuring individual rights, meaning separate legislative, executive and judiciary, similar to consensual merchant-dominated government of maritime oligarchies; Venice, Bruges, Antwerp, Amsterdam, post-1688 England and antiquity's 'merchant houses' in Tyre, Sidon, Carthage, Miletus and Athens, as William Temple pointed out in 1673.[9] Locke's 1690 *Essay Concerning Human Understanding* argued for freedom of thought and religious belief two years after the Revocation of the Edict of Nantes. In *Letters on Toleration* (1689–92) he wrote, 'the business of laws is not to provide for the truth of opinions but for safety and security of the commonwealth and…man's goods and services'; trading communities' principles and practice, unlike continental Europe's, Ming and Mughal oppression.

Amsterdam tolerated Jews and dissenting Protestant sects, exposing its people to various liberal theologies. Franciscus van den Enden for example, from the 1650s to 1671, argued for a radical, democratic state where religious leaders played no role, citizens having civil, political and legal equality, freedom of speech, religion and opinion, its leaders elected for limited terms by well-educated men and women.[10] Baruch Spinoza (1632–1677) was grandnephew of Abraham de Spinoza, a hide and cloth merchant who fled Portugal to Nantes in the 1590s, then in 1616 Amsterdam, importing Portuguese fruits and nuts. Freethinking Baruch did not believe in the soul's immortality and that there is no reward or punishment after death, ideas, he thought, used by religious leaders to exert control. He believed that Jews were not God's chosen people, but God 'is equally well disposed to all', that the *Torah* was not written by Moses, not divinely-inspired and that God is identical with Nature.[11]

Christian Huygens (1629–1659) argued that light consisted of waves and began grinding lenses in 1655. He helped develop calculus and invented pendulum clocks in 1657, improved upon during the next decade by Thomas Tompion in London and developed balance spring watches. Understanding focal length and spheres, he produced more effective telescopes, explained Saturn's rings and greater understanding of the solar system. Baruch Spinoza, also a lens grinder, complimented by many scientists for his telescopes and microscopes,[12] agreed with Hobbes about living under a sovereign power ruling in the subjects' interests, guided by reason with the peoples' will, the outcome of a stable, prosperous state whose citizens had a sense of civic virtue.[13] Free of thought-crushing Church power, maritime-influenced people continued to experiment. Dissection, aided by instrument makers in Leiden and London, became a growing skill. Delft's Antonie van Leeuwenhoek (1623–1723) improved microscopes, first described single-cell organisms, muscle fibres, bacteria, sperm and blood flow in capillaries; the father of microbiology.

An English visitor to Amsterdam thought it 'superior in riches' to Venice. It controlled Baltic grain, was strong in fishing, had market gardens, dairy herds, selective breeding and canal distribution. Its people were well-fed while famines still affected peasants in continental Europe. In 1669 public street lighting was introduced. With better lifestyles, wages and literacy levels they led in intellectual enquiry, sciences and every significant technology, often working with English scientists and technologists. Temple admired the liberty 'the Dutch value so much,' especially 'of talking openly whatever they thought upon, the public affairs, both of their own state and their neighbours.' Catholics, Jews and many dissenting sects practiced their faiths openly. The Earl of Shaftesbury recommended England follow suit to attract skilled workers.[14] Many continental observers however, viewed it as a 'seedbed of theological, intellectual and social promiscuity,' a threat to absolutist authority, especially as Holland was a centre for printing and publishing; books, newssheets and pamphlets in many languages, to spread through Europe.[15] Unknown in continental Europe, women had numerous rights; inheritance, bequeathing and signing commercial contracts. Some became designers, painters, engravers, writers and actresses, the first appearing on stage in 1655. Respectable women walked out unaccompanied, engaging in discussions, held hands with men, exchanged kisses on meeting and parting, but not sexual freedom in anti-hierarchical Calvinist society.

Appointed the King's Surveyor of Works (1669) to rebuild London after the Great Fire, Christopher Wren was responsible for 51 churches. Nicholas Hawksmoor, employed by him in 1679, worked with him from 1684 to 1700 on many projects. The apogee of Wren's reputation was St. Paul's design and rebuilding. He also worked on Greenwich's Royal Naval College and Royal Observatory, Trinity College Cambridge library, Chelsea Hospital, Whitehall, Kensington Palace, Hampton Court, Temple Bar, St. James' Piccadilly, St. Mary le Bow, St. Brides Fleet Street and many more. The Monument, built by Royal Surveyor Wren and City Surveyor, Robert Hooke, a monument to the Great Fire was also for scientific experiments, the central shaft used for pendulum, gravity, barometric pressure experiments and as a telescope. Hawksmoor worked with Sir John Vanbrugh on Blenheim Palace, solely on various Oxford and Cambridge colleges and London churches. Grinling Gibbons (1648–1721), born and educated in Rotterdam of English parents, his father a merchant, became the finest wood carver. Known from 1680 as the 'King's

Carver', he specialised in decorative garlands for mirrors, furniture, church and palace walls, and worked on some Wren building interiors; Windsor Castle, St. Paul's, St. James' Piccadilly and other London churches. The best Dutch artists moved to England in the 1672 disaster year, as the market in maritime art moved to where maritime trade was gaining most momentum.

It was widely recognised that maritime trade and knowledge advancement went hand-in-hand. England's destiny, wrote Thomas Sprat in 1667, was not only to be 'mistress of the Ocean, but the most proper seat for the advancement of knowledge,' because London commanded 'a large intercourse with all the earth.'[16] Isaac Newton in the Royal Society from 1679 and Edmund Halley's work on comets revolutionised intellectual history. Newton's *Principia Mathematica* (1687) described physical laws of the universe and the earth, explained by the same principles and laws. It fundamentally changed perceptions to a rational god who created the world based on physical laws. God, like kings, were no longer arbitrary monarchs.[17] The Royal Society concentrated more on profitable and practical inventions, technological prowess a prime objective. Its largest committee was by far the mechanical,[18] their experiments introducing improved clocks and optical instruments. Robert Boyle concentrated on mining and metallurgy, Robert Hooke and William Petty, who had studied in Leiden and other Dutch universities, with shipbuilding, pumps, engines and dyeing cloth. Until 1661, importing cochineal and logwood was banned to promote local woad. This was reversed and Petty, Boyle and Hooke presented papers on textile dyeing, industrial application of science, the culmination of Francis Bacon's pioneering methodology. Boyle advised using seafarers and travellers to collect specimens in new areas. Henry Oldenburg from Bremen became the Royal Society's secretary, liaising with Huygens, Spinoza and other European, mainly Dutch scientists and philosophers, sending them Boyle's essays on gas expansion laws. Thomas Savery in 1698 patented a steam engine, demonstrating it to the Royal Society in 1699.

Barometers were in every laboratory. John Ray catalogued plants, animals and insects in *Historia Generalis Plantarum* between 1686 and 1704, classifying almost 19,000 species of plants, thanking God he was born in the age of 'philosophy, solidly built upon the foundations of experiment.' Microscopes discovered protozoa and bacteria, telescopes the vastness of the cosmos and explorers uninhabited lands, deserts and forests with strange life-forms, no longer explained by the doctrine that life was created by God for man. Colbert's *Académie des Sciences* by contrast was managed by the Crown, dependent on fickle patronage. The Royal Society was driven by enthusiastic, inquisitive individuals. The result was accelerating English patents, 31 in the 1660s, 51 in the 1670s, 53 in the 1680s, 102 in the 1690s.[19]

Much second-half century economic discussion was foreshadowed by Thomas Mun, (1571–1641) an EIC director. His *England's Treasure by Foreign Trade*, written about 1630, only published in 1664, explained that the 'means... to increase our wealth and treasure is by foreign trade...to sell more to strangers yearly than we consume of theirs in value,' in short, a favourable trade balance.

He wrote of England's wool, iron, lead, tin, hides, etc. as its 'natural wealth' and England's overdependence on cloth manufacture and export. Increasing quality of life engendered optimism about increased trade. John Evelyn in 1674 wrote that because of the seas, 'the earth...seems from the very beginning to have been disposed for traffick and commerce.'[20] A 1675 Royal Society paper calculated that it cost the same to carry coal 15 miles overland and 300 on water. Maths, popular among intellectuals and gentry in the 1640s, continued to be seen as key to knowledge advancement and statistics for economic purposes. Petty, who saw enrichment in a bigger population involved in trade, industry and shipping, in 1676 published *Political Arithmetic*, 'the art of reasoning by figures upon things relating to the government,' demonstrating that a 'small country and few people may be equivalent in wealth and strength to a far greater people and territory,' a foretaste of Adam Smith and Douglas North, comparing Holland with France's ten-times higher population, but a ninth of the merchant fleet and a quarter of its foreign trade, double its interest rate and negligible foreign assets. Petty identified wind power and internal waterways as engines of economic growth, religious toleration, an advantage for skilled immigration, clear property rights, efficient legal system and sound banking for economic enterprise.

Improvement, agricultural control, managing nature, improving pasture, animals, vegetables and New World experiments in tobacco and sugar, often ascribed to a Protestant ethic, economically desirable and a moral imperative,[21] is rooted in the maritime imperative; problem-solving. Economic writings on commercial maritime affairs increased as the national interest, export and trade, often previously hidden in dynastic rhetoric, came to the fore. In 1676, Andrew Yarranton wrote *England's Improvements by Land and Sea. To Outdo the Dutch Without Fighting*, advocating flax cultivation, linen manufacture and connecting England's rivers, such as the Severn and the Thames. Gregory King's *Natural and Political Observations* (1696) explored government matters, tax revenues, national income, population etc. by using Petty's quantitative methods with increasingly available data, that a quarter of land was not agriculturally exploited. He estimated per capita revenues of England and France similar but the Netherlands 2.5-times larger, drawing figures from personal observation and tax records.

The hallmark of the continuing upsurge and diversity in scientific and artistic enquiry was the freedom to think and publish. In 1688 Halley produced a map of ocean trade winds, in 1698 sailed on a crown-sponsored voyage to investigate magnetic variations, which produced a map for navigators in 1701. Many had more free time and because of scientific advances, information and opportunity. By 1700 many households had pendulum clocks, unknown 50 years earlier. Libraries were fashionable. People no longer looked to the ancients as the source of scientific, artistic, and intellectual wisdom. John Ray thought, 'the ancients excel the moderns in nothing but acuteness of wit and elegancy of language...as for painting and sculpture and music and architecture some of the moderns I think do equal, if not excel the best of them...but in natural history and experimental philosophy we far transcend them...in astronomy, geography and chronology we excel them much.'[22] History was studied. Clarendon's *History of the Rebellion and Civil Wars in England* written at the turn of the century was followed by John Smith's edition of Bede's *Ecclesiastical History* and Gibson's work on the *Anglo-Saxon Chronicle*. They were self-confident, increasingly aware of the nature of the universe.

Sixteenth and early-17th-century English legislation against witchcraft was gradually ignored. Prosecutions reduced, as more rational explanations for behaviour of poor, ignorant old women were found, the last 'witch' executed in 1685. Charles II used the 'royal touch' on an estimated 90,000 people, a supposed divine cure for scrofula, a type of tuberculosis.[23] William and Mary refused to perform such superstitious rituals. Anne was the last to do so. Jan Hodde in Amsterdam solved the problem of assets and liabilities, the balance sheet of a worldwide business in one currency on a fixed date. Aphra Behn, pioneering English woman author, wrote *Oroonoko, or the Royal Slave* in 1688, a noble negro she met in Surinam. Adapted for the theatre it played throughout the 18th century, the precursor of abolitionist humanitarian thought. Continental Europe however, was dominated by fear, ignorance, superstition, variable harvests, subsistence, epidemics, unaltered husbandry methods, increasingly subject to domineering lords, absolute monarchs, serfdom and crippling tax. The centre of power, money and intellect had swung decisively from the Mediterranean to maritime north Europe and was swinging from Holland to England.

Meanwhile, in the late-1680s, Castile's economy and administration totally collapsed. Only raw wool was exported. Two-thirds of the treasure fleet was controlled by foreigners. Its cultural luminaries were dead; Gracian 1658, Velasquez 1660, Zurbaran 1664 and Murillo, whose paintings of ragged street children questioned its priorities, the last in 1682. Elliot blames the Church which, 'had little to offer a passive population but an unending succession of sedatives in the form of Te Deums, processions, solemn masses and heavy ceremonial...the rights of the Church had denigrated into mere formalism, its dogmas into superstition,' finding hope in 'the peripheral provinces,' where Catalans looked to the Americas as a possible replacement for their lost Mediterranean markets.[24]

Chapter 37

Changing Baltic Trade Patterns

The first half 17th-century Baltic arguably overtook the Mediterranean as Europe's densest shipping market. Politically it was dominated by Sweden, commercially by Dutch interests in Swedish industry, in trade by exports of grain and naval stores. Dutch ships sailed full inbound and outbound, dominating inter-Baltic trade while competitors often sailed inbound in ballast. Sweden naturally tried to reduce Dutch dependency. Its 1645 Navigation Act applied higher tariffs to foreign vessels, so its iron, copper, pitch and tar exports, hitherto carried mainly in Dutch ships were gradually replaced by Swedish, the aim of the 1648 Swedish Tar Company. With her copper and iron ore mines adjacent, exports were routed via Stockholm, controlling 75% of Swedish trade. Like Denmark, she had ambitions beyond the Baltic. The 1649 Swedish Africa Company established a fort in Guinea, but all depended on Dutch capital. Unlike the 1600–1650 period, between 1650 and 1700, the Dutch share of inter-Baltic trade fell. Sweden's, Denmark's and England's rose. The Dutch share of Baltic exports held up well but the most significant development was that naval stores overtook grain. How and why did that happen and with what consequences?

Riga, now Latvia's capital, was Sweden's second port. Its hinterland, Poland, Lithuania and Russia exported grain, leather and timber, generating far more customs revenue than in Russia's only western outlet, Archangel. It imported French and Portuguese salt, textiles, fish and wine. Sweden's economic growth fuelled Russia's desire for a Baltic port. Sweden's German ports gave it harbour-toll revenues on north-south rivers. The Dutch, anxious that if Sweden expanded and took Danzig, it could threaten her trade, needed Sweden, Denmark and Poland to be relatively weak, ironically what the Hansa had wanted. As always, Denmark aimed to maximise Sound dues. The English wanted unimpeded access.

The Baltic's 1633–1649 wheat and rye exports were the largest until the 19th century, causing 1640s shortages of Amsterdam canal barges. But English cultivable areas had been expanded by Dutch drainage engineers. Furthermore, the 1663, 1670 and 1689 Corn Laws encouraged grain production and export. So English grain exports replaced some Baltic exports, previously Poland's economic engine. Consequently, the average annual number of ships passing the Sound declined from 2,038 in the century's first half to 1,634 in the second. Between 1640 and 1690, Dutch ships' share of these declining volumes increased; in rye from 66% to 83%, salt 50% to 80%, cloth 42% to 64%, herring 64% to 82%, Rhenish wine 77% to 95%.[1] However, the fastest growing Baltic and Norwegian trade was shipbuilding's raw materials. Trans-Atlantic bulk trades needed more ships. French and English navies grew fast. Burgeoning demand meant increasing Swedish and Norwegian timber and Swedish tar, hemp and iron bar exports. Ships had miles of hemp line and tons of hemp canvas. Without tar, planks deteriorated faster. These cargoes increasingly came from Swedish Livonian ports. Between 1675 and 1700, Riga's exports were almost double Danzig's,[2] previously the largest Baltic port, whose export share declined from 40% early in the century, to under 20% in 1700.

These trends were not evident mid-century. Thus, Sweden's Charles X invaded Poland in 1655, targeting Danzig, and Denmark attacked Sweden. The Dutch sent the fleet in 1656 and Sweden withdrew. In 1658, Charles claiming the right to keep foreign fleets out of Swedish waters, attacked Copenhagen again. The Dutch again sent a fleet, forcing retreat. In the 1660 treaty, Sweden agreed not to discriminate against foreign ships. It still needed Amsterdam's capital and financial markets, while Dutch traders profited from Swedish iron ore, copper and weapons' industries, importing munitions, founding iron forges, glass manufacturing, financing mines and shipping Baltic grain. England's economic growth meant increasing Swedish iron imports, its merchants at Narva prospering, but the Dutch still dominated.

In 1667 Sweden set high duties on salt and wine imports in foreign ships unless of the cargo's country, similar to England's Navigation Acts. The Bank of Sweden, formed in 1668, indicated commercial health. War again broke out between Sweden and Denmark. Brandenburg joined, claiming much of Swedish Pomerania. The Dutch again forced Swedish retreat in 1679. Thereafter relations and trade improved, as Sweden realised how precarious its hold over its scattered territories really was, especially Pomerania. Only French intervention against Brandenburg in 1676 got its possessions restored. By 1700, Sweden's protectionist policies meant it had almost 750 ships, mostly coastal, out of a Baltic total of about 2,000. Narva's importance increased as hemp and timber exports grew, especially deals and masts, the most valuable timber export, up to 290 a year. From 1690, Armenian merchants switched Persia's silk supply from Archangel to Narva and Reval, benefitting Sweden, emphasising Russia's lack of a Baltic port.[3]

Before 1650 Konigsberg's Lithuanian hinterland gave significant flax and hemp exports, but Riga benefited most from increased demand. Its merchants invested in tanneries, foundries, rope making and shipbuilding. Frederick William of Prussia (r. 1640–1688) learnt from Baltic ports that religious toleration worked, from the large but weak Polish-Lithuanian state, that it needed a large standing army. It produced Prussia's mix of toleration and militarism, ruled by Junkers, agrarian, social conservatives and cultural philistines, whereas Konigsberg's burghers were defenders of the law, restricting central government power.[4]

Czar Peter in 1697 toured Germany, England, Venice, Vienna and especially Holland to learn about modern shipbuilding. He also targeted Azov on the Black Sea in 1695–96, but a Baltic port was prioritised. In 1700, all Sweden's enemies fought her in the Great Northern War; Poland, Russia, then Denmark-Norway and in 1717, Brandenburg and Hanover, coveting Oder estuary ports. The war's cause was mainly the changed Baltic trade patterns, especially Narva's increasing importance, its Russian-origin cargoes and customs duties benefiting Sweden and secondly regional resentment against Swedish power. Poland wanted Sweden's Livonia, north German states control of their tolls, Denmark to regain Schleswig-Holstein and Scania. Poland besieged Riga, Denmark marched into Swedish Schleswig-Holstein and Peter attacked Narva, building the fort at the River Neva's mouth, which became St. Petersburg in 1703, his 'window on the west,' the war far from finished.

Sweden initially did well, repulsing all except Peter, who also attacked Poland and Saxony. He eventually defeated Sweden deep inside Polish territory at Poltava in 1709. Hostilities stopped shipping through the Sound from 1710 to 1722. Sweden refused to concede, even after Russia followed up with a naval victory in 1714, occupied Livonia and raided Sweden. Her small population proved insufficient in prolonged war. In the 1721 Treaty of Nystad, she lost southern Pomerania including Stettin and the Oder to Brandenburg-Prussia, Bremen and Verden to Hanover. She retained Wismar and northern Pomerania. Finland, captured by Russia was returned, but Livonia went to Russia, including Viborg, Novgorod, Reval, Narva and Riga. St. Petersburg rather than Narva was developed. Less exposed, it gave river access, and with planned canals, strong regional transport. So important, it was made Russia's new capital. Peter encouraged foreign artisans and technicians to settle. Russians trained in Holland for shipbuilding, France and Austria for military training. Industrial companies were established. At the 1721 inauguration ceremony Peter was offered the title 'Father of the Fatherland, Emperor of all Russia, Peter the Great.' His chancellor said he 'brought us out of the darkness of ignorance onto the world stage of glory, from non-existence...to existence.'[5] He was Russia's right man at the right time. The 'window on the west' was Ivan the Terrible's and Richard Chancellor's invention, but the export growth of naval stores gave Peter the opportunity to fulfil Ivan's aim.

Chapter 38

Mercantilism?

Many 17th-century histories describe European trade policy as 'mercantilist', after Adam Smith's 1776 *Wealth of Nations* description of commerce in his lifetime and before. Explanations of what it means vary widely; that 'a nation's wealth was measured by the amount of gold and silver it possessed'[1] or Navigation Act protection, restrictions on foreign ships, attempts to monopolise or dominate trade at competitors' expense, restraint of manufactured goods import and encourage their export. But Smith, against restraint, <u>praised</u> the Navigation Acts as helping expand the merchant fleet and aid national defence. Some think it includes planting colonies, bans on foreign ships, high tariffs, subsidising shipping, manufacturing and exports. One says 'politically-orientated privateering' was part of mercantilism,[2] another that 'the exchange of raw materials for manufactures remained the mercantilist ideal.'[3] Some think Napoleon's bullionist economic policy or modern EU protectionism, mercantilist. Most concentrate on European states but Sanjay Subrahmanyam applies it to 17th-century Bengal, 'as an ideology wherein the state behaves like a merchant.'[4] Braudel thought the word gave 'coherence it could never have had' and quotes approvingly another historian's phrase, 'one of the vaguest and most irritating 'isms' in the language',[5] but uses it to cover policies pushing states 'toward modernity...by different routes in different stages.'[6] Norman Davies sums up, it 'has meant many things to many men.'[7] It is therefore unhelpful. One disapproving historian has described it as 'invented retrospectively to give order to a confused situation' and 'a straw man, to be cut down by the knight of free trade,'[8] another sensibly that 'protectionism' is more meaningful.[9]

Sixth to 1st-century BC wars for Mediterranean trade routes, a 13th-century Aragonese Navigation Act, frequent 14th-century Castilian grain and livestock export bans, competition between Pisa, Genoa and Venice, between the Hansa, Baltic states, Dutch and English show trade protection was not new and attempted in different ways. Unless they had the ships and power to make bans or Navigation Acts effective, they did not work, as delusional Ming and Spanish New World exclusionists proved. France's Louis XI in the 1460s tried to ban foreigners from importing spices to protect southern French galleys for spice monopoly, but Venetians, Genoese and Florentines continued pepper, ginger and sugar imports via Marseilles, not then part of France.[10] The 1381 English Act required English traders to ship goods in English ships, modified a year later with an exception, if none were available. Acts in 1485 and 1489 required Gascon wines and Toulouse woad be imported in English ships. One in 1516 declared all licenses granted to disregard the law void. Acts of 1532 and 1541 declared them still operating, with maximum freight rates charged by English shipowners.[11]Another in 1562 required goods carried between English ports to be in English ships. James I issued Orders in Council with the same aim. They were all ineffective because England did not have enough merchant ships or strong enough navy. So, 1651's Navigation Act was not new in legal intent. What was new was that shipping and merchant interests were for the first time of real importance to England's economy, ignored by James and Charles, and put centre stage by the 1649 republican government, which meant confronting Dutch maritime hegemony. English customs had long provided that imports and exports in foreign-built ships bear a small extra duty, the 'Aliens Duty', stabilised in 1660 at 1.75% of the cargo's official value, tweaked in 1673 and 1690. The bulk of English shipping <u>volume</u>, rather than value, was coal, for which foreign ships, mainly Dutch, almost disappeared after 1660.[12]

In a period of rapidly expanding trade, with Dutch dominating, from 1649 England's republican leaders assisted its merchants better. Europe increasingly depended on worldwide cargoes. Sugar, tobacco, tea, coffee, saltpetre and Indian textiles were added to early spice obsessions, hence the increased importance of merchant power. Post-1649 English leadership implemented policies in the national interest, not her monarch's vanity. Olivares and Colbert realised the importance of foreign trade and Colbert of colonies, but they were culturally unable to create a free merchant class when government-led. Yet even this imperfect trade orientation was not appreciated in wider Spanish and French circles. The origins of the modern French policy of state-owned 'national champions' derives from Colbert. Dutch and English models were different from each other. It is better to understand each nation's differences in their approach to maritime trade, partly reflected by their geographic and cultural contexts. Oxenstierna was interested in collecting Baltic tolls, later Swedish leaders in controlling shipping. Some were involved in industrial investment to promote trades, which could be controlled. The Dutch and Sephardim tended to embrace all such entrepreneurial activities, absent in Castile after the 1400s, thwarted in Catalonia, and confined to mainly Protestant-dominated French ports. Spanish and French aristocrats looked down on trade, the English married into it. For Dutch maritime provinces, it was their raison d'etre.

The term 'mercantilism' also ignores widespread differences in economic thought. Correlation between bullion, prosperity and power was axiomatic in early-modern Europe. Thomas Mun (1571–1641) however, attacked bullionism and defended the EIC. Others criticised <u>any</u> monopoly. Bullion export, Mun argued, was fine as long as the value of imports were of greater value. A nation's wealth could not be measured by one form of exchange. By contrast, Thomas Bowdler who served in overseas embassies wanted to discourage Asian ventures due to bullion <u>and</u> sailor losses in favour of concentration on the Americas to 'raise another England' against Spain 'without waste of treasure…and…mariners', the high mortality rate of settlers of little consequence in contrast to mariners.[13] Mun argued more powerfully that bullion for spices and cotton cloth profits financed the purchase of more bullion.

The EIC, he concluded, was 'the means to bring more treasure into this realm than all the other trades of this kingdom.' The alternative was to buy expensive Dutch pepper and continental linens. This was the start of progressive economic thought about international trade. William Bernstein shows well before Adam Smith, similar economic theories were aired, highlighting Roger Coke (1628–1703), who saw that wealthy Holland imported nearly everything and poor Ireland exported far more than it imported. There was more to national wealth than the balance of trade. Charles Davenant explained the benefits of cheap imports outweighed damages done to domestic employment and that protectionism encouraged domestic inefficiency. Henry Martyn's *Considerations upon the East India Trade* (1701) argued that a nation's wealth was defined by how much it consumed.[14] Holland consumed 'every country's manufactures. English cloth, French wines, Italian silks...If these things were not riches, they would not give their bullion for 'em.' Weavers' lost jobs meant their efforts should be directed more profitably.[15] William Petty also wanted investment rather than bullion hoarding. These influential writers don't fit bullionist definitions of mercantilism. Roman emperors also worried about bullion outflow, but were also reconciled by desirable imports.

The very different Portuguese, Spanish, English, French, Dutch and competing Baltic nations, not to mention Gujaratis, Tamils, Makassars, Fujianese, etc., were driven by diverse sets of geographical and cultural factors, not the least of which is that in Asia, 16th and 17th-century Europeans were gradually penetrating an ancient, extensive, voluminous, rich, elaborate trade network. In the Americas they were dealing with a vast landmass virtually denuded of people. Sixteenth-century Portuguese, Spanish, Dutch and English thought monopolies necessary where exercising sovereign functions, dealing with foreign rivals and local powers, but England's privileged Merchant Adventurer monopoly was unconcerned with English dyeing and finishing, declining due to Netherlands' protection, accentuated because of reliance on Antwerp, preventing wider merchant participation, which was unleashed after 1649.

Competitive trans-Atlantic trade gave London and outer ports dynamism. Dutch Atlantic trade was a WIC monopoly. How can there be a unified 'ism' for this ad-hoc state of affairs? In the Baltic, unarmed fluyts traded unmolested except in war but in the Mediterranean, armed convoys were necessary and the EIC and VOC employed large, heavily-armed Indiamen. Newfoundland and Caribbean competition also meant heavier, armed ships were necessary. While the Dutch professed *Mare Liberum* they hypocritically tried to monopolise, kept the Scheldt closed, set out to destroy Portuguese trade, used violence and intimidation to discourage the EIC, Javan and Makassar competition, damaging previous freer, indigenous trade; a far cry from Grotius's call to 'boldly fight, not only for thine own liberty, but for liberty and freedom of all mankind.' Moreover, the VOC and EIC, seemingly similar national champions, pursued different policies, the VOC an aggressive, rigid monopolistic model which gradually ossified, while after 1674 the EIC allowed their employees to engage in third-party trade, which being more dynamic, ate away VOC's intra-Asian trade. Second-half 17th-century maritime trade in Asia and the Atlantic proved Peter de la Court's 1662 comment, 'Commerce desires to be free,'[16] but the Dutch persisted with monopolies.

In England the EIC, RAC and Levant Company were regularly criticised for monopolistic inefficiency, but there were axes to grind. The Levant Company criticised the EIC because it lost out to superior EIC's Indian cloths, thus hijacked illogical bullionist arguments. The Puritan-minded were uneasy with new brightly-coloured fashions. Impoverished silk and wool weavers opposed EIC imports. Wars after 1689 were paid for mainly by a land tax, splitting English politics into rural Tories, who saw merchants draining England of bullion for imported frivolous Indian fashions and merchant Whigs who fronted progressive economic thought.

Trade was a complex interplay of merchants, chartered companies, guilds, shipowners, industrialists and free-trade champions like planters, all acting according to their interests. Competitive advantage was on everyone's agenda, although with Spanish taxing its manufactured exports as its raw materials sold abroad, subsidised on foreign ships and Louis XIV's contradictory policies, some was misguided. Sixteenth-century English monopolies were increasingly criticised as volumes rose. Already a 1645 English pamphlet read, 'Nothing [is] more pernicious and destructive to any kingdom or commonwealth than monopolies. Trade…is like dung which being kept close in a heap or two stinks, but being spread abroad, it doth fertilise the earth and make it fructible.'[17] Davenant expressed growing English consensus when in *An Essay on the East India Trade*, he wrote 'trade is in its nature free…[it] finds its own channels and best directs its own course and all laws to give it rules and directions may serve the particular ends of private men but are seldom advantageous to the public.'[18] Josiah Child's *A New Discourse of Trade* noted 'we have…increased less in those trades limited to companies than in others where all his Majesty's subjects have equal freedom to trade.'[19] In short, independent companies outperformed monopolies. For individuals risking their lives in the Caribbean and North America it was counter-productive to force them into a monopoly.

The Hansa had gone through a similar dynamic; the encouragement of trade, nurtured and protected in the 12th century but no longer appropriate with rapidly expanding volumes and competing Dutch, English and Baltic states. Denmark wanted control of the Sound. Newly independent, ambitious Sweden eyed opportunity in Livonia and newly liberated Muscovy wanted its own Baltic port. Dutch and English monopoly companies, created to trade beyond north Europe, were challenged by free traders. Nothing was static, but a recurring pattern of competition and conflict, because of maritime trade's growth. Any protective system invites competition. National interest was often perceived in terms of exclusion of foreigners in trade but most ports were inclusive; Dorestad, Bruges, Antwerp, Amsterdam, Livorno and London. Lubeck and Hamburg dealt with post-Hansa decline in different ways. Hamburg allowed foreign traders of any religion to settle, a similar social structure to Amsterdam and London, with 50–60% of its merchants foreign. The Bank of Hamburg was founded in 1619, encouraged by English Merchant Adventurers, Portuguese and Dutch merchants. It developed insurance, financial facilities, a large merchant fleet and its population rose steadily.

Lubeck, in contrast, did not allow foreigners to trade equally. In 1688 William Carr explained 'the reason of the decay of trade in Lubeck was chiefly the inconsiderate zeal of their Lutheran ministers who persuaded the magistrates to banish all Roman Catholics, Calvinists and Jews and all that dissent from them in matters of religion, even the English Company too, who all went and settled in Hamburg,'[20] which rapidly replaced Lubeck as the region's largest port, and a major 18th-century sugar, rice, coffee, tea and tobacco entrepot, eroding Amsterdam's position. Konigsberg also only allowed local merchants to trade until 1736. The term mercantilism does not help us understand these dynamics, nor the crucial role of Jews, Phoenician heirs in Egypt, Carthaginian in Iberia and its diaspora, or other minorities; Huguenots, Quakers, and in Asia, Jains, Tamils, Gujaratis and Armenians.

Iberian anti-Semitism and expulsions in the 7th and 15th-16th centuries hurt its economy, directly benefiting enemies. Religious bigotry hurt Venice and Lubeck. Heavy-handed Spanish rule in Flanders enriched England's economy with Flemish migrant textile workers. France's expulsion of Huguenots was an equally profound act of self-harm in the name of Catholic uniformity, which hobbled economic vigour, enriching competitors. Jewish traders were profoundly influential in Europe and the Americas, over-contributing to Portuguese, Dutch and English success.

The RAC abandoned slave trading in 1731 for Guinea's ivory and gold, resulting in the British monetary unit the Guinea, and was dissolved in 1752. Apart from the EIC, all monopolistic English trade companies withered. The Merchant Adventurers were the first, the Eastland Company had its privileges curtailed in 1673. By the 1720s it was a dining club.[21] The Levant Company survived until 1754 because of south and east Mediterranean dangers. None of this fits a consistent 'ism.' Competition energises; monopoly leads to complacency. Restrictions weaken. Castile's American monopoly had no hope of success. The Hudson Bay Company and RAC were unable to fulfil demand and French Caribbean islands were forbidden from developing rum to protect their brandy industry, so was developed elsewhere; random examples of a general truth. By 1700 it was clear the Dutch were weakening, the WIC and VOC ossifying. English monopolies' disappearance, except the EIC, signalled a new world of energetic private companies, especially in the Atlantic. English traders because of valuable Indian trade and vast Atlantic opportunities were energised. Momentum was with them. Seventeenth-century maritime-orientated nations promoted trade, leading to increasingly free, tolerant societies.

Nations, ports and merchants attract trade in different ways. Mercantilism as a catch-all word for all these complexities will not do. As trade grew and was seen to be wealth creating, governments wanted their share. Colbert integrated commercial motives into French traditional, land-grabbing foreign policy. The inevitable clash with commercial maritime powers led to the huge growth of navies, hence the Baltic's increased importance for naval stores, despite grain export decline. All states were increasingly aware of maritime trade's value and used naval power to protect it, attack their competition and reduce piracy. Instead of an 'ism' we should instead think of multiple variations in the way that states protected, encouraged, or discouraged trade, which most eventually thought important. The English competition model in the Atlantic endured far into the future, as did the state-owned French national champion model.

The age of mercantilism is supposed to have ended with Adam Smith's 1776 *Wealth of Nations*, which ushered in free or freer trade, yet this was about the time in India when the British defeated the French and began to take monopoly advantage, overturning previously competitive access to Indian weavers. Furthermore, in today's supposedly freer trade, China and Germany are committed to trade surpluses. China subsidised exports until its entry into the World Trade Organisation in 2001. It probably still does. Emerging 20th-century economies, Japan, South Korea, Taiwan and China pursued similar policies of protecting home markets, subsidising producers, managing currencies and imposing unnecessary regulations and delays on imports, so 17th-century economies should similarly be seen as <u>emerging economies</u>. It is however, not quite that simple. The US, the world's strongest economy, promoter of free trade, has protected its coastal trade since 1920 by the Jones Act. Canada, India and Indonesia also do so and France's cabotage laws protected French-flagged ships until the 1970s. The EU, the US and Japan subsidise expensive domestic agriculture at the expense of cheaper imports. The supposedly free trade loving EU's tariffs are not designed primarily as revenue generating, but set at just the right percentages to exclude foreign imports. Today's world economy cannot be easily generalised, any more than the 17th century, indeed any age. 'Mercantilism' gives undeserving unity to myriad trade policies born of numerous geographical, cultural, historical and political factors.

Chapter 39

End-Millennium Perspective

The world of 700 was cleft in two. Europe was depopulated, poor, with little meaningful maritime trade; Asia accelerated already thriving maritime trade over vast distances in a huge variety of goods, perishables, necessities and luxuries. That a corner of north Europe a thousand years later turned the tables so decisively, dominating European and Atlantic commercial shipping and was of growing importance in Asian trade was partly its achievement, partly self-inflicted. Early Europeans in Asia thought Malacca as big as Amsterdam and London, with well-developed financial systems and low interest rates,[1] yet by 1700 there was no Asian equivalent, despite intra-Asian trade still being the richest and most voluminous. The year 1700 does not mark in any way a take-over. There were only 114 English civilians in Madras, 1,200 in Calcutta, 700–800 in Bombay, all living modestly. European ships in intra-Asian trade had mixed, mainly local crews. EIC Indian factories borrowed from Indian merchant bankers. Dejima was tiny, Macao small, Goa and Batavia a little larger,[2] but Europeans were energetic intruders, stimulating and developing networks, gradually gaining ground.

Apart from Mongols not attacking Europe, concentrating instead on Persia, Mesopotamia, India and China, there were four key periods; China's private trade ban in 1372, its withdrawal of naval power in 1432, Portuguese Indian Ocean entry in 1498 and the 1649–1700 period. Coxinga's maritime empire was destroyed by hubris. Ottoman and Safavid empires peaked, China, Japan and Korea, virtually closed. Aurangzeb's wars were collapsing Mughal power, leaving Indian maritime polities fragile. Mataram with little maritime interest, conquered other Javanese lands, damaging its ports and shipping, but when beset by rebellion, became a VOC client. Governor General Speelman in 1677 noted 'the eastern Javanese of Mataram, besides their great ignorance at sea, were now completely lacking in vessels of their own.'[3] Bantam tried to develop an indigenous merchant fleet but VOC conquest in 1682–1684 ended that prospect. All Asia's potentially strong maritime powers disintegrated, self-destructed or self-isolated, while England's merchant momentum in the Atlantic, Baltic and Asia and crucial political reform established firm foundations for further trade growth.

Between 1640 and 1700 English exports increased from £2.5 million to £4.5 million but re-exports from negligible amounts to nearly £2 million, with colonial production far beyond English needs, its re-exports nearly a third of all exports.[4] Indian textiles were two-thirds of EIC imports, mainly re-exported,[5] paid for with silver. Between 1615 and 1700 English tobacco imports rose from

50,000 lbs. to 38 million lbs., two-thirds re-exported.[6] By 1700 half of England's Caribbean sugar and 60% of tobacco imports[7] were re-exported as European demand increased.[8] English imports from Asia and America rose from zero before 1600, about 7% in 1621 to 34% in 1700.[9] By 1700, 30% of imports and 15% of exports were Indian and American.[10] England was Europe's great entrepot. After 1689 anyone in England could export cloth. In 1700 cloth exports were freed from customs duty and were rivalled in value by re-exports of calicoes, silks, tobacco and sugar.[11] Iron and copper were allowed to be exported anywhere except France. Landowners were encouraged to dig for tin, lead, iron and copper. After 1690 statutes encouraged gin distillation from English grain. French brandy imports were banned. In 1689, customs duty on grain exports was removed. They rose quickly. Gregory King in 1696 thought successful merchants had higher incomes than lesser gentry.

As Dutch were economically invigorated by war with Spain, so was England under merchant-driven government by war with the Dutch and France. In the 1670s, following Cromwell's reconnoitring, English warships used Port Mahon and Cadiz to revictual and refit. In 1689 there were 15 joint-stock companies worth £0.9 million. By 1695 there were 150 worth £4.3 million.[12] Naval investments were double France's, which retrenched 50% between 1693 and 1695. Instead, commerce raiding was its naval strategy. English naval yard workers increased 20% between 1654 and 1687, over 475% in the following 15 years![13] The navy became England's largest industry. With merchant interest paramount, it protected maritime trade. Its 22,000 men in 1689 rose to 48,500 in 1695. The 1690s Plymouth dockyard commanded the Channel approach. After the 1693 Smyrna convoy disaster, the House of Commons attached a provision to the 1694 Land Tax bill allocating 43 ships for trade protection, virtually a second navy. The Lords agreed, establishing a precedent of Commons control of money bills and naval support.[14] England's Board of Trade and Plantations in 1696 replaced Privy Council Committees, liaising between traders and Admiralty on convoy protection. As J.H. Plumb explains, 'the more complex trade is, the more involved financial structure, the greater the need for political stability.'[15] By 1700, the financial, economic and political infrastructure of a complex trading nation was established. After the development of life insurance, creation of the Bank of England and National Debt, land was not necessarily the best investment. Increasingly trade was, no longer restricted to privileged, well-connected people in exclusive, regulated monopoly companies.

The United Provinces' land wars with France damaged it. Dutch Indian Ocean aggressiveness enunciated by Coen, echoed by Van Diemen's 'the Company's trade in Asia cannot subsist without territorial conquests', was ultimately detrimental to it. Peter de la Court's 1662 *Interest of Holland* stated that war was prejudicial and peace beneficial, because by 1648, they were so successful that they were virtually everyone's enemy and needed peace. They established coffee plantations in Java and Surinam but failed to fully appreciate tea's possibilities and lost opportunities to trade with China after the Manchu conquered Taiwan. By 1700 the EIC imported about 100,000 lbs. of tea. But despite reverses, Dutch overseas trade in 1699 reached the high-water mark attained 50 years earlier.[16] Peter the Great wanted to study Dutch shipbuilding in 1697. In 1700 its whaling and fishing industries employed 260 ships and 14,000 seamen.[17] Double-entry book-keeping, developed in early-14th-century Genoa, had not spread quickly. Although early-17th-century Stadtholder Maurice applied it for state finances, many merchants including the VOC did not use it,[18] nor keep consolidated accounts. VOC President Johannes Hudde's 1680's planned overhaul was never implemented, losses hidden by territorial administration expenses. Its 2,500 Asian employees of 1625 rose to a bloated 13,000 in 1700 as EIC employees nibbled away at its inter-Asian network.[19] Spices and pepper reduced from 75% of VOC returns in 1620 to 33% in 1670, 23% in 1700. In 1650 VOC Europe-bound ships carried by value 50% pepper and 18% spices, by 1700 only 11% each, silks and cottons 50% and dyes, copper, tea and coffee 4–8% each.[20] Europe's merchants changed world trade dynamics.

All VOC employees from the top down traded unofficially. VOC accounts were easily manipulated with little secrecy, especially in Bengal and Japan.[21] Opium, Bengal's main illegal private trade, cost three-times more in Batavia.[22] VOC Indian factories had profitable cotton cloth trades to Batavia, the largest VOC export to the Netherlands after the 1680s. A third of their cloth imports in 1697 were Bengali, more than the EIC, both profiting from re-exports, exceeding home consumption, although the VOC's lead was shrinking fast.[23] Coromandel cottons as early as 1612 were described as the VOC's 'left arm', spices its 'right arm', starting better than the EIC but in the last quarter of the century, Aurangzeb's wars around Golconda shook its hold, and the EIC surpassed it in capital recourses. The VOC's 'left arm' withered.[24] Profitable VOC Japan trade declined after the silver export ban. Dutch relative decline was partly due to Anglo-Dutch wars but mainly French aggression. Only in hindsight was the 1621–1654 concentration on Brazil a mistake. When driven out they had insufficient Caribbean colonies. WIC monopoly was also far less energetic and effective than England's many private companies, also easier to appreciate in 1700 than 1650. But in 1707 the Zaandam region still had over 60 shipyards with 306 vessels being built.[25]

After 1663 Spain bought slaves for South America via the WIC in Curacao, considered less strategically threatening than England or France. Commodities followed, leading to a Dutch entrepot at Tucacas, northwest Venezuela supplying inland settlements. Sephardic Jacob Senior (c 1660–1718), most active in developing it, received most goods from Amsterdam's Abraham Fundas.[26] By 1700 Curacao was a gateway to Spanish America and trading centre for cocoa, tobacco, indigo, sugar, hides and coffee, a ship-repair and financial centre. Surinam's coffee, sugar, cacao and cotton were South America's most productive. In 1700 Curacao had about 80 ships, many Sephardic owned,[27] but under WIC direction, lacked the vitality of English private trade. In the United Provinces with the Heren XVII gentrifying, the nobility adopted French culture and language. Dutch painting quantity and quality declined.

Portugal heavily depended on Brazil's sugar customs revenue, but Bahia complained against penal export duties, which they said had encouraged English and French Caribbean sugar.[28] Seemingly on the verge of collapse in 1691, Portugal recovered as European demand increased. Anglo-French war caused Portugal's wine exports to grow. Alluvial gold found in Brazil's Minas Gerais region in the 1690s also steadied Portugal's economy, as it conquered Angola, ensuring slave supply. In Asia it retained only Timor, Macao, Goa, Daman and Diu. Sweden, at the height of its territorial powers had increasingly valuable naval stores, although early English colonists had taken hemp seeds to North America, allowing it to export cordage, cloth, canvas, sacks, etc. Sweden's iron bar exports to Holland had been 3,000 tons in the late-1620s, 11,000 in 1650. Much of the 1680's 27,000 tons went to England, by 1700, half of its 30,000, in English and Swedish ships, only a quarter to the Dutch.

Sixteenth-century English trade had been mainly in high-value goods. Bulk cargo supporting shipping, played little part in its economy, employed little capital. Much was controlled by privileged monopolies, although fishing was important. Seventeenth-century growth was based mainly shipping coastal and overseas coal, timber, then tobacco and sugar as mass demand was created and became England's fastest growing industry. Tonnage multiplied nearly seven-fold as the population doubled. Consequently, national income rose impressively.[29] Merchant shipping by 1700 was one of England's largest employers, driving London's population growth; seamen, warehousemen, stevedores, victualling, building, repairing, all of which required services. Anglo-French wars after 1689 meant more modest growth than 1649–1689 but after 1680 contemporary literature on shipping's problems died away reflecting successful fightback against the Dutch and shipping's growing significance in England's economy.[30]

Its most significant commercial change and that of greatest value was the growth of trans-Atlantic trade and re-exports. In 1660 trans-Atlantic trade was 4% of England's total trade, in 1700, 20%.[31] Asia was drawn in as Indian cloth was sold in the Caribbean and North America. Shipping and capital made London a major financial centre with shipyards, warehouses and wharves. Its merchant fleet grew from 115,000 tons in 1629 to 323,000 in 1702.[32] Collapsing sugar and tobacco prices enabled affordability. London was the leading tobacco processor and sugar refiner. England bleached, finished, dressed and dyed cloth to the highest standards, enabling it to achieve full value. But it was less dependent on it. Its export value against total export value fell from 75% in 1660 to 50% in 1700. The American market stimulated cotton, silk, shoe, hat, glass and iron industries. Large ships meant economies of scale. Stowage improved, loading and discharging times shortened. By 1700 London manufactured telescopes, clocks, navigational instruments; Europe's leading instrument maker. In 1500, Europe's political, cultural and economic hub was the Mediterranean. By 1700 it was Amsterdam and London, the momentum with London. In 1550 London was still small and economically backward. By 1700 it was a world city, home to industrious immigrants, created by economic, political and from 1517, religious competition. From a 50,000 population in 1550, 125,000 in 1603 it rose to 550,000 in 1700,[33] with two-thirds of England's trade, 70% of trans-Atlantic imports, 15% of which remained in London, the rest distributed, encouraging road investment.[34] Whilst post-1649 developments were crucial, credit must also go to Thomas Cromwell and William Cecil, who tried countering entrenched monopoly earlier.

Exeter, Bristol, Liverpool, Newcastle, Hull, Whitehaven, Glasgow and Kings Lynn grew. West coast ports were well-located for growing trans-Atlantic trade. In Liverpool sugar refineries emerged. In 1694 the Mersey was widened and in 1700 dock building started.[35] Glasgow imported sugar, iron bars, tobacco, indigo and skins in locally-owned, English, American and Irish ships, encouraging processing industries.[36] In 1669 a Glaswegian built the 'East Sugar House' operated by a Dutch master boiler. North, South and West Sugar Houses followed, using local coal for boiling. Bristol's customs increased ten-times between 1614 and 1687 with increasing Portuguese trade, access to developing Midlands' industry, before sugar refining, tobacco and slave trading took off. As England's second largest town and port, 240 ships a year called in 1668. Pepys thought it 'in every respect another London.'[37] Its redistributed cargo benefited north Devon's and Cornish ports.[38] In 1698 African trade was opened up on payment of a 10% levy on African exports to subsidise the RAC. In 1700 it had 500 ships carrying 100,000 slaves, 30,000 tons of sugar and had eight African forts, but private traders were more dynamic. In 1712 the trade became free and it ceased to function by 1730.[39] The age of the regulated company and merchant guilds without joint capital was, the EIC apart, over. As London's 17th-century population doubled and coal consumption grew six-fold, colliers increased from a 73-ton average in 1606 to 248 tons in 1700, employing thousands; 'the nursery of seamen'.[40] The use of coal in brewing, dye making, salt boiling, sugar and other industries entailed experimentation with coal grades and furnace types, leading to coal use in brick and pottery making. One in three Bostonians invested in shipping. Its fleet matched Bristol's.[41] Economic progress made literacy levels rise, especially in ports, but not the French interior, Mediterranean and eastern Europe.[42]

France's rising military power was based on a large population and resources, but unable to embrace diversity, it was commercially restricted. Merchants' sons preferred careers as officials, army officers, clerics or lived off investments and property, unlike 17th-century Dutch merchants' sons following their fathers into the business. Similar to Venice's commercial nobility, they increasingly transformed into a landed class from the 1690s, hindering economic development. This 'noblesse de robe' of judicial and administrative offices, urban property, government bonds and agricultural lands, meant capital became increasingly unproductive. Spain was worse. One estimate has 8% of adult males in the priesthood in Philip IV's reign.[43] There was nothing like the numerous English pamphlets and books vigorously debating trade policy. Offices were bought; a means of enrichment and an increasing revenue source. The opposite developed in England after 1649. Investment opportunities grew, becoming competitive with the Dutch by 1700.

Dutch commercial power faded, its population and land small, increasingly preoccupied with territorial gains in Asia. English economic power based on liberating maritime merchant potential increased astonishingly quickly, despite demographic disadvantage. North American self-governing communities became a strength. In Asia, Srivijaya's and Majapahit's collapse, Mongol conquest, the Ming ban, Mataram's decline, Japan's self-isolation, Coxinga's maritime empire's failure and Aurangzeb's self-defeating bloodbath meant no Asian naval power could protect Asian shipping.

In these thousand years however, there are constants. Whatever the political narrative, even in war, merchants continued trying to provide goods where there was demand, including grain in famines. Jewish, Muslim and Christian merchants, even in Crusader states, cooperated. In the Indian Ocean, diversity and cooperation was standard. Various political mentalities concerning maritime trade have been monitored; those distrusting it, those trying to ban it, those self-isolating, those attempting control through national monopolies and those giving merchants freedom and encouragement. The latter naturally embraced toleration, representation and liberty. To repeat Pirenne's point; trade flourishes 'when unhindered' by princes. The millennium revolution happened because northern European states largely encouraged it, stutteringly from the 11th century, eventually putting it to the forefront of policy, making them increasingly wealthy and militarily powerful. Merchants were always mobile; whether Jew, Omani, Yemeni, Chinese, Gujarati, Tamil, Flemish, Huguenot, Portuguese or English. It is a worldwide, ageless phenomenon.

In India, the southward march of intolerant, continental Islam hindered merchants. Chinese merchants, individually talented and entrepreneurial, were constrained by princes' intolerance. Towards the end of this thousand years, Asian and Mediterranean land powers obstructed or ignored trade. In northern Europe, France frustrated the Netherlands. Eastern Europe's free 15th-century peasants were enserfed in the 16th. They lost mobility, rights to marry freely and free themselves, performing six days compulsory labour a week, driven by food demand and noble's ability to oppress.[44] Inland western Europe escaped it, but there were hundreds, probably thousands of revolts, riots, insurrections and disturbances in France with peasants in constant conflict with landlords.[45]

Northern Europe's triumph was partly fortuitous. Destructive steppe nomad invasions were not directed at Europe, as in the 2nd-5th centuries, but Mesopotamia, China, India and Anatolia. As a result, no Asian power successfully resisted European penetration and no Mediterranean state could compete. The Black Sea could have played a similar role to the Baltic, but Ottoman aggression neutered Mediterranean development. The Baltic, potentially vulnerable to eastern attack, became a commercial powerhouse in multiple commodities, sold to north Europe and beyond. Baltic trade was vital in catapulting northern Europe into global trade pre-eminence. English and Dutch merchants gained expertise in seafaring, fishing, ship design, trade knowledge and finance. Competition between Hansa, Denmark, Sweden, Dutch, English and competing Baltic ports, intensified around choke points. Atlantic fishing was also extremely influential. But geographical determinism alone cannot account for extraordinary people and their decisions; countless Fujianese, Tamil, Gujarati, Makassar, Jewish, Venetian, Genoese, Portuguese, English and Dutch merchants and important political leaders, Al-Mansur, Jayanasu, Godfred of Denmark, Song dynasty emperors, Hongwu, Paramesvara, Ivan IV, Elizabeth I, Cromwell, Downing, Coxinga and William of Orange for example. Nevertheless, the theme of continental against maritime mentalities played out in these years as clearly as Spartans-Athenians, Phoenicians-Egyptians, between Charlemagne and Frisia and Denmark, between Castile and Catalonia-Aragon, Castile-driven Spain and the United Provinces, Portugal and Spain, France and England, Song and Ming, Mughals against Gujaratis and Tamils, inland against coastal China. Throughout history, continental mentality has held back, sometimes destroyed the maritime dynamic, which in 1700 emerged strongly, partly fortuitously, in northwest Europe, the unlikeliest outcome viewed from the perspective of 700.

Chapter 40

American Maritime Commerce
before Columbus

Innovative sea-traders had settled the Americas and produced civilisations from deep antiquity. The incubator for subsequent South and central American civilisations was Peru's Caral-Supe. Like the Chimor or Chimu successors, they used the Humboldt current's bounty, greened the desert, importing fertile soil, directing irrigation canals including aqueducts, made intricate ceramics, gold and silver ornaments and valued spondylus shells from warmer waters further north, used in rituals and as ornaments and jewellery. Their most important deity was the Sea Goddess. They painted and etched fish on ceramics, but were destroyed in the 1460s by the Inca.

Ecuadorians were long-distance maritime traders. By 100 BC they established maritime commercial routes from Chile to Mexico, introducing metallurgy, pioneered by the Moche. Guilds of traders organised deployment of large balsa log rafts. Pizzaro's chief pilot in 1526 captured one off Ecuador's coast, carrying 20 men and trade goods, including silver objects from tiaras to tweezers.[1] One was described as 'very thick and long wooden logs which are soft and light in the water as cork. They lash them very tightly together with a kind of hemp rope and above them they place a high framework so that the merchandise...do not get wet. They set a mast in the largest log in the middle and hoist a sail and navigate all along this coast. They are very safe vessels because they cannot sink or capsize, since the water washed through them.'[2] They were ideal for long-distance transport.

They traded with significant Amazonian settlements, found by the first Europeans. In 1542 Francisco de Orellana, sailing the Amazon, searching for El Dorado, wrote, 'the further we went, the more thickly populated and the better did we find the land. There were many roads here that enter into the interior of the land and many highways. Inland from the river to a distance of six miles, more or less, there could be seen some very large cities, glistening white and besides this, the land is as fertile and as normal in appearance as our Spain.' He was impressed with the large population behind palisades, their good health, the colour of their clothes and pottery, which he said compared with the finest from Malaga. No later travellers confirm this picture because of a near-extinction pandemic, perhaps 90–95% from smallpox, measles and other diseases for which they had no immunity.[3] As forest was cleared in the 1980s, evidence of these roads connecting towns and villages appeared, some over 50 metres across, in straight lines forming an integrated regional grid. It had been densely-populated with people using sophisticated astronomical and mathematical knowledge.

Andean civilisations influenced all those of south and central America. The Olmec calendar began in 3114 BC. In the fertile Coatzacoalcos River Valley, their economy was based on agriculture, river transport and trade in iron ore, jade, schist, obsidian, mirrors, tools, weapons, small figurines and jewellery. They were apparently in contact with northern Peru's Chavin, a jaguar cult common to both, and may have introduced maize, exchanged for cocoa. The evidence is scarce and mainly about leaders and wars rather than trade. There is little evidence of sea travel, which doesn't mean it didn't happen, and its trade did facilitate knowledge transfer to other Mesoamerican and Andean cultures. Around 2000 BC there was a migration from South America into the Caribbean. Trade between islands and with the mainland was in large dug-out canoes.

Columbus said Caribbean natives were seafarers. He reported a large Taino trading dug-out canoe with 12 rowing benches, about 40 feet long for 24 rowers plus passengers and cargo in 1492 from northeast Cuba. One was described as 79 feet long, built by Carib and Taino tribes, who knew Florida's Calusa and Maya. The Carib, cannibals who migrated from South America about 1000, undertook long sea voyages to capture people. Florida's Calusa who, according to a Spanish account, attacked a Spanish ship in eight war canoes, probably traded along the coast and reached Cuba while Taino traded inter-island.[4]

The older Mayan civilisation traded over a far wider area with other Mesoamerican cultures including Peru with many precise links between Mayan and Andean ideas.[5] Much Maya trade was by sea. Starting in the 9th century BC, they encompassed modern southeast Mexico, Guatemala, Belize, parts of Honduras and Salvador, a diverse political, social and economic area, bound together by shared culture and ideology. They had Mesoamerica's only fully-developed system of writing, mathematics, astronomical skills, place-value numeration and calendar, especially during the so-called classic (600–900) and post-classic periods (1200–1521) when there was great cultural interaction and maritime trade across Mesoamerica as far south as Panama in pottery, cotton, obsidian, cacao, vanilla, basalt, honey, beeswax, natural dyes, shells, hides and salt, and for elites, jaguar and other skins, macaw feathers, jade, gold and turquoise. Wealthy merchants supplied commodities and slaves to towns which had massive public construction projects. 'The Chontal Maya had developed naval engineering, metallurgy, tool design, woodworking and shipbuilding capabilities that enabled them to construct the large, composite, seaworthy vessels. Their accomplishments in mathematics and astronomy enabled the Chontal Maya to develop a sophisticated method of celestial navigation for their overseas voyages.'[6]

Unlike Taino and Caribs who hollowed out their dug-outs with fire and stone tools, Maya developed efficient bronze cutting tools to build vessels. Drawings show a high prow and stern, an extended freeboard, pointed paddles and uniquely in the Caribbean, a steering oar, planked craft with rudders and cabins, also propelled by sails.[7] Columbus described an eight-foot wide trading canoe with cargo from Mexico with a central awning 'like that which the Venetian gondolas carry' which 'gave complete protection against the rain and waves' carrying cotton mandles and shirts embroidered and painted in various designs and colours and 'crucibles for smelting ore.'[8] Their bronze axes, adzes, chisels and drills, made from copper and tin from mountains far from Mayan lowlands, were sold in markets.[9] Their long-haul voyaging influenced Caribbean and Florida tribes' games, totems, religious icons, ceremonial garments, pyramid temples and depictions of their gods, a knowledge exchange due to planned voyages.[10] Finding no tradeable goods in Florida, many stayed, enjoying a higher status, perhaps as priests, spreading Maya culture. In navigation they used the sun and wave patterns, as Polynesians did, and at night, a dark void in the sky, a familiar charted map, unlike Europeans, who used the pole star. Their mathematical data was recorded in two of their only three surviving books. Many of their buildings were celestial observatories[11] predicting orbital paths of stars, planets and constellations.

From their Yucatan peninsula heartland, they shipped inland products from ports such as Tulum, Zaman-Ha, Pole, Xen-Ha, Muyil and Cozumel. Northeast Yucatan's Tulum, south of Cancun, was at its height in the post-classic age, probably also important earlier. Its speciality was obsidian for tools and weapons, traded over central America and Mexico. Copper, ceramics, incense burners, salt and textiles were traded and dispersed inland up the Rio Motagua and Rio Usumacinta-Pasion systems, south to Caribbean islands as far as Antigua, where Mayan jade sites are found, north to Florida, where they introduced corn and Georgia where they mined gold. The connection survives in the name Miami, after the Mayaim tribe who lived around Lake Okeechobee near the Mayayuaka and Mayaka.[12] Vista Alegre, north of Cancun was probably another port from 800 BC to the mid-16th century. Archaeologists have identified over 75 trade goods. The Maya deity Ek Chuah was associated with trade. On Columbus's fourth voyage, a Mayan eight by fifty-foot-long canoe carrying passengers and cargo was seen.

As European diseases decimated the population, mobile Mayan traders spread them. Tulum survived for about 70 years after Spanish arrival, another 100 before all Maya lands were Spanish controlled, because unlike Inca and Aztec empires, there were many Maya polities, which fiercely resisted. Church and government officials deliberately destroyed their texts. In 1531 they eradicated 600 Mexican temples and 20,000 idols, valuable cultural heritage. Historians thus only deal with scraps of information. The last polity was suppressed in 1697, an ignominious end to what apparently was a culturally rich civilisation. Many questions remain unanswered, but Mesoamerica's most culturally advanced society was maritime, destroyed by Europe's then premier continental one. Isolation meant it developed no further. There was no equivalent of the Jain-Phoenician knowledge-transfer, Eurasian history's seminal event.[13]

Glossary

Ballast	Heavy material loaded into a ship to increase steadiness and draft (i.e. sit lower in the water), especially when **ballasting**, or **in ballast** (i.e. empty of cargo), to the loadport.
Bill of Lading	A receipt for the cargo prepared by the supplier/shipper and signed by the carrier to prove he has received the cargo. Also, a 'document of title', proof of ownership of the cargo, therefore to whom the cargo should be delivered and evidence of the terms of the conditions for the contract of transport. (See below)
Charter Party	A contract for transport of cargo by sea between shipowner and charterer.
Cog	Medieval European single-masted cargo ship.
Entrepot	Port where goods are received for onward shipment.
Factory	Place/enclave where factors (merchants) lived and traded.
Fluyt	Late-16th-century Dutch pine-built, simply-rigged cargo ship, which reduced building and running costs, thus highly competitive.
Funduq	Factory, as above, in Arabic, Fondaco in Venetian, Funnaco in Sicilian.
Freight Rate	Agreed payment by the charterer of a ship to the shipowner, usually per ton of cargo, occasionally lumpsum.
General Average	Rules for division of damages in a maritime accident on the principle that when a sacrifice is made to save the interests of all parties involved in a voyage, the party making the sacrifice must be compensated by all parties who stand to benefit from the sacrifice.
Herring buss	Late-16th-century ship which caught, salted and packed herring.
Hire	Agreed payment by the charterer of a ship to the shipowner on a daily basis.
Kontor	Hansa trading station/factory.
Kra Isthmus	Narrowest section of the Malay Peninsula, used to tranship goods before the Malacca and Sunda Straits were used.
£ s d	Signs for English money units. Pounds, shilling and pence; 20 shillings in one pound, 12 pence in a shilling
Sixty-fourths	Lowest division of ship ownership, to spread risk and enable capital formation.

Notes

In Memory
1. Bloomberg Businessweek.
   The Highjacking of the Brillante
   Virtuoso 2017

Introduction
1. Tawney (ed) p 37
2. ibid p 41
3. Lopez pdf p 57
4. Pirenne 1915 p xv
5. Braudel 1984 p 30
6. Taleb p 17
7. ibid pp 5, 216
8. Scott 2019 p 30
9. Braudel 1982 p 582
10. Marshall 1993 pp 19–20
11. Beckwith p 502
12. ibid p 213
13. Ferguson p 98
14. Pye p 87
15. Bartlett p 19
16. ibid p 23
17. Pye p 168
18. Marshall 1993 p 131
19. Tawney (ed) pp 95–99
20. Lopez pdf p 67
21. ibid p 68
22. Fernandez-Armesto 2010
    pp 122–124

Chapter 1
1. Collins 2021 pp 31–35
2. Paine p 310
3. Ebrey p 120
4. ibid
5. Hourani p 62
6. Guy

7. ibid
8. Francopan p 92
9. Munoz pp 135–137
10. ibid p 139
11. ibid pp 140–141
12. Zakharov
13. Munoz pp 144–145
14. Bowring p 63
15. Hall p 28
16. ibid p 32
17. Adelaar
18. Hourani pp 76–77
19. Bernstein p 86. Levathes p 39
20. Gungwu in Tracy 1990 (ed) p 402
21. Wade pp 239–240

Chapter 2
1. Collins 2021 pp 160–163,
   189–196, 198–199, 270–272
2. *Koran* 2:164
3. ibid 16.14
4. ibid 30.46
5. Hourani p 64
6. Lopez and Raymond pp 410–411
7. Hourani p 76
8. Hobson pp 176–179
9. Lopez and Raymond pp 27–29
10. Sanyal p 140
11. Hall p 14
12. ibid p 16
13. Hourani p 78
14. ibid p 98
15. Nanji in Ray (ed) pp 84–96
16. Hourani pp 119–120
17. Chaudhuri p 98
18. Nanji in Ray (ed) p 96
19. Mukund p 150

20. Hall p 141
21. Hourani p 82
22. Mukund pp 41–42
23. ibid pp 63–64
24. Sashadri in Kulke et. al. (ed) pp 107–108
25. ibid p 68
26. ibid p 117
27. ibid p 118
28. Susanti in Kulke et. al. (ed) pp 229–230
29. Seshadri in Kulke et. al. (ed) pp 118–119
30. Told to me by an Arwi colleague, Syed Cader in Dubai in 2011
31. Ray in Ray (ed) p 39
32. Wade pp 250–251
33. Hourani p 80
34. Wells pp 171–172
35. Paine p 266
36. Pearson p 99
37. ibid p 79
38. Abu-Lughod p 203

Chapter 3
1. Pirenne 1915 pp 2–3
2. Pye pp 140–141
3. ibid pp 150–151
4. Wickham 2005 pp 682–683
5. Fleming p 195
6. Pye pp 30–31
7. ibid p 45
8. Latouche p 140
9. Milne p 35
10. Jones p 169
11. Wood 1981 pp 94, 79–80
12. Jones p 103
13. ibid p 199
14. Pye p 92
15. Jones pp 98–99
16. Latouche p 233
17. Jones p 171
18. Cunliffe 2008 p 460
19. Wells pp 178–179, 219–232
20. Cunliffe 2001 p 493

21. Latouche pp 215–216
22. Wickham 2009 p 478
23. Jones pp 199–200
24. Bloch p 53
25. ibid p 55
26. Milne p 40
27. Jones p 107
28. Collins 1991 pp 332–334
29. Bloch p 17
30. Latouche p 222
31. Pye p 78
32. Wood 1981 p 170
33. ibid
34. Cunliffe 2017 p 453
35. Cunliffe 2008 p 460
36. Abu-Lughod pp 80–81
37. Wickham 2009 p 458
38. ibid p 465
39. Bloch p 145
40. Pirenne 1915 p 11
41. Wood 1981 p 170
42. Cunliffe 2008 p 459
43. Jones p 95
44. McLynn p 2
45. Collins 1991 p 77
46. Holland p 125

Chapter 4
1. Wickham 2005 p 818
2. Cunliffe 2017 p 396
3. Abulafia 2011 pp 256–257
4. Purcell and Horden p 162. Lopez and Raymond pp 31–32
5. Abu-Lughod p 157
6. Abulafia 2011 pp 248–249
7. Lopez and Raymond pp 35–36
8. Cunliffe 2008 p 452
9. Latouche p 282
10. Cunliffe 2008 p 441
11. ibid. King p 72
12. Herrin p 150
13. Cunliffe 2008 p 445
14. Lopez 1976 pp 65–66
15. Wickham 2009 p 356

16. Herrin p 125
17. Wells pp 234–239

Chapter 5
 1. Davies 2011 p 119
 2. Abulafia 2011 p 253. Wickham 2005 pp 732–723
 3. Wickham 2009 p 230
 4. Abu-Lughod pp 219–223
 5. Braudel 1982 p 556
 6. Latouche pp 264–265
 7. Braudel 1982 p 558
 8. Lopez and Raymond pp 57–58
 9. Wickham 2009 p 231
10. Norwich 1997 p 28 note 2
11. Cunliffe 2008 p 457
12. Lopez 1976 p 63. Lopez and Raymond pp 38–41
13. Norwich pp 31–32
14. Kurinsky Part 1
15. Abulafia 2011 p 253
16. Lambert p 114
17. Norwich 1997 p 50

Chapter 6
 1. Kulke in Prakash and Lombard (ed) p 24
 2. The date is disputed. See Munoz p 151 note 88. Most accept 1016
 3. ibid p 153
 4. Munoz p 155
 5. Ebrey p 141
 6. Hartwell p 369
 7. ibid p 384
 8. Yoshinobu pp 24–25
 9. Kulke in Kulke et. al (ed) p 5
10. Sen in Kulke et. al. (ed) p 66
11. Wade pp 232–233
12. Yoshinobu pp 31–33
13. Abulafia 2019 p 240
14. Yoshinobu pp 36–37
15. Ebrey p 144
16. Yoshinobu pp 181–182
17. Curtin p 110
18. Yoshinobu p 100

19. Wade p 229
20. ibid p 223
21. Yoshinobu p 212
22. Wade p 258
23. ibid p 239
24. Hobson p 217
25. Yoshinobu p 9
26. Wade pp 224–229
27. Clark
28. Yoshinobu p 48
29. ibid p 45
30. ibid p 160–163
31. ibid p 61
32. Waley-Cohen pp 39–40
33. Yoshinobu p 88
34. Vainker
35. Yoshinobu p 185
36. ibid pp 185–187
37. ibid p 27
38. Clark
39. Yoshinobu pp 192–193
40. Wade p 243
41. Pearson in Tracy (ed) 1991 p 103
42. Sakhuya and Sakhuya in Kulke et. al. (ed) p 87
43. Sashidri in Kulke et. al. (ed) p 124
44. ibid pp 129–130
45. Kulke in Kulke et. al. (ed) p 6
46. Mukund p 118
47. ibid p 119
48. ibid p 139
49. Susanti in Kulke et. al.. (ed) pp 235–236
50. Wade p 248–249
51. ibid p 249
52. Kulke in Kulke et. al. (ed) p 9
53. Wade p 256
54. Devare in Kulke et. al. (ed) p 182
55. Munoz p 164. Kulke in Kulke et. al. (ed) pp 11–12
56. Kulke in Kulke et. al. (ed) p 12
57. Kulke and Rothermund pp 125–126
58. Kulke in Kulke etc. (ed) p 13
59. ibid

60. Karashima in Kulke et. al. (ed) pp 138–139
61. Mukund pp 98–103
62. ibid p 106
63. ibid pp 148–151
64. Karashima in Kulke et. al. (ed) p 50. Mukund p 152

Chapter 7
1. Goitein pp 33–34
2. ibid p 18
3. Kearney p 73
4. Bramoule pp 127–135
5. Goitein pp 10–13
6. ibid pp 18, 52–54
7. Goitein in Cook (ed) p 55
8. Goitein p 21
9. ibid p 60
10. Braudel 1982 p 528
11. Abulafia 2011 p 265
12. Goitein p 158
13. ibid p 159
14. Goitein in Cook (ed) pp 55–58
15. Goitein p 103
16. ibid pp 27, 64. Paine p 246
17. Goitein pp 70–71
18. ibid p 61
19. ibid p 73
20. ibid p 238
21. ibid pp 164–165
22. ibid p 168
23. ibid p 167
24. ibid p 168
25. ibid p 169
26. ibid p 110
27. ibid p 127
28. ibid p 45
29. ibid p 44
30. ibid
31. ibid pp 44–45
32. ibid pp 45–46
33. Goitein in Cook (ed) p 55
34. Gotein pp 318–319
35. Abulafia 2011 pp 280–281
36. Lopez 1976 p 64
37. Norwich 1977 p 70
38. Lopez pdf p 56
39. Pirenne 1925 p 93
40. Fleming pp 300–303
41. McLynn p 7
42. Bartlett p 9
43. McLynn p 121
44. Jones pp 148, 157
45. Pirenne 1925 p 98
46. Hoskins p 101
47. Pirenne 1925 pp 116–119
48. Latouche p 259
49. McNiel and Houser p 77
50. Pye pp 177–178

Chapter 8
1. Margariti p 27
2. Goitein and Friedman p 630 note 23
3. Ghosh pp 174–177
4. ibid p 157
5. Abulafia 2019 p 264
6. Roy pp 39–40
7. Margariti p 114
8. ibid p 88
9. ibid p 140
10. ibid p 195
11. ibid p 162
12. Ray (ed) pp 130, 140
13. Margariti pp 166–169
14. ibid p 124
15. Abulafia 2019 pp 184–186
16. Ghosh pp 255–256
17. ibid p 260
18. ibid p 284
19. Karashima in Kulke et. al. (ed) pp 148–149
20. ibid p 149
21. Margariti p 163
22. Abu-Lughod p 204
23. Goitein and Friedman pp 727–730
24. ibid pp 553, 561 notes, 564
25. Goitein and Friedman pp 653–655
26. Margariti p 155
27. Goitein in Cook pp 182–183

28. Abu-Lughod p 227
29. Bramoulle pp 133–134
30. Margariti pp 152–153
31. Labib
32. Chaudhuri in Tracy (ed) 1991 p 431
33. Bernstein p 129
34. Paine p 365
35. Risso p 46

Chapter 9
1. Bartlett p 293
2. ibid p 184
3. Abulafia 2011 pp 290–291
4. Goitein p 45
5. Norwich p 85
6. ibid
7. Bartlett p 186
8. Abulafia 2011 p 298
9. ibid pp 299–301
10. ibid pp 301–303
11. ibid
12. Abulafia 2011 p 298
13. Lopez and Raymond pp 217–218
14. Valerian
15. Lopez and Raymond pp 384–387
16. Valerian
17. Simonsohn
18. Goitein p 70
19. Kurinsky Fact Paper Part 1
20. Lopez and Raymond p 255
21. Milne p 70
22. Rose 2011 p 62
23. Lloyd p 6
24. Lewis and Runyan pp 116–117
25. Bartlett pp 191–192
26. ibid p 17
27. ibid p 195
28. Milne p 89
29. ibid pp 79–80
30. Wickham 2016 p 141

Chapter 10
1. Bartlett p 196
2. Madden

3. ibid
4. ibid
5. Morris p 27
6. King p 97
7. ibid p 82
8. De Lara
9. ibid
10. Elliot 1963 p 26
11. Davies 2011 p 186
12. King p 82
13. Lopez pdf p 56
14. ibid p 58
15. ibid
16. ibid p 59
17. ibid p 61
18. ibid p 64
19. Lopez 1976 pp 166–167
20. O'Connell in Blockmans et. al. (ed) p 112
21. Spufford pp 181–187
22. ibid p 378
23. Abulafia 2011 p 354
24. Lopez 1976 pp 144–145
25. ibid pp 139–140
26. ibid pp 140–141
27. ibid p 166
28. Krondl p 53
29. Bartlett p 119
30. ibid p 180
31. Kurlansky 2002 p 117
32. Cunliffe 2017 p 476
33. Menard in Tracy (ed) 1991 p 236
34. Lloyd p 7
35. ibid p 13
36. ibid p 22
37. Milne p 93
38. ibid p 108
39. Warren p 140
40. ibid pp 288–294
41. Lloyd pp 26–27
42. ibid p 29
43. ibid pp 37–38
44. Rose 2018 pp 17–18
45. Tawney (ed) pp 6–7
46. Lloyd p 64

47. Spufford p 202
48. Braudel 1982 p 82
49. Abu-Lughod p 59
50. Spufford p 146
51. Lloyd p 144–145
52. ibid pp 79–80
53. ibid pp 39–40
54. Spufford p 12
55. Childs p 152
56. Cunliffe 2017 p 494
57. Pye p 222
58. ibid p 226

Chapter 11
1. Yoshinobu pp 8–9
2. ibid p 199
3. ibid p 205
4. Abulafia 2019 p 244
5. Wade pp 229, 234, 238
6. Clark
7. ibid
8. Kulke in Prakash et. al. (ed) p 31

Chapter 12
1. Munoz p 253
2. Kulke in Kulke et. al. (ed) p 5
3. Abulafia 2019 p 155
4. ibid p 157
5. Abu-Lughod p 336
6. Munoz pp 259–262
7. Soon in Miksic and Low Mei Gok. Chapter 4
8. Wade p 241
9. Soon in Miksic and Low Mei Gok p 78
10. ibid
11. Paine p 350
12. Abulafia 2019 p 247
13. ibid p 248. Bowring p 107
14. Wade pp 226–227
15. ibid p 235
16. Lee in Kulke et. al. (ed) pp 242–243
17. ibid p 243
18. Paine p 350

19. Abulafia 2019 p 218
20. Abu-Lughod p 166
21. Mackintosh-Smith p 264
22. ibid pp 223–224
23. Jakarta Post 13 May 2011

Chapter 13
1. Malouf
2. Abu-Lughod pp 189–191
3. ibid pp 192–193
4. Braudel 1966/1995 p 187–188
5. Mackintosh-Smith p 268
6. Gelber p 66
7. Marshall p 66
8. Gelber p 65
9. Marshall pp 65–66
10. ibid p 69
11. ibid pp 79–80
12. ibid pp 165–167
13. ibid p 170
14. ibid pp 180–181
15. Kearney p 92
16. Runciman 3 p 353
17. ibid p 365
18. ibid pp 397–402
19. Fernadez-Armesto 2009 p 13
20. Runciman 3 p 474
21. Abu-Lughod p 47
22. Lopez 1976 p 111
23. Levi. Hobson p 186
24. Hobson p 187–188
25. Abu-Lughod p 169

Chapter 14
1. Kulke and Rothermund p 122
2. Mackintosh-Smith p 167
3. ibid p 176
4. ibid pp180–183
5. Boyd p 51
6. Pye p 125
7. Boyd Chapters 1–4
8. Mackintosh-Smith p 233
9. ibid p 87
10. ibid pp 90–91
11. ibid pp 98–99

12. ibid p 215
13. ibid p 222
14. ibid p 223
15. ibid p 221
16. ibid p 226
17. ibid p 223
18. ibid p 227
19. Lopez and Raymond p 359
20. ibid pp 375–377
21. Lopez ibid p 417
22. Ferguson 2011 p 21–22
23. ibid p 23

Chapter 15
1. Levathes p 34
2. Gungwu in Tracy (ed) 1990 p 406
3. ibid p 407
4. Dreyer p 170
5. Gilbert and Reynolds p 63
6. Dreyer p 106
7. Menzies *1411*
8. Dreyer p 148
9. ibid p 54
10. ibid p 67
11. Pearson p 86
12. Dreyer p 163
13. Woo-keun pp 225–227

Chapter 16
1. Braudel 1993 p 198
2. Risso p 67
3. Brook pp 113–16
4. Abulafia 2019 p 268
5. Ray in Prakash etc. (ed) p 40
6. ibid pp 40–41
7. ibid p 44
8. ibid pp 41–42

Chapter 17
1. Spufford p 397
2. ibid pp 398–399
3. Lopez pdf p 66
4. Piccinno in Blockmans et. al. (ed) p 162
5. di Cosmo

6. Spufford p 152
7. di Cosmo
8. Mackintosh-Smith p 102
9. ibid pp 111–112
10. Piccinno in Blockmans et. al. (ed) p 164
11. ibid p 168
12. ibid p 169
13. Cunliffe 2017 p 508
14. Spufford pp 237–239
15. ibid p 250
16. ibid pp 271–272
17. O'Connell in Blockmans et. al. (ed) p 106
18. Spufford p 270
19. Lambert p 118
20. Krondle p 15
21. Origo pp 99–100
22. Abu-Lughod p 126
23. ibid pp 126–127
24. Norwich pp 269–270
25. O'Connell in Blockmans et. al. (ed) p 110
26. ibid p 109
27. ibid p 112
28. Lambert p 122
29. O'Connell in Blockmans et. al. (ed) p 107
30. Norwich p 272
31. Braudel 1984 pp 120–121
32. Spufford p 389
33. Elliot 1963 p 31
34. Origo p 126
35. Luis in Blockmans et.al. (ed) p 218
36. Lopez pdf p 57, Trivelatto
37. Origo p 40
38. ibid p 74
39. ibid p 139
40. ibid p 365 note 6
41. ibid p 133
42. ibid p 75
43. ibid p 71
44. ibid p 73
45. ibid p 102

46. Elliot 1963 pp 32–35
47. Spufford p 402
48. O'Connell in Blockmans et. al. (ed) p 110
49. ibid p 111
50. Christ in Blockmans et. al. (ed) pp 132–133
51. Abu-Lughod p 246 note 22
52. Norwich p 341
53. King p 101
54. Morris pp 59, 136
55. O'Connell in Blockmans et. al. (ed) p 113
56. King p 116
57. ibid pp 113–114
58. O'Connell in Blockmans et. al. (ed) p 115
59. Spufford p 404

Chapter 18
1. ibid p 172–173
2. Jenks in Blockmans et. al. (ed) pp 42–51
3. Abu-Lughod pp 100–101 note 19
4. Spufford p 318
5. Abu-Lughod p 89
6. ibid p 90
7. Spufford p 291
8. Power p 3
9. Braudel 1982 p 393
10. Lloyd p 139
11. ibid p 99
12. ibid p 104
13. Power p 13
14. Rose 2018 pp 63–70
15. Lloyd pp 171–172
16. ibid p 185
17. Rose 2011 p 65
18. ibid p 66
19. Boyd pp 6–7, 29–31
20. Seward p 24
21. ibid p 32
22. Childs p 21
23. ibid p 6
24. ibid p 30

25. Rose 2011 p 69
26. Braudel 1982 p 393
27. Lloyd p 215
28. ibid p 225
29. Rose 2018 pp 77–78
30. Power p 57
31. Lloyd p 251
32. Childs p 80
33. Cunliffe 2017 pp 544–545
34. Bartlett p 193
35. Abulafia 2019 p 430
36. ibid p 446
37. Pedersen
38. Zins pp 17–19
39. Milne p 133
40. Childs pp 169–170
41. Power p 13
42. Cunliffe 2017 p 509
43. Davies 2011 p 131
44. ibid p 133
45. ibid p 136
46. Spufford pp 403–404
47. Childs p 50
48. ibid p 58
49. Kowaleski in Blockmans et. al. (ed) p 398
50. Rose 2011 p 73
51. Ramsey p 48
52. Abulafia 2019 p 459
53. Zins p 9
54. Sobecki
55. Pye pp 239–240
56. Davies 2011 pp 348–349
57. Wubs-Mrozewicz in Blockmans et.al. (ed) p 255
58. Jenks p 2
59. ibid p 10
60. ibid p 47
61. ibid pp 16–23
62. ibid pp 12–13
63. ibid pp 14–15
64. ibid p 47
65. Hair and Law in Canny (ed) p 244
66. Trenchant in Blockmans et. al. (ed) p 362

67. Kurlansky 1999 p 51
68. Kowaleski in Blockmans et. al. (ed) p 383
69. Morris p 67
70. Kowaleski in Blockmans et. al. (ed) p 400
71. ibid p 402
72. Milne p 158
73. Elton p 50
74. Milne p 160
75. Sicking and Neele in Blockmans et. al. (ed) p 371
76. ibid p 374
77. Hinton p 1
78. Childs p 83
79. Spufford pp 376–379, 388
80. ibid p 380
81. ibid pp 387–388

Chapter 19
1. Pearson p 83
2. Pearson p 104, Curtin p 130
3. Pearson pp 83–84
4. Fernandez-Armesto 2009 p 259. Ray in Ray (ed) p 142
5. Fernando-Armesto 2009 p 263
6. ibid p 211
7. Abulafia 2019 p 231
8. Abu-Lughod pp 19, 258, 363

Chapter 20
1. Thomaz in Prakash et. al. (ed) pp 122–123
2. Hall p 106
3. Curtin Chapter 7
4. Spufford p 340
5. Boxer 1969 pp 29–30
6. Hobson p 136
7. Braudel 1984 p 143
8. Boxer 1969 p 30
9. Hair and Law in Canny (ed) p 244
10. Pagden in Canny (ed) p 49

Chapter 21
1. Krondl p 15
2. Crowley 2015 pp 96, 102

3. Pearson p 122
4. ibid p 124
5. Hall p 195
6. Thomaz in Prakash et. al. (ed) pp 135–136
7. Xavier pp 16–17
8. ibid pp 35–36, 125
9. Margariti p 207
10. Boxer 1969 pp 73–74
11. Bowring p 170
12. Abulafia 2019 pp 214–216
13. Pearson in Tracy (ed) 1991 p 72
14. Subrahmanyam in Prakash et. al. (ed) pp 62, 66–68
15. Pearson p 121
16. Pearson in Tracy (ed) 1991 pp 77–78
17. van der Wee in Tracy (ed) 1990 p 29
18. Boxer 1969 pp 52–56
19. Xavier p 18
20. Pearson p 98
21. Pearson in Tracy (ed) 1991 p 97
22. ibid
23. Krondl p 138
24. Thomaz in Prakash et. al. (ed) pp 140–142
25. Andrade and Miranda in Blockmans et. al. (ed) p 343
26. Risso p 80
27. Curtin p 145
28. ibid p 142
29. Thomaz in Prakash et. al. (ed) p 156
30. ibid p 157
31. Risso p 81
32. Spufford p 350–375
33. Crowley 2008 p 288
34. Arruda in Tracy (ed) 1991 pp 373–375
35. Parker p 11
36. Boxer 1969 p 105
37. Parry p 32

Chapter 22

1. Pye p 305
2. Zins p 55
3. McCusker pp 259–321
4. Elton p 121
5. Tawney (ed) p 143
6. Elton pp 190–192
7. Davis 1973 p 12
8. Hinton p 2
9. Sicking and Neale in Blockmans et. al. (ed) pp 366–371
10. www.balticconnections.net Part 3
11. Tawney (ed) p 138, 207
12. ibid p 153
13. Davis 1962/1972 pp 1–2
14. Zins p 145
15. ibid p 146
16. Davis 1962/1972 p 4
17. Elton pp 333–334
18. Zins p 35
19. Ramsey p 73
20. Longworth p 88
21. ibid p 104
22. ibid pp 128–149
23. Zins p 169
24. Tawney (ed) pp 288–289
25. Ramsey p 156
26. Tawney (ed) p 217
27. ibid p 202. Elton p 249
28. Lambert p 149
29. Scott 2019 p 58
30. Zins p 55
31. Scott 2019 p 75
32. Wubs-Mrozewicz in Blockmans et. al. (ed) p 256
33. Boxer 1965 p 7
34. Davis 1973 p 43
35. Boxer 1965 p 5
36. de Vries pp 161–162
37. de Vries and van der Woude pp 198, 232–233
38. Jacks p 22
39. ibid p 24
40. Kotilaine p 297

Chapter 23

1. Luis in Blockmans et. al. (ed) p 218
2. Elliot 1963 pp 39–40
3. Simonsohn
4. Braudel 1966/1995 p 118
5. Crowley 2008 p 29
6. Marshall in Canny (ed) pp 264–284
7. Braudel 1966/1995 p 812
8. Matsuki p 176
9. ibid p 177
10. ibid p 178
11. Durstelar
12. Blockmans and Wubs-Mrozewcz in Blockmans et. al. (ed) p 474
13. Brady in Tracy (ed) 1991 p 132
14. Avraham
15. Braudel 1965/1995 p 817
16. Crowley 2008 p 42
17. Braudel 1965/1995 p 882
18. Lambert p 136
19. Kurinsky Fact Paper 6
20. Kurinsky Fact Paper 41
21. ibid
22. Crowley 2008 Ch 18
23. Elliot 1963 p 241
24. Crowley 2008 p 282
25. Elliot 1963 p 249
26. Lambert p 144
27. Braudel 1965/1995 p 808
28. ibid p 128
29. ibid p 129
30. Kuncevic in Blockmans et. al. (ed) p 147
31. ibid p 146
32. Abulafia 2010 p 439

Chapter 24

1. Elliot 1989 p 10
2. ibid p 15
3. Elliot 2006 p 21
4. ibid p 110
5. Elliot 1989 p 11
6. Phillips in Tracy (ed) 1990 pp 83–84

7. Elliot 1989 p 20
8. ibid p 19
9. Elliot 2006 p 95
10. Ramsey p 58
11. Latimer p 11
12. Martin and Parker p 55
13. Hair and Law in Canny (ed) pp 246–247
14. Curtin p 150
15. Parker p 19
16. Martin and Parker p 70
17. Kurlansky 1999 pp 58, 50–51
18. Martin and Parker p 72
19. Zins pp 56–57
20. Martin and Parker p 99
21. ibid p 102
22. Padfield pp 25–26
23. Martin and Parker pp 29, 34–37
24. ibid p 223
25. Elliot 2009 p 26
26. ibid p 37
27. Milton p 17
28. ibid p 6
29. Keay p 4
30. Milton p 59
31. ibid p 63
32. ibid p 88
33. Guillot in Prakash et. al. (ed) p 166
34. Parker in Tracy 1991 (ed) p 179
35. Borschberg in Miksic and Low Mei Gek (ed) Chapter 7
36. Boxer 1965 p 26
37. Curtin p 153
38. Boxer 1965 p 23
39. Elliot 2006 p 100
40. Hair and Law in Canny (ed) pp 251–252
41. ibid pp 254–255

Chapter 25
1. Braudel 1966/1995 pp 623–624
2. Ramsey p 69
3. Parry in Cook (ed) p 226
4. Tawnwy (ed) p 328
5. ibid p 202

6. Braudel 1966/1995 pp 138–143
7. Davis in Cook (ed) p 195
8. Braudel 1966/1995 pp 625–627
9. Collins 2021 pp 111–114
10. Braudel 1966/1995 p 243. His figures from 1900 but implied for millennia.
11. ibid pp 245, 328
12. ibid p p 329–331
13. ibid p 592
14. ibid p 600
15. Boxer 1965 p 22
16. Braudel 1966/1995 pp 491–493
17. ibid p 1240

Chapter 26
1. Borah p 94
2. ibid p 2
3. ibid p 4
4. ibid p 5
5. ibid pp 51–56
6. ibid p 94
7. ibid p 81
8. ibid p 100
9. ibid p 106
10. ibid p 85
11. Barrett in Tracy (ed) 1990 p 248
12. Gungwu in Tracy (ed) 1990 p 412
13. Waley-Cohen p 58
14. Borah p 95
15. ibid p 121
16. ibid p 122
17. ibid p 123
18. ibid p 125
19. Braudel 1982 p 547
20. Bernstein p 202
21. Borah p 126
22. Elliot 2006 p 111
23. Flynn in Tracy (ed) 1991 p 333
24. Bernstein p 202

Chapter 27
1. Zahedieh p 26
2. Tawney (ed) pp 326–327
3. ibid p 327

4. Hill 1961 pp 38–40
5. Wilson p 107
6. Braudel 1982 p 419
7. de Vries p 122
8. Bernstein p 223
9. Davis 1962/1972 p 9
10. Wilson p 52
11. ibid p 53
12. ibid p 38
13. Tawney (ed) p 279
14. Wilson p 71
15. Childs pp 7, 84
16. Wilson p 54
17. ibid pp 52–53
18. ibid p 54
19. ibid p 45
20. Scott 2011 p 34
21. Royal and McManamon p 123
22. Davis 1967 p 35
23. ibid p 29
24. Boxer 1965 p 48
25. Scott 2011 pp 58–59
26. Horn in Canny (ed) p 183
27. Parker pp 16–17
28. Butel p 90
29. Elliot 2006 p 24
30. ibid p 131
31. ibid p 134
32. ibid
33. ibid pp 24–28
34. ibid p 112
35. Davis 1962/1972 p 315
36. Latimer p 85
37. Barker
38. Elliot 2006 p 216
39. Horn in Canny (ed) p 177
40. Pope
41. Davis 1962/1972 p 10
42. Pope
43. ibid
44. Latimer p 72–73
45. Butel in Tracy (ed) 1990 p 142
46. Parker Chapter 1
47. Beckles in Canny (ed) p 222
48. Parker pp 36–37
49. ibid p 43

Chapter 28
1. Al-Qasimi pp 16–17
2. ibid p 19
3. Milton p 248
4. Guillot in Prakash et. al. (ed) p 171
5. Risso p 81
6. Hobson p 155
7. Marshall in Canny (ed) p 264
8. Lewis p 52
9. Steensgaard in Tracy (ed) 1990 p 123
10. ibid p 124
11. Lewis p 52
12. Subrahmanyam in Prakash et. al. (ed) pp 69–70
13. Marshall in Canny (ed) p 276
14. Subrahmanyam in Prakash et. al. (ed) pp 70–75
15. Braudel 1982 p 593

Chapter 29
1. Wilson p 7
2. *Hamlet* Act 5 Scene 2
3. Pryor 2011 pp 131–132
4. Braudel 1984 p 365
5. Brook p 8
6. Nadler p 26
7. ibid p 42
8. Jardine pp 237–238
9. Elliot 1989 p 234
10. Timothy Brook's thesis in *Vermeer's Hat*
11. Wilson p 121
12. ibid p 347

Chapter 30
1. Elliott 1990 p 121
2. de Bruyn Kops p 2
3. ibid
4. Wilson 2009 p 8
5. Boxer 1969 p 108
6. de Vries p 132
7. Klooster in Kagan and Morgan (ed) pp 34–35
8. Fedorwicz p 191

9. Elliot 1989 p 124
10. ibid p 134
11. ibid p 179
12. ibid p 258
13. Wilson 2009 p 367
14. Latimer p 52
15. Butel p 117
16. de Bruyn Kops p 6
17. ibid
18. ibid pp 31–32
19. Parker p 27
20. van der Kraan 2009 p 9
21. van der Kraan 2004
22. Elliot 1989 p 238
23. Kotilaine p 321
24. de Bruyn Kops p 35
25. Boxer 1965 p 30
26. Bowring p 195
27. ibid p 201
28. van der Kraan 1999 p 85

Chapter 32
1. Scott 2019 p 161
2. Unger 1984, 2006
3. Brook p 74
4. ibid p 79
5. Padfield p 67
6. ibid
7. Hill 1970 p 126
8. Jardine p 336
9. Scott 2019 pp 123–124
10. ibid p 124
11. ibid p 131
12. Hill 1970 p 127
13. Rodger p 5. Firth p 234
14. Roger p 5
15. ibid p 7
16. ibid
17. ibid p 3
18. Hill 1970 p 144
19. Braddick in Canny (ed) p 288
20. Sawyers
21. Boxer 1965 p 95
22. Al-Qasimi pp 29–30
23. Firth p 363

24. Davis 1962/1972 pp 12–13
25. Hill 1970 p 150
26. Firth pp 366–367
27. ibid p 371
28. Latimer p 128
29. Davis 1962/1972 p 316
30. Keay p 127
31. Kurinsky Fact Paper 41
32. Nadler p 114
33. Coulton
34. Firth p 374
35. Abulafia 2011 pp 489–90
36. Hill 1970 p 159

Chapter 33
1. Clements p 63
2. Curtin p 167
3. ibid p 168
4. ibid
5. ibid p 169
6. ibid p 170
7. ibid p 172
8. Clements p 111
9. Hung
10. Clements pp 133–134
11. ibid p 160
12. ibid p 161
13. Hung
14. ibid
15. Brook p 170
16. Hung

Chapter 34
1. Davis 1962/1972 p 14
2. Wilson p 163
3. Zahedieh p 27
4. Hill 1961 p 185
5. Davis 1962/1972 p 217
6. ibid p 292
7. Zahedieh p 28
8. Price in Marshall (ed) p 79
9. Landsman in Canny (ed) pp 356–357
10. Elliot 2006 p 149
11. Zahedieh p 23

12. Hill 1961 p 187
13. Boxer 1965 p 48
14. Levi
15. Pearson p 164
16. ibid p 166
17. Haynes p 84
18. ibid
19. ibid pp 35–39
20. ibid p 84
21. ibid
22. Hair and Law in Canny (ed) p 256
23. Freely p 194
24. Jardine p 332
25. Israel in Canny (ed) p 432
26. Klooster in Kagan and Morgan (ed) pp 37–38
27. Ben-Ur in Kagan and Morgan p 154
28. Hill 1970 p 150
29. ibid p 246
30. Davis 1962/1972 p 53
31. Scott 2019 p 130
32. Jardine p 335
33. Parker p 122
34. ibid p 125
35. Latimer p 163
36. ibid p 172
37. ibid p 182
38. Richardson in Marshall (ed) p 445
39. Wilson p 171
40. Parry p 33
41. Butel p 125
42. Boxer 1965 p 103
43. Wilson pp 168–169
44. Braudel 1984 pp 189–190
45. Mikosch
46. ibid
47. ibid
48. Braudel 1982 p 240
49. Hoppit p 53
50. Butel p 122
51. Braudel 1982 p 193
52. Trivellato
53. Butel pp 128–129
54. ibid p 129
55. Butel in Tracy (ed) 1990 p 160
56. Hill 1961 p 188
57. ibid p 191
58. Israel in Canny (ed) p 436
59. Padfield p 117
60. Davis 1962/1972 p 225
61. ibid p 316
62. ibid p 18
63. Davis in Cook (ed) p 195

Chapter 35
1. Prakash in Prakash et. Al. (ed) p 236
2. ibid pp 236–237
3. Al-Qasimi p 31
4. Steensgaard in Tracy (ed) 1990 pp 124–125
5. Zahedieh in Canny (ed) p 413
6. Keay p 169
7. ibid p 170
8. ibid p 142
9. ibid p 177
10. ibid p 168
11. Latimer p 241
12. Zahedieh pp 283–284
13. Parker p 128
14. Menard in Tracy (ed) 1991 pp 254–259
15. Elliot 2006 p 135
16. Hoppit p 20
17. Israel in Canny (ed) p 440
18. Rodger p 13
19. Kenyon p 165
20. Hoppit p 25
21. Dunn in Canny (ed) p 465
22. Hill 1970 p 248
23. Hill 1961 p 227
24. Elliot 2006 p 220
25. ibid p 221
26. Elliot 1989 p 263
27. Steensgaard in Tracy (ed) 1990 p 136
28. Lambert p 190
29. ibid p 191, 200
30. Steensgaard in Tracy (ed) 1990 p 127

31. Hoppitt p 26
32. ibid pp 99–100
33. Davis1962/1972 p 316
34. ibid
35. Hill 1961 p 230
36. Zahedieh p 41
37. Davis 1962/1972 pp 338–362
38. Zahedieh p 20
39. ibid p 10
40. ibid p 281
41. ibid p 105
42. ibid p 88
43. Elliot 2006 pp 113–114
44. Zahedieh pp 95–96
45. ibid p 99
46. Kurinsky Fact Paper 41
47. Kurinsky Fact Paper 6
48. Kurinsky Fact Paper 41
49. Zahedieh p 138
50. ibid p 155
51. Davis 1967 p 35, Horn in Canny (ed) P 183
52. Zahedieh p 184
53. Davis 1962/1972 pp 61–65
54. ibid pp 66–67
55. ibid p 83
56. ibid pp 102–104
57. Sheridan in Marshall (ed) p 399
58. Zahedieh pp 229–230
59. ibid p 287
60. Parker pp 145–146, 165
61. ibid p 198
62. Hill 1961 p 236
63. Zahedieh in Canny (ed) pp 408–409
64. ibid p 416
65. Hill 1961 p 228
66. Padfield p 168
67. Wilson p 167
68. Braudel 1982 p 453

Chapter 36
1. Beckles in Canny (ed) pp 230–231
2. Weir in Canny (ed) p 384
3. Hill 1961 p 159

4. ibid pp 161–163
5. Wilson p 187
6. ibid p 230
7. ibid p 232
8. ibid p 234
9. Scott p 123
10. Nadler p 122
11. ibid pp 155–158
12. ibid pp 216–217
13. ibid p 400
14. Padfield p 68
15. ibid p 69
16. Drayton in Marshall (ed) p 232
17. Hill 1961 p 261
18. Wilson p 186
19. ibid p 187
20. Scott 2011 p 30
21. Thomas p 254
22. Hoppit p 201
23. ibid p 60
24. Elliot 1963 pp 369–370

Chapter 37
1. Stoye p 145
2. ibid
3. Kotilaine p 332
4. Davies 2011 pp 359–360
5. Longworth p 150

Chapter 38
1. Bernstein p 257
2. Thomaz in Prakash and Lombard (ed) pp 116–117
3. Zahedieh in Canny (ed) p 412
4. Subrahmanyam in Prakash et. al. (ed) p 51
5. Braudel 1981 p 542
6. ibid p 543
7. Davies 1997 p 523
8. Hoppit pp 192–193
9. Ogg p 98
10. Spufford p 402
11. Davis 1962/1972 p 301
12. ibid p 311
13. Canny in Canny (ed) p 19

14. Bernstein p 258
15. ibid p 259
16. Braudel 1984 p 205
17. Zahedieh pp 42–43
18. ibid pp 43–44
19. ibid p 8
20. Brand and Muller (ed) p 56
21. Hinton p 161

Chapter 39
1. Bowring p 198
2. Braudel 1984 pp 495–497
3. Boxer 1965 p 219
4. Davis 1973 p 32
5. ibid p 34
6. ibid p 35
7. Davis 1967 pp 35–36
8. Davis 1973 p 36
9. ibid
10. Zahedieh in Canny (ed) p 399
11. Davis 1973 p 37
12. Scott 2019 p 224
13. Hill 1961 p 230
14. Rodger p 159
15. Plumb p 3
16. Boxer 1965 p 118
17. ibid p 121
18. Braudel 1982 p 574
19. Pearson p 148
20. de Vries p 135
21. Boxer 1965 pp 225–227
22. ibid p 228
23. ibid p 197
24. ibid p 224
25. Boxer 1965 p 323

26. Kagan and Morgan pp 15–16
27. ibid p 14
28. Boxer 1969 p 154
29. Davis 1962/1972 pp 388–389
30. ibid p 391
31. Zadedieh p 287
32. Davis 1962/1972 p 27
33. Scott 2019 p 39
34. Zahedieh p 290
35. Wilson p 179
36. ibid p 180
37. ibid p 179
38. Kennerley etc. (ed) p 28
39. Hair and Law in Canny (ed) p 259
40. de Vries p 167
41. ibid p 408
42. ibid p 199
43. de Vries pp 217–218
44. Braudel 1982 pp 265–270
45. ibid p 495

Chapter 40
1. Hosler p 20
2. ibid p 25
3. Documentary
4. Peck pp 1–4
5. Kearsley pp 176 and 810
6. Peck p 1
7. Rissolo
8. ibid p 10
9. ibid pp 11–13
10. ibid pp 14–15
11. ibid pp 25–27
12. Daniels
13. Collins 2021 pp 189–196

Select Bibliography

Abulafia, David; *The Great Sea: A Human History of the Mediterranean*; Oxford; Oxford University Press; 2011
—— *The Boundless Ocean: A Human History of the Oceans*; London; Penguin Books; 2019
Abu-Lughod, Janet L; Before European Hegemony. The World System AD 1250–1350 (1989)
Al-Qasimi, Sultan bin Mohammad; Power Struggles and Trade in the Gulf 1620–1820 (1999)
Barker, Rosalin; The Rise of an Early Modern Shipping Industry. Whitby's Golden Fleet 1600–1750 (2011)
Bartlett, Roger; The Making of Europe. Conquest, Colonisation and Cultural Change. 950–1350 (1993)
Beckwith, Christopher I; Empires of the Silk Road. A History of Central Eurasia from the Bronze Age to the Present (2009)
Bernstein, William; A Splendid Exchange. How Trade Shaped the World (2008)
Bloch, Marc; Feudal Society (1961)
Blockmans, Wim, Krom, Mikhail and Wubs-Mrozewi, Justyna; The Routledge History of Maritime Trade Around Europe 1300–1600 (2017)
Borah, Woodrow Wilson; Early Colonial Trade and Navigation between Mexico and Peru (1954)
Bowring, Philip; Empire of the Winds. The Global Role of Asia's Great Archipelago (2019)
Boxer, C.R; The Dutch Seaborne Empire (1965)
—— The Portuguese Seaborne Empire (1969)
Boyd, Douglas; April Queen. Eleanor of Aquitaine (2004)
Brand, Hanno (ed): Trade, Diplomacy and Cultural Exchange: Continuity and Change in the North Sea and Baltic c. 1370–1750 (2006)
Braudel, Fernand; The Mediterranean and the Mediterranean World in the Age of Philip II (2nd edition 1966/translated 1995)
—— The Wheels of Commerce (1982)
—— The Perspective of the World (1984)
Brand, Hanno and Muller, Leos; The Dynamics of Economic Culture in the North Sea and Baltic Region (2007)
Brook, Timothy; Vermeer's Hat. The Seventeenth Century and the Dawn of the Global World (2009)
Butel, Paul; The Atlantic (1999)

Canny, Nicholas (ed); The Origins of Empire (1998)

Chaudhuri, K.N.; Trade and Civilisation in the Indian Ocean (1985)

Childs, Wendy R; Anglo-Castilian Trade in the Later Middle Ages (1978)

Clements, Jonathan; Pirate King. Coxinga and the Fall of the Ming Dynasty (2004)

Collins, Nick; How Maritime trade and the Indian Subcontinent Shaped the World. Ice Age to Mid-Eighth Century (2021)

Collins, Roger; Early Medieval Europe 300–1000 (1991)

Cook, M.A. (ed) Studies in the Economic History of the Middle East (1970)

Cunliffe, Barry; Facing the Ocean. The Atlantic and its Peoples (2001)

—— Europe Between the Oceans 9000 BC-AD 1000 (2008)

—— On the Ocean. The Mediterranean and the Atlantic From Prehistory to AD 1500 (2017)

Crowley, Roger; Empires of the Sea (2008)

—— Conquerors (2015)

Darwin, John; After Tamerlane (2008)

Davies, Norman; The Isles (1999)

—— Vanished Kingdoms. A History of Half-Forgotten Europe (2011)

—— Europe (1994)

Davis, Ralph; The Rise of the English Shipping Industry in the 17th and 18th Centuries (1962/1972)

—— English Overseas Trade 1500–1700 (1973)

de Bruyn Kops, Henriette; A Spirited Exchange; The Wine and Brandy Trades between France and the Dutch Republic in its Atlantic Framework 1600–1650 (2007)

de Vries; Jan and van der Woulde, Ad; The First Modern Economy. Success, Failure and Perseverance of the Dutch Economy 1500–1815 (1997)

de Vries, Jan; The Economy of Europe in an Age of Crisis 1600–1750 (1976)

Dreyer, Edward; Zheng He. China and the Ocean in the Early Ming Dynasty 1405–1433 (2007)

Ebrey, Patricia Buckley; Cambridge Illustrated History of China (1996)

Elliott, J.H.; Imperial Spain (1963)

—— Spain and its World 1500–1700 (1989)

—— Empires of the Atlantic World. Britain and Spain in America 1492–1830 (2006)

Elton, G.R; England Under the Tudors (1955)

Fedorwicz, J.K.; England's Baltic Trade in the Early Seventeenth Century (1980)

Ferguson, Niall; Civilisation. The West and the Rest (2011)

Fernandez-Armesto, Felipe; Civilisations. Culture, Ambition and the Transformation of Nature (2001)

—— 1492. The Year Our World Began (2010)

Firth, Sir Charles; Oliver Cromwell and the Rule of the Puritans in England (1900)

Fleming, Robin; Britain after Rome. The Fall and Rise 400–1070 (2010)

Frankopan, Peter; The Silk Roads. A New History of the World (2016)

Freely, John; Children of Achilles: The Greeks in Asia Minor since the days of Troy (2009)

Ghosh, Amitav; In an Antique Land (1992)
Gilbert, Erik and Reynolds, Jonathan T; Trading Tastes. Commodity and Cultural Exchange to 1750 (2006)
Goswami, Chhaya; Globalisation Before its Time. The Gujarati Merchants from Kachchh (2016)
Goitein S.D.; A Mediterranean Society (1967)
Goitein S.D. and Freidman, Mordechai; India Traders of the Middle Ages. Documents from the Cairo Geniza 'India Book' (2011)
Hall, Richard; Empires of the Monsoon. A History of the Indian Ocean and its Invaders (1996)
Haynes, Douglas E.; Rhetoric and Ritual in Colonial India. The Shaping of a Public Culture in Surat City 1852–1928 (1991)
Herrin, Judith, Byzantium. The Surprising Life of a Medieval Empire (2007)
Hill, Christopher; God's Englishman. Oliver Cromwell and the English Revolution (1970)
—— The Century of Revolution 1603–1714 (1961)
Hinton, R.W.K.; The Eastland Trade and the Common Weal in the Seventeenth Century (1959)
Hobson, John M; The Eastern Origins of Western Civilisation (2004)
Holland, Tom; Millennium (2008)
Hoppitt, Julian; A Life of Liberty? England 1689–1727 (2000)
Hourani, George F.; Arab Seafaring in the Indian Ocean in Ancient and Early Medieval Times (1963)
Hoskins, W.G; The Making of the English Landscape (1955)
Jacks, David; Market Integration in the North and Baltic Seas 1500–1800 (2004)
Jardine, Lisa; Going Dutch. How England Plundered Holland's Glory (2008)
Jenks, Stuart; Robert Sturmy's Commercial Expedition to the Mediterranean 1457/8 (2006)
Kagan, Richard and Morgan, Philip; Atlantic Diasporas. Jews, Conversos, and Crypto-Jews in the Age of Mercantilism 1500–1800 (2009)
Kearney, Milo; The Indian Ocean in World History (2004)
Kearsley, Graeme R.; Inca Origins: Asian Influences in Early South America in Myth, Migration and History (2003)
Keay, John; The Honourable Company. A History of the East India Company (1991)
Kennerley, Alison, Doe, Helen and Payton, Philip' The Maritime History of Cornwall. An Introduction (2014)
Kenyon, J.P.; The Stuarts (1958/1970)
King, Charles; The Black Sea. A History (2004)
Kotilaine, J.T.; Russia's Foreign Trade and Economic Expansion in the Seventeenth Century: Windows on the World (2004)
Kurlansky, Mark; Cod (1999)
—— Salt (2002)
Kulke, Hermann and Rothermund, Dietmar; A History of India (2016)

Kulke, Hermann, Kesavapany K, Sakhuja, Vijay (ed); Nagapattinam to Suvarnadwipa. Reflections on the Chola Naval Expeditions to Southeast Asia (2009)

Krondl, Michael; A Taste of Conquest (2007)

Lambert, Andrew; Seapower States. Maritime Culture, Continental Empires and the Conflict that Made the Modern World (2018)

Latimer, Jon; Buccaneers of the Caribbean (2009)

Levathes, Louise; When China Ruled the Seas (1994)

Lloyd, T.H.; The English Wool Trade in the Middle Ages (1977)

Longworth, Philip; Russia's Empires. Their Rise and Fall from Prehistory to Putin (2005)

Lopez, Robert S; The Commercial Revolution of the Middle Ages 950–1350 (1976)

Lopez, Robert S and Raymond, Irving W; Medieval Trade in the Mediterranean World. Illustrative Documents (1955)

Mackintosh-Smith, Tim (ed/transl); The Travels of Ibn Battutah (2002)

Margariti, Roxani Eleni; Aden and the Indian Ocean Trade (2007)

Marshall, P.J.; The Eighteenth Century (ed) (1998)

Marshall, Robert; Storm in the East. From Ghengis Khan to Kublai Khan (1993)

Martin, Colin and Parker, Geoffrey; The Spanish Armada (1988)

McLynn, Frank; 1066 The Year of the Three Battles (1988)

McNeill, William and Houser, Schuyler; Medieval Europe (1971)

Miksic, John N. & Low Mei Gek, Cheryl-Ann; Early Singapore 1300s-1819 (2004)

Milne, Gustav; The Port of Medieval London (2003)

Milton, Giles; Nathaniel's Nutmeg (1999)

Morris, Christopher; The Tudors (1955)

Morris, Jan; The Venetian Empire. A Sea Voyage (1980)

Mukund, Kanakalatha; The World of the Tamil Merchant (2012)

Munoz, Paul Michel; Early Kingdoms of the Indonesian Archipelago and Malay Peninsula (2006)

Nadler, Steven; Spinoza. A Life (2nd edition 2018)

Norwich, John Julius; A History of Venice (1977)

Ogg, David; Europe and the Ancien Regime 1715–1783 (1965)

Origo, Iris; The Merchant of Prato (1957)

Padfield, Peter; Maritime Supremacy and the Opening of the Western Mind (2000)

Paine, Lincoln; The Sea and Civilisation. A Maritime History of the World (2014)

Parker, Mathew; The Sugar Barons (2012)

Parry, J.H; Trade and Dominion (1971)

Pearson, Michael; The Indian Ocean (2003)

Plumb, J.H.; The Growth of Political Stability in England 1675–1725 (1977)

Pirenne, Henri; Medieval Cities (1925)

—— Early Democracies in the Low Countries (1915)

Purcell, Nicholas and Horden, Peregrine; The Corrupting Sea (2000)

Prakash, Om and Lombard, Denys (ed); Commerce and Culture in the Bay of Bengal 1500–1800 (1999)

Pryor, Francis; The Birth of Modern Britain (2011)
Pye, Michael; The Edge of the World. How the North Sea Made Us Who We Are (2014)
Ramsey, Peter; Tudor Economic Problems (1963)
Ray, Himanshu Prabha (ed); Bridging the Gulf. Maritime Cultural Heritage of the Western Indian Ocean (2006)
Risso, Patricia; Merchants and Faith (1995)
Rodger, N.A.M.; The Command of the Ocean. Naval History of Britain 1649–1815 (2004)
Rose, Susan; The Wealth of England. The Medieval Wool Trade and its Practical Importance 1100–1600 (2018)
—— The Wine Trade in Medieval Europe 1000–1500 (2011)
Runciman, Steven; A History of the Crusades 1.2.3 (1951, 1952, 1954)
Sanyal, Sanjeev; Land of the Seven Rivers. A Brief History of India's Geography (2012)
Scott, Jonathan; How the Old World Ended. The Anglo-Dutch-American Revolution 1500–1800 (2019)
—— When the Waves Ruled Britannia. Geography and Political Identities 1500–1800 (2011)
Seward, Desmond; A Brief History of the Hundred Years War (2003)
Sobecki, Sebastian I; The Sea and Medieval English Literature (2008)
Southern R.W.; The Making of the Middle Ages (1953)
Spufford, Peter; Power and Profit. The Merchant in Medieval Europe (2002)
Stoye, John; Europe Unfolding 1648–1688; 1969
Taleb, Nassim Nicholas; Anti-fragile. Things that Gain from Disorder (2012)
Tawney, R.H. (ed); Studies in Economic History: The Collected Papers of George Unwin (1927)
Thomas, Keith; Man and the Modern World, Changing Attitudes in England 1500–1800 (1983)
Thrupp, Sylvia; *The Merchant Class of Medieval London 1300–1500*; The University of Michigan Press; 1948
Tracy, James D. (ed); The Rise of Merchant Empire. Long-Distance Trade in the Early Modern World 1350–1750 (1990)
—— The Political Economy of Merchant Empires. State Power and World Trade 1350–1750 (1991)
van der Kraan, Alfons; Murder and Mayhem in Seventeenth Century Cambodia. Anthony van Diemen v King Ramadhipati I (2009)
Waley-Cohen, Joanna; The Sextants of Beijing. Global Currents in Chinese History (1999)
Warren, W.L.; King John (1961)
Wickham, Chris; The Inheritance of Rome. A History of Europe from 400 to 1000 (2009)
—— Framing the Early Middle Ages (2005)
—— Medieval Europe (2016)
Wilson, Charles; England's Apprenticeship 1603–1763 (1965)

Wilson, Peter H.; Europe's Tragedy (2009)
Wood, Michael; The Story of India (2007)
Woo-keun, Han; The History of Korea (1970)
Xavier, P.D.; Goa. A Social History 1510–1640 (2nd edition 2010)
Yoshinobu, Shiba; Commerce and Society in Sung China (1970)
Zahedieh, Nuala; The Capital and the Colonies. London and the Atlantic Economy 1660–1700 (2010)
Zins, Henryk; England and the Baltic in the Elizabethan Era (1972)

Articles

Adelaar, K.A.; East Barito: Who were the Malayo-Polynesian Migrants to Madagascar? pressfiles.acu.edu.aie
Avraham, Alexander; 'Sephardim'; *The YIVO Encyclopedia of Jews in Eastern Europe*; The Institute of Jewish Research
Bramoulle, David; Fatimids and the Red Sea (969–1171) *British Foundation for the Study of Arabia. Monographs* (2012)
Clark, Hugh R; Muslims and Hindus in the Culture and Morphology of Quanzhou from the Tenth to the Thirteenth Centuries (*Journal of World History* 6 No 1 (1995) 49–74)
Coulton, Barbara; 'Cromwell and the "readmission" of the Jews in England 1656'; *Cromwelliana – The Journal of the Cromwell Association*; 2001
Daniels, Gary C; 'Were the Maya Mining Gold in Georgia?'; Lost Worlds; http://lostworlds.org/maya-mining-gold-georgia/; 2011
De Lara, Y.G.; The State as Enforcer in Early Venetian Trade; A Historical Institutional Analysis (2005)
Di Cosmo, Nicola; 'Mongols and Merchants on the Black Sea Frontier in the Thirteenth and Fourteenth Centuries: Convergence and Conflicts'; *Mongols, Turks, and Others: Eurasian Nomads and the Sedentary World*; Amitai, Reuven, Biran, Michal (ed); Brill's Inner Asian Library; Vol. 11; 2005
Dursteler, Eric; Commerce and Coexistence. Veneto-Ottoman Trade in the Early Modern Era (2002)
Goitein, S.D.; New Light on the beginnings of the Karim Merchants *Journal of Economic and Social History of the Orient* August 1957
Guy, John; The Phanom Surin Shipwreck, a Pahlavi Inscription and their Significance for the History of Early Lower Central Thailand *Journal of the Siam Society* Vol 105, 2017
Hartwell, Robert M; Demographic Political and Social Transformation of China 750–1550. *Harvard Journal of Asiatic Studies* Vol 42 No 2 1982 pp 365–442
Hosler, Dorothy; Ancient Maritime Trade on Balsa Rafts. An Engineering Analysis *Journal of Anthropological Research* Volume 64 (2008)
Hung, Ho-fung; 'Maritime Capitalism in Seventeenth Century China. The Rise and Fall of Koxinga Revisited'; The Johns Hopkins University; Working Paper October 2000
Kurinsky Samuel; *Hebrew History Foundation Fact Paper*. The Judaic Origins of Venetian Glass Part 1 (www.hebrew history.info)

—— Glass Making, A Jewish Tradition Part III Flint Glass and the Jews of Genoa *Fact Paper 6*

—— The Da Costas, A Remarkable Sephardic Family *Fact Paper 41*

Labib, Subhi Y; Capitalism in Medieval Islam *Journal of Economic History* March 1969

Leroy, Beatrice; 'The Jews of Navarre'; *Hispania Judaica*; Vol.4; 1985 pp 17–54

Levi, Scott C; Asia in the Gunpowder Revolution. *Oxford Research Encyclopedia of Asian History (2018)*

Lewis, Dianne; British Trade to Southeast Asia in the Seventeenth and Eighteenth Centuries Revisited. *New Zealand Journal of Asian Studies* 11.1 June 2009

Lopez, Robert S; The Culture of the Medieval Merchant (pdf-Medievalist.net)

Madden, Thomas F.; Venice, the Papacy and the Crusades Before 1204 (Saint Louis University)

Malouf, Amin; 'The Crusades through Arab Eyes (1985)

Matsuki, Eizo; The Crimean Tatars and their Russian Captive Slaves. An Aspect of Muscovite-Crimean Relations in the 16th and 17th Centuries'; The Mediterranean World; 2006

McCusker, J.J.; The Demise of Distance. The Business Press and the Origins of the Information Revolution in the Early Modern World *American Historical Review* 2005/2 pp 259–321

Mikosch, Elizabeth; 'The Manufacture and Trade of Luxury Textiles in the Age of Mercantilism'; The Institute of Fine Arts, New York University; *Textile Society of America Symposium Proceedings*; Vol. 612; 1990

Peck, Douglas T.; The Little-known Scientific Accomplishments of the Seafaring Chontal Maya from Northern Yucatan

Pedersen, Frederick; Trade and Politics in the Medieval Baltic. English Merchants and England's Relations to the Hanseatic League 1370–1437 (2006)

Pope, Peter; Adventures in the Sack Trade. London Merchants in the Canada and Newfoundland Trades 1627–1648, *The Northern Mariner* VI January 1996

Power, Eileen; The Wool Trade in English Medieval History. *The Ford Lectures* (1939)

Rissolo, Dominique; 'The Ancient Maya and the Rise of Maritime Trade'; *Exploring the Hidden World of the Maritime Maya 2011*; NOAA Ocean Exploration; 2011

Royal, Jeffrey R and McManamon, John M; Three Renaissance Wrecks from Turkey and their Implications for Maritime History in the Eastern Mediterranean *Journal of Maritime Archaeology* 4(2):103–129 (2009)

Sawers, Larry; 'The Navigation Acts Revisited'; *The Economic History Review*; Vol. 45, No. 2; 1992 pp 262–284

Simonsohn, Shlomo; 'International Trade and Italian Jews at the Turn of the Middle Ages'; The Italia Judaica Jubilee Conference; *Brill's Series in Jewish Studies*; Vol.48; 2013; pp 223–238

Trivellato, Francesca; 'Discourse and Practice of Trust in Business Correspondence during the Early Modern Period'; Economic History Workshop; Department of Economics, Yale University; 2004

Unger, Richard W; Changing Energy Regimes and Early Modern Economic Growth (2006)

—— Energy Sources for the Dutch Golden Age; peat, wind and coal *Research in Economic History* (1948)

Vainker, Shelagh; Production and Trade of Porcelain in China 1000–1500. *Ashmolean Museum of Oxford 2006 Conference Paper*

Valerian, Dominique; 'Ifriqiyan Muslim Merchants in the Mediterranean at the end of the Middle Ages'; *Mediterranean Historical Review*; Vol. 14, No. 2; December 1999; pp 47–66

van der Kraan, Alfons; Anthony van Diemen. From Bankrupt to Governor General 1593–1636 *The Great Circle, Journal of the Australian Association for Maritime History* Volume 27 No 1 (2005) and Part 1 Volume 26 No 2 (2004)

—— 'Baptism of Fire: The van Goens Mission to Ceylon and India 1653–54 Part 2'; *The Great Circle: Journal of the Australian Association for Maritime History*; Vol. 21, No. 2; 1999; pp 73–108

Wade, Geoff; An Earlier Age of Commerce in South East Asia 900–1300 *The Journal of Southeast Asian Studies* June 2009

Zakharov, Anton O.; The Sailendras Reconsidered. *Institute of South Asian Studies Working Paper* 12 August 2012

Documentary
BBC Natural History Unit, Unnatural Histories. Ep. 3 Amazon 23 June 2011

Press
Bloomberg Businessweek; The Hijacking of the Brillante Virtuoso (2017)

Index